CUBA IN TRANSITION

Volume 13

Papers and Proceedings of the

Thirteenth Annual Meeting
of the
Association for the Study of the Cuban Economy (ASCE)

Coral Gables, Florida
August 7–9, 2003

(ISBN 0-9729551-2-7)

Cuba in Transition volumes may be purchased from:

Association for the Study of the Cuban Economy
P.O. Box 0567
McLean, Virginia 22101-0567

Email: publications@ascecuba.org or antoniog@att.net

Information on availability of volumes and book order forms are available at publications@ascecuba.org or antoniog@att.net

PREFACE

This volume of *Cuba in Transition* brings together papers and selected commentaries presented at the Thirteenth Annual Meeting of the Association for the Study of the Cuban Economy, which took place August 7-9, 2003, in Coral Gables, Florida. As with previous volumes, this collection of papers and commentaries covers a wide range of topics related to Cuba's economy and society: the current economic situation, macroeconomics, foreign investment, the external sector, tourism, agriculture, transition issues, governance and the role of civil society, legal issues, and demography.

The theme for the Thirteenth Annual Meeting was "Cuba's External Sector: Developments and Challenges." We heard presentations from invited speakers on Cuba's external debt and on status and prospects of hemispheric economic integration as well as many papers and commentaries on a variety of issues relevant to the interests of the Association's membership. We also held a special half-day session on August 7, entitled "Propuestas para la democracia desde Cuba," which brought together prominent speakers to discuss several proposals to create a democratic society in Cuba that have emerged from the island. We will issue the presentations made at this session as the third volume of the ASCE Occasional Studies.

In March of this year, the Cuban Government struck at the heart of an emerging civil society composed of independent journalists, economists, and human rights activists, jailing 78 of them and condemning them to sentences as long as 28 years. Among those arrested and sentenced were three distinguished members of ASCE, Marta Beatriz Roque Cabello, sentenced to 20 years imprisonment, Arnaldo Ramos Lauzurique, 18 years, and Oscar Espinosa Chepe, 20 years. They were arrested without justifiable cause, not allowed to defend themselves, and their property was confiscated. ASCE dedicated the Thirteenth Annual Meeting to them and to the other men and women unjustly imprisoned by the Cuban regime because of their dedication to freedom and human rights.

On behalf of the Board of Directors of ASCE, I would like to take this opportunity to thank Jorge Pérez-López for preparing and editing this volume of *Cuba in Transition*. I also would like to thank the Institute for Cuban and Cuban-American Studies of the University of Miami for its cooperation at the annual meeting and its contribution in support of this volume's publication.

Beatriz C. Casals
ASCE President

IN MEMORIAM

Arturo Pino Navarro (1923-2003)

Arturo Pino Navarro, an active member of ASCE, passed away in Miami on December 18, 2003. A graduate of the Universidad de la Habana in 1945 with the degree of Ingeniero Agrónomo, Arturo Pino dedicated his professional life to public service, first in Cuba and later in the United States and Latin America. He started his professional career in Cuba in the Ministry of Agriculture and in 1951 became administrator of the Contramaestre office of the newly-established Banco de Fomento Agrícola e Industrial de Cuba (BANFAIC). In 1959 he was appointed General Manager of BANFAIC and Vice-Minister of Agriculture. He left Cuba in 1960 and became a consultant to the Organization of American States (OAS) and a staff member of the Inter-American Development Bank (IDB), where he worked for 25 years. He held several important positions at the IDB, including Chief of the Agricultural Planning Section, Chief of several Operations Divisions, and representative of the IDB in Honduras and Costa Rica. He was also a consultant to the Banco Centroamericano de Integración Económica (BCIE). Arturo Pino was an active member of the Colegio de Ingenieros Agrónomos de Cuba en el Exilio and was instrumental in the preparation by that organization of a two-volume work titled *Desarrollo Agrícola de Cuba* (Miami, 1992 and 1994), to which he also contributed a chapter on agricultural credit in a Cuba of the future. He was a frequent speaker on topics related to agricultural development in Cuba and in Latin America. Those of us who knew him will remember him for his professionalism and integrity. May our esteemed colleague rest in peace.

Rodolfo A. Carrandi

TABLE OF CONTENTS

THE CUBAN ECONOMY IN 2002-2003

Jorge F. Pérez-López[1]

The amount of information on the current condition of the Cuban economy available as of mid-2003 is very limited in comparison to what had become customary in recent years. Not available at this time are: (1) the official statistical yearbook for 2002 or a preliminary statitistical summary; and (2) the report of the Banco Central de Cuba for 2002. Moreover, the analysis of the performance of the economy for 2002 by the Comisión Económica para América Latina y el Caribe (CEPAL 2003); based on statistics provided by the Cuban government, has more statistical gaps than has been the case in recent years.[2] Adding to the dearth of information on the current economic situation is the March 2003 government crackdown on independent journalists that has reduced substantially—although not eliminated altogether—the flow of news and analysis from non-government sources within the island.

RECENT ECONOMIC PERFORMANCE

Speaking to the National Assembly of People's Power (ANPP) in December 2002, Deputy Osvaldo Martínez, President of the ANPP's Commission on Economic Affairs, reported that the nation's gross domestic product (GDP) had grown by 1.1 percent in 2002, lower than the projected 3.0 percent, but nevertheless it had been a stellar year for Cuban economic development. He said:

... 2002 was a year of low growth but high development. Low growth with respect to the gross domestic product, and high development with respect to setting the essential bases for integral human development that transcends the narrow confines of mercantile transactions and goes beyond the conceptions of development that exist in the neoliberal, globalized world, affected by a deep economic crisis and even more affected by a crisis in human values (Martínez 2002).

This view was echoed by Minister of the Economy and Planning José Luis Rodríguez, who in his end-of-the-year address to the ANPP recalled that

In more than one occasion, *compañero* Fidel has referred to the deficiencies of the GDP as a measure of the economic development of a nation. .... The entirely justified criticisms [of the concept of GDP] made by *compañero* Fidel are more poignant in the case of Cuba because this international methodology, in addition the deficiencies of GDP itself, underestimates our performance in relation to other countries given the higher percentage of free and subsidized services in Cuba as well as that measure's inability to capture properly the moral values created by a society like ours ... (Rodríguez 2002).

Notwithstanding the effort to deflect the attention from the anemic economic performance by criticizing the measure, it is evident that the economy stag-

---

1. This paper expresses strictly the personal views of the author.

2. CEPAL also produces a very brief preliminary analysis of the performance of each economy in the Latin American and Caribbean region typically released in December as part of a larger CEPAL publication. The December 2002 publication has a section on Cuba. See CEPAL (2002).

nated in 2002. The prospects for 2003 are equally gloomy.

Macroeconomic Performance

Beginning with 2001, Cuba rebased its national accounts statistics to 1997 (1981 had been used as the base year for nearly two decades). In addition to changing the price base and presumably rebalancing components of GDP to reflect their relative importance in 1997, the revision also included other changes: (1) introducing measures of activity in the banking and insurance sector; (2) changing the methodology for imputing rents for privately-owned dwellings; (3) incorporating additional data from the tourism sector; and (4) expanding coverage of production by self-employed workers and by households (ONE 2002, pp. 85-86). As a result of the rebasing and of other methodological changes, a long-term GDP series is not available (the Official Statistical Office has only recalculated GDP on the new basis back to 1996). Thus, it is no longer possible to compare recent GDP levels to those of earlier periods, e.g., to 1989 and earlier, to assess the extent to which current Cuban GDP levels compare with those before the economic crisis of the 1990s. Compounding the problem in making comparisons over time is the fact that levels of GDP in the new series are significantly different—roughly 60 percent higher—than those for the earlier series.[3] Annual growth rates are also somewhat different between the two series, although for the four years (1997-2000) for which growth rates are available based on both series, the cumulative growth rates are very close (16.1 percent for the 1997 series v. 16.3 for the 1981 series).

As discussed above, GDP in 2002 reportedly rose by 1.1 percent (and GDP per capita by 0.8 percent), the third consecutive year of declining GDP growth rates, suggesting a stagnant economy (Table 1). Cu-

ban officials (Martínez 2002) blamed the weak economic performance in 2002 on external economic shocks and adverse climatic conditions: the slowdown in world tourism after the September 11 terrorist attacks, adverse terms of trade for oil and sugar, the world economic slowdown and U.S. economic sanctions, as well as three hurricanes (Michelle in November 2001 and Isidore and Lili in 2002).[4] This assessment is echoed by CEPAL (2002, p. 94), stating that the growth slowdown was attributable to "external and climatic mishaps (*adversidades*)." Cuban officials and CEPAL thus hold harmless wrong-headed Cuban economic policies and lack of policy reforms, contrary to the views of other analysts within and outside the island who have posited that external factors did not cause the slowdown of the economy of 2001-2002 but instead aggravated an already existing problem: the malaise of the domestic economy (Mesa-Lago 2003, p. 23).

Table 1. Key Macroeconomic Indicators, 1997-2002

	1997	1998	1999	2000	2001	2002
GDP Growth Rate (%)	2.7	0.2	6.3	6.1	3.0	1.1
GDP/capita Growth Rate (%)	2.3	0.3	5.9	5.7	2.6	0.8
Gross Capital Formation/ GDP (%)	16.2	14.4	13.6	14.3	13.3	12.0
Growth in Consumer Prices (%)	1.9	2.9	-2.9	-3.0	-0.5	7.0
Money Supply/GDP (%)	41.1	40.6	38.8	38.0	42.0	45.2
Budget Balance/GDP (%)	-2.0	-2.4	-2.3	-2.4	-2.5	-3.4
Unemployment Rate (%)	7.0	6.6	6.0	5.5	4.1	3.3

Source: CEPAL (2002, 2003); Rodríguez (2002).

Gross capital formation (investment) declined by 9.2 percent in 2002. The ratio of investment to GDP was 12.0 percent in 2002, down from 14.3 percent in 2001. This ratio was much lower than in the 1980s, when it was in the range of 25 percent. Investment in 2002 was concentrated in the following

---

3. See Espinosa Chepe (2003a) for some puzzles in the rebased statistical series.

4. According to CEPAL (2002, pp. 94-95), hurricane Michelle inflicted damages estimated at 1.9 million pesos (6.3 percent of GDP), while the damage inflicted by Isidore and Lili has been estimated at 800 million pesos (2.7 percent of GDP). Minister Rodríguez (2002) has stated that hurricane Michelle damaged about 180,000 dwellings, destroying over 18,000, and affected electricity, transportation and telecommunications infrastructure, crops and industrial facilities; meanwhile, hurricanes Isidore and Lili damaged over 92,000 dwellings and destroyed over 17,000, and affected roads, electricity and telecommunications infrastructure and tobacco and citrus plantations.

Table 2. Physical Output Indicators, 1996-2002

	1996	1997	1998	1999	2000	2001	2002[a]
Sugar (thousand MT)	4528	4252	3229	3783	4059	3530	3605
Oil (thousand MT)	1476	1438	1658	2104	2621	2773	3500
Natural gas (million cubic m)	19	37	124	460	574	595	585
Nickel (thousand MT)	54	62	68	66	71	76	76
Plantains (thousand MT)	539	382	462	493	581	679	496
Citrus (thousand MT)	690	835	745	795	959	957	459
Corn (thousand MT)	144	203	177	238	273	299	299
Tobacco (thousand MT)	31	31	38	31	32	32	32

Source: ONE (2002); CEPAL (2003); Rodriguez (2002).

a. Estimated.

sectors: oil and gas production, electricity generation, tourism, priority social programs and housing.

In the mid-1990s, the Cuban government was successful in stabilizing the economy, bringing down inflation and a mushrooming government budget deficit. In 2002, however, macroeconomic instability seemed to be reappearing. After several years of price stability (actually, deflation in 1999-2001), consumer prices rose by 7 percent in that year. At the end of 2002, the money supply was estimated at approximately 45 percent of GDP, up from 42 percent a year earlier.

The budget deficit in 2002 reached 3.4 percent of GDP, compared to 2.5 percent a year earlier and 2.4 percent for several previous years. Minister of Finance and Planning Millares (2002) attributed the deficit to extraordinary expenses associated with hurricanes Isidore and Lili as well as substantial increases in budgeted expenditures on education, public health, pensions, culture, arts, sports, and science and technology.

Despite the adverse economic conditions, unemployment reportedly fell in 2002 to 3.3 percent from 4.2 percent a year earlier. Three observations regarding this very low, and declining, unemployment rate are in order: (1) the reported unemployment rate refers to open unemployment and therefore masks the severe underemployment that exists in the island. CEPAL estimated measures of "equivalent unemployment"—open unemployment plus underemploy-

ment—for the mid-1990s in the range of one third of the labor force (the open unemployment at that time was in the 7-8 percent range); (2) not counted as unemployed in 2002 are the roughly 320,000 persons engaged in "urban agriculture," tending to garden plots located within and in the outskirts of cities and the nearly 120,000 high school drop out youths who have been enrolled in the "schooling as a job" program; and (3) also out of the labor force are over 7,000 youths that have been tapped to be trained as social workers.

Sectoral Economic Performance

Sugar: Sugar production increased by 2 percent in 2002 over 2001, from 3.530 million tons to 3.605 million tons (Table 2). Production in 2002 was about 9 percent below the average 3.970 million tons produced in 1996-2000 and 56 percent below the 8.121 million tons produced in 1989. During the 2001-2002 sugar *zafra*, which ended in June 2002, 104 sugar mills were in operation and 52 were idle (Varela Pérez 2002).

Oil: Oil production, a sector that has attracted a great deal of foreign investment, continues to be a star performer. In 2002, oil and gas production reached the historical high of 4.1 million tons of oil equivalent, a 20 percent increase over the 3.4 million tons produced in 2001 ("Rompen petroleros" 2002).[5] Oil production rose by 26 percent to 3.5 million tons, while natural gas production fell from 595 to about 585 million cubic meters. According to

---

5. In a feat of accurate forecasting, in early August 2002, Cuban officials were already predicting that production of oil and gas would reach 4.1 million tons and represent an increase of 20 percent over 2001 (Oramas 2002).

Table 3. Key Tourism Sector Statistics

	1998	1999	2000	2001	2002	% change 2002/01
Tourists (thousands)	1416	1603	1774	1775	1686	-5.0
Hotel rooms (thousands)	29.1	33.4	35.4	37.7	40.0	6.1
Room occupancy rate (%)	64.0	60.0	60.7	58.0	57.0	-1.7
Gross income (million USD)	1759	1901	1948	1840	1769	-3.9
Income/tourist-day (USD)	174.3	173.2	168.6	153.5	150.7	-1.8

Source: CEPAL (2003).

Minister Rodríguez, 74 percent of the electricity produced in 2002 was generated using domestic crude. Cuba has invested about 1 billion pesos to modernize and reconvert thermoelectric plants to use domestic crude. Plans are for up to 90 percent of electricity to be generated from domestic crude.

Nickel: Nickel production in 2002 was basically unchanged from 2001, at about 75,600 metric tons. Foreign-invested Nicaro Nickel again set a new historical production record (Rodríguez 2002). Production in 2002 exceeded nominal production capacity, suggesting that additional increases in production are not feasible without an increase in investment.

Non-sugar Agriculture: In the non-sugar agricultural sector, particularly severe were a 50 percent decline in citrus and a 27 percent decline in plantain output in 2002. Both of these crops were damaged by high winds associated with the hurricanes that affected the island in 2001 and 2002. Output of tobacco and corn were essentially unchanged in 2002 compared to 2001, while output of *viandas* (excluding plantains) reportedly rose by 5 percent. Also rising, by an unspecified amount, was production of vegetables (*hortalizas*). According to Minister Rodríguez (2002), production of animal feed "stabilized" in 2002, so that Ministry of Agriculture production of pork increased by 27 percent and of eggs by 16 percent. These production increases refer only to production by the state sector and therefore do not reflect output growth at the national level.

Minister Rodríguez (2002) admitted that food production was still not sufficient to meet national needs. Daily food consumption in 2002 was estimated at 2,916 calories and 76.8 grams of protein per capita, roughly the same levels of 1989.

Tourism: After several years of double-digit growth, the Cuban tourism sector slumped in 2001 as a result of world economic slowdown compounded by the aftermath of the terrorist attacks of September 11. In 2001, the number of tourist arrivals barely surpassed arrivals in 2000 (1.775 million tourist arrivals in 2001 compared to 1.774 million in 2000) and revenue from tourism fell by 108 million dollars or 5.5 percent (Table 3).

In mid-2002, Tourism Minister Ferradaz stated that tourist arrivals in the first quarter of 2002 were 14 percent below the previous year. To stimulate travel by Europeans, Cuba authorized the use of euro in all international tourism facilities (since June 2001, use of the euro had been authorized in Varadero); more than 55 percent of tourists traveling to Cuba originated from Europe ("Ministro admite" 2002).

The World Tourism Organization, in an early report of the performance of the industry in 2002, reported that Cuban tourist arrivals were off by 6.7 percent from a year earlier ("World Tourism" 2003). A subsequent report by the same organization indicated that tourist arrivals in 2002 were 1.686 million, 5 percent under 2001 ("Short-Term" 2003). The figure in this latter report matches up with the tourist arrivals figure reported by CEPAL (2003) and with the 5 percent decline in the tourism sector that Minister Rodriguez (2002) reported for 2002. Gross tourism revenue in 2002 has been reported at $1,769 million, 3.9 percent below the level in 2001. Revenue per tourist-day fell by 1.8 percent in 2002, to $150.7, the fourth consecutive year of decline in this important indicator (Table 3).

Despite the slump, construction of the tourism infrastructure continued to grow in 2002, with the number of hotel rooms suitable for international tourism

Table 4.   Key External Sector Indicators, 1996-2002

	1996	1997	1998	1999	2000	2001	2002
Merchandise exports (million pesos)	1866	1819	1512	1496	1675	1661	1446
Merchandise imports (million pesos)	3569	3987	4181	4349	4796	4788	4128
Merchandise trade balance (million pesos)	-1704	-2186	-2669	-2853	-3120	-3127	-2682
Foreign investment (million pesos)	82	442	207	178	448	39	100
Remittances (million dollars)	744	791.7	813.0	798.9	740.4	812.9	820
Hard currency debt (million dollars)	10.465	10.146	11.209	11.078	10.961	10.893	10.900
Exchange rate (pesos for one U.S. dollar)	19	23	21	20	21	26	26

Source: 1996-2001: ONE (2001, 2002). 2002: Merchandise exports, imports and trade balance from Espinosa Chepe (2003b); foreign investment from Triana Cordoví (2003); remittances and hard currency debt from CEPAL (2003); exchange rate from Rodríguez (2002).

reaching 40,000 at the close of the year. The occupancy rate in 2002 was 57 percent, compared to 58 percent a year earlier (Table 3). The share of domestically-produced goods and services within the inputs of the tourism sector repeatedly reached 68 percent in 2002 (Rodríguez 2002).

EXTERNAL SECTOR

The condition of the external sector continued to be critical in 2002. Exports of goods and services were down from 2001 and consequently imports of goods and services had to be severely restrained. Foreign investment recovered from 2001 and remittances continued to play a critical role in providing resources in convertible currency. The foreign debt in convertible currency rose slightly and Cuba again faced difficulties in meeting foreign debt servicing obligations and sought further concessions from key creditors. The unofficial dollar-peso rate of exchange remained at 26 pesos to the dollar. Table 4 brings together estimates of key indicators of the performance of the external sector culled from several sources.

Trade

As of mid-2003, there are still no official statistics on Cuba's foreign trade in 2002. However, Cuban officials reported in February 2003 that merchandise exports in 2002 declined by 13.6 percent from 2001 (to about 1,446 million pesos) and merchandise imports by 14.0 percent (to about 4,128 million pesos). The merchandise trade deficit was nearly 2.7 billion

pesos, about 400 million pesos higher than the merchandise trade deficit in 2001 (Espinosa Chepe 2003b).[6]

Meanwhile, based on official statistics, CEPAL (2002) has estimated that exports of goods and services in 2002 amounted to 4.3 billion pesos, down by 6.5 percent from the 4.6 billion recorded in 2001. Two factors contributed importantly to the fall in the value of exports of goods and services in 2002: (1) the reduction in the number of tourists and in revenues from tourism; and (2) weak international market prices for sugar, which were about 20 percent below the average price in 2001.[7] As shown in Table 5, the top 5 merchandise export markets for Cuba in 2001 were Russia (Russia continues to be the main importer of Cuban sugar), three members of the European Union and China. As discussed above, Europe is also the source of most tourists, thereby highlighting the importance of relations with Europe for the Cuban economy.

Imports of goods and services fell sharply in 2002, to under 4.8 billion pesos from 5.5 billion pesos in 2001 (CEPAL 2003) or by 14 percent. The oil bill in 2002 exceeded $1 billion (Rodríguez 2002), as oil world market prices rose during the year from about $20 to $26 per barrel (World Bank 2003) and supplies from Venezuela—under a bilateral arrangement—suffered disruptions. Despite increases in domestic oil production, imports still accounted

---

6. CEPAL (2003) reports slightly different merchandise export and import figures: 1,436 million pesos for exports and 4,160 million pesos for imports.

7. The average world market price for sugar in 2002 (International Sugar Agreement, ISA, daily price, raw, f.o.b. and stowed at greater Caribbean ports) was 6.9 cents/pound, compared to 8.6 cents/pound in 2001. See World Bank (2003).

Table 5. Merchandise Trade and Top-Five Trading Partners, Exports and Imports (million pesos)

	1997	1998	1999	2000	2001
Merchandise exports	1819.1	1512.2	1495.8	1675.3	1660.6
Russia	303.2	355.3	302.8	324.6	402.6
Netherlands	39.1	53.1	93.0	116.8	333.9
Canada	249.9	230.2	229.2	278.0	227.8
Spain	170.4	141.1	159.4	150.2	188.6
China	97.2	81.9	49.5	80.5	70.8
Merchandise imports	3987.3	4181.2	4349.1	4795.6	4787.8
Venezuela	432.7	385.6	451.5	898.4	951.5
Spain	497.0	608.2	721.8	743.2	693.9
China	248.3	336.5	432.2	443.8	547.8
Canada	264.5	321.0	339.6	311.1	362.4
Italy	231.9	253.2	264.1	296.6	297.9
Merchandise balance	-2162.8	-2669.0	-2853.3	-3120.3	-3172.2

Source: ONE (2002), pp. 133-138.

for 55-60 percent of Cuba's oil consumption.[8] As is clear from Table 5, Venezuela was Cuba's top source of merchandise imports in 2001 and most likely continued to hold this position in 2002 by virtue of its position as main provider of Cuba's oil imports. Spain, Canada and China, three of Cuba's top-five markets for exports, were also among the top-five Cuban suppliers in 2001.

In 2002, Cuba imported about $255 million worth of products from the United States, primarily agricultural commodities (Jordan 2003). Pursuant to the terms under which these transactions were authorized by the United States,[9] Cuba had to pay in cash for them and such purchases therefore represented a serious drain on foreign exchange holdings. Purchasing from the United States on a cash basis in an environment of foreign exchange shortages and when credits for agricultural imports are available from other countries does not make sense unless the motive for the transactions is to whet the appetite of U.S. agricultural exporters to enlist their support in modifying the U.S. trade embargo.

Balance of Payments

As with trade in goods and services, there are no official statistics on the balance of payments for 2002.

CEPAL (2003) has estimated some of the main components of the balance of payments; these are reported in Table 6 together with official balance of payments statistics for 1996-2001.

According to CEPAL, the deficit in trade of goods and services reached 513 million pesos in 2002, much lower than in previous years. Factor payments were estimated at 600 million pesos. These outflows were compensated, to a large extent, by current transfers (mostly personal remittances), estimated at 820 million pesos in 2002. Based on a survey of remittances senders and other sources, the Inter-American Development Bank (IDB 2003) has estimated that remittances to Cuba amounted to $1.138 billion in 2002, 22 percent higher than the roughly $890 million the same source estimated was remitted in 2001. If these latter estimates turn out to be correct, they would mean that remittances to relatives and friends in Cuba played even a larger role in addressing the serious foreign exchange shortages in the island.

According to the CEPAL estimates, the deficit in the current account of the balance of payments in 2002 was roughly 293 million pesos. CEPAL estimates that capital flows into the island during 2002 amounted only to 300 million pesos, for a positive

---

8. The lower foreign oil dependency ratio is from Oramas (2002) and the higher from CEPAL (2003).

9. The legislation that authorizes certain U.S. exports to Cuba is the Trade Sanctions Reform and Export Enhancement Act (TSRA) of 2002.

Table 6. Balance of Payments (in million pesos)

	1997	1998	1999	2000	2001	2002
Current Account	-436.7	-392.4	-461.8	-776.0	-552.7	-293
Goods and services	-745.5	-756.7	-746.6	-894.2	-863.4	-513
Goods (net)	-2264.5	-2688.8	-2909.3	-3117.2	-3076.2	-2724
Exports	1823.1	1540.2	1456.1	1676.8	1661.5	1436
Imports	4087.6	4229.0	4365.4	4876.7	4838.3	4160
Services (net)	1519.0	1932.1	2162.7	2223.0	2212.8	2211
Factor income	-482.9	-448.7	-514.1	-622.2	-502.2	-600
Current transfers	791.7	813.0	798.9	740.4	812.9	820
Capital Account	457.4	409.4	484.9	805.4	594.5	300
Long-term capital	786.9	632.7	209.9	1018.4	367.2	
Foreign investment	442.0	206.6	178.2	448.1	38.9	
Other	344.9	426.1	31.7	570.3	328.3	
Other capital	-329.5	-223.3	275.0	-213.0	227.3	
Change in reserves	-20.7	-17.0	-23.1	-29.4	-41.8	-7

Source: 1997-2001: ONE (2002), p. 130; 2002: CEPAL (2003).

change in reserves of 7 million pesos. There is very little information on the composition of capital flows in 2002. However, Cuban economist Triana Cordoví (2003, p. 10) has reported that foreign direct investment in 2002 reached $100 million and 24 new joint ventures were established, a significant increase from the $34 million in foreign direct investment in 2001 (according to official data in Table 5, foreign direct investment in 2001 was nearly $39 million).

Debt

As reported in Table 4, Cuba's debt in convertible currency rose slightly in 2002, to 10.9 billion dollars. There is no detailed information on Cuba's creditors in the latter year, but in 2001 more than 19 percent of the debt was with Japan and about 15 percent with Germany.[10] CEPAL (2003) estimates that 32.4 percent of the debt consisted of export credits backed by government guarantees, 26.0 percent were bank loans and deposits, and 17.0 percent were government-to-government loans.

Cuba has been in technical default of its foreign debt since the early 1980s and therefore its borrowing has been limited to supplier credits and short-term loans with very high interest rates. As of mid-2002, Cuba's main short-term creditors were France ($548 mil-

lion), Netherlands ($302 million), Spain ($300 million), Germany ($140 million) and Italy ($105 million) (Triana Cordoví 2003, p. 9). China reportedly committed $400 million in long-term loans to Cuba in April 2001 ("Cuba's Foreign Debt" 2002).

In 2002-2003, Cuba encountered difficulties in meeting repayment terms *vis-a-vis* key trading partners. According to the U.S.-Cuba Trade and Economic Council, "throughout 2002 and throughout 2001, the government of the Republic of Cuba and government-operated companies failed to maintain payment schedules on commercial debt, commercial debt guaranteed by government agencies, and government-to-government obligations in countries including Canada, France, Spain, Mexico, Japan, Chile, and Brazil, among other countries" (USCTEC 2003, p. 2). Thus,

- In October 2002, Cuba defaulted on a $750 million refinancing agreement with Japan's private sector pursuant to a refinancing agreement signed in 1998 ("Cuba's Economy" 2003).

- Mexico is seeking repayment of approximately $400 million owed by the Cuban government to the Banco Nacional de Comercio Exterior (Ban-

---

10. According to the Banco Central de Cuba (2002), 33.9 percent of Cuba's debt in 2001 was denominated in U.S. dollars; 19.2 percent in Japanese yen; 14.7 percent in German deutsche marks; 9.4 percent in Eurodollars; 6.4 percent in Swiss francs; 4.4 percent in Canadian dollars; 3.5 percent in British pounds; 3.0 percent in Spanish pesetas, 1.3 percent in French francs; and 4.2 percent in other currencies.

comext); the loan dates to the early 1990s and was restructured ˙ recently at Cuba's request ("México quiere" 2003). Cuba reportedly missed a payment in June 2002 ("Cuba's Economy" 2003).

- Cuba is in arrears on $100 million short-term credit lines from Panamanian banks and trading companies ("Cuba's Economy" 2003).

- France's export financing agency, COFACE, has suspended Cuba's $175 million credit line because of Cuba's failure to make repayments; this line of credit was used in the past to finance French exports to Cuba of agricultural products and capital goods ("Cuba's Economy" 2003).

- In 2003, Cuba had the worst repayment record within Spain's creditors. Cuba accounts for nearly one-third (32.5 percent) of Spain's overdue debts from sovereign nations ("Cuba es el primer" 2003).

- As of February 2003, Cuba owed Venezuela $266 million pursuant to the Integral Cooperation Program between the two countries signed in 2000. Cuba imports Venezuelan oil under the agreement. The debt includes $127 million already in arrears (Ventura Nicolas 2003).

POLICY DEVELOPMENTS

Cuba's high water mark with respect to economic policy experimentation and reform was the early 1990s, when several initiatives that promoted a modicum of economic liberalization were put in place. Since the financial sector reform of 1997, no new policy initiatives of significance have been implemented and, in fact, the Cuban government has deliberately eroded the impact of some of the earlier reforms through bureaucratic means and gone back on others to reestablish state control over the economy. An announcement by the Cuban Central Bank in July 2003 that thenceforth state enterprises would be

prohibited from making transactions among themselves in U.S. dollars and would have to change any U.S. dollar balances they held into "convertible pesos," was seen by analysts as a way to reverse a key measure reluctantly taken in the early 1990s—the legalization of the use of the U.S. dollar—and might signal a return to centralized direction of the economy ("Cuba starts" 2003; Frank 2003a).

Some analysts anticipated that the VI Congress of the Cuban Communist Party, scheduled for October 2002,[11] would generate some economic liberalization steps that might revitalize the economy. However, as of mid-2003, the VI Party Congress has not been held and no firm convocation date has been announced. In a subtle criticism of the lack of reforms, Cuban economist Triana Cordoví (2003) asked rhetorically whether the means (*resortes*) that had brought about economic growth since the mid-1990s (he mentions increases in tourism and oil production, creation of an internal market based on foreign currency, attraction of foreign investment and mobilization of domestic savings associated with financial sector reform) had been exhausted and wondered if new approaches were needed to revitalize the economy.

Since the mid-1990s, then, the policy of the Cuban government has been to make no additional economic liberalization concessions and stay the course of orthodox socialism. The recent economic initiatives—e.g., urban agriculture and the restructuring of the sugar industry (see below)—fit this mold of paralysis of economic reforms. Changes in the economic leadership suggest a hardening of the line against further reforms.

Urban Agriculture

The National Urban Agriculture Program started in 1994 as a response to the dire need for food and the lack of transportation and housing necessary to redeploy urban unemployed workers to the countryside

---

11. Following the practice of the communist countries, Cuba held major Congresses of its communist party at five-year intervals beginning in 1975. These party congresses typically evaluated developments during the previous five-year period and set out policy guidance and goals for the next. The most recent such congress, the V Congress of the Cuban Communist Party, was held in October 1997 and the VI Congress was expected in October 2002.

to work in agricultural activities (75 percent of the Cuban population resides in urban areas). Since then the program has grown by leaps and bounds and become an important producer of food.

At the end of 2002, organized urban agriculturalists controlled about 35,800 hectares of land growing fresh vegetables and herbs in over 4,000 organoponics (raised beds filled with organic matter), 8,600 intensive vegetable gardens, 180,000 small plots and 300,000 backyard plots, the latter coordinated through the local Committees to Defend the Revolution (CDR) (Madruga 2003; Companioni and Ojeda Hernández 2002). Output from the National Urban Agriculture Program in 2002 was estimated at 3.1 million tons of fresh vegetables, and urban agriculture employed 320,000 workers throughout the island (Rodríguez 2002).

Sugar Industry Restructuring

In June 2002, Cuba announced a plan to restructure the sugar agroindustry that contemplated very significant reductions in sugarcane lands, the number of sugar mills and overall industry employment. According to the plan (Valenzuela 2002), about half of the roughly 2 million hectares devoted to sugarcane would be shifted to other crops and the existing 156 sugar mills would be disposed of as follows:

- 71 mills, those with the highest efficiency and the lowest production costs, would continue to produce sugar;

- 14 mills would produce only enriched molasses; and

- 71 mills would be permanently shut down. Seven of these mills would be converted into tourism facilities and the remaining 64 would be demolished and their equipment used as spare parts for other mills.

Although there are no precise statistics on the number of workers affected by the restructuring plan, analysts estimated that approximately 100,000 workers—roughly evenly split between field and mill workers—would be affected. General Rosales del Toro, Sugar Industry Minister, stated in 2002 that the restructuring plan was intended to maintain an industry capable of producing about 4 million tons of sugar per annum, roughly the average production volume during the special period, but with higher efficiency, lower costs, higher profitability, and making a greater contribution to the national economy (Varela Pérez 2002b).

Economic Leadership Reshuffling

A number of changes and reassignments within the Cabinet suggest dissatisfaction with the performance of the economy:

- In October 2002, Construction Minister Juan Mario Junco del Pino was dismissed from his post and replaced by then Vice Minister Fidel Fernando Figueroa de la Paz. Normally, no explanation about personnel changes is provided, but in the case of Junco del Pino, the Cuban media stated that "this decision responds to the fact that the organization failed to meet the anticipated results under his direction, and to the need for this sector—notwithstanding being affected the material restrictions facing the nation—to reach higher quantitative and qualitative results under more demanding management and higher levels of discipline, organization and control" ("Castro destituye" 2002).

- Minister of the Economy and Planning José Luis Rodríguez was dropped from the Council of State in March 2003, and replaced in this key policy-making body by Francisco Soberón, President of the Cuban Central Bank ("El gobierno mantiene" 2003). Earlier in the year, 4 of the 6 vice ministers responding directly to Minister Rodríguez were dismissed ("La Habana sustituye" 2003). As of mid-2003, Rodríguez remained at the helm of the Ministry of the Economy and Planning, however.

- Minister of Transportation Alvaro Pérez Morales was dismissed in mid-June and replaced by Manuel Pozo Torrado ("Destituyen" 2003; Batista 2003).

- At about the same time, Minister of Finance and Prices Manuel Millares, who held the post since 1995, suffered the same fate and was replaced by

Georgina Barreiro ("Cae el titular" 2003; "Designan nuevo" 2003; Batista 2003).

Although the new appointees are younger than their predecessors, there is no reason to expect that their appointment signals new policy directions. In fact, the new appointees are viewed as being loyal to President Castro and perhaps less open to reform than their predecessors. One analyst described the new appointees as follows: "They're baby dinosaurs. Their thinking is old guard, but they just happen to be younger" (San Martin 2003).

2003 PLAN AND PERFOMANCE

Cuban officials anticipated that 2003 would also be a challenging year with respect to economic performance. The economic goals for 2003 set out by Minister Rodriguez (2002) included:

- overall GDP growth target of 1.5 percent;

- focus investment on the energy sector: reconverting power plants to use domestic oil, oil exploration, construction of oil pipelines and conversion from oil to natural gas in commercial application;

- oil and gas production to increase by 16.8 percent, to over 4.7 million tons oil equivalent;

- at least 92 percent of electricity to be generated from domestic oil;

- nickel output to increase by 4.4 percent, to 78,900 tons;

- sugar production to be set at "levels that will offer the largest rates of return taking into consideration the behavior of world market prices" and increases in the production of sugar derivatives;

- increase in the production of agricultural products from lands shifted out of sugar cane production; 3 percent overall increase in non-sugar agricultural production, recovery of production of plantains and citrus and increases in the production of *viandas* and vegetables;

- construction of about 2,000 additional rooms for tourists and increase in the number of tourists as large as possible given conditions in the international market.

- The 2003 budget anticipated a deficit of 1.074 billion pesos, about 3.4 percent of GDP (Millares 2002).

As of mid-2003, some information was available on the performance of the sugar and tourism sectors.

- According to unofficial sources, sugar production in the 2002-2003 *zafra* was in the range of 1.9 to 2.0 million tons (Frank 2003b). (Sugar production of 2 million tons would mean a 45 percent decrease from 2002 and the lowest production volume since 1912.[12]) The 2002-2003 *zafra* lasted 180 days and 71 sugar mills operated producing sugar, with 14 others producing molasses (Carralero Hernández 2003). A Sugar Ministry official attributed the dismal results of the 2002-2003 harvest to three factors: (1) lack of financing; (2) management problems, including failing to react adequately to the changes brought about by restructuring; and (3) excess rainfall. Cuban officials are banking on the rebound of the industry in the 2003-2004 sugar harvest, dubbed *la zafra de la restructuración* (Martori 2003).

- Tourism Minister Ferradaz reported that tourist arrivals in the first half of 2003 were 16 percent ahead of 2002, suggesting that the total for the year would approximate 1.9 million tourists ("Aumentarán" 2003).[13] This assessment is con-

---

12. Cuba first produced over 2 million tons of sugar in 1912. At the time, demand for Cuban sugar was stimulated by the disruption to the European sugar beet industry associated with World War I and the Cuban industry expanded eastward to the provinces of Camagüey and Oriente. Production remained above the 2 million-ton mark for the next 90 years.

13. The Cuban press (Comellas 2003) reported the arrival of the one-millionth tourist of the year 2003 on June 29, one month earlier than in 2002. This is consistent with the 16 percent growth rate in tourist arrivals reported by Minister Ferradaz for the first half of 2003.

sistent with information from the World Tourism Organization indicating that tourist arrivals for the first four months of 2003 were 19 percent higher than in 2002 ("Short-Term" 2003). Optimism about the recovery of the Cuban tourism industry is also evident in Spanish firm Sol Meliá's decision to continue with its expansion program in the island, including three hotels under construction ("Sol Meliá" 2003).

CONCLUDING REMARKS

The condition of the Cuban economy in 2002-2003 can be characterized by: (1) stagnation; (2) foreign exchange crisis; and (3) policy paralysis.

Undoubtedly, 2003 will be another challenging year for the Cuban economy, with external sector pressures continuing to mount and a leadership intent on refusing to implement needed reforms. As if economic reforms were a luxury only to be undertaken by flourishing economies, CEPAL (2003, p. 3) predicts:

Taking into consideration that the shortage of foreign exchange will increase in 2003, the implementation of measures that would deepen the institutional and structural reforms that began in the 1990s—such as the gradual elimination of exchange rate and price system duality, the consolidation of macroeconomic adjustment, the liberalization of self-employment and the resumption of foreign investment in the real estate sector—will be delayed.

Writing in the spring of 2002, Peters (2002, p. 10) was pessimistic about the prospects for further economic reforms: "Based on the current economic policy discussions in Cuba, it seems highly unlikely that a new round of economic reforms would be adopted in the near term. It therefore seems very likely that the partially met challenges of Cuba's unique brand of socialism will be faced by the island's next generation of economic policy makers." A year later, Peters' pessimism about further reforms seems still valid, although the economic environment—particularly with regard to the external sector—is less auspicious than what Cuba faced in 2002.

BIBLIOGRAPHY

"Aumentarán capacidades para el turismo en Cuba." 2003. *Granma* (16 July).

Banco Central de Cuba. 2002. *Informe Económico 2001*. La Habana: BCC (May).

Batista, Carlos. 2003. "Aprietos económicos anuncian un verano difícil." La Habana, AFP, *El Nuevo Herald* (24 June).

"Cae el titular de finanzas." 2003. AFP, La Habana. *El Nuevo Herald* (22 June).

Carralero Hernández, Alfredo. 2003. "Concluyó la zafra azucarera 2002-2003." Agencia de Información Nacional, La Habana (23 June), http://www.ain.cubaweb.cu/secciones.economia1.htm.

"Castro destituye a un ministro." 2002. EFE, La Habana. *El Nuevo Herald* (10 October).

Comellas, Miguel. 2003. "One millionth tourist arrives." *Granma International Digital* (30 June), http://www.granma.cu/ingles/2003/junio/lunes30/26turista-p.html.

Comisión Económica para América Latina y el Caribe (CEPAL). 2003. *Cuba: Evolución Económica Durante 2002 y Perspectivas para 2003*. LC/MEX/L.566. Santiago: CEPAL (24 July).

Comisión Económica para América Latina y el Caribe (CEPAL). 2002."Cuba," pp. 94-96 in *Balance preliminar de las economías de América Latina y el Caribe, 2002*. Santiago: CEPAL (December).

Companioni, Nelso, and Yanet Ojeda Hernández. 2002. "The Growth of Urban Agriculture." Pp. 220-236 in Fernando Funes, et al., editors, *Sus-*

tainable Agriculture and Resistance. Oakland, California: Food First Books.

"Cuba es el primer país de la lista de morosos de España." 2003. Europa Press, Madrid (May 15).

"Cuba starts to ease out the dollar." 2003. BBC News (21 July).

"Cuba's Economy in the Doldrums." 2003. Staff Report, Cuba Transition Project, University of Miami, Issue 43 (June 18).

"Cuba's Foreign Debt Crisis." 2002. _Focus on Cuba,_ Cuba Transition Project, University of Miami, Issue No. 19 (19 August).

"Designan nuevo Ministro de Finanzas y Precios." 2003. La Habana, AIN (21 June) http://www.ain.cubaweb.cu/jun2103cmministro.htm

"Destituyen en Cuba a Ministro de Transporte." 2003. AP, La Habana. _Yahoo Noticias_ (20 June).

Espinosa Chepe, Oscar. 2003a. "Anuario Estadístico 2001: Una inexplicable modificación," _Encuentro en la red_ (15 January), http://arch.cubaencuentro.com/economia/2003/01/15/11510.html

Espinosa Chepe, Oscar. 2003b. "Se agrava la crisis del comercio exterior cubano." La Habana, Cubanet (4 March). http://www.cubanet.org/CNews/y03/mar03/04a9.htm

Frank, Marc. 2003a. "Adiós al dólar en las empresas estatales," El Nuevo Herald (22 July).

Frank, Marc. 2003b. "Cuba raw sugar output seen nearing 2 million tonnes." Reuters, La Habana (14 May).

Frank, Marc. 2002. "Cuba Boosts GSP by Switching Price Base to 1997." Reuters (July 19), http://www.lanuevacuba.com/nuevacuba/notic-02-7-2110.htm

"El gobierno mantiene intacta la cúpula de poder y hace cambios en la dirección económica." 2003. AFP, La Habana. In _Encuentro en la red_ (10 March), http://www.cubaencuentro.com/sociedad/noticias/20030310/5b9b763fb0b75be24c15e85e5d4d7498.html

Inter-American Development Bank (IDB). 2003. _Sending Money Home: An International Comparison of Remittance Markets._ Washington: Inter-American Development Bank, Multilateral Investment Fund (February).

Jordan, Pav. 2003. "Aumenta el comercio entre EEUU y Cuba pese a las restricciones." Reuters, Mexico. Yahoo Noticias (17 February).

"La Habana sustituye a cuatro altos cargos de la Economía." 2003. _Encuentro en la red_ (4 March), http://www.cubaencuentro.com/sociedad/noticias/20030304/5d4bb46dc0a2c8e3641836cbfb0c54a2.html

Madruga, Aldo. 2003. "Acercar los alimentos a la mesa." _Granma_ (7 January).

Martínez, Osvaldo. 2002. "La hermosa paradoja de la economía cubana en 2002." _El Economista de Cuba Digital,_ http://www.eleconomista.cubaweb.cu/2002/nro188/188.406.html

Martori, Raquel. 2003. "Procurarán mejorar la próxima zafra azucarera." EFE, La Habana. _El Nuevo Herald_ (7 July).

Mesa-Lago, Carmelo. 2003. _The Slowdown of the Cuban Economy in 2001-2003: External Factors or Domestic Malaise?_ Coral Gables: Center for Cuban and Cuban-American Studies, University of Miami.

Mesa-Lago, Carmelo. 2001. "The Cuban Economy in 1999-2001: Evaluation of Performance and Debate on the Future." Pp. 1-17 in _Cuba in Transition—Volume 11._ Washington: Association for the Study of the Cuban Economy.

"México quiere que La Habana salde la deuda." EFE, Mexico. _El Nuevo Herald_ (3 July).

Millares, Manuel. 2002. "Lo importante es el ser humano y su desarrollo integral." Granma (23 December). http://www.granma.cubaweb.cu/2002/12/23/nacional/articulo02.html

"Ministro admite una baja en el turismo." 2002. Associated Press, La Habana. *El Nuevo Herald* 23 July). http://www.miami.com/mld/elnuevo/news/world/cuba/3714672.htm

Núñez Betancourt, Alberto. 2002a. "Incrementará Cuba presupuestos para educación, salud y seguridad social." *Granma* (21 December) http://granma.cubaweb.cu/2002/12/21/nacional/articulo11.html

Núñez Betancourt, Alberto. 2002b. "Reafirma Cuba que ampliará sus programas sociales en el 2003." *Granma* (21 December) http://granma.cubaweb.cu/2002/12/21/nacional/articulo12.html

Oficina Nacional de Estadísticas (ONE). 2002. *Anuario Estadístico de Cuba 2001*. La Habana: ONE.

Oficina Nacional de Estadísticas (ONE). 2001. *Anuario Estadístico de Cuba 2000*. La Habana: ONE.

Oramas, Joaquín. 2002. "Crece en más del 20% la extracción de petróleo en el 2002." Granma Internacional Digital (5 August). http://www.granma.cu/espanol/agosto02/lu5/32crece-e.html

Pérez-López, Jorge F. 2002. "The Cuban Economy in an Unending Special Period." Pp. 507-521 in *Cuba in Transition—Volume 12*. Washington: Association for the Study of the Cuban Economy.

Peters, Philip. 2002. *Survival Story: Cuba's Economy in the Post-Soviet Decade*. Arlington, Virginia: Lexington Institute.

Rodríguez, José Luis. 2002. "Informe sobre los resultados económicos del 2002 y el plan económico y social para el año 2003." http://www.cubagob.cu/des_eco/discursojlranpp.htm

"Rompen petroleros cubanos récords de extracción de crudo." 2002. *Granma* (25 December). http://www.granma.cubaweb.cu/2002/12/25/nacional/articulo12.html

San Martin, Nancy. 2003. "Castro shuffles posts as Cuban economy sags." *The Miami Herald* (14 July).

"Short-Term Tourism Data." 2003. *WTO World Tourism Barometer*, vol. 1, no. 1 (June).

"Sol Meliá prosigue plan de expansión." 2003. *El Nuevo Herald* (26 June).

Triana Cordoví, Juan. 2003. "La economía cubana en el 2002." Octavo Seminario Annual de la Economía Cubana. La Habana: Centro de Estudios de la Economía Cubana, February.

U.S.-Cuba Trade and Economic Council (US-CTEC). 2003. *2003 Commercial Highlights*. New York. http://www.cubatrade.org.

Valenzuela, Lídice. 2002. "Seguridad para los azucareros." *Trabajadores* (18 July) http//www.trabajadores.cubaweb.cu/2002/julio/18/portada/seguridad.htm

Varela Pérez, Juan. 2002a. "Fue un duro batallar de los azucareros." *Granma* (1 June) http://www.granma.cubaweb.cu/2002/06/01/nacional/articulos08/html

Varela Pérez, Juan. 2002b. "Vamos a moler la caña que económicamente se justifique." *Granma* (23 August) http://www.granma.cubaweb.cu/2002/08/23/nacional/articulos09/html

Ventura Nicolas, Patricia. 2003. "Cuba adeuda al país $266 millones." *El Universal* (Caracas) (8 March), in *Cubanet* (11 March), http://www.cubanet.org/Cnews/03/mar13/11o8.htm

World Bank. 2003. *Commodity Price Data Pinksheet* (May). http://www.worldbank.org/prospects/pinksheets/pink0503.htm

"World Tourism in 2002: Better than expected." 2003. World Tourism Organization Press Release, (27 January). http://www.world-tourism.org/newsroom/Releases/2003/jan/numbers2002.htm

WHY CAFTA?

Isaac Cohen

One of the main questions raised by the ongoing trade negotiations between the United States and five countries of Central America—Costa Rica, El Salvador, Guatemala, Honduras and Nicaragua—is why these very small economies have decided to negotiate a free trade agreement (the Central American Free Trade Agreement, known as CAFTA) with the biggest and most powerful economy in the world?

A second related question has to do with the reasons why these negotiations are happening now. After all, economic relations between the United States and Central America are almost two centuries old. However, never before, due to different reasons, the possibility had emerged of signing a multilateral free trade agreement between these economies.[1]

Finally, a third question has to do with some of the main lessons that can be drawn from the way these negotiations are taking place.

This essay tries to answer these questions by means of a brief review of the present state and prospects of the ongoing negotiations.

WHY NEGOTIATE?

The main justification for a small economy, or a group of smaller economies, to undertake a negotiation of a free trade agreement (FTA), or any other form of economic integration, is to overcome the limitations that the smallness of the market imposes on their growth and development. The central purpose is to attain the economies of scale that smaller markets do not allow.[2] Additionally, there are gains from the efficiency brought about by the increased competition generated by wider markets.

These are some of the most obvious benefits, derived from opening these economies, because the smallness of their markets has often led to the creation of one, or at the most two companies, which enjoy the exclusive privilege of supplying almost captive demand for their products. Those who are familiar with the economic history of Central America know that one brewery or one cement factory, for instance, has dominated these small markets without challenge, for many years.

Smaller economies negotiate FTAs because by widening and deepening their markets they become more capable of attracting foreign investment. Therefore, beyond the gains from increased trade generated by economic integration, other more dynamic benefits justify market expansion as an instrument to attract foreign investment.

---

1. With the breakdown of the multilateral trading system in the thirties, each of the five Central American governments signed bilateral, Reciprocal Trade Agreements with the United States. These agreements remained in force until the fifties, when the first steps were taken to initiate the process of Central American economic integration. ECLAC (1991, pp. 97-197).

2. The smallness of the individual Central American markets was the main argument used by the Economic Commission for Latin America and the Caribbean (ECLAC) to promote, in the early fifties, the adoption by the Central American governments of a program of economic integration. The proposal was contained in a document drafted by ECLAC's Mexico Office and presented by Raul Prebisch, then Executive Secretary of ECLAC, to the first meeting of the Central American Cooperation Committee, held in Tegucigalpa, Honduras, in August 1952. See ECLAC (1952).

The second, relatively more peremptory, objective that justifies the decision to negotiate FTAs by smaller economies, has to do with their trading partners. By definition, smaller economies that participate in international trade are "price takers." They do not have the capacity to create, or influence decisively, the conditions under which they participate in trade relations. Usually, these conditions are set by the dominant players in international trade, or by the "principal suppliers," as they have been traditionally known. For this reason, smaller economies have to exhibit an exceptional capacity to adapt to circumstances created by others, in order to obtain the benefits of international trade.

For the Central American economies, since it was their main trading partner—the United States—who decided to engage in the negotiations, they had to stand ready to negotiate once the opportunity to do so became available. Because the worst case scenario, for any small economy, is to be left out of those negotiations made possible by the disposition to negotiate of the principal players in the international trading system.

Contrary to common past perceptions, negotiations between asymmetrical trading partners are no longer perceived as having a predetermined outcome in favor of the bigger and more powerful participant. Fear of this zero-sum outcome inspired in the past a loud rhetoric of confrontation between North and South, in great measure inspired by the fact that no possibilities were perceived of achieving mutually beneficial outcomes through negotiations.

With the end of the Cold War and the emergence of one international economy, the search for these mutually beneficial outcomes has now moved beyond the rhetoric of confrontation to the negotiating table. Although some manifestations of the North-South confrontation sometimes still flare, these are better understood as part of the accepted posturing that normally precedes and accompanies the process of negotiation.

Finally, precisely because they cannot determine the conditions in which they trade, smaller economies need to actively engage in trade negotiations in order to increase their capacity to import, and therefore, their capacity to grow. Today, there is a wider recognition that imports are the main motivation to engage in international trade. The vision of a trade policy aimed at increasing exports to achieve a positive trade balance, for its own sake, is no longer dominant. In today's interdependent world economy, exports are one of the means to enable an increased capacity to import the necessary raw materials, capital goods and technologies that are essential for economic growth. In Paul Krugman's words, "imports, not exports, are the purpose of trade. That is, what a country gains from trade is the ability to import things it wants. Exports are not an objective in and of themselves" (Krugman, 1997, p. 120).

WHY NOW?

A second set of questions has to do with why the CAFTA negotiations are happening now. Given the relatively small influence that the Central American economies exercise in the international trading system, the answer to this question must be found elsewhere. The main factor that explains why these negotiations are happening now has to do with a gradual and significant change in the commercial policy of the United States.

After the end of the Second World War, among the central objectives of U.S. commercial policy was to support a multilateral trading system, which in 1948 led to the creation of the General Agreement on Tariffs and Trade (GATT). Under the conditions expressed in Article XXIV of the GATT, the United States supported, but refrained from participating in, regional or subregional processes of trade liberalization, such as what is today the European Union and, after some hesitation, the economic integration of Central America. One outstanding exception to this policy was a free trade agreement with Israel, which entered into force in 1985, mainly inspired by strategic reasons.

What has changed is this reluctance by the United States to engage in trade agreements that involved selected parties rather than concentrating on trade liberalization through the multilateral global trading system embodied in the GATT. Today, the United States is actively involved in trade negotiations of all sorts, bilateral (as those that led to bilateral agreements with Chile and Singapore—or plurilateral (as those ongoing with the five Central American economies and with the rest of the Western Hemisphere or those in the early 1990s that led to the North American Free Trade Agreement, NAFTA).

This policy shift started gradually, in 1965, with the entry into force of the agreement between Canada and the United States that was known as the Auto Pact, to regulate trade in automobiles and auto parts. The Auto Pact was so successful that by 1986, when negotiations were started for an FTA between the United States and Canada, automobile-related trade between the two countries represented one-third of their bilateral trade. The Canada-U.S. FTA entered into force in 1989 and formalized one of the most intense trading relationships existing between any pair of countries. No other pair of countries trade as much as the United Sates and Canada; today, more than one billion U.S. dollars in goods and services cross (both ways) the Canada-U.S. border each day.

In 1991, when it was announced that Mexico and the United States were about to open negotiations for a trade agreement, similar to the Canada-U.S. FTA, the Canadian government proposed to join the negotiation, thus transforming the originally-intended bilateral negotiation, into a multilateral undertaking. The concern that led to Canadian participation in what later became the NAFTA was avoiding the emergence of what has been called a "hub and spoke" type of trading arrangement (Wonnacott, 1991). The risk was that should the United States negotiate an FTA with Mexico after already having one with Canada, the United States would become a "hub" linked through bilateral agreements to different "spokes," with the spokes not having trade relations among themselves. The hub would, therefore, become the most attractive location to invest because it would have access to the spokes, while investment in the spokes would be confined to each one of them. By contrast, a multilateral arrangement, where all the parties liberalize trade among themselves, would allow more trade between the spokes, and a wider distribution of some of the dynamic benefits of trade liberalization.

NAFTA entered into force in 1994 and almost immediately began generating remarkable results. For instance, in a few years, Mexico displaced Japan as the second largest trading partner of the United States and investment flows responded accordingly. Besides the fact that it was the first trade agreement signed by the United States with a developing country, NAFTA also became the main manifestation of the adoption by the United States of a trade policy no longer based exclusively on multilateral global liberalization. Regional, subregional and even bilateral trade agreements were perceived as "building blocks" in the path toward what remained the ultimate objective of worldwide trade liberalization.

As stated in the 1995 *Economic Report of the President* of the United States, "when structured according to principles of openness and inclusiveness, regional blocs can be building blocks rather than stumbling blocks for global trade and investment. Seen in this light, carefully structured plurilateralism is a component rather than an alternative to U.S. multilateral efforts" (Council of Economic Advisers, 1995, pp. 213-214).

This meant that, henceforward, the United States would engage in all sorts of negotiations, with individual countries or groups of trading partners, to sign FTAs conceived as building blocks in the process of global trade liberalization. This policy has been characterized as "competitive liberalization," whereby the United States is willing to negotiate FTAs with those who are willing to do so. In the words of U.S. Trade Representative Robert Zoellick, through FTA negotiations, the United States is "spurring a competition in liberalization" (Zoellick, 2003).

With the exception of the U.S.-Jordan FTA, no bilateral or plurilateral negotiations were completed during the administration of President Clinton, because the Congress had not granted the President authorization to negotiate trade agreements. Only with the approval by the Congress of the United States, in August 2002, of what is known as "trade promotion authority (TPA)," formerly known as "fast track authority," several negotiations were activated, including the Doha Round within the World Trade Organization (WTO). Additionally, bilateral negotiations have been successfully completed with Chile and Singapore. Meanwhile, negotiations for the Free Trade Area of the Americas (FTAA) have moved into a more decisive phase and negotiations with the five Central American governments to create the CAFTA, have been evolving consistently toward completion by the end of 2003. Standing in line are negotiations with Morocco, Australia, the countries of the South African Customs Union (Botswana, Lesotho, Namibia, South Africa and Swaziland), Bahrain, the Dominican Republic and Colombia.

Finally, this change in policy and the consequent flurry of negotiations that it has unleashed, have not happened without generating acute criticism from detractors. Among them, the most intense criticism has come from defenders of the global trading rules embodied in the WTO.

Columbia University Professor Jagdish Baghwati, one of the most outspoken critics of bilateral and regional FTAs, has been called "the prime warrior for free trade." In testimony presented to the United States House of Representatives in April 2003, Professor Bhagwati claimed that it is among politicians that there is a preference for bilateral FTAs, while "a vast majority of economists consider them a plague on the world trading system" (Bhagwati, 2003).

The proliferation of partial, as opposed to global, trade agreements has created what Professsor Bhagwati characterizes as "a massive systemic problem," whereby trade "preferences have multiplied worldwide through varying tariff schedules based on origin and also with varying rules of origin." According to Professor Bhagwati, this is better described as a "spaghetti bowl problem, with preferences like noodles crisscrossing all over the place" (Bhagwati, 2002). Professor Bhagwati is also critical of the policy of "competitive liberalization," promoted by U.S. Trade Representative Robert Zoellick, arguing that it does not contribute to multilateral trade liberalization. "As the bilaterals multiply," Professor Bhagwati holds, "the willingness to invest more lobbying effort into pushing the multilateral envelope begins to weaken." Ambassador Robert Zoellick has responded to such criticism arguing that perhaps the critics live "in a world where everybody will agree at once to

open their markets, but that's not the world that I see out there" (King, 2002).

SOME LESSONS FROM CAFTA

One of the salient lessons that can be drawn from the undergoing CAFTA negotiations has to do with the quite extraordinary and unprecedented fact that the five Central American governments are participating as a group. It is extraordinary and unprecedented because this has not been the case until now. Even when these five governments have negotiated trade agreements together, they have made it very clear that such agreements would not apply bilaterally. This is the first time that these five governments are negotiating a trade agreement that will be enforced multilaterally. Therefore, in the ongoing trade negotiations with the United States, by contrast with other recent negotiations, the Central American governments are participating with an unprecedented degree of cohesion.

The process of Central American economic integration, which began in the fifties, has yet to lead to the emergence of a common commercial policy among the participants. The negotiations with the United States represent the very first time that these five governments attempt to negotiate an agreement that will be enforced multilaterally, rather than bilaterally, as it has been the case with other agreements negotiated recently by the Central American governments.

Several factors explain this outcome. For the Central American economies, the United States is their main trading partner, representing about half of all their international trade, and their main source of foreign direct investment. Furthermore, almost 75 percent of all Central American exports to the United States already enjoy duty free access, on account of the preferences unilaterally granted under the Caribbean Basin Initiative (CBI) and other preferences. However, these preferential arrangements are temporary and require periodic reauthorization by the Congress of the United States.

By contrast, an FTA between the United States and Central America will institutionalize, and therefore make more stable, the rules that govern an already intense and profound trade relationship. The sum of imports and exports between the United States and Central America amounted in 2002 to more than US$20 billion. Foreign direct investment from the United States amounted to more than US$3 billion in 2001.

In 2002, the Central American countries together represented a market for U.S. exports of more than US$10 billion, which ranks the region 17th—between Malaysia and Switzerland—as a market for U.S. exports. Individually, the five Central American countries ranked between 31st and 69th among markets for U.S. exports. For all these reasons, an observer has concluded that, for the Central American governments, the negotiation of a free trade agreement with the United States represents "the mother of all trade negotiations."

Another important lesson which can be drawn from the ongoing negotiations relates to the compatibility of the Central American economic integration process, which has existed for almost half a century, with the FTA they are negotiating with the United States.

Even without a formal agreement, trade relations between Central America and the United States are relatively more profound and intense. As noted above, trade relations with the United States represent half of all Central American foreign trade. By contrast, trade relations among the Central American countries represent around one third of their total foreign trade.

The process of Central American economic integration needs to be adapted and upgraded to make it compatible with the potential widening and deepening of the relationship with the United States. Otherwise, there is a risk that the countries of Central America will become more interdependent with the United States, at the expense of their relations. As a consequence, intra-Central American relations may become rarefied, as relations with the United States intensify.

Several issues demand attention within the Central American integration process. A few examples are presented here, to illustrate the sort of adaptation that will be necessary to achieve compatibility between both trade agreements.

- First and foremost is the common external tariff. If it is the intention of the Central American governments to continue acting as a group, at least in their trade relations with the United States, it will be necessary to complete the common external tariff, which according to optimistic estimates already covers around two thirds of all tariff items. Otherwise, it will be necessary to streamline and tighten the very relaxed rules of origin which prevail within the Central American integration process. Based on an honor system, present rules of origin require a sworn statement by the producer that the goods have been produced in Central America. These rules of origin need to be upgraded, at least to bring them to the same level of formality as the rules of origin that will be agreed in the CAFTA.

- A second issue that will need revision is the dispute settlement procedure that has been agreed among the Central American countries. Both the CAFTA and the Central American dispute settlement procedures should coexist harmoniously, each serving as mechanisms for solving disputes that will emerge between the Central American governments themselves and with the United States.

Be it as it may, these adaptations and adjustments to the Central American integration process will have to be done after the conclusion of the CAFTA negotiations. In the meantime, perhaps the Central American governments can agree on a general principle whereby they are willing to extend to each other the same concessions that they will grant to the United States. This general principle will assure that the process of Central American integration, at least, will not lag behind the process of liberalization that will be unleashed by the approval of the CAFTA.

REFERENCES

Bhagwati, Jagdish, 2002. *Free Trade Today.* Princeton, Princeton University Press.

Bhagwati, Jagdish, 2003. Testimony before the U.S. House of Representatives, Committee on Financial Services, Subcommittee on Domestic and International Monetary Policy, Trade and Technology. Washington, D.C. April 1.

Council of Economic Advisers, 1995. *Annual Report.* Washington, D.C., U.S. Government Printing Office.

ECLAC, 1952. *Informe preliminar del Secretario Ejecutivo de la Comisión Económica para América Latina sobre integración y reciprocidad en Centroamérica* (E-CN.12-AC.17), August 1.

ECLAC, 1991. *A Collection of Documents on Economic Relations Between the United States and Central America 1906-1956.* Santiago, Chile, United Nations.

King, Neil, 2002. "Trade Envoy: Small is Beautiful," *The Wall Street Journal*, October 25.

Krugman, Paul, 1997. *Pop Internationalism.* Cambridge, MIT Press.

Wonnacott, Ronald J., 1991. *The Economics of Overlapping Free Trade Areas and the Mexican Challenge.* Toronto, C.D. Howe Institute and Washington D.C., National Planning Association.

Zoellick, Robert B. 2003. "Our Credo: Free Trade and Competition," *The Wall Street Journal,* July 10.

CHILE'S TRADE POLICY AND THE CHILE-UNITED STATES FREE TRADE AGREEMENT

Alfie Antonio Ulloa Urrutia

The recent signing by Chile of several international trade agreements—a free trade agreement (FTA) with the United States and agreements with the European Union, the European Free Trade Association (EFTA) and Korea—as well as the launch of negotiations with Singapore and New Zealand, have definitely placed Chile at the vanguard of trade integration. The wide scope of the agreements and the importance of the partners suggests that Chilean trade policymaking has reached a high-water mark, pursuing a trade policy strategy that began to be implemented at the turn of the 1990s.

The negotiation of bilateral trade agreements is only one strand of Chile's trade policy. In fact, the Chilean trade policy strategy is based on "three principles":

- Unilateral liberalization and development of the internal market.

- Active multilateral and regional participation (World Trade Organization, Free Trade Area of the Americas, Asia Pacific Economic Forum, etc.).

- Wide and aggressive bilateral negotiations.

THE STRATEGY OF THE "THREE PRINCIPLES"

In the mid-1970s, the economic authorities of the Chilean Military Government rejected the logic of import substitution industrialization (ISI). Their view was that the internal market would grow sufficiently for efficient performance and to allow pro-

ductive sector specialization. At that time (1973), the average Chilean tariff was about 100%. There were also large variations in tariff levels across commodities, reflecting the logic of offering each sector the level of protection that would guarantee their income-yield capacity. Internationally isolated after the military coup and surrounded by a state of general autarky in the region resulting from the general application of ISI, the bilateral option was impossible. Thus if Chile lowered its tariffs, it would do it for efficiency gains, but "in exchange for nothing" with respect to the protection tariff structures of other countries. More than an integration policy, Chile's elimination of tariffs was a microeconomic reform that eliminated internal distortions caused by protectionism.

Unilateral

When the democratic government took over in 1990, Chile's customs tariff was 15% for all goods. The process of opening to international competition had hit several economic sectors hard, but shifting demand for local products for demand for imports made feasible the reallocation of resources toward the exporting sector. Exports had grown at rates exceeding 10% a year, reaching in 1990 a volume five times larger than in 1975. Convinced of the soundness of the unilateral strategy, the democratic government decided to expand it and, in 1991, lowered the general tariff from 15% to 11%. Around that time, the first opportunities for bilateral agreements surfaced, as the international community was getting ready for the Uruguay Round of the General Agreement on

Tariffs and Trade (GATT), which gave rise to the present World Trade Organization (WTO).

Multilateral

The key role of the WTO in the liberalization of world trade is not at issue: world trade liberalization can only be obtained by means of multilateral agreements. The greatest success of the WTO to date has been to develop a series of basic rules to regulate world trade and a mechanism to resolve disputes. These rules are the result of many international negotiations, culminating with the Uruguay Round Agreements in 1994. The strength of the rules is evident as they have been strong enough for the institution to withstand the failures in Seattle (1999) and Cancún (2003). Chile incorporates effectively the WTO as a center piece of its trade policy strategy, but not as an exclusive element. For this reason, Chile has negotiated and will continue to negotiate free trade agreements with partners ready to advance in reciprocal liberalization, within the general framework of the WTO. In this way, when world trade liberalization via the WTO occurs, Chile will have already "arrived" at its main markets.

Bilateral

Chile was the first country to react positively to the "Initiative for the Americas"[1] proposed by President George Bush, who in an official visit to Chile (1991) was talking about a bilateral free trade agreement (FTA). Nevertheless, more than a decade and three governments have passed before signing it, if we consider that, on the same year of Bush's visit, the experts were starting to meet to explore the long road that culminated with the signing of a Chile-U.S. FTA in December 2002. It was under the first Clinton Presidency, when the North American Free Trade Agreement (NAFTA) between the United States, Canada and Mexico came into force, that the first step was taken to start a liberalizing agenda de-signed to make a free trade area within the 34 democratic countries of the hemisphere. Soon came the First Summit of the Americas and with the launching of the negotiations toward a "Free Trade Agreement of the Americas" (FTAA), the ship of hemispheric trade integration seemed to be arriving to port.

Unfortunately for Chile and others, the negotiation of new free trade agreements beyond NAFTA required that the United States Congress bestow the authority on the Executive to negotiate such pacts: the so-called "fast track" or Fast Track Trade Negotiating Authority, more recently known as Trade Promotion Authority (TPA). This law specifies the subject matters and the objectives in each for U.S. negotiators. The Congress in exchange guarantees a fast Congressional consideration process, without amendments and within an established timeframe. The U.S. Congress, after authorizing the Executive to negotiate NAFTA and the Uruguay Round Agreements, denied for eight years the authority to sign new treaties.[2]

Chile's exports are widely distributed: the United States, Europe, Asia and Latin America each represent about 20%. This composition of exports imposed the challenge of negotiating agreements with all the continents, because concentrating on a single partner would have had created enormous trade diversion. For this reason, while the United States could not negotiate because of lack of fast track authority, Chile entered into FTAs with NAFTA partners that did not impose this requirement, with Central America and all its neighbors (simpler agreements), and also associated with MERCOSUR, ALADI and APEC. Table 1 summarizes this impressive process of negotiations.

Concurrently with these negotiations, Chile continued participating actively in the WTO and in 1998[3]

---

1. The initiative was announced in 1990, just after the FTA between U.S.A. and Canada (1989). It was a development agenda which included economic, trade and political aspects, emphasizing peace, democracy and prosperity as regional objective. It was an updating of the Monroe Doctrine of "America for the Americans" in a wide political-economic sense.

2. The authorization that Clinton received during his first term resulted in the implementation of the Uruguay Round Agreements and the NAFTA. It expired in June 1994 and was only given to George W. Bush in August 2002.

3. With the explicit objective of avoiding the trade diversion generated as the result of the associate membership in MERCOSUR

Table 1. Chilean Trade Agreements

Multilateral Agreements	Date	Observations
APEC	November 1994	Asia Pacific Economic Cooperation. Regional agreement under negotiation
FTAA	December 1994	Free Trade Agreement of the Americas. Regional agreement under negotiation.
WTO	January 1995	Uruguay Round of the WTO (Doha Round under negotiation).

Bilateral Agreements	Date in Force	Observations
Mexico	January 1992	Economic Complementarity Agreements under ALADI.
Bolivia	July 1993	
.Venezuela	July 1993	
Colombia	January 1994	
Ecuador	January 1995	
Peru	July 1998	
Argentina	May 2000	
MERCOSUR	October 1996	Chile became an associate member rather than a full member.

Free Trade Agreements	Signed	Entry into Force
Canada	December 1996	July 1997
Mexico	April 1998	August 1999
Central Americaᵃ	December 1999	January 2002
European Unionᵇ	April 2002	February 2003
Korea	October 2002	Under consideration by the Chilean Parliament.
United States	June 2003	
EFTAᶜ	June 2003	

Note: An FTA with Singapore and New Zealand is under negotiation. Bilaterals with Panama and Cuba have been waiting for approval by the Parliament for several years.

Source: DIRECON

a. Costa Rica, El Salvador, Guatemala, Honduras, Nicaragua.
b. Austria, Belgium, Denmark, Finland, France, Germany, Greece, Holland, Ireland, Italy, Luxembourg, Portugal, Spain, United Kingdom.
c. Sweden, Norway, Iceland, Lichtenstein.

went even further to open its market by lowering the tariff in force (11%) by one percentage point per year, to reach in 2003 the 6% general tariff in force today.[4]

CHILE—UNITED STATES FTA

A few days before the summit at Florianopolis (November 2000) at which MERCOSUR and Chile were going to discuss a common strategy to confront the United States in the FTAA, a formal announcement of the re-initiation of FTA negotiation between Chile and the U.S. was made. President Clinton had only a few months left in the White House and Lagos had only been a few months in La Moneda. The first round of talks occurred some time after the announcement, even though the real initiation of the

negotiations had to wait until the new Bush administration team was in place. There were negotiations every month during the whole year 2001, even though Fast Track had not been authorized. Fast track was approved—by the closest of margins—in August 2002,[5] precipitating the closing of the negotiations in December.

Understanding the FTA text is not an easy task. As any law, it is constructed and dominated by legal concepts that specify details that will govern the relationship between the partners. The composition of the negotiating teams (50-60 per country) was heavily weighted in favor of lawyers and economists from different public departments within the two governments.

---

4. The non-preferential tariff.

5. There also was a discussion about this in Chile, because there was great concern in the Chilean agricultural sector about negotiating an agreement with a power that had just approved a very large package of agricultural subsidies. Additionally, the restrictions that the Trade Promotion Authority legislation imposed on the executive left the negotiation capacity very limited. With respect to the debate in the United States, just remember that three votes in the Senate and one in the House approved the FTA.

Table 2.   Chapters in the Chile-U.S. FTA

I. Initial Provisions	XIII. Telecommunications
II. General Definitions	XIV. Temporary Entry for Business Persons
III. National Treatment and Market Access for Goods	XV. Electronic Commerce
	XVI. Competition Policy, Designated Monopolies, and State Enterprises
IV. Rules of Origin and Origin Procedures	XVII. Intellectual Property Rights
V. Customs Administration	XVIII. Labor
VI. Sanitary and Phytosanitary Measures	XIX. Environment
VII. Technical Barriers to Trade	XX. Transparency
VIII. Trade Remedies	XXI. Administration of the Agreement
IX. Government Procurement	XXII. Dispute Settlement
X. Investment	XXIII. Exceptions
XI. Cross-Border Trade in Services	XXIV. Final Provisions
XII. Financial Services	

Table 3.   Tariff Reductions for Chilean Exports to the United States

Category	Total (000US$)	%	Agriculture (000US$)	%	Industry	%
Immediate	2,756,482	87.0	865,309	84.0	1,891,173	88.5
2 years	246,542	7.8	—	0.0	246,542	11.5
4 years	5,996	0.2	5,698	0.6	298	0.0
8 years	17,420	0.5	17,401	1.7	19	0.0
10 years	248	0.0	207	0.0	41	0.0
12 years	141,508	4.5	141,508	13.7	—	0.0
Total	3,161,196	100.0	1,030,123	100.0	2,138,073	100.0

Source: DIRECON, Rosales (2003).

The 24 chapters of the legal text (Table 2), some of them generic and others specific, cover 19 issues, grouped into seven general areas of negotiation: 1) Market Access; 2) Trade Remedies; 3) Customs Rules and Standards; 4) Services; 5) Investment; 6) Labor; and 7) Environmental Issues.

Market Access

The most significant outcome is the total elimination of protective tariffs and other restrictions on mutual trade over a twelve-year period. This longer period is only applicable to the agricultural sector, because in two years all non-agricultural trade will be free. Table 3 shows the schedule for phase out of the tariffs.[6] As it was anticipated, the most important sensitivities were in the agricultural sector, where full liberalization requires a 12-year period.

Nuovissimos

That the Chile-U.S. FTA is up to date with the millennium is evident in the commitments on Electronic Commerce, the first agreement in the world with a chapter that maintains cyberspace free of protective tariffs and barriers. Both countries commit not to apply protective tariffs to digitalized products, which could be sent by electronic means or that are transmitted through other means.

The chapter on Government Procurement is an extraordinary achievement in the negotiation and maybe the only one that can be guaranteed as pure business creation with respect to Chile. Since the 1930s, the *Buy American Act* prohibits the U.S. Federal Government from buying foreign goods. The only way to change such obstacle to trade and for Chile to accede with certainty to this enormous and previously blocked market is by means of this Chapter. The

---

6. The only exception with respect to the United States is tobacco. Sugar has a special tariff mechanism in both countries.

agreement actually extends coverage beyond the Federal Government and to several States.[7]

Controversial

No part of the agreement was discussed as intensely as Labor and Environmental issues. Chile did not want to negotiate them as part of the Agreement, and preferred a "parallel" solution along the lines of the agreement signed with Canada, following the NAFTA model.[8] The local business community anticipated a disaster if these topics were handled within the agreement and even the Chilean-North American Chamber of Commerce was opposed to it. The final result shows the political importance of this issue in the United States. This chapter was not effectively negotiated until Congress approved TPA (which includes it as a *sine qua non* requirement). At the end of the day, there is a Labor chapter in the agreement, and fines (of up to US$20 million) and commercial business sanctions (as a last measure) are included.

The parties maintained their right to set labor standards, consistent with international labor standards of the International Labor Organization (ILO). Both countries agreed to effectively enforce their own laws in five specific areas: freedom of association; collective bargaining; working conditions; forced labor; elimination of child labor and minimum age to work.

On environment, the commitments are the same regarding effective enforcement of environmental laws, even though there are no minimum international standards. Summarizing, any "action or inaction" with respect to the application of domestic environmental laws is susceptible to a lawsuit, if it harms trade. Neither party can relax environmental laws to promote trade or attract investment. The Environmental chapter includes an annex with specific cooperation programs between both countries.

The main impact of these obligations will fall on the Chilean Congress. This new factor will have to be considered before any modification in labor or environmental norms. The corresponding authorities will also need to be transformed, since they are the ones in charge of enforcing the law.

Services

Chile assumed a commitment to open widely the services market, across borders (e.g. Electronic Commerce), as a result of physical movement of the seller or the buyer (Temporary Entrance), or because of presence in the territory of the other country to provide it (Investment). There are commitments of "regulatory equality," independent of the provider's origin; this means the regulator can not discriminate because of nationality and must maintain the same requirements. Commitments regarding transparency were also included. Thus both countries must consult with each other before changing regulatory matters and their views must be taken into account.

The assumed commitments on investment ensure the protection of foreign investments within a defined and predictable framework, with the same rights and requirements than national investments. In addition, the investor's rights are clearly defined, avoiding frivolous demands of "dreamers" and demands against the State like the ones that destabilized NAFTA through claims of indirect expropriation. It is expected that the commitments assumed by Chile, granting greater certainty and credibility to the protection and equal treatment of investments, will attract higher levels of U.S. investment.

Capital Flows

Another particularly complex topic was resolved during the last days of the negotiations: the attributions of the Central Bank of Chile in the regulation of capital flows. The topic is important for Chile, because

---

7. Total expenditures of the U.S. Government in 1998 were US$1.49 trillion, 32% of the GDP. Federal expenditures on goods alone were US$35.5 billion and at the state level US$94.5 billion.

8. This, together with the elimination of antidumping, were the most explicit, most important objectives for the Chilean authorities, although it is not known if it was done for strategic reasons or for conviction. Antidumping is one of the defense mechanisms that the United States uses and that it can continue applying to Chile since it was not limited in the FTA, although it was limited in the U.S.-Canada FTA.

in order to avoid the volatility of speculative, short-term capital flows, the Chilean monetary authority applied a reserve requirement that made more difficult the movement of such capital. The last time it was applied, between January 1996 and June 1998, the requirement was 30%, to be reduced to 10%, and then to 0%. Even though at the time of the negotiations the requirement is not applied (in other words, a reserve requirement of 0% was applied) the ability to apply such requirement is one of the attributions that the law grants to monetary authorities.

The dispute became a great political and academic issue. Chile's Finance Minister, Nicolás Eyzaguirre, former Research Director of the Central Bank, traveled to the deciding meeting in Washington. His counterpart was John Taylor, U.S. Under Secretary of the Treasury. It was a question of principle for the United States that there be no restrictions on the capital movements of its investors. Chile did not want to diminish the faculties of the Central Bank and preferred to maintain the ability of the monetary authorities through the tools already available.

The result was a "creative" formula to preserve both positions. The Central Bank kept most of its attributions and can impose restrictions on capital flows for one year without having to give explanations or compensation. It can also keep them for another year, but then the U.S. may challenge it through the Dispute Settlement mechanism of the agreement. Chile could then establish a cash reserve for two years and, starting the second year, a Panel could determine if the measure "substantially affects transfers."[9]

CONCLUSIONS

It took twelve years for Chile to finalize a Free Trade Agreement with the United States. But Chile did not waste time during the prolonged negotiations. Chile signed agreements with all of Europe, its Latin American neighbors, and South Korea, reaffirming its leadership as an open economy and its development policy based on export growth. Thus, it diversified its trading partners and avoided its dependency in any of them. At the same time, it grew impressively and consolidated its position as the country with the lowest investment risk in the region.

With the same degree of patience, Chile will have to wait another twelve years to see the complete elimination of U.S. protective tariffs, quotas and other barriers as a result of the FTA. This long time only applies to 4.5% of bilateral trade (agricultural trade) because industrial tariffs will disappear after the second year of implementation of the agreement.

The impact of the FTA on the Chilean economy is uncertain in magnitude, but no doubt positive. The elimination of U.S. tariff and other protections and the certainty of zero tariffs in the future, will add value to exports and will diversify the products basket in the short and medium term. The effect on investment can be even greater: as of right now, any U.S. company that wishes to invest in Latin America will see in Chile a much more solid and attractive partner than in any other country in the region.

These achievements are outstanding. It is now in the private sector's hands to take advantage of the opportunities the government has opened for them through the negotiation of a Chile-U.S. Free Trade Agreement.

---

9. The regulations of the Monetary Authority refer to the formal market. Thus, an argument can be made on whether there is a substantial impediment to transfers.

REFERENCES

Banco Central de Chile. "Comercio entre Chile y los Estados Unidos," Trade Statistics, February, 2001.

Chomo, Grace. "Free Trade Agreements between Developing and Industrialized Countries: Comparing the U.S.-Jordan FTA with Mexico's Experience under NAFTA." U.S. International Trade Commission Working Paper, 2002.

Frankel, Jeffrey and Romer, David. "Does trade cause growth?" *The American Economic Review*, Vol. 89-3, 1999.

Harrison, Glenn, Rutherford, Thomas and Tarr, David. "Trade Policy Options for Chile: A Quantitative Evaluation." The North-South Agenda Papers, May, 1997.

Harrison, Glenn, Rutherford, Thomas and Tarr, David, "NAFTA, MERCOSUR and additive regionalism in Chile: A quantitative evaluation," Washington, D.C., 1997.

Larraín, Felipe and Coeymans, Juan E., "Efectos de un Acuerdo de Libre Comercio entre Chile y Estados Unidos: Un enfoque de equilibrio general." *Cuadernos de Economía*, No. 94, December, 1994.

Meller, Patricio. *Un siglo de economía política chilena (1890-1990)*. Ed. Andrés Bello. Santiago, 1998.

O.D.E.P.A. "Inserción de la agricultura chilena en los mercados internacionales." Working Paper, No. 3, Santiago de Chile, December, 2001.

Rodrik, Dani. *Institutions for High-Quality Growth: What They are and How to Acquire Them*. Working Paper 7540. NBER, February, 2000.

Rodrik, Dani. "Trade Policy Reform as Institutional Reform." 2000, available at http://ksghome.harvard.edu/~.drodrik.academic.ksg/Reform.PDF

Rosales, Osvaldo. "El TLC Chile-Estados Unidos," 2003, available at www.direcon.cl/frame/acuerdos_internacionales/documentos/TLC-AMCHAM-abril2003.pdf

Rutherford, Thomas and Tarr, David, "Regional Trading Arrangements for Chile: Do the Results Differ with a Dynamic Model?" Trade Division, Word Bank, April, 1999.

Sáez, Sebastián. *Estrategia y Negociación en el Sistema Multilateral de Comercio*. Ed. Dolmen. Santiago, 1999.

Sáez, Sebastián and Valdés, Juan Gabriel. "Chile y su política comercial 'lateral.'" *Revista de la CEPAL*, No. 67, Abril, 1999.

OUTPUT AND PRODUCTIVITY IN CUBA: COLLAPSE, RECOVERY, AND MUDDLING THROUGH TO THE CROSSROADS

Ernesto Hernández-Catá

More than a decade after the collapse of central planning in most former communist countries and the disintegration of the USSR, Cuba remains an "island of socialism" in the Caribbean sea, 90 miles from the United States. All along, and in spite of massive economic difficulties, the survival, of "socialism" has been the authorities' explicit objective. So far they have achieved their goal through a combination of political determination, some good and some very bad economic policies, and a steep deterioration in the living standards of the Cuban population. This paper tries to explain the behavior of output and productivity in Cuba in the period since 1989, with particular emphasis on the role of macroeconomic and structural policies, and attempts to provide some basis for evaluating the outlook for the Cuban economy under alternative policy scenarios.

MACROECONOMIC DEVELOPMENTS SINCE 1989: A BRIEF OVERVIEW

This remarkable and turbulent period of Cuban economic history can be broken down into three distinct phases.[1]

- Collapse and brute force policy response, 1989-1993. This first phase begins when Gorbachov, facing serious difficulties of his own, slashed the generous subsidies that the USSR had been providing to Cuba, notably the subsidy on Soviet oil

deliveries. Beginning in 1991, a triumphant but cash constrained-Russia under Boris Yeltsin dismantled what remained of the former Soviet Union's massive plan of assistance to Cuba. The Cuban government's response was blunt. Price controls were tightened, with the predictable result that rationing, queues, and power shortages became more widespread. Trying to maintain social spending and granting large subsidies to loss-making enterprises, the government ran increasingly large budget deficits that were financed predominantly by monetary expansion. This resulted in a growing monetary overhang as many prices remained under administrative control, and skyrocketing inflation in black markets. Domestic output and productivity collapsed, and so did household consumption and capital formation. The value of the Cuban dollar fell sharply in the black market

- Reform and stabilization, 1994-96. In this phase, a new strategy is implemented that combines (i) macroeconomic stabilization (a sharp fall in the fiscal deficit though deep cuts in government expenditure including social spending and subsidies to enterprises, and an absolute decline in the money supply); and (ii) structural reforms (creation of basic cooperative units and free farmer's markets in agriculture, legalization

---

1. This period is curiously referred to by the Cuban officials as the "special period" (*período especial*).

27

of self-employment and de-criminalization of the holding and use of U.S. dollars). Abruptly, output and labor productivity stopped falling in 1994 and recovered strongly in 1995-96. The fiscal deficit plunged, inflation vanished from both official and parallel markets, the monetary overhang shrank, and the peso appreciated in the unofficial market.

• Backtracking and muddling through, 1997-2001. The measures introduced in 1993-94 were clearly successful from an economic point of view. From the perspective of the government, however, they had created political problems. The incomes of the self-employed, some of the private farmers, and some in the tourist-related sector, including prostitutes, rose much faster than the wages of state employees, which had fallen dramatically in real terms during the early 1990s. In response, the government failed to pursue the reforms and even backtracked in some areas, for example by increasing the taxation of self-employment activities.

Can these developments be explained? There is, in fact, not much of a mystery about the first phase. First, the elimination of Soviet subsidies on sugar and nickel imports from, and fuel exports to, Cuba was a massive negative terms-of-trade shock for both households and enterprises. Second, the end of Russian loans to Cuba and the corresponding fall in Cuba's foreign saving led to a steep decline in domestic investment. Third, the collapse of trade arrangements with the CEMA disrupted Cuba's foreign trade and curtailed supplies of materials and capital goods to domestic enterprises. These events prompted a bad policy response that led to increasing distortions, rationing, and a massive increase in the budget deficit. All the ingredients for a deep economic crisis appeared to be present.

In a previous paper,[2] hereafter referred to as "Mirage or Reality," I considered three possible explanations

for the economic recovery in the second phase: (a) that the recovery never took place and was a mere statistical fabrication; (b) that it reflected the keynesian effects of demand-side shocks; and (c) that it resulted from the macroeconomic and structural measures adopted in 1993-94. The paper concluded that there was little empirical support for the first two hypotheses, while the third one seemed to be consistent with the evidence. In particular, the slashing of subsidies to loss-making enterprises helped to bring down the deficit, the money supply, inflation in some sectors, and the monetary overhang in others. Private employment surged with the creation of agricultural markets and the self-employment sector, absorbing the workers released by troubled state enterprises and still allowing for a decline in unemployment. I will argue that continued growth in 1998-2001 reflected the lagged effects of reform and stabilization and could have been much higher had it not been for the lack of perseverance, and in some cases the backtracking on structural policies. Macroeconomic policy, so far, has remained appropriately cautious.

The conclusions of "Mirage or Reality" seemed consistent with the data and with theory, but the scope for empirical analysis was severely constrained by the data set used.[3] The analysis relied mostly on a Dennison-style "growth accounting exercise" to show that the drop in investment in the first half the 1990s had made a significant contribution to the decline in real GDP. But it also concluded that much of that decline, and much of the subsequent rise beginning in 1994, was "accounted" for by movements in residual total factor productivity (TFP). The paper provided some evidence from panel regressions for all the transition countries including Cuba, of a correlation between these movements and the size of the non-state sector. But the paucity of data precluded a rigorous analysis of the effect of other policy variables, so that much of the swings in TFP continued to reflect the "measure of our ignorance."

---

2. See Hernández-Catá (2001).

3. The study relied mostly on annual aggregate GDP, saving, investment, and monetary/fiscal data from 1989 to 1998 for a total of only 10 annual observations.

This paper relies on a more extensive database provided by the sectoral national account and wage/employment data to extend the analysis of "Mirage or Reality." The main objectives of the paper are:

1. To estimate, on the basis of time-series/cross-section regressions, a sectoral model of the Cuban economy's supply side.

2. To use the model to analyze the contribution of exogenous shocks and shifts in policy-related variables to changes in TFP and output during the past decade or so. These variables include the rationing of energy; the discount on the peso in the parallel foreign exchange market; the subsidization of loss-making enterprises; and the share of growth of non-state employment.

3. To perform model simulations of the possible evolution of potential GDP on the basis of alternative assumptions about economic policy.

THE DATA

These objectives require a substantial increase in the number of observations in comparison with that used in the earlier paper. To that effect, this paper relies on the data for nominal and real GDP, average monthly wages and employment broken down by productive sectors. This data is provided in the *Anuario Estadístico de Cuba, 2000*[4] for the period 1994-2000. Estimates of GDP deflators by sector can be obtained by dividing nominal GDP by the corresponding constant 1981 price series. The data can be backdated to 1985 (for GDP and price deflators) and to 1989 (for employment and wages) on the basis of the Economic Commission for Latin America's *La economía cubana: Reformas estructurales y desempeño en los noventa* (CEPAL 2000). More complete definitions and sources of data are provided in Annex 1.

To sum up, a complete set of output, employment, and price-wage data is available from 1989 to 2000 (12 years). With seven sectors, this yields a total of 84 observations. The relatively small "financial institutions" sector and the large and heterogeneous "others" sector[5] were excluded from the regressions for two reasons: (i) production data in those sectors is probably based on scaled up input data and not on measures of physical output; and (ii) the discontinuity beginning in 1994 between CEPAL and official Cuban statistics is particularly large for those sectors. Still, the use of sectoral, as opposed to economy-wide, data allows for a large increase in degrees of freedom.

A visual inspection of the data set reveals a number of "stylized facts":

- As shown in Table 1, total GDP, as well as GDP in most sectors, peaks in the late 1980s (agriculture, transportation, industry and total GDP) or in 1990 (construction and electricity). Output then contracts in all these sectors and reaches a trough in 1993 (industry and electricity) or in 1994 (agriculture, construction, aggregate GDP). The commercial sector, where output had started to decline already in 1986, also bottomed out in 1994. All these sectors recovered strongly in the next few years and stabilized in the late 1990s. The pronounced u-shaped pattern of output in most sectors is illustrated in Figure 1.

- Employment is a lagged indicator of economic activity. In most key sectors (industry, construction, transportation and commerce) state employment begins to fall in 1989 and continues to decline beyond the trough in GDP (Table 2). State sector employment finally bottoms out in 1995 (in construction and transportation) or in 1996 (agriculture and commerce). Industrial employment reaches its trough later, in 1998.

- Employment in the non-state sector is very small until 1993. It surges in 1994-96 and then stabilizes at around 25% of total employment (Table 3).

4. Referred to hereafter as *AEC* (2001).

5. This sector, officially labeled "social, communal and personal services," includes education, public health, R&D expenditure, and military and security spending.

Figure 1. Cuba: Real GPD in U-Shaped Sectors

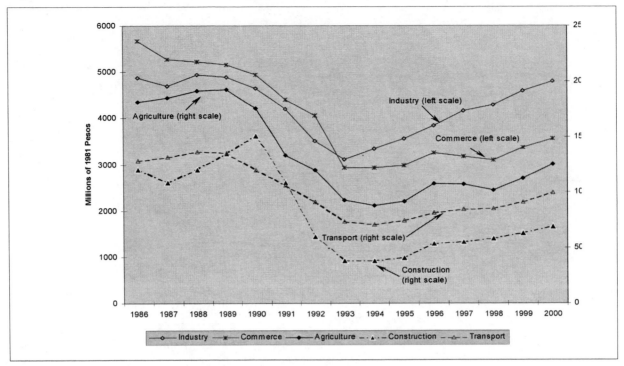

Table 1. Cuba: Real GDP by Sectors

Year	Total	Agriculture	Industry	Construction	Transport	Commerce	Electricity	Mining	Finance	Other
					(millions of pesos, at 1981 prices)					
1986	20385	1813	4869	1205	1283	5661	367	114	1642	3431
1987	19934	1852	4691	1085	1319	5271	391	119	1653	3552
1988	20644	1916	4943	1207	1363	5224	414	117	1682	3778
1989	20960	1925	4887	1350	1353	5151	452	123	1729	3992
1990	20349	1756	4640	1508	1202	4936	455	92	1760	4000
1991	18415	1335	4200	1085	1059	4396	427	82	1807	4025
1992	16591	1197	3507	604	912	4050	378	106	1722	4116
1993	14332	925	3104	386	733	2936	335	96	1699	4118
1994	12868	879	3341	384	709	2935	350	98	492	3681
1995	13185	916	3555	412	748	2985	384	152	484	3548
1996	14218	1075	3835	539	813	3251	398	177	519	3611
1997	14572	1074	4155	556	845	3176	422	182	545	3619
1998	14754	1018	4291	588	855	3090	427	184	599	3703
1999	15674	1123	4595	632	912	3370	430	186	637	3790
2000	16556	1253	4794	693	995	3551	468	213	671	3918
					(percent of total GDP)					
1989	100%	9%	23%	6%	6%	25%	2%	1%	8%	19%
1993	100%	6%	22%	3%	5%	20%	2%	1%	12%	29%
1994	100%	7%	26%	3%	6%	23%	3%	1%	4%	29%
1997	100%	7%	29%	4%	6%	22%	3%	1%	4%	25%
2000	100%	8%	29%	4%	6%	21%	3%	1%	4%	24%

Source: See Annex 1.

Table 2. Cuba: Employment in the State Sector

Year	Total	Agriculture[a]	Industry[b]	Construction	Transport[c]	Commerce[d]	Electricity[e]	Mining	Finance[f]	Other[g]
					(Thousands of workers)					
1989	3527	736	686	319	236	435	41	34	65	976
1990	3569	785	685	310	233	431	41	39	65	981
1991	3579	831	663	305	229	420	40	40	66	985
1992	3542	838	655	288	215	416	43	43	57	989
1993	3470	846	646	232	198	413	44	40	55	995
1994	3034	815	569	180	179	333	42	32	49	836
1995	2917	675	513	179	177	314	34	22	37	966
1996	2961	683	520	180	185	318	35	24	37	979
1997	3003	752	472	192	169	351	41	43	53	932
1998	3007	733	459	179	175	355	46	47	48	965
1999	3005	714	513	167	157	375	51	21	54	952
2000	3005	714	513	168	157	375	51	21	54	952
					(Percent of total state employment)					
1989	100%	23%	18%	6%	6%	11%	1%	1%	1%	33%
1993	100%	25%	16%	6%	6%	12%	1%	1%	2%	31%
1994	100%	24%	15%	6%	6%	12%	2%	2%	2%	32%
1997	100%	24%	17%	6%	5%	12%	2%	1%	2%	32%
2000	100%	24%	17%	6%	5%	12%	2%	1%	2%	32%

Source: See Annex 1.

a. Includes fisheries and hunting
b. Includes sugar refining
c. Includes warehousing and communications
d. Includes hotels and restaurants
e. Includes gas and water supply
f. Includes real estate and services to enterprises.
g. Includes public administration, defense, education, research and development, public health, culture and sports, and other services.

Table 3. Employment in the Non State Sector

Year	Total[a]	Total[b]	Agriculture	Mines	Industry	Electricity	Construction	Commerce	Transport	Finance	Other	Residual[c]
						(Thousands of workers)						
1991	...	255	138	2	45	3	21	29	16	4	507	-510
1992	...	280	130	4	50	3	22	33	17	5	547	-531
1993	...	343	142	4	59	4	21	38	19	5	553	-501
1994	...	671	163	6	113	8	36	66	21	10	592	-344
1995	702	688	160	3	122	8	42	74	27	9	229	14
1996	707	686	159	0	121	8	42	74	23	9	228	21
1997	740	721	182	7	114	10	46	85	20	13	225	19
1998	789	768	189	6	118	12	46	91	24	12	248	21
1999	868	842	198	22	124	15	41	107	24	15	271	26
2000	892	865	224	30	102	2	37	99	38	1	307.	27
						(Share of total non-state employment)						
2000	100%	97%	25.9%	3.4%	11.8%	0.3%	4.2%	11.4%	4.3%	0.1%	35.5%	3.1%

Source: AEC (2001), CEPAl (2000), and author's calculations.

a. Includes mixed entreprises
b. Excludes mixed entreprises
c. Includes mixed entreprises and, before 1994, the discrepancy between AEC (2001) and CEPAL (2000) data.

- Average real wages[6] in the state sector drop continuously from 1991 to 1995 (by more than one half in industry, construction and commerce) and rise slowly thereafter.

- The rate of inflation (based on the GDP deflator) increases rapidly in 1993 and 1994, falls by about half in 1995 and remains very low, or negative, thereafter. Sectoral prices rise sharply from 1992 to 1995, particularly in industry and agriculture) and stabilize thereafter. The exception is electricity and gas where prices are kept stable through rationing. Unofficial indexes of free and black market prices show a much sharper acceleration in 1993-94 and a steep decline thereafter.

THE MODEL

The model seeks to explain the supply side of the economy by combining three equations for each sector: a production function, a labor supply function, and a demand for labor function.

In each sector, the **production function** is assumed to be of the Cobb-Douglas variety:

$$Y_{it} = N_{it}^{\alpha} K_{it}^{1-\alpha} A_{it} \qquad (1)$$

where Y is real GDP (1981 prices) N is effective employment, K is the capital stock and A is total factor productivity. The subscript i denotes the sector (see Table 1) and the subscript t the year (t=1989 to 2000). Using lower case letters to represent natural logarithms, equation (1) becomes

$$y_{it} = \alpha \, n_{it} + (1-\alpha) \, k_{it} + a_{it} \qquad (2)$$

The **labor supply function** expresses employment in the state sector as a log-linear function of the real wage $(w-p_c)$—the nominal wage rate divided by the consumption deflator—and n* the average worker's maximum daily work capacity times the potential labor force. The parameter θ represents the relative preference of workers for consumption over leisure.

$$n_{it} = \theta \, (w - p_c)_{it} + n^{*}_{it} \qquad (3)$$

Equation (4) assumes that household income consists only of wages. The assumption is realistic in that Cuban households do not receive interest, dividends or capital gains since state enterprises are not allowed to issue equities or bonds. The assumption is restrictive, however, in that some households in Cuba do receive foreign currency transfers from their relatives or acquaintances abroad; since 1994, these transfers can be used to purchase goods in "dollar stores."

The **demand for labor** reflects maximization of enterprise profits subject to the constraint imposed by the production function (1), which implies the equality of the marginal productivity of labor and the real wage rate $(w_i - p_i)$ where p_i is the GDP deflator for sector i.

$$y_{it} - n_{it} = ln(\alpha) + w_{it} - p_{it} \qquad (4)$$

Combining equations (3) and (4) and substituting into the production function (2) gives the **aggregate supply function** for each productive sector.

$$y_{it} = v_i + (1-\alpha) \, k_{it} + \beta \, n^s_{it} + \beta \, (p-p_c)_{it} + \alpha/(1-\alpha) \, n^{*}_{it} + a_{it} \qquad (5)$$

where $\alpha\theta = \beta/(1+\beta)$, and v_i is a sector-specific constant. Equation (5) provides the general form of the estimated equations presented in Table 4.

STATISTICAL ISSUES AND REGRESSION RESULTS

Before moving to the measurement of factor inputs and TFP, there are a number of data issues that must be confronted. First, there is a significant discontinuity in the employment and national accounts data derived from CEPAL (for 1989-1993) and those taken from the *AEC* (for 1994-2000). To deal with this problem, the regressions include a dummy variable (d) equal to one from 1994 to 2000 and to zero otherwise. It is used in the equations reported in Table 4, both in additive form, and multiplied by the state employment and relative price variable. This is not an ideal solution, however, because the dummies could be picking up effects other than the statistical discontinuity. In particular, since 1994 was the first

---

6. Based on the GDP deflator.

Table 4. Panel Regression Results for Sectoral Supply Functions[a]

Variable:	State employment n^s	Relative price $p - p_c$	Non-state sector proxy $\sigma(n^{ns}-n^s)$	Exchange rate premium x	Real subsidies s	Power consumption c_E	1994 dummy d	dummy X state employment $d\,n^s$	dummy X relative prices $d\,(p-p_c)$	Adjusted R-squared
(Equation)										
(a)	0.289 (1.49)						0.886 (3.41)	-0.179 (3.78)		0.954
(b)	0.247 (1.42)	-0.925 (5.80)					1.176 (4.29)	-0.16 (3.97)	1.012 (4.66)	0.957
(c)	0.247 (1.42)	-0.925 (5.80)					1.18 (4.29)	-0.165 (3.99)	1.011 (4.66)	0.969
(d)	0.385 (2.30)	-0.823 (5.45)	1.407 (3.48)				1.001 (3.88)	-0.07 (1.61)	0.771 (3.61)	0.973
(e)	0.452 (3.36)	-0.542 (4.21)	1.171 (3.60)	-0.430 (6.38)			1.115 (5.34)	-0.154 (4.87)	0.656 (3.82)	0.983
(f)	0.444 (3.39)	-0.59 (4.64)	0.964 (2.91)	-0.280 (2.96)	-0.159 (2.15)		0.987 (4.65)	-0.159 (5.12)	0.737 (4.29)	0.984
(g)	0.152 (1.49)	-0.412 (4.33)	0.681 (2.81)	-0.086 (1.16)	-0.064 (1.66)	0.609 (7.97)	0.78 (4.98)	-0.11 (4.68)	0.72 (5.77)	0.991

a. The dependent variable in all equations is the natural logarithm of real GDP. Figures in parenthesis below the coefficients are t statistics. Each equation includes a constant term and a set of 6 sectoral dummies. The sample includes 84 observations.

full year of reform, the dummy variables could be capturing the effects on TFP and GDP growth of omitted structural change variables, including the emphasis on state enterprise profitability after 1994.

Labor and Capital Inputs

Measurement of the non-state sector. It would have been desirable to explain separately output in the state and non-state (private and cooperative) sectors. Unfortunately, real GDP data by type of ownership are available only for the overall economy. It is possible, however, to obtain employment data disaggregated both by type of production and by ownership (see Annex 1). On this basis, a variable was constructed[7] and used in the regressions to take some account of the rapid rise in the non-state sector after the measure taken in 1993-94. The coefficient of this variable is positive as expected (total output increases

when the share of the more productive non-state employment rises) and consistently significant.

Employment in state enterprises. Ideally, the variable n should represent the effective labor input defined as the number of employed adjusted for the average number of hours worked and the effort supplied by the average worker. This is important in Cuba, as it was in other communist countries in the past. Because of the government's reluctance to create open unemployment, state enterprises tend to react to a fall in demand not by firing workers but by cutting real wages, to which workers react by lowering the number of hours worked (through absenteeism, goofing off, or giving up second jobs). Unfortunately, data for hours worked, overtime, and shifts, is not available in Cuba, and data for work effort does not exist. Thus, a key aspect of the cyclical behavior of labor markets cannot be analyzed.

---

7. This variable is the difference between the logarithms of non-state and state employment ($n^{ns}-n^s$) multiplied by the share of non-state employment into total employment ($\sigma = N^{ns}/N$).

In table 4 the coefficient of the state employment variable (β) implies values of $\alpha\theta$ between 0.13 and 0.33 for 1989-93 and between 0.08 and 0.24 for 1994-2000 (the second range is obtained by using the coefficient of the multiplicative dummy). The coefficient α cannot be identified from the estimated supply function. But even assuming a fairly high income elasticity of labor supply (say, $\theta = 1$) the estimates of α would average about 0.20. This is unusually low by the standards of econometric studies in other countries, and particularly given the tendency of estimated production functions in the United States to reveal the opposite problem: a high labor coefficient of 1 or more.[8]

Relative prices. The most disturbing result stemming from Table 4 is the negative (and strangely significant) value of the coefficients for the relative price variable in 1989-93. For 1994-2000, the coefficient is positive and ranges from 0.08 to 0.23, not way out of line with the coefficients of the state employment variable. But there is no reason why the estimate for the previous period should have a negative sign. It could be that the labor market equations are misspecified, for reasons suggested earlier, that the dummy variables are messing up the results, and/or that the true underlying production function is not Cobb-Douglas.

Capital stock. While *aggregate* investment data is available for the whole economy from 1989 on, investment *by sector* is available only from 1994. These data were used to build sectoral capital stock variables that in turn were used to estimate supply functions for the seven sectors for the shortened period 1994-2000. However, the estimated coefficients of the capital stock variables were statistically insignificant. This is probably because the data are not good (among other things, data for individual sectors do not differentiate between business fixed investment, residential construction, and inventory accumulation.

Total Factor Productivity (TFP)

TFP is defined as the set of economic, technological administrative and political variables that affect the organization of economic activity for given values of labor and capital. In particular, TFP includes the effect of policy variables, and is therefore the central part of the present study. In addition to the non-state sector labor differential (which is included as a statistical adjustment given the unavailability of non-state GDP data), four key variables were used:

Exchange rate premium on the U.S. dollar (x_t). This variable is the log-difference between the parallel market exchange rate and the official market rate between the peso and the U.S. dollar. Variables of this sort are frequently used in empirical studies of growth in developing countries as proxies for the intensity of distortions.[9] In the Cuban case it may capture, among other things, the effects of price controls. In Table 4, the coefficient of the variable x is negative and significant, except in equation (f) where its t-value is lowered by the high correlation between x and the energy consumption variable.[10]

Real government subsidies (s_t). The specific variable used here is the real value of government subsidies provided to loss-making enterprises. The role of this variable is not to capture the *direct* effects of these subsidies on state enterprise production (subsidies for losses, just as taxes on profits, do not affect the firm's profit maximization plan) but rather to capture the general effects of soft-budget constraints on overall enterprise productivity. In effect, these subsidies keep unprofitable enterprises alive, thus absorbing scarce resources that could otherwise be used

---

8. In reviewing possible explanations for this high value of the estimated labor coefficient, Berrnake and Parkinson (1991) suggest three possibilities: a bias due to technological shocks, a bias due to labor hoarding, and the effect of increasing returns. The first two explanations are relevant to the Cuban case (the Soviet oil shock of the late 1980s /early 1990s, and the tendency for labor hoarding by state enterprises). Yet the estimated values of α derived from Table 4 seems very low.

9. The subscript t indicates that the exchange premium changes over time but is the same for all productive sectors.

10. Every sector of the economy confronts the same exchange rate premium, so that the sectoral index i can be omitted. The same holds for government subsidies, in this case because data by sector is not available.

Table 5.   Cuba: Growth Accounting and Medium-Term Scenarios

Period	(a) 1990-93	(b) 1994-96	(c) 1998-01	Medium term scenarios (d) Reform	(e) Current policy
(Average annual rates)					
Actual real GDP growth	**-10**	**3**	**5**	**10**	**-2**
(Contributions to the growth of real GDP, in percentage points at annual rates)					
Input growth	**0**	**-3**	**-2**	**1**	**1**
Capital formation	0	-2	-2	2	0
State employment growth	0	-1	0	-1	1
Total factor productivity growth	**-8**	**10**	**5**	**9**	**-3**
Changes in exchange rate premium	-2	2	0	1	-2
Non-state sector growth	0	2	0	7	0
Changes in power consumtion	-5	3	3	0	0
Subsidies to loss making entreprises	-1	3	2	1	-1
Other variables, including unexplained residual	-2	-4	2	0	0

Source: Regression coefficients from Table 4; and author's estimates.

more efficiently by other (state or non-state) enterprises. They also convey to firms in general the message that enterprise managers need not work hard to cut losses by increasing productivity, because in any event they will be bailed out at the expense of the budget. The estimated coefficient of subsidies is thus expected to be negative, and this is confirmed by the results in Table 4, even though significance drops in equation (f), probably because of multicollinearity.

Electricity consumption in real terms (c^E_t). In the late 1980s the Soviet Union suspended shipments of heavily subsidized oil to Cuba in exchange for sugar[11] Forced to satisfy its oil requirements (which accounted for the bulk of its energy use) by buying in the world market at market prices, and given the critical shortage of foreign exchange it was experiencing, the Cuban government decided to ration energy supplies to both households and enterprises. For the latter, the result was a massive adverse technological shock that resulted in generalized output cuts. As expected, the coefficient of the variable c^E_t in Table 4 is positive, meaning that a decrease in the oil quota assigned

to a particular sector or enterprise results in a contraction of output.

CAN WE EXPLAIN THE 1990s?

The coefficients reported in Table 4 were used to perform a backward looking growth exercise for the three sub-periods within the so-called "special period":

- The period of contraction (1989-93) associated with the end of Soviet aid and characterized by a steep fall in output.

- The period of recovery (1994-96), following the stabilization and liberalization measures adopted in 1993-94.

- The period of "muddling through" (1997-2000) characterized by the cessation of further structural reforms (and even the backtracking in some areas), but with continued emphasis on macroeconomic stability.

The results are summarized in Table 5. For every year in the sample, the contribution of each explanatory variable was calculated by multiplying the per-

_____

11. As well as the additional supplies of oil that Cuba could sell in the open market to obtain foreign exchange.

centage change in that variable by the corresponding estimated coefficient. For example,

$$C(X_t) = \gamma \, \Delta \, ln(X_t) = \gamma \, \Delta \, x_t$$

Where $C(X)$ is the contribution of variable X to the growth of real GDP in year t, and γ is the estimated coefficient of x from Table 4. Since no estimated coefficient was available for the capital stock, the contribution of capital was take from the growth accounting exercise reported in "Mirage or Reality."

In the **period of contraction,** the fall in domestic production averaged 10 % a year and reflected a steep decline in total factor productivity. More than half of this decline was accounted for by the rationing of power supply following the end of Soviet subsidies. The other part resulted from a bad policy response that increased distortions (as evidenced by the widening of the exchange rate premium) and weakened incentives for enterprise reform (as reflected in a rise in subsidies). Capital and labor made no contribution to the change in GDP during that period.

In the **period of recovery (1994-96)** positive growth was restored in spite of a decline in net capital formation. TFP surged at an annual rate of 10 percentage points following a broad improvement in policies. First, much of the sharp decline in the government deficit during that period resulted from a *cutback in subsidies* to cover enterprise losses, which tightened budget constraints and improved incentives in the state sector. Second, *the exchange rate premium narrowed* substantially following the legalization of the U.S. dollar, some price decontrol, and the reduction in monetary financing due to a sharply reduced government deficit. This contributed 2 percentage points to the growth of output in 1994-96. Third, *the rise in the non-state sector* following the measures taken in 1993-94 also contributed 2 percentage points to the average growth rate of real GDP during

the recovery. Altogether, these three policy variables contributed seven percentage points to annual GDP growth, with most of the increase concentrated in 1994. Finally, the *supply of electric power* rose owing to an increase in both imports and domestic production of oil.[12] It should be noted that the model over-predicts real GDP growth in 1994-96, as the identified policy variables are more than sufficient to account for growth in that period. The post reform recovery was a reality, not a mirage.

From **1998 to 2001** real GDP expanded at an average annual rate of 5 %.[13] This is not bad by the standards of developing countries in general (4.6% during that period) and much better than the average for Latin American countries (1.8%). The expansion was more than accounted for by continued growth in TFP and reflected a further increase in the supply of energy and additional reductions in government subsidies. However, the contribution of capital formation was negative, as it had been since 1992. The key question in these circumstances is: can the expansion of potential GDP be sustained? Of course, there is plenty of scope for TFP to grow at a fast pace. But this would require price and exchange system liberalization and, most critically, privatization. There is still some scope for reducing subsidies—not those to cover enterprises losses, but those to finance differentials between free market and regulated prices. However, a further increase in the supply of energy will depend on the vagaries of the world oil price (and of subsidized Venezuelan shipments), as domestic oil production appears to have tapered off.

WHERE IS CUBA GOING?

The recovery that started in 1994 is running out of space. The structural reforms that fueled the recovery in its early years have been essentially interrupted, capital formation continues to shrink, and the benefits from macroeconomic stabilization have been

---

12. From 1989 to 1993 imports of petroleum and products fell by more than 60% from 13.1 million metric tons (mt) to 5.5 million mt while the rise in domestic oil production was small. As a result, total supply of petroleum and products fell from 13.8 to 6.6 milllion mt. By contrast, from 1993 to 2001 total supply increased by 35% (to 8.9 million mt) as both imports and domestic production rose.

13. This period includes an out-of-sample year (2001) in which the model over-estimated growth by just under one percentage point. Perhaps this is because the economy was affected by two exogenous shocks in that year: hurricane Michelle, and the effects on Cuba's tourism of the events of September 11.

largely absorbed. Therefore, barring new structural change, further positive growth of <u>actual</u> GDP, stemming for example from a rise in tourist receipts or a policy-induced expansion of domestic demand, would soon bump against the constraint of a falling *potential* output. The result could be a resumption of inflation in free and black markets and the temptation to tighten price controls. More likely, as has already happened since 2001, it will take the form of a rise in the demand for imports. Given the lack of official international reserves and the authorities' insistence on maintaining the fixed official exchange rate at par with the dollar, this would manifest itself in two ways: the further tightening of import controls; and the depreciation of the peso in the parallel market.

The simulation results shown in columns (d) and (e) in Table 5 suggest what might happen over the medium-term (around three years) under two very different policy assumptions. Column (e) illustrates the case of **unchanged policies**: real GDP would decline at an annual rate of 2% even though the negative contribution of investment would stop, as the exchange rate premium on the dollar would likely widen with the tightening of import and price controls. The energy situation is assumed to remain unchanged although, of course, this would remain an area of vulnerability. Furthermore, any decline in remittances from Cubans abroad would compromise the authorities' already difficult task of repaying its foreign obligations. More generally, the bleak prospects for national income raises questions about the government's ability to fund its domestic and foreign liabilities, including the payment of pensions to an ageing population.

The consequences of a **shift in policy towards reform** are illustrated in column (d) of Table 5. In this scenario, real GDP would grow at an average annual

rate of 10 percent.[14] TFP would surge and the contribution of capital formation would turn positive. The non-state sector would expand from 25% to 40% (measured in terms of the sector's share in total employment), still well below the shares already achieved by many transition countries from China and Vietnam to Hungary and Poland. Exchange rate unification and the elimination of government subsidies would make a further contribution to the growth of TFP and output.

In spite of significant problems with the availability and consistency of data, the empirical results presented in this paper seem strong enough to support some important conclusions.

- Economic policies matter a great deal.

- The cessation of Soviet aid coupled with a terrible policy response sent the economy into a tailspin in the first half of the 1990s.

- The liberalization and stabilization plan of 1993-94 brought about the resumption of positive growth. The recovery was real—not a statistical trick.

- The Cuban economy is approaching the crossroads. Without new supply-side measures, continued recovery is likely to be thwarted as the gap between potential and actual GDP continues to narrow. Never has the policy choice been so clear: continued policies mean, at best, stagnation and debt services difficulties. Further backtracking on structural reforms would be a recipe for disaster, particularly if macroeconomic stability is given up. By contrast, a decisive reform plan would reinvigorate the Cuban economy and set the stage for a lasting improvement in the living standards of the population, after so many years of economic deprivation.

---

14. A formidable performance by revolutionary Cuban standards, but not greatly out of line with recent growth in developing Asia (around 6% at annual rate) and among the transition countries of the former Soviet Union (an average of more than 7% in 2000-2001).

REFERENCES

Anuario Estadístico de Cuba 2000 (2001). La Habana, Cuba.

Bénassy, Jean-Pascal (1993). "Nonclearing Markets: Microeconomic Concepts and Macroeconomic Applications," *Journal of Economic Literature,* Volume XXXI (June)

Bernake, Ben S., and Parkinson, Martin L. (1991). "Procyclical Labor Productivity and Competing Theories of the Business Cycle," *Journal of Political Economy*, Vol. 99, Number 3 (June).

Comisión Económica para América Latina (CEPAL) (2000). *La economía cubana: Reformas estruc-*
turales y desempeño en los noventa. Fondo de Cultura Económica, Mexico.

Comisión Economica para América Latina (CEPAL) (2002). "Cuba: Evolución económica durante 2001." United Nations. LC/MEX/L.525

Hernández-Catá, Ernesto (2001). "The Fall and Recovery of the Cuban Economy in the 1990s: Mirage or Reality?" International Monetary Fund *Working Paper* 01/48.

Nordhaus, William D. (2002). "Productivity Growth and the New Economy," *Brookings Papers on Economic Activity,* No. 2.

ANNEX 1
DEFINITIONS AND SOURCES OF VARIABLES

A_{it} = **Total factor productivity (TFP).** A vector of variables including changes in the exchange rate premium, in electrical power consumption, in subsidies to loss making enterprises and in the non-state sector.

C_E = **Consumption of electricity**, in gi ga-watt hour. *AEC,* Cuadro VII.15 for industry, construction, agriculture, transportation, and aggregate consumption. For the commercial sector, electricity consumption was estimated by subtracting household consumption (Cuadro VII.10) from "other" sectors in cuadro VII.15..

N = **Total employment** in thousands of workers. *AEC,* Cuadro V.2. for 1994-2000; and *CEPAL* (2000) for 1989-1993.

N^s = **Employment in state entities,** in thousands of workers. *AEC,* Cuadro V.3. for 1994-2000; and *CEPAL* (2000) for 1989-1993.

N^{ns} = **Employment in the non-state sector,** in thousands of workers. Includes self-employed, agricultural private sector, cooperatives, and mixed enterprises. Sectoral data obtained by subtracting, for each sector, state employment (Ns) from total employment (N).

P = **Implicit GDP deflator**. Sectoral data calculated by dividing, for each sector, nominal GDP by real GDP. *AEC (2001)* for 1994-2000; and *CEPAL* (2000) for 1989-1993.

P_c = **Personal consumption deflator**. Data calculated by dividing, for each sector, nominal private by real private consumption. *AEC (2001)* for 1994-2000; and *CEPAL* (2000) for 1989-1993.

S = **Government subsidies** for state enterprise losses. *AEC (2001)* cuadro IV.4. for 1994-2000; and *CEPAL* (2000) for 1989-1993. Deflated by the aggregate GDP deflator.

T = **Government revenue**, in millions of pesos. *AEC (2001)* Cuadro IV.4. for 1994-2000; and *CEPAL* (2000) for 1989-1993. Deflated by the aggregate GDP deflator.

W^s = **Average monthly wage in state entities,** in pesos. *AEC,* Cuadro V.5. for 1994-2000; and *CEPAL* (2000) for 1989-1993.

X = **Exchange rate premium** on the U.S. dollar. *CEPAL* (2002), Cuadro 21.

Y = **Gross domestic product (GDP)** in constant 1981 prices. *AEC,* Cuadro III.1. for 1994-2000; and *CEPAL* (2000) for 1989-1993.

EL DESEMPLEO EN CUBA

Manuel García Díaz

Uno de los aspectos que más resalta la propaganda del régimen castrista como un gran logro, junto con la educación y la salud pública, es la erradicación del desempleo masivo prevaleciente hasta 1959. "Ya se señaló que el desarrollo social ha sido acaso el mayor logro de las últimas décadas de Cuba ... El índice de desempleo[1] disminuyó de 20% en 1958 a menos del 8% en 1989" (CEPAL, 2000a, pág. 69). Era de esperar que con la catástrofe económica que comienza en los primeros años de la década del 90 del pasado siglo se incrementase la tasa de desempleo. Sin embargo, según el mismo libro (CEPAL, 2000a, pág. 253) la tasa de desempleo en los años 1989-1998 osciló entre el 6,1% (mínimo alcanzado en 1992) y el 7,9% (en 1989 y 1995). Al referirse a estas cifras dice: "Ahora bien, la política ocupacional ha evitado que la tasa de desempleo siga aumentando...Sin embargo, gran parte de la población ocupada ha debido bajar sus niveles de productividad y califica como subutilizada" (CEPAL, 2000a, pág. 252). Más asombroso aún resulta el dato contenido en el "Informe sobre los Resultados Económicos del 2002..." leído por el Ministro de Economía y Planificación, José Luis Rodríguez. Según dicho informe, la tasa de desempleo en el 2001 fue de 4,1%, y en el 2002 se redujo al 3,3% (Rodríguez, 2002).

Tales cifras del desempleo en Cuba, como demostraremos en lo que sigue, han sido falseadas con el evidente objetivo de ocultar la verdadera situación catastrófica del empleo en Cuba.

El análisis que realizaremos no tiene como primera prioridad demostrar la manipulación de tales estadísticas por el gobierno cubano. Perseguimos el objetivo primordial de develar el volumen del desempleo con que se enfrentará el gobierno que inicie la transición al mercado. Consideramos que este problema, si tenemos en cuenta lo ocurrido con el empleo en todos los países de Europa Central y Oriental que han emprendido el tránsito hacia el mercado, devendrá en uno de los principales problemas que tendrá que enfrentarse. Parece imprescindible que desde los primeros momentos de dicho tránsito se tenga una medida confiable de la verdadera magnitud del desempleo y de su probable comportamiento. Intentemos develar la real magnitud del desempleo en la economía cubana en los momentos actuales. Examinemos las cifras disponibles.

LA MAGNITUD REAL DEL DESEMPLEO

Para emprender el análisis que haremos del desempleo resulta conveniente examinar algunas de las serias anomalías que hemos encontrado en las cifras estadísticas sobre tal cuestión. Tales anomalías parecen ser parte de una operación, no de maquillaje, sino de

---

1. Índice de desempleo o Tasa de desempleo es el % de Población Económicamente Activa que no trabaja. Por su lado, según el Comité Estatal de Estadísticas, la Población Económicamente Activa "Está integrada por el total de ocupados en la economía, más los desocupados que buscan empleo. Comprende a todas las personas que contribuyen a la oferta de trabajo para producción de bienes y prestación de servicios en sentido general, incluyendo no sólo a los empleados en el período que se informa, sino también a los que buscan empleo. Se excluyen de ésta, los estudiantes, amas de casas y personas en otros quehaceres del hogar, así como los retirados y pensionados" (CEE 1990, Págs. 78–79).

verdadera cirugía estética, a los fines de ocultar la verdadera situación del paro en la Isla. Las cifras a que nos referimos son las oficiales del gobierno cubano, publicadas por sus organismos gubernamentales o por CEPAL[2] en varios de sus informes sobre la situación económica cubana.

Los datos y cifras a las que nos referimos, además de las más arriba mencionadas Tasas de Desempleo, son los siguientes:

- El *Anuario Estadístico de Cuba, 1990*, en su página 57 dice que la población en edad laboral (mujeres entre 17 y 54 años y hombres entre 17 y 59 años) en 1989 asciende a 6.278.697 personas.

- En las estimaciones hechas por CEPAL de la población en Cuba (CELADE, 1999b), se muestra que la población en edad laboral (acorde con la definición oficial cubana de tal indicador) asciende, para ese mismo año 1989, a 5.980.400 personas.

- En el Anexo Estadístico del libro de CEPAL, *La Economía Cubana. Reformas Estructurales y Desempeño en los Noventa*, en la Tabla No A.46, se dice que la población en edad laboral (17 años o más) asciende, también para ese mismo año, a 7.739 miles de personas. ¡Casi millón y medio de personas de más que el *Anuario Estadístico de Cuba* y un millón ochocientas mil más que los estimados de CELADE! Más sorprendente aún resulta esta cifra, ya que en la tabla A.68 de ese mismo libro se dice que la población en edad laboral en Cuba, en 1989, ascendió a 6.279 miles de personas.

- Según tales estadísticas de CEPAL (2000a), la tasa de desocupación en el año 1989 ascendió al 7,9% de la población económicamente activa, poco más de 370 mil personas en paro. En los años más críticos de la década (1992 y 1993), cuando el PIB se redujo, según el gobierno cubano, al 60% del alcanzado en 1989, el paro, en lugar de aumentar, se redujo al 6,1% (283 mil personas) en 1992 y al 6,2% (285 mil personas) en 1993. En el último año recogido en tales estadísticas, 1998, la cifra de desempleados ascendió a 307 mil (6,6%) del total. Estas cifras, por supuesto, suscitan suspicacias.

- A tales dudosas cifras de desempleo hay que sumarle lo siguiente. De acuerdo con las cifras oficiales, el empleo creció, de 1995 al año 2000, en casi 800 mil personas, en una época de cantidades muy reducidas de inversiones y de restricciones al trabajo por cuenta propia. Si comparamos estas cifras con las correspondientes al período 1975-1989, resulta lo siguiente: en estos catorce años las inversiones brutas en el sector estatal civil ascendieron a 50.462 millones de pesos (las inversiones netas correspondientes ascendieron a 30.395 millones de pesos), y en esos mismos años se incrementó la ocupación en 1,047 millones de personas, es decir, se invirtieron (brutos) 48.200 pesos por cada nuevo puesto de trabajo.[3] Según los citados datos del gobierno cubano, en el período 1995-2000 la inversión bruta ascendió a 6.993 millones de pesos, y se incrementó el empleo en 780 mil personas, es decir, se invirtieron (brutos) 9.200 pesos por puesto de trabajo[4] (el 19% de lo que "costaba" crear un puesto de trabajo en el período 75-89). Además, si queremos conocer lo que realmente se invirtió en la creación de nuevos puestos de trabajo, debemos calcular la inversión neta: Para ello, a los 6.993 millones de inversión bruta se le resta la depreciación, que a finales de la década de los 80 ascendía a unos 2.200 millones de pesos anuales (1.433,4 millones anuales de promedio en el período 75-89); resulta entonces que la inversión bruta es insuficiente incluso para la reposición de los bienes de capital que causan baja, es decir, la inversión neta es negativa.[5]

---

2. CEPAL, como reconoce en todos sus documentos sobre la economía cubana, solamente utiliza los datos oficiales del gobierno cubano y algunas estimaciones que hace a partir de tales datos, es decir, estimaciones basadas en las cifras oficiales del gobierno cubano.

3. Cifras calculadas por el autor a partir de los datos de CEE (1990).

4. Cifras calculadas por el autor a partir de los datos de CEPAL (2001).

5. El desmantelamiento de la mitad de los ingenios azucareros es una demostración palpable de la veracidad de esta afirmación.

Tabla 1. Población en Edad Laboral, Económicamente Activa y Ocupada (miles de personas) según CEPAL 2000a

	Población en Edad Laboral	Población Económicamente Activa	Población Ocupada Total	Total de Desocupados y Tasa de Desempleo (%)
1989	7.739	4.728	4.356	372 (7,9%)
1990	7.892	4.742	4.394	348 (7,3%)
1991	8.007	4.737	4.374	363 (7,7%)
1992	8.110	4.635	4.352	283 (6,1%)
1993	8.210	4.597	4.313	285 (6,2%)
1994	8.253	4.496	4.195	301 (6,7%)
1995	8.289	4.526	4.169	358 (7,9%)
1996	8.331	4.515	4.172	343 (7,6%)
1997	8.368	4.606	4.283	322 (7,0%)
1998	8.400	4.646	4.339	307 (6,6%)

Fuente: CEPAL 2000a, Tabla A.46.

Podemos concluir, por tanto, que las cifras oficiales de los años 90, tales como los de la Tabla No. 1, son, sencillamente, increíbles, en el sentido estricto de no creíbles. Tales milagrosos resultados (crear puestos de trabajo sin nuevas inversiones), de los cuales no se encuentra evidencia alguna en ningún otro país del mundo, inducen a dudar de la veracidad de las cifras oficiales expuestas en los documentos del gobierno cubano o en las mencionadas publicaciones de CEPAL.

Comencemos por la Población en Edad Laboral (PEL). Este indicador, para Cuba, comprende a la población femenina entre 17 y 54 años, y a la población masculina entre 17 y 59 años. Veamos las cifras disponibles en la Tabla No. 2. En la primera columna aparece la PEL según Juceplan (1977); en la segunda, según CEE (1990), en la tercera, según la Tabla A.46 de CEPAL 2000a; en la cuarta, según Organización Internacional del Trabajo (OIT), 2003.

Como se puede apreciar, resulta la tremenda diferencia entre las cifras de CEPAL 2000a y las de las demás fuentes. Si llevamos tales cifras a una gráfica (Gráfica No. 1), resulta posible apreciar mejor las características de la diferencia señalada.

¿Cuál puede ser la causa de la diferencia entre el libro de CEPAL y el *Anuario Estadístico de Cuba*, a pesar de que ambas, según reconoce CEPAL, deben proceder de la misma fuente?[6] ¿Por qué tal diferencia, a pesar de que existe un estimado previo independiente, hecho por la propia CEPAL[7] que indica que la cifra de 7,7 millones es exagerada? ¿Se trata simplemente de un error?

Para nuestros cálculos posteriores proponemos utilizar los datos reales y los resultados de los pronósticos de población que aparecen en CELADE 1999a, según los cuales la PEL sería la indicada en la Tabla No. 3.

En la Gráfica No. 2 se muestra la congruencia entre ambos tramos (1975-1989 y 1990-1998). Como se evidencia en dicha gráfica, la Población en Edad Laboral estimada mantiene en la década de los 90 la tendencia a aumentar, aunque su crecimiento es ahora menor.

Emprendamos ahora la tarea de esclarecer el indicador Población Económicamente Activa (PEA). En la llamada a pié de página No. 1 se muestra el concepto de PEA que se aplica en Cuba. Es preciso señalar que en dicha definición aparece una frase que hay que resaltar: "incluyendo también a los que buscan em-

---

6. Como se dice en la Presentación del Anexo Estadístico del libro de CEPAL 2000a, las cifras básicas proceden de fuentes gubernamentales cubanas, complementadas con algunas estimaciones propias "... a fin de ofrecer un panorama de lo más acorde posible a una visión global de la economía cubana" (CEPAL, 2000a, Pág. 675).

7. Las estimaciones hechas por CELADE 1999a.

Tabla 2.   Versiones de la Población en Edad Laboral. (mil personas)

AÑO	PEL (Juceplan)	PEL (CEE)	PEL (CEPALª)	PEL (OIT)
1960	3.527,7			3.570
1961	3.510			
1962	3.518,4			
1963	3.544,3			
1964	3.570,2			
1965	3.623,8			
1966	3.761			
1967	3.858			
1968	3.951,4			
1969	4.042,1			
1970	4.164,2			4.034
1971	4.216,6			
1972	4.287			
1973	4.363,5			
1974	4.430,6			
1975	4.489	4.476,2		
1976		4.545,2		
1977		4.641,7		
1978		4.753,5		
1979		4.880,5		
1980		4.972,6		
1981		5.067,6		
1982		5.213,6		
1983		5.364,1		
1984		5.518,7		
1985		5.661,9		
1986		5.863,1		
1987		5.994,6		
1988		6.140,2		
1989		6.278,7	7.739	
1990			7.892	6.882
1991			8.007	
1992			8.110	
1993			8.210	
1994			8.253	
1995			8.289	6535
1996			8.331	
1997			8.368	
1998			8.400	
1999				
2000				6.634

a.   Según la Tabla A.46 de CEPAL (2000a).

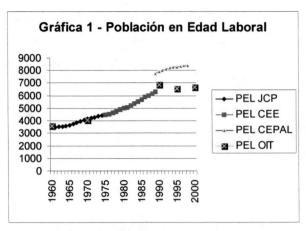

Gráfica 1 - Población en Edad Laboral

Gráfica 2 - Población en Edad Laboral

Tabla 3.   Población Económicamente Activa (mil personas)

Año	PEL	Año	PEL	Año	PEL	Año	PEL
1975	4.476,2	1981	5.067,6	1987	5.994,6	1993	6.530,3
1976	4.545,2	1982	5.213,6	1988	6.140,2	1994	6.574,5
1977	4.641,7	1983	5.364,1	1989	6.278,7	1995	6.606,9
1978	4.753,5	1984	5.518,7	1990	6.319,2	1996	6.639,5
1979	4.880,5	1985	5.661,9	1991	6.411,6	1997	6.660,1
1980	4.972,6	1986	5.863,1	1992	6.472,3	1998	6.668

Fuente: Tabla elaborada por el autor con los datos de CEE (1990) para los años 1975-1989 y de CELADE 1999a para los años 1990-1998.

pleo." ¿Qué significa esto en un país en el que el empleo, aún en las empresas privadas que allí funcionan, lo provee, con carácter de monopolio, el gobierno? ¿Cuál es el significado de tal frase, en un país en el que durante muchos años estuvo vigente una Ley contra la Vagancia? Tal indefinición tiene, entre otras, la siguiente consecuencia: la cifra de Población Económicamente Activa puede ser manipulada, a capricho, por el gobierno. Pero, es que de tal cifra depende el resultado que se obtenga de la Tasa de Desempleo, pues dicha tasa es, en el caso cubano, la parte de la PEA que no trabaja (expresada en %). Por supuesto, dicha cifra resulta muy importante (sobre todo, para la propaganda).

En la Gráfica No. 3 reflejamos las series de Población Económicamente Activa, de 1975 a 1989 según CEE 1990; de 1989 a 1998 según CEPAL 2000a; y estimados para varios años, desde 1960 hasta el 2000, elaborados por la Organización Internacional del Trabajo (OIT, 2003)

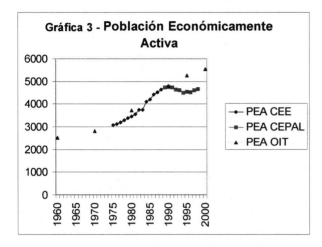

La gráfica muestra, con claridad meridiana, cómo los valores de la Población Económicamente Activa que aparecen en la Tabla A.46 de CEPAL 2000a difieren radicalmente, sin que haya causas que lo justifiquen, de la tendencia que prevaleció hasta ese momento, tendencia que subyace también en los estimados de la OIT, el comportamiento de los cuales concuerda plenamente con el de los datos reales expuestos en CEE 1990.

¿Qué importancia tiene el cálculo más exacto posible de la Población Económicamente Activa? ¿Qué implicaciones puede tener la existencia de distintas versiones de este Indicador para Cuba?. Si tomamos el que aparece en la Tabla A.46 de CEPAL 2000a, entonces en 1998 se tuvo una Tasa de Desempleo de 6,6%. Sin embargo, podemos también intentar realizar el cálculo a partir del estimado de Población Económicamente Activa elaborado también por CEPAL, pero en otro material, CELADE 1999. Según este estimado de CELADE la Población Económicamente Activa en Cuba en el año 2000 sería 5.240 miles de personas.[8] Interpolando, para el año 1998, tal indica-

dor ascendería a 5.138 miles de personas. Si se toma esa cifra, los desempleados en ese año serían 799 mil personas, y la tasa de desempleo en ese año ascendería a 15,6%.

Otra alternativa de cálculo, como vimos más arriba, es la siguiente: se toma la Población en Edad Laboral que hemos estimado anteriormente (6.668 miles de personas en 1998) y se mantiene la Tasa Global de Participación (Población Económicamente Activa dividida por Población en Edad Laboral) que a esta cifra corresponde en 1989, el 75,3%. Entonces los desempleados en el año 1998 serían 682 miles de personas, equivalente a una Tasa de desempleo del 13,6%.

Podemos seguir realizando cálculos alternativos, partiendo de cifras más veraces que las de CEPAL 2000a, y llegaríamos siempre al mismo resultado: el desempleo en la Cuba actual es muchísimo mayor que el reflejado en las publicaciones del gobierno y reflejadas en los análisis que hace CEPAL de la situación económica de la Isla. Tal certeza, y la necesidad de conocer con mayor precisión el posible paro cuando comience el tránsito hacia una economía de mercado, recomiendan realizar un cálculo más objetivo. Para ello haremos lo siguiente:

Partiremos de la Población en Edad Laboral estimada por CELADE 1999a, que, como vimos más arriba, parece ajustarse bien al comportamiento real anterior de ese indicador. Haremos un estimado de la Tasa de Actividad (% de la PEL que conforma la Población Económicamente Activa) para el período 1990-2000. Con esas dos series de cifras haremos el estimado de la Población Económicamente Activa en los años 1990-2000.

De CEE 1990 obtenemos los datos de PEL y PEA, para los años 1975-1989, que nos permiten calcular la Tasa de Actividad, valores que presentamos en la Tabla No. 4

En los años a partir de 1990, según los informes del propio gobierno castrista, no parecen haberse dete-

---

8. Recuérdese que el estimado de la Población en Edad Laboral de CEPAL correspondiente al año 1989 era inferior al del Comité Estatal de Estadísticas de Cuba en casi 300 mil personas.

Tabla 4. Cálculo de la Tasa de Actividad

Año	Población en Edad Laboral (mil personas)	Población Económicamente Activa (mil personas)	Tasa de Actividad
1975	4476,2	3072,9	0,68649748
1976	4545,2	3127,1	0,68800053
1977	4641,7	3196,2	0,68858392
1978	4753,5	3282,9	0,69062796
1979	4880,5	3375	0,69152751
1980	4972,6	3452,2	0,69424446
1981	5067,6	3552,9	0,70110111
1982	5213,6	3735,4	0,7164723
1983	5364,1	3749,1	0,69892433
1984	5518,7	4109,7	0,74468625
1985	5661,9	4201,2	0,7420124
1986	5863,1	4405,8	0,75144548
1987	5994,6	4513,9	0,75299436
1988	6140,2	4620,8	0,75254878
1989	6278,7	4728,2	0,75305398

Fuente: Tabla elaborada por el autor con datos de CEE 1990.

Tabla 5. Población Económicamente Activa Estimada (Miles de personas)

Año	Población en Edad Laboral	Población Económicamente Activa	Tasa de Actividad
1990	6.319,2	4.794,5	0,75871698
1991	6.411,6	4.900,9	0,76437398
1992	6.472,3	4.983,9	0,77003398
1993	6.530,3	5.065,5	0,77569398
1994	6.574,5	5.137,0	0,78135398
1995	6.606,9	5.199,7	0,78701398
1996	6.639,5	5.263,0	0,79267398
1997	6.660,1	5.317,0	0,79833398
1998	6.668	5.361,0	0,80399398
1999	6.675,2	5.404,6	0,80965398
2000	6.685,4	5.450,7	0,81531398

Fuente: Tabla elaborada por el autor.

riorado las condiciones que parecen determinar la disposición de los individuos a acceder a un trabajo, tales como la calificación de las personas en edad laboral, los niveles de educación, la salud pública, etc. Por tanto, en lo referido a la Tasa de Participación, lo más lógico es suponer que se mantiene su tendencia anterior. Con los datos de la cuarta columna podemos calcular, por regresión lineal, la tendencia de variación de la Tasa de Actividad.

En efecto, los cálculos realizados nos indican que la ecuación

TASA DE ACTIVIDAD = -11,095 +0,00566·AÑO

es una buena aproximación a la realidad, con R = 0,931, y R cuadrado corregida igual a 0,858. Además, tanto la regresión como la constante y el coeficiente de la variable AÑO tienen muy altos niveles de significación. El incremento anual promedio de la Tasa de Actividad es igual a 0,00566. A partir de este resultado podemos calcular, para los años 1990-1998, los valores de la Tasa de Actividad que aparecen en la cuarta columna de la Tabla No. 5:

Tales Tasas, aplicadas a la Población en Edad Laboral, nos han permitido calcular la Población Económicamente Activa, en este caso, a partir de cifras que se ajustan mejor a la realidad anterior y, por tanto,

más creibles. Los resultados de tal cálculo aparecen en la tercera columna de la Tabla No. 5.

Si dibujamos en una gráfica (Gráfica No. 4) los valores reales de la Población Económicamente Activa, desde 1975 hasta 1989, los valores estimados por nosotros para los años 1989-2000, y los valores que aparecen en la Tabla A.46 de CEPAL 2000a, se podrá apreciar claramente como los dos primeros tramos coinciden en su tendencia, mientras que el tercero, sin que existan causas que lo justifiquen, se desvía de la tendencia natural de dicha variable.

Adicionalmente, como datos relevantes que confirman la bondad de nuestras estimaciones, podemos señalar que los estimados de este indicador por la Organización Internacional del Trabajo ascienden a 4.792 miles de personas para el año 1990 y 5.267 miles para el año 1995. Por su lado, los estimados de

Tabla 6. Empleo y Desempleo 1994-2000[a]

Año	Población Económicamente Activa (miles)	Tipo de Desempleo (%)	Total de Desempleados (miles)	Total de Empleados (miles)
1994	4.496	6,7	301	4.195
1995	4.526	7,9	358	4.169
1996	4.515	7,6	343	4.172
1997	4.606	7,0	322	4.283
1998	4.646	6,6	307	4.339
2000	5.242[b]	5,5[c]	288	4.954

Fuente: Tabla elaborada por el autor con datos de CELADE (1999), CEPAL (2000) y CEPAL (2001).

a. Las cifras de los años 1995 y 2000 se calcularon de los datos de CEPAL (1999) y CEPAL (2001), partiendo de la población económicamente activa y el tipo de desempleo para calcular el total de empleados. Las cifras de los años 1994 y 1999, con los datos de CEPAL (2000) y CEPAL (2001), partiendo de la cifra de empleo y el tipo de desempleo para la población económicamente activa y el desempleo.

b. Según CEPAL (2002b).

c. Según CEPAL (2000).

CELADE, que aparecen en el *Boletín Demográfico* No. 64, ofrecen el valor estimado para el año 1995 de 4.987,8 miles de personas como Población Económicamente Activa, mucho más cerca del estimado nuestro que del de CEPAL 2000a.[9]

Pasemos ahora a calcular las cifras de desempleo. Para ello tomaremos, a falta de otras y ante la ausencia de posibilidades para comprobarlas y corregirlas, las cifras oficiales del gobierno cubano sobre empleo total que aparecen en los materiales de CEPAL.

Las cifras que queremos contrastar son las tasas de desempleo y el total de desempleados en Cuba, para el año más reciente posible. Según las estadísticas oficiales del régimen en el año 1992 ese fenómeno afectaba al 6,1% de la población económicamente activa,[10] alcanzando la cima en el año 1995, cuando llegó al 7,9%. Analicemos estos números a partir de las cifras oficiales que ofrece el gobierno castrista, que aparecen en la Tabla No. 6.

Estos cálculos, que arrojan una cifra (oficial) de 307 mil desempleados en 1998 y de 288 mil en el año 2000 tienen, como basamento, la cifra oficial de población económicamente activa (que aparece en la primera columna de la Tabla No. 6), la cual, como

hemos demostrado, está muy lejos de la cifra real. Llamamos la atención sobre el supuesto incremento del empleo en los años 1999 y 2000: según tales cifras, se incrementó en 615 mil personas en dos años, lo cual es, sencillamente, imposible.

A los fines de prever la situación que encontrará el gobierno que dirija la transición hacia el mercado, propongo, como cifra más cercana a la realidad, tomar a la calculada por nosotros, que coincide con las estimaciones de la Organización Internacional del Trabajo y del Centro Latinoamericano de Demografía, y que aparecen en la segunda columna de la Tabla No. 5. Los resultados aparecen en la Tabla No. 7.

El total de desempleo abierto ascendía a casi un millón cien mil personas en 1998. Como se dijo más arriba, resulta imposible que durante los dos años siguientes, 1999 y 2000, se hayan creado más de seiscientos mil empleos. Suponiendo que se pudiera mantener el ritmo de incremento de empleados de los cuatro años anteriores y dados los ínfimos montos de las inversiones anuales, durante los años 1999 y 2000, a lo sumo, se pudieron crear entre 20 y 30 mil nuevos empleos anuales. Por lo que, lo más probable, es que el desempleo abierto en el año 2000 sea de más de un millón de personas.

---

9. En relación con el estimado de CELADE, vale señalar que toma, como punto de partida, valores inferiores a los reales para los años 1980 (3.429,3 frente a 3.452,2 real) y 1985 (3.962,4 frente a 4.201.2 real), por lo que es lógico que su estimado para el año 1995 resulte ligeramente inferior al calculado por nosotros.

10. Se trata de la relación entre desempleados (población económicamente activa desempleada) y la población económicamente activa, y no sobre población en edad laboral (población en edad laboral que no trabaja).

Tabla 7. El Desempleo Abierto Actual en Cuba

Año	Población Económicamente Activa (miles)	Total de Empleados (miles)	Total de Desempleados (miles)	Tasa de Desempleo (%)
1994	5.137,0	4.195a	942,0	18,3
1995	5.199,7	4.169a	1.030,8	19,8
1996	5.262,0	4.172a	1.090,0	20,7
1997	5.317,0	4.283a	1.034,0	19,4
1998	5.361,0	4.339a	1.022,0	19,1
2000	5.450,7b	4.954c	496,7	9,1

Fuente: Tabla elaborada por el autor.

a. Según CEPAL (2000a).

b. Según la Organización Internacional del Trabajo (2003) esta cifra es 5.552 miles de personas, según la cual la Tasa de Desempleo sería 10,8%.

c. Cifra calculada a partir de CEPAL (2000 y 2002b).

A la cifra del desempleo abierto (alrededor de un millón de personas) habría que sumarle el desempleo encubierto. De este último se puede hacer un cálculo aproximado. Si se hubiera mantenido la productividad del trabajo de 1989,[11] el PIB (a precios constantes) del año 1998 se hubiera podido producir con 3.432 trabajadores, es decir, unos 907 mil menos que los realmente empleados. Si esa cifra se la sumamos a la del empleo abierto, estimada en un millón de personas, resulta que el desempleo en el año 1998 alcanzó a más de dos millones de personas. En relación con la verosimilitud del cálculo que hemos realizado del desempleo oculto podemos señalar que, según CEPAL (2000a, Pág. 253), el desempleo encubierto en el año 1998, causado por la brecha de productividad respecto a 1989, era equivalente a una tasa de desempleo del 25,1%. Esta tasa, aplicada a la Población Económicamente Activa de 4.646 (CEPAL, 2000a, Tabla A.46), equivale a un desempleo de casi 1,2 millones de personas.

A lo anterior habría que agregar varios cientos de miles de personas, que hoy aparecen empleadas pero que, cuando se produzca el cambio político hacia la democracia en la Isla, devendrán en desempleados (llamémosles desempleo latente). Nos referimos al inmenso aparato militar y represivo y a la abultada burocracia del aparato de gobierno y del partido comunista cubano.

La cantidad de personas empleadas en los órganos militares y de orden interior puede ser estimada por la diferencia entre la Población Ocupada Total (CEPAL, 2000a, Tabla A.46) y la Población Ocupada Civil total (CEPAL 2000a, Tabla A.1). La diferencia entre estas dos cifras era de 690 mil en 1989, y de 585 mil personas en 1998 Con toda seguridad, los órganos de defensa y orden interior de Cuba, en condiciones de democracia, requerirán muchísimas menos personas que las que empleadas por el régimen castrista. Se puede entonces suponer que, con el paso a la democracia y a una economía de mercado, el desempleo latente pudiera aportar al desempleo abierto unas 400-500 mil personas.

En fin, el desempleo abierto, más el desempleo encubierto, más el desempleo latente, puede superar la cifra de 2,5 millones de personas.

EL DESEMPLEO Y LA TRANSICIÓN AL MERCADO

Hechas tales aclaraciones, abordemos ahora el problema global del desempleo que enfrentará Cuba en los próximos años.

Recordemos que este era uno de los más graves problemas del país en los años 50. En el período de gobierno castrista realmente se hizo un gran esfuerzo para liquidar este mal. Sin embargo, al subordinar los criterios económicos a los políticos, además de medidas adecuadas para su liquidación, como la realización un amplio plan de inversiones, se tomaron medidas que, más que resolver el problema, lo ocultaban. Ejemplo de ello fue la política practicada a principio de los años 60 de jubilación forzosa masiva

---

11. Lo cual supone, en los marcos del análisis que estamos realizando, que en ese año no había desempleo oculto, lo cual no es cierto.

de personas que, independientemente de la edad que tuvieran, aún en plenitud de facultades físicas e intelectuales, habían cumplido los 25 años de trabajo. También los afanes políticos de "resolver" el problema llevó al sobre-empleo (o empleo encubierto), fundamentalmente en las actividades de servicios no destinados a la venta, como forma de ocultar el desempleo. Así, en aquellos años (hasta 1989), no se reconocía la existencia del desempleo como problema para el país, aunque si se reconocía la existencia de problemas de empleo en algunas provincias orientales. Es con la debacle de los años 90 que, ante la imposibilidad de ocultar un fenómeno masivo y manifiesto, se reconoce la existencia del desempleo.

Dado el objetivo de este trabajo, cual es el intento de reflejar algunas de las características estructurales materiales que se encontrarán los que tengan de dirigir el tránsito hacia una economía de mercado, lo que interesa en este momento es la cifra de desempleados: admitamos que en la Cuba actual, en lo que se refiere al desempleo abierto, dicha cifra es, como se vió más arriba, de alrededor de un millón de personas. Además, el desempleo oculto (el encubierto más el latente) puede aportar un millón y medio más de desempleados.

Si esas son las cifras, y bajo los siguientes supuestos:

- en el período 2000-2010 la población económicamente activa crecerá en más de 190 mil personas (Ver Tabla N° 23a de CELADE 1999),

- las cifras de inversiones en Cuba en estos años siguen siendo tan pequeñas como lo han sido a partir del año 1990, hecho muy probable dada la política económica del régimen castrista, de modo que se creen anualmente entre 20 y 30 mil nuevos puestos de trabajo,

- no se reduce más la cantidad de trabajadores por cuenta propia,

- el gobierno que emprenda el tránsito hacia el mercado tendrá que enfrentarse de inmediato a un paro masivo superior a un millón personas,[12]

al cual se le puede incorporar, en un breve plazo, más de 1,5 millones adicionales,

no parece ser realista partir del supuesto (optimista) de que no ocurrirá lo que parece una regularidad de los países que transitan hacia el mercado: el cierre de capacidades productivas y la conversión masiva de empleados en desempleados. Dadas las magnitudes del desempleo encubierto y latente en la Cuba actual, parece imposible evitar que se reproduzca tal fenómeno. De ser acertados estos cálculos, la situación prevista sólo puede ser calificada de catástrofe social.

¿Qué alternativas tiene el gobierno cubano actual de reducir o frenar el paro masivo? Una primera alternativa de "solución" es mediante el incremento del empleo innecesario, con el consecuente aumento de la presión inflacionista y el descenso de la productividad. ¿Es ello posible? Ya se ha hecho en anteriores ocasiones. Desde el punto de vista económico es una política suicida, pero si se considera como alternativa a la luz de la máxima del gobierno actual, "la economía debe supeditarse a la política," es altamente probable que ello ocurra. Lo que ocurrirá, sin duda, es que el actual desempleo encubierto no se reducirá por la vía de la reducción del personal empleado; la única vía que pudiera hacer que esa cifra se redujera es la del incremento de la productividad del trabajo. Hay que contar con que, para el gobierno cubano, siempre es preferible incrementar las "prestaciones sociales" a los desempleados mediante esta forma encubierta en lugar de hacerlo abierta y directamente. Luego, en lugar de que el desempleo encubierto se reduzca, es más probable que en los próximos años éste siga aumentando, con el fin de intentar "reducir" la tasa de desempleo abierto.

Otra alternativa para reducir el desempleo en las condiciones actuales sería que, de nuevo, se amplíen los márgenes para el trabajo por cuenta propia, medida que se ha tomado en otras ocasiones pero que es, como sabemos, altamente indeseable para el gobierno castrista. En esta vía se puede enmarcar la posibilidad, mediante la liberalización de las relaciones estado-productor en el sector agropecuario, de generar

---

12. Cálculos menos optimistas elevan la cifra por encima del millón y medio de personas.

una gran cantidad de nuevos puestos de trabajo que pudieran ser creados sin necesidad de grandes inversiones.

Por otro lado, dada la política del gobierno castrista en relación con las inversiones extranjeras, parece probable que en los próximos años éstas alcancen volúmenes tales que contribuyan sustancialmente a la creación de nuevos puestos de trabajo. Además, parece poco probable que gobiernos de otros países o instituciones internacionales sean fuente de créditos para el desarrollo.

Ante tales perspectivas, hay que hacerse la siguiente pregunta: ¿Dispone la economía cubana actual capacidad para incrementar 200 mil puestos de trabajos anuales hasta el 2010 de modo que pueda asimilar parte del desempleo más el incremento de la población en edad laboral que se incorpore a la actividad económica del país? La consecuencia de la respuesta obvia es que en los próximos años existe una altísima probabilidad de que el paro se incremente. Lo más probable es, por tanto, que el comienzo del tránsito hacia el mercado se haga a partir de un paro real de alrededor de más de un millón de personas, al cual, muy rápidamente, se comenzarán a incorporar los más de un millón y medio de desempleados encubiertos y latentes que hoy existen.

Bajo el supuesto de un cambio de régimen en el futuro inmediato, el gobierno de transición se tendrá que enfrentar con tal fenómeno del desempleo masivo: situación social extremadamente crítica que ha sido generada por el régimen castrista. Por un lado, un paro masivo de más de un millón de personas, por otro, un paro encubierto y latente que, por la lógica del mercado y de la entronización de la democracia, por los imprescindibles cambios institucionales y por la necesidad de reducir los gastos innecesarios, aflorará como paro descubierto. La situación generada durante el castrismo, saldrá a la superficie.

Sin embargo, es altamente probable que se le atribuya la culpa al nuevo gobierno, y se le asocie a la política de transición. Ello ocurrirá con mucha probabilidad ya que, sea cual sea la política de transición al mercado, por su propia naturaleza (de modo que realmente se promueva la transición hacia el mercado), provo-

cará el cierre de instalaciones productivas y de "servicios" gubernamentales. La población, como ha ocurrido en otros países en transición hacia el mercado, asociará el desempleo al cierre de empresas. Ello, en condiciones democráticas, servirá de caldo de cultivo para que se incremente la nostalgia por el régimen anterior. Esta situación ha sido típica en todos los países en transición de Europa del Este, con la "atenuante" de que el socialismo real en aquellos países ni fue consecuencia de movimientos populares ni se realizó con la presencia de caudillos con un alto respaldo popular (excepto, para ambos casos, la revolución rusa de 1917). En Cuba se presentaría la misma situación, pero agravada por la presencia de las dos circunstancias señaladas. Luego, sería muy saludable para el período de tránsito que se avecina, que se encuentren soluciones a este fenómeno demográfico. Por supuesto, soluciones que no comprometan a la política de transición ni por la vía de frenar o ralentizar las reformas necesarias para evitar conflictos sociales, ni por la vía de enfrentar el conflicto y arriesgarse a que, mediante los mecanismos democráticos, el poder pase a manos de grupos menos interesados en la transición.

En tales circunstancias, hay que tomar en cuenta que el incremento del desempleo en la década del 90 está causado, en no poca medida, por el cierre de muchas instalaciones productivas, al desaparecer los mercados de los países del Comité de Ayuda Mutua Económica (CAME). Por un lado, la brusca caída de los suministros, por otro, la desaparición de compradores de sus productos de exportación, llevó al cierre de muchas instalaciones o a la drástica reducción de sus escalas de producción. La posible existencia de capacidades productivas ociosas, aunque se trate de instalaciones con algún retraso tecnológico, pudiera ser un factor que ayude a la solución del problema del desempleo, pues puede reducir la necesidad de nuevas inversiones para crear puestos de trabajo. Por supuesto, tal posibilidad está condicionada por las siguientes cuestiones. En primer término, ¿existe mercado para esas producciones? Como he demostrado en otro lugar (ver García, 2002), el volumen de producción de Cuba está muy condicionado por el volumen de exportaciones, por lo tanto, los mercados a los que se refiere esa interrogante son, fundamentalmente, exteriores. En caso de que puedan existir tales mercados ¿el nivel tecnológico de esas instalaciones ociosas sería suficiente para producir bienes que compitan en ellos o que puedan competir en el mercado doméstico bajo barreras proteccionistas admisibles? Suponiendo que las respuestas a las anteriores preguntas son positivas, ¿se utilizarían tales capacidades con la eficiencia requerida para producir bienes y servicios a precios competitivos? Muchas son las interrogantes que surgen, pero una cosa debe quedar absolutamente clara: las inversiones permiten crear puestos de trabajo, pero estos devienen en puestos empleos efectivos si se vende lo que en ellos se produce. En el caso de Cuba, los incrementos de la producción dependen mucho del incremento de las exportaciones; luego, la creación de miles de nuevos puestos de trabajo, que permitirían la eliminación del paro masivo, sólo es posible si se incrementa la exportación de bienes y servicios.

Aún la situación más optimista induce a pensar que el gobierno de transición no podrá evitar que el paro, durante los primeros años, alcance cifras que pondrán en peligro la estabilidad social. Hay pues que pensar en soluciones alternativas, como pudiera ser la emigración temporal. En este sentido, países como los Estados Unidos, España y, en menor medida, otros miembros de la Unión Europea, pueden, a los fines de ayudar al tránsito hacia el mercado y la democracia en Cuba, acordar con este último país la acogida temporal de contingentes de trabajadores cubanos que vayan a esos países para un tiempo limitado, con el compromiso expreso de regresar a Cuba al término de "su contrato." Convenios de migraciones temporales controladas pueden aliviar considerablemente las presiones que el desempleo pueda ejercer sobre el gobierno de transición.

Por supuesto, la única vía real de solución de tan grave problema social es la creación masiva de nuevos puestos de trabajo, para lo cual se requerirá un flujo estable y grande de nuevos capitales que permitan, por un lado, recuperar el máximo posible de las capacidades de producción hoy existentes y que, por falta de materias primas, materiales, combustibles y partes y piezas de repuesto, se encuentran paralizadas; por

otro, que permita crear nuevos puestos de trabajo con un nivel tecnológico adecuado. Recordemos, una vez más, que la liberalización del trabajo por cuenta propia y de la producción agropecuaria parece que pudieran aportar un potencial de considerables dimensiones para la creación de decenas de miles de nuevos puestos de trabajo que no requerirían grandes inversiones de capital.

Pero la magnitud del problema es tan considerable que parece imposible hallar una solución rápida a tal problema. Se pudiera presentar el siguiente escenario:

- Una población total de alrededor de 11,5 millones de personas;

- De ellas, casi 7 millones en edad laboral;

- Unos 5,5 millones de personas activas económicamente, es decir, que trabajan o que quisieran trabajar;

- Un empleo, en el peor de los casos, de alrededor de 3 millones de personas, y en el mejor, de alrededor de 4 millones, es decir, entre 1,5 y 2,5 millones de personas desempleadas y que quisieran trabajar;

- Desde el punto de vista social se tendría entre 3 y 4 millones de personas en edad laboral sin fuente de sustento propia;

- Con ello, se tendría una tasa de desempleo de más del 27% (o 45%, en el peor de los casos) en relación con la población económicamente activa;

- Cada persona que trabaja tiene que generar ingresos para el sostenimiento de 3 – 4 personas;

- Todo ello en un país de muy baja productividad y con escasas (por no decir nulas) posibilidades de ahorro.

De tal modo se nos plantea una cuestión muy delicada, que podrá ser dilucidada solamente cuando la economía cubana se encuentre en una situación normal: ¿son suficientes los recursos naturales, productivos y humanos del país para sustentar a una población de 11 millones de habitantes?

BIBLIOGRAFÍA

Centro Latinoamericano y Caribeño de Demografía CELADE, (1998), *Boletín Demográfico* N1 62, Internet.

Centro Latinoamericano y Caribeño de Demografía CELADE, (1999), *Boletín Demográfico* N1 64, Julio 1999, Internet.

Centro Latinoamericano y Caribeño de Demografía CELADE, (1999a), *Boletín Demográfico* N1 63, Enero 1999, Internet.

Centro Latinoamericano y Caribeño de Demografía CELADE, (1999b), *Boletín Demográfico* N1 66, Julio 1999, Internet.

Comisión Económica para América Latina CEPAL (2000a), *La Economía Cubana: Reformas Estructurales y Desempeño en los Noventa*. Segunda Edición, Fondo de Cultura Económica, México.

Comisión Económica para América Latina CEPAL (1997), *La Economía Cubana: Reformas Estructurales y Desempeño en los Noventa*. Primera Edición. Fondo de Cultura Económica, México.

Comisión Económica para América Latina CEPAL (2000), "Cuba: Evolución Económica Durante 1999," Internet.

Comisión Económica para América Latina CEPAL (2001), "Estudio Económico de Cuba 2001," internet.

Comité Estatal de Estadísticas (1990). *Anuario Estadístico de Cuba 1989*, Comité Estatal de Estadísticas de Cuba, La Habana.

García Díaz, M. (2002), "Parasitismo económico y su impacto en el tránsito hacia el mercado," *Cuba in Transition—Volume 12*, Association for the Study of the Cuban Economy, Washington, D. C.

Junta Central de Planificación Juceplan (1977), "Reconstrucción y Análisis de las Series Estadísticas de la Economía Cubana 1960-1975," Dos Tomos, Ed. JUCEPLAN, La Habana.

Organización Internacional del Trabajo (2003), Laborsta, Internet.

Rodríguez, J. L. (2002), "Informe sobre los Resultados Económicos del 2002 y el Plan Económico y social para el año 2003 leído por el Diputado José Luis Rodríguez, Ministro de Economía y Planificación," Internet.

WHAT IF U.S.–CUBAN TRADE WERE BASED ON FUNDAMENTALS INSTEAD OF POLITICAL POLICY? ESTIMATING POTENTIAL TRADE WITH CUBA

Matthew McPherson and William Trumbull

In our analysis, we compare several methods for estimating the unrealized U.S.-Cuban trade potential in the context of the gravity trade model. We are the first to focus on the Hausman-Taylor method for out-of-sample trade projections, and find that this seldom-used method to be the superior choice. The Hausman-Taylor method eliminates the heterogeneity bias that plagues ordinary least squares (OLS) estimation and the correlation between included variables and the individual error term that introduces bias in random-effects estimation. Further, unlike fixed-effects estimation, the Hausman-Taylor method allows for the inclusion of time-variant explanatory variables.

The U.S.-Cuban trade relation provides a unique opportunity to estimate trade potentials. The economic relationship between the United States and Cuba was very strong prior to the socialist period. Sixty-seven percent of Cuban exports and 70 percent of imports were with the United States in 1958.[1] The U.S. was also the main source of both private and official capital for Cuba.[2] Since the Cuban revolution and the subsequent U.S.-imposed economic sanctions, trade between the two countries has been effectively eliminated, at least until recently (in the case of agricultural exports to Cuba). In addition to analyzing competing estimators based on their economic properties, the unrealized trade potential between the U.S. and Cuba allows for a more practical assessment. The final trade potential estimates should be comparable to those of similar countries in the region, as well as the historical (pre-1959) U.S.-Cuban trading pattern.

The gravity trade model is the obvious choice for this analysis; since the early 1960s it has been utilized to estimate trade flows.[3] The Model is based on the assumption that trade can be explained by size (GDP or GDP per capita), distance (physical distance and/or various measures of economic distance), and other measures of preferences (common border, common language, etc.). In various forms, it has been applied in studies analyzing the border effect on trade,[4] as well as estimating the impact of currency unions, preferential trading agreements, free trade agreements, and removing trade barriers.[5]

---

1. United Nations Economic Commission for Latin America (ECLAC), *Economic Survey of Latin America, 1963* (New York: United Nations, 1965), p.273.

2. *Economic Impact of U.S. Sanctions with Respect to Cuba*: Chapter 3: "Overview of the Cuban Economy and the Impact of U.S. Sanctions," U.S. International Trade Commission, February 2001.

3. See Tinbergen (1962) and Poyhonen (1963).

4. See, among others, Helliwell (1998); Helliwell and Verdier (2001); Wolf (2000); and Anderson and Wincoop (2003).

5. See Pakko and Wall (2001).

In predicting trade potential, the gravity model has been used in two different ways. The first strategy is based on in-sample predictions.[6] In this method, the country pair(s) under examination is included in the sample. The residual is then interpreted as the difference between potential and actual bilateral trade relations. Recent research has been critical of this approach. In the context of trade potential between EU and former COMECON countries, Egger (2002) shows that large systematic differences between residuals among country groups are not found when the proper estimation technique (one with white-noise residuals) is used. Egger (2002) suggests "that any systematic difference between observed and in-sample predicted trade flows indicates misspecification of the econometric model instead of unused (or overused) trade potentials."

The second strategy, and the one employed here, is the out-of-sample approach. The gravity trade model is estimated excluding the trade flows of interest. The model's parameters are then used to project natural trade relations between countries outside the sample. The difference between the observed and the predicted trade flows can be interpreted as unrealized trade potential. This approach is similar to that used in Wang and Winters (1991), Hamilton and Winters (1992), and Brulhart and Kelley (1999).

As alluded to earlier, the choice of estimation technique is extremely important in correctly estimating trade potentials. The most common techniques used to estimate the gravity trade model has been questioned in recent literature. Among others, Cheng and Wall (2002) demonstrate that OLS estimation of the gravity model is susceptible to heterogeneity biases. That is, if trading partners are heterogeneous in ways not accounted for in the model, and if that heterogeneity is somehow related to the variables that are included in the regression, then the resulting estimates will be biased. They suggest the fixed-effects estima-

tor based on a data panel, that is, cross-sectional observations on two or more years.

Fixed-effects estimation allows for individual effects by estimating a separate intercept for each country pair. However, this technique does not allow for the inclusion of time invariant variables. Their effect on trade is captured by country-pair-specific constant terms. "This modeling assumes that there are fixed pair-specific factors that may be correlated with levels of (trade) and with the right-hand-side variables. It is in this sense fixed-effects modeling is a result of ignorance: we do not have a good idea which variables are responsible for the heterogeneity bias, so we simply allow each trading pair to have its own dummy variable."[7] This estimation method has severe limitations when estimating potential trade flows using the out-of-sample technique. Much information needed for an accurate prediction of potential trade flows is contained in the country-specific constant terms. Estimation of a constant for out-of-sample countries is problematic, and at best ad hoc.

Another method that allows for the inclusion of individual effects is the random-effects estimator. Random-effects has the added benefit of the inclusion of time-variant variables. This specification is based on the assumption that individual effects can be included as part of the error term; however, this method is susceptible to bias if there is correlation between these effects and the regressors. This is often the case empirically. Nonetheless, it has been used as an alternative to fixed-effects estimation when the effect of time-variant explanatory variables is of importance or when no bias has been detected.[8]

Hausman and Taylor (1981) suggest an alternative that combines the beneficial aspects of both the random-effects and fixed-effects estimators. The major shortcoming of the random-effects model is the assumption that the included explanatory variables are uncorrelated with the error term. The Hausman-Taylor method is an instrumental-variable technique

6. See Baldwin (1994) and Nilsson (2000).

7. Wall (2000).

8. See Baldwin (1994), Gros and Gonciarz (1996), Matyas (1997), and Egger (2000)

that uses only information already contained in the model to eliminate the correlation between country-specific effects and the error term. Unlike the fixed-effects estimator, this approach does not necessitate the elimination of time-invariant explanatory variables. Egger (2002) is the first to apply this approach to the gravity model in his critique of in-sample trade potential estimation.

In our analysis, we employ the out-of-sample approach to estimating the trade potential between the U.S. and Cuba. We compare the OLS, fixed-effects, random-effects, and Hausman-Taylor estimation of the gravity trade model and provide substantial evidence that the Hausman-Taylor estimator is the superior choice in this setting.

The remainder of the paper is organized as follows. The next section contains a detailed description of the methodology used and a description of our data set. In the following section, we summarize results. The last section concludes and offers ideas for future research.

DATA AND METHODOLOGY

We estimate the gravity model separately using four different techniques: OLS, fixed-effects (FE), random-effects (RE), and the Hausman-Taylor method (HTM). The OLS (equation 1), fixed-effects (equation 2), and random-effects (equation 3) estimators are straightforward and are as follows:

$$Y_{ijt} = \alpha_0 + \beta' X_{ijt} + \delta Z_{ij} + \varepsilon_{ijt} \qquad (1)$$

where α_0 is an overall constant and ε_{ijt} is a mean zero error term;

$$Y_{ijt} = \alpha_{ij} + \alpha_0 + \beta' X_{ijt} + \varepsilon_{ijt} \qquad (2)$$

where α_{ij} is a specific country-pair effect between trading partners and captures the effect of all time invariant variables;

$$Y_{ijt} = \alpha_0 + \beta' X_{ijt} + \delta Z_{ij} + \varepsilon_{ijt} + \mu_{ij} \qquad (3)$$

where μ_{ij} is a country-pair-specific disturbance term, $E[\mu_{ij}] = 0$, $Var[\mu_{ij}] = \sigma_\mu^2$, and $Cov[\mu_{ij}, \varepsilon_{ij}] = 0$.

We define the independent variable, Y_{ijt} as imports of country i from country j in year t. The data set contains annual trade flows[9] between 101 trading partners (see Appendix A) for the time period 1996 to 2000. Numerous individual trading pairs were eliminated due to missing data, and the final data set consists of 9,230 country pairs. This translates to 46,150 trade-flow observations over the five-year period.

The explanatory variables are divided into two groups, those that change through time and those that are constant. $X'_{ijt} = [x_{it} \, x_{jt} \cdots]$ is a 1 x 9 row vector of country-specific variables that change through time. These include the standard-gravity model variables: GDPs per capita, and populations of both countries.[10] We also include a measure of economic freedom for each country, the Heritage Foundation's Index of Economic Freedom. In this index, a higher value indicates less economic freedom. High levels of economic freedom are associated with low levels of governmental, social, and/or political barriers to trade. Therefore, we expect negative coefficients for these variables. In addition, we include the absolute value of the difference of the two trading partners' freedom index and trade freedom index scores.[11] The coefficients of the freedom index variables are expected to be negative; the closer two

---

9. Trade statistics were obtained from Statistics Canada's World Trade Analyzer dataset.

10. These data were obtained from the World Bank's Development Indicators Database.

11. These data were obtained from the Heritage Foundation / Wall Street Journal Index of Economic Freedom. http://www.heritage.org.

countries are in terms of their freedom level, the more likely they are to trade. Lastly, we include a variable to indicate both countries' membership in a preferential trading agreement.[12] Member countries enjoy the benefits of reduced transaction costs (such as tariffs), which would presumably lead to higher levels of trade.

Z'_{ij} = is a 1 x 4 row vector of time-invariant country-pair-specific variables. These include the direct-line distance between capitals and common border.[13] We also include dummy variables for past or present communist affiliation. We include a variable that takes on the value of one if both of the trading parties have past communist affiliation and zero elsewhere. A different indictor variable takes on the value of one if both trading partners are not former communist countries.

The Hausman-Taylor method is an extension of the random-effects estimator. The main assumption of the Hausman-Taylor method is that the explanatory variables that are correlated with μ_{ij} can be identified. Equation (3) is augmented as follows:

$$Y_{ijt} = \alpha_0 + \beta'_1 X 1_{ijt} + \beta'_2 X 2_{ijt} + \delta_1 Z 1_{ij} + \delta_2 Z 2_{ij} + \varepsilon_{ijt} + \mu_{ij} \quad \textbf{(4)}$$

where X1 are the variables that are time varying and uncorrelated with μ_{ij}; X2 are time varying and correlated with μ_{ij}; Z1 are time invariant and uncorrelated with μ_{ij}; and Z2 are time invariant and correlated with μ_{ij}.

The presence of X2 and Z2 is the cause of bias in the random-effects estimator. The strategy proposed by Hausman and Taylor (1981)[14] is to use information already contained in the model to instrument for the problematic variables, X2 and Z2. Hausman and Taylor show that the needed set of instrumental variables can be constructed as follows:

The group mean deviations of X1 and X2 can be used as instrumental variables. This is based on the same logic as the fixed-effects estimator. The transformation to deviations from the group means removes the part of the disturbance term that is correlated with X2. By definition, Z1 is uncorrelated with the error term and can therefore be included in the set of instrumental variables. The final set of instrumental variables is the group means of X1. The availability of these variables as instruments is not intuitive, but an econometric explanation is provided by Hausman and Taylor. The model is identified as long as the number of variables in X1 is greater than the number of variables in Z2.

Table 1.   Explanatory Variables Correlation with α_{ij}

Abs. value of difference in freedom score	-0.03656	Free score of country j	-0.09886
Preferential trading agreement	0.137837	Abs. value of diff. in trade free. score	-0.05967
Population of Country i	-0.25808	Common Border	0.11425
Per capita GDP of country i	0.029789	Distance	-0.13366
Freedom score of country i	-0.04824	Both countries Communist	0.071595
Population of Country j	-0.23059	Both countries non-communist	-0.03242
Per capita GDP of country j	0.113887		

12. This variable is based on World Trade Organization records. It includes properly notified and recognized customs unions, free trade agreements, and service agreements. The included agreements are EC, BANG, ASEAN, ECO, GCC, LAIA, SPARTEC, MERCOSU, CEFTA, EFTA, CARICOM, CACM, CIS, BAFTA, NAFTA, PATCRA, CER, EAC, CEMAC, WAEMU, MSG, COMESA, SAPTA, and AFTA.

13. These data were obtained from *Direct-Line Distances International Edition.*

14. This strategy is explained in detail in Greene (2002, pp. 303 to 309).

The selection of the variables that should be included in X2 and Z2 is not obvious. Hausman and Taylor (1981) base their selection on economic intuition. In our model, intuition alone does not point to a set of variables. We propose a process to select the set of variables to instrument that goes beyond economic intuition. The goal is to identify the variables that are correlated with the individual effects. If the Hausman-Taylor method is being considered, then the random-effects estimator has been shown to contain bias. The fixed-effects model, however, includes the proper modeling of the individual effects. Therefore, we estimate the fixed-effects estimator; this gives us an individual-specific constant term for each country in the sample. We then test for correlation between this term and the explanatory variables. Table 1 shows the correlations for each explanatory variable and α_{ij}. The variables separate into three groups, variables with high, medium, and low correlation. The relatively high-correlation group (over 0.1 in absolute value) includes border, distance, population of country i, population of country j, membership in a preferential trading agreement, per capita GDP of country j, and the freedom index score of country j. The medium-correlation (0.05 to 0.1 in absolute value) group is much smaller, and includes the absolute value of the difference-in-trade-freedom score and both countries having a communist history. The low-correlation group contains variables with correlations of less than 0.05 in absolute value. This group includes the absolute value of the difference-in-freedom score, per capita GDP of country i, the freedom-index score of country i, and both countries having a non-communist history.

Given the restriction for identification of X1 being greater than Z2, the selection of variables to instrument for is not difficult. We select the variables from the high correlation group as follows: Z2 (border and distance) and X2 (population of country i, popula-

tion of country j, membership in a preferential trading agreement, per capita GDP of country j, and the freedom-index score of country j). In this way, we have been able to identify the variables that are correlated with the individual effects in the data.

RESULTS

The results will be discussed in three sections. First, we will summarize the various economic tests to determine the appropriateness of each of the estimators. Next, the parameter estimates will be discussed, and finally, estimates of U.S.-Cuban trade flows will be given based on each estimator.

Comparison of the Estimators' Econometric Properties

Past research has shown that OLS is susceptible to heterogeneity bias. An examination of our residuals confirms the presence of heterogeneity bias in our data, as well. Figure 1 contains the residuals from OLS estimation. When graphed against imports, the residuals form a clear pattern. As the magnitude of the trade flow increases, the errors are positive and increasing. At low levels of trade, the residuals are consistently negative. In contrast, Figures 2-4 contain the residuals from the fixed-effect, random-effect and Hausman-Taylor methods, respectively. It is clear that for each of these estimation techniques, the heterogeneity bias is eliminated.

The next step in selecting the appropriate estimator is to use an F-statistic to test for individual and time effects. If individual effects are present, then OLS is not appropriate and another method that allows for individual effects (fixed-effects, random-effects, or the Hausman-Taylor methods) should be selected. We find strong evidence indicating the presence of individual effects[15] and evidence against time (or period) effects.[16] The results of the F-tests and the presence of heterogeneity bias are clear evidence against

---

15. We use a F[9228,36903] statistic to test if all of the individual effects are equal across groups. The test statistic of 212.91 is far larger than the critical value, and the we can conclude that there are indeed individual effects in the data and OLS estimation is not appropriate.

16. The F[4,46126] statistic value of 0.74 is fair less than the critical value of 2.37, indicating that there are no significant trade flow differences across periods that are not accounted for by our explanatory variables.

the use of OLS, suggesting that a more appropriate estimator should allow for individual effects.

Figure 1. OLS Residuals Vs. Trade Flows

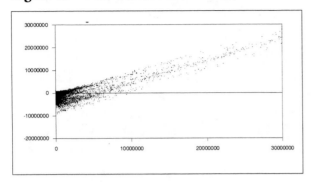

Figure 2. Fixed Effects Residuals Vs. Trade Flows

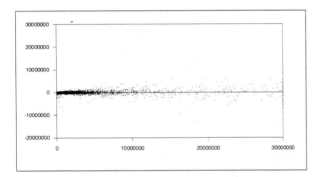

Figure 3. Random Effects Residuals Vs. Trade Flows

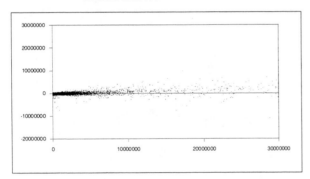

Next, we test to determine if there is correlation between included variables in the model and the error terms. If correlation is detected, the random-effects estimator can be eliminated as a possible estimation

Figure 4. Hausman Taylor Residuals Vs. Trade Flows

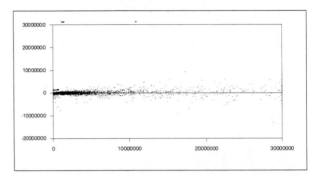

technique. First we perform a Hausman (1978) test comparing the fixed and random-effects estimators.[17] We conclude that there is correlation between the included variables and the error terms, and therefore fixed-effects is a better choice than random-effects.

An additional Hausman (1978) test is conducted using the fixed-effects and the Hausman-Taylor methods to determine if the instrumental variable technique has eliminated the correlation that plagued the random-effects estimator.[18] We find that the correlation has been removed, and conclude that, of the two alternatives considered here, the Hausman-Taylor estimator is the better choice. That is, the problematic correlation between variables included in the model (X2 and Z2) and the individual component of the error term that introduced bias into the random-effects estimator has been removed through the use of instrumental variables.

Comparison of Parameter Estimates

Table 2 contains the parameter estimates of the gravity model using the four different estimation techniques (equation 1-4). As expected, the parameter estimates for the fixed-effects and Hausman-Taylor methods are very similar. This confirms that we are able to separate the effects of time-invariant variables using the Hausman-Taylor estimator without compromising the parameter estimates of the time-varying variables. Comparing the parameter estimates for

---

17. A test statistic of 34.45 is far larger than the critical value of a chi-squared with 8 degrees of freedom.

18. A test statistic of 12.63 (less than the critical value of 15.51) indicates the hypothesis that the individual effects are uncorrelated with the other regressors in the model cannot be rejected.

Table 2. Parameter Estimates

	OLS	Fixed Effects	Random Effects	HTM
Constant	317,314	-841,485	345,434***	-43,340
	(1.43)	(na)	(1.97)	(0.42)
Per Capita GDP 1	65.29***	65.55***	66.76***	69.03***
	(24.32)	(18.48)	24.33	(20.74)
Per Capita GDP 2	32.68***	30.60***	46.90***	30.88***
	(15.30)	(8.62)	(17.09)	(8.86)
Population 1	2.32***	9.14***	2.86***	8.79***
	(19.41)	(10.21)	(11.52)	(10.06)
Population 2	2.23***	8.21***	2.67***	8.20***
	(18.64)	(9.17)	(10.76)	(9.32)
Freedom Index 1	-141,370***	-52,394*	-87,627***	-62,040**
	(3.35)	(1.83)	(3.28)	(2.22)
Freedom index 2	-57,117	-46,904*	-113,297	-46,363*
	(1.37)	(1.65)	(4.26)	(1.66)
PTA	932,245***	49,858	139,744***	52,512
	(12.97)	(1.14)	(3.29)	(1.22)
Abs Value Diff. of freedom index	-96,470**	-79,603***	-84,072***	-69,204***
	(2.32)	(3.43)	(3.74)	(3.07)
Abs Value Diff. trade freedom index	-183,298***	-8,755	-4,676	-10,211***
	(9.07)	(1.46)	(0.80)	(1.74)
Distance	-44.42***	NA	-72.11***	-150.36
	(9.08)		(7.37)	(0.67)
Border	2,716,386***	NA	2,949,867***	10,304,392
	(20.73)		(10.45)	(1.44)
Both Communist	-48,283	NA	-214,213	-1,508,357***
	(0.24)		(0.50)	(2.84)
Both Non-Communist	-44,503	NA	123,779	1,000,108***
	(0.84)		(1.12)	(3.78)

* indicates significant at the 10 percent level.
** indicates significant at the 5 percent level.
*** indicates significant at the 1 percent level.

the fixed and random-effects estimators shows that if the random-effects estimator were chosen under the premise that the time-invariant variables is crucial to the analysis, the time-varying parameter estimates would be compromised. Specifically, the parameter estimates for population of country i, per capita GDP of country j, population of country j, the freedom-index score of country j, and membership in a preferential trading agreement are quite different for the fixed and random-effects estimators.

Further, the Hausman-Taylor method is able to provide statistically significant parameter estimates for 2 out of the 4 time-invariant variables. Therefore, we are able to successfully estimate the effect of time-invariant explanatory variables that, under fixed-effects

estimation, would be consolidated in the country-specific constant term. In addition, it is of particular interest to note that the distance and common border variables are not statistically significant. This is consistent with the results of Egger (2002) who also finds the effect of distance (as measure by physical distance between capitals and the border) effect to be insignificant. These results clearly call into question the use of this type of measure in gravity-model estimation.[19]

It is also interesting to note that membership in a preferential trading agreement has a statistically significant effect for the OLS and random-effects methods, but not for the Hausman-Taylor or fixed-effects methods. In many cases, countries that enter a pref-

---

19. Trumbull (2001) summarizes a number of issues related to the use of this measure of distance and border.

Table 3. Cuban Trade Flow Estimates by Estimation Type

	Estimate	95% Confidence Interval	Estimate	95% Confidence Interval
A. OLS	Imports		Exports	
Year				
1996	1,354,908	[-6,762,607 to 9,472,424]	1,523,017	[-6,594,510 to 9,640,545]
1997	1,462,515	[-6,655,101 to 9,580,133]	1,629,358	[-6,488,272 to 9,746,988]
1998	1,571,952	[-6,545,610 to 9,580,133]	1,729,639	[-6,387,936 to 9,962,714]
1999	1,688,375	[-6,429,229 to 9,806,051]	1,845,034	[-6,272,653 to 9,962,722]
2000	1,848,099	[-6,269,428 to 9,965,627]	1,990,788	[-6,126,753 to 10,108,330]
B. Fixed Effects	Imports		Exports	
Year				
1996	4,024,424	NA	2,754,679	NA
1997	4,100,862	NA	2,885,695	NA
1998	4,174,603	NA	3,007,260	NA
1999	4,252,269	NA	3,135,709	NA
2000	4,361,280	NA	3,299,206	NA
C. Random Effects	Imports		Exports	
Year				
1996	1,513,684	[230,458 to 2,796,911]	2,017,902	[734,483 to 3,301,321]
1997	1,594,054	[309,757 to 2,878,352]	2,126,521	[842,025 to 3,411,017]
1998	1,670,630	[385,838 to 2,955,422]	2,230,692	[945,701 to 3,515,683]
1999	1,758,607	[472,673 to 3,044,542]	2,345,102	[1,058,962 to 3,631,241]
2000	1,876,644	[590,235 to 3,163,052]	2,495,620	[1,209,006 to 3,782,234]
D. HTM	Imports		Exports	
Year				
1996	2,345,872	[844,687 to 3,847,058]	3,569,360	[2,040,670 to 5,098,051]
1997	2,423,123	[919,057 to 3,927,189]	3,705,048	[2,171,309 to 5,238,787]
1998	2,497,002	[990,308 to 4,003,696]	3,829,399	[2,291,443 to 5,367,355]
1999	2,575,938	[1,066,562 to 4,085,313]	3,963,048	[2,420,286 to 5,505,809]
2000	2,685,940	[1,173,612 to 4,198,269]	4,129,894	[2,582,666 to 5,677,122]

erential trading agreement have similar characteristics. In the random-effects and OLS specifications, this variable may be capturing effects that are included in the individual effects in the properly specified models (fixed-effects and Hausman-Taylor methods).

Trade Flow Estimates

Table 3 contains trade-flow estimates. We apply the out-of-sample technique to calculate these estimates. The out-of-sample approach to estimating trade potential between the U.S. and Cuba is straightforward for the OLS, random-effects, and Hausman-Taylor estimators and is calculated as follows:

$$\hat{Y}_{ijt} = \hat{\alpha}_0 + \hat{\beta}' X_{ijt} + \hat{\delta} Z_{ij} \qquad (5)$$

The parameter estimates for OLS and random-effects have been shown to be biased; however, the Haus-

man-Taylor method parameter estimates are not and we are therefore able to use the out-of-sample method of trade projections and include time-invariant variables.

In the case of the fixed-effects estimator, the approach is much more complex, and relies on the ad hoc assignment of an individual dummy variable for the U.S.–Cuba trading pairs. The trade flow estimate is achieved as follows:

$$\hat{Y}_{ijt} = \hat{\alpha}_{ij} + \hat{\alpha}_0 + \hat{\beta}' X_{ijt} \qquad (6)$$

The constants from equation (6), can be recovered using the OLS normal equations as follows:

$$\hat{\alpha}_0 = \bar{\bar{Y}} - \bar{\bar{X}}' \beta \qquad (7)$$

$$\hat{\alpha}_{ij} = (\overline{Y_{ij\cdot}} - \overline{\overline{Y}}) - (\overline{X_{ij\cdot}} - \overline{\overline{X}}) \qquad (8)$$

where the individual specific mean is

$$\overline{Y_{ij\cdot}} = \frac{1}{n} \sum_{t=1}^{T} Y_{ijt}; \quad \text{and the overall mean is}$$

$$\overline{\overline{Y}} = \frac{1}{nT} \sum_{ij=1}^{n} \sum_{t=1}^{T} Y_{ijt}.$$

The same notation is followed for X. All of the needed information is present in the data set except for $\overline{Y_{ij\cdot}}$ for Cuba. As a proxy, we substitute the individual-specific mean for the Dominican Republic, the country that arguably most closely matches Cuba. This underscores the ad hoc nature using the out-of-sample method with the fixed-effects estimator.

Table 3 contains the trade flow estimates for each technique, along with the 95 percent confidence interval for the estimation.[20] The OLS and random-effects estimates are very similar, and tend to be less than those of fixed-effects and Hausman-Taylor methods. Although the parameter estimates are very similar for the fixed-effects and Hausman-Taylor estimators, the trade projections are quite different. This highlights the benefits of using the Hausman-Taylor method, which yields a more precise estimate than fixed-effects due to the inclusion of more explanatory variables. In addition, the Hausman-Taylor method does not require an ad hoc specification of the individual specific constant term for Cuba.

Table 4 places the trade-potential projections in both historical and regional perspective. The trade flow percentages included in this table are based on the assumption that 50 percent of the trade projected between the U.S. and Cuba would displace existing Cuban trade.[21] In the case of imports, the OLS and random-effects estimators consistently underestimate

Table 4. Country Comparison of Percentage Trade with the United States, 2000

Country	Imports	Exports
Cuba OLS*	52	69
Cuba FE*	74	84
Cuba RE*	52	73
Cuba HTM*	61	82
Cuba in 1958**	70	67
Argentina	16	11
Barbados	33	3
Bolivia	20	26
Brazil	21	23
Colombia	26	40
Costa Rica	39	41
Dominican Republic	62	77
Ecuador	25	36
El Salvador	35	14
Guatemala	41	31
Haiti	56	61
Honduras	77	33
Jamaica	41	17
Mexico	68	85
Nicaragua	25	31
Panama	40	11
Paraguay	13	2
Peru	20	25
Uruguay	13	6
Venezuela	29	55

* Assumes 50 percent trade displacement.
** United Nations Economic Commission for Latin America (ECLAC), Economic Survey of Latin America, 1963, (New York: United Nations, 1965), p.273.

the U.S.-Cuban trade flow (52 percent) as compared to the historical US-Cuban trading pattern (70 percent) and that of the Dominican Republic (62 percent), the country most like Cuba in the region. The projections based on fixed-effects estimation (74 percent) seem to be more reasonable, but overestimate the level of imports. On the other hand, the Hausman-Taylor method produces estimates that are nearly identical to regional trading patterns (61 percent compared to 62 percent for the Dominican Re-

---

20. A confidence interval is not included for the fixed-effects estimator projection due to the ad hoc estimation procedure.

21. For reference, Appendix B contains the percentages of trade that would be with the U.S. assuming various levels of displacement. Determining the amount of trade that would be displaced by U.S. trade is a complicated issue, and beyond the scope of this paper. The USITC, *Economic Impact of U.S. Sanctions with Respect to Cuba*, circumvented this issue with the ad hoc assumption that US-Cuban trade should be restricted to a percentage of current Cuban trade levels. We feel this specification is overly simplistic and the assumption naive.

public) and very similar to the historical U.S.-Cuban relationship.

In terms of Cuban export projections, each of the estimation techniques produce estimates that are reasonably close to those of the regional trading patterns and the historical relation between the U.S. and Cuba. However, the fixed-effects and Hausman-Taylor estimators produce projections considerably higher than those of the OLS and the random-effects estimators.

It is important to keep in mind that the Hausman-Taylor and the fixed-effects methods are the only estimators that properly model the individual effects in the data. The consistently lower projections of the OLS and random-effects estimators may be due to the various forms of bias introduced with these methods. Based on the historical Cuban data and trading patterns of the region (especially the Dominican Republic), we conclude that the Hausman-Taylor estimator produces the most plausible trade potential predictions. In addition, the Hausman-Taylor method is the only estimator with projections that are reasonable for both imports and exports.

CONCLUSION

In our analysis, we compare several methods for estimating the unrealized U.S.-Cuban trade potential in the context of the gravity-trade model. We find the seldom-used Hausman-Taylor method to be the superior choice for estimating trade flows using the out-of-sample approach. The Hausman-Taylor method is ideal because it allows for the inclusion of time-invariant variables in trade projections and circumvents the problem of an ad hoc estimation of the country-specific dummy variable needed for a projec-

tion based on the fixed-effects estimator. In addition, based on a Hausman (1978) specification test comparing the Hausman-Taylor method and the fixed-effects estimator, the Hausman-Taylor method proved to be a superior specification given our data. Examining the trade potential projections of the various estimators in both historical and regional contexts, it is clear that the Hausman-Taylor estimator produces more plausible projections than the OLS, random-effects, and fixed-effects estimators. This result holds for both Cuban imports and exports.

This research could be extended in a number of ways. First, our results, combined with those of Egger (2002), call into question the use of physical distance and border in the gravity model, at least in their current forms. The use of the distance between the capitals or economic centers of two countries does not seem to reflect important issues involved in the likelihood of trade, such as transportation costs and political environment. Variables that better capture economic distance or actual transportation costs seem to be better suited to measure the distance between potential trading partners. Therefore, there is room for improvement in this area. In addition, the border variable could be improved. For example, the addition of length of border may prove informative.

Further, an interesting topic for future research is the amount of trade displacement that would occur if the U.S.-Cuban trading relationship were based on economic fundamentals and not political policy. That is, to what extent would free trade between the U.S. and Cuba merely substitute for trade already occurring with Europe? We leave this topic for future research.

REFERENCES

Anderson, J.E. and Wincoop, E., 2003. "Gravity with Gravitas: A Solution to the Border

Puzzle." *American Economic Review,* 93 (1), 170-92.

Baldwin, R., 1994. In: *Towards an Integrated Europe,* Center for Economic Policy Research, London.

Brulhart, M. and Kelly M., 1999. Ireland's Trading Potential with Central and Eastern European

Countries: A Gravity Study. *Economic and Social Review*, 30 (2), 159-74.

Egger, P., 2000. "A note on the proper econometric specification of the gravity equation."*Economic Letters*, 66, 25-31.

Egger, P., 2002. "An Econometric View of the Estimation of Gravity Models and the Calculation of Trade Potentials."*World Economy*, 25 (2), 297-312.

Greene, W., 2002. *Econometric Analysis*. New York: Prentice Hall.

Gros, D. and Gonciarz, A., 1996. "A Note of the Trade Potential of Central and Eastern Europe." *European Journal of Political Economy*, 12, 709-21.

Hamilton, C.B. and L.A. Winters,1992. "Opening Up International Trade with Eastern Europe." *Economic Policy* 14, 77-116.

Hausman, J., 1978. "Specification Tests in Econometrics." *Econometrica*, 46, 1251-1271.

Hausman, J. and W. Taylor, 1981. "Panel Data and Unobservable Individual Effects." *Econometrica* 49, 1377-1398.

Helliwell, J.F., 1998. *How Much Do National Borders Matter?* Brookings Institute, Washington D.C.

Helliwell, J.F. and Verdier, J., 2001. "Measuring International Trade Distances: A New Method Applied to Estimate Provincial Border Effects in Canada." *Canadian Journal of Economics*, 34 (4), 1024-41.

Matyas, L. 1997. "Proper Econometric Specification of the Gravity Model." *The World Economy*, 20 (3), 363-368.

Nilsson, L., 2000. "Trade Integration and the EU Economic Membership Criteria." *European Journal of Political Economy*, 16 (4), 807-27.

Pakko, M.R. and Wall, H.J., 2001. "Reconsidering the Trade-Creating Effects of a Currency Union." *Federal Reserve Bank of St. Louis Review*, 83 (5), 37-45.

Poyhonen, J., 1963. "A Tentative Model for Volume in Trade Between Countries." *Weltwirtschaftliches Archiv*, 90, 91-113.

Tinbergen, J., 1962. In: *Shaping the World Economy: Suggestions for an International Economic Policy*, Twentieth Century Fund, New York.

Trumbull, W., 2001. "Imperfect methodology but the right results? The USITC Report on the Economic Impact of U.S. Sanctions with Respect to Cuba." *Cuba in Transition—Volume 11*, 105-109.

Wall, H.J., 2000. "Gravity Model Specification and the Effects of the Canada-U.S. Border." *Federal Reserve Bank of St. Louis Working Paper*, 2000-024A.

Wang, Z.K. and Winters, L.A., 1991. *The Trading Potential for Eastern Europe*. discussion paper, 610, Center for Economic Policy Research, London.

Wolf, H.C., 2000. "(Why) Do Borders Matter for Trade." *Intranational Macroeconomics*, 112-28.

Appendix A.   Country List

Algeria	Egypt	Jordan	Philippines
Angola	El Salvador	Kenya	Poland
Argentina	Ethiopia	Korea Republic	Portugal
Australia	Fiji	Kuwait	Saudi Arabia
Austria	Finland	Madagascar	Senegal
Bahamas	France	Malawi	Sierra Leone
Bahrain	Gabon	Malaysia	Singapore
Bangladesh	Germany	Mali	South Africa
Barbados	Ghana	Malta	Spain
Belgium-Lux	Greece	Mauritania	Sri Lanka
Benin	Guatemala	Mexico	Sudan
Bolivia	Guinea	Morocco	Suriname
Brazil	Guyana	Mozambique	Sweden
Burkina Faso	Haiti	Nepal	Switzerland
Burundi	Honduras	Netherlands	Tanzania
Canada	Hong Kong	New Zealand	Trinidad Tbg
Chile	Hungary	Nicaragua	Tunisia
China	India	Niger	Turkey
Colombia	Indonesia	Nigeria	Uganda
Congo	Iran	Norway	UK
Costa Rica	Ireland	Pakistan	Uruguay
Cyprus	Israel	Panama	USA
Denmark	Italy	Papua N Guinea	Venezuela
Dominican Rp	Jamaica	Paraguay	Yemen
Ecuador	Japan	Peru	Zambia
			Zimbabwe

Appendix B.   Estimated Cuban Trade with U.S. by Percent Trade Displacement (Year 2000 in Billions of Current US $)

A. Exports

	OLS		FE		RE		HTM	
Displacement	Total	%US	Total	%US	Total	%US	Total	%US
0%	$3.8	53%	$6.5	72%	$4.3	58%	$5.9	70%
25%	$3.3	60%	$6.1	77%	$3.8	65%	$5.5	75%
50%	$2.8	69%	$5.6	84%	$3.4	73%	$5.0	82%
75%	$2.4	82%	$5.2	91%	$2.9	85%	$4.6	90%
100%	$2.0	100%	$4.7	100%	$2.5	100%	$4.1	100%

B. Imports

	OLS		FE		RE		HTM	
Displacement	Total	%US	Total	%US	Total	%US	Total	%US
0%	$5.2	35%	$8.2	58%	$5.3	36%	$6.1	44%
25%	$4.4	42%	$7.3	65%	$4.4	42%	$5.2	51%
50%	$3.5	52%	$6.5	74%	$3.6	52%	$4.4	61%
75%	$3.4	54%	$5.6	85%	$3.4	55%	$3.5	76%
100%	$3.4	54%	$4.8	100%	$3.4	55%	$3.4	79%

CUBA'S ENVIRONMENT: TODAY AND TOMORROW—AN ACTION PLAN

Argelio Maldonado

Worldwide, Cuba's tropical forests and maritime areas are recognized as rich storehouses of biodiversity. Historically, these treasures have not enjoyed any type of significant societal and governmental commitment aimed at habitat conservation. Furthermore, since 1960, they have suffered from further degradation as a result of a failed Soviet-style approach to economic development. Based on a number of sources, we can conclude that in the context of any future political transitional process:

- A great deal needs to be done regarding the long-term damage already done to Cuba's terrestrial habitats.

- The maritime habitats present an excellent opportunity for long-term conservation and sustainable development efforts.

- True success depends on all involved stakeholders accepting that Cuba's environment has an economic value that is not free for the taking, thus, requiring enlightened regulatory oversight.

- Cuba's poverty must be addressed, particularly among surrounding local communities, as part of any effort aimed at recovering and preserving the island's diverse habitats and unique species.

- A detailed action plan is needed based on outreach and consensus to leverage this unique opportunity to conserve and restore Cuba's environment, thus making it a permanent aspect of the island's national reconstruction strategy.

CUBAN ENVIRONMENTAL OVERVIEW

The Cuban government presented its "National Environmental Strategy," in 1997 at the United Nations Earth Summit in New York. This document clearly defines past mistakes, as detailed below:

> There have been mistakes and shortcomings due mainly to insufficient environmental awareness, knowledge and education, the lack of a higher management demand, limited introduction and generalization of scientific and technological achievements, the still insufficient incorporation of the environmental dimension in the policies, development plans and programs and the absence of an integrative and coherent judicial system (Houck and Rey Santos, 1999).

The same National Environmental Strategy document goes on to identify soil degradation, deforestation and pollution as key environmental issues. After the U.N. meeting, three editions of *Panorama Ambiental de Cuba* (1998, 1999 and 2000), have pointed out the same problems plus increasing salinity, the deterioration of sanitation due to poor waste water treatment and decaying sewage systems, and the loss of endemic species, one of Cuba's most important and abundant natural assets.

Cuba's fresh water system (rivers/lakes/aquifers) has very serious problems. Under Castro's policy of *voluntad hidráulica*, which called for not a single drop of fresh water to "be lost" to the ocean, the government has built over 1,000 large and small dams throughout the entire island, covering 1.4% of Cuba's territory. The results are similar to what has happened in Pakistan's Indus delta over the last 50 years.

Table 1.   Cuban Marine Conservation Priorities

	Area (km²)	Coastal System	Source of Threat	Conservation Urgency	Priority
North Central	16866	Mangrove Islands	Development	H	H
Gulf of Batabanó	27873	Mixed	Overfishing, pollution, tourism, development	M	H
S.E. Cuba	24422	Mixed	River dams, fishing, industrial waste	M-H	H

More specifically, although the benefits to Cuban agriculture are clear in terms of increased irrigated land (close to 1 million hectares), the ecological effect has been quite negative in terms of lowering the water's oxygen level and increasing salinity. Dams have also blocked the dispersal of sediment and fresh water runoff over mangrove areas, contributing to a 30% average reduction of mangrove coverage and biodiversity loss. (*Panorama Ambiental de Cuba, 2000*). Another factor contributing to the increased salinity is the excessive use of aquifer waters for urban consumption and wells for irrigating sugar and citrus crops.

Cuba's major preservation opportunity revolves around its almost pristine coral reefs, which protect a good portion of its coastline. Unlike true barrier reefs, the lagoons behind Cuba's reef are very shallow. In most cases, these wide lagoons, together with the long archipelagos of small coral cays that lie on their outer edges, have protected the reefs from the adverse impact of land-source pollution. Presently, only short stretches of coast are heavily urbanized or industrialized, thus, pollution tends to be localized. Although a significant degree of organic pollution is present in major bays, it is thought to affect only a small portion of Cuba's reefs. Also, it should be noted that there has been extensive exploitation of black coral for jewelry production. In 1998, coral bleaching was reported to have been severe on all coasts, although bleaching-related mortality was low (World Atlas of Coral Reefs).

As previously mentioned, the majority of these reefs lie offshore in long tracts that resemble barrier reefs, separated from the main island by broad lagoons. The longest is the North Central system, which runs along the north coast from the Archipelago de Sábana to the Archipelago de Camagüey. On the south coast, the Jardines de la Reina reef stretches from Trinidad to Cabo Cruz and is considered to be among the healthiest in the Caribbean. This system and the

Batabanó system enjoy the largest and most diverse shelf habitat in the Caribbean, plus mangroves and extensive seagrass beds

The Nature Conservancy and the University of Miami published in 1999 an analysis of 57 coastal systems in the Central Caribbean in an effort to set marine conservation priorities. Three of the eight ecoregions in Cuba were judged to be of the highest priority (see Table 1). These three systems harbor diverse habitats as well as encompassing 40% of all coastal mangroves in the Central Caribbean, or close to 6,000 km. Fortunately, some coastal areas are already protected, such as the Punta Francés National Park, on the west coast of Cuba's Isle of Youth. The Wildlife Conservation Society helped get it designated as a United Nations World Heritage site, thereby protecting its endangered black coral.

The island's initial post-1958 economic development model was based on the takeover of most private agricultural land, the implementation of the Soviet centralized planning model of large state farms, and the consolidation of small farms into agricultural cooperatives. This model required large land areas, oil-driven mechanization, river damming, and heavy use of agrochemicals. Little regard was given to soil husbandry in terms of compaction, erosion and loss of fertility (Funes et al, 2002). This exploitative approach, the use of marginal land for cultivation and inadequate environmental management of resources are some of the root causes of Cuba's serious habitat degradation, salinity and soil desertification. This was confirmed by Cuba's own *Panorama Ambiental de Cuba, 2000*, which noted that 15% of Cuba is affected by salinity and 43% by erosion.

The good news is that despite Cuba's 500 years of environmental resource misuse, the island is somewhat better than its Caribbean neighbors due to the lack of sustained economic development and a sharp reduction since the early 1990s of agrochemical usage. In addition, the government has attempted to reverse past logging damage. Since the early 1960s, a large reforestation project was initiated, with particular emphasis on large monoculture plantations, resulting in (as in the case of Chile) a substantial increase in Cuba's forested area to 21% by the 1990s, but a reduction of native tree coverage. More recently, the Cuban government has realized the economic potential of its biodiversity and has started to take necessary steps toward preservation. Still, although Cuba claims that areas with some type of protection encompass 22% of the national territory, many of these 236 so-called ecological preserves are simply "paper parks," allowed to stagnate due to the lack of resources and enforcement.

Cuba's Flora and Fauna: Rich Biodiversity and High Endemism

According to Dr. Michael Smith of Conservation International, when compared to the United States and Canada combined, Cuba has 12 times as many mammal species, 29 times as many amphibian and reptile species, 39 times as many bird species and 27 times as many vascular plant species, on a per hectare basis. Also, Cuban endemism, which refers to the exclusive presence of species in a specific location, is quite high (Smith, 1995). For instance, 52% of plants are endemic to the island. As unique habitats were eliminated for the sake of increased sugar, citrus, coffee, rice and cattle production, Cuba's rich biodiversity and endemism have been and continue to be pressured. For perspective, based on a 1994 report from the World Conservation Monitoring Centre, among Cuba's 6,500 plant species (for comparison, North America has 18,000), 1,149 are threatened.

Animal species have been less studied, although they also show high levels of endemism and dwarfism. Cuba has a small number of vertebrates (54), as well as 350 birds, 121 reptiles and 46 species of amphibians. Of these, 128 are at a critical, endangered or vulnerable level. Cuba's best known endangered species, *Crocodylos rhombifer,* is one of 23 crocodile species in the world and has one of the most geographically restricted distributions. Its only habitats are some remote marshy zones of Zapata. Cuba enjoys a notable biodiversity in mollusks—2,940 species have been identified, of which 1,400 are terrestrial and include the critically endangered *Polymita* tree snail. These snails have magnificent colors and designs and over 80% of them are endemic. For perspective, France has only 400 species of mollusks (Lopez Vigil, 2001). The island also shelters, among its many dwarf species, the world's smallest scorpion and smallest bird, the bee hummingbird.

Poverty in Cuba

Cuba is broke, with a per capita foreign debt ($3,000) that is one of the largest in the world and a Moody's credit rating of Caa1, which is considered to be "speculative grade." The balance of payments account deficit continues to worsen, further increasing devaluation pressures. Rather than following China's and Russia's example and conducting their foreign policy in pragmatic terms, for ideological reasons Cuba has refused to deal with the IMF. Thus, at this point, a long-term solution via debt renegotiations is not an option, thus eliminating future foreign funding. In addition, with the highest ratio of population over 60 years of age (14%) in Latin America, Cuba faces the long-term challenge of caring for a fast-increasing aging population (21% by 2020), placing further pressure on its limited finances (González, 2002).

Since 1959, the Cuban revolution has accomplished significant gains in providing the poor with a social safety net in terms of education and health, although a serious housing shortage persists. However, Cuba has failed miserably in creating a dynamic economy capable of generating individual wealth. Over a forty-year period, the island has gone from one of Latin America's wealthiest countries to one of the poorest. For perspective, in 1958, Cuba and Chile's per capita incomes were about the same (Table 2). During the 1960-2000 period, Cuba faced a number of years of negative gross domestic product (GDP) growth, and the result for the average Cuban has been dismal. For perspective, Chile's per capita income grew 28 times vs. Cuba's 5 times during the 1960-2000 period. Unfortunately, economic indicators are not improving. The latest indices show sugar production, tourism, new home construction, electric power generation, etc. are trending down.

Table 2. Cuba and Chile— Selected Comparisons

Year	Country	GDP (million U.S. dollars)	Population (thousands)	Per Capita GDP (U.S. dollars)
1958	Cuba	$2360	6631	$356
	Chile	$2580	7165	$360
2000	Cuba	$19200	11000	$1760
	Chile	$153100	15160	$10100

Source: Corzo (2003).

The Cuban government, with its *libreta de racionamiento* (ration card), has attempted to provide its population with a minimal 7-10 days caloric input each month. For instance, on a monthly basis, each person is only entitled to 2.7 kilograms (kg) of rice, 2.2 kg of sugar, 0.5 kg of beans, and 450 grams of chicken, as well as a liter of milk for children under seven years of age. This forces Cubans to complement their nutritional needs by either purchasing expensive food on the black market or shopping in the agromercados, which operate under market-driven conditions, or via bartering. The combination of low monthly salaries (average 221 pesos, about $10US at the unofficial exchange rate used by government-operated foreign exchange outlets), limited allotments of subsidized food, and relatively high prices for the available non-subsidized food forces people in Cuba to steal and engage in other anti-social activities. According to a 2001 study by Cuba's Centro de Investigaciones Psicológicas y Sociológicas (CIPS), more than 90% of Cuban households are involved in some type of illicit activity to complement the State's food and clothing allotment (Vicent, 2003).

Poverty and Conservation

We can conclude without fear of contradiction, that the average Cuban citizen is very poor. Survival skills include the social institution of *"resolver"* (stealing from the government) which leads to activities such as cutting down trees for fuel, and selling endangered species such as the Cuban parrot and *Polymitas* for profit (Linden, 2003). The economic situation has tremendous significance in the development of any future environmental strategies in Cuba. Just as in the poorest areas of Brazil, Ecuador, the Philippines or Africa, we must be aware of the effect of surrounding poverty and institutionalized individual behavior

on the development, execution and success of any specific program aimed at preserving biodiversity.

In other words, if poor Cubans are not provided with alternative income opportunities, conflicts and local opposition will develop to the creation of ecological preserves and other conservation efforts. The development of a viable environmental strategy for the tomorrow's Cuba must incorporate a significant element of sustainable development in order to neutralize the surrounding poverty via income raising measures. A continuation of resource exploitation will bring a further downward cycle of environmental degradation combined with worsening poverty. The best example of this phenomenon in the Caribbean is Haiti, which has very little (1%) of its original forest cover and deep poverty.

Any future conservation strategy must also reflect a clear understanding of the today's Cuba. It must clearly recognize and address the past misuse and exhaustion of natural resources (water, forests, etc.) as a tool of the State's failed fast-track economic development efforts and clearly define how these terrestrial environmental effects should be reversed. The good news is that the lack of coastal development, in particular, presents an excellent opportunity to do things differently in Cuba. For instance, Cuba could easily leverage the almost pristine coral reefs and coasts, which lend themselves to a Belize-like ecotourism-based strategy, and avoid the mistakes and excesses of places such as Cancún and the Spanish Mediterranean coast.

Looking ahead, care must also be taken to avoid falling into the trap represented by any type of short-term-oriented free market approach that calls for unregulated foreign investment. The future of Cuba's environmental sustainability depends on changing its 500-year old mindset, where environmental resources and services are considered to be free for the taking by locals and/or foreigners simply interested in making a quick profit. On the other hand, if done properly the island's well endowed environment can become a permanent asset in any future economic strategy where tourism will surely play a key role. This will require enlightened regulatory oversight and dialogue with the business world to encourage economic growth while assuring conservation.

INDICATED ACTION

Our intention is to create a conservation Trust Fund whose main strategic thrust will be to rescue, defend, and preserve the scientific, cultural, economic, and aesthetic values of Cuba's unique national natural assets for the benefit of current and future generations. This will be accomplished by establishing an efficient, science-based not-for-profit organization. This private organization will provide a stable and non-political source of funds for environmental education, biodiversity conservation, and sustainable programs aimed at combating poverty.

Working with an initial two-year Phase I, the Trust Fund's first activities would focus on preparing to deal with future political changes that should create a more amenable scenario for truly independent local environmental groups and their conservation projects to prosper. In addition, the Cuban government should not only allow independent conservation trust funds to support conservation efforts, but also allow Cuban citizens and government officials to serve on their boards. During the first year, the proposed Trust Fund's objectives are modest, attempting to:

• Start generating the outreach and bridge building needed to build consensus.

• Increase short term resources for biodiversity research and legal regulations;

• Create the necessary infrastructure to go after U.S. federal funds as well as financial support from conservation-oriented donors that should become available after a regime change;

• Work with the opinion makers (media, etc.) to increase public awareness via education regarding the importance of preserving Cuba's biodiversity due to its socioeconomic, cultural and aesthetic values.

• Create a website that will seek to educate the reader about the status of the Cuban environment and serve as a link to related web-destinations.

The Trust Fund will be based on four pillars essential to its success: (1) a clear strategic vision, (2) transparent governance, (3) efficient financial/operational procedures, and (4) a consultative approach among all key stakeholders. In addition, and probably most important to its success and credibility, is that this new Trust Fund must be able to tap into the Cuban-American community's desire to help revitalize the Motherland. The proposed Trust Fund should begin working with a select group within the Cuban-American community as well as key opinion makers in Washington, conservation organizations and the Cuban media in South Florida. The media must play a vital part in selling, emotionally and objectively, the idea of the importance of conserving Cuba's natural resources.

There is a political aspect to the proposal beyond Phase I that requires further discussion at all levels beyond a normal environmental project. In order to move beyond Phase I's focus on science and education, the Trust Fund must generate very clear operating criteria. More specifically, it will not move from Phase I to Phase II until the Cuban political system allows truly independent NGOs to operate and obtain support from outside funding sources. In addition, it is important that transparent regulation and oversight exist.

The effort to create the Trust Fund should be divided into four distinct steps:

Step I: Independently Define Cuba's Present Situation and Conservation Efforts

Since the mid-19th century, Cuba has had excellent scientific libraries and biodiversity collections such as the one located in Cienfuegos that were shared with a number of foreign institutions. Close cooperation between Cuban and U.S. scientists existed prior to 1959, although very little took place during the subsequent 30 years. Since 1990, a limited opening permitted U.S. and Cuban scientists to collaborate, and as a result, a number of documents that provide a basis for understanding the present environmental situation have been published. In addition, Tulane University has done a great deal of work regarding Cuba's Environmental Law and Environmental Defense and is working with Cuban scientists conducting basic research and co-sponsoring workshops aimed at maritime conservation. We intend to include all of these materials plus the findings from the research described below in a website.

Step I should start with a relatively quick gap analysis aimed at reviewing existing research literature regarding the status of Cuba's environment and its unique species, which will highlight knowledge gaps. The analysis should be followed with aerial and satellite imagery aimed at assessing the current situation and changes since the l960's. Based on preliminary work done by Díaz-Briquets and Pérez-López, this initial analysis would include examining Cuba's: (1) forest cover, with particular emphasis on desertification, salinization and forest make-up, including inroads by the pest plant *marabú;* (2) coastal areas, with particular emphasis on pollution in bays and estuaries, the effect of the *Dique Sur* infrastructure in the southern region of Havana and the effects of *pedraplanes* (earthworks) connecting a number of cays along the northern coast; (3) industrial consequences of the sugar industry (particularly waste and the aquifers), as well as nickel strip mining and overall industrial pollution plus, (4) dams and how they have affected the flow of fresh water and surrounding habitats.

As demonstrated by the World Wildlife Fund in *The Root Causes of Diversity Loss* (Wood, et al, 2000), in the face of the variety of factors simultaneously affecting biodiversity, it is essential to have a comprehensive and holistic approach to conservation analysis that looks beyond the local level. By following this approach, we can gain an understanding of the complex social, economic and political linkages that underlie local, national and global socioeconomic root causes of habitat loss. Therefore, it is critical that a root analysis aimed at better understanding Cuba's habitat loss and degradation is also fielded, incorporating the following elements:

- Post-Castro reverse migration and anticipated increased consumption;

- Current poverty and social inequality;

- Present and future public policies, markets and local political empowerment;

- Expected social change and development biases;

- Current environmental legal structure and its implementation.

Step II: Define Trust Fund's Initial Working Group Membership and Strategic Plan

The envisioned initial working group will be small and limited to those key strategic players willing and able to fully participate and support this effort in terms of time, funds and resources. This group will be composed of representatives from (1) the Cuban-American community (will provide funding), (2) a corporation (will provide a bridge to the business world), (3) a major conservation NGO (will provide resources, know-how, and contacts), (4) a Florida-based university (will provide context to the science and education effort), and (5) the Cuban-American media (will provide public support). Once the group is formed, its initial priorities will involve approving the Trust Fund's vision statement and strategy as well as its initial conservation and preservation priorities.

Long-term, the Trust Fund's main objective would be to carefully select local NGOs and provide them with a permanent, independent, and non-political source of support and income. The conservation projects could be either government or privately sponsored as long as they contribute in a sustainable manner to solving environmental issues and poverty elimination. Complementary support will be provided by the Trust Fund to local communities and NGOs in order to strengthen their own organizations and help them build their own capabilities.

Step III: Execute Funding Strategy Needed to Support Plan

The short-term, two-year funding objective will be to obtain $200,000 in order to pay for the knowledge gap and root cause analyses, as well as legal and outsourced administrative costs and the development and support of a website. Long term, the funding strategy would initially revolve around the creation of a matching three-year $1 million sinking fund to be followed by the creation of an endowment (value to be determined) to support conservation projects. Summarized below are the preliminary elements of a fund raising strategy aimed at obtaining the initial $100,000 in private donations matched with an additional $100,000 from other sources. This will be followed later by the establishment of a $1 million three-year sinking fund.

Cuban-American Community: An understanding of the importance of the Cuban-American community's role in this funding strategy is critical. Despite its relatively small size (4% of all Hispanics) and recent arrival to the U.S., the Cuban-American community's financial and political clout is considerable. This political influence can be quantified in terms of four members in the U.S. Congress, one Cabinet secretary, plus key jobholders in the Bush and previous Democratic administrations. Aside from the Jewish-American PAC juggernaut, the Cuban-American National Foundation is the second largest ethnic PAC in the nation. This combined influence will be refocused into obtaining significant American and foreign support (including environmental) for a post-Castro Cuba.

Despite legal restrictions, in 2000, Cuba received $720 million in remittances from the Cuban diaspora, more than the $453 million generated by sugar, Cuba's number one export. For a perspective of the magnitude of the remittance, the nearly $4 billion in cumulative remittances during the 1989-2000 period was twice the accumulated foreign direct investment for the same period. More recently, according to the Inter-American Development Bank, Cuba's remittance grew to $1.1 billion in 2002, despite the world economic slump. If only 1% of this significant individual funding capacity could be redirected to the environment, much could be accomplished by not only preserving its maritime treasures, but also rescuing Cuba's degraded terrestrial habitats for the benefit of future generations.

U.S. Conservation Foundations: There are presently about 60 U.S. foundations focusing on biodiversity conservation in Latin America; however, only a few are active in Cuba because of regulatory issues. This low ratio, combined with a keen interest in Cuba, suggests a significant upside potential to broaden the funding sources by eventually tapping the non-participating foundations. Our strategy is to approach a grantor institution, before the current Treasury restrictions are eliminated, with a proposal to help address Step I via a matching seed grant of $100,000. Once the restrictions are eliminated, this would be followed with a broader request in order to fund future stages.

Corporations: The corporate focus will be both national and international. Prior to 1959, Cuba had an extensive array of foreign corporations (Citibank, Shell, Sears, etc.) operating in the island. Given the appropriate legal and political scenario, it is reasonable to expect that these and other foreign firms will be attracted to return to Cuba. This group should be the core from which we will create a group similar in purpose to Conservation International's (CI) Center for Environmental Leadership in Business, which is an independent unit within CI, having its own executive board focused on establishing cooperation between the corporate world and CI.

According to CI, the Center "promotes business practices that reduce industry's ecological footprint, contributes to conservation and creates value for the companies that adopt them. The result is a net benefit for the global environment and for participating companies." Our strategy would call for a similar approach by focusing on the industry segments (banking, mining, agriculture, etc.) with the largest environmental risk. The plan behind the Center will be based on understanding the prospective sponsor's corporate needs and making certain that this group has a voice, rather than transforming it into an opponent early-on in the Cuban transition.

Bilateral Development Assistance Agencies: Following positive political changes in Cuba, a primary thrust for U.S. government funds could be the USAID and the new Millenium Challenge Account (MCA), assuming it is fully funded by Congress. The MCA represents a new approach to providing development assistance and it is the only significant source (over $1 billion a year) of new foreign aid available to poor countries. The goal of the MCA is to reduce poverty by significantly increasing the economic growth trajectory of recipient countries. Alternate sources for major long term funding would be the two units within the World Bank—the Global Environment Facility and the International Finance Corporation—as well as the Inter-American Development Bank, which fund specific sustainable development, poverty alleviation and conservation projects.

Others: As explained above, the Trust Fund's initial priorities would be to work with foundations whose charters emphasize poverty reduction and biodiversity conservation, corporations, the Cuban-American community and bilateral assistance agencies. In addition, the Trust Fund will explore other more sophisticated sources of funding such as Cuba's debt restructuring, and CDM CO_2 projects under the Kyoto Protocol. For instance, a good example of a carbon sequestration scheme, aimed at reducing deforestation, is Costa Rica's Protected Areas Program. Also, the Trust Fund will work closely with the future Cuban government to propose and help implement tax revenue generating strategies (trust land tax, purchase development rights, usage fees, etc.) and privatization schemes aimed at supporting conservation, similar to those implemented in South Africa. Regarding water pollution, schemes such as Colombia's successful market-driven Watershed Cap and Charge Program should be carefully evaluated as an alternative to command and control regulations (Black-Arbeláez, 2001).

POST-CASTRO ENVIRONMENTAL RELATED DYNAMICS

Based on the author's own experiences in developing a "Return-to-Cuba 1981 Business Strategy," for a major bank, it is important to remember that even after Castro there could be a number of environmental unfriendly scenarios. Indeed, the Bank analysis developed and evaluated 15 possible scenarios that incorporated multiple socioeconomic, political, human rights variables plus legal issues such as labor, bankruptcy, securities, antimonopoly, and other laws. The analysis concluded that only 1/3 of the scenarios merited a strong investment commitment. Still, if we assume a scenario where independent NGOs can prosper, outside foreign support can take place, and environmental regulations are clear, a number of dynamics must be addressed.

Credible Science-based Dynamics

An early priority of the Trust Fund will be to encourage and develop a reliable, independent science information base capable of painting an accurate and credible picture of Cuba's present environmental problems and opportunities. It is important to not only understand the root causes and severity of habitat degradation and specie extinction, but also prioritize the needed preservation and restoration requirements. It should be noted that Cuban and foreign scientists have already done a great deal in identifying a number of sites and endemic species that merit protection, as well as identifying its environmental problems. The expected lack of government resources for its own scientists as well as park support should be solved via the use of outside bilateral help, a worldwide funding strategy, partial privatization, ecotourism, and other sustainable economic development efforts.

Most Cubans, whether they reside on the Island or abroad, tend to perceive nature as either infinite or having little value. In other words, the environment is under-valued because it is not perceived as scarce and/or irreplaceable. As part of the process of selling this plan to a broader audience and in setting priorities, it is important to generate the necessary credibility that the environment has not only social, cultural and aesthetic value, but also real economic value that will be critical in Cuba's future reconstruction. Thus, going forward the Trust Fund must seek to generate the economic facts necessary for promoting long-term conservation.

Once conditions are favorable to conducting research that compares sustainable development vis-á-vis resource exploitation, the Trust Fund must seek out expert help in order to be able to determine the fully loaded net marginal benefit of the preserved areas using a sustainable market-based approach. Examples of this approach were summarized in 2002 (Balmford et. al., 2002) in five different countries (Malaysia, Cameroon, Thailand, Canada and Philippines). The evaluation quantified benefits of tourism, carbon sequestration, sediment control, water supply for agricultural and household use, net of administrative expenses. The resulting data was compared to the opportunity cost of not exploiting the natural resource. In each instance, the benefits were larger than the opportunity cost of avoiding habitat conversion. Furthermore, it should be noted that the net result did not include aesthetic and cultural values, preserved biodiversity, air quality, etc.

Political and Socioeconomic Dynamics

Also, it will be essential to understand the expected post-Castro political and socioeconomic dynamics as well as corruption. These elements could affect the future preservation of Cuba's maritime treasures as well as the recovery process of its degraded terrestrial habitats. The South African experience (Fearnhead, 2003) teaches that any future national preservation strategy will have to deal with: (1) increased demands by the impoverished local population for meaningful economic benefits and political empowerment; (2) the need to support the creation of local, independent NGOs; (3) the expected increased interest by outside investors looking for quick get-rich investments using (or abusing) Cuba's natural resources; and (4) the full implementation of Cuba's environmental law, including needed amendments.

Economic Dynamics

From an economic standpoint, when attempting to evaluate the potential overall net effect of structural adjustment loans on the environment, the Trust Fund should be in a position to assist policy makers in evaluating past experience. More specifically, once Cuba is able to have access to the World Bank and the IMF for economic aid, these organizations in return will surely prescribe structural adjustment loans. These adjustment packages are aimed at increasing productive efficiency and economic growth by liberalizing the economy. Historically, environmentalists have opposed these programs claiming they trigger rapid resource depletion and increased poverty.

According to the World Bank (Wheeler, 2001) the overall effect of adjustment programs is unclear. With respect to the usual exchange rate policy recommendations, adjustment packages have in fact had a deleterious effect on the environment by (1) increasing deforestation rates and (2) stimulating the expansion of erosive crops. Conversely, fiscal policies have had mixed results, with the elimination of subsidies and cuts in public services generating both positive and negative effects on the environment.

Legal and Regulatory Dynamics

Future Cuban policymakers, when designing a pluralistic environmental strategy, will probably use a mix of market-based and command-and-control based elements in order to protect the environment. Command-and-control is a regulatory approach that relies on standards of varies types, such as ambient, emission, and technological (Field, 1994). Meanwhile, the market-based approach uses market tools such as taxes, subsidies, and credible emissions permits to achieve the same purpose.

In the context of Cuba's realities, both approaches have pros and cons that must be critically assessed before implementation. Market-based has the cost advantage of seeking out static efficiency by equating marginal abatement cost across sources. Command-and-control's standards also achieve emissions reduction but at an undesirable higher cost. Market-based has the advantage of providing strong incentive to innovate pollution technology in the long-run; while this efficiency is only partially met under command-and-control standards. Nevertheless, command-and-control has the advantage of depending on less complex monitoring and usually has a simpler implementation (Pérez, 2001).

In addition to whatever strategy regulatory policy makers choose to follow, it is important to understand the future legal and environmental regulatory implementation challenges facing Cuba. For perspective, in 1989 President George H. Bush gave a speech in Budapest pledging U.S. assistance for environmental recovery in East Europe. According to Ruth Greenspan Bell, from Resources for the Future, support from the United States and Western Europe was considerable and helped the Easter European countries develop new environmental laws as vehicles for social change. However, implementation of these laws has lagged, particularly in those countries with citizens that are suspicious of laws in general. Thus, she suggests that there should be greater emphasis on implementing conservation projects that are rooted in cultural value systems, traditions, or community needs.

71

Caribbean Ecoregion Dynamics

The fact that Cuba is an island facilitates any future conservation strategy due to the absence of threats from neighboring countries. Still, it is important to note that grantors and concerned outside parties will judge any effort by the Trust Fund in the context of the Caribbean, given its rich biodiversity and Hot Spot designation. Thus, aside from Cuba's conserva-tion/poverty linkage, which has already been described in detail, it is important to keep in mind cross-boundary policy linkages as well as the ability to replicate any proposed program beyond Cuba. This should not present a problem to the Cuba of tomorrow given its deep scientific talent pool that will help Cuba's future case for funding among grantor institutions.

BIBLIOGRAPHY

Balmford, Andrew et al., "Economic Reasons for Conserving Wild Nature," *Science*, vol. 297, 9 August, 2002: 950.

Bell, Ruth Greenspan, " Legitimacy, Trust and the Environmental Agenda: Lessons from Armenia." *The Environmental Law Reporter* 30 (2000): 10771-10777.

Bell, Ruth Greenspan and Clifford Russell, "Environmental Policy for Developing Countries," *Resources*, Spring 2002.

Black-Arbeláez, Thomas. "Economic Instruments and Environment," *The Andean Center for Economics in the Environment* 1, no. 4 (2001).

Clark II, Edwin H., Jennifer A. Haverkamp, and William Chapman. *Eroding Soils: The Off-Farm Impacts*. Washington D.C.: The Conservation Foundation, 1985.

Clissold, Gillian Gunn, "Cuba Today," Center for National Policy U.S. Cuba Policy Project, April 2002.

Cole, Daniel H, *Instituting Environmental Protection: From Red to Green in Poland*. New York: St. Martin's Press, 1998.

Cole, Daniel H., and Peter Z. Grossman, "When is Command-and-Control Efficient? Institutions, Technology, and the Comparative Efficiency of Alternative Regulatory Regimes for Environmental Protection," *Wisconsin Law Review* 5 (1999): 887-938.

Corzo, Humberto, "Comparación estadística del producto interno bruto (pib) cubano durante la Cuba republicana y la Cuba de hoy," 10 February 2003, http://www.neoliberalismo.com/Archivo-01/compara.htm.

Díaz-Briquets, Sergio and Jorge Pérez-López, *Conquering Nature: The Environmental Legacy of Socialism in Cuba*. Pittsburgh: University of Pittsburgh Press, 2000.

Dinerstein, Eric et al., *A Conservation Assessment of the Terrestrial Ecoregions of Latin America and the Caribbean*, Washington D.C.: The World Bank in association with WWF, 1995.

Doubilet, David, "Midnight in the Forbidden Garden of the Queens," *PADI*, November/December 2002.

Fearnhead, Peter, *The South African National Parks Concessions Programme: A Pioneering Public-Private Partnership for Commercially Sustainable Conservation*. Washington D.C.: International Finance Corporation, April 2003.

Field, B., *Environmental Economics*. New York: McGraw-Hill, 1994.

Funes, Fernando et al, *Sustainable agriculture and resistance: Transforming food production in Cuba*. Oakland: Food First Books, 2002.

Gonzalez, Edward, *After Castro: Alternative Regimes and US Policy*. Institute for Cuban-American Studies: University of Miami, 2002.

Houck, Oliver A. and Orlando Rey Santos. *Cuban Environmental Law: The Framework Environmental Law and an Index of Cuban Environmental Legislation.* Edited by Jerry Speir. New Orleans: Tulane, 1999.

Linden, Eugene, "The Nature of Cuba," *Smithsonian*, May 2003.

López Vigil, María, "Cuba Campaign: Twenty Issues for a Green Agenda," Global Exchange, 5 October 2001, http://www.globalexchange.org/campaigns/cuba/sustainable/lopez100501.html.

McConnell, Virginia, Margaret Walls, and Elizabeth Kopits, "A Market Approach to Land Preservation," *Resources*, Spring 2003.

Mellor, John W, "Poverty Reduction and Biodiversity Conservation: The Complex Role for Intensifying Agriculture," WWF—Macroeconomics Program Office, October 2002.

Olson, D. et al., *Freshwater biodiversity of Latin America and the Caribbean: A conservation assessment.* Washington D.C.: Biodiversity Support Program, 1999.

Panorama Ambiental de Cuba 2000. La Habana, CITMA, 2001.

Pérez, Andrés, "Evaluation of the Advantages and Shortcomings of Market-based Instruments and Command-and-Control Regulation," research paper, University of Chicago, 2001.

Sealey, Kathleen Sullivan and Georgina Bustamante. *Setting Geographic Priorities for Marine Conservation in Latin America and the Caribbean.* The Nature Conservancy, 1999.

Situación Ambiental de Cuba 1998. La Habana, CITMA, 1999.

Smith, M.L., "Cuban biodiversity: an opportunity for complementarity and cooperation," *The Environment in the U.S., Cuban Relations: Opportunity for Cooperation.* Washington: Inter-American Dialogue, 1995: 13-21.

Stevens, William K., "Unusual U.S.-Cuban Team Maps Island's Hidden Cornucopia of Life," *The New York Times*, 1 October, 1991: C4.

Vicent, Mauricio, "Subsistir en Cuba," *El País*, 11 May 2003.

Wheeler, P.K., "Structural Adjustment and Forest Resources: The Impact of World Bank Operations," public research working paper, Washington D.C.: The World Bank Development Research.

Wood, Alexander, Pamela Stedman-Edwards, and Johanna Mang ed., *The Root Causes of Biodiversity Loss.* Earthscan Publications Ltd., 2000.

RECRUITMENT OF SCIENTISTS AND DEVELOPMENT OF INTERNATIONAL FUNDING RESOURCES IN POST CASTRO CUBA

Larry Daley

The objective here to solicit input, gather information, identify sources of funding and ideas to support science and scientists in a post-Castro Cuba.

IDENTIFICATION OF POTENTIAL SOURCES OF FUNDING

This is the most straight-forward of all these matters. And it boils down to a shopping list of public and private funding sources (see Box 1).

SUPPORT FOR GRANT PREPARATION IN POST CASTRO CUBA

Some kind of infrastructure will be necessary to allow scientists in Cuba to ready themselves for the changed circumstances, and to prepare grant and negotiate collaborations. It is important that such infrastructure be pluralistic and transparent so as to avoid capture by any group seeking to use it a base to control scientific funding, or impose ideological or other restraints.

COLLABORATION WITH U.S. AND OTHER SCIENTISTS

There are a number of scientists from the U.S. and abroad who already work or envision working in Cuba. There are other scientists who, for one reason or another, cannot do research in Cuba; these must not be excluded.

One of the potential sources of conflict is that the present Cuban government seeks to capture and to a great extent succeeds in using visiting scientists' work for propaganda purposes and to milk their funding resources to the benefit of the Castro regime. Anecdotal accounts of such conflicts have been reported, one might rationally expect a full accounting of this to emerge on regime change. This leaves memories of such harm.

One notable result of these policies of the Castro government has been to limit academic advancement in U.S. universities of Cuba specialists who are critical of the present regime. Some rather shameful cases of this have come to my attention recently.

On the other hand there is a large reservoir of good will towards Cuban scientists and the scientific opportunities that the Island offers. It is suggested that at least the most rabid of Castro ideologues be gently retired, that old contacts with scientists overseas, including in the United States, be strengthened and new scientific contacts promoted.

SOLICITATION OF SCIENTIFIC SUPPORT FOR CUBAN STUDIES IN THE U.S. AND ABROAD

Hopefully with the help of Cuban-Americans in Congress, legislation can be prepared and approved to qualify Cuban nationals and Cuban-Americans for this funding and perhaps even develop a set aside for collaborative efforts with U.S. scientists.

PROBLEMS AND CONFLICT RESOLUTION IN TRANSITION

Building and Rebuilding Scientific Facilities and Research Reserves: It appears that much of what

Box 1.   Names of Funding Agencies and their Web Site Addresses (from IRIS Search)

- Academy for Educational Development, National Security Education Program (NSEP), David L. Boren Graduate Fellowships, http://www.aed.org/nsep/
- American Sociological Association, Minority Fellowship Program, http://www.asanet.org/
- Council on International Educational Exchange, John E. Bowman Travel Grants, http://www.ciee.org/scholarships.cfm?subnav=Students
- Council on Social Work Education Minority Fellowship Program, Mental Health/Substance Abuse Clinical Fellowship Program (MHSACFP) Clinical Fellowship Program, http://www.cswe.org/programs/MFP/MFPNews/index.htm
- Earthwatch Institute, Research Program, Field Research Grants, http://www.earthwatch.org/research/proposals.html
- Institute of Current World Affairs (The Crane-Rogers Foundation) Fellowships, http://www.icwa.org/
- Institute of International Education, Benjamin A. Gilman International Undergraduate Scholarship Program, http://www.iie.org/gilman/
- National Security Education Program (NSEP), David L. Boren Undergraduate Scholarships, http://www.iie.org/nsep/
- Interior (Department of), National Park Service, Canon National Parks Science Scholars Program for the Americas, http://www.nature.nps.gov/canonscholarships/
- International Council on Monuments and Sites (ICOMOS), US/ICOMOS International Summer Intern Program, http://www.icomos.org/usicomos/
- National Science Foundation, Directorate for Social Behavioral and Economic Sciences, Office of International Science and Engineering (INT), Americas Program Joint Seminars and Workshops, http://www.nsf.gov/pubsys/ods/getpub.cfm?nsf03559
- International Research Fellowship Program (IRFP), http://www.nsf.gov/pubsys/ods/getpub.cfm?nsf02149
- Reynolds (Christopher) Foundation, http://www.creynolds.org/
- Social Science Research Council Cuba Grant Competition http://www.ssrc.org/

one sees in Cuba today are facilities left from pre-Castro times, looted ecological reserves, residues of Soviet aid projects, and display laboratories with little in-depth reality. Remedies are going to take money and time.

Coping with Habits of Downwardly-Directed Autocratic Action and a Culture of Informers: There must be recognition that there are going to be conflicts in such circumstance. Conflict resolution is thus going to be a priority. The perceptions of scientists in Cuba have been severely distorted by autocratic (that is an understatement) abuses of leadership.

Scientific opportunity in Cuba is still and perhaps more so in recent months tied to loyalty to present government. While abuses by present government have left a great yearning for freedom, they have also left scars and habits of downwardly directed autocratic action, and a culture of informers. This matter will have to be addressed.

Coping with Rivalries in a Small Universe: One must also realize that even in the United States, academic rivalries are common and with some frequency lead to bitter "turf" battles. In the U.S. such "turf" battles are mitigated by the complexity and independence of research organizations and plethora of funding sources. Thus in the United States, science advances steadily, if untidily, despite rivalries.

However, in a post Castro Cuba the "universe" of science will be much smaller and aggressively ambitious individuals will play a much larger role. Therefore mechanisms to challenge these individuals to do good science without harming rivals will be of more importance that in the far larger "world" of science in the U.S. Good funding will help ameliorate this but tact and dispersion of rivals will be needed.

When to start is not clear, going to Cuba now is not as safe as it was until recently and then it there were problems. It is most probably that conferences to this end will have to be funded and held in this country. This can be started now.

CONCLUSION

Planning for funding of science in post-Castro Cuba is essential. As the present leadership regime "ages" and desperately plans for its own continuance, planning for real change and which faces "real realities" becomes increasingly important. In the field of science facing such realities is also essential. Good planning is essential and urgent. Coping with the aftermath of Castro manipulation and oppression is necessary but will be most difficult. Discussion and preparation of plans must start now.

THE TOURISM INDUSTRY IN THE CARIBBEAN AFTER CASTRO

Art Padilla[1]

The Caribbean Sea is home to the world's largest assemblage of small and mini-states, a mixture of large to small islands with a wide fusion of languages, religions, ethnic groups, and customs (Thomas 1988). This pattern of development reflects the influences of colonization and settlement: four major European empires, as well as the United States and the former Soviet Union, historically have operated in the region. Within this sociological and political context, tourism has grown amazingly rapidly over the last two decades, but, as will be seen, very unevenly. The Caribbean has become the most tourist-penetrated region in the world: according to Tourism Satellite Account estimates, tourism across the Caribbean accounts for roughly 20 percent of all exports and capital formation, and 16 and 17 percent of regional employment and GDP, respectively (WTTC 2002) Between 1970 and 2000, fueled in the main by North American and European travelers, Caribbean stayover tourist arrivals increased nearly five times, from 4 to 19 million annually, and the region's share of the world total rose from 2.2 to 2.5 percent (CTO 1991, 2001; U.S. Department of Commerce 1993). Tourism is now the most critical source of revenue for all of the 30 or so countries and destinations in the region.

At the same time, the Caribbean region is one of the world's most peculiar tourist areas because its largest nation and fastest growing tourist destination, Cuba, remains an international enigma, a sort of Jurassic Park of communism at the doorstep of the United

States. The trade and travel embargo imposed by the United States on most of its own citizens, along with Castro's peculiar socialistic regime and the lack of modern infrastructure in Cuba, effectively prevent or seriously discourage the travel of U.S. residents and of others as well (US International Trade Commission 2001).

For the first two decades of Castro's rule (during the 1960s and 1970s), tourism in Cuba was essentially non-existent, viewed by the Cuban regime as a western vice inconsistent with socialistic goals (Thomas 1998; Schwartz 1997; Espino 1991 and 1995). During this period other destinations in the region began an expansion of their tourism, taking advantage of not only the void left by Cuba but also the rising North American and European affluence; the advent of economical jet travel; the influx of foreign hotel investment encouraged by tax concessions; and the large-scale expansion of aid-financed transport infrastructure (McElroy and de Albuquerque 1998). However, the collapse of the Soviet Union and the loss of over US$6 billion in annual support from Russia forced Cuba's regime to turn to tourism as a replacement industry (Espino 2001; Gordon 1997). The allure of Cuba's natural charms (Linden 2003) and its status as a curiosity turned Cuba into one of the fastest growing tourist destinations in the world, growing from an estimated 300,000 in 1989, the year of the collapse of the Soviet Union, to over 2 million visitors today arriving annually from Europe, Canada, and other regions. But with Castro in his

---

1. The author thanks the Fulbright Foundation and the Atlantic Philanthropies for their support.

late 70s now, and with notable—if inconsistent—sentiment in the U.S. Congress to eliminate the trade and travel embargo,[2] many destinations as far away from Cuba as Bermuda, and as close as Key West, Florida, are expressing increasing concern about the impact of the opening of Cuba to tourism and travel in a new, fundamentally different social and economic context (Ausenda 2002; "Tarnished" 2000).

The purpose of this paper is to analyze and explore the likely scenarios and winners and losers to the opening up of Cuba to full-blown tourism. It approaches the problem by: (1) analyzing the historical record to see what lessons the past may bring; (2) reviewing and developing estimates and projections of tourist inflows into Cuba; and (3) presenting qualitative evidence from detailed interviews with CEOs and managers of the largest hotel and resort chains now doing business in Cuba and in the Caribbean. The brief historical overview at the beginning of the paper is done to gain insights into the nature of tourism in Cuba and the Caribbean and to focus on the forces likely to affect tourism in the Caribbean in the near future. The paper then proceeds to examine future scenarios for Cuba and the likely impacts of new Cuban "products" that will be introduced into this mature industry.

TOURISM AND INVESTMENTS IN CUBA AND IN THE CARIBBEAN BEFORE 1959

Historical data for world or Caribbean tourism are often difficult to obtain, anecdotal, and usually not particularly accurate. But there are two notable exceptions: the useful and out-of-print books published in 1943 and 1959, respectively, by Armando Maribona, a prolific and widely traveled Cuban author who specialized in travel and tourism (Maribona 1943 and 1959). Both books contain rich historical information about the travel industry and provide contemporaneous insights about the early days of tourism in Cuba, the Caribbean, and other parts of the world.

As the largest island in the region (or more accurately, an archipelago, of 114,000 square kilometers), Cuba has always been among the leaders in Caribbean tourism and in fact has undergone three tourism cycles: one in the mid- and late 1920s; a second one in the 1950s; and the third after the collapse of the former Soviet Union in 1989. This latter period has already lasted longer that either of the two previous ones (both of which, incidentally, ended with the overthrow of the existing government), reflecting the current importance of tourism to the Cuban economy. During the first fling with tourism in the "Roaring 20s," Cuba's image as a tourist destination underwent major transformation. Articles of that time in travel magazines described Havana in lyrical terms, referring to its climate and its Afro-Cuban music in provocatively sensual ways (Schwartz 1997; Williams 1925; Frank 1926). In a crescendo of spectacle and promotion, all in close association with U.S. promoters and investors, each event outdid the previous one:

- U.S. President Calvin Coolidge visited in January of 1928 and opened the 6th Pan American Conference (Maribona 1943; Schwartz 1997). Pan American Airways timed its inaugural Key West-to-Havana flights for the event.

- *The New York Times* extolled Havana's cleanliness and friendliness and even suggested to the fun-loving mayor of New York City, James J. ("Jimmy") Walker, to take some lessons from Cuba.

- In February of 1928, Charles Lindbergh arrived with his airplane, the Lone Eagle, to promote the new commercial flights between Florida and Cuba.

- In 1929, Amelia Earhart opened the new terminal at the Havana Airport.

- Irénée Du Pont, president of the Du Pont chemical company in the early 1920s and a friend of Cuban President Gerardo Machado, was con-

---

2. In mid-2003, for example, the U.S. Congress had two pieces of legislation pending: one would prohibit the U.S. President from regulating travel to or from Cuba by U.S. citizens and another would completely lift the trade embargo with Cuba.

verting the Varadero beach (90 miles or 140 kilometers east of Havana) into an exclusive resort.

The Great Depression of the 1930s changed the Western world and with it the hopes for continued growth of tourism in Cuba: in 1928 visitors spent some US$26 million in Cuba (about US$300 million in 2002 dollars), but this fell to under US$10 million by 1932. In 1933, Cuban President Machado was overthrown and tourism revenues totaled under US$5 million (Schwartz 1997). In spite of these reversals, many continued to encourage tourism in Cuba and elsewhere in the Caribbean as a way to diversify the economy. For example, in 1935, U.S. President Franklin Delano Roosevelt observed to visiting officials from Cuba that certain kinds of tourism would attract U.S. citizens and would help diversify Caribbean economies:

> Cuba must pay greater attention to tourism...while avoiding tourism based on gambling, horse racing, and casinos, [because] it has great possibilities...with its climate, with its beach at Varadero, with its historic sites, and its natural beauty that serve as sure incentives to families ["honest persons"] from the United States (translated from Maribona, 1943).

Tourism was on a very different scale after World War II compared to tourism today. While the tourism numbers for Caribbean destinations for the 1950s appear low in comparison to today's figures, they were not especially low when compared to those of other nations at the same period. The figures for the 1950s in Table 1 were derived from the Maribona accounts (Maribona 1959, 1943) but they must be viewed as illustrative estimations rather than as hard and accurate figures because there is no easy way to verify them. They underscore that while tourism was growing rapidly, it was still on a different level or scale during the 1950s than it is today. Cuba lost market share in the Caribbean tourist market shortly after World War II, mostly due to a lack of adequate hotels, but it was rapidly regaining it by the early 1950s. In terms of arrivals, Cuba was above all the other Caribbean destinations by 1955, which is particularly significant given the revolutionary turmoil and continuous barrage of terrible publicity that existed about the island. For example, *The New York*

Times reported in March of 1957 that two young men from New Jersey vacationing in Havana had been caught in the crossfire between anti-Batista forces and the police. Both were hit as they watched from the door of their hotel, and one of them, Peter Korenda, died on the way to a hospital. A year later, in February of 1958, Argentinean car racer and world champion Juan Manuel Fangio was kidnapped by "26 de Julio" rebels and prevented from racing in a highly publicized Grand Prix race in Havana. Fangio later would have words of praise for the captors, much to Batista's chagrin and to the further detriment of tourism in Cuba. The race went off as scheduled but was ended prematurely when a car crashed into the grandstand killing four and injuring scores (Schwartz 1997).

One may also glean from Maribona's work that tourist per capita spending during the mid-1950s in the Caribbean ranged from a high of US$225 in Bermuda to under US$100 in Trinidad and Tobago, with the average around US$130-150. (This would be approximately US$975 in today's dollars and compares to the 2000 range of between US$400 at Haiti and Belize to over US$2,200 at the Turks and Caicos and an average of slightly more than US$1,000 per arrival). Pan American Airways had regular flights to Cuba, Jamaica, Puerto Rico, and Nassau from Miami and New York, and these were becoming more frequent in the late 1950s, particularly to Cuba. Already hotels in St. George, Bermuda, were experimenting with "all inclusive" concepts, offering rooms and food for US$6 per person per room, and Cuba was offering packages that included airfare, ground transportation, food, drinks, and overnight hotel stay. Nassau had 4,000 rooms and its government pledged that it would not permit high-rise buildings and enforce a 45-foot height limit. Most of Jamaica's hotels and guest houses were in the beaches of Montego Bay in the late 1950s, although the country was actively seeking investments to expand its existing 3,500 hotel rooms. Puerto Rico's tourist arrivals came mostly from New York and other neighboring states and in 1958 had some 2,800 hotel rooms, mostly in the San Juan area. Unlike the tourists going to Cuba, who were in the main U.S. citizens who

Table 1.   Number of Non-Resident Tourist Arrivals for Selected Countries

Country	1950	1956 (or 1957)	Estimated expenditures (1957)	2001
England	NA	1.18 m.		25.5 m.
France	2.8 m.	3.31m.		76.5 m.
Greece	NA	157,000		13.6 m.
Italy	7.7 m.	12.67 m.		39.0 m.
Spain	1.0 m.	3.0 m.		49.5m.
USA		973,693		45.5 m.
Caribbean				
Barbados	NA	17,829	US $ 2.1 m.	507,086
Bermuda	88,000	120,984	US $26.8 m., 80 % US citizens	274,983
Cuba	180,014	381,600	US $ 57.2 m., 90 % US citizens	1,774,541
Dominican Republic	14,796	48,040	US $ 7.3 m.	2,868,915
Haiti	13,679	68,000	US $ 8.6 m.	110,000
Jamaica	74,892	161,386	US $ 29 m.	1,276,516
Mexico	NA	611,500		19.8 m.
Nassau (Bahamas)	45,371	192,480	US $28 m., 94 % US citizens	1,428,209
Puerto Rico	64,507	207,583	US $ 29.5m.	1,219,531
Trinidad and Tobago	64,290	103,000	US $ 9.3 m.	383,101
Virgin Islands	20,295	99,563	US $ 11.6 m.	609,646

Source: Maribona, *Turismo en Cuba* (1959) and Caribbean Tourist Organization and World Tourism Organization (various editions).

Notes: In several cases, the data include both stayovers and excursionists. Mexico's numbers are for the entire country and not just for its more recent Caribbean destinations. The data for the "Virgin Islands" exclude the British Virgin Islands for consistency purposes. And the numbers for Italy clearly seem high in comparison to those of other European nations.

stayed in hotels and other tourist accommodations, many of the "tourists" in Puerto Rico were returning Puerto Rican-Americans, and a large fraction of them stayed in private residences with relatives or friends (Maribona 1959).

In the 1950s, very few hotel accommodations could be found outside of Havana. The famous Varadero beach area had fewer than 300 hotel rooms, with most of them at the Internacional, a hotel of some 160 rooms frequented mostly by Cuban vacationers (Maribona 1959). In fact, despite record government revenues and public project spending during the late 1940s, the connecting road to Varadero from Havana (the Vía Blanca) was not even completed as late as 1950 (Maribona 1959). Batista, aware of the shortage of hotel rooms in Cuba and inspired by the example of Las Vegas, Nevada, decided to create a statutory incentive in 1955 to generate more tourism: a casino would be allowed in any hotel with an investment of at least US$ 1 million (Schwartz 1997). In an attempt to mitigate criticism about gambling and corruption, the law also would set aside a portion of the expected casino revenues for charitable works under the direction of Batista's wife, Marta Fernández.

Even though Havana had a reputation for gambling, in fact only three locations were involved in this activity prior to 1955, and then only on a relatively small scale: the internationally-known Tropicana nightclub; the Sans Souci, which offered gamblers crap games and bingo; and the Montmartre, a Cuban-owned hotel/casino patronized mostly by wealthy Cubans but later owned by Meyer Lansky (Schwartz 1997; Johnston 1958). But the 1955 law changed this, and changed it dramatically and quickly, even if for only a brief four-year period before Castro arrived. After the law was passed, the Hotel Nacional, originally built in 1930 during the first tourism period in Cuba, was thoroughly renovated and its International Casino, operated by Wilbur Clark (who also ran the Desert Inn in Las Vegas, Nevada) opened. In addition to these four, a few other hotels with gambling were added in the short space of two or three years: the Sevilla-Biltmore; the Riviera (which was supposed to be the hotel in the famous *Godfather II* movie scene, but in fact the scene was filmed in Santo Domingo's El Embajador Hotel), also associated with Meyer Lansky, a long-time Batista associate and gambling "expert" from Florida; the Capri; and the Havana Hilton (now the dilapidated

Havana Libre[3]), completed eight months before Castro arrived and formerly operated by the Hilton Hotels International under a lease from its owner, the Cuban Federation of Gastronomic Food Workers Union (Crespo 1999; Schwartz 1997).

During the brief months that marked this second tourism period, these establishments attracted international stars such as Nat "King" Cole, Maurice Chevalier, Edith Piaf, Dorothy Lamour, and Jimmy Durante. The gambling operations were rather miniscule in comparison to today's standards in Las Vegas, Nevada, or Atlantic City, New Jersey, or Monte Carlo. For example, the International Casino at the Hotel Nacional had just seven roulette wheels, one crap (dice) game, and 21 slot machines ("one armed bandits"). The mammoth Tropicana, a huge, 36,000 square-meter, modernistic nightclub, with seating for 1,750 people, had just 10 gaming tables and 30 slot machines (Mallin 1956). And as rapidly as it had grown in a few short years, tourism was still not a large part of the Cuban economy (or the Caribbean economies either); sugar was still king, with tobacco a distant second (Thomas 1998).

THE CUBAN REVOLUTION'S IMPACT

By 1958 tourism in Cuba had already begun to decline dramatically and would decline further after Castro's arrival the following year. Tourism was not in fact a major economic influence and with the support of the Soviets, who badly wanted a communist outpost at the borders of the United States, it would not be viewed as important. It was, in effect, a dispensable "vice" that brought dependency with capitalist nations and undesirable cultural influences, in the eyes of the new regime (Askari et al. 2003; Espino 2000; Schwartz 1997). In fact, the annual Soviet assistance to Cuba at its peak has been conservatively estimated at US$6 billion in 2003 U.S. dollars (Peréz-López 2001), which is more than three times the foreign currency currently provided by both the remittances (approximately US$ 850 million) from Cuban-Americans (Suro et al. 2003) and by the current tourism industry (net revenues of US$1 billion,

generously assuming that Cuba retains 50 % of the tourism revenues after imports of food, managerial human capital, and other leakages).

The turmoil in Cuba during the early 1960s—including the Bahía de Cochinos invasion (April 1961) and the missile crises of 1961 and the larger one of October, 1962—was not particularly good for tourism anywhere in the Caribbean (Interview with Fernando Rainieri, former Minister of Tourism, Dominican Republic, June 2001). But slowly the other Caribbean destinations began to develop to take advantage of the void left by Cuba and to build the business alliances and the infrastructure that would enable them to take advantage of the coming growth in tourism in the region. At first, the investments and the tourist flows began to grow in Puerto Rico (in the Condado area of San Juan) and also in the "Mayan Riviera" of Cancún and Cozumel, Mexico, the Virgin Islands, and Jamaica. The Dominican Republic, now the tourism leader in the Caribbean, was also experiencing political and social turmoil after the assassination of its long-time dictator Rafael L. Trujillo in May 1961. As a result, the Dominicans were not able to get themselves organized for nearly two decades and did not begin their tourism efforts in earnest until the late 1970s.

In 1970, just prior to the explosion in tourist arrivals in the Caribbean, around 4 million tourists traveled to the region. By 1975, this total had grown to 5.5 million and then to just under 7 million in 1980. Puerto Rico (1.6 million), the Bahamas (1.2 million), and Bermuda (492,000) were the leading destinations at the beginning of the 1980s. Current leader Dominican Republic, just beginning its impressive growth, stood at the back of the region with 301,000 arrivals in 1980, a tenth of its present levels. Cuba had just over 100,000 arrivals, one twentieth of its total in 2002.

Shortly after the Castro regime took hold, government policies led to casino closings and to the use of hotels as vacation retreats for loyal workers. Many of the visitors during the 1960s and 1970s were either

---

3. The view from its 360-degree lounge on the top floor remains the best in Havana.

journalists or Eastern Bloc communists on government-paid Cuban vacations who were invited to visit "model" communities, schools, hospitals, or other places where socialist achievements could be displayed. Between the mid-1960s and mid-1970s, only about 3,000 foreign visitors traveled to Cuba each year. Part of Castro's struggle against Batista possibly involved a revulsion against the excesses of mass tourism and the inequity between the haves and the haves not, so the regime's turn against tourism perhaps should have been expected (Aeberhard 2002).

The fall of communism in Eastern Europe in 1989 and the disintegration of the former Soviet Union in 1991 were monumental events for the world and for Cuba, which had been receiving an amazing US$6 billion per year (2003 dollars) in foreign assistance from Russia, one-fourth of Cuba's GDP. Castro put it succinctly for once: "To speak of the Soviet Union's collapse is to speak of the sun not rising." The economic collapse that followed was on a level with the Great Depression of the 1930s, as the Cuban economy contracted by one-third within two years (González 2002; Pérez-López 2001). Cuba began a desperate search for a replacement industry. Reluctantly, Castro turned to tourism as neither sugar nor tobacco nor nickel mining would provide the needed foreign exchange (Espino 1991; Weintraub 2000). In the past, said Castro, "we feared that tourism would defile us, but tourism is gold" (Aeberhard 2002, 77).

Three decades earlier, Batista had turned to foreign investors in an attempt to build hotels and infrastructure to attract the dollars left by tourists and now Castro would have to do the same thing. The process actually began before the collapse of the Soviet Union with the creation of INTUR (National Institute of Tourism) in 1976, run by the Cuban military, and in 1982, Law Decree No. 50 authorized foreign investments through joint ventures. Nine years later, in May of 1990, the first joint-venture hotel opened

in Varadero beach: the Cubanacán/Sol-Meliá with an initial investment of US$87 million by Spain's Meliá chain. Shortly thereafter, German, Jamaican, and Canadian hotel interests opened joint ventures as well.

CARIBBEAN TOURISM TRENDS SINCE THE 1980S

The growth in tourism in Cuba is shown in Table 2, which depicts the increases in hotel rooms in selected countries and destinations in the Caribbean. Meanwhile, Table 3 presents the market shares of tourist arrivals in the Caribbean by five-year intervals. The focus here is on those destinations most likely to be affected by the opening of Cuba to U.S. tourists, determined on the locations that attracted the highest shares of U.S. tourists in 2002 (see Box 1).[4] Table 3 chronicles the dramatic changes that have taken place in less than 20 years: Cuba and the Dominican Republic have increased their market share impressively while Caribbean tourism as a whole has also been increasing markedly.

Table 2. Hotel Rooms in Selected Caribbean Destinations, 1990 and 199

Country	1990	1999	% change
Bahamas	13475	14153	5 %
Cuba	12868	34300	167 %
Dom. Rep.	15782	51412	226 %
Cancún/Cozumel	20500	28566	39 %
Jamaica	16103	23067	43 %
Puerto Rico	8250	11635	41 %

Source: Caribbean Tourism Organization.

The evidence from the time regressions (the natural logarithm of arrivals is the dependent variable and time is the independent) at Table 4 tell a more detailed story about this history of growth, one of great unevenness in the Caribbean basin since 1985. For the region as a whole, tourist arrivals increased at over 5.4 % per year over the 1985-2002 periods (da-

4. To simplify the exposition, remaining destinations are grouped into three categories, defined by the five-year average level of per tourist spending: Rest of Caribbean (ROC) Upscale; Rest of Caribbean Medium; and Rest of Caribbean Low. Upscale destinations were those where on average tourists spent more than US$1,300 per tourist for the 1996-2000 period; middle scale between US$900 and US$1,250; and low scale between US$350 and US$850).

Table 3. **Market Shares of Tourist Arrivals in the Caribbean by Five-Year Intervals**

	1985-1989	1990-1994	1995-1999	2000-2004
Bahamas	17	12	10	9
Cuba	3	4	8	10
Dominican Republic	6	12	14	17
Mexico	18	17	17	15
Jamaica	8	8	8	8
Puerto Rico	5	6	6	7
ROC—Upscale	17	12	10	10
ROC—Middle scale	18	20	17	16
ROC—Low scale	8	9	10	8

ROC=Rest of the Caribbean. "Upsca;e," "middle scale" and "low scale" refer to the level of tourist spending.

Source: Caribbean Tourism Organization.

Box 1. **Most Popular Caribbean Destinations of U.S. Tourists (% market share in 2002)**

- Cancún/Cozumel (20%)
- Bahamas (14%)
- Puerto Rico (13%)
- Jamaica (11%)
- Dominican Republic (9%)
- U.S. Virgin Islands (6%)
- Aruba (5%)
- Cayman Islands (3%)
- Bermuda (3%)
- Netherlands Antilles (3%)
- Rest of the Caribbean (16%)

Source: Calculated from CTO and WTO data.

ta availability determines the dates included here) but at 7.1 % per year for the first part of that time (1985 to 1993) and 2.9 % for the second part of the period (1994 to 2002).

The decline in the rate of growth between these two periods in part reflects the influence of the September 11 terrorist attacks, but there are notable differences among the various destinations that remain even after accounting for that event (Crespo and Suddaby 2002).

- The three fastest growing destinations over these two decades have been Cuba, Dominican Republic, and Puerto Rico, but all but Cuba and the upscale destinations as a group in the rest of the Caribbean (ROC-upscale, which includes Antigua, Barbados, Bermuda, Turks and Caicos, and U.S. Virgin Islands) have experienced notably lower growth rates during the second half of this period.

- The Dominican Republic's unsustainable growth rate of 21.2 % between 1985-1993 drops to 7.5 % between 1994-2002; Aruba's from 16.8 % to 1.7 %; Puerto Rico's from 12.7 % to 5.1 %; Mexico's (Cozumel and Cancún) from 5.3 % to 0.8 % (not statistically different from zero); Jamaica's from 7.9 % to 2.0 %.

- Overall, excluding the two fastest growers (Cuba and Dominican Republic) the growth rate has gone from 5.7 % to 1.0 %. Only Cuba's rate as well as the rate for the ROC-upscale destinations have accelerated, over these two time frames; Cuba's annual growth rate went from 11.8 % in the 1985-1993 interval to 14.1 % for the 1994-2002 period and the ROC-upscale from 2 to 2.2 %.

- Tourism growth in the Dominican Republic, led by the Punta Cana region in that country, has once again accelerated, increasing at nearly 20 % annual rate for the first half of 2003. In addition, the upscale destinations as a group have maintained their position over these two decades, although within this group losses by Bermuda have been offset by the gains of the Turks and Caicos and U.S. Virgin Islands. It may be that some of the more upscale destinations are better insulated against the sharp growth of the "all inclusive" tourist areas by the nature of their clientele that demands a differentiated product. Aruba seems to be the biggest loser between the first period and the second.

Although the new tourist industry in Cuba has grown impressively, reaching over 2 million arrivals annually, it has not been the panacea everyone thought: the rigid, bureaucratic controls of the re-

Table 4. Regressions: Natural Log of Tourist Arrivals as a Function of Time

Country	1985 to 2002			1985 to 1993			1994 to 2002		
	β	% annual change	Adj. R sq.	β	% annual change	Adj. R sq.	β	% annual change	Adj. R sq.
Aruba	0.0768	8.0	0.797	0.1550	16.8	0.942	0.017	1.7	0.476
Bahamas	0.0046	0.5	0.113	0.0080	0.8	0.176	-0.0120	-1.2	0.271
Cuba	0.1401	15.0	0.975	0.1114	11.8	0.952	0.1321	14.1	0.863
Dominican Rep.	0.1265	13.5	0.900	0.1926	21.2	0.847	0.0720	7.5	0.911
Mexico	0.0401	4.1	0.701	0.0513	5.3	0.983	0.0084	0.8	0.018
Jamaica	0.0489	5.0	0.881	0.0763	7.9	0.866	0.0200	2.0	0.829
Puerto Rico	0.0808	8.4	0.935	0.1200	12.7	0.952	0.0494	5.1	0.894
ROC- Upscale	0.0151	1.5	0.502	0.0195	2.0	0.119	0.0213	2.2	0.242
ROC- Middle scale	0.0011	0.1	0.501	0.0014	0.1	0.119	0.0009	0.1	0.242
ROC-Low scale	0.0570	5.9	0.825	0.0900	9.4	0.942	0.0050	0.5	-0.112
Total	0.0523	5.4	0.938	.0684	7.1	0.989	0.0282	2.9	0.569
Total less Cuba and DR	0.0372	3.8	0.865	0.055	5.7	0.970	0.0101	1.0	0.175

Notes: All estimated coefficients () are significant at the .001 level except for Bahamas (all periods), which are significant at the .10 level, and for Mexico and ROC- Low scale (94-02) and ROC-Middle scale(85-93), which are not significant.

ROC= "Rest of Caribbean" and "upscale," "middle scale," and "low scale" refer to the level of tourist spending. Annual percentage change calculated by raising e to the ß power.

gime are inefficient and make hotel managers into hotel "operators" (Interview with regional vice president of Spanish hotel chain, June 2003). It has created ideological problems for the regime because its "apartheid" tourism prohibits Cubans from going to the tourist resorts without foreign currency. In the past, for example, there have been up to three military/police check points on the road to the Varadero resorts to ensure that Cuban citizens are not entering. Prostitution has exploded, some of it highly organized, leading the regime to put on stringent controls to try to prevent it (Bruni 2001; Clancy 2002; Davidson 1996). It has not been the revenue generator anticipated because a large, but ultimately indeterminate, amount has inevitably "leaked out" of the nation through imports of needed inputs to the process, such as food, furniture, and oil. It is estimated that the leakage rate, including profit-sharing with the hotel chains and the value of goods and services imported for the tourism enterprise, exceeds the 40 to 50 % rate that applies to most of the Caribbean destinations and may approach 75 %. This would mean that only one of every four dollars spent by tourists on their vacations in fact remain in Cuba. Expensive infrastructure had also to be put in place or renovated and this further reduced the net gain of

foreign currency. Finally, the human resource element has been a problem as the workers have not been as prepared as needed, all leading to one of the lowest "return" rates, estimated at 10 % for Cuba, compared to between 50 and 80 % for other destinations in the Caribbean (Simon 1995; Martin de Holan and Phillips 1997)

A TRANSITION FOR CUBA?

The purpose of this paper, as noted at the outset, is not to speculate about regime change in Cuba but rather to develop a method through which to analyze possible, if not probable, outcomes. Myriad articles and books already exist on the political aspects of regime change in Cuba, and it is difficult, if not impossible, to explore the post-Castro Caribbean tourism industry without some discussion about possible transition events (Gonzalez 2002). Castro's regime has outlived ten U.S. presidents and even more predictions about his demise over the last 44 years, but it is also true that Castro is approaching 80 and there are biological imperatives. Put differently, even a ten-year planning horizon is not overly long for a nation planning the thoughtful growth of its tourist sector.

In terms of possible scenarios, one may draw limited lessons from experiences of nations in Eastern Europe and of the Dominican Republic and perhaps Vietnam, China, and Iraq (Åslund and Hewko 2002). However, there are fundamental differences between Cuba and Eastern European or Asian nations (Stein and Kane-Hanan 1996). The most obvious—and perhaps most important—difference is distance from the United States; only 90 miles (145 kilometers) separate the two. The histories of Cuba and the United States are closely interlaced and richly described in various books and biographies. Their economies were really one prior to Castro: in 1959, the value of U.S. investment in Cuba was greater than it was for any other Latin American nation except for Venezuela (owing to large investments there by American oil companies), but on a per capita basis, the value of U.S. enterprises in Cuba was over three times larger than anywhere else in Latin America (Thomas 1998).

Unlike the situation in the former Communist nations in Europe, Cubans have had and continue to have close ties to people in the United States. They are intimately familiar with North American culture and trends. Even after nearly a half-century of communism, there are obvious signs of these connections. For instance, the main road to the crowded Varadero beach resorts from Havana is dubbed "Calle Ocho" by local Cubans, in honor of the main street of the Cuban American community in Miami, Florida (Zúñiga 1998). This situation existed in the 1950s and before, when Cuba's nearness to the U.S., along with its large middle class, meant that it was relatively easy for Cubans to obtain many items not readily available elsewhere: Cuba in the 1950s had more telephones per capita (26 per 1000) than any other Latin American country except Argentina and Uruguay; more radios and far more television sets than any other Latin American country and most other nations as well (56 TVs per 1000, compared to 19 for Argentina and 43 for Italy). Cuba also had more cars per capita than all other Latin American nations except Venezuela (25 per 1000 in Cuba versus 29 in Venezuela). A radio station in Havana that played American "pop" music devoted Saturday afternoon broadcasts to the songs of Elvis Presley. And although it would be difficult to prove, there were possibly more Cuban millionaires (in U.S. dollars)

than "anywhere south of Dallas" (Thomas 1998, 1111); Havana in 1954 bought more Cadillacs than any other city in the world (Ruiz 1968) Transport costs were small between the U.S. and Cuba, and there were no foreign exchange problem as dollars and pesos were entirely interchangeable. As Thomas observes in his encyclopedic work on Cuba: "North Americans had always been more popular in Cuba than in Mexico or other countries" (Thomas 1998, 1059). These factors all suggest a relatively rapid reunification after a regime change.

It is also clear that in the short term, any form of change, whether due to the lifting of the embargo and the travel restriction or due to some form of regime change, will involve distortions and upheavals. To say the least, no nation has "hit the ground running" following a regime featuring a long-term dictator like Castro, Trujillo, Hussein, or Franco. Additionally, Cuba will require time to move to a place from which it can compete in global markets and this would be very difficult, if not impossible, under the current regime. How long this period of upheaval lasts depends in part on how power is transferred and on the likelihood and manner of foreign interventions.

And after a transition, the form government in Cuba could, in theory, remain the same as it is now or it could move toward democracy and openness and free markets. If the current socialistic system somehow remains in place, whether or not Castro is in power, then this outcome is likely to have the least impact on Cuba's tourism and on the rest of the Caribbean (Simon 1995). Why would this be the case?

Cuba's current tourism strategy of price leadership or low-cost leadership requires that both its prices and its costs be lower than those of its competitors. The absence of economic competitive rivalry in the communist model, the lack of supporting industries, and, more generally, the economic inefficiencies inherent in a communist regime, suggest that it could not compete very effectively in the long term against places like the Dominican Republic for U.S. tourists (Martin de Holan and Phillips 1997). Even if Cuba didn't have to import most of the inputs used for tourism, they would still be *producing* these inputs with a socialist cost structure and *pricing* them at competitive world prices. Foreign investment would continue to be made difficult by myriad regulations and bureaucratic policies that exist within an amazingly deteriorated economy; foreign ownership would continue to be prohibited; capitalism and private enterprise would be hindered; and tourists would be kept physically and artificially apart from most Cubans.

Relations with the U.S., the potential source of the largest and wealthiest market for tourism, would remain uncertain, particularly if Castro were to remain in power, even absent the embargo. At the same time, a transition after Castro leaves the scene that keeps the present system largely intact, while possible, is not considered likely by many experts outside Cuba and even by some inside Cuba as well (though this latter group is understandably much less vocal and reticent to put their thoughts in print) in a new community of nations that encourages democracy, freer trade, and freedom of expression and travel (Martin de Holan and Phillips 1997; Gonzalez 2002; Stein and Kane-Hanan 1996; Weintraub 2000).

As suggested above, lifting the travel restrictions without any substantive change in the regime or its policies toward economic liberalization is likely to have the least effect on the larger Caribbean tourism market. As Weintraub has observed about the market-democracy nexus: "Democracy exists *only* in market economies, but markets do not by themselves assure democracy. I certainly do not wish to push the market/democracy connection in Cuba while Castro remains in power, but this surely will be a key consideration once he is gone" (Weintraub 2000, 339).

Some current competitors and government officials from neighboring islands and destinations surprisingly dismiss Cuba's future impact on the Caribbean tourism industry by pointing to the island's current economic system and by asserting that it will be a long time before Cuba becomes an attractive investment opportunity.[5] Such a position is understand-

able if one travels to Cuba and focuses on how Cuban hotels are currently managed and operated and on the uncertainty in the regime's future. At the same time, the foregoing analyses underscore that Cuba could become a formidable tourist destination very rapidly and could attract great sums of foreign investment in the process. Even with its current inefficiencies and with Castro's erratic behavior toward tourism, internal dissidents, and foreign investment, and more importantly, without American tourists and American investors, Cuba is nonetheless closing rapidly on the Dominican Republic as the top destination in the Caribbean.

Therefore, if or when circumstances shift toward democracy and free markets after a period of transition and upheaval after Castro (and toward a new constitution that allows for private enterprise and that recognizes private ownership), it would not be unreasonable to imagine that a welcoming investment environment would quickly materialize. Only then would a true expansion of the tourism industry in Cuba begin in earnest. It is this democratic scenario with free markets and a new constitution that recognizes private property and other freedoms that I deem most likely, and it is the one also that would have the greatest impact on tourism. Efforts toward product differentiation and consumer segmentation would need to be supported by a strong infrastructure and by an integrated marketing and communication effort, things that Cuba presently cannot provide and that many investors are not willing to supply under the current economic system.

COMPETITIVE ANALYSES

Assuming the democratic scenario prevails, what are the likely consequences on tourism in Cuba and their impact on other destinations? Under conditions of stable and free markets and of democracy, Cuba could offer several kinds of tourism "products," some of which would be unique in the Caribbean. But it is fruitful to distinguish among these different products because their impacts will be different on the other

5. But see discussion below about author's interviews during 2003 with resort owners and managers and government officials from Spain, Turks and Caicos, Dominican Republic, Belize, and Puerto Rico.

destinations and on Cuba's own success. More specifically, Cuba could be involved in three categories of products into the Caribbean tourism market (Lilien, Kotler, and Moorthy 1992).

New Product Innovation

This would entail tourism products that are new both to the Caribbean market and to Cuba. These types of activities would be truly new and different classes of services that would compete against other classes of existing offerings. Examples would be short ferry services from Key West to Havana where tourists could bring their cars to drive in Cuba; fast-speed ferry boats (hovercrafts, similar to the ones in Capri, Italy) from Key West and Miami to Havana; city tourism, capitalizing on the city of Havana and its vast resources and architectural styles. The unique proximity of Cuba to the United States would be a real advantage, along with the mystique of the island and its history: Hemingway, mojitos, *I Love Lucy*.

New Brands

This would represent efforts of a destination to add its own entry to an established product class already in existence in the industry. It would entail services or products new to Cuba but not particularly new to the market (the Caribbean tourism industry). Consumers recognize the new brand as part of the established product class, and less learning has to take place compared to the case of new product innovation. Cuba has already experience with all-inclusive resorts run by European owners, but new resorts and hotels would surely open catering to a massive United States market. Many American tourists are not particularly interested in all-inclusive experiences and tend to make their own travel planning. Europeans who travel to the Caribbean in the main arrange their travel through large tour operators (Interviews with hotel CEOs and managers, June 2003).

With the right investments, Cuba could easily move into the more upscale and specialized market segment, catering to more elite customers with higher levels of expectations about service and performance. Cuba currently has no entries in this segment of great appeal to many potential U.S. visitors. Ecotourism opportunities in Cuba, one of the most bio-diverse places in the world, will compete with those of other nations in the area and even in places in Central America like Costa Rica (Linden 2003). Cruise ship visitors would be another new brand that could compete successfully with several other island destinations (particularly Puerto Rico) and Cuba's proximity to Miami and its size and plentiful deep harbors could make it a major destination for cruise ships. The latter two offerings would not be in the same class of revenue production as other, more massive forms of tourism.

New Model or Style

This would involve the introduction of a product only marginally new to Cuba and to the Caribbean region and is immediately recognized and understood by consumers as simple extension of the existing product line. Cuba, as the largest nation in the Caribbean has tremendous opportunities to expand and to offer "new models" of the same basic product in its various keys and smaller islands, some of which, of course, are the size of several other Caribbean countries.

Products in these three categories will compete differently with different nations and destinations:

- the totally new products may generally be expected to attract a new class or type of visitors to the Caribbean but may also compete with other destinations to varying degrees. These new offerings will tend to increase overall visitors to the Caribbean basin;

- the second class of products, new products to Cuba but not new to the Caribbean, will be expected to compete with selected, mostly upscale destinations in other islands such as the Turks and Caicos and Bermuda; and

- the products that simply extend Cuba's existing product line will tend to compete with comparable, middle-and-down destinations and will tend to depress prices due to increases in supply offered.

The preceding discussion, along with the evidence shown in Table 3 and 4, suggests that Cuba in theory and in practice could compete with every destination in the Caribbean. The converse is not true: not every

Table 5.   Estimates of U.S. Tourist Arrivals in Cuba After a Lifting of Travel Restrictions

Organization	Year	Estimate of U.S. Arrivals	Diversion Rate	Impact on US or Caribbean tourism
US Int'l Trade Comm.	2001	100-350K total U.S. citizens	Negligible	Cites Pto. Rico
Center Int'l Policy	2002	3.2 million total U.S. citizens	50%	Not mentioned
Cuba Policy Foundation	2002	1 m. in first year; 2.8 m in 5 years plus 100K/500K in cruise/ferry passengers	80%	Not mentioned

Source: 1) U.S. International Trade Commission, The Economic Impact of U.S. Sanctions With Respect to Cuba, USITC Pub. 3398. February 2001. .2) Robyn, E., et al. Impact on the U.S. Economy of Lifting Restrictions on Travel to Cuba. Center for International Policy. Washington, DC. 2002. 3) Sanders, E. and P. Long. Economic Benefits to the U.S. from Lifting the Ban on Travel to Cuba. Cuban Policy Foundation. Washington, DC. 2002.

destination in the Caribbean will be able to compete with some of the products that Cuba could offer. The curiosity factor for Cuba and its proximity to the United States will likely be significant variables and "early sales" are likely to have a major impact on its tourism arrivals and on those of competitors. This curiosity factor would be mitigated by a lack of adequate infrastructure and by the extent of turmoil associated with a change in government in Cuba. Nonetheless, one would expect a "sales" profile that rises sharply in the early stages of product introduction, then peaks, and falls off to some equilibrium level. A crucial element in where this equilibrium levels settles will be the ability of other Caribbean destinations to lure back repeat visitors as well as the competitive reactions and countermoves of key rivals in the region.

ANALYSIS OF IMPACT

The possible opening of Cuba is of interest to a surprisingly large number of groups and organizations, given the island's small population (about 11 million) and its ultimate economic potential. Each of these groups, of course, has its own particular concerns or self-interests, but one consequence has been an impressive number of studies and reports published on not only the effects of the embargo but also forecasting what will happen when Cuba rejoins the global economy. Three recent reports are pertinent to the extant analysis and their results are summarized in Table 5.

All three are carefully done and contain solid information. The most thorough and comprehensive of the three was the one conducted by the U.S. International Trade Commission staff in response to a request from the U.S. Congress, House Committee on Ways and Means, to examine and report on the economic impact of U.S. sanctions on Cuba (U.S. International Trade Commission 2001). The ITC report used a gravity model to estimate the effects of sanctions on bilateral trade and on tourism. The other two were prepared by the Brattle Group (Robyn et al. 2002) and by analysts at the University of Colorado-Boulder (Sanders and Long 2002) in response to requests by the Center for International Policy and by the Cuban Policy Foundation, respectively, organizations that have in the past expressed concerns about the travel and trade embargo against Cuba.[6]

In each of these reports, an effort is made to forecast the various effects on trade and tourism of the elimination of the embargo. Regarding tourism, assumptions are made regarding not only the overall future demand for tourism in the Caribbean—a difficult task indeed—but also the amount of tourism business diverted by Cuba away from other Caribbean destinations. The ITC's report, not surprisingly, shows the smallest effect on tourism. This is because their study considers the impact of eliminating the embargo within the context of the present Castro regime and its business and social policies. Still, their range of 100,000 to 350,000 additional U.S. tourists each year over the number that now travel there may

6. The board of the Cuban Policy Foundation, chaired by former U.S. Secretary of State William Rogers, and which had been a strong advocate for the elimination of the U.S. embargo, resigned en masse as a protest against the imprisonment of political dissidents in Cuba in the Spring of 2003.

be a bit conservative, even if the regime does not change its policies. About 8 million U.S. citizens traveled in 2002 as stayover tourists to one (or more) of the destinations in the Caribbean. Thus, the ITC estimate would represent 6.2 % of the U.S. tourists who traveled to the Caribbean, a much lower "market share" of U.S. tourists than they had during the 1950s. The ITC report does not mention a diversion impact away from other destinations, and even though its estimates of additional U.S. travelers are modest, it nonetheless notes that the potential impact is of considerable concern to Puerto Rico.

The other two reports estimate larger numbers, but it is not clear what assumptions they make about the kind of regime and economic system that would exist in Cuba when the embargo is lifted. For example, the Sanders and Long report has three "scenarios," including one where all travel and trade restrictions are eliminated by the United States and any company would be free to make investments (Sanders and Long 2002). But the report does not state, for instance, whether private ownership would be allowed or whether "joint ventures" between the Cuban regime and the investors would be mandatory. Such inefficient restrictions have caused many investors from nations that don't have an embargo against Cuba not to invest in Cuba because they can get a higher return elsewhere without the headaches. The European Union has recently noted these concerns ("Foreign investment" 2002). These two reports are also silent about the impact that the opening of Cuba would have on other Caribbean nations and destinations.

Nonetheless, their estimates are useful because they may represent an approximation to the situation that may exist in the Caribbean if Cuba changes its economic and political system and rejoins the global economy at some juncture. The Sanders and Long report project under their most favorable forecast that nearly 3 million U.S. citizens would travel to Cuba annually as stayover tourists. This seems to be based on their (undocumented) assertion that Cuba's market share of Caribbean tourism was between 18 and 21 % in the 1950s. (Table 1 above, based on Maribona's 1959 book and other sources, suggests a

market share closer to 30 % for Cuba in 1956). Additionally, based on a questionnaire sent to travel agent "experts," they estimate that half of the U.S. tourists who will go to Cuba would be drawn away from other Caribbean destinations. Under this set of assumptions, nearly one out of every five U.S. tourists now going to one of the other islands would be lured away by Cuba (1.5 million out of the current total of 8 million). This would be a major problem for some destinations.

The third report (Robyn et al. 2002) estimates that 3.2 million U.S. tourists would visit Cuba post-embargo, but it is also silent about the impacts on other islands and the kind of regime and economic system that would exist after the restrictions are lifted unilaterally by the U.S. Their estimates are based on the patterns of travel back to the Dominican Republic by Dominican-Americans (whom they believe are the "most comparable group" among the Caribbean "emigrants" to Cuban Americans) and on the travel patterns of Canadians to Cuba as a percentage of the Canadian population. Specifically, they assumed that Cuban Americans would, on average, return to visit friends and relatives at about 80 % of the rate of Dominicans. And since 0.97 % of all Canadians, or 308,000, traveled to Cuba in 2000, they adopted that same rate and applied it to the U.S. population of 280 million: one per cent of 280 million generates the 2.8 million U.S. tourists to Cuba. The study conducted for the Center for International Policy also assumes that 80 % of the U.S. travelers would be diverted from other islands, which amounts to 2.6 million U.S. tourists, or 32 % of the total currently traveling to the Caribbean.

Lest these numbers seem overly optimistic, in fact similar growth has been witnessed in the Caribbean in recent years. During the decade of the 1990s, for example, the number of hotel rooms in the Dominican Republic increased by 36,000, or 126 %, and the number of stayover (non-resident, foreign) arrivals by 2 million; tourists to the Cancún and Cozumel destinations in Mexico have also increased dramatically since 1990 (Padilla and McElroy 2003). Cuba, which is about 85 % the size of England and three times larger than the Dominican Republic, currently has over 42,000 hotel rooms and could realistically add the same number of rooms within a 5-10 year time frame, particularly if the political and economic conditions existed that welcomed foreign, and especially U.S., investments.

In this quasi-zero-sum game, however, where one nation gains and others lose to a greater or lesser extent, it is curious that neither of the two latter studies examines the losses of the other islands as a result of the gains by Cuba. These major economic losses surely would affect the demand for U.S. goods and services negatively, just as the Cuban gains might increase demand. Similarly, while U.S. air carriers may experience an increase in demand for travel to Cuba, they would experience drops in air traffic due to decreased air travel to the other islands from which tourists would be diverted. More importantly, the reports are silent about the certain countermoves that will be made by other Caribbean destinations as tourism expands in Cuba. While one may quibble about underlying assumptions or omissions, these three major reports are reasonable given their assumptions. According to these "best guesses," when Cuba opens up there may be between 350,000 and 3.2 million additional U.S. tourists traveling there each year. A significant fraction, up to 80 %, of Cuba's additional traffic is expected to come from existing U.S. tourism to other islands. The diverted totals are likely to number between 2 and 3 million U.S. tourists, or between 25 and 35 % of the total U.S. tourists, and some destinations are likely to be much more vulnerable than others. But can anything else be said about the impact that Cuba will have on the Caribbean?

First, since the opening up of Cuba will affect the U.S. tourist market most heavily, it is useful to examine the current market shares of U.S. tourists in the Caribbean and consider the destinations with high percentages of American tourists. Box 1 shows the favored Caribbean destination of U.S. travelers in 2002; excluded are areas within the United States—such as Florida—that would be directly affected,

both positively and negatively, by the opening of Cuba.[7] Considering just the "traditional" Caribbean destinations, four out of every five American tourists last year went to one of the top seven destinations: Cancún/Cozumel, Bahamas, Puerto Rico, Jamaica, Dominican Republic, U.S. Virgin Islands, and Aruba. All except one destination, the Dominican Republic, had a very large proportion of U.S. tourists as a percent of all tourist arrivals in their destinations. However, the Dominican Republic is making concerted efforts, with great success particularly in the Punta Cana region, to attract more Americans to their resorts and has been making some inroads into the market share in this segment of the industry. (Interviews with President Hipólito Mejía, June 2003).

Therefore, a change in policy that allows U.S. citizens to travel freely to Cuba is likely to have the greatest impact on this set of destinations, with some qualifications:

- Much of Puerto Rico's travel involves Puerto Rican Americans going back home to visit friends and relatives (VFR). Unfortunately, disentangling VFR trips from other trips made by "regular" tourists is a challenge, given the data available. (The information presented herein attempts to do so and has adjusted the data using a variety of sources to reflect comparable numbers from destination to destination). The extent to which Puerto Rico's tourism is based on VFR travel will determine the level of exposure of that destination.

- The diversification of tourists that exists in the Dominican Republic also will insulate it somewhat from an opening of Cuba but, still, over 700,000 U.S. tourists travel there annually and the island is trying to attract more U.S. tourists and to move away from the all-inclusive focus of the past.

- Cancún and Cozumel cater to the largest number of U.S. tourists, and that region of México

7. According to a recent report to the Florida Commission on Tourism, 43 % of intended Florida vacationers are interested in going to Cuba and 21 % of them are interested in the Cuba vacation as a replacement for the Florida vacation (Pitegoff 2002).

has grown rapidly in the last 20 years though as shown above (Table 2) the last decade has been slow and hotel occupancy is down. Most of Cuba's and the Dominican Republic's tourism is "all inclusive," while Cancún's is not and this difference contributes to some differentiation in that destination (Crespo and Suddaby 2000). Additionally, many Mexican nationals go to Cancún in the summer months, unlike the situation in either Cuba or the Dominican Republic.

- Jamaica has been holding on to market share, neither gaining nor falling back, on the strength of its local tourist industry and its managerial leadership in the all-inclusive resort industry. Reports of persistent crime and dissatisfaction with "garrison" tourism, as Jamaicans call it, point to some vulnerability.

- The Bahamas has already been losing market share, depends on the U.S. market heavily, and is in an increasingly vulnerable position.

- Bermuda and the Cayman Islands have been losing market share and are also vulnerable. Bermuda's upscale image and relative distance from the Caribbean proper may allow it to differentiate its products further, but this will take careful marketing efforts and concerted planning.

- Aruba, which enjoyed large rates of growth up until the mid-1990s and which caters to a largely U.S. market, has seen its growth slow down dramatically in the last few years.

- U.S. destinations such as Key West and to a lesser extent, Miami, could be affected. Key West could benefit in some ways (departure point for ferries) but could also be vulnerable. The Florida Keys Tourist Development Council has already set up an "Opening Cuba Committee" and it is considering ways to keep tourism thriving, perhaps by making Key West an attractive stopover for Cuba-bound tourists or a pleasant side trip for those who decide to travel there directly.

- Smaller Caribbean destinations are not specifically listed in Table 2 or Box 1 but some of them, such as the Turks and Caicos, Barbados, and Belize, have recently been losing some market share and could be vulnerable to some of the new products that Cuba might offer, such as more upscale tourism and ecotourism.

The strategic group maps (see Charts 1-4) add a visual perspective to the foregoing discussion and highlight the changes in the Caribbean market and the gains made by Cuba and the Dominican Republic. Strategic maps are widely used in the strategic management literature and essentially show three dimensions in two-dimensional space. On the vertical axis, the average level of the destination is shown, broken out by "low scale," "middle scale," and "upscale" based on the average tourist spending at the destination. The horizontal axis shows the language spoken at the destination. The circles represent destinations, and the size of the circles represents the total number of arrivals or the size of their market share. This way of presenting the data enables one to see where the rivals are within this competitive space. Comparing the 1985-89 pentad with those of 1990-94 and 1995-1999 and 2000-04 (data for 2003 and 2004 were projected based on time trends by the author so there would be four full pentads of comparison) clearly shows the movement over time and the rise of Cuba and Dominican Republic.

Finally, interviews were conducted by the author during summer of 2003 with one dozen CEOs and senior managers representing most of the European hotel chains now in the Caribbean and in Cuba. These structured interviews ranged over all aspects of the operations and finance of hotel management and strategy. They support several observations:

- Over half of the CEOs and managers interviewed expected Cuba to have a major impact; the CEO of the Sol-Meliá chain (which has the largest presence in Cuba) termed it an "avalanche." Others were not so sure, principally because there is so much uncertainty about how any transition event would end up, but most felt that repeat business would be crucial for destinations like Jamaica and the Dominican Republic: customer loyalty is seen as a key success factor in retaining market share.

Figure 1.   Strategic Group Map of Tourist Arrivals, 1985-1989

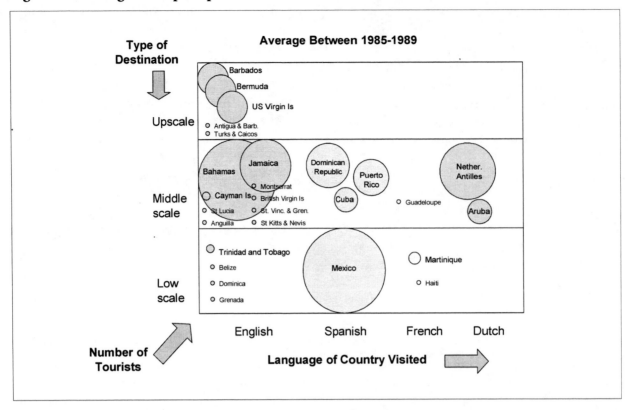

Figure 2.   Strategic Group Map of Tourist Arrivals, 1990-1994

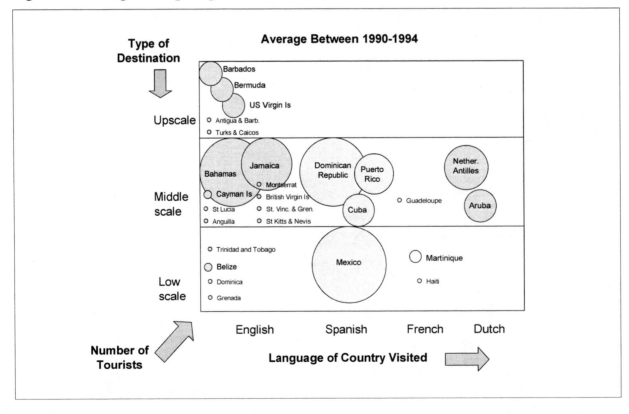

Figure 3.   Strategic Group Map of Tourist Arrivals, 1995-1999

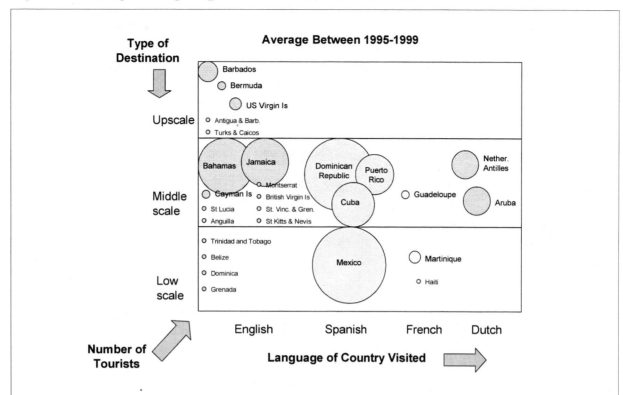

Figure 4.   Strategic Group Map of Tourist Arrivals, 2000-2004

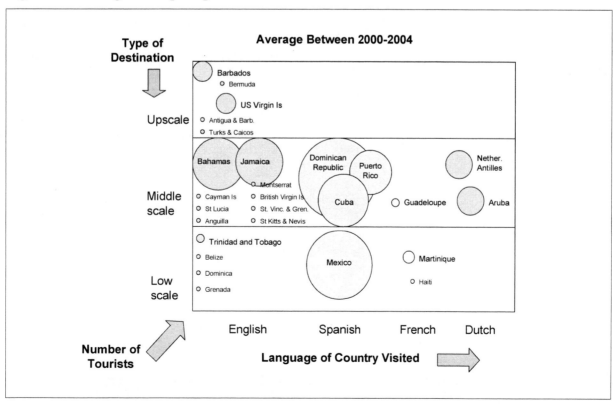

- Second, the clear sense emerged from the interviews that Cuba's system would have to change dramatically in order for any "avalanche" to begin. "It is just too hard to do business there. We are really just operators of hotels; we're not managers or owners." These comments tend to lend support to the conservative estimates of the U.S. International Trade Commission (2001) report cited earlier.

- Third, there is, according to the majority of the managers and owners, a "herd" mentality in the hotel industry: when one or a few investors go in, they all want to follow quickly. One CEO noted the reason he entered the Caribbean market was because "the rest of those guys were already there." The implication is that when Cuba opens up and the politics and economy stabilize, investments are likely to increase rapidly to take advantage of emerging opportunities.

CONCLUSIONS

George Bernard Shaw said that we learn from history that we learn nothing from history. The history of Caribbean tourism, however, offers many lessons. The first lesson is that Cuba has been and will continue to be a major force in the Caribbean tourism industry. Another is that the United States and Cuba have a long history of trade and cultural relations and the opening of Cuba to U.S. tourism will have a major impact on the Caribbean tourism industry on which all of the destinations in the region increasingly depend for their economic well-being. And, as seen above, two of Cuba's three tourism periods have ended with the collapse of the government. If the Castro regime is eventually replaced by a democratic one with a new constitution that recognizes private property rights and free markets, then Cuba's impact could be, as one hotel chain CEO observed, an avalanche.

Certain Caribbean destinations are more vulnerable than others to Cuban tourism. The Mexican resorts in Cancún and Cozumel as well as Aruba, Bahamas, Bermuda, Jamaica, Puerto Rico, and the Dominican Republic are all, for various reasons, at risk of significant downturn during the early stages of the opening of Cuba and possibly beyond. Thoughtful resort

managers and government officials likely to be affected should begin to plan their strategies and countermoves now. These planning activities should involve at a minimum better data collection and analyses; strengthened marketing efforts, particularly in the U.S. markets, focusing on product differentiation and specialization; active exploration of alliances with other Caribbean destinations; and greater attention to the quality of their infrastructure and their environments.

At the same time, there are reasons for concern with Cuba's own opening its tourism to U.S. travelers. First, it would be naïve to think that investors who have built amazingly expensive properties in other islands will simply watch Cuba siphon off tourists without any response. Competition based on price, airline flight availability and convenience, and on marketing will surely increase. Destinations that continue to offer value within the context of safe, clean, and interesting surroundings will do best with the U.S. and other markets.

Second, the history of mass tourism is one of ebb and flow and "trendiness" and of social, environmental, and political challenges. Cuba's future tourism development, if not thoughtfully and carefully planned, could head in the same direction as have some others in the ecologically fragile Caribbean area and in other islands across the globe. For example, the overbuilding in the Puerto Plata region of the Dominican Republic, a booming tourist destination in the 1980s, has caused significant problems and tourist arrival declines in recent years. The Punta Cana area in the Dominican Republic is now the Caribbean's hottest destination as measured by its amazing growth and its surrounding publicity, but there are troubling signs there of environmental and crowding problems that could change conditions within a few years.

Third, Cuba's novelty and associated curiosity factor will be a real advantage during the early months after its opening, and repeat business will be crucial to other destinations. Cuba has to be prepared to deal with the expected responses of competitors: price competition, alliances with airlines and hotel chains and tour operators, new and improved products.

Finally, the various governments in the Caribbean basin should invest a small portion of their receipts from tourism to obtain better data. This would include appropriate and timely information not only about tourist arrivals and numbers of hotel rooms, but also about the environment, crime, and other social and economic impacts and consequences of tourism. Trade organizations like the Caribbean Hotel Association and the Caribbean Tourism Organization, as well as a few government agencies in various countries, have pioneered data collection activities but the Caribbean region desperately needs more accurate information about its most important industry.

REFERENCES

Aeberhard, D. 2002. *Insight Guides: Cuba.* Singapore. Insight Print Services.

Askari, H., J. Forrer, H. Teegen, and J. Yang. 2003. *Economic and Strategic Impacts of U.S. Economic Sanctions on Cuba.* Occasional Paper Series, George Washington University (February 24).

Åslund, A. and J. Hewko. 2002. "Lessons for Cuba after communism." *The Christian Science Monitor* (June 24).

Ausenda, Becky. 2002. "Cuba's Dangerous Allure." *Bermuda Sun* (August 21). <http://www.bermudasun.bm/archives/2002-08-21/01News08>

Bruni, F. 1999. "Island of Forbidden Fruits." *The New York Times* (August 8).

Bruni, F. 2001. "Bush administration showing willingness to enforce law on visiting Cuba." *The New York Times* (August 5).

Caribbean Tourism Organization. 1991. *Caribbean Tourism Statistical Report.* St. Michael, Barbados: CTO.

Caribbean Tourism Organization. 2002. *Caribbean Tourism Statistical Report, 2001-2002.* St. Michael, Barbados: CTO.

Central Intelligence Agency. 2002. *The World Fact-Book 2002.* <http://www.cia.gov/cia/publications/factbook/index.html>

Clancy, M. 2002. "The globalization of sex tourism and Cuba: A commodity chains approach." *Studies in Comparative International Development* 36:63-88.

Clarke III, I., K. Micken, and H. S. Hart. 2002. "Symbols for Sale…at Least for Now: Symbolic Consumption in Transition Economies." *Advances in Consumer Research* 29:25-30.

Conway, D. 1995. "The New Tourism in the Caribbean: Reappraising Market Segmentation." In Gayle D. and J. Goodrich, eds., *Tourism Marketing and Management in the Caribbean*, pp. 167-177. London, Routledge.

Crespo, N. 1999. "Forty Years After: A Candid Recount of Experiences at Tourism Destinations in Cuba." *Cuba in Transition—Volume 9.* Washington: Association for the Study of the Cuban Economy, 370-385.

Crespo, N. and C. Suddaby. 2002. "Impact of September 11 on Tourism Activities in Cuba and in the Caribbean." *Cuba in Transition—Volume 12.* Washington: Association for the Study of the Cuban Economy, 354-359.

Davidson, J. 1996. "Sex tourism in Cuba." *Race and Class* 38:39-48.

Díaz-Briquets, S. and J. Pérez-López. 2003. *The Role of the Cuban-American Community in the Cuban Transition.* Cuba Transition Project (CTP), Institute for Cuban and Cuban-American Studies, University of Miami.

Divisekera, S. 2003. "A Model of Demand for International Tourism," *Annals of Tourism Research* 30(1): 31-49.

Espino, M. 1991. "International Tourism in Cuba: An Economic Development Strategy?" *Cuba in Transition—Volume 1*. Miami: Association for the Study of the Cuban Economy, 193-220.

Espino, M. 1995. "Tourism development in socialist Cuba." In Gayle, D.J. and J. Goodrich eds., *Tourism Marketing and Management in the Caribbean*. London: Routledge, 100-110.

Espino, M. 2000. "Cuban Tourism During the Special Period." *Cuba in Transition—Volume 10*. Washington: Association for the Study of the Cuban Economy, 360-373.

Espino, M. 2001. "Cuban Tourism: A Critique of the CEPAL 2000 Report." *Cuba in Transition—Volume 11*. Washington: Association for the Study of the Cuban Economy, 343-349.

"Foreign investment in Cuba falls, EU wants reform." 2002. Reuters (July 8, 2002).

Frank, W. "Habana of the Cubans." *New Republic*, June 1926, 140.

Gayle, D.J., and J.N. Goodrich, eds. 1993. *Tourism Marketing and Management in the Caribbean*. London: Routledge.

Gonzalez, E. 2002. *After Castro: Alternative Regimes and U.S. Policy*. Cuba Transition Project (CTP), Institute for Cuban and Cuban-American Studies, University of Miami.

Goodrich, J. 1995. "Health-care tourism in the Caribbean." In Gayle, D.J. and J. Goodrich. eds. *Tourism Marketing and Management in the Caribbean*. London: Routledge, pp122-128.

Gordon, J. 1997. "Cuba's Entrepreneurial Socialism." *The Atlantic Monthly* (January): 18-30.

Hall, D. 1995. "Tourism development in Cuba." In Harrison, D. (ed), *Tourism in the Less Developed Countries*. London: Wiley 102-120.

Harrison, D. (ed). 1995. *Tourism in the Less Developed Countries*. London: Wiley.

Hays, D. 2002. Statement at Hearing on U.S. Trade Policy with Cuba, Senate Committee on Commerce, Science and Transportation, Sub-Committee on Consumer Affairs, Foreign Commerce, and Tourism (May 21). <http://www.canf.org/News/archived/020521newsd.htm>

Jebodsingh, L. 2001. "Cuba: A Market Profile." Arthur Anderson, posted on Hotel Online. <http://www.hotel-online.com/Trends/Andersen/2001_CubaProfile.html>

Johnston, W. 1958. Letter to the Commissioner of Customs, Division of Investigations, U.S. Bureau of Customs, by the U.S. Treasury Representative in Charge of Cuba. (March 27). <http://cuban-exile.com/doc_276-300/doc0288.htm>

Kirkpatrick, D.D. 2003. "U.S. Halts Cuba Access by Educational Groups. *The New York Times* (May 4).

Latell, B. 2003. *The Military in Cuba's Transition*. Cuba Transition Project (CTP), Institute for Cuban and Cuban-American Studies, University of Miami.

Lilien, G., P. Kotler, and K. Moorthy. 1992. *Marketing Models*. Englewood Cliffs, New Jersey: Prentice Hall.

Linden, E. 2003. "The Nature of Cuba." *Smithsonian* (May) 34:94-106.

López, F. 2003. "Disciplina y control, absolutas prioridades para el turismo." *Granma* (March 8). <http://www.granma.cubaweb.cu/2003/03/09/nacional/articulo11.html>

Macaulay, J.F. 1994. "Tourism and the transformation of Cuba." *Cornell Hotel and Restaurant Administration Quarterly* (June) 35(3):16-21.

Mallin, J. 1956. "Havana Night Life" (unpublished article). <http://cuban-exile.com/doc_201-225/doc0211.htm>

Manning, R. 1965. "Hemingway in Cuba." *The Atlantic* (August).

Maribona, A. 1943. *Turismo y Ciudadanía*. La Habana, Cuba: Alrededor de America.

Maribona, A. 1959. *Turismo en Cuba*. La Habana, Cuba: Lex.

Martin de Holan, P. and N. Phillips. 1997. "Sun, sand, and hard currency: Tourism in Cuba." Annals of Tourism Research 24: 777-795.

Mathers, S. and G. Todd. 1993. "Tourism in the Caribbean." The Economist Intelligence Unit. London, Special Report No. 455.

McElroy, J.L. and K. de Albuquerque. 1998. "Tourism Penetration Index in Small Caribbean Islands." Annals of Tourism Research 25:145-168.

O'Reilly, A. 1995. "Tourism in the Bahamas - An appraisal." In Gayle, D.J. and J.N. Goodrich (eds). *Tourism Marketing and Management in the Caribbean*. London: Routledge, 31-40.

Padilla, A. and J. McElroy. 2003. "Tourism Development in the Dominican Republic: An Application of the TPI" (unpublished manuscript).

Pattulo, P. 1996. *Last Resorts: The Cost of Tourism in the Caribbean*. London: Latin American Bureau.

Pérez-López, J. 2001. "Waiting for Godot: Cuba's Stalled Reforms and Continuing Economic Crisis." *Problems of Post-Communism* (November-December):44-45.

Perry, J.M., J.W. Steagall, and L.A. Woods. 1997. "Cuban Tourism, Economic Growth, and the Welfare of the Cuban Worker." *Cuba in Transition—Volume 7*. Washington: Association for the Study of the Cuban Economy, 141-149.

Phillips, R. 1960. *Cuba: Island of Paradox*. New York: McDowell and Obelensky.

Pitegoff, B. 2002. Cuba: An Updated Strategic Analysis. Research Department, Visit Florida. Presented to Florida Commission on Tourism, December 12, 2002.

Radu, M. 2002. *The Cuban Transition: Lessons from the Romanian Experience*. Cuba Transition Project (CTP), Institute for Cuban and Cuban-American Studies, University of Miami.

Sanders, E. and P. Long. 2002. *Economic Benefits to the Unites States from Lifting the Ban on Travel to Cuba*. Center for Sustainable Tourism, Leeds School of Business, University of Colorado.

Simon, F. 1995. "Tourism Development in Transition Economies." *Columbia Journal of World Business* 30: 26-39.

Robyn, D., J. Reitzes, and B. Church 2002The Impact on the U.S. Economy of Lifting Restrictions on Travel to Cuba. The Brattle Group Washington, DC. Retrieved from: http://www.brattle.com/_documents/Publications/Presentation523.pdf.

Ruiz, R. 1968. *Cuba: The Making of a Revolution*. Amherst: University of Massachusetts Press.

San Martin, N. 2003. "Rules Changed on Cuba Trips: Some Stiffer, Others Relaxed." *Miami Herald* (March 25), pp. 3A.

Sanders, E. and P. Long. 2002. *Economic Benefits to the United States from Lifting the Ban on Travel to Cuba*. Center for Sustainable Tourism, Leeds School of Business, University of Colorado.

Schwartz, R. 1997. *Pleasure Island: Tourism and Temptation in Cuba*. Lincoln, Nebraska: University of Nebraska Press.

Stein, M. and L. Kane-Hanan. 1996. "Cuba—Tourism as a Replacement Industry." Arthur Anderson, posted on Hotel Online (Summer 1996). <http://hotel-online.com/Trends/Andersen/Cuba_TourismIndustry_Spring1996.html>.

Suro, R., S. Bendixen, B.L. Lowell, and D. Benavides. 2003. *Billions in Motion: Latino Immigrants, Remittances and Banking*. Philadelphia, Pennsylvania: Pew Hispanic Center and the Multilateral Investment Fund.

"Tarnished Key West: Island's Tourist Trade Could Suffer as Cuba Opens Up." 2000. Reuters (January 11), <http://abcnews.go.com/sections/travel/DailyNews/cuba_keywest000111.html>.

Thomas, C. Y. 1988. *The Poor and the Powerless: Economic Policy and Change in the Caribbean.* New York. Monthly Review Press.

Thomas, H. 1998. *Cuba or the Pursuit of Freedom.* New York. Plenum Press.

Travieso-Diaz, M. 2002. *Alternative Recommendations for Dealing with Confiscated Property in Post-Castro Cuba.* Cuba Transition Project (CTP), Institute for Cuban and Cuban-American Studies, University of Miami.

U.S. Bureau of the Census. 2002. International Database. Washington, DC: International Programs Center. <http://landview.census.gov/ipc/www/idbnew.html>

U.S. Department of Commerce. 1993. *Tourism in the Caribbean Basin.* Washington, DC: U.S. Travel and Tourism Administration.

U.S. Department of State. 1998. *Zenith and Eclipse: A Comparative Look at Socio-Economic Conditions in Pre-Castro and Present Day Cuba.* Re-leased by the Bureau of Inter-American Affairs (February 9, Revised June 2002).

U.S. International Trade Commission. 2001. *The Economic Impact of U.S. Sanctions With Respect to Cuba.* USITC Publication 3398 (February).

Van Doren, C.S. 1993. "Pan Am's legacy to world tourism." *Journal of Travel Research* 32:3-12.

"Wary Partners: Cuba and the EU Trade and the Single Party." 2003. *The Economist* (March 20).

Weintraub, S. 2000. "Cuba's Trade Policy After Castro." *Cuba in Transition—Volume 10.* Washington: Association for the Study of the Cuban Economy, 337-341.

Williams, H. *The Emerald Isle of Cuba.* Travel. November 1925, 7-9.

World Travel and Tourism Council. 2002. *The Travel and Tourism Economy 2002: Special End of Year Update.* London: WTTC. http://www.wttc.org (accessed 23 January 2003).

Zúñiga, J. 1998. "Cuba: The Thailand of the Caribbean, An Unauthorized Report." Independent Journalists' Cooperative (June 18). Havana, Cuba.

COMMENTS ON "THE TOURISM INDUSTRY IN THE CARIBBEAN AFTER CASTRO" BY PADILLA

Nicolás Crespo

In his paper "The Tourism Industry in the Caribbean after Castro," Art Padilla makes his case. His historical analysis of the tourism industry in the Caribbean and particularly in Cuba reflects an exhaustive research effort on the growth of the industry in the region.

Cuba's impressive tourism industry development in just over ten years can only be compared to the postwar development of the tourism industry in the Mediterranean coast of Spain. Coincidentally, the extraordinary efforts and subsequent success of the Cuban and Spanish tourism industries was triggered by comparable catastrophic economic reasons. Spain and Cuba embraced the support of and allied with the tyrannical regimes of foreign powers that aspired to dominate the World. After these regimes were defeated, democracy began to emerge. As economic support that was based on politics and ideology disappeared, Spain and Cuba turned to tourism as the quickest way to recover from their past. Spain and Cuba re-discovered their most important renewable economic resource, tourism.

Padilla's compilation of prognosis of the future of the tourism industry of the Caribbean by experts is presented in his paper in an orderly and systematic fashion. He also touches on the current marketing strategies of Cuba and other Caribbean destinations and suggests strategies for retaining their current number of visitors and revenues as well as programs for future growth and improvement of their competitive position in the region.

Cuba has attained in more than a decade, a hotel inventory totaling 40,000 rooms. Like the Dominican Republic, Cuba achieved spectacular growth without the contribution of U.S. investors and visitors. However, during the last five years, the Dominican Republic has increased its efforts to penetrate the American market and the newly-built products are geared to satisfy the demands of American tourists. Despite the expansion in the tourism industry in Cuba, the "Big Island's" peculiar type of state capitalism has failed to provide benefits to the majority of its inhabitants, except, in a minimal way to those privileged to have a job within the hospitality industry.

PROFITABILITY

Padilla cites estimates of profitability of Cuba's tourism industry by several credible and responsible authors. Sometimes there are discrepancies when figures and statistics are presented without taking the time factor into consideration. In other cases the comparison of data is affected by changes in methodology or misinterpretation of trade or industry terminology.

The three principal entrepreneurial parties in the Cuba tourism development scene are: (1) the Foreign Investor (lender); (2) the Foreign Operator; and (3) a Cuban Corporation. e.g., Cubanacán, Gaviota, Horizontes, etc. Considering that the economy of Cuba is centralized, the accounting of revenue and expenses related to joint ventures, particularly those in hospitality and tourism activities, is incredibly convoluted. To simplify matters, we will use an example from one of the principal Spanish investors/operators in the Island.

Asset Cost

The cost of a hotel from the Cuban Corporation's point of view is a fictitious figure that comprises: (1) the labor and materials originating in Cuba, valued in dollars at standard world prices; and (2) the imported materials and equipment, valued at actual dollar cost. This total cost is used to calculate the amortization at the time of calculating profits shared by the Foreign Operator and the Cuban Corporation. Cuba profits greatly from the difference between the fictitious cost and the actual salary expense and cost of locally produced materials.

Management

Regarding the management of hotel operations, where a Foreign Operator is involved, the Cuban Corporation controls the accounting of hotel revenues from a centralized office. Labor expense is allocated to the hotel accounts in U.S. dollars, although it is paid out in pesos by the government labor agency that pays directly to the worker. Salaries, even when expressed in dollars, represent about one third of the standard salaries in the rest of the Caribbean. (Salary and other compensation in the Caribbean averages 35-40 % of total revenue, while the comparable percentage in Cuba is only 10-11%.) The higher cost of imported materials and supplies acquired and paid in hard currency is offset by the lower salary cost, even when expressed in U.S. dollars.

To summarize how entrepreneurial parties benefit from tourism:

- the Foreign Investor gets paid interest and loan amortization from the operating profits before profit distribution to the Foreign Operator and the Cuban Corporation (by the way, loans are unsecured).
- the Foreign Operator normally obtains compensation in the form of management fees and profits that are similar to comparable operations outside Cuba. This is attributed to the low labor cost in Cuba.
- the Cuban Corporation benefits from the labor manipulation scheme and dollar valuation of the

locally produced materials. They create a profit margin unique in the industry, although there are known previous cases in Jakarta and Bali in Indonesia.

This simplified analysis is intended to explain the mechanics of Cuba's apparent success in the tourism industry through the exploitation of its work force.

COMPETITIVE ANALYSIS

I fully share Padilla's decision to limit his analysis to the "democratic scenario." Otherwise, the crystal balling could become a major Monte Carlo roulette exercise.

In addition to its natural resources and exotic allure of the destination, Cuba's proximity to the affluent and populated east and south coasts of the U.S. and the potentially easy access to its eleven international airports are its main competitive advantages when compared to the rest of the Caribbean.

Cuba is already planning for the American market. For example, a planned world-class multi-use resort development in Jibacoa and the introduction of the Paradisus upscale brand of Melia's all-inclusive hotels. Cuba is opening new properties and refurbishing others at the rate of 2,000/3,500 rooms per year. Cuba is also depending on the current 40,000-hotel room inventory and is seriously planning development of meeting and convention facilities to accommodate an international clientele.

ANALYSIS OF THE IMPACT OF U.S. TOURISM

The three studies mentioned by Padilla have their own merits and do not require further addressing. However the estimate of 3.2 million additional visitors from the United States calculated by the Center for International Policy deserves some analysis.

Taking the Ministry of Tourism's published data for 2002, we have calculated the number of hotel rooms necessary to accommodate 3,200,000 additional visitors from the United States. We assume that the visitors from other sources already traveling to Cuba will remain unchanged. We used the same occupancy rate and the same average length of stay reported for 2002. In addition we made similar calculations using a 90% occupancy rate. The detailed methodology is set out in the annex.

Our calculations indicate that in order to accommodate 3,200,000 additional tourists, Cuba would require between 98,000 and 116,000 hotel rooms. At the current rate of 3,500 new hotel rooms opened per year, it would take 16.6 to 21.8 years to build an additional 58,000 to 76,000 rooms. (With its current 40,000 rooms, Cuba could accommodate 469,000 additional visitors by elevating its occupancy rate to 90% on an annual basis.) The seasonal patterns of the region and profile of tourism makes it practically impossible to attain higher occupancy overall. Regarding air transportation for the additional visitors, we have not factored the additional flights and equipment required for its airlift. We also have not addressed the significant cost of building the additional rooms, estimated at between $4.3 billion and $5.7 billion, based on an average cost of $75,000 per room.

CARIBBEAN COMPETITION

While Cuba prepares for the advent of American visitors by developing new products and converting existing properties to satisfy the quality and standards demanded by the American traveler, other Caribbean destinations are also planning to strengthen their market position and products for the future. This will continue irrespectively of Cuba's obtaining access to the American market.

The following selected projects are on the planning stage or under different stages of development in the Caribbean. Our selection was made in view of the competitive nature of each project in the Caribbean region.

Cap Cana, Dominican Republic

The Cap Cana project is positioned as a luxury resort/residential community and encompasses 29,000 acres overlooking five miles of stunning beaches on the eastern coast of the Dominican Republic. Even though Cap Cana is only 15 minutes from Punta Cana International airport and a number of first class resorts, its immediate area has a very low population density and a pristine natural environment. The project comprises eight hotels; golf courses and marinas; real estate components such as single and multifamily units; and other amenities such as equestrian

activities, polo, tennis, a 5,000-seat open-air amphitheatre and a world class European style casino.

Puerto Rico Convention Center

The 580,000 square feet convention center will be a part of a large-scale district development project encompassing a 500-room headquarter hotel, offices, residential, retail, restaurant and other urban development uses. It is a private and public sector project offering attractions and facilities for convention participants, business travelers, tourists, as well as local residents. The convention center itself promises to rank on a par with the world's leading convention centers in both design and functionality. The $416 million convention center will position Puerto Rico as a major destination in the Caribbean for conventions, trade shows, consumer shows and conferences targeting North America, Latin America and the Caribbean convention markets.

Puerto Rico currently has approximately 12,800 rooms, and through innovative tax incentive and financial programs, continues to support new hotel development. In 2002, $427 million were invested in in new hotel and resort development, including six major hotels and resorts and the aforementioned convention center.

Cartagena de Indias, Colombia

The Baru Island Resort planned for Cartagena, Colombia, consists of 3,225 acres on the island of the same name. The peninsula became an island after the construction of the Canal del Dique during the Spanish colonial period to provide Cartagena a waterway to the interior or the country through the Magdalena River.

The initial phase of the master plan calls for a marina, an 18-hole golf course, golf clubhouse, a hotel and a variety of real estate components. The whole plan calls for an additional hotel and golf course and marina and real estate components of diverse size and price up to 2,600 units. Other amenities will be added as the project progresses.

Quintana Roo, Mexico

In addition to the mature developments in Cancun, Isla Mujeres and Cozumel, the Mundo Maya and the Riviera Maya resorts, south of Cancun, continue their rapid development. The governments of Mexico, Guatemala and Belize are creating a special cultural passport for tourists to move around different spectacular Mayan ruins with minimum hassle.

As an example of new niche marketing, two hotels opened in this area to cater to a special segment of the market: the obese or oversized traveler. Doors and elevators are wider and bedding has been redesigned as well as the bathrooms. Beach chairs are made of wood to accommodate the extra weight of the customers. Restaurants provide buffet service and its chairs are 60 percent wider and stronger than usual.

The Atlantis, Paradise Island, Bahamas

The Atlantis plans a major expansion of this successful mega resort that currently comprises 2,300 rooms, a marina, casino, 38 restaurants, spectacular aquarium and 11 exhibit lagoons, and a wide range of amenities.

CONCLUSION

In conclusion, and with the assistance of my crystal ball, I believe that the tourism avalanche to Cuba will not occur, at least not abruptly as forecasted, as the

existing room supply is inadequate to accommodate such a number of new visitors to Cuba. I hope that the tourist "avalanche" will be gradual, more like a blow of snowflakes and driven first by ethnic tourism, business travelers and the price conscious traveler in search of a good value and curious about this new exotic destination. Some of the small island competitors that cannot afford an adequate promotional budget, will suffer relatively more from growth of Cuban tourism than the bigger islands with an established critical mass of rooms and significant marketing and promotion budget.

There are many elements that have to be in place to ensure a successful tourism industry, from airlift to trained staff to availability of infrastructure necessary to support the development of lodging facilities tailored to the U.S. market. Cuba, as the largest of the islands in the Caribbean with its numerous and varied unexplored natural tourism resources, eventually will claim its natural position in the Caribbean region. However, this will not happen instantly or in the immediate future after Castro.

APPENDIX
METHODOLOGY FOR ESTIMATING IMPACT OF TOURISM INCREASES

To estimate necessary additions to the physical plant of Cuban hotels to accommodate an additional 3,200,000 visitors originating in the United States, we have started out with official Cuban statistics for 2002 issued by the Ministry of Tourism. They are:

- Current number of rooms: 40,000
- Visitors (arrivals):1,836,716
- Average stay (days): 6.6
- Occupancy rate: 76%
- Rooms to open in 2003: 3,500

As shown in Table 1, in order to accommodate the additional 3,200,000 new visitors, Cuba will need 98,139 new rooms (at 90% occupancy rate) or 116,195 rooms (at the 76% occupancy rate attained in 2002). This would mean between 58,139 and 76,195 new rooms. These estimates of new rooms needed translate into an investment of between $4.3

Table 1.   Estimated Impact of the Addition of 3,200,000 Visitors to the Cuban Tourism Market (based on 2002 statistics)

| | 2002 | After Addition of 3,200,000 Visitors | |
		At 76% Occupancy	At 90% Occupancy
Rooms	40,000	116,195	98,139
Visitors	1,683,716	4,883,716	4,883,716
Average Days of Stay	6.6	6.6	6.6
Available Room Nights	14,600,000	42,411,217	35,813,917
Occupied Room Nights	11,168,998	32,232,525	32,232,525
Unused Room Nights	3,431,002		
Equivalent Visitors at 90%	469,000		

Source: Ministry of Tourism, Phoenix Hospitality and Consulting Corporation

and $5.7 billion at an average cost per room of $75,000.

TAXATION LEVELS IN CUBA—AND OTHER TOPICS OF RHETORICAL INTEREST

Nicolás Sánchez[1]

This article is written as a result of a trip that the author made to Cuba in March 2003. Some of the non-economic aspects of the trip are brought out in an article that has been published elsewhere.[2] The economic topics that follow are those that arose in conversations with people from Cuba, or with the students who accompanied the author to Cuba. While these topics require the need to make some reference to scholarly materials, the weight of the arguments depends more on rhetoric than on scholarly discourse (that would include the statistical testing of hypotheses).

The author found the need to engage others in rhetorical arguments, highly dependent on language, in order to understand the ideas that he heard in Cuba. Some persons may find this approach to argumentation new and even confusing, just like the author did while he was in Cuba. However, the author would now argue that one needs to master this approach to understand discourse about Cuba, even abroad (in Western countries). Hence this article is a call for clarity, rationality and consistency in the use of language.

It is divided into four sections. The first describes the effective use of language, from a rhetorical point of view, by a Cuban professor at a university in Matan-zas, and how the questioning of that language led to a different conclusion. The second illustrates how the meaning of words can be so corrupted that many people in Cuba actually believe that their taxation levels are close to zero. The third section deals with the emotional issue of the American embargo—or blockade, as it is known in Cuba; it tries to demonstrate how the complexity of the issue is obfuscated by language. The final section deals with how Cubans abroad perceive the issue of Cuban independence; it suggests, but does not prove, that we are all slaves to the history we read.

This article is written in the hope that it is read by both faculty and students contemplating trips to Cuba, by Cuban scholars in Cuba and outside of Cuba, and by Cuban nationals. It touches on a variety of controversial topics that should be addressed by anyone interested in Cuban history and culture.

AN INFINITE NUMBER OF BOOKS

The group of students and faculty that went to Cuba visited the Camilo Cienfuegos University, just outside the city of Matanzas. The group was welcomed by a professor who gave a detailed history of the university. This individual made the point that prior to the Revolution there were only four universities in Cuba, whereas now (in the year 2003) there are fifty

---

1. The author would like to thank his colleague Miles Cahill, and one of his daughters, Irene Leonor Sánchez, for very useful comments.

2. Nicolás Sánchez, "Reflections on a Recent Trip to Cuba," *The Fenwick Review* (The Independent Journal of Opinion at the College of the Holy Cross), Vol. X, No. 3, May 2003.

universities on the island; in fact, the government's goal for the future is to create a university in every municipality, for a total of over one hundred and fifty universities. This was, of course, a strong rhetorical argument in support of the educational achievements of the Cuban Revolution: fifty is clearly greater than four, and one hundred and fifty is three times an order of magnitude than fifty. The students were very impressed with these numbers.

At the conclusion of the presentation, the author asked for the approximate number of books at this particular university, which has about eight thousand students. Instead of answering the question, the professor commented on the difficulty of obtaining books in Cuba. But he made the point that with access to the Internet, the need for books in a modern library is somewhat limited. This argument resonated with the students, since most of them have grown accustomed to writing research papers based on what they find on the Internet.

The group was given total access to the university. It soon discovered that the computer lab available to students consisted of eight computers. When the students in the group tried to send simple e-mail messages to the United States, they were frustrated. It took one student 30 minutes to do so, another gave up after 45 minutes of trying, and the rest did not bother to try. The group found no other computer access for students at the university, although it later became known that Cuban faculty had their own access to the Internet, which they might share with some of their students. (The reader can obtain more information about this university by logging on to www.umcc.cu.)

The author then met with one of the librarians and asked for an approximate count of books in the library. First, the librarian informed him that the library was divided into three sections: technical-scientific, humanities and social sciences. Then the librarian turned towards the collection in the technical-scientific section and declared with complete confidence: "Well, you can see for yourself: *we have an infinite number of books in this library* (emphasis added)." After visiting all three sections, the author's own estimate was that the number of books available

was no more than 12,000, with the technical-scientific section possessing the largest share.

It is important to note that the above librarian did not appear to be sarcastic or completely committed to the Revolution, since an older child of this individual was already living in the United States. But the nature of the argument is very significant. If we take the word infinity to mean what it usually means, then this individual demonstrated cognitive dissonance, for it is simply impossible to hold an infinite number of standard-sized books in a fairly small finite space. That was precisely what the individual was stating. While this individual might be unique in all of Cuba, the response illustrates the difficulties that the author confronted when he tried to make people address certain topics that would be of interest to economists.

It is obvious that if individuals (like students, or people doing research work) fail to make conceptual distinctions as to what a university is all about, then the "truth" of academic discourse depends on the way that language is used or misused. To the author, it does not make sense to count as equals his college, which has a collection of half a million volumes in its library and widespread student access to the Internet, and the Camilo Cienfuegos University, which has fewer volumes in its library than many high school libraries in the United States and no effective access to the Internet. The argument is even stronger when the comparison involves research universities in the United States. Hence, the number of universities in Cuba now or in the future is hardly an argument in favor of the educational achievements of the Revolution.

The paucity of books in Cuban libraries can be appreciated with the following figures. The library of the Cuban Academy of Sciences has slightly more than 100,000 books and pamphlets and 60,000 serials. This library was founded in 1864. A newer library, founded in 1979 and devoted to the study of tobacco, has 958 books, 5,300 bound periodical volumes, 611 reports, 15 manuscripts, 43 patents, 2 microfiche and 2 reels of microfilm. On the other hand, the Cuban National Library has a respectable 2.22 million volumes.[3]

TAXATION LEVELS IN CUBA

The author found well-educated people in Cuba who honestly believe that taxation in Cuba is minimal. People actually told the author that the only income that was heavily taxed in Cuba was that generated through the *paladares* (private restaurants), the few private hostels that can collect dollars, and foreign enterprises that exist in partnership with the Cuban government. The owners of *paladares* with whom the author talked to were in fact quite resentful of the levels of taxation, claiming that they reached 40% or higher. What, then, is the level of income taxation in Cuba?

Before this issue is addressed, it might be useful to explain the meaning of "income" in economics. This term is equivalent to the value of production of goods and services, or the value of output that is produced in an economy over a period of time, usually one year. The reason that the word "income" is used is that ultimately all output accrues to someone in the form of income; the one exception is depreciation charges, since some of the goods produced need to be used to replace old capital equipment.

There are three ways of calculating income or output: first, by adding the "value added" that has been contributed by each industry or sector of the economy; second, by taking into account all the expenditures on "final" goods and services by consumers, businesses, government and the foreign sector; and third, by determining the income that the various factors of production have earned as a result of their productive activities. All three approaches yield the same result

using different procedures. In the income approach, however, sometimes it is difficult to determine how income accrues to individuals. For example, suppose that labor and capital together produce some output, but this output is fully taxed by the government. The government can then turn around and either assign the output to producers and/or non-producers, or give money transfers to producers and/or non-producers so that these transfers can be used to purchase either these goods or other goods.

Gross Domestic Product (GDP), then, is the standard measure of the value of output within a country. In Cuba, per capita GDP is now in the neighborhood of $2,000 (in U.S. currency).[4] Given that approximately 45% of the population is economically active, the average GDP per worker is $4,444. From this figure, one should subtract income or output produced by the capital that belongs to foreigners, since the goal is to calculate taxation rates *for Cuban workers*. Foreign investment in Cuba has been estimated at $2.5 billion,[5] and assuming that this investment yields the extraordinarily high pre-tax return of 25%, one can calculate[6] that the $4,444 should be reduced by 3%,[7] leaving a Gross National Product (GNP) per capita of $4,310.

One then needs to subtract 10% for depreciation from this figure,[8] a part of production that would never accrue to any worker; this leaves an amount of $3,880 for Net National Product (NNP) per worker. Normally, indirect business taxes would then be subtracted and government subsidies to firms would be added, but since one is trying to calculate taxes on

3. These figures are taken from the 1997 edition of the *Directory of Special Libraries and Information Centers*, New York, Gale Publishers, 1997.

4. The *2003 World Development Report*, in Table 1a, footnote h, gives an estimate of between $746 and $2975 for the year 2001. The 2003 *Britannica Yearbook* gives an estimate of $1,700 for 1999. Hence a $2,000 estimate for the year 2002 or 2003 appears reasonable.

5. See Claes Brundenius, "Whither the Cuban economy after recovery? The reform process, upgrading strategies and the question of transition," *Journal of Latin American Studies* (May 2002), Vol. 34, no. 2, p.368.

6. $2.5 billion times .25 is $625 million. Since GDP per capita was estimated at $2,000 and there are 11 million persons in Cuba, total GDP is about $22 billion. Dividing $625 million by $22 billion is 2.8%, and the number has been rounded up to 3%.

7. Income generated by Cuban nationals abroad might reduce the 3% figure, but the author found no available data to make the correction. Whether the correct figure is 3%, 2% or 1% does not make a difference in the final results.

8. This assumes a depreciation rate close to that of the United States. This is really an over-estimate, since the capital equipment of Cuba is quite old and a significant amount of it should have been depreciated in full.

the income of Cuban workers, this correction will not be made. Hence, with no correction made to NNP per worker, the $3,880 equals what is called National Income (NI) per worker.

In traditional income accounting, corporate profits minus dividends, net interest paid by business firms, and contributions to social insurance are subtracted from NI, and then personal interest income received from government, and transfers payments to persons are added to NI: the result is Personal Income. This, minus personal taxes, gives rise to Disposable Personal Income. Here, however, a different approach will be used, since several of the above categories (like profits and dividends) do not apply in the case of Cuba.

Continue by assuming that 70% of National Income would accrue to workers as salaries, and 30% of National Income would accrue to those who own capital.[9] In Cuba, however, the only "return to capital" that accrues directly to the people is the housing services provided by the housing stock, which is *de facto* (if not *de jure*) under the "ownership" of current occupants. The author estimates these housing (or properly speaking, shelter) services to be about 20% of the (potential) salary income of the working population; this would amount to $543 a year for the average worker.[10] If correct, this means that in Cuba an average household made up of two adult workers and two children receives $1,086 in shelter services per year.

It has recently been reported in the American press ("Los expertos predicen año difícil para la economía," *The Miami Herald*, at www.elherald.com, posted on Friday June 6, 2003) that the Centro de Estudios de la Economía Cubana, in Cuba, estimated that the average yearly salary for workers was $120 (again, in U.S. currency). If we add $543 in direct shelter services (which are part of NNP) to $120 paid in cash to workers, this comes up to $663 of yearly income to workers. It then follows that the average taxation rate on the *total* income of workers (salary plus potential returns to capital) in Cuba is approximately 83 percent of income [($3880-$663)/$3,880].[11]

To round down the number, one can argue that taxation on *total* income in Cuba is 80%. It may be interesting to note that Bulgarian government expenditures were 77.3% of Gross National Product in 1991,[12] during the transition from communism to a "democratic, constitution and welfare state" regime in that country.[13] Hence a central government expenditure and taxation figure for Cuba of 80%, assuming a balanced budget, does not appear unreasonable. This simply indicates that the Cuban government controls 80% of the income generated by the workers *and* the capital stock (that supposedly belongs to the workers). The government does so by providing transfer payments and direct services to the population at large (including the workers, of course); these embrace monetary transfers for social insurance, meals at work places, subsidized utilities, educational services, medical attention, etc. The figure may be an over-estimate if the underground economy is a large part of the Cuban economy, but this issue is not addressed in this paper. Nor does this paper address the whole issue of the taxation of remittances sent by the exile community, which are in the neighborhood of $800 million a year. These funds are pure transfers from abroad and do not rep-

---

9. This is an approximation for the coefficients of a typical Cobb-Douglas production function. See Charles I. Jones, *Introduction to Economic Growth*, London, W. W. Norton & Company, 1998, pp. 41-45.

10. Shelter expenditures in the U.S. were approximately 15% of median income during the 1980s. See various issues of the *Statistical Abstract of the United States*. The 20% figure is used because one would expect significantly higher expenditures on shelter in a poor country.

11. The taxation rate on salary alone is much higher, at 96%, but given the large return on the housing capital stock that is received directly by the average household, it appears that this higher rate is quite misleading.

12. The figure comes from the *World Development Report 1993*, published by the World Bank, p. 259.

13. See the 1992 *Britannica Yearbook*, p. 421.

resent output that is either produced in Cuba *or* abroad by Cuban-owned assets or nationals.[14]

It should now be clear why traditional accounting practices were not followed once the Net National Product per capita was determined. Workers receive salaries and substantial direct services in the form of shelter: these add up to a figure that can be called Earned Disposable Income. Everything else that workers and others in the population get is a direct or an indirect transfer, which the government is able to provide because of the many hidden taxes on salaries and returns to capital.[15]

Someone might argue that as long as income produced by the Cuban people is returned to them (or to some deserving group) as transfers, this whole discussion about taxes is irrelevant. There are serious flaws with this assessment, for the following reasons: (a) it is clear that in democratic countries taxation levels are part and parcel of the political discourse, and that people do in fact limit the power of government officials in the allocation of resources; (b) there is a vast literature in economics demonstrating that existing taxation schemes are inefficient, leading to what is called "dead-weight" losses; (c) hidden taxation, as practiced in Cuba and other communist regimes, makes it especially difficult to make rational economic decisions; (d) those individuals benefiting from transfers coalesce into interest groups that lobby for ever-greater benefits, thereby ratcheting up the tax rates; (e) those persons facing ever higher taxes, in turn, seek to engage in tax avoidance rather than productive activities; and (f) the recipient of transfers never observe and appreciate the true sacrifice that taxpayers make.

The 80% taxation figure is a very different figure from the one that is normally quoted in Cuba: practically zero by the average person.[16] How is it that people in Cuba feel that they face minimal taxation? A variety of answers seem plausible. First, people are not explicitly told, nor do they receive formal documentation to the effect that they face an extraordinarily high tax rate. (Neither do the Europeans, but at least they are aware through the political process that the value-added tax, VAT, is quite large. In personal conversations with Swedes, the author has found that at least the *immigrants* to this country are fully aware of the extremely high taxation rates in that country. Swedish government expenditures were 44.2% of Gross National Product in 1991,[17] and they have been in the range of 40% to 45% for years. Yet the implied taxation rate in Sweden, again assuming a balanced budget, is about one half that of Cuba.) Second, people in Cuba live in a society that has accepted that the state owns the capital stock; hence one can assume that the people correctly understand—even when they do not correctly state—that the returns to capital (except for shelter) accrues to the state and not to individuals. Third, the Cuban state provides a great variety of goods and services at either very low prices or at zero prices, and these goods and services would have been purchased anyway if the people had not been taxed at such high rates.

Whatever the appropriate explanation, the author's experience in Cuba was very perplexing (except with one journalist who was working as a business entrepreneur in Varadero; while this individual did pay taxes on his dollar earnings, he was fully aware of the

---

14. As mentioned in footnote 6, it was not possible to determine the income of Cuban nationals abroad. The group learned at the Camilo Cienfuegos University that when university faculty members travel abroad to work, their contracts are negotiated by the university, which gets to keep part of the foreign earnings. Cuba sends medical teams and athletes—including baseball players—abroad, and the author assumes that similar arrangements are made by other governmental institutions.

15. It is widely recognized that taxation is well hidden in communist countries; this has given rise to serious political difficulties for transition governments, as they try to make government taxation transparent. See Jorge Martinez-Vazquez and Robert M. McNab, "The tax reform experiment in transitional countries," *National Tax Journal* (June 2000), Vol. 53, No. 2 for a comprehensive discussion of this issue.

16. The difficulty that Cubans have had in understanding and accepting taxation had long been noted in a 1996 article in *The Economist*, entitled "Cuba's two nations: or, why dollars are dangerous," April 6, 1996, Vol. 339, No. 7960.

17. The figure comes from the *World Development Report 1993*, published by the World Bank, p. 259.

hidden taxes charged by the government). People simply did not know how to respond when told that they paid more than minimal taxes. The usual response was that the government gives them the goods and services for free, or at subsidized prices. When asked, "how does the government gain access to these goods and services—is it not through taxation?" the respondents were truly baffled by the question.

Language, of course, plays tricks on everyone. Even in the United States, people talk about public education being "free"; the difference is that when people are challenged ("how does the government pay for this free education?") most individuals are painfully aware of local property taxes and are willing to concede that there is no such thing as a "free lunch."

Even Cuban scholars in the United States seem to have a bit of difficulty in conceptualizing the connection between taxation levels, educational opportunities and medical care in Cuba. The achievements of the revolution are stated in terms of access to education and the improvements in health that have resulted from "free" medical services. Somehow, people fail to ask "at what cost to the taxpayer?" as if that was not a relevant question. Would people in the United States want "free" education and "free" health care at 80% average taxation rates on *total* income? Why is this powerful rhetorical question never asked by scholars or in the American press?

At best, Cuban scholars in the United States provide budget expenditures that are devoted to education; but these expenditures are not representative of educational costs[18] (even ignoring opportunity costs). Utilities for schools are subsidized; transportation to schools is subsidized; health care and retirement benefits for teachers are subsidized; the schools' food purchases involve subsidized prices; and the list can go on and on. The same is done with expenditures on health care.[19] The costs of medical personnel are

many times the reported expenditures by the state: hence the reported expenditures are invalid measures of costs. What scholars need to do is an accurate cost-benefit analysis of education and health care.[20] Also, they need to ask people in Cuba if the choices made for them by the government, *given the true costs of the services*, are the choices they themselves would make.

One final anecdote will illustrate the frustration that the author felt in Cuba when he raised the tax issue. The group visited an agricultural cooperative just outside Havana. The morale of the workers seemed quite high. When asked about taxation, the chief officer said that the cooperative paid only a 5% sales tax on goods sold and a 5% tax on inputs purchased from the government. When pressed further, however, the officer revealed that the government took possession of part of the crop, the cooperative members consumed directly another part, a percentage of the crop had to be sold at subsidized prices dictated by the government in government stores, and the remainder was sold in open markets, where the 5% sales tax applied. The cooperative also received direct assistance from some European governments (helping to build a fence and helping to acquire some machinery). Given the complexity of the arrangement (including possibly subsidized input prices) it is evident that calculating the tax rate for this cooperative would be a most difficult task. However, the only "taxes" that were recognized by the officer were the sales and purchase taxes previously mentioned. The author honestly believes that the officer was not in any way trying to hide the higher effective rates of taxation: she simply did not understand the question as people in the United States would understand the question.

There exists, then, a substantial gap between what people in Cuba collect as income or housing services and what gets reported as production in the form of GDP. The difference between these two figures must

---

18. See, for example, Manuel E. Madrid-Aris, "Education's Contribution to Economic Growth in Cuba," *Cuba in Transition— Volume 10* (2000), pp. 342-351.

19. A recent informative, yet flawed analysis from an economic perspective is that of Felipe Eduardo Sixto, "An Evaluation of Four Decades of Cuban Health Care," *Cuba in Transition—Volume 12* (2002), pp. 325-343.

20. Such an analysis would use shadow prices to calculate costs and willingness to pay to calculate benefits.

be accounted mainly by a variety of indirect taxes that accrue to the government, which in turn uses various subsidy schemes to make people feel that the government provides "free" or minimal-cost commodities. People in Cuba fail to grasp how the process works, and hence insist that taxes on *total* income are minimal. The head of the government in Cuba is, in effect, Santa Claus, who miraculously distributes income or output to the population.

THE BLOCKADE EXPLAINS EVERYTHING

Even the most casual visitors to Cuba, if given the opportunity to talk to anyone, come to understand the difficult economic conditions that people there face. Tourists are accosted for money and illegal trade (especially in cigars and prostitution). A visitor to a food distribution center will find bare shelves. Children embrace anyone who gives them money or goods. Personally, the saddest experience that the author had was finding a child who had no knowledge as to what toothpaste was for. People in Cuba engage visitors freely in conversations about the difficult economic times that they face; their inability to find what Americans call over-the-counter drugs and simple toys for children are recurrent complaints by the population.

This, however, does not translate into criticism of government policy—quite the contrary. For when asked why they face these problems, the respondents *reluctantly* (as if trying to avoid conflict with American visitors) answer that it is due to the American blockade.

The author tried to initiate discussions on this issue but found it rather difficult to proceed. First, people in Cuba really believe that the United States effectively prevents other countries from selling goods and services to Cuba. Second, the people have no notion of the staggering foreign debt that Cuba owes to the rest of the world. The 2003 *Britannica Yearbook* lists a figure of $11 billion. This, however, does not include the debt to Russia or the former Soviet Union, which has been estimated at $20 billion.[21] And third,

the results of the so-called blockade are so obvious to ordinary Cubans—there are no goods to purchase when using Cuban currency—that the blockade is the *sui generis* explanation for their troubles. This point of view was repeated many times to the group by government officials, and the students initially found the explanation quite convincing. There seems to be nothing more appealing than a simple argument for a humanitarian catastrophe.

The explanation is also appealing because the American embargo has in fact caused some difficulties to the Cuban economy. In the early years of the Revolution, it made it much more difficult and costly to replace existing industrial machinery in Cuba. Also, since the United States was the closest trading partner that Cuba could possibly have had, transportation costs for Cuba were increased whenever Cuba traded with other countries. However, forty-four years after the Revolution, both of these arguments have lost their currency.

Many basic necessities that are scarce in Cuba today—such as clothing and shoes—are purchased *abroad* by Americans: this means that despite the transportation costs, people in the United States find it cheaper to buy these goods in Asia. The same would apply to people in Cuba today if (and this is the big if) they had the financial resources to buy those goods anywhere. Hence, while the transportation cost argument retains some validity (particularly with respect to food) it is invalid for a wide range of goods that both Cubans and Americans should find themselves buying in cheaper Asian markets. With regard to industrial machinery, the argument is now obsolete. After forty-two years of a trade embargo, Cuba has had enough time to replace all of its manufacturing capital stock from countries other than the United States. That it has not done so is an indication of its inability to trade elsewhere, for the simple reason that it has lacked enough output to conduct mutually beneficial trade. The Cuban economic

---

21. The $20 billion figure was reported by *The Economist* years ago, in the article "Cuba's two nations: or why dollars are dangerous," April 6, 1996, Vol. 339, No. 7960.

problem is lack of Cuban output and not the American embargo.

There is, however, another route to defend the importance of the American embargo on the Cuban economy: Cuba cannot sell tourist services to Americans, at least to the extent that it would like. This argument is valid as far as it goes, but does not go far enough. The embargo cannot be lifted, according to the Cuban Liberty and Solidarity Act of 1996, until Americans assets confiscated in Cuba are returned—or, conceivably, compensation for them is provided. It was the policy of the Revolution to break with the American economic hegemony in the island: "Yankees go home" was the battle cry of the Revolution—stated in much more unpleasant language. This attitude remains, and there is simply no willingness in Cuba to accept the return of properties or to provide compensation for them. The Helms-Burton Act is universally despised.

Cubans seem to believe that they had the right to take these foreign properties and that, under current conditions, confiscated housing taken from former Cuban nationals (which provides them with a significant part of their income) now belongs to them. The author is convinced that the Cuban revolution was consolidated through the confiscation of property. In a sense, almost everyone was made a partner in confiscation, and no one today has the moral authority to declare that what the government did was wrong and detrimental to economic growth. No one, of course, realized the long-term consequences of what was being done (such as the destruction of the vibrant construction industry in the cities) but that is not surprising. Cuban history since independence has been one where both democratic and dictatorial regimes have followed market-destructive policies[22] (especially with regard to labor legislation[23]).

What the author found surprising was that the American students, with whom the embargo issue could and was discussed openly, generally came out on the side of the Revolution. Some of their arguments are instructive. For example, some students argued that the American Revolution ended up confiscating the properties of English partisans, an argument that is factually correct: 80,000 British loyalists who fled to Canada had their property expropriated.[24] Hence, if the Americans could do this to the English, then the Cubans could also do the same to the Americans.

Students also brought into the discussion the confiscation of native American lands by the English. This was helpful, in the sense that if such confiscation was illegal and deserving of compensation, wouldn't one have to determine the legality of Cuban confiscation of Cuban-owned and American-owned properties? But the confiscation of native American lands was brought in to demonstrate the exploitative nature of the founders of the United States. Since the Americans are the exploiters and the bad guys, the confiscation of property needs no justification. End of argument.

Well, not quite the end of the argument. Students accept the idea of American exploitation because they lack a good understanding of *how* wealth originates. While it is true that the United States is rich in natural resources (and hence "natural" wealth), it can be made clear to students that wealth originates with technical change and the introduction of know-how into productive processes. Students can be reminded that all modern conveniences arise because people in this country, Europe and Japan have learned to develop knowledge and have incorporated that knowledge into physical processes and commodities. Television sets, for example, are technical ideas embodied in a physical medium. Once the students understand

---

22. The economic absurdities of the 1940 Constitution are exposed by Jorge A. Sanguinety, "Implicaciones de la Constitución del 40: Lecciones para el Futuro," *Cuba in Transition—Volume 12* (2002), pp. 369-381.

23. The economic and political power of labor unions in Cuba prior to the Revolution is usually ignored by commentators. An excellent discussion of this topic can be found in Chapter XCVI of Hugh Thomas, *Cuba: The Pursuit of Freedom*, New York, Harper & Row, 1971.

24. See Antroy A. Arreola, "Who's isolating whom?: Title III of the Helms-Burton Act and compliance with international law," *Houston Journal of International Law* (Winter 1998), Vol. 20, No. 2, p. 353.

that, they become reluctant (in most cases) to give away their own potential contributions to wealth in the form of ideas, and the so-called exploitation by the West and Japan of poor societies takes on a more problematical nature. One can ask the students point blank: what was it that Cuba contributed to the development of modern technologies? One plausible answer is the telephone, but this invention was not patented and the telephone was re-invented elsewhere years later. The Italian Antonio Meucci, who invented the telephone in Cuba in 1849, never received the credit or the financial rewards.[25] In addition, one can argue with them that the economic arrangements that are incorporated in legal systems impact the productive activities of nations. If socialism as a way of organizing production has failed in Eastern Europe, what makes a person confident that it will succeed in Cuba? The response to that question, by the organizer of the trip to Cuba, was that Cuba only needed more time. Language, then, can be used cleverly to cast doubt on the strength of a powerful argument. This can be illustrated with another example.

Students in Cuba were struck by the great disparity in the quality of housing that they observed in Havana. To some, this disparity justified the re-distributive policies of the Revolution. Interestingly, some of the more radical students came to believe that the Revolutionary elite had simply displaced the old bourgeoisie in terms of control over the better-quality housing. Others justified current conditions on the basis that equality did not preclude hierarchical differences, which were necessary to continue the work of the Revolution. This suggests that hierarchical differences do not directly translate into *de facto* inequalities. It seems more reasonable to argue that, in both the old and the new Cuba, class differences have translated into differences in access to goods and services. In addition to housing, one can mention access to travel: in the pre-Revolutionary days few people could travel abroad because few people could afford to do so, while in Revolutionary days

foreign travel is restricted to those who are part of the governing elite (except for those who are subsidized by relatives abroad).

Traveling within Cuba is both costly and difficult, given the state of the transportation system. The roads are there but carry minimal traffic. This has had an important consequence which is relevant to the discussion of this section: Varadero is not seen by the great majority of the population. Travel books state that 18,000 Cubans live permanently there. Varadero is the best argument against the idea that the so-called blockade accounts for Cuban poverty. Hundreds of first class facilities have been built for the foreign tourists, American goods can be purchased most everywhere, and even the music of well-known exiles (Celia Cruz, Gloria Estefan) can be heard in public places. Where, then, is the famous American blockade that supposedly prevents economic prosperity? The students were too concerned with enjoying the beach to pay much attention to this argument. The disparity between Cuban and tourist facilities became much more evident to the students in a different context, near the Viñales Valley. At a tourist attraction, a grandiose painting on the rocks depicting native Taino Indians and prehistoric dinosaurs side by side required millions of gallons of paint. The students spontaneously argued that the paint could have been better used for the dilapidated buildings of Havana.

The American embargo, or blockade, as it is known in Cuba, is the government's explanation for the economic hardships found in the island, and the people of Cuba generally find this argument convincing. No one bothers to explain to them how or why the embargo arose, and no one there questions Cuba's right to confiscated property. Many American students buy into these arguments, and their beliefs are only shaken when they see islands of abundance within Cuba, catering to the tourist sector, or when they see that income inequalities remain, particularly in housing and foreign travel. Those who want the embargo

---

25. This obscure fact is hardly ever mentioned in standard encyclopedias; the one exception is The *MacMillan Visual Desk Reference*, New York, 1993, Section 3161, entitled "Time frame of modern communications."

lifted fail to answer a simple question: When will Cuba pay what it owes to the rest of the world? In the recent past, Cuba has traded with many capitalist countries (Canada, Japan and Western European countries) and has left many bills unpaid. Why should American banks extend credits to a country that is so much into debt?[26]

Are these rhetorical questions, or questions that take into account Cuba's minimal potential for economic growth, given that it lacks the technical know-how and legal institutions to make its economy work? The answer, of course, depends on perspective, for Cuban nationals are in desperate need of American help. Many of their relatives and friends abroad side with them. Cuban scholars abroad also remain hopeful that Cuba's problems can be overcome, if and when the appropriate transition to democracy and a market economy takes place.

COGNITIVE DISSONANCE IN CUBA AND ABROAD

The author has thus far presented three cases where cognitive dissonance arose: a librarian who thought that a finite and quite small number of books added up to infinity; people in Cuba who really believe that taxation levels are quite low, despite the fact that their whole life is dependent on government transfers; and many American students and the great majority of Cubans who take seriously the argument that the so-called blockade is responsible for poverty in Cuba, despite the opulence of Varadero and other tourist spots. How is it possible to explain this cognitive dissonance or situation where people believe things that contradict one another?

One answer, of course, is that language has been used in such a way that the cognitive dissonance is only *apparent* but not *real*. The librarian might really want to use language in such a way that the achievements of the Revolution are presented in the most favorable light; Cubans might really have a peculiar definition of taxation; and the word "blockade" might be an icon that captures the animosity of some American students and many Cubans towards the U.S. government.

Much can be said for this argument because people are influenced by the history that they read and absorb, which is always presented from a particular point of view. Thus everyone, almost by definition, could be motivated to fall into a language trap that gives rise to at least the *appearance* of cognitive dissonance. History, as we know it, is generally written by the winners of some revolution. Since everyone can be made proud of their own history (unless the history is written by the winners of a recent counter-cultural Revolution, as seems the case in the United States) this pride is sufficiently powerful to make people overcome the uneasy feelings that arise when they state or imply a contradiction. One final example from Cuba will illustrate this point.

On the trip to Viñales, as the bus left the Western outskirts of Havana, the tour guide proudly noted a complex of new buildings that house a Cuban university catering to foreign students. She made the point, once again, that education to these students was provided for free. When the author pointed out (again!) that nothing is free, and that the tour guide herself had to pay taxes that served to house and feed these foreign students, the tour guide became visibly

---

26. It has been argued by the U.S. Chamber of Commerce and many business interests that the embargo should be lifted. But one must recognize that American business interests do not care about who pays the final bill, but rather care for the extension of bank credits that will allow others to purchase their goods. The final bill, in the case of sales to Cuba, will be most likely paid for by the American taxpayers. It is remarkable, then, that politicians (who should side with the taxpayers they represent) end up siding with business interests that might fund their political campaigns. An argument for the lifting of the embargo *can be made on humanitarian grounds* (even by people who are motivated by self or family interests) since conditions in Cuba is truly deplorable. But if one believes that the Cuban political system will not yield to economic reforms, then the interests of taxpayers should be taken into account. Moreover, since taxes can be used to help poor Americans, the humanitarian argument turns on who is more deserving of economic aid—poor Cubans or poor Americans? The answer to this question is fairly obvious, to the American voter and taxpayer. The failure of the Cuban-American community to understand this trade-off has the potential of alienating some sectors of the American public, especially the poor and other minority members who are potential recipients of government aid.

upset. People do not like to hear things that injure their pride. The tour guide, like most people in Cuba, refuses to believe that she pays any significant amount of taxes, and is a strong believer in the achievements of the Revolution.

So it occurred to the author to conduct a "thought experiment," to discover if cognitive dissonance or possibly a language trap extended to himself and his scholarly friends. The thought experiment begins with a question: would it make sense for Puerto Rico to become an independent nation?

Most scholars are aware that Puerto Rico has received huge amounts of American subsidies over the years. They are aware that U.S. corporations have established themselves there, providing much needed know-how to the island and training opportunities to large segments of the population. Scholars know that Puerto Ricans who cannot find employment in the island can easily move to the United States mainland and find employment, good educational opportunities, or at the very least collect substantial welfare payments. Puerto Rico has had a relatively peaceful political climate throughout most of the twentieth century. Puerto Rico did not have a war for independence against Spain in the nineteenth century,[27] as Cuba did, and the assets of its wealthier classes were not burned to the ground. Puerto Ricans have an income per capita that is several times that of Cuba today. Hence, on economic grounds, one can easily argue that Puerto Rican independence does not make sense. Whatever other grounds might exist for independence, it seems obvious that the economic grounds have always weighed more heavily in Puerto Rican hearts, since independence has been repeatedly voted down by the electorate.

The thought experiment now continues with another set of questions. Did the *total* war of independence in Cuba against Spain make sense? Most Cuban citizens and Cuban exiles would answer in the affirmative.[28]

Did the elimination of the Platt Amendment and U.S. supervision of Cuban affairs make sense? Similar response. Did U.S. corporations in Cuba before the Revolution bring to the island highly needed technical know-how? While the answer might depend on whether the Cubans live in Cuba or in exile, the author is not so sure. A good number of exiles, years ago, resented American participation in the Cuban economy and would have given a negative response, just like their countrymen in Cuba are likely to do today. Now, however, most exiles and a small but growing number of Cuban nationals would love to see American participation in the Cuban economy. It is also important to state that Cuba has experienced 100 years of independence marred by political violence, attributed to one or another faction; not surprisingly, the resulting instability has been a factor contributing to poor economic performance.

The final question in this thought experiment is this: does it make economic sense for Cuba to be an independent nation? The author suspects that most Cubans abroad would answer in the affirmative, while holding simultaneously that Puerto Rico should not be independent. Is this a sign of cognitive dissonance? Have Cubans abroad been manipulated by those writing the history of another Revolution—the one for Cuban independence?

The current Revolution is using language that obfuscates the conditions and choices that people in Cuba face. But this argument is too easy to make for those who live abroad. Maybe, just maybe, all Cubans were the children of another Revolution that also obfuscated the conditions and choices that Cubans made in the past. Has the time come, for example, for Cuban scholars to distance themselves from the promoters of *total* war (which was how the wars of independence were conducted) because these wars were destructive of the civil society of Cuba in the nineteenth century? Has the time come to accept that in the modern world wealth originates from technical

---

27. Puerto Rico had only minor rebellions of short duration.

28. Carlos Manuel de Céspedes, who began the wars of independence, said: "Better... that Cuba should be free even if we have to burn down every vestige of civilization." Quoted in Hugh Thomas, *Cuba: The Pursuit of Freedom*, New York, Harper & Row, 1971, p. 255. Chapters XXI and XXVII of this book explain how the wars were conducted.

know-how and Cuba has no possibility of standing alone as an independent nation? Has the time come to accept that Cubans might need outsiders to act as good-faith arbiters in their political squabbles that repeatedly turn deadly?

The author does not know the answers to the above questions, but his trip to Cuba has forced him to consider them. He hopes that other potential visitors to Cuba will also take them seriously, and that these questions lead to reasonable discussions among people of good faith. Finally, the author wants to make clear that his questions are not rhetorical devices that might help to justify the American annexation of Cuba. First, Cubans need to make their political decisions freely, through a democratic process and from an initial state of political independence. Second, and more importantly, other viable alternatives make much more sense. One is the integration of Cuba to a Spanish federation of autonomous regions, based on the democratic principles and practices that currently prevail in Spain (and which did not exist at the time that Cubans fought bravely for Cuban independence). Another is the integration of Cuba to a Caribbean federation of states, loosely resembling the United States but significantly smaller (including all the Caribbean islands that wish to participate and, hopefully, the Central American nations plus Colombia and Venezuela). A third alternative might be provided by an inspired reader of this article, guided by Providence. In the short-run, every one (including the author) wants to see a free, independent, peaceful, prosperous and democratic Cuba; but can such an entity endure without changing the parameters that history and circumstances have placed upon the Cuban Republic? Let the reader find his or her own answer.

SCHOOLING VS. HUMAN CAPITAL: HOW PREPARED IS CUBA'S LABOR FORCE TO FUNCTION IN A MARKET ECONOMY?

Luis Locay

A transition to a market economy is always challenging, especially when it also involves the struggle out of underdevelopment. Sometime in the future Cuba will probably be involved in such a transition. Almost everyone agrees the task will be most difficult, but many observers of the Cuban economy point out that one thing the Island has going for it is a fairly well-educated labor force. Increases in education and literacy are among the "achievements of the revolution" that are frequently proclaimed by the Cuban regime and its supporters.

High education coexists, however, with low productivity. In 2001 the United States government ranked Cuba above only Haiti in all of Latin America and the Caribbean in purchasing power adjusted per capita income (*World Factbook*, 2002). These two apparently contradictory characteristics of Cuba's labor force are normally reconciled by attributing the low productivity to the misuse of productive resources, including labor, by government planners. Under this view Cuba has high levels of human capital, so the earning potential of its labor force in an efficient market-oriented system is high. This conclusion is based on an extrapolation to Cuba of the relationship between schooling and earnings observed in market economies. The forces that have shaped the skills of Cuba's labor force, however, are much different than

in market economies, so this extrapolation may be unwarranted.

Formal education and informal on-the-job training are the primary ways individuals acquire the various skills that are collectively referred to as human capital. As with physical capital, the return to human capital can be in the form of direct consumption or it can be indirect through higher earnings. In market economies individuals (or their families) receive most of the benefits and face many of the costs (including opportunity costs) of their investments in human capital. It is not surprising therefore, that in making schooling and occupational choices (how long to stay in school, what field to study, what occupation to go into) potential earnings plays an important role. The end result is that proxy measures of human capital such as years of schooling and years of work experience are strongly related to earnings.

The formation of skills in Cuba's command economy has been guided by a very different process from that found in more market-oriented economies.[1] Decisions have not been made by individuals guided by market determined wages and prices. Cuba's distributions of skills and occupations have, for the most part, been shaped by the same planners who have either been uninterested in using Cuba's resources efficiently, or unable to do so. Presumably they have

---

1. Madrid-Aris (2000) finds that increases in education, though large, contributed little to economic growth in the period 1963-88.

been guided by the same political concerns that have guided their production decisions, so it may well be the case that Cuba's current distributions of skills and occupations are quite different from the distributions that will prevail once Cuba makes a transition to a market economy. If the two distributions are very different, and it is difficult to transition from one to the other, then it amounts to saying that Cuba's current levels of schooling and work experience overstate the country's human capital.

As an example, consider a twenty-year professional in the area of physical education. This is a field whose high current numbers are almost certainly not sustainable in a future market-oriented economy. Such an individual may well not find employment in his profession in a post transition Cuba. His basic education is a general form of human capital that is useful in most jobs in a modern economy, but his post-secondary education and on-the-job training may have generated fairly occupation specific human capital. If this is so, our hypothetical individual may be a college graduate with 20 years of work experience on paper, but his human capital is really closer to that of an 18-year-old high school graduate.

To suspect that there may be a mismatch between current skills and those that will prevail in a future market economy is quite different from knowing what specific fields will expand and which will contract. Knowledge of what the occupational and skill distribution will be *does not exist today*. To claim otherwise is to fall into the central planner's fallacy: the belief that armed with the "facts" an intelligent analyst can determine what markets will do. Yet it would seem that such knowledge is necessary if we are to compare Cuba today with what it will be in the future. This task is not possible, even with much better data than currently exists. We can, however, ask a related, but more modest question: does the distribution of occupations and skills in Cuba today resemble those in more market-friendly Latin American countries? More precisely, could we pick Cuba out from a sample of Latin American economies on the basis of broad occupational and schooling categories? If Cuba is not an outlier on the basis of broad categories, it does not necessarily imply that its skill and occupational distribution is close to what it will be under a market system, since it is possible that it is an outlier if narrower categories are used. But if Cuba is an outlier under such broad comparisons it would suggest that the necessary adjustments may be considerable, and that optimism for a future transition due to Cuba's high level of human capital should be tempered.

The first section of this paper describes some of the major changes in Cuba's labor market in the 1990s. The second section is the heart of the paper. There I compare Cuba's labor force with those of more market-oriented Latin American economies. The basic finding is that Cuba's skill and occupational distribution tends to be an outlier, so that its transition to a market economy may be more difficult than one would expect from looking at overall levels of education. I conclude with a few findings using more disaggregated data that support the conclusion that Cuba's levels of education overstate its levels of human capital, and I raise additional concerns about the quality of its labor force and the problems that may pose to a future transition.

THE CUBAN LABOR MARKET IN THE 1990s

By the 1980s, Soviet assistance to Cuba was enormous, perhaps as much as one third of national output.[2] Between 1989 and 1992 this assistance came to an abrupt end, sending Cuba into its worse economic crisis since the Castro government came to power. Despite initial resistance to making any structural changes, toward the end of 1993 the government was forced to implement limited reforms in order to avert disaster. The events surrounding these reforms are

---

2. Madrid-Aris (1997) reports that Soviet subsidies during 1980-84 accounted for 33% of Gross Material Product, while Hernández-Catá (2000) estimates that subsidized prices and credit averaged 15% of Gross Domestic Product during 1986-90 if converted at the official exchange rate of 1 peso per US$.

Table 1. Selected Cuban Labor Statistics (thousands)

	1989	1994	1995	1996	1997	1998
Total Labor Force	4,728	4,496	4,526	4,515	4,606	4,646
% of working age population	76.1	67.5	67.8	67.9	69.2	70.0
Civilian Labor Force	4,039	4,141	3,948	3,970	4,028	4,061
% of working age population	65.0	62.2	59.1	59.7	60.5	61.2
Total Government Employment	4,127	3,524	3,409	3,401	3,453	3,440
% of labor force	87.3	78.4	75.3	75.3	75.0	74.0
Civilian Government Employment	3,437	3,169	2,831	2,856	2,875	2,855
% of civilian labor force	85.1	76.5	71.7	71.9	71.4	70.3
Mixed Enterprises	-	82	72	85	109	131
% of civilian labor force	0	2.0	1.8	2.1	2.7	3.2
Cooperatives	65	324	349	348	339	329
% of civilian labor force	1.6	7.8	8.8	8.8	8.4	8.1
Total Private	164	264	326	312	357	418
% of civilian labor force	4.1	6.4	8.3	7.9	8.9	10.3
Unemployed	372	301	357	343	323	307
% of civilian labor force	9.2	7.3	9.0	8.6	8.0	7.6

Source: From data in ECLAC (2000) and *Anuario Estadístico de Cuba*, 2002.

well document and will not be discussed here in any detail.[3]

In late 1993 the Cuban government began implementing a series of policies that would stabilize the economy and result in modest recovery. The new policies decriminalized the possession and use of hard currency, and legalized transfers of dollars from abroad as well as a limited form of self-employment. State farms were converted into cooperatives, and farmers' markets, where many products could be sold at free market prices, were legalized. Foreigners were allowed to own property, and government employment was reduced. Over the period 1993-2000 real GDP grew 29.3%, while in per capita terms growth was almost 26%.

Despite the modest nature of the reforms of 1993-94, the Cuban leadership became concerned about the expansion of the private sector and in 1996 the process of liberalization ended and was even somewhat reversed. Taxes and fees were sharply increased, and fines were imposed. Economic recovery slowed. Many of the new entrepreneurs were driven out of business, or into the informal sector. By 2000 GDP and GDP per capita were still 12% and 17% below

their respective 1989 levels.[4] Since September 11, recovery appears to have slowed further.

After initial resistance following the collapse of the Soviet, the Cuban government reduced state employment and allowed the appearance of a small, but significant, private sector that could absorb some of the displaced workers. Other displaced workers were employed in government joint ventures with foreign firms, mostly in the tourism sector. These firms have to hire their workers through a government employment agency. The salaries of such workers are paid in dollars to the government agency, which then pays the workers in pesos at an exchange rate of one-to-one. The market exchange rate has not fallen below 20 pesos per dollar since holding and using dollars was legalized, so the effective tax rate has been 95% or higher.[5] Some reduction in state employment also appears to have been achieved through early retirement and probably an increase in the informal sector.

Table 1 shows the behavior of the labor force and of government and private sector employment for the period 1989-98. From 1989 to 1998 total government employment fell by about 687,000 workers, and the civilian government workforce by about

---

3. For a good summary of the events and policies of this period see Hernández-Catá (2000).

4. Again, according to Mesa-Lago (2001) GDP was 21% and GDP per capita 25% below their respective 1989 levels.

5. This does not take into consideration under-the-table payments or gratuities the workers may receive.

583,000. The bulk of the decline followed the reforms of 1993-94.[6] The state sector's share of employment fell from about 95% to 79%. This decline in government employment was accounted for mostly by increased employment in other sectors. Most state farms were converted into cooperatives (264,000), which though having some autonomy, are far from being private enterprises. Employment in mixed enterprises, the joint ventures between the government and foreign firms mentioned above, increased by 131,000 workers. ECLAC considers both of these sectors part of the private sector, while the government considers the bulk of the mixed enterprise employment part of the state sector.[7] I believe it is useful to keep them separate. The true private sector, made up for the most part by the self-employed and by small farmers, increased by 254,000. The remaining decline in public sector employment was accounted for by declines in the labor force (82,000). Unemployment was actually lower in 1998 than in 1989 (a decline of 65,000).

The data in Table 1 does not adequately account for informal activity, so the relative decline of the state sector may be understated. During the period covered in Table 1, for example, the size of the working age population rose (by 424,000) and university enrollments fell (by 140,000).[8] Together with the declining size of the labor force, these numbers suggest an increase in the informal sector. Furthermore, there is anecdotal evidence that at least some government employees work at their official job only a fraction of the day, devoting much of their time to informal market activity. Other observers claim, however, that this effect is modest. While they agree that underemployment is huge, they claim it is difficult for

government employees to turn free time into informal market activity. It is also frequently claimed that the formal self-employed report only a fraction of their income (the usual number is one half), so that many in the formal sector may also be acting informally. Though it may not accurately measure the division of employment between the public and private sectors, Table 1 probably does indicate general trends.

Prior to 1993 wages played a very small role, if any, in determining the occupational and skill distributions of the Cuban labor force than they would have if the country had had a market economy. The reason being that Cuba's command economy did not rely very much on prices to allocate jobs or schooling. The government decided what jobs would have to be filled, what fields of study would be offered, and so forth. The end result was a wage structure with little relationship to productivity, a characteristic of the public sector to this day. Mesa-Lago (2000), for example, reports ratios of highest to lowest wages of only 4.9:1 and 4.5:1 in 1979 and 1987, respectively. Table 2 shows monthly average product per worker by sector and monthly salary of public employees. In 1989 the public sector made up almost the entire economy. Even excluding financing, insurance, real estate and business services, which I suspect includes the rental value of owner-occupied housing (see data appendix), the two variables are negatively correlated, though not significantly different from zero.

While the wages of government employees appear to understate productivity differences in government enterprises, the difference in earnings between private sector and government workers after 1993 almost certainly exaggerates the productivity differences between the two sectors. According to Mesa-Lago (2002) the poorest private farmers tend to have incomes that are three or four times those of doctors or university professors, while owner's of *paladares*, the

---

6. The figures in Table 1 imply a very sharp decline in the non-civilian government workforce occurred in 1994, followed by a large increase in 1995. I wonder if a reclassification of workers is partly responsible.

7. Political and social organizations are included in government employment.

8. The data are from ECLAC (2000). For women working age is defined as 17-54 and for men 17-59.

Table 2. Average Product and Salary, 1989 (in pesos)

Sector	Monthly Average Product per Worker	Monthly Salary
Agriculture, Forestry, Hunting, and Fishing	243	187
Mining and Quarrying	368	206
Manufacturing	578	183
Electricity, Gas, and Water	1024	200
Construction	331	199
Wholesale/Retail Trade, Restaurants, and Hotels	861	164
Transport, Storage, and Communications	485	207
Community, Social, and Personal Services	387	194
Financing, Insurance, Real Estate, and Business Services	2031	203
Average	463	188

Source: Computed from data in ECLAC (2000)

small home restaurants, can make much more.[9] Such earnings disparities probably overstate the differences between wages in the two sectors. As stated previously, many public employees do very little actual work, and private economic activity, whether practiced formally or informally, has substantial risks and costs that require that a compensating differential be paid. Even taking these considerations into account, the earnings differences between the private and public sector appear to be quite large. Such earnings differentials could not be maintained in the absence of severe restrictions on occupational choice. Most professionals, for example, are not allowed to practice their profession in the private sector. It is widely believed that such restrictions, coupled with the distortions in wages between the two sectors, have contributed significantly to the sharp decline in university enrollments that will be mentioned below.

COMPARISONS WITH OTHER COUNTRIES IN LATIN AMERICA

I begin the comparison of Cuba with other Latin American countries by looking at the distribution of employment by sector. Countries can differ considerably in their distribution of employment by sector due to their levels of economic development and their comparative advantages. To mitigate this problem, the comparison below excludes the two sectors most sensitive to the level of economic development and to comparative advantage: (1) agriculture, forestry, hunting and fishing, and (2) mining and quarrying. Table 3 shows the distribution of employment for selected countries and years among the remaining sectors. Data availability, completeness and consistency determined the choice of countries and years. As can be seen, Cuba in 1997 had lower than average employment in trade and in financial and other services.[10] The last column of Table 3 shows the sum of the *relative* deviations (not including the "not specified" category) from the mean occupational distribution of the countries in the table, excluding Cuba's state sector. Let s_{ij} be country j's share of employment in sector i, and s_i be the sample average share in sector i. The relative deviation for country j in sector i, is defined as $d_{ij} = |s_{ij} - s_i| / s_i$. The sum of the d_{ij}'s over all sectors is the measure of total relative deviation that appears in the last column of Table 3. As can be seen, Cuba's economy deviates the most from the sample mean. Cuba's state sector deviates even more than the economy as a whole.

The results of Table 3 may be just a fluke. After all, employment by sector could vary considerably even among market economies. Table 4 shows similar results, however, for major occupational categories. As can be seen, Cuba is heavy with professional and administrative personnel, but relatively light on clerical and service workers. Once again Cuba deviates the most from the mean distribution of employment by

---

9. These salaries correspond to March and April of 2002. Some of the magnitudes appear implausible and may reflect confusion between gross and net earnings Nevertheless, the differences are so huge that even with considerable error they still suggest incredible distortions. Similar numbers are found in Mesa-Lago (2000).

10. I chose 1997 for comparison because it was the year for which data for the other countries was most commonly availabe.

Table 3. Employment Distribution by Sector (% employed, excluding (1) agriculture, forestry and fishing, and (2) mining and quarrying)

Countries	Manufac-turing	Electricity, Gas, and Water	Construc-tion	Wholesale/ Retail Trade, Restaurants, and Hotels	Transport, Storage, and Communica tions	Financing, Insurance, Real Estate, and Business Services	Community, Social, and Personal Services	Not Specified	Deviation from Sample Average
Chile (1997)	19.1	0.7	10.8	21.6	8.9	8.3	30.6	0.0	1.80
Colombia (1997)	20.7	0.6	6.3	25.8	7.5	9.5	29.3	0.4	1.62
Cuba (1997)	21.5	1.9	8.7	16.0	6.9	2.4	42.5	0.0	2.53
Ecuador (1997)	16.7	0.4	6.5	30.6	6.2	4.9	34.6	0.1	1.30
El Salvador (1997)	21.9	1.0	9.1	29.1	6.3	2.0	30.6	0.0	1.17
Honduras (1997)	27.6	0.5	6.7	30.0	3.6	3.2	28.5	0.0	2.16
Paraguay (1996)	15.1	0.7	7.3	35.3	5.5	5.0	31.0	0.0	1.16
Uruguay (1995)	18.9	1.4	7.6	20.6	6.0	6.5	38.9	0.0	1.31
Venezuela (1995)	15.9	1.0	9.5	26.4	7.3	6.6	33.2	0.2	0.83
Average	20.2	1.0	8.1	25.0	6.3	5.0	34.2	0.1	1.54
Cuba, Public Sector (1997)	24.4	2.2	8.7	14.4	5.3	1.8	43.3	0.0	3.34

Source: *Statistical Abstract of Latin America*, Vol. 36 and ECLAC (2000)

Table 4. Employment Distribution by Major Occupational Category (% employed)

Countries	Professional, Technical and Related Workers	Administrative and Managerial Workers	Clerical and Related Workers	Service Workers	Other Workers	Deviation from Sample Average
Chile (1997)	9.0	3.5	14.4	13.0	60.1	1.06
Colombia (1997)	14.1	1.8	12.6	17.8	53.6	1.25
Cuba (1997)	21.4	7.8	4.6	15.4	50.8	2.32
Honduras (1997)	6.4	2.3	4.1	10.4	76.8	2.15
Panama (1997)	12.9	6.3	10.3	16.2	54.4	0.75
Paraguay (1994)	8.9	4.0	8.1	17.8	61.1	0.66
Uruguay (1995)	11.5	4.1	14.2	18.2	52.1	0.80
Venezuela (1995)	12.3	3.4	10.2	14.8	59.4	0.29
Average	12.1	4.1	9.8	15.5	58.5	1.16

Source: *Statistical Abstract of Latin America*, Vol. 36 and ECLAC (2000)

sector using the same measure of total relative deviation used in Table 3.

The countries selected for Table 4 are the ones that had complete and consistent data. Table 5 shows employment distribution for a larger set of countries, but only for three occupations for which complete and comparable data were available. Again, Cuba deviates the most from the sample average.

Given that professional and technical personnel make up such a large portion of Cuba's workforce, it is instructive to explore the distribution of fields of study of post-secondary school students. This is done in Table 6, which shows the distribution of enrollments for various countries for selected years.[11]

Given the importance the Cuban government places on the training of doctors, it is not surprising that Cuba has by far the highest percentage of majors in health care. Perhaps not as well known is that it also

---

11. I followed the definitions of fields of study used by Chile. In some cases this required extrapolating from previous years. A country, for example, may report a single figure for law and social science majors for the year in Table 6, but break down the number in a previous year. In such cases I assumed that the division between the two fields was the same in the two years.

Table 5.   Employment Distribution by Major Occupational Category (% employed)

Countries	Professional, Technical and Related Workers	Administrative and Managerial Workers	Clerical and Related Workers	Deviation from Sample Average
Bolivia (1996)	13.9	4.1	4.2	0.93
Chile (1997)	9.0	3.5	14.4	0.97
Colombia (1997)	14.1	1.8	12.6	1.28
Costa Rica (1997)	10.9	4.5	7.4	0.44
Cuba (1997)	21.4	7.8	4.6	2.67
Dominican Republic (1997)	4.7	1.4	4.5	1.61
El Salvador (1997)	8.9	2.1	4.6	1.01
Honduras (1997)	6.4	2.3	4.1	1.26
Mexico (1997)	13.4	2.1	5.8	0.88
Panama (1997)	12.9	6.3	10.3	1.26
Paraguay (1994)	8.9	4.0	8.1	0.39
Peru (1997)	9.2	0.8	5.9	1.20
Uruguay (1995)	11.5	4.1	14.2	0.96
Venezuela (1995)	12.3	3.4	10.2	0.35
Average	11.0	3.4	8.2	1.1
Sources:				

Source: *Statistical Abstract of Latin America*, Vol. 36 and ECLAC (2000)

has the highest percentage of education students. Together, health care and education accounted for over 60% of post-secondary students. At the other end, Cuba had the lowest percentage of business students, again not a surprising result. As with the occupational distributions, Cuba's distribution of majors deviates the most from the average distribution of Latin American countries in the sample. What's more, Cuba's deviation is likely understated because the "other or not specified" category was not used in the calculations. This was the fourth largest category for Cuba (almost 8% of enrollment), and it consisted entirely of physical fitness majors.

During the 1990s, post-secondary school (mostly university) enrollments in Cuba fell dramatically. They went from 242,434 in 1990 to only 102,598 by 1998. The decline in enrollments, together with a distribution of majors heavily skewed toward education, medicine and physical education, as shown Table 6, means that in some fields Cuba will be producing few professionals. If we rank the countries in Table 6 from lowest (1) to highest (16) in majors per person, we find that Cuba's average weighted average rank, where the weights are the fraction of each major in the entire sample of countries, is only 5.2. In several fields only Haiti had fewer majors per person, and the Haitian data is for 1989. In two fields that many would consider important for a successful tran-

sition to a market economy, business and technology, Cuba ranks second and third lowest, respectively.

Table 7 compares post-secondary enrollments in Cuba with those of the most market-oriented economy in Latin America, that of Chile. The data for the two countries are not exactly comparable. Cuba's include all post-secondary students, while Chile's exclude graduate students and post-graduates. Consequently, Chile's numbers are undercounted by about two or three percent. Fields are not defined exactly alike, though for the ones shown there are considerable similarities in the titles used.

Cuba's big lead in education and medical students declines throughout the 1990's, so that by 1998 both countries are close in terms of enrollments per 1,000 persons in these two fields. In technology and business, however, Chile's lead in 1990 grows dramatically, so that by 1998 Chile has more than six times as many students per capita than does Cuba in these two fields. In total students Cuba's slight lead in 1990 is completely reversed by 1998. In that year Chile had almost three times as many undergraduates per 1,000 persons as Cuba had post-secondary students per 1,000 persons.

CONCLUSIONS

We saw in the previous section that Cuba's employment distributions by very broad industry and occu-

Table 6. Distribution of University Enrollments by Major (% enrolled)

Country					Majors						Deviation from Sample Average
	Ed-ucation	Human-ities	Art and Archi-tecture	Law	Social Science and Mass Communication	Commercial and Business Administration	Natural Sciences	Health Care	Tech-nology	Agriculture, Forestry and Fishery	
Argentina (1994)	1.6	8.3	7.0	16.2	5.9	20.1	9.4	13.7	13.0	3.4	4.6
Bolivia (1991)	0.7	2.0	3.1	12.4	9.2	17.7	7.6	19.8	18.6	2.5	3.3
Brazil (1994)	11.6	8.3	2.1	11.5	12.8	19.1	8.4	9.3	10.2	2.4	3.0
Chile (1996)	7.7	6.0	6.6	5.0	14.3	18.9	2.4	5.6	25.7	7.7	5.8
Costa Rica (1994)[a]	15.6	3.8	3.1	5.4	7.2	18.6	5.6	6.1	9.2	2.2	2.6
Cuba (1996)	34.2	1.7	1.4	2.0	2.6	4.0	2.6	26.3	12.7	4.9	7.8
Ecuador (1990)	24.8	0.6	2.9	8.2	14.8	17.5	3.6	11.5	12.5	2.7	3.7
El Salvador (1996)	0.2	10.9	4.4	7.1	9.8	23.6	14.9	12.5	14.7	1.7	5.1
Haiti (1989)	3.4	14.1	0.0	14.9	2.4	30.3	6.3	12.4	11.8	4.4	6.5
Honduras (1994)	12.6	1.4	1.3	12.4	5.3	22.5	5.3	11.7	15.7	3.8	2.6
Mexico (1994)	11.7	1.0	5.2	9.9	9.0	24.4	7.3	7.9	20.8	1.4	3.0
Nicaragua (1995)	11.6	1.2	2.0	16.3	6.3	19.6	9.2	11.1	18.7	2.0	3.3
Panama (1994)[a]	12.1	7.6	5.8	5.1	12.0	29.0	5.1	4.2	17.7	1.1	4.3
Peru (1991)[a]	11.4	1.5	1.7	9.2	13.2	19.2	5.4	11.4	17.3	4.6	2.4
Uruguay (1996)	17.0	0.0	9.1	14.6	21.9	5.6	6.2	13.5	7.6	3.7	6.2
Venezuela (1988)	21.1	1.1	1.5	7.0	7.5	21.2	4.9	9.5	15.9	3.8	3.3
Average	12.3	4.3	3.6	9.8	9.6	19.5	6.5	11.7	15.1	3.3	4.2

Source: Computed from data in *Statistical Abstract of Latin America*, Vol. 36

a. Universities only.

Table 7. Enrollments per 1,000 Persons, Chile and Cuba

		1990	1991	1992	1993	1994	1995	1996	1997	1998
Technology	Chile	5.1	4.9	5.4	5.8	5.8	6.0	6.5	6.7	7.4
	Cuba	3.5	3.3	3.1	2.6	2.0	1.6	1.4	1.3	1.2
Business	Chile	4.2	3.8	4.3	4.8	4.8	4.8	4.7	4.4	4.5
	Cuba	1.3	1.1	0.8	0.6	0.5	0.4	0.5	0.5	0.7
Education	Chile	1.9	2.0	1.9	1.8	1.8	1.8	1.8	1.8	2.0
	Cuba	10.5	9.2	7.2	5.3	4.4	3.8	3.5	3.2	3.2
Agricultural Sciences	Chile	1.4	1.4	1.8	2.0	2.0	1.9	1.9	2.0	1.9
	Cuba	1.0	0.9	0.8	0.8	0.7	0.6	0.5	0.4	0.4
Natural Sciences and Mathematics	Chile	0.5	0.5	0.5	0.5	0.5	0.5	0.6	0.6	0.6
	Cuba	0.6	0.5	0.5	0.5	0.5	0.5	0.4	0.4	0.4
Medicine	Chile	1.1	1.1	1.1	1.1	1.2	1.2	1.4	1.5	1.6
	Cuba	3.6	3.5	3.6	3.4	3.1	2.7	2.5	2.3	2.2
Total	Chile	18.7	18.5	20.7	22.5	23.0	23.8	24.8	25.4	26.5
	Cuba	22.8	20.9	18.3	15.2	12.9	11.1	10.1	9.5	9.2

Source: Computed from data in *Statistical Abstract of Latin America*, Vol. 36

pational categories deviate more from the means of a group of Latin American economies than any other country in the sample. Because of the broad definitions used here, it is to be expected that differences between Cuba and the other countries are actually greater. I do not know of the existence of more disaggregated data that could be used to explore this proposition, but there is some evidence on the allocation of professional talent that supports it.

As is well known, Cuba has one of highest, if not the highest, number of doctors per capita in the world. The general public may view having a large number of doctors as a good thing, but that is only because they ignore the opportunity costs of doctors. Not only are doctors expensive to train, but the individuals that become doctors are usually capable of being quite productive in other occupations. No doubt, such ignorance of economics has been exploited by the government, as it widely proclaims Cuba's many doctors as a great achievement of the revolution.

It can be argued that in a market economy there will tend to be under investment in education in general and in medical training in particular. This is why a high number of doctors in a developing economy us usually viewed as a good thing. It shows that such a country is successfully countering this tendency toward under investment. Beyond a certain point, however, the social return to an additional doctor is lower than the social cost. With a level of doctors per capita that is several times that of richer countries in the region with comparable or better levels of life expectancy, Cuba almost certainly has gone well beyond the point of optimality (ECLAC, 2000).[12] Rather than an indication of success, the high number of doctors is a sign of pathology. Regardless of efficiency, Cuba's high number of doctors will likely not be sustainable in a more market-oriented economy.

Another example of Cuba's peculiar allocation of professional and technical talent is found in the number of scientist, engineers, technicians and auxil-

iary personnel devoted to research and development. In 1995 Cuba had 44,119 such persons engaged in non-military research and development (*Statistical Abstract of Latin America*, 2001). This may well be the highest level in Latin America, though we cannot be certain because the data differ somewhat across countries. It is certainly the case, however, that Cuba has by far the highest number of research personnel per 1,000 inhabitants. When one considers the very low productivity of the Cuban economy, it appears likely that once again the Cuban government is pursuing an agenda with respect to its occupational assignments that has little to do with economic efficiency.

In the previous section we saw that Cuba's distribution of post-secondary fields of study also deviated the most from the average for a sample of Latin American countries. Cuba had unusually high concentration of students studying medicine, which is consistent with its extremely high number of doctors per capita. The most common major has been education, and not surprisingly, Cuba has a very high number of elementary and secondary schoolteachers. ECLAC (2000) reports that in 1996 Cuba had the lowest and second lowest number of students per elementary and secondary schoolteacher, respectively, in all of Latin America and the Caribbean. Medicine and education, along with physical fitness, have accounted for much of post-secondary education in Cuba. While the fraction of students in these fields has declined slightly, it remains high. In 1990 69% of post-secondary students were in one of these three fields. By 1998 it had only declined to 65%. The absolute number of students in these fields fell sharply, of course, because post-secondary enrollments fell by more than 50% over this period.

The high number of professionals in these three fields poses some significant problems for a future transition to a market economy. First, the numbers of persons in these fields are almost certainly unsustainable in a more market-oriented system. Second,

---

12. Cuba has more than twice the number of doctors per capita than the United States has, and more than four times as many as Barbados, Chile and Costa Rica, all of which have equal or higher life expectancies.

the training in these fields is probably not easily applied to other occupations. Together, these two conditions suggest that professionals in these fields may become a serious obstacle to future market-friendly reforms. This is especially true of the field of education. The profession is one of the most ideologically sensitive in Cuba, in which Marxist ideology is an important part of the educational content. This "knowledge" is not very useful in teaching outside a Marxist society, it is useless in any other profession in a market economy, and it is likely to be a hindrance in a future democratic Cuba. Many teachers produced by the current regime, therefore, are of suspect quality and have training which may not be very desirable in a future Cuba even in the field for which they were trained. Doctors, on the other hand, may find that being able to practice in a the private sector, even in one with enormous excess supply, is still better than working for the public sector under current conditions. Unlike teachers, Cuban doctors are likely to have skills that are valuable in other countries. I expect many Cuban doctors to emigrate if the opportunity presents itself.

The high number of professionals in medicine, education and physical education, along with sharply declining post-secondary school enrollments, implies that professionals in other fields are few in number and falling or not growing very rapidly. This is especially important in business and technology, where a comparison with the most market oriented economy in Latin America, Chile, highlighted Cuba's lack of students in these areas. Business education is a particular concern, not only because of the low number of students and the low number of trained personnel, but also because one cannot but be skeptical of the quality of business education they are receiving. Opportunities for on the job training are probably also very limited. Anecdotal evidence confirms the scarcity of persons trained in business administration, especially in marketing, finance, management, and to a lesser degree accounting, where recent efforts are being made to increase the number of accountants. Not surprisingly Cuba's distribution of employment by industry (excluding agriculture and mining) shows it to have below normal percentage of workers in trade and finance (Table 3). At the same time Cuba has an unusually high percentage of administrative personnel, something not unusual for bureaucratic systems. The number of administrators and managers will almost certainly fall in a transition to a market economy. More problematic is that their managerial and administrative skills, like those of many teachers, may not transfer well to the private sector. From the ranks of public managers and administrators may well come some of the strongest opposition to future reform.[13] What is more, they will be in positions to sabotage the reform process from within.

Besides the question of the disparity between the current skill distribution in Cuba and the distribution that would prevail in a market economy, there is the question of the quality of the existing skills. In some professions ideological purity is the paramount consideration. The classic example is probably teaching. When a characteristic other than ability is used in the selection process, ability suffers. In some fields, such as business, the educational expertise may be lacking, and the opportunities for practicing severely limited. Depreciation of skills for lack of use may be a serious problem, even in professions where the initial skills acquired were fine. This is happening not only to those professionals who have abandoned their fields to work in the private sector, but also to many in the public sector. Extensive underemployment has led many professionals to do the work of mid-level technicians—electrical engineers doing the work of electricians is an example—which also leads to a depreciation of human capital. A related problem arises because in some fields Cuban industry is quite primitive and there are insufficient opportunities to apply and develop new knowledge. A good example of this problem is agriculture, which because of a lack of inputs, especially fuel, has been reverting to a pre-industrial state. According to knowledgeable observers, two industries where Cuban workers are well trained by international standards are mining and tourism.

---

13. See Locay and Ural (1995).

These are two industries subject to international competition and under foreign management.

Some economists outside of Cuba also worry to what extent fundamental skills and values useful in a market economy may have been eroded. Many of the features that have characterized the Cuban economy under the Castro regime—the lack of connection between performance and pay, the evasion of responsibility, the lack of incentives for risk taking, the view of the law as something to be gotten around—have led to patterns of behavior that would be highly dysfunctional in a market economy. The question that cannot be answered at this time is to what extent these harmful attitudes that have developed over the past forty years will linger once a transition to a market system begins in earnest.

One of the supposed bright spots in Cuba's future prospects, its well-educated labor force, does not seem so bright on closer inspection. This should come as no surprise, for why should we expect a system that has failed miserably in terms of efficiency in every other aspect of the economy to have done a good job in educating and allocating its workforce?

REFERENCES

Economic Comission for Latin America and the Caribbean (ECLAC), 2000. *La economía cubana: Reformas estructurales y desempeño en los noventa.* Fondo de Cultura Económica, Mexico.

Hernández-Catá, Ernesto, 2000. "The Fall and Recovery of the Cuban Economy in the 1990's: Mirage or Reality." *Cuba in Transition—Volume 10.* Association for the Study of the Cuban Economy, Washington, D.C.

Locay, Luis and Ural, Cigdem, 1995. "Restitution vs. Indemnification: Their Effects on the Pace of Privatization." *Cuba in Transition—Volume 5.* Association for the Study of the Cuban Economy, Washington, D.C.

Madrid-Aris, Manuel, 1997. "Growth and Technological Change in Cuba." *Cuba in Transition—Volume 7.* Association for the Study of the Cuban Economy, Washington, D.C.

Madrid-Aris, Manuel, 2000. "Education's Contribution to Economic Growth in Cuba." *Cuba in Transition—Volume 10.* Association for the Study of the Cuban Economy, Washington, D.C.

Mesa-Lago, Carmelo, 2000. *Market, Socialist, and Mixed Economies: Comparative Policy and Performance—Chile, Cuba, and Costa Rica.* The Johns Hopkins University Press, Baltimore.

Mesa-Lago, Carmelo, 2001. "The Cuban Economy in 1999-2001: Evaluation of Performance and Debate on the Future." *Cuba in Transition—Volume 11.* Association for the Study of the Cuban Economy, Washington, D.C.

Mesa-Lago, Carmelo, 2002. "Crecientes disparidades económicas y sociales en Cuba: Impacto y recomendaciones para el cambio." *Cuba Transition Project.* Institute for Cuban and Cuban-American Studies, University of Miami, Coral Gables, FL.

Statistical Abstract of Latin America, vol. 37, 2001. James W. Wilkie, ed.. UCLA Latin American Center Publications, University of California, Los Angeles.

World Factbook 2002. http://www.cia.gov/cia/publications/factbook/

EL MOVIMIENTO SINDICAL INDEPENDIENTE DE CUBA: ACTUALIDAD Y DESARROLLO

Joel Brito y Christopher Sabatini

Hace algún tiempo se viene aceptando como un hecho la crisis que sacude al sindicalismo mundial como un actor más dentro de la sociedad, lo que lesiona sin duda los legítimos derechos e intereses de los trabajadores y de sus organizaciones. El caso de Cuba no escapa a esta crisis. La Confederación de Trabajadores de Cuba (CTC), fundada en 1939, fecha en que se realizó su primer congreso, llamada la Central de Trabajadores de Cuba (CTC) desde 1961, es considerada hoy en día por la mayoría de los trabajadores cubanos la organización de masas más comprometida con el gobierno, utilizada por éste para instrumentar y llevar a la práctica las indicaciones que emanan del Partido Comunista.

La profundización desde hace algunos años de la crisis económica, política, social e ideológica, unida a la falta de libertades y de representatividad de los genuinos intereses de la clase obrera por parte de la CTC, el alejamiento acelerado de ésta de las problemáticas fundamentales que afectan a los trabajadores, su inmovilismo y compromiso con el gobierno, han sido sin duda las causas que han compulsado el surgimiento y ulterior desarrollo del Movimiento Sindical Independiente. En los ultimos años el crecimiento del sector independiente sindical es notable no solamente en términos de número de organizaciones y actividades, sino también por los sectores representados, el crecimiento en la membresía, la calidad de las actividades, y la evolución de su reconocimiento, nacional e internacional. Sin embargo, existen todavia una serie de retos para la consolidación de un sector sindical representativo, democrático, activo, y con amplia representación internacional. Los dirigentes y activistas de este movimiento, que vienen jugando un papel determinante en la oposición pacífica y civilista al gobierno totalitario de la isla, han sido blanco desde el inicio del mismo de provocaciones, golpizas y encarcelamientos en un esfuerzo desesperado por parte de los órganos represivos del régimen de ahogarlos y silenciarlos

LA LEGISLACION LABORAL ACTUAL EN CUBA

En los Estatutos de la CTC se puede leer: "La CTC y los Sindicatos reconocen abierta y conscientemente la dirección superior del Partido Comunista de Cuba, como destacamento de vanguardia y máxima organización de la clase obrera, acogen, hacen suya y siguen su política." En la Ley 49, Código del Trabajo, del 28 de diciembre de 1985, en los artículos 15 y 16 hacen referencia explicita a la existencia y a la afiliación de los trabajadores a la CTC y a sus Sindicatos Nacionales.

El Decreto Ley 67, De la Organización de la Administración Central del Estado, del 19 de abril de 1983, en su artículo 61 " le confiere a la CTC la representación legal e institucional de los trabajadores cubanos."

En los últimos 13 años la Republica de Cuba, ha recibido en 10 ocasiones, señalamientos de la Comisión de Expertos en Aplicación de Convenios y Recomendaciones de la Organización Internacional del Trabajo (OIT) referidos a Observaciones Individuales sobre el Convenio 87 "Libertad Sindical y Protección del Derecho de Sindicalización." Dos ejemplos en los que se pueden leer:

- Año 2003: La Comisión recuerda que sus comentarios anteriores se referían a: (1) la necesidad de suprimir del Código de Trabajo de 1985 (artículos 15 y 16) la referencia a la "Central de Trabajadores"; (2) la necesidad de modificar el decreto-ley número 67 de 1983 (artículo 61) que confiere a dicha Central el monopolio de la representación de los trabajadores del país ante las instancias gubernamentales; y (3) la recomendación del Comité de Libertad Sindical en la que se solicita al Gobierno que reconozca ciertas organizaciones sindicales.

- Año 1997: La Comisión insiste en que tomando en cuenta el contexto unipartidista y de una sola central sindical, el Gobierno debería garantizar en la legislación y en la práctica el derecho que tienen todos los trabajadores de constituir libremente organizaciones profesionales independientes, tanto a nivel de base como de central, y fuera de toda estructura sindical existente, si así lo desearen.

Es evidente que el gobierno cubano no cambiará de sus leyes la mención explícita a una sola Central, la cual en la práctica funciona como un departamento estructural del Comité Central del Partido Comunista de Cuba, cuya función fundamental es movilizar, controlar, dirigir e instruir políticamente a los mas de tres millones de trabajadores del sector estatal afiliados a ella y a sus 19 Sindicatos Nacionales.

Los principales órganos de dirección de la CTC son: el Secretariado Nacional, el Comité Nacional y el Consejo Nacional.

- **Secretariado Nacional** cuenta con 17 Miembros, todos militantes del Partido Comunista de Cuba, su secretario general Miembro del Buró Político y del Consejo de Estado, 3 Miembros del Comité Central del Partido, 6 integrantes de la Asamblea Nacional del Poder Popular (Parlamento Cubano). Entre sus funciones según los estatutos están: "la dirección del trabajo cotidiano del movimiento sindical. Entre una y otra reunión del Comité Nacional de la CTC sus decisiones son de obligatorio cumplimiento para todos los organismos y organizaciones de base que se le subordinan." Es elegido por un período de cinco años. Se reúne cada 15 días.

- **Comité Nacional** cuenta con 50 miembros y esta integrado por los 19 Secretarios Generales de los Sindicatos Nacionales, los 15 Secretarios de las CTC en las provincias y por algunos Jefes de Departamentos de la CTC y personalidades de la vida política, social y cultural, todos son militantes del Partido Comunista de Cuba. Sus reuniones son cada dos meses y a las mismas participan dirigentes del Buró Político, del Consejo de Estado, de las Fuerzas Armadas, el Ministerio del Interior, Ministros y representantes de organizaciones de masas.

- **Consejo Nacional** cuenta con 250 Miembros, se debe reunir dos veces al año, hace mas de dos que no se reúne, es un organismo decorativo, que esta integrado por todos los secretarios municipales de la CTC (162), Buroes Sindicales de importancia, los secretarios generales de los Sindicatos Nacionales y las provincias. Todos son miembros del Partido Comunista de Cuba.

Los sindicatos oficiales, lejos de defender los intereses de los trabajadores, constituyen un instrumento represivo del gobierno para impedirles la defensa de sus demandas y la realización de su justa aspiración a disfrutar de bienestar por medio de su trabajo. Los dirigentes de la CTC oficialista y sus sindicatos ramales son cuadros políticos del Partido Comunista, son en la práctica empleados del gobierno.

RESTRICCIONES AL SINDICALISMO INDEPENDIENTE

Los derechos sindicales son definidos por la OIT como: "Un conjunto de todos los derechos y libertades que son indispensables a la existencia y al funcionamiento eficiente de sindicatos democráticos capaces de defender y promocionar los intereses de los trabajadores y trabajadoras. Normalmente, un movimiento sindical legítimo y democrático se desarrollará en lugares en donde los derechos humanos fundamentales sean respetados y garantizados."

El Estado cubano continúa prohibiendo la creación de sindicatos independientes, lo cual no sólo viola sus obligaciones internacionales, sino también sus propios principios, consagrados en la Constitución de la República y el Código del Trabajo, ya que éstos establecen el derecho de reunión y asociación de los trabajadores, aunque de forma muy ambigua y declaran que las organizaciones sociales "gozan de la más amplia libertad de palabra y opinión, basados en el derecho irrestricto a la iniciativa y a la crítica." Por supuesto más adelante precisa que éstos no pueden ser ejercidos "contra la existencia y fines del Estado socialista, ni contra la decisión del pueblo cubano de construir el socialismo y el comunismo."

Los juegos de palabras muy usuales en la legislación y documentos elaborados por el gobierno ponen al relieve que en Cuba no puede existir el derecho de libre asociación y de crear sindicatos independientes, ya que estas organizaciones evidentemente no estarían supeditadas a los intereses del Estado patrón, ni guiadas sus funciones por el Partido Comunista.

Las principales limitaciones que enfrenta el desarrollo del Movimiento Sindical Independiente adicionales a las que les impone el régimen, están dadas por:

- No se ha logrado extender el movimiento a todos los sectores económicos, a los diferentes segmentos poblacionales y a todas las provincias.

- No se ha podido lograr un proceso de movilización popular y coordinación política en la toma de decisiones y acciones que debe ir dando el sindicalismo independiente como parte activa de la disidencia interna, para forzar cambios hacia la democracia.

- Ha existido en ocasiones falta de liderazgo, experiencia, capacidad movilizativa y recursos materiales y financieros para enfrentar tan complejo proceso en el enfrentamiento al régimen.

- La diversidad de organizaciones sindicales pudiera limitar el alcance del trabajo a corto plazo, por lo que habría que trabajar en función de garantizar la unidad en el seno de las diversas organizaciones. Al gobierno le interesa la división dentro de este movimiento, ya que es más fácil penetrar-

los y tratar de desacreditarlos al tildarlos de grupúsculos contrarrevolucionarios.

- La labor divulgativa aun es insuficiente, hay que lograr que se conozca internacionalmente lo que ellos como movimiento hacen por los trabajadores cubanos y cómo se enfrentan a las políticas gubernamentales.

- La capacitación sindical es deficiente, se debe trabajar en función de fortalecerla para formar dirigentes sindicales capaces de influir en la comunidad y en los colectivos obreros, con una verdadera capacidad de liderazgo, esta labor en la actualidad esta muy lejos de cumplir con su objetivo.

- Proceso lógico de cansancio y agotamiento ante las posibilidades reales de cambio, lo que ha contribuido que en los últimos cinco años el 60 % de los fundadores del movimiento sindical se encuentren en el exilio. El gobierno utiliza muchas veces toda su presión para sacarlos del país, lo que sin duda hace que el movimiento se debilite y pierda experiencia, aunque a veces gana en dinamismo. Nuevas ideas y ejecutivos jóvenes llenos de deseos de ejecutar cambios en el país asumen tareas de dirección dentro del sindicalismo.

- La reciente ola represiva del gobierno llevó a la condena de 7 dirigentes sindicales y la intromisión de dos agentes de la Seguridad del Estado destapados en los juicios contra sus compañeros de trabajo. Se puede precisar que dentro de la policía política existe una Sección llamada Organismos de Masas que es la encargada de realizar todas las tareas de espionaje, penetración, captación y análisis de la información sobre la temática sindical.

Algunas estadísticas que reflejan la política de hostigamiento del gobierno contra el Movimiento Sindical Independiente, en los últimos 18 meses.

En el año 2003:

- Encarcelamiento de 7 dirigentes sindicales, condenados a 150 años. Según el gobierno la causa esta tipificada en la Ley 88 como "Actos contra la independencia o la integridad territorial del estado cubano." Los juicios fueron realizados en un entorno judicial parcializado, como ha sido la práctica en los últimos 44 años, carentes de garantías y con indicaciones precisas del máximo jefe de gobierno de sancionarlos a penas ejemplarizantes. Constan en nuestro poder muchas de las sentencias así como testimonios de familiares que dan fé de ésto y en muchos casos calificaron los juicios como "un circo."

- Durante los meses de marzo y abril le fueron decomisados u ocupados a los miembros de este movimiento computadoras, faxes, teléfonos, libros de literatura universal, manuales de capacitación obrera, Normas Internacionales del Trabajo, denuncias de violaciones laborales, llevando a la desarticulación total de 4 bibliotecas con literatura laboral y sindical.

- En el reciente libro *Los Disidentes*, publicado por la Editora Política del Comité Central del Partido Comunista de Cuba, en 10 ocasiones se hace mención a la labor de la Federación Sindical de Plantas Eléctricas, Gas y Agua (Federación Sindical) de apoyo al desarrollo del Movimiento Sindical. Por supuesto son utilizados epítetos y afirmaciones que están bien alejados de la realidad.

En el año 2002:

- 16 acciones de abusos, golpizas, negación de prestación de servicios médicos contra sindicalistas independientes encarcelados.

- 52 acciones de golpizas, amenazas, detenciones y negación de empleo a sindicalistas independientes.

- 84 trabajadores de diferentes sectores de la economía que han sido expulsados por sus opiniones políticas, su enfrentamiento a la administración y al partido comunista

- 33 acciones reportadas de represalias contra trabajadores por cuenta propia, los cuales conforman el creciente, pero hostigado sector informal.

- 65 acciones de la policía política en la intercepción y desconexión de llamadas telefónicas, violación y decomiso de correspondencia, así como de literatura sobre el tema sindical y laboral.

- Decomiso por la Aduana General de la Republica de 300 ejemplares de la Revista LUX, en los aeropuertos internacionales de Ciudad de La Habana y Santiago de Cuba.

- Sometido a fuerte interrogatorio por la Seguridad del Estado y advertido de sanciones de privación de libertad una de las personas que de forma trimestral servía de valija entre la Federación Sindical que forma parte de la red de solidaridad en exilio para derecho laboral en Cuba y las organizaciones del Movimiento Sindical.

- Infestadas de virus informáticos en varias ocasiones las computadoras de la Federación

EL DESARROLLO DE LOS SINDICATOS INDEPENDIENTES

Si bien es cierto, que la reciente ola represiva afectó en gran medida el desarrollo del Movimiento Sindical y muchos de los objetivos de trabajo tuvieron que ser diferidos, el proceso de cambio hacia la democracia, aunque difícil, es inevitable y cada día más cercano.

El Consejo Unitario de Trabajadores Cubanos (CUTC), organización fundada en La Habana el 14 de julio de 1995, por un valioso grupo de sindicalistas entre los que se destacan Pedro Pablo Álvarez Ramos, Lázaro Cuesta Collazo, Carmelo Díaz Fernández y Vicente Escobal Rabeiro, es uno de los pilares con que cuenta el Movimiento dentro de Cuba. Datos expuestos por su ejecutivo a los fines de 2002 situaban la cifra de los afiliados en el orden de los 3500, con representación en 14 provincias del país.

En sus documentos se puede leer "Nuestro Consejo tiene representaciones establecidas en todo el territorio nacional, y ha solicitado su registro como organización sindical independiente en las instancias correspondientes del estado, sin haber recibido respuesta a nuestra solicitud. Nos acogemos a los derechos consagrados en el Convenio 87 de la OIT sobre la libertad sindical, el Convenio 98 sobre la libertad de asociación y en la Declaración Universal de Derechos Humanos."

En todo este proceso de desarrollo se debe destacar el hecho de la afiliación del CUTC a la Central Latinoamericana de Trabajadores (CLAT) y la Confederación Mundial del Trabajo. Despues de la ola represiva, la CLAT jugó un gran papel ante la 91 Conferencia Internacional de la OIT donde denunció los hechos acaecidos en contra de los dirigentes sindicales en Cuba que eran miembros de su organización afiliada.

Otra de las organizaciones obreras es la Confederación de Trabajadores Democrática de Cuba (CTDC), cuya formación data del 25 de marzo de 1992. Esta organización se ha caracterizado por un fuerte enfrentamiento al gobierno, sus dos principales dirigentes en la actualidad se encuentran cumpliendo 40 años de prisión. En los últimos 10 años, unos 30 dirigentes sindicales de la misma han cumplido años de prisión o se han visto obligados a emigrar.

Así también la Unión Sindical de Trabajadores Independiente de Cuba, cuya constitución data de 1994. Su trabajo se ha limitado a realizar denuncias, su alcance en afiliación limitado, el ejecutivo tiene experiencia y se ve una recuperación con la definición de objetivos comunes con el resto de las organizaciones.

En septiembre de 1998, se fundó en La Habana la Federación Sindical de Plantas Eléctricas y Anexos de Cuba, esta organización que devino en el 1999 en la Confederación Obrera Nacional Independiente de Cuba, tiene asociado dos proyectos importantes: la Agencia Sindical de Prensa Lux InfoPress y un Instituto de Investigaciones Socio-Laborales. Ha encaminado su trabajo a la denuncia antela OIT de las violaciones de las Normas Internacionales del Trabajo y a investigar temas como el impacto en los trabajadores cubanos de la inversión extranjera, los accidentes de trabajo y las enfermedades profesionales. El trabajo de afiliación ha estado dirigido sectorialmente a captar trabajadores de la salud, educación, turismo, industria química y la administración publica.

Ya en el año 2000 y hasta la fecha mantiene la Federación Sindical de Plantas Eléctricas y Anexos de Cuba relaciones de trabajo e intercambio de informaciones con: Asociación de Trabajadores por Cuenta Propia, Central Sindical Cristiana (Independiente), Federación de Plantas Eléctricas, Gas y Agua de Cuba (Granma), Sindicato Libre de Trabajadores Cubanos, Sindicato de Conductores de Bici Taxis, Central Sindical Cristiana y 8 delegaciones provinciales del Centro Nacional de Capacitación Sindical y Laboral (CONIC), que suman mas de 4000 afiliados en el país.

En los últimos años el movimiento sindical independiente ha logrado lo siguiente:

- El Movimiento Sindical ha desarrollado cinco cursos básicos de capacitación, en diferentes modalidades, que han abarcado a unos 200 dirigentes y trabajadores.

- La creación del Centro Nacional de Capacitación Sindical y Laboral, cuya labor está dirigida a elevar la capacitación de los dirigentes sindicales para educar a los trabajadores cubanos en los derechos laborales y sindicales internacionalmente reconocidos y en la organización de sindicatos libres, cooperativas de trabajadores y otras formas de libre asociación para que de esta forma puedan defender de mejor manera, los derechos que de forma diaria son violados por el gobierno. Sus objetivos esenciales estarán dirigidos ha promover la labor de educación obrera y sindical, a través de talleres, conferencias, cursos directos, distribución de Normas Internacionales e intercambio con funcionarios de la OIT, sindicalistas del mundo libre y académicos. El primer seminario nacional con la asistencia de sindicalistas internacionales tuvo que ser suspendido el mes de abril de 2003 ante la ola represiva desplegada por el gobierno.

- Se ha publicado dentro de la Isla el boletín *Trabajador Cubano*, con ediciones limitadas de unos 300 ejemplares. Es el único de su tipo que circula en Cuba y en estos momentos no se ha podido restablecer su impresión y distribución por razones obvias.

- Han desarrollado por dos años consecutivos eventos nacionales bajo el asedio de la Seguridad del Estado, donde se han adoptado acuerdos de trascendencia para el desarrollo del sindicalismo cubano.

- El Instituto ha desarrollado una excelente labor de captación de datos y denuncias para ser enviados a la OIT, a la vez que ha desarrollado investigaciones sobre diversos temas vinculado a la realidad sindical y laboral.

- Introducción en el país en los últimos 18 meses de 4500 revistas LUX.

- La agencia sindical de prensa Lux InfoPress ha enviado hacia al exterior como promedio anual 1500 despachos con noticias, denuncias y artículos sobre la realidad de los trabajadores cubanos.

- Se ha multiplicado la labor de afiliación con la peculiaridad que los afiliados no necesariamente tienen que romper con su afiliación con la oficialista CTC, en aras de preservar al trabajador de despidos por cuestiones políticas.

- Trasmisiones radiales (104 horas anuales) haciendo énfasis en los derechos de los trabajadores y organizaciones sindicales internacionalmente reconocidos, así como con denuncias y artículos procedentes de la en la voz de corresponsales y colaboradores de la Federación Sindical.

OPORTUNIDADES PARA EXPANDIR EL APOYO A LOS SINDICATOS INDEPENDIENTES

El gobierno de la Republica de Cuba es signatario de 88 convenios en la OIT. En el año 1959 ya Cuba tenía firmados 65 convenios, entre ellos los fundamentales, y se destacaba por los avances en el terreno laboral y sindical. En los últimos 13 años las estadísticas de la OIT, muestran lo siguiente:

- 54 observaciones individuales de la Comisión de Expertos en Aplicación de Convenios y Recomendaciones.

- 11 observaciones individuales de la Comisión de Aplicación de Normas de la Conferencia Internacional del Trabajo.

- 11 sumisiones a las autoridades competentes.

- 7 informes del Comité de Libertad Sindical.

Con fecha 11 de Junio de 2003, la 91 Conferencia Internacional de la OIT adoptó una resolución de condena al gobierno de la Republica de Cuba, la cual no ha tenido precedentes en la historia. La resolución, es muestra que la comunidad internacional continúa ganando conciencia de la falta de libertades y de violaciones flagrantes del derecho internacional que comete el gobierno cubano contra los trabajadores, su movimiento sindical y el pueblo en general. En síntesis la declaración de la comisión expresa:

- Imposibilidad de un pluralismo sindical.

- No reconocimiento de organismos sindicales independientes, así como amenazas, detenciones y presiones contra sindicalistas.

- La importancia del pleno respeto de las libertades civiles para el ejercicio de los derechos sindicales.

- Instó al Gobierno a que modifique en breve plazo la legislación y la práctica nacionales para reconocer el derecho de los trabajadores de constituir las organizaciones que estimen convenientes en un clima de plena seguridad.

- Urgió al Gobierno a que tome medidas inmediatas para la liberación de los sindicalistas detenidos y el reconocimiento de las organizaciones sindicales.

- Pidió al Gobierno que acepte una misión de contactos directos con miras a verificar la situación "in situ."

Con posterioridad a esta resolución, la Confederación Internacional de Organizaciones Sindicales Libres (CIOSL) envió una carta fechada el 11 de Julio, firmada por su secretario general el Sr. Guy Rider a Fidel Castro en la que se puede leer al final de la misma:

> La CIOSL le exhorta a tomar todas las medidas necesarias para proceder a la liberación inmediata de los compañeros encarcelados y mientras tanto, para que se mejoren las condiciones inaceptables de detención. Además, nuestra organización, llevará a cabo una campaña internacional entre sus afiliadas y alertará a todos los organismos internacionales para obtener su liberación incondicional.

El 10 de Julio, el Sr. Luis Anderson, el presidente de la Organización Regional Interamericana de Trabajadores ORIT, la filial latinoamericana de la CIOSL, también se dirigía a Castro en una misiva en términos muy firmes en la que le exponía:

> La CIOSL/ORIT en representación de sus 45 millones de trabajadores/as afiliados en todo el continente, reafirma su condena ante la imposibilidad de que en su país se puedan ejercer con plenitud los derechos sindicales, lo cual en nada contribuye a la superación de la complicada situación social y económica de miles de trabajadores/as cubanos/as. En tal sentido demanda la liberación inmediata de todas las personas detenidas por intentar ejercer sus derechos. Especialmente solicita de su gobierno el respeto a la libertad sindical en su país, que facilite el funcionamiento de organizaciones sindicales independientes, así como el libre ejercicio de las libertades democráticas para toda la población, tal como está contemplado en los diferentes tratados internacionales, suscritos por la República de Cuba.

En el transcurso de los meses de marzo y abril de 2003 diferentes personalidades del mundo sindical se dirigieron al gobierno cubano en términos de rechazo y pidiendo el respeto a la Libertad Sindical. Se destacan: Central de Trabajadores de Venezuela, AFL-CIO, AFT, Confederación Mundial del Trabajo, la CLAT, Confederación General Italiana del Trabajo, Unión General de Trabajadores y Comisiones Obreras de España y Central General de Trabajadores de Guatemala.

Ante el rechazo mundial, la posición de la CTC como apéndice del gobierno ha sido de atrincheramiento y ataque, primando un total divorcio con la realidad. Muestra de ellos son misivas dirigidas por Pedro Ross a José Maria Fidalgo, Secretario General de Comisiones Obreras de España, y más reciente la de Leonel González al Sr. Juan Somavia, Director General de la OIT.

CONCLUSIONES Y RECOMENDACIONES

Hoy mas que nunca se ve un avance del Movimiento Sindical en Cuba, con metas y objetivos de trabajos precisos y definidos. También se observa por primera vez en 44 años, como sindicatos de diferentes vertientes ideológicas han convergido en la necesidad de señalarle al gobierno cubano la falta de libertad sindical y la necesidad inaplazable del respeto a los más elementales derechos universalmente reconocidos.

- Creemos que es necesario fortalecer la labor de solidaridad con los trabajadores y sindicalistas cubanos, a través de campañas internacionales y acciones coordinadas e inteligentes, fundamentalmente en Europa con organizaciones como la Unión de Sindicatos Europeos y la CIOSL y en América Latina coordinar esfuerzos con la ORIT y la CLAT.

- Comunicarles por escrito a todos los gobiernos y empresas radicadas en Cuba, o con inversiones, así como a las principales organizaciones sindicales de esos países, la resolución de la OIT sobre el tema de la falta de Libertad Sindical. Por otra parte, las posibles implicaciones que tendrían para los inversionistas en una futura Cuba democrática y con un movimiento sindical independiente las violaciones de otros convenios como son el 95, 98, 111 y 122.

- Para la 92 Conferencia de la OIT en Junio del 2004, trabajar en función de elaborar un reporte bien detallado de las todas las violaciones en materia laboral y sindical que ha cometido Cuba en los últimos años y coordinar esfuerzos comunes con organizaciones amigas para que acompañen denuncias en materia de Libertad Sindical.

- Continuar de forma gradual el incremento del apoyo material y financiero de varios actores en solidaridad al movimiento a los diferentes grupos sindicales existentes en el país y coordinar con ellos acciones como se ha estado realizando hasta el momento.

THE CUBAN EXTERNAL SECTOR IN 1989-2002: SOME OBSERVATIONS ON ACHIEVEMENTS, FAILURES AND CHALLENGES

Rolando H. Castañeda[1]

Cuba's economic transformation in the 1990s cannot be considered the solution to the formidable challenge of substantially modifying the current productive structure of the economy in order to achieve development. Despite the changes, the reconstruction of the Cuban economy is an incipient process with a high level of indeterminacy. To put it simply, it is a challenge awaiting resolution.

— Pedro Monreal (2002b, p. 29).

esos resortes, los cuales no están realmente agotados, …si exhaustos y requieren de nuevas condiciones de funcionamiento ..

— Juan Triana Cordoví (2002, p.12).

Cuban economic debates seem to have their own cycles. For stretches of time they may disappear, only to reappear later covering the same old ground. Cuba's economy, which had rebounded in the 1990s after a dramatic fall in 1990-1993, is once again in difficulty, due to lack of proper and sufficient reforms.

In 2002, Pedro Monreal (2002a) edited a book where a group of Cuban academics and researchers (Julio Carranza, Pedro Monreal, Lázaro Peña, among others) presented significant critical analysis of the external sector policies and development strategy of the Cuban authorities during the 1990s. They pointed out several limitations of the then-current policies

and proposed future prescriptions to improve the existing situation.

I consider their basic criticisms valid, but their prognosis is only a limited and succinct first step in the right direction, insufficient to address Cuban external sector problems. Specifically, they neither propose to use sufficient market mechanisms and practices—unlike what China, Vietnam and the former socialist European countries have done quite successfully—nor propose to change the emphasis on import substitution strategy as the foundation of the country's economic development strategy. Contrary to Triana's statement (above), the Cuban external sector strategy is both worn out and exhausted, but he is quite right that 2003 will be "a difficult year."

The purpose of this paper is to offer alternative observations on the nature, extent and trends of transformations of the external sector of the Cuban economy in 1989-2002. The paper also reviews policy adjustments made by the authorities and their major achievements, failures and challenges for the future.

The paper is organized as follows. The first section offers a general overview of the problems in the external sector at the beginning of the 1990s and the

1. The author appreciates Armando Linde's comments at the 2003 ASCE Annual Meeting and Jorge Pérez-López's editing. The author is very concerned for our ASCE colleagues in jail: Marta Beatriz Roque Cabello, co-author of "The Fatherland Belongs to All" and President of the Cuban Institute of Independent Economists, her deputy Arnaldo Ramos Lauzarique, and Oscar Espinosa Chepe.

pressing need for new policies and reforms. The second section examines the key developments and trends in the external sector in 1989-2002. The third section discusses the nature and scope of the policies and reforms implemented by the government throughout this period, their major achievements and failures, and their impact on the performance of the external sector and of the economy at large. The fourth section considers some important lessons learned from external sector reforms in the transition countries and Latin America during the 1990s, especially from the successful Chilean experience. The fifth section presents some observations regarding the required transformation of external sector policies to boost the rate of growth of the economy. The last section contains some concluding remarks.

THE EXTERNAL CONTEXT IN THE EARLY 1990s AND THE NEED FOR NEW EXTERNAL POLICIES AND REFORMS

Since the First Congress of the Cuban Communist Party in December 1975, the industrialization of the country and the centralized and socialist organization of the economy were defined as the foundations of the development strategy of the country. During this period, Cuba relied on subsidized exports to the former European socialist countries and considerable external aid from the Soviet Union.[2] Additionally, Cuba relied on outdated and energy-wasting forms of technology from the socialist countries. After the political changes in Europe in the early 1990s, the impossibility of continuing to rely on subsidized exports, external aid and energy-wasting technology made unfeasible the expansion of this inward development strategy and even its operation.

By the beginning of the 1990s Cuba had already experienced real GDP stagnation since 1985, a moratorium of its convertible currency external debt since 1986, an abrupt end to the substantial aid in the form of trade subsidies[3] and automatic soft trade deficit financing,[4] and the tightening of the U.S. embargo. Almost 80% of its trade was with CMEA countries. Therefore, Cuba faced the urgent task to adjust its international economic relations and to reallocate its trade in a context of limited access to foreign aid and international financing.

The stagnation in real GDP since 1985 reflected the limits of the extensive growth model that had been in effect, the end of the economic liberalization measures adopted in the early 1980s that eliminated the use of most market mechanisms and practices, and the increasing vulnerability of the external sector. The extensive growth model resulted in low efficiency, required a high level of external aid and subsidies and implied a high-income elasticity of imports. The measures introduced in 1986, in the framework of the infelicitously-termed "Campaign for the Rectification of Errors and Negative Tendencies," eliminated most liberalization measures, put the economy under tighter central control, and made worst the difficult external situation. As a result, the economy suffered from profound distortions, and inefficiencies were paramount.

Ludwig von Mises in his 1922 book *Socialism* established the impracticality of a socialist economy, demonstrating that it is impossible to have proper economic calculation and incentives; to be more precise, to ascertain the real costs and results of economic activities under a socialist economy. Furthermore, Cuba faced the impediments of poor accounting, financial and management practices that reduced even more the reliability of information (Peña, 2002, pp. 106-107) and the opposition to change that arises

---

2. Cuba's poor economic performance is partially the result of the mismanagement of billions of rubles of Soviet subsidies and aid. Massive transfer of resources does seem to be a curse rather than a blessing, as it imposes a heavy drag on long-run economic growth. But the real curse of this transfer was not so much that it incited the infamous "Dutch disease"—the misallocation of resources away from tradable sectors. Rather, it was that it allowed a series of pathologies—rent seeking, patronage, corruption, and plunder—that corrode vital domestic public institutions and undermine governance.

3. CEPAL (2001) considers it a change in terms of trade.

4. Any bilateral trade deficit was financed almost automatically by the Soviet Union and re-exports of surplus Soviet oil shipments to Cuba served to finance trade with the West in hard currency.

from any centralized bureaucracy, impediments that slow and even prevent economically and socially beneficial changes to be made in state-owned enterprises. The wide distortions and the existence of multiple exchange rates and price systems magnified these impediments.[5]

The great challenge for the Cuban authorities in the early 1990s was to understand the profound implications of the key changes and to articulate the necessary adjustments to overcome them strategically in order to recover the viability of the Cuba economy in a new international context.

DEVELOPMENTS AND TRENDS IN THE EXTERNAL SECTOR, 1989-2002

The Current Account of the Balance of Payments

In 1989-2002, exports of goods and services fell by 29% and imports of goods and services by 44%, resulting in a decline in the economy's openness index (as measured by the ratio of the value of exports of goods and services to GDP) from 0.30 in 1989 to 0.14 in 2002, and of the import coefficient (ratio of the value of imports to GDP) from 0.43 in 1989 to 0.16 in 2002 (see Table 1). There was also a marked decline in the gross investment rate; it fell from 0.162 in 1997 to 0.120 in 2002 (see Table 1) and it is likely that it diminished from approximately 0.30 in the early 1990s to 0.162 in 1997.

Vis-à-vis the rest of the world, Cuba derives its potential competitive advantage from its natural resources: land well suited for sun-and-sand tourism; the cultivation of particular crops like tobacco; minerals deposits like nickel and cobalt; and low wage rates of a skilled labor force. However, Cuba suffers a relative shortage of capital. The concept of intra-industry trade extends the principle of competitive advantage to include finer differences in endowments

of specific elements of human capital and technological capability. However, potential competitive advantage does not always convert into effective or realized competitive advantage, in the case of Cuba due to the problems of lack of adequate information in a socialist economy without market prices, inflexible bureaucracy and out-of-date business administration practices, accentuated by the lack of proper accounting and financial practices.

Gross mismanagement of traditional export sectors, such as agriculture, poor marketing across all sectors, and price distortions, meant that some sectors and sub-sectors with obvious strengths and advantages in relative factor endowments, contributed little or nothing to exports. It would be dangerous and incorrect to assume anything close to a maximal response to policy changes.

Basic products, the typical export basket of underdeveloped countries (sugar, nickel, tobacco, fish products and citrus), dominate Cuban exports, making export revenues highly sensitive to changes in commodity prices. Due partially to an overvalued Cuban peso pegged to the U.S. dollar, the dollar value of exports of goods increased only 26% in 1993-2002, one of the worst performances in Latin America. With the exception of tobacco, minerals and other minor products, the rest of the Cuban export sectors performed poorly. This poor export performance has been aggravated by unfavorable changes in terms of trade since 1997. Imports of goods increased from $1,984 million in 1993 to $4,161 in 2002 (see Table 2); part of this increase is attributed to the tourism sector, however, and total imports of goods in 2002 were still only 51% of their 1989 level.

In addition to an export sector lacking dynamism during 1993-2002, another characteristic of Cuban

---

5. This first economy encompasses all of the gross inefficiencies of socialism. Nearly everything ordinary Cubans must buy, including sugar, is rationed. Store shelves are empty and people either do without or improvise things to keep them going. That is why Cuba is frozen in time, a land of steam-powered locomotives and 1957 Fairlanes. The second economy serves some foreign markets and Western tourists providing luxury hotels and other modern installations at beaches, off-limits to ordinary Cubans. The third sector is the absolutely essential underground economy, despite the fact that it is illegal. Socialism holds that buying and selling in a market setting is evil and exploitative, and refers to it as speculation. Yet, this is the only market open to ordinary Cubans that do not have access to dollars and actually works. If it were not for the underground market, many Cubans could not purchase necessities like cooking oil and other basic foods, not to mention luxury goods such as footwear and clothing.

Table 1.   Cuba: Main Economic Indicators, 1989-2002

	1989	1990	1991	1992	1993	1994	1995	1996	1997	1998	1999	2000	2001	2002
Gross domestic product (GDP)[a]	19.8	19.8	16.7	15.6	15.8	19.4	21.9	23.3	23.4	23.8	26.1	28.2	29.4	29.8
Annual rate of growth of real GDP	1.5	-2.9	-9.5	-9.9	-13.6	0.6	2.5	7.6	2.5	0.2	6.3	6.1	3.0	1.1
Investment/GDP	49.4	49.5	29.6	13.7	9.6	9.7	12.8	14.6	16.2	14.4	13.6	14.3	13.3	12.0
Exports of goods and services[b]	5993	5940	3563	2522	1968	2542	3036	3795	3974	4132	4311	4791	4616	4272
Exports/GDP	0.30	0.30	0.21	0.16	0.12	0.13	0.14	0.16	0.17	0.17	0.17	0.17	0.16	0.14
Imports of goods and services[b]	8608	8017	4702	2737	2339	2849	3674	4213	4720	4889	5057	5685	5479	4785
Imports/GDP	0.43	0.40	0.28	0.18	0.15	0.15	0.17	0.18	0.20	0.21	0.19	0.20	0.19	0.16
Gross sugar production[c]	7329	8124	7536	6947	4084	3862	3133	4367	4155	3159	3715	3886	3581	3652
Extra official exchange rate[d]	NA	7.0	20.0	35.0	78.0	95.0	32.1	19.2	23.0	21.0	20.0	21.0	26.0	26.0
Foreign visitors[e]	NA	340	424	461	546	619	746	1004	1170	1416	1603	1774	1775	1686
Gross income from tourism[b]	NA	243	402	550	720	850	1100	1333	1543	1759	1901	1948	1856	1768
Total external debt in convertible currency[f]	6.1	6.6	6.8	6.4	8.8	9.1	10.5	10.5	10.1	11.2	11.1	11.0	10.9	10.9
Terms of trade index (1993=100)	184	198	128	95	100	121	131	120	123	118	98	87	87	79
Purchasing power of exports index (1993=100)	385	386	224	149	100	124	118	150	153	129	117	113	117	100
Debt/GDP	0.31	0.33	0.41	0.41	0.56	0.47	0.48	0.45	0.43	0.47	0.43	0.39	0.37	0.37

Note: In 2003 the Cuban National Statistical Office (Oficina Nacional de Estadísticas) changed the real GDP series from one based on 1981 prices to 1997 prices and adjusted some figures; however, it did not present series for the whole 1989-2002 period. As a result, the author estimated figures for GDP and investment for 1989 to 1996 based on previous trends in official figures published by CEPAL (2001 and 2002). Obviously, the investment rates for 1989 and 1990 are excessively high and are not realistic.

Source: CEPAL (2001, 2002, 2003).

a.   Billon Cuban pesos
b.   Million U.S. dollars
c.   Thousand tons
d.   Pesos for US$1
e.   Thousands of visitors
f.   Billion dollars; excludes foreign debt with former CMEA members

exports was their relative reliance on low level processing of natural resources and the stagnation of the efforts to expand export activities with greater value added and technological complexity.

There were some notable changes in the composition of exports, mainly reflecting developments in sugar, nickel and cobalt, tobacco, fish and seafood, and other goods. Sugar represented 66% of total exports of goods in 1993 but only 33% in 2002; meanwhile, nickel and cobalt exports increased from 12% to 34%, and tobacco from 6% to 16%. Nickel and cobalt exports increased at annual average rate of growth of 14.7% and tobacco at 13.7% during 1993-2002.

The sugar agroindustry has been lagging due to both technological obsolescence and low agricultural and industrial yields. Sugar production decreased 50% in 1989-2002 (see Table 1) and faces a major crisis. Making this sector competitive again would require high levels of investment as well as fundamental

changes to correct price distortions. Sugar has been used as collateral to cover short and medium term loans made to Cuba by international capital markets, and its availability or scarcity strongly influences the country risk evaluations of the Cuban economy.

The sugar industry, downsized in 2002, expected a gloomy 2.0 million ton output for the 2003 harvest season, the lowest production on record in 90 years, or since 1920. As Peña (2002, p. 108) indicates, total cost per ton of Cuban sugar in the period 1990-1995 was above the average cost on the world market (US$434.0 vis-à-vis US$360.8). Furthermore, his data shows that during the 1980s, Cuban production costs were higher than those of its global competitors (Australia, Brazil and Thailand). The persistent organizational and inefficiency problems of the sugar sector have contributed to the rise in financing costs. The reforms of the 1990s were limited and were not accompanied with the exigencies imposed by the

Table 2. Cuba: Balance of Payments, 1989-2002 (Million U.S. dollars)

	1989	1990	1991	1992	1993	1994	1995	1996	1997	1998	1999	2000	2001	2002
Current Account Balance	-3001	-2545	-1454	-420	-372	-260	-518	-167	-437	-392	-462	-776	-552	-293
Trade Balance	-2615	-2076	-1138	-215	-371	-308	-639	-418	-746	-757	-747	-894	-863	-513
Exports of Goods and Services	5993	5940	3563	2522	1968	2542	3036	3795	3974	4132	4311	4791	4616	4272
Goods	5400	5415	2980	1779	1137	1381	1507	1866	1823	1542	1496	1675	1661	1435
Sugar	3913	4313	2259	1220	752	748	704	957	845	605	471	458	551	474
Nickel & Cobalt	486	388	231	214	142	196	417	427	415	342	394	573	438	489
Tobacco & Tobacco Products	80	111	113	94	71	71	101	107	158	189	201	160	261	225
Fish and Seafood	126	97	125	104	68	99	121	125	127	103	96	87	79	Na
Other Goods	795	506	252	147	104	267	164	250	278	312	308	414	340	Na
Services	593	526	584	742	832	1160	1528	1929	2151	2592	2855	3114	2954	2836
Imports of Goods and Services	8608	8017	4702	2737	2339	2849	3674	4213	4720	4889	5057	5685	5479	4785
Goods	8140	7417	4234	2315	1984	2353	2992	3657	4088	4197	4365	4877	4838	4161
Services	468	600	468	422	355	497	683	556	632	660	692	808	640	625
Net Transfers	-48	-13	18	43	263	470	646	744	792	813	799	740	813	829
Remittances	Na	Na	Na	Na	Na	Na	537	630	670	690	700	Na	Na	Na
Donations	Na	Na	Na	Na	Na	Na	73	87	88	47	42	Na	Na	Na
Other Transfers	Na	Na	Na	Na	Na	Na	36	27	34	76	57	Na	Na	Na
Factor Services	-338	-456	-334	-248	-264	-423	-525	-493	-483	-449	-514	-622	-502	-666
Capital Account Balance	4122	2621	1421	419	356	262	596	174	457	409	485	805	595	300
Direct Investment	NA	NA	NA	NA	54	563	5	82	442	207	178	448	39	100
Global Balance	1121	76	-33	1	-16	2	79	8	21	17	23	29	42	-60

Source: CEPAL (2001, 2002, 2003)

highly competitive conditions of the sugar international market.

The development of services exports partly reflects normalization of this sector after it was neglected until the 1990s. Services exports increased continuously up to 2000, boosted by higher earnings from tourism and transport. Tourism became the most dynamic sector of the economy or the growth engine during the "Special Period," with over 23.1% average annual growth in 1990-2000. Services exports dropped by 9% in 2000-2002 (see Table 2). The accelerated growth of tourism in 1990-2000 was based on the so-called sand and sun tourism predicated on an intensive use of natural resources, where Cuba's competitive margins are relatively greater and more sustainable, despite competition from the Caribbean. It also depended significantly on the European and Canadian tourists, who have a preference for escaping from the harsh winter months.

Gross income from tourism replaced sugar as the main source of foreign exchange in 1994. This was due both to the rapid expansion of tourism and to the contraction in sugar production and exports. However, the direct import component of tourism is around 75% vis-à-vis 25% in sugar.

Imports have been repressed by the slow export expansion and the chronic external debt crisis. The shrinking share of machinery and equipment in total imports—reflected in the collapse of the investment rate, which is very low and decreased in 1990-2002—results in part because a large part of the import bill (at least 20% of the total) has gone to finance oil imports.

The deficit of trade in goods and services, or the trade balance, increased steadily from US$371 million in 1993 to US$894 million in 2000, but then it decreased to US$863 million in 2001 and to US$513 million in 2002, as tourism and foreign direct investment (FDI) declined.

Net transfers, mainly personal remittances from Cubans living abroad, and especially in the United States, to family and friends in the island have been positive and remain a major source of financing since 1993, when they substantially increased due to the legalization of foreign exchange holdings (see Table 2). Net transfers have surpassed other sources of income, like sugar, FDI or net income from tourism, since 1998. Net transfers increased US$263 million in 1993 to US$829 million in 2002, or at average annual rate of 13.6%; however, they have remained almost flat since 1998.

Deficits in factor services have increased, as a consequence of rising indebtedness and profit repatriation of FDI, from US$264 million in 1993 to US$666 million in 2002 (see Table 2), or at average annual rate of 10.8%.

The growth of the aggregate current account deficit in the 1990s reflected the interaction of economic recovery, structural factors, external shocks, erroneous development strategy and insufficient economic reform measures. Structural domestic factors seem to explain the disappointing export performance. Macroeconomic policies temporarily exacerbated imbalances up to 1993 due to the lack of a proper stabilization policy, with correction eventually being made through policy measures and/or adjustments triggered by the GDP and export contraction in 1990-1993.[6] Unfortunately, expansionary fiscal/monetary policies in the face of poor external performance have been used again since 2001.

The current account deficits reflect a net transfer of resources from abroad that has helped to boost domestic economic activity. In other words, in the absence of the deficits, the economic recovery would have been slower than it has been. The long-term concern is that current account deficits, especially those largely financed by foreign debt, are unsustainable. However, reducing the deficits could lower short-term recovery prospects under current conditions.

Deficits can be a normal part of the development process, but the key is to distinguish between good and bad deficits. Good deficits are those that arise from external borrowing used to invest in productive assets, which will eventually produce a return to service and pay off the debt. Bad deficits are those used to finance current economic activity (consumption) and will lead eventually to default. To reduce the risks of non-sustainable current account deficits, FDI is preferred to debt financing.

Evolution of the Terms of Trade

Cuba's terms of trade noticeably worsened after 1997, partly because the world market price of major international commodities—except for oil and some metals—fell while the average dollar prices of manufactured goods exports remained unchanged or increased slightly. Cuba's purchasing power of exports index worsened from 153 in 1997 to 100 in 2002, a decline 35%. Concurrently, the terms of trade index steadily deteriorated from 123 in 1997 to 79 in 2002, or a 36% decline, which explains the behavior of the purchasing power of exports index.

The lower the degree of openness of a country's economy, dependence on a few commodity exports, and weakness of institutions, the larger its exposure and vulnerability to variations in the terms of trade. Since 1997, Cuba has been subject to sharp terms of trade fluctuations leading to a reduction of exports and, hence, of output recovery. The adjustment to the terms of trade shock requires either an economic slowdown (or recession) or a modification in relative prices, implying an increase in the price of tradables relative to the price of nontradables; that is, a depreciation of the real exchange rate and some expenditure switching.

Evolution of Capital Inflows and of the External Debt

Capital inflows fell more than tenfold from US$4,122 million in 1989 to US$356 million in 1993 as the soft financing from the CMEA disappeared while Western capital markets remained relatively closed. Subsequently, capital inflows averaged US$454 million per annum in the period 1994-2002 (see Table 2). Therefore, Cuba was only able to finance an average current account deficit of US$429

---

6. The government implemented a sharp decrease in the fiscal deficit through deep cuts in government spending including social expenditures, capital formation expenditures and subsidies to enterprises, as well as an absolute reduction in the money supply.

million in 1994-2002 vis-à-vis US$3,001 million in 1989 and US$2,545 million in 1990. The current account deficit was further reduced to only US$293 million in 2002.

The potential for FDI to stimulate economic growth is well recognized. Among other ways, it can supplement domestic savings, improve the allocation of resources, and act as a conduit for new technologies and know-how. For Cuba, burdened by decades of socialist technological backwardness, FDI can facilitate the process of modernization, economic reform, and enterprise restructuring and help improve international competitiveness. According to CEPAL (2001, p. 1), in 2000, joint ventures with foreign investors generated around 6% of output, produced 16% of total exports of goods and services, and provided direct employment for 33,000 workers.

FDI averaged US$212 million in 1993-2002 but dropped to US$39 million in 2001and US$100 million in 2002. Europeans and Canadians, Cuba's leading source of investment capital, have grown increasingly frustrated with the government's bureaucracy and arbitrariness in dealing with investors. European embassies in Havana jointly presented a detailed list of suggestions and grievances to the Cuban government in 2002. However, Cuba's foreign investment minister, Marta Lomas told diplomats that "Cuba is not changing the rules" and that European businessmen "knew them [the rules] when they arrived."[7]

For Cuba, opening the economy to Western capital inflows has meant excessive indebtedness in good times—when economic growth improved international perceptions of creditworthiness and interest rate spreads were low—and a sharp reversal of inflows in bad times—when adverse shocks caused severe deterioration of international perception of creditworthiness and interest rate spreads were high. However, insufficient (ex ante) accumulation of foreign reserves, lack of access to additional sources of liquidity, and the sudden stop of capital inflows resulted in default of external obligations in 1986 and chronic balance of payments problems with Western countries.

For countries in default, the normalization of relations with official (the Paris Club) and commercial (the London Club) creditors is generally a precondition for reentering international credit markets. Certain types of investors are legally prohibited from lending to countries in default, if they are not already deterred by a country's balance of payments prospects. However, some short-term lenders extend cash at high yields even in the absence of fundamental reforms.

Due to the lack of structural reforms, the difficult situation in the early 1990s and the numerous obstacles to be overcome, Cuba has failed to create the conditions for attracting sustained and increasing foreign capital inflows and even suffered setbacks. Cuba has been only able to attract funds temporarily. On April 1, 2003, Moody's classified Cuba's credit ratings as Caa1 or Caa2—"speculative" and "demonstrate very weak creditworthiness relative to other issuers"—because of chronic delinquencies and mounting short-term debts.[8] Also, the Economist Intelligence Unit classified Cuba's sovereign debt risk as D and currency risk as C.

In October 2002, Cuba defaulted on a US$750-million refinancing agreement with Japan's private sector after having signed a debt restructuring accord in 1998. Japan, Cuba's single largest creditor, had expected to see the first payments in 2003 on part of the US$1.7 billion owed to Japan by Cuba. According to one Japanese creditor, "[The Cuban government] told us...there was no way they could make the scheduled payments next year [in 2003]." Francisco Soberón, president-minister of the Banco Central de Cuba, admitted as much: "The proposed conditions

---

7. Statement by Cuba's foreign investment minister, Marta Lomas, as quoted by European sources in "Foreign investment in Cuba falls, EU wants reform," Reuters, Havana, July 8, 2002.

8. Moody´s Latin American Rating Lists as of April 1, 2003, at www.moodys.com.br/pdf/LARL%20April.pdf.

are absolutely impossible for us. They would cause a social explosion."[9]

Also, in October 2002, Cuba suspended all payments on US$380 million owed to Bancomext, the Mexican government's export financing bank. According to Bancomext, "First, the Cuban government unilaterally cancelled debt guarantees that took years to negotiate. Then they missed a multimillion dollar June 2002 payment without even giving an explanation."[10]

Cuba's oil bill debt with Venezuela's Petróleos de Venezuela S.A. (PDVSA) rose to US$266 million by May 2003. CUPET, Cuba's state-owned and operated oil company has fallen behind on payments to PDVSA repeatedly since Cuba and Venezuela signed a trade agreement in October 2000. PDVSA supplies approximately 35% of the island's oil under generous financing terms that amount to a 25% price subsidy over five years. Due to the value of oil exports, Venezuela is now Cuba's leading trade partner.

In 2002, Cuba fell into arrears on US$100 million in short-term credit lines from Panamanian banks and trading companies based in the Colon Free Zone. Cuba has traditionally circumvented the U.S. trade embargo by sourcing American consumer goods and technology through Panama-based suppliers. Panamanian lenders have also helped to finance Cuba's sugar crop in recent years.

In May 2003, Spain acknowledged—in response to a parliamentary inquiry—that Cuba is Spain's top foreign debtor government, presently in default on an estimated US$816 million. France's export financing agency, COFACE, has suspended Cuba's US$175million credit line after Cuba fell more than a year behind in repayment of annual loans for the purchase of French agricultural products and capital goods in 2001. The Italian government withdrew a proposed US$40 million aid package in early June 2003 in response to Cuba's crackdown on internal dissents. The Cuban government had already accumulated a short-term debt of US$73 million with Italy. Italy, which assumed the presidency of the European Union (EU) in July 2003, has called for an EU embargo on all non-humanitarian assistance to Cuba.

Cuba's worsening foreign exchange constraint and foreign debt problems have brought about a reprioritization of key commercial relationships. Mexico, Canada and Spain have all lost Cuban trade share to a diverse assortment of emerging economic partners in Latin America (Brazil and Venezuela), Asia (China, Malaysia and Vietnam), Europe (Belgium and Germany), and the Middle East (Iran and the Muslim world at large).

The Strengthening of the U.S. Embargo in the 1990s

In 1961, under the Kennedy Administration, the U.S. imposed a comprehensive embargo against Americans who wanted to trade with, travel to, or invest in Cuba. In 1992, the U.S. enacted the Cuban Democracy Act, the so-called Torriceli Law, that tightened the embargo and changed its focus from U.S. national security to promoting political reform within Cuba. It prohibited U.S. subsidiaries in third countries to trade with Cuba and stipulated that ships that load and unload merchandise in Cuban ports are banned from entering U.S. ports for a period of 6 months from the date of arrival in Cuba. This latter provision increases Cuba's freight costs and delays delivery of traded goods.

In 1996, the U.S. enacted the Cuban Liberty and Democratic Solidarity Act, the Helms- Burton Law. This law imposes extra-territorial penalties on foreign companies and citizens that traffic in property that Cuba expropriated from U.S. citizens, hindering foreign investment flows to Cuba.

The U.S. embargo has been ineffective, inconsistent and counterproductive. Therefore, it cannot be

---

9. Statements by an anonymous Japanese creditor and by Francisco Soberón, head of the Central Bank of Cuba, as quoted by Marc Frank, "Cuba said to miss Japan, Mexico debt payments," Reuters, Havana, October 25, 2002.

10. Ibid.

blamed for the deficient performance of the Cuban external sector. Economic theory and practice indicate that unilateral economic sanctions have never worked and are ineffective.[11] This has held true in the case of Cuba despite the fact that the island is only ninety miles from the U.S. shore. The embargo only adds some additional freight and financial costs to imports or reduces the net revenues from exports. Despite the embargo, American goods can be found in the dollar stores in Cuba, and some Cuban products, like medicines, are available in the United States.[12]

The U.S. embargo is inconsistent because the United States allows around US$800 million to flow annually from Cuban-Americans or Cubans living in South Florida to their families in the island. Additionally, Cuban-Americans and Americans are visiting Cuba in record numbers. More than 200 U.S. universities and research centers have been licensed by the Treasury Department to lead trips to Cuba. About 150,000 Americans visited with such permission in 2002. Another estimated 50,000 slipped into Cuba illegally from third countries. In 2000, U.S. lawmakers carved an important exemption in the trade embargo by legalizing the sale of food and medicines. Since then, U.S. companies have sold nearly $200 million in corn, rice, and other commodities to the island.

Finally, by pointing to the U.S. "blockade," Cubans, whose affection for the American way of life (individual freedoms and prosperity) is very strong, are taught by the authorities that the embargo is clear proof that the United States wants to promote misery in Cuba, that it is using economic deprivation to promote political change, and that the United States must be regarded as their enemy, responsible for the

poor economic situation instead of the flawed socialist system and erroneous economic policies in place. Furthermore, they are an excuse for the regime's economic ineptitude and repression. Since the breakup of the USSR, and with the maintenance of the embargo, it is the Cuban people who suffer the costs of the sanctions.

POLICIES AND REFORMS IN 1990-2002 AND THEIR IMPLICATIONS

The Cuban authorities managed to halt the striking decline in GDP from 1990-1993, maintained positive growth of GDP for nine consecutive years (1994-2002), substantially modified the country's international relations based on new products and markets, and attained greater macroeconomic stability. The "extra official" exchange rate appreciated almost steadily from 1994 to 1999. However, Cuba still faces chronic disequilibrium in the balance of payments and has not been able to generate self-sustained growth.

The partial recoveries of the external sector and of the economy since 1994 have been significant but insufficient achievements. Utilization of existing capacity is still below 1989 levels in most agricultural and manufacturing activities (see Table 3); GDP is below 1985 or 1989 levels (a retrogression of more than 17 years); and GDP growth became less dynamic over the last four years. In summary, Cuba has been trapped in low and declining living standards since 1985 due to misguided development strategy and policies and persistent external bottlenecks.

The internal economic reforms initiated since the breakup of the Communist trading bloc are based on the premise of maintaining government control of the economy. Some required changes have been in-

---

11. "Although sanctions clearly create suffering in many places, how often have they achieved the desired goal? In Myanmar, Iraq, North Korea, and Cuba, despotic regimes not only survived the imposition of sanctions, but became more despotic. These regimes were able to blame foreigners for domestic hardships, even when it was their own policy mistakes and human rights abuses that caused the crises. Indeed, sanctions weaken an economy and public health, but do not necessarily make it more likely that a despotic regime will collapse. Sanctions purportedly undermine the regime by causing widespread unrest and by reducing the government's power base and tax collections. But sanctions also weaken the ability of the private sector to finance an opposition, tend to cut off the domestic opposition from international sources of support, and reduce, rather than increase, international awareness of the abuses taking place" Sachs (2003).

12. Elaine de Valle, "Crece el tráfico de medicamentos desde Cuba," *El Nuevo Herald*, September 30, 2003.

Table 3. Selected Indicators of Agricultural and Industrial Physical Output, 1989-2002 (Thousand tons)

Indicators	1989	1990	1992	1993	1994	1995	1996	1997	1998	1999	2000	2001	2002	2002/ 1989
Rice	532	474	358	177	387	396	673	614	441	567	462	589	609	1.14
Citrus	1,016	1,016	787	645	540	585	690	835	744	795	959	157	488	0.48
Milk	1,131	1,034	622	586	636	638	640	651	655	618	614	621	605	0.53
Eggs	2,673	2,727	2,331	1,512	1,647	1,542	1,12	1,632	1,416	1,753	1,722	1,525	1,682	0.63
Nickel and Cobalt	47	41	32	30	27	43	54	62	68	66	71	77	75	1.60
Oil	718	671	882	1,107	1,299	1,471	1,476	1,457	1,658	2,104	2,621	2,780	3,546	4.94
Sugar 96°	7,579	8,445	7,219	4,246	4,017	3,259	4,529	4,318	3,271	3,274	4,058	3,748	NA	a 0.46
Cigars	304	318	295	208	186	192	194	214	264	285	246	339	224	0.73
Electricity (GWh)	16	15	12	11	12	12	13	14	14	14	15	15	16	1.00
Cement	3,759	3,289	1,134	1,049	1,085	1,456	1,438	1,701	1,713	1,785	1,633	1,334	1,376	0.37
Fertilizers	898	833	178	95	136	217	241	184	156	138	118	93	93	0.10

Source: CEPAL (2001, 2003)

a. CEPAL (2001, 2003)

troduced into the system on a limited and piecemeal fashion and are allowed only as long as their consequences remain under central control.

Tourism, remittances, FDI, and short-term commercial credits have only partially substituted for the massive external subsidies and aid from the former Soviet Union. Exports—primarily of basic commodities—have declined since 1996. An elementary type of tourism has been developed, but the international political and economical setting is not favorable to its continued expansion due the events after September 11, 2001, to the recent confrontations with the Italian and Spanish governments—countries where 17% of tourists originate—and the economic slowdown in Europe. The government also does all it can to prevent that tourism activities would have spillover effects to the rest of the economy.

During 1990-2002, the main policies of the government for the external sector were: (1) maintain the strategy of import substitution and a central command economy as the foundations of the development strategy, with very limited use of market mechanisms and practices; (2) maintain an overvalued official exchange rate and ration available foreign exchange; (3) encourage dollarization of the economy to boost up remittances; (4) promote tourism and FDI in joint ventures to expand exports and to have access to foreign markets, technology and capital; (5) decentralize firms, up-grade their business practices

and allow some export firms to have privileged access to the foreign exchange they generate; (6) make selective payments and arrangements on the external debt; and (7) stretch the period of external adjustment to reduce social costs.

Despite the major global changes since the breakup of the Soviet Union, Cuba's leadership has continued to insist on a centrally-controlled economy and import substitution as viable ways into the future and to maintain that it is the American "blockade" rather than the inefficiency of the inward socialist and centrally controlled system that is the prime culprit behind Cuba's economic problems. As we indicated above, this in not the case, and only a poor excuse.

The development policy of the external sector in place in 1994-2002 would have to be modified significantly to promote high and self-sustained development in the future. Cuba needs a strategy for a successful international insertion. A small country like Cuba lacks alternatives outside an export-oriented strategy based on the intensive use of market mechanisms and practices, as China, Vietnam and former socialist European countries have done quite effectively. Only through exports expansion and application of market mechanisms, can Cuba obtain the resources necessary for investment and continuous economic expansion based on productivy increases related to specialization, economies of scale, and learning by doing.

Cuba cannot have both a fixed exchange rate pegged to the U.S. dollar and an independent fiscal/monetary policy, as it had in 1990-1993 and more recently in 2001-2003. These inconsistent macroeconomic policies have been accentuated by Cuba's lack of openness to trade, high dependence on basic commodities and services, and low external liquidity.[13] For a pegged exchange rate to work on a sustainable basis it must be set at realistic levels, and there must not be actual or potential external debt problems and there has to be economic policy credibility. As a result of Cuban wrong and inconsistent macroeconomic policies, there has been an almost unrelenting increase in the spread of the interest rate that Cuba has to pay in international credit markets as a result of perceptions of the country's deteriorated ability to service its debt and the real possibility of default (CEPAL, 2001, p 138, as well as Moody's and the Economist Intelligence Unit's worsening credit ratings as of April 2003 and September 2003, respectively).

The lack of a market-established and unified exchange rate also obstructs the determination of Cuban costs and prices truly comparable to those in the world market, affects the Cuban economy as a whole and has influenced the marked decline of the sugar industry. Forward and backward linkages need to be stimulated through a unified exchange rate, to overcome the phenomenon of a few dynamic exporting sectors based on natural resources amid a stagnant overall economy, and to foster the spillovers to the rest of the economy

Cuba only has liberalized FDI partially. Major obstacles that still exist are the reluctance to allow ownership of land or capital, the bureaucratization of procedures for foreign investment authorization, the selection by the government of the employees of joint ventures, and a system of remuneration of workers whereby wage rates paid by foreign investors to the government employment agencies are ten times what the workers are paid. Also, FDI is unlikely to be attracted to Cuba in significant amounts be-

cause the protection of property rights is arbitrary and weak, and the institutional framework for market-based activity is deficient. FDI in Cuba has outgrown its institutional underpinnings. This is not surprising, as access to high quality investment funds, is often conditional on the implementation of structural reforms that favor market mechanisms and practices and sound macroeconomic policies.

It is sound policy to change the norms, regulations and economic organization and management systems in state-owned enterprises in order to adapt the country to the new circumstances under which is currently developing (CEPAL, 2001, p. 4). Nevertheless, to be effective, enterprise reform should occur in the context of a deep transformation of the economy and not of increasing distortions, controls and backtracking from further reforms.

It is very important to encourage remittances to increase the level of economic activity in Cuba. However, the restrictions on the use of the remittances for consumption purposes should be eliminated as soon as possible because they act as a disincentive to increasing remittances.

The practice of selective payments on the external debt has increased the risk and uncertainty of foreign lending and investment in Cuba. Specifically, it has increased both the interest rates that Cuba has to pay for short-term loans and has reduced the quality of investment that can be attracted.

The slow and piecemeal external sector reforms have not only slowed the change towards the market but also have slowed the rate of economic recovery and have had resulted in high welfare costs by discouraging production of tradables, increasing major distortions in the domestic markets, reducing employment and worsening the income distribution.

What is truly amazing, in retrospect, is that the pattern of development that emerged from the policy decisions of the 1990-1993 crises has represented an essential continuity, rather than a significant trans-

---

13. Changes in the exchange rate of a major trading partner relative to the dollar might bring unexpected and undesirable change in the effective domestic real exchange rate.

formation of the previous pattern. Unfortunately, Cuba's economic policies have not been focused on development or on adjusting the economy to the new international environment and conditions, but rather on preserving Castro's specific view of socialism and his absolute power.

STRATEGIC LESSONS FROM THE EXTERNAL SECTOR REFORM OF THE 1990s AND FROM THE SUCCESSFUL CHILEAN EXPERIENCE

The experiences of Central European, former Soviet Union and Latin American countries in the 1990s shows the critical role of macroeconomic policies and exchange rate management in making foreign trade reform (or trade liberalization) sustainable and part of an effective pro-growth strategy. In several of these countries, notable progress toward more open foreign trade regimes and faster export growth failed to translate into real expansion of output, productivity and employment. In this context, it is not surprising that unemployment, poverty, and income inequality increased.

One of the key purposes of trade reform is to promote economic growth by capturing the static and dynamic gains from trade through increased productivity—more efficient use of resources—and a shift in resources from inefficient to efficient activities and sectors; greater external competition among previously protected firms to change their behavior and performance; an increase in the flow of knowledge and investment, and ultimately a faster rate of capital formation and technical progress. Barriers to trade and anti-export bias reduce export growth below potential. Import controls are likely to reduce efficiency, although they protect the balance of payments at the same time in the short run.

Countries with well-functioning markets and a better human resource base benefit more from productivity gains resulting from trade reform than countries with less well-functioning markets. This explains the need for broad and in-depth systematic reforms to liberalize prices and wages, implementation of sound accounting and financial practices, and reduction of the bureaucratic regulations in state owned enterpris-

es so that they will be to react to the new policy environment.

The presumption is that trade reform will raise the growth of exports and imports, but the implications for the trade balance and the balance of payments are ambiguous because this depends on the relative impact of trade liberalization on export and import growth, and on what happens to the prices of traded goods. Trade reform may promote growth from the supply side, but if the balance of payments worsens, growth may be negatively affected from the demand side because the payments deficits resulting from trade reform are unsustainable and need to be rectified by relative price (real exchange rate) adjustments.

Studies of trade reform in developing countries have paid a lot of attention to its impact on export performance, economic growth, employment, wage inequality and income distribution, but very little to its impact on imports, the balance of trade and the balance of payments. These are equally important areas of analysis because if trade reform leads to faster growth of imports than exports, it can have serious implications for the balance of payments of countries that may constrain growth below their productive potential. That is to say, while trade reform may promote growth from the supply side through a more efficient allocation of resources, it may constrain growth from the demand side unless a balance between imports and exports can be maintained through exchange rate adjustment or deficits can be financed through sustainable capital inflows.

Santos-Paulino and Thirlwall (2002) examined a sample of 22 developing countries—from four continents, with over 450 observations—that had undergone extensive trade policy reforms over the period 1972-1997. They paid particular attention to identifying the year when significant liberalization was embarked on and constructed time series for the duties applied to exports and imports over the period of analysis (used as measures of liberalization). They reached the following six main conclusions:

• First, reductions in export and import duties significantly affected the growth of exports and imports, with the impact on import growth being greater. For a one percentage point reduction in duties, exports grew by just under 0.2%, while imports grew by between 0.2 and 0.4%.

- Second, the impact of a more liberalized trade regime, in all its manifestations, independently of duty reductions, raised import growth by more than exports. Evidently, it was easier for importers to import than for producers to reallocate resources to the tradables sector and to develop export markets. Compared to the pre-liberalization regime, the process of liberalization raised export growth by just under 2%, while import growth has increased by between 2 and 9%.

- Third, liberalization increased the income elasticities of demand for imports and exports by roughly equal amounts, but the price elasticity of demand for imports increased more than for exports. Fourth, the pure effect of trade liberalization, independent of duty changes, worsened the trade balance by over 2% of GDP, but the impact on the current account of the balance of payments was less, worsening by approximately 0.8% of GDP on average. The effects of liberalization on the trade balance and balance of payments were similar across the regions of Africa, East Asia, Latin America and South Asia, in the sense that all regions suffered deterioration.

- Fifth, the impact of liberalization differed according to whether countries started highly protected or not. The positive effect of liberalization on import growth, and the adverse effects on the trade balance and balance of payments, were all greater in the more highly protected countries.

- Sixth, it appears that liberalization had a positive effect on income growth, but the balance of trade consequences might reduce growth below what might otherwise had been if a balance between exports and imports had been maintained.[14]

Therefore, the policy conclusion is that countries that have promoted trade liberalization need to take great care in the nature and sequencing of the liberalization of exports and imports to achieve a better balance between export and import performance. Liberalization for liberalization's sake that leads to a massive flood of imports, without a corresponding rise in exports, will be counterproductive because, except for countries able to run payments surpluses, all deficit countries ultimately become balance of payments-constrained in their growth performance.

The transition from a restrictive to an open trade regime can also impose short-term adjustment costs through efforts to restore macroeconomic stabilization, such as reductions in fiscal deficits, that could hurt the country's already weak infrastructure.

Even a relative strong export performance might not result in faster economic expansion, because the benefits of trade liberalization can be more than offset by policies that work against sustainable outward orientation. To promote a sustainable macroeconomic environment, countries have to deal with transition and adjustment costs in a balanced and consistent manner. For that reason, it is also very important to adopt exchange rates and other complementary policies that help keep competitiveness and outward orientation.

Export expansion needs to be fast enough to allow the economy to grow at the maximum potential rate allowed by its supply-side productive potential, while keeping the current account deficit to a level that can be financed on a sustainable basis. Capital account liberalization could result in large capital inflows with the undesired appreciation of the real exchange rate. To discourage short-term inflows and to prevent an excessive appreciation of the domestic currency, Chile and Colombia, successfully enforced tax and reserve requirements on foreign credits and deposits during the 1990s. Argentina is now establishing controls to prevent short-term capital inflows.

---

14. In a study of Latin American countries, Khan and Zahler (1985) found that the balance of trade effects had serious consequences for the growth of output.

Table 4. Central European Transition Countries: Movements of the Real Effective Exchange Rate, 1992-1997[a]

	Real Effective Exchange Rate using Industrial Producer Prices					
	1992	1993	1994	1995	1996	1997[b]
Bulgaria	100	117.1	98.9	109.4	103.3	114.6
Czech Republic	100	117.9	122.0	125.4	132.6	136.0
Hungary	100	105.9	100.6	96.0	98.9	108.9
Poland	100	107.4	103.1	107.4	111.4	109.2
Romania	100	106.7	115.8	115.3	114.4	123.5
Slovakia	100	116.7	119.1	123.4	128.6	136.6

	Real Effective Exchange Rate using Consumer Prices					
	1992	1993	1994	1995	1996	1997[b]
Bulgaria	100	154.8	146.9	174.1	156.2	188.1
Czech Republic	100	122.3	130.4	136.4	147.4	153.5
Hungary	100	110.5	109.7	104.6	107.6	115.7
Poland	100	107.6	108.0	114.9	125.5	130.5
Romania	100	141.2	151.9	149.3	135.3	146.6
Slovakia	100	118.9	123.6	129.5	134.8	144.1

Source: *Economic Indicators for Eastern Europe, Monthly Release (1994-1997).* Basle: Bank for International Settlements, Monetary and Economic Department.

a. Trade-weighted indices 1992=100, vis-à-vis 21 industrial countries, based on industrial producer prices (PP) and consumer prices (CP).

b. Cumulative data from January up to latest observation (September 1997).

The costs of real appreciation should not be underestimated, particularly in a context of rapid trade liberalization, because the key prices of labor relative to capital, of exports relative to imports, and of tradables relative to nontradables depend on the evolution of real exchange rates. Some policy mixes could led to a significant real appreciation of the domestic currency, spiraling current account deficits, a major increase in the external debt, and eventually to a foreign exchange and financial crisis. Krueger (1997) warns of the dangers of trade liberalization that is not accompanied by competitive exchange rate policies. In other words, a realistic exchange rate is key to protect domestic firms from imports and gives domestic firms greater incentives to export during a trade liberalization process.

Drabek and Brada (1998) show that trade liberalization followed up by current account and capital account liberalization in six Central European nations (Bulgaria, the Czech Republic, Hungary, Poland, Romania, and Slovakia) led to major appreciations of the real exchange rates (see Table 4) and, hence, to a reversal of some trade liberalization measures. In other words, in these six transition countries, trade liberalization was not sufficient to keep competitive real

exchange rates that allow continuous export and economic growth. The concurrent sharp appreciation in the real effective exchange rate added considerably to the growth of domestic demand for imported consumer goods. Moreover, the appreciation of the exchange rate, combined with higher domestic inflation than foreign inflation, forced up the level of interest rates, thus attracting foreign capital, which also stimulated the growth of domestic aggregate demand. Increased flexibility in real exchange rate appears to be the only and sensible choice because any form of fixed value or peg may be quite vulnerable to a sudden loss of credibility, which is quite likely in the transition process to a market economy. Therefore, managed floating with inflation targeting seems the best alternative for small economies, like Cuba, given the need to manage the availability of scarce foreign liquidity and to keep a competitive real exchange rate.

Accumulation of foreign liquidity is also a necessary complement. This policy prescription was advanced and developed by Goldstein (2002) and has been fruitfully adopted by an increasing number of Latin American countries in recent years.

Another ingredient of successful outward-oriented policies is complementary measures for the elimination of the anti-export bias characteristic of the former import substitution model. Since the mid-1980s, Chile has successfully applied a variety of administrative instruments to promote exports aggressively: simplified tax rebates, temporary admission of imports, tariff deferrals on exporters' capital goods, and corrections of informational market failures (Agosin, 1999).[15]

An export policy focused on providing information, supporting marketing abroad, and facilitating access to export finance and insurance can help diversify production. ProChile[16] confirms that this is quite possible. In this regard, an active commercial diplomacy geared to securing market access, identifying new opportunities, and counteracting trade restrictions can help expand exports. Government agencies can also assist firms, especially small and medium-sized businesses, to deal with issues such as technology diffusion and innovation, and with human resource development.

In addition, other key policies geared to foster productivity are needed to reap the full benefits of international specialization and the dynamic gains from trade liberalization, in a world characterized by persistent and significant failures in markets for technology, credit and human capital, considering that technology is not a public good and the process of acquiring technological capabilities is not automatic. The combination of outward orientation based on a realistic exchange rate with technology and industrial policies may encourage greater exploitation of dynamic scale economies in the presence of market failures in technology, international trading information and financial markets, factors that according to Nobel Laureate Stiglitz (1996) helped to explain the superior growth performance of East Asia vis-à-vis Latin America.

Fostering export growth for sustained economic growth also requires designing a comprehensive strategy on the basis of building and maintaining adequate physical infrastructure. Chile has been able to develop an impressive economic infrastructure (roads, airports, etc.) through public concessions to the private sector since the mid-1990s.

FUTURE EXTERNAL POLICY CHALLENGES

The lack of fundamental economic and institutional reforms in Cuba and the overvalued exchange rate explain the unsatisfactory export performance in recent years and the dependence on permanent transfers from external sources in 1994-2002. Proper policies prevent pitifully poor performance but negligence and irresponsibility inevitability lead to loss of standard of living. The limited recovery was made possible by Cuban natural competitive advantages in a few goods and services, the enormous economic slack prevailing in the first years of the 1990s, and took place simultaneously with deepening dualism and shrinking of the capital formation. Increased external financing will not be useful and successful unless proper institutions, practices, and adequate policies are in place.

Cuba still has to adjust to the new, more competitive international context. The lack of enough foreign exchange is a main stranglehold for production and investment in the economy. Cuba's notable competitive strength based on its most potentially advantageous factor, its skilled labor force, is not currently used in an intensive manner and it is discouraged by the artificially high wage policy of the gov-

15. Chile's post-1983 strategy has relied on an outward orientation based on a large real depreciation supported by appropriate fiscal and monetary policies, a bit of support for non-traditional exports in agro-industry, saving mobilization through pension privatization, and discouragement of short-term capital inflows.

16. ProChile is the Chilean Trade Commission, an agency within the Chilean Ministry of Foreign Affairs. Its role is to support and advance Chilean business interests in the global marketplace by assisting in the development of the export process. ProChile is active in establishing international business relationships, fostering the exchange of goods and services, attracting foreign investment and forging strategic alliances. It serves as a source of market research, international trade data and leads for the export industry for both foreign and Chilean firms alike. Though ProChile seeks to stimulate and diversify the country's export base in general, special emphasis is given to promoting non-traditional products.

ernment by charging the foreign enterprises in dollars but paying the Cuban workers in pesos. The overall situation presents challenges that require bolder initiatives and much less dogmatism in several areas as some Cuban academics and researchers have correctly pointed out (Monreal, 2002a).

Based on the strategic lessons learned from the experiences in transitions economies and in Latin America in the 1990s, Cuba needs three main systematic, broad and in-depth policy reforms tailored to its own capabilities, constraints and opportunities: (1) institutional reforms to use more the market mechanisms and practices,[17] (2) trade liberalization, and (3) a competitive and flexible exchange rate. The proposed reforms will raise enormously Cuba's growth potential and make it more resilient, faster and less vulnerable. Also, they will reduce the mismanagement and weakness of state-owned enterprises due to lack of foreign competition and proper information for sound business decisions; open significantly the economy to external trade, reducing the worst inefficiencies of an inward orientation in a small economy; diminish considerably the dependence on a few basic commodity exports and reduce the export vulnerability to terms of trade shocks; decrease the reliance and dependence on foreign savings and lay the foundations for a higher investment rate; and will reduce the fragility of the external debt profile.

These three fundamental policy reforms, but particularly a competitive and flexible exchange rate, will also allow Cuba freedom in the choice of fiscal-monetary policy mix. However, they will require other complementary administrative and export promotion policies to transform faster external growth into better economic performance as the successful Chilean experience has clearly shown since the mid-1980s.

CONCLUDING REMARKS

The partial recoveries of the external sector and of the economy in 1994-2002 were based on three main pillars: (1) the continued intensive use of natural resources to expand Cuba's export base of goods and services, (2) the access to remittances from Cubans living abroad, and (3) moderate access to foreign direct investment (FDI), mainly in tourism, tobacco and mining, and short-term foreign credits. However, these revenues could in no way compensate for the massive Soviet subsidies and aid to the Cuban economy. The new pattern of development and of international insertion is insufficient to achieve Cuba's economic and social development goals over the long term and to insure a permanent improvement in the standard of living of the population. The Cuban economy remains anemic and below its 1985 level despite some recovery since 1994.

With the decline of sugar, tourism and FDI already felt in 2001 and 2002 and most other economic indicators pointing downward, including an increase of inflation, the Cuban economy is on a new downturn. In 2003 the country's balance of payments has been in its worst shape in several years and can only be expected to benefit partially from the improving international economic situation. The government's erroneous policy responses have been a tightening of controls (including foreign exchange controls)[18] and trying to increase social spending with the predictable results of increasing and widespread scarcities and distortions as evidenced by the increasing exchange rate premium, as well as expanding budget

---

17. The establishment of the most basic of these mechanisms and practices, and a fair level playing field can be expected to unleash a flurry of new investments and entrepreneurship, to spur productive dynamism, as well as to lower regulatory burdens and corruption, as they did in the early 1980s and in 1994-1995. Both experiments with market mechanisms, incentives and practices were quite successful in Cuba and brought immediate results (Hernández-Catá, 2003). Aslund and Johnson (2003) consider that small and medium enterprises have played a key role in the successful transitions in Poland and Hungary and explain 50 to 60 percent of their GDP today.

18. Managers and foreign enterprises doing business in Cuba are in an uproar over the government's move in July to introduce foreign exchange controls for state-owned enterprises. They were ordered to hand over their dollars and were ordered from now on to buy dollars from the Central Bank for their imports and debt payments and local purchases from joint ventures in Cuba. Foreign suppliers and businesses in Cuba that sell products to the state-owned enterprises complained that they will face further delays of over two weeks in collecting payments and arrears from the cash-strapped state. Local analysts and businessmen say the measures were taken by the government in response to the hard currency crunch it faces due to a stagnant economy and scarce foreign investment.

deficits that are being financed predominantly by monetary expansion and decreasing capital formation. Therefore, the main ingredients for a new economic crisis are present.

The inadequate policies for the external sector are responsible for the unsatisfactory developments in 1990-2002 and have adverse implications for the sustainability of current economic recovery and financial inflows. Once again, an inward development strategy for a small country has been exposed as an economic loser. The failure of exports of goods and services to expand, as expected, under the current institutional and policy conditions and development strategy, risk the continuation of economic recovery. Given the small size of the Cuban economy it is unfeasible to function as a closed economy and without market mechanisms and institutions.

Prospects in the short and medium term are bleak. The current strategy appears to be crumbling, like the buildings in old Havana so many times mentioned in Zoé Valdés' novels. Nevertheless, Castro hangs on to his wishful vision, in spite of the hard-nosed analysis made by the island's academics and researchers on the island, hoping for some turn of fate and blaming the U.S. embargo for the downturn. It is hard for him even tacitly to admit a mistake. But the island's academics and researchers cannot follow his irresponsible lead. Sooner or later they must address questions about this policy and strategy.

Although there is no agreed road map, Cuba needs a new development strategy tailored to its own capabilities, constraints and opportunities to open its economy, to make reforms to be more competitive and efficient, and to develop more goods and services for export that will permit increasing and sustained growth. Cuba also needs to increase and diversify its export basket and improve its debt/GDP ratio to reduce its external vulnerability. As discussed above, trade liberalization is very important but it is not a panacea. In order to work it must supported by sound macroeconomic and exchange rate policies, fundamental institutional changes addressing the lack of market mechanisms and practices, and other pro-export domestic policies.

REFERENCES

Manuel R. Agosin, "Comercio y Crecimiento en Chile," in *Revista de la CEPAL*, 68, 1999, pp. 79-100.

Anders Aslund and Simon Johnson, *Small Enterprises and Economic Policy,* Working paper, Sloan School, MIT, April 22, 2003.

Julio Carranza, "The Cuban Economy during the 1990s: A Brief Assessment of a Critical Decade," in Pedro Monreal (editor), *Development Prospects in Cuba: An Agenda in the Making*, London: University of London, 2002, pp. 30-44.

Comisión Económica para América Latina y el Caribe (CEPAL), *The Cuban Economy: Structural Reforms and Economic Performance in the 1990s*, LC/MEX/R.746/Rev. 1, 2001.

Comisión Económica para América Latina y el Caribe (CEPAL), *Cuba: Evolución Económica durante 2001*, LC/MEX/L.465, 21 de mayo de 2002.

Comisión Económica para América Latina y el Caribe (CEPAL), *Cuba: Evolución Económica durante 2002 y Perspectivas para 2003*, LC/MEX/L.566, 24 de julio de 2003.

Zdenek Drabek and Joseph C. Brada, *Exchange Rate Regimes and the Stability of Trade Policy in Transition Economies*, World Trade Organization, Staff Working Paper, July, 1998.

Morris Goldstein, *Managed Floating Plus*, Policy Analyses in International Economics 66, Washington, DC: Institute for International Economics, 2002.

Paul Hare, *Trade Policy during the Transition. Lessons from the 1990's,* July 2000.

Ernesto Hernández-Catá, "Output and Productivity in Cuba: Collapse, Recovery, and Muddling Through to the Crossroads," in this volume.

M. S. Khan and R. Zahler, "Trade and Financial Liberalization given External Shocks and Inconsistent Domestic Policies," *IMF Staff Papers,* March 1985.

Anne Krueger, *Nominal Anchor Exchange Rate Policies as a Domestic Distortion,* NBER, Working Paper No. 5968. Cambridge, Mass: 1997.

Anne O. Kruger, "Trade Policy and Development: How We Learn," *American Economic Review,* March 1997.

Will Martin, *Trade Policy Reform in the East Asian Transition Economies,* World Bank, Working Papers, No.2535, January 2001.

Frederic Miskin and Klaus Schmidit-Hebbel, *One Decade of Inflation Targeting in the World: What Do We Know and What Do We Need to Know?,* NBER, Working Paper 8397, Cambridge, Mass, 2001.

Pedro Monreal (editor), *Development Prospects in Cuba: An Agenda in the Making,* London: University of London, 2002a.

Pedro Monreal "Export Substitution Reindustrialization in Cuba: Development Strategies Revisited," in Pedro Monreal (editor), *Development Prospects in Cuba: An Agenda in the Making,* London: University of London, 2002b, pp 9-29.

Lázaro Peña, "The Sugar-Cane Complex: Problems of Competitiveness and Uncertainty in a Crucial Sector," in Pedro Monreal (editor), *Development Prospects in Cuba: An Agenda in the Making,* London: University of London, 2002, pp. 96-118.

Jeffrey Sachs and Felipe Larrain, "Why Dollarization is More Straitjacket than Salvation," *Foreign Policy,* No 116, 1999, pp. 80-92.

Amelia Santos-Paulino and A.P. Thirlwall, *The Impact of Trade Liberalisation on Export Growth, Import Growth, the Balance of Trade and the Balance of Payments of Developing Countries,* University of Kent, June 2002.

Andrea Schaeter, Mark Stone and Mark Zelmer, *Adopting Inflation Targeting: Practical Issues for Emerging Market Countries,* IMF Occasional Paper 202, Washington: International Monetary Fund, 2002.

Jeffrey Sachs, "Re-Thinking Trade Sanctions," in *Project Syndicate,* July, 2003 (http://www.project-syndicate.org/commentaries/commentary_text.php4?id=1283&m=series).

Joseph E. Stiglitz, "Some Lessons from the East Asian Miracle," *World Bank Research Observer,* 11, no. 2, 1996, pp. 151-177.

Verónica Silva, *Estrategia Comercial Chilena en los Años Noventa,* CEPAL Serie Comercio Internacional 11. Santiago: Comisión Económica para América Latina y el Caribe, 2001.

Juan Triana Cordoví, *El desempeño económico en el 2002,* Centro de Estudios de la Economía Cubana, 2002.

BRIDGING THE GAP: IMF AND WORLD BANK MEMBERSHIP FOR SOCIALIST COUNTRIES

Daniel P. Erikson

Over the last two decades, a range of socialist and post-communist countries have become successfully integrated into the international financial system. This has occurred as the globalization of the world economy has increased the relevance of the international financial institutions (IFIs) as key arbiters of economic policy, the guardians of macroeconomic stability, and the leading resources for knowledge and technical advice on development issues. In particular, the International Monetary Fund (IMF) and the World Bank have played a central role in stemming financial crises and aiding in the economic transition of the post-communist countries of Eastern Europe and the former Soviet Union. While there are a range of other institutions that play a role in the international economic system—including regional development banks, the World Trade Organization, and various United Nations agencies—the IMF and the World Bank have been at the center of the major economic developments and the key institutional gatekeepers for countries that desire full participation in the global economy. Aside from granting access to financial resources, a country's membership in the IMF and World Bank facilitates access to funds from regional development organizations and provides an important signal to foreign investors that seek a stable economic climate. Although the free-market economic policies promoted by the IMF and World Bank occasionally come under fire,

and the development strategies they promote remain a work in progress, the international financial institutions are undeniably vital actors in managing the global economy and promoting economic development. Countries as diverse as China, Vietnam, and the former Soviet Union have recognized this and sought out membership in the IFIs.

At first glance, socialist countries with centrally planned economies may seem to have little common ground with market-based institutions such as the IMF and World Bank. Indeed, many socialist and communist countries remained outside the international financial system for many years, and some, such as Cuba and North Korea, remain non-members today. However, the active participation of the Soviet Union in the original Bretton Woods conference in 1944, and the challenge of including socialist economies was an important consideration during the initial development of these institutions. As a result, there is little doubt that participants at the Bretton Woods conference were willing to accept socialist countries as members, and the resulting Articles of Agreement contain no formal obstacle that would prevent a communist or socialist country from joining the IMF and the institutions of the World Bank Group.[1]

The international financial system was conceived at the end of World War II to promote financial and

---

1. Joseph Gold, *Membership and Non-Membership in the International Monetary Fund* (Washington, D.C.: International Monetary Fund, 1974), p. 141.

monetary stability, aid in reconstruction, and broaden the reach of the market system by offering trade and market access to all countries. Initially consisting only of the IMF and World Bank, this system expanded to include the General Agreement on Tariffs and Trade in 1948 (which became the World Trade Organization in 1995). The IMF and World Bank are often referred to as the "Bretton Woods twins," and they share the same basic rules of governance (including weighted voting power), annual meetings, and a common development committee that advises their governors. The IMF was to provide exchange rate stability while the mission of the World Bank focused on long-term development, acting as an intermediary between the financial markets and developing countries, and providing favorable financing for development projects. In addition to their financial activities, the IMF and World Bank are engaged in establishing conditions for lending, providing surveillance of the monetary system, and generating intellectual contributions to understanding the processes of development and how policies can be improved.[2]

While the IMF is a single institution, the World Bank consists of a group of organizations in addition to its core component, the International Bank for Reconstruction and Development (IBRD). The IMF is the gatekeeper to the Bretton Woods twins. All countries must join the IMF before becoming a member of the World Bank and its affiliates; and no country has joined the IMF and declined membership in the World Bank. Furthermore, membership in the IBRD is required before a country can join the World Bank's four other affiliates: the International Development Association (IDA), International Finance Corporation (IFC), the Multilateral Investment Guarantee Agency (MIGA), and the International Center for the Settlement of Investment Disputes (ICSID). Each of these organizations was created in the decades following the Bretton Woods

convention to address needs beyond the original mandate of the IBRD. In addition to the IMF and World Bank group, other important economic actors include the regional development banks for Africa, the Americas and Asia, which supplement the main IFIs by providing loans and grants to aid development at the regional level.

In this universe of economic organizations, there are unique challenges facing the relationship between the IMF and World Bank and centrally planned economies. The first question is purely economic—countries with socialist economic systems may lack any meaningful relationship between the price of their exports and the domestic costs of production, or conversely, between the internal price of imports and foreign export prices. Under such a scenario, exchange rates are meaningless as instruments to allocate resources effectively, although some authors have argued that the Articles have been written in such a way to bypass this problem in socialist countries.[3] While the IMF may allow economic practices that are inconsistent with the Articles to persist for extensive periods, economic reform of a centrally planned economy will continue to be a continuous point of dialogue. In consultations, IFI officials can be expected to urge the benefits of eliminating multiple exchange rates and other practices inconsistent with the charter of the IMF.

Aside from the exchange rate price dilemma, the issues of transparency and information sharing can present a problem for countries used to keeping their economic data close to the vest. Article VIII of the IMF lists "furnishing of information" as one of the general obligations of members, and specifies several types of economic information including national income, price indices, buying and selling rates for foreign currencies, exchange controls, and international balance of payments and investment positions.[4] Many centrally planned economies prefer not to

---

2. Timothy King, "Requirements for Participation in the International Monetary Fund and the World Bank," *Soviet and Eastern European Foreign Trade*, vol. 26, no. 2, Summer 1990, p. 286.

3. Gold, 142.

4. *IMF Articles of Agreement*, Article VIII, Section 5.

share that information for security reasons, fear of demonstrating economic weakness, insufficient capacity to collect data, corruption, or bureaucratic competition. This was especially true during the Cold War period, but even today centrally planned economies often closely protect their economic data or use methods of dubious international validity.

Despite the potential economic and policy hurdles that can complicate IMF and World Bank membership for socialist and communist countries, the historical record shows that the primary obstacles to IFI accession have often been political. In particular, the Cold War created an environment where the Washington-based IMF and World Bank were political instruments of the West, with the United States as the most important shareholder. By contrast, most socialist and communist countries were bound together by their own trade and security arrangements, such as the Council for Mutual Economic Assistance (CMEA). This geopolitical division resulted in several important disincentives with regard to socialist members in the IFIs. On the side of communist countries, an ideological commitment to socialism precluded membership in institutions representing the "neoliberal international system," especially when there was little interest in market reform. Furthermore, there was trepidation about the political ramifications of joining an institution where the United States was both the largest shareholder and the leading proponent of the "international will" expressed through these organizations. Of course, from the perspective of the West, there was little interest in integrating and providing development finance for avowed enemies of the democratic world, especially with regard to the Soviet Union.

Nevertheless, the IMF has in practice admitted applicants with state-controlled economies, including Romania in 1972, and Hungary and Poland in 1982 and 1986 respectively. There were several rationales for socialist countries to join the IMF, and while the desire to incorporate more market mechanisms may not have been the primary motivation, this decision often led to some level of economic opening. Aside from the ability to borrow from the IMF to ease balance-of-payments bottlenecks, countries that join

also improve the perception of their creditworthiness among foreign investors, leading to an increase of foreign direct investment. Access to research and technical expertise can also be an incentive, as well as the political desire to stake a claim in some of the world's key financial institutions. In the case of the People's Republic of China, for example, the desire to replace the Taiwanese government as the representative of China's seat at the IMF and World Bank was undoubtedly an additional motivator.

Furthermore, many countries regard IMF membership as a necessary step in order to gain access to the World Bank's development loans. The World Bank's focus on development—including through its corollary institutions like the International Development Association, which provides concessional lending for projects and programs in poor countries—often makes this the more attractive of the Bretton Woods twins. Socialist countries that are wary of the IMF requirements and conditionalities may nonetheless join to gain access to World Bank resources. In fact, as mentioned above, no country has joined the IMF and subsequently declined membership in the World Bank. More importantly, accession to the IFIs is an important stepping stone for countries to begin the process of opening to the world economy, especially after achieving political and economic reconciliation with the United States, a global economic power and key backer of these institutions.

IFI GOVERNANCE AND THE MECHANICS OF MEMBERSHIP

Despite the complexity of political and economic issues involved, the mechanics of accession to the International Monetary Fund and World Bank are quite straightforward. Since the IMF is the gatekeeper for membership in the Bretton Woods institutions, the process for joining the IMF is both the most rigorous and requires the most information. Once a country is admitted to the IMF, membership to the World Bank only requires approval of the Board of Governors and payment of the determined subscription. In order to become a member of the IMF, an applicant must meet three basic eligibility requirements: it must be a country; be in control of its foreign affairs; and capable and willing to assume the responsibilities of membership. Occasionally the IFIs will make exceptions to engage with regions outside their membership, as in the case of the Palestinian Authority, which receives support though it is not a country and thus not a member. Normally, however, if an applicant meets these three conditions, then upon submitting an application for membership to the Fund, the country receives a mission of IMF staff who will visit and collect the necessary data to prepare a background paper that describes the economy in detail and sets forth a recommended share for the country that is consistent with the relative positions of other countries. While the admission process requires a separate vote by the governors of the two organizations, after acceptance by the IMF a country only needs to accept responsibility for the World Bank's obligations up to the amount of its subscription and pay a small proportion of that amount to the Bank.

Once this first stage is completed, the Executive Board of the IMF establishes an ad hoc committee of 6 to 8 Executive Directors that is constituted on the recommendation of the Managing Director. This committee will consider the applicant's initial quota in the Fund as well as other standard terms and conditions of membership. Once the committee agrees to an initial quota, the chairman of the committee—typically one of the Fund's major shareholders—will contact the applicant to find out whether the government is in agreement with the findings of the committee. Once the applicant agrees, the chairman of the committee sets forth a report of recommendations for approval by the Executive Board. If approved, the proposed quota and related terms of membership are submitted to the Board of Governor's for a vote in the form of a Membership Resolution. A vote on membership requires a majority of Governors holding at least 85 percent of the votes in the Fund, and must be approved by a majority of votes cast. In practice, however, all membership decisions are made by consensus, and the membership vote is a pro forma decision, not an opportunity for open debate on the potential new member. After membership has been approved, applicants typically have six months to complete the required legal paperwork; once the documents are approved by the Fund,

then a signing ceremony is arranged whereby the country becomes a formal member of the IMF. New members must appoint a Governor and Alternate Governor to the IMF's Board of Governors, posts typically held by the country's Minister of Finance or President of the Central Bank.

For communist countries, it is the juxtaposition of two central tenets of the membership process that can create frustration for those interested in IMF and World Bank accession. First, there is no inherent formal obstacle for membership by a socialist country—even one that has not undergone systemic reform. In theory, this means that the door should be open for application at any time. Second, although the rules allow for a member to join with only 85 percent vote of the shareholders, in practice all membership decisions are made by broad consensus. During the Cold War, and even today, it can be expectedly difficult to achieve consensus among the 185 member countries of the IMF and World Bank. However, in practice, it has typically been the United States—backed by its 18 percent voting share that effectively constitutes veto power over major decisions in IFI policy—that has helped to determine what consensus is in many key matters facing the international financial system.

In this context, the experiences of China, Russia, and Vietnam illustrate important lessons for Cuba and remaining socialist countries that may, at some point, contemplate accession to the IMF and World Bank. The People's Republic of China joined the Fund and the Bank as a communist country in 1980, while the Republic of Vietnam initially joined in 1956 but was replaced by its socialist successor in 1976 after reunification. Russia was an initial participant in the Bretton Woods conference but did not join the international financial institutions until 1992, after its communist political and economic system had already unraveled. While the following case studies demonstrate that each of these socialist countries experienced an idiosyncratic process of accession to the IMF and World Bank, there are several main themes that run through their experiences. First, in all cases, membership in the IFIs has been accompanied by significant economic reform; in no instance did a country become more heavily dependent on central-planning or more resistant to market mechanisms after joining the IFIs. Second, the pace of reform varied widely; Russia engaged in rapid transition to a market-based economy, while China and Vietnam opened their economies but remained essentially socialist states. Third, the timetable for mending the bilateral relationship with the United States greatly affected both the pace of accession as well as the trajectory of the subsequent relationship with the IFIs. Although each process of insertion into the international financial system was beset by its own unique circumstances, the experiences of China, Russia, and Vietnam all hold important lessons for Cuba.

CHINA'S ROBUST PARTNERSHIP WITH THE IFIs

China was both an initial signatory at the Bretton Woods conference in 1944 and a founding member of the IMF when the Article of Agreements entered into force on December 27, 1945. However, when the Chinese revolution led to communist control of mainland China in 1949, nationalist leader Chiang Kai-shek withdrew to the island province of Taiwan, which had only recently been released from half-a-century of Japanese rule. Taiwan occupied China's seat at the IMF and World Bank from the 1950s through the 1970s, as the island was seen as an important bulwark against communist expansionism. This arrangement resulted in occasional tension within the IFIs, as some countries rejected the legitimacy of the Taiwanese government to represent the seat of China. For example, at each annual meeting of the IMF's Board of Governors between 1950 and 1954, Czechoslovakia raised a challenge to the credentials of the governor from the Republic of China, as Taiwan was officially known, on the grounds that the country lacked authority to appoint a governor. The socialist People's Republic of China (PRC) registered its displeasure with the arrangement from the very beginning. In 1950, the foreign minister of the PRC sent a cable to the IMF's managing director, stating that the mainland government was the sole le-

gal authority and that no other delegate was qualified to represent China in the Fund.[5] While the situation nevertheless endured for nearly thirty years, Taiwan eventually ceased borrowing from the international financial institutions, sensing the increasing precariousness of its position within the system.

In the late 1960s, Washington and Beijing began to develop closer ties to counter perceived Soviet expansionism, and in 1971, China's seat on the United Nations Security Council was taken over by the mainland government, thus removing Taiwan from the U.N. The historic visit of President Richard Nixon to Beijing in 1972 set the stage for closer relations between the U.S. and China, and rekindled the communist country's interest in taking over Taiwan's position at the IMF and World Bank. The People's Republic of China subsequently expressed interest in IMF and World Bank membership in 1973, when IMF officials received a cable at the annual meeting in Nairobi demanding the immediate expulsion of the "Chang Kai-shek clique."[6] However, when Bretton Woods officials asked if China would be interested in replacing Taiwan, the country did not follow through with an application. In 1976, China issued another protest in the annual meeting in Manila, but again did not apply for membership.

However, the restoration of diplomatic relations between the U.S. and China in 1979 dramatically reduced the key political obstacle to China's accession to the IMF. In the run-up to membership, the United States transformed into a strong supporter of China's effort to join the international financial institutions. Nonetheless, there were significant doubts at the IMF as to whether the country would be capable to producing acceptable economic statistics, especially given the near absence of information after the late 1950s, owing in part to the upheaval of the Cultural Revolution. In order to address this concern, China began publishing a large amount of economic data in mid-1979 to build its case for membership. In April 1980, China joined the IMF in a decision that ended

---

5. Gold, 67.

6. Larry Gurwin and Stanley Wilson, "How Big a Splash Will China Make?," *IMF/World Bank IV*, September 1980.

Taiwan's thirty-one years of representation in the IFIs. Taiwan had represented China in the IMF since 1949, as one of 140 members.[7] The executive directors of the IMF voted to make the People's Republic of China a member, with a quota of 550 million special drawing rights (SDRs),[8] valued at about $700 million at the time.[9] According to the late Thomas Leddy, then-assistant secretary of the treasury, the United States backed the decision: "The United States position was to welcome and support the People's Republic of China's entry into the fund."[10]

As a result of this decision, China had to accept a number of conditions that the IMF requires of its members, including a complete survey of its economy, and annual consultations with the IMF under Article IV of the institutional charter. China's decision to join the IMF was thought to reflect its desire to enhance its international political position and guarantee access to large amounts of relatively inexpensive development credit. According to one observer, "The prime reason why China is keen to join is straightforward. China needs to achieve the Four Modernizations and understandably wants to obtain those funds on the most advantageous terms."[11] Membership benefited China in several concrete ways, including the ability to use various "special facilities" of the IMF; gaining access to IMF assistance in the case of difficulties in balance-of-payments; sharing in the profits of the IMF's gold auction; and improving its creditworthiness with commercial banks and export credit agencies.[12]

China's decision to join also had two favorable side effects: enhancing the country's credit-worthiness in the eyes of the private banking sector and increasing the diplomatic isolation of Taiwan. China's entry into the IMF hinged on a compromise forged between China and Taiwan about the return of Taiwan's subscription to the Fund and the subsequent restitution of the subscription in gold.[13] Taiwanese officials, anticipating the possible expulsion, had already eliminated any clauses from loan agreements that required IMF membership and boosted international reserves to nearly $7 billion.[14] While establishing the quota can often be the most contentious element of negotiating new membership, in China's case this was avoided by merely taking over Taiwan's financial position. China's decision to join was seen as an economic decision with important political implications, and it was widely interpreted as a policy decision to become an active member of the international community. IMF membership was closely followed by membership in the World Bank and sometime later in the Asian Development Bank (ADB). At the time of its acceptance, China became the largest communist country to be a member of the IMF.[15] Other communist countries included Vietnam, Cambodia, Laos, Romania, and Yugoslavia. In addition, China's membership came at a time when there was growing global demand for IMF and World Bank resources, and China's large claim on these resources meant less for other countries. However, in practice, China only used the IMF's financial resources once, in the mid-1980s. It was a first tranche-drawing, with limited conditionality, that was repaid on time a few years later.

---

7. "China Admitted to IMF," *New York Times*, 18 April 1980.

8. SDRs are an international reserve asset created by the countries of the IMF in order to support the expansion of world trade and economic development. SDRs were originally intended to supplement the gold and U.S. currency reserves, but today mainly serve as a unit of account for the IMF.

9. Oscar E. Naumann, "China Joins International Monetary Fund," *Journal of Commerce*, 18 April 1980.

10. "China Admitted to IMF."

11. Gurwin and Wilson.

12. Gurwin and Wilson.

13. Anthony Rowley, "Compromising on a Gold Cache," *Far Eastern Economic Review*, Vol. 108, April 25, 1980, p. 85.

14. Gurwin and Wilson, 176.

15. "Changing the Power Balance," *Far Eastern Economic Review*, Vol. 108, April 25, 1980, p. 85.

Although China joined both the IMF and World Bank, its relationship with the latter institution has proved to be the more robust partnership over the last twenty years. According to a written history of the World Bank, "in the first few years the Bank's role was primarily a didactic one of educating a cadre of senior Chinese officials in new economic ideas and technical systems."[16] In the process of moving from a centrally planned economy to a socialist market economy, China has intensively engaged several development agencies, including the World Bank, as well as active relations with the IMF, Asian Development Bank, and the Bank for International Settlements. However, the World Bank has emerged as China's pre-eminent development partner, with China as the largest client of the Bank since 1993, and the Bank as the biggest single source of long-term foreign capital.[17] The World Bank's programs in China were allocated about half for transportation and energy, a quarter for agriculture, a sixth for industry and finance and ten percent for education.[18] The portfolio is considered to be very high quality, with projects that are well implemented and a correspondingly low failure rate. In fact, China's creditworthiness has increased to the point that the country is no longer eligible for IDA loans, the concessional source of financing that is an attractive element of World Bank membership for lower-income countries.

As a member of the international financial institutions, Chinese authorities have set clear parameters on policy conditions from the very beginning of the relationship. In one memorandum from a 1984 meeting with the Chinese delegation, the World Bank official noted that Minister of Finance Wang Bingjian "explained China's view that assistance to developing countries should be unconditional . . . [T]his did not mean that the Bank could not offer advice and ideas. The World Bank could put these forward and they would be considered if they were useful. But the Bank should not impose its views."[19] China also set a policy of linking its IBRD borrowing to its IDA allocation that lasted until the late-1990s. In addition, the issue of Taiwan remained a constant source of friction between China and the World Bank, due to the long-standing sensitivities regarding what China regards as its renegade province. China, for example, demand that references to Taiwan be deleted from Bank documents or be rephrased as "Taiwan Province, China."[20] Evidently, the Bank felt that it had little option but to accommodate China on this point, lest the entire relationship be soured. Another set of issues arose regarding the relationship of China and India; boundary disputes between the two countries would resurface in discussions on how the countries were geographically represented in Bank documents. Furthermore, China's accession and subsequent use of IDA grants meant that less was available for India, especially during periods when the IDA coffers were declining.

After normalization of China's relations with the United States in the late 1970s, politics occasionally reemerged to influence IFI decisions relating to the country. Most notably, the Tiananmen Square massacre in 1989 prompted the U.S. to strongly pressure the World Bank to condition its lending arrangement on the respect for political liberties and human rights. The World Bank and other multilateral agencies froze dealings with China as a result of Tiananmen. Shielding the Bank's programs from the political fallout was a major priority for Bank staff at this time. The IFIs resisted these entreaties more successfully than in many other cases; perhaps because China's sheer size produces a form of pragmatism not necessary with smaller countries such as Vietnam or, certainly, Cuba. Nevertheless, the crackdown in Chi-

16. Devesh Kapur, John P. Lewis, and Richard Webb, *The World Bank: Its First Half Century* (Washington, D.C.: The Brookings Institution, 1997), p. 24.

17. Presentation by Pieter Bottelier, "China and the International Financial Organizations," 1999.

18. Kapur et al., 24.

19. Kapur et al., 24.

20. Kapur et al., 25.

na did provoke limited repercussions, and some World Bank affiliates, such as the International Finance Corporation, did not resume investment in China until 1991.

Nevertheless, the partnership between the World Bank and China has been recognized as one of the most successful, as measured by the effectiveness of Bank projects in China and the fulfillment of the country's fiscal responsibilities. This success is ironic when one considers the fact that U.S. economic aid to Asian countries in the 1950s was geared to prevent "another China" by alleviating the poverty of the rural peasantry thought to be at high risk for communist mobilization.[21] A review of China's accession and subsequent relationship with the IMF and World Bank reveals both the advantages and the continuing challenges of having such a large, communist country take part in the international financial system. In 1980, China still had a great deal to learn about how the IFIs worked, especially with regard to substitution accounts, gold equivalents, SDR allocations, and the specifics of conditionality. In addition, there was considerable concern about China's ability to generate economic statistics that met IMF standards, as well as the willingness to share this information. (Some communist countries, such as Romania, had worked out confidentiality agreements with the IMF that restricted access to sensitive economic information.) By joining the IMF and World Bank and working through these issues, China both engaged in targeted economic reform at home while claiming an active role in the international economic community. In 2001, China finally became a member of the World Trade Organization. In retrospect, China's accession to the IMF and World Bank marked an important step towards substantial market-oriented reform, greater insertion in the global economy, and asserting itself in the larger international political arena. However, the relative absence of dysfunction in China's relations with the IFIs was by no means as-

sured, as demonstrated by the experiences of Russia and Vietnam with the international financial system.

RUSSIA, THE IFIs, AND POST-COMMUNIST TRANSFORMATION

The Soviet Union—like China and Cuba—was a participant in the Bretton Woods meetings in 1944 that led to the creation of the IMF and World Bank. However, the Soviet Union was the only country represented at the conference that did not become a member of the IFIs for nearly 50 years. Most participating countries were either original members or joined shortly thereafter; the second longest holdout from the original conference, Liberia, joined in 1962. Although the Soviet Union ultimately declined to join, there is no doubt that the existence of such a large and influential communist state was taken into account by the leading architects of these international institutions. In April 1942, an early draft of the White Plan, which outlined the purpose of the proposed institutions, discussed the possible membership of USSR in detail: "No restrictions as to membership should be imposed on grounds of the particular economic structure adopted by any country . . . [T]o exclude a country such as Russia would be an egregious error. Russia, despite her socialist economy could both contribute and profit by participation . . . If the Russian Government is willing to participate, her counsel in the preliminary negotiations should be as eagerly sought as that of any other country, and her membership in both Fund and Bank equally welcome."[22] Similarly, an advanced draft of the Keynes Plan referred to the case of the USSR, stating that "[t]he position of Russia, which might be a third founder, if she can be party to so capitalist-looking an institution, would need special consideration."[23]

While the final versions of the Bretton Woods proposals contained no statement pertaining to the membership of the USSR, Russia continued to play in a role in the consultative process in 1943 and

---

21. Kapur et al., 112.

22. Gold, 129.

23. Gold, 129.

1944, and the head of the Russian delegation was one of four vice-chairmen of the Bretton Woods conference. Several historians have concluded that Russia's active participation in the process undoubtedly played a role in the decision to draw the charters of the Fund and the Bank broadly enough to encompass communist and socialist countries, even though the Soviet Union ultimately declined to join. While the Soviet government never set forth a formal refusal to join the IMF, several factors may have led to this decision. These may have included dissatisfaction with the formula for voting power, reluctance to release economic data, concerns about the transparency of the Fund's governance, and resistance to the Fund's views on economic and monetary policy.[24] Despite these concerns, there is no doubt that the Bretton Woods agreements were designed so that socialist countries could become members, and that this was primarily guided by the desire to accommodate the Soviet Union. As one analyst has noted, some of the Fund's Articles of Agreement "contain certain clauses that are completely unexplainable but from the angle of some Soviet idiosyncrasy."[25]

In the intervening decades, there was no formal contact and little informal communication between the Soviet Union and the IMF and World Bank. The heightened tensions of the Cold War prevented any type of policy dialogue and contributed to an atmosphere of mutual suspicion. This remained true even while the international financial institutions incorporated a growing number of communist members, including China, Vietnam, and several of the republics of Eastern Europe. However, in 1990, the economy of the Soviet Union began to unravel at the same time as the body politic lurched towards democracy. As a result, Soviet membership in the IMF and World Bank reemerged as a possibility.

Three interlocking narratives dominated the run-up to Russia's accession to the international financial institutions. First as the once super-power teetered both politically and economically on the edge of dissolution, the relationship of Russia to its fifteen republics presented a major legal and technical obstacle to membership in the IMF and World Bank. Finalizing the structure of the Soviet Union's successor—the Russian Federation—was essential to the decision of incorporating it into membership. Second, the question of economic reform in Russia became paramount; the United States pressed a clear interest in having Russia join the international financial system, but some also called for the country to abandon communism as a pre-requisite to succession. However, the desire to stabilize the government of Mikhail Gorbachev meant that quick action to help the Russian economy might in fact provide credit to sustain the communist system in the short-term, something that was anathema to conservative elements in the United States. Third, the issue of Soviet membership arose at a time when the United States was considering a major quota increase to the IMF. The convergence of these two sensitive issues complicated Russia's path to membership due to resistance by congressional conservatives who equated IFI support for Russia with extravagant foreign aid. This was a hot button issue in early 1992, and something that then President George H. W. Bush was reluctant to confront directly in an presidential election year unfolding amidst a recession.

The approach phase between the Soviet Union and the international financial institutions originated with the Houston Economic Summit of July 1990. At this gathering, the leaders of the G-7 countries—with the support of President Gorbachev—asked the IMF, World Bank, Organization for Economic Cooperation and Development (OECD), and the European Bank for Reconstruction and Development (EBRD) to initiate a collaborative study of the Soviet economy. This effort was expressly intended to provide recommendations for reform, guide external aid efforts, and prepare the Soviet Union for membership in the IFIs.[26] However, even behind this appar-

---

24. Gold, 134.

25. Gold, 142.

26. *Assisting Russia's Transition: An Unprecedented Challenge* (Washington D.C.: The World Bank, 2002), p. 6.

ent consensus, some shareholders retained lingering concerns. Japan, for example, was concerned that locking itself into a single aid strategy with Western countries would reduce its leverage to negotiate the return of the northern territories from Russia.[27] The United States was similarly cautious to embrace its old enemy, while West Germany and France were keen to extend substantial immediate aid to Gorbachev. As a result, the IMF-led study of the Russian economy represented a compromise that allowed some nations to proceed with bilateral aid while opening an economic policy dialogue between the Soviet Union and the IFIs, and by proxy, the United States.

Steps towards formal membership in the IMF and World Bank followed in mid-1991. On August 19, a coup by Soviet hard-liners led to the end of Soviet communism when Russian President Boris Yeltsin managed to rally Russian nationalism and passed a decree banning Communist party activities on Russian soil. Gorbachev resigned from the Communist Party shortly thereafter, thereby ending Communist control and setting in motion the dissolution of the Soviet Union. As a result, that month the World Bank approved the concept of "associate" membership for the Soviet Union, which entitled the country to technical assistance. However, this was quickly followed by a recommendation to approve $30 million in World Bank funds to support a program including research on the Soviet economy, and training of Russian personnel.[28] In September 1991, U.S. Treasury Secretary Nicholas Brady openly criticized the slow pace of the IMF in granting special membership status to the Soviet Union. Later that month, IMF officials proposed reductions in USSR arms expenditures to apply to economic needs; at that time Soviets had formally applied for full membership in IMF, and associate status soon followed at both the IMF and World Bank.

Due to the fast pace of events in the Soviet Union and the sensitive issues facing the IMF, World Bank and U.S. government in Washington, there was a strong push to move ahead with ties to Russia even though many principle issues of membership remained unresolved throughout 1991. In particular, the months between the "Group of Seven" summit in London in July and the October meetings of the IMF and World Bank in Bangkok proved to be critical both to the fate of the Soviet Union and to the process of IFI accession. On July 15, the Soviet Union applied for full membership in the IMF.[29] On October 5, 1991, the Managing Director of the IMF and President Gorbachev signed an agreement on the "special association" between the USSR and the IMF. This agreement provided for the IMF to examine economic developments in the USSR in a manner consistent with Article IV consultations[30]; the provision of technical assistance; Soviet representation at Executive Board meetings concerning the USSR or world economy as a whole; Soviet participation in IMF annual meetings. In return, the Soviet Union was required to provide regular economic data to the IMF consistent to that collected by member countries; allow for the IMF to establish a permanent office in Moscow and provide diplomatic immunity for IMF staff, and potentially contribute to the cost of Fund services. This special association status was intended to be in place until the USSR became a full member or the agreement was terminated by either party.[31]

While the World Bank's Articles of Agreement do not allow for the type of "special association" status granted by the IMF, the World Bank did sign a Technical Cooperation Agreement with Moscow on

---

27. Kenji Kitahara, "Japan Uneasy Over Economic Aid to Moscow," *The Daily Yomiuri*, July 2, 1990.

28. "A Bank Role for the Soviets," *The Journal of Commerce*, August 26, 1991.

29. Karl-Heinz Kleine and Ernst Thien, "The Role of the IMF and the World Bank in the Former Eastern Bloc Countries," *Intereconomics*, January/February 1992, p. 23.

30. Article IV consultations.

31. Kleine and Thien, 23.

November 15, 1991. This accord, signed by Bank president Lewis Preston and Gorbachev, allowed for the World Bank to provide technical assistance to the Soviet Union or its republics prior to membership. This included exchanges of the progress of the assistance program, and the establishment of a World Bank office in Moscow with the concomitant immunities and privileges for its staff. The technical assistance itself included advice on economic management and reforms, creation of a social security network and food aid assessment, advice in the fields of privatization, agriculture and energy, and personnel training. This agreement was underwritten by a $30 million trust fund established by the Bank's executive board, and financed by the institutions' net income.[32]

The associate membership and technical cooperation agreements paved the way for much more extensive consultations between IMF and World Bank staff and all fifteen republics of the Soviet Union. IMF missions began to travel frequently to the USSR, with five separate missions to Moscow alone in November and December of 1991.[33] The mission teams gathered economic data and negotiated technical assistance and stabilization and reform programs, which would lead to analytical reports similar to regular Article IV consultations with other IMF members. In particular, the IMF was responsible for developing reliable assessments of the external financing requirements of Russia and the other republics. However, there was also a perception gap on the side of Russia. Senior administrators in the USSR tended to focus on the issue of IMF membership through a quite narrow focus on the material costs and benefits, such as concern that payment of the IMF quota would deplete Russia's monetary reserves.[34] As a result, little weight was given to the non-material benefits of membership, such as an improved perception for foreign investment or access to research and technical expertise. In addition, there was considerable trepidation about several aspects of joining the Fund, including the use of the U.S. veto, the impact of stabilization programs on the Soviet economy, and the need to release economic data previously regarded as sensitive.[35]

For the international financial institutions, the dissolution of the Soviet Union and subsequent accession of all fifteen states was a watershed moment that fundamentally changed the way that the IMF and World Bank operated. The sheer size of the task, historic nature of the transition, and complexity of the economic issues involved, forced the IFIs to dramatically reorient their thinking towards the challenges facing transition economies. In December 1991, the IMF created a new area department called European II to work exclusively with the Baltic States and former members of the USSR. Over the course of a few months, the IMF radically reoriented its staff to this challenge, increasing from 2,000 to 2,200 employees and assigning 150 to work full-time on the ex-Soviet Union.[36] (In 2003, this department was eliminated and the fifteen countries were absorbed into other departments.)

In January 1992, a major stumbling block to Russia's accession was cleared when the IMF determined that the former Soviet republics would have a quota set at 4.5 percent of the global total, leaving Britain and France in their joint fourth-place position behind the United States, Japan, and Germany.[37] On April 27, 1992, the IMF formally offered membership to Russia, enabling the rich G-7 countries to release $24 billion in aid unveiled by President Bush and Chan-

---

32. Kleine and Thien, p. 26.

33. Richard D. Erb, Deputy Managing Director of the International Monetary Fund, Remarks at the Conference on European Security and Regional Stability, Institute for Foreign Policy Analysis, Washington D.C., January 24, 1992.

34. Goergy Matyukhin, "The Union of Soviet Socialist Republics and Other Socialist Countries in the International Monetary and Financial System," *Journal of Development Planning*, Vol. 20, 1990, p. 273.

35. Matyukhin, 273.

36. Steven Greenhouse, "Point Man for the Rescue of the Century," *New York Times*, April 26, 1992.

37. Ben Laurence, "IMF Clears the way for ex-Soviet States," *Guardian*, January 24, 1992, p. 24.

cellor Helmut Kohl on April 1 at the London summit.[38] The package included $4.5 billion in aid from the IMF and World Bank in 1992, a $6 billion fund to stabilize the ruble, $2.5 billion in debt deferral and $11 billion in direct bilateral aid from wealthy countries.[39] The IMF accord was required not only for the multilateral aid, but most of the other components of the aid package. Of the fifteen Soviet republics, all but Azerbaijan were offered membership in the IMF at the 1992 Spring meetings, and the World Bank followed suit with all but Azerbaijan and Turkmenistan. (In both cases the delays were attributed to incomplete paperwork, and they joined subsequently.) The aid effort to the former Soviet republics represented by far the most ambitious undertaking in the history of the IMF. The Russian Federation joined the IMF on June 1, 1992; its accession to the World Bank followed on June 16. The IMF and World Bank made $1.6 billion available to Russia in mid-1992 with virtually no conditions, as authorized by their practice.[40]

However, the IMF also needed a capital increase of $60 billion, which had been provisionally approved by the membership in 1990 but had failed to fully materialize when the U.S. Congress balked at the $12 billion share due from the United States. President Bush favored the capital increase but did not want to go on record asking Congress to support it due to the political sensitivity surrounding foreign aid prior to the 1992 election. However, many Congressional Democrats were only willing to support an increase after a specific request by the White House; otherwise, they feared, they were being asked to take responsibility for effectively voting for aid for Russia, and face the political fallout alone. This unresolved issue shadowed most of Russia's membership negotiations, until President Bush finally conceded the point and formally took a stand in favor of the capital increase for the IMF.

In retrospect, Russia's accession to the international financial institutions was characterized by an abbreviated period of non-lending assistance, from the fall of 1991 to the summer of 1992, followed by massive disbursements of aid. After reviewing the years 1991 to 2001, the World Bank's Country Assistance Evaluation report concluded that Russia would have benefited from a strategy oriented around analytical and advisory services with only limited financial support during the period from 1992 to 1998, instead of the large volumes of adjustment lending that were actually released.[41] World Bank assistance to Russia was rated unsatisfactory from 1992 to 1998. To facilitate Russia's transition, the Bank focused on helping to build the institutions of a market economy, develop the private sector, and alleviate the social costs of transition. The Bank committed 55 loans for $12.6 billion through 2001; at that time $7.8 billion had been disbursed and $2.4 billion cancelled. However, as described in the evaluation report, "at the behest of the international community, the Bank rushed the processing of many projects, both for investment and general budget support, even though the prospects for their success were highly uncertain. These high-risk/high-payoff operations did not succeed... Bank advice and lending played a positive but marginal role in the design of policies and in their implementation until 1998."[42] However, the report notes that some members of the World Bank group—such as the IFC and MIGA—were resistant to external pressure, selected their interventions carefully, and accrued an impressive record of technical assistance and service.

The Soviet Union, like China, only joined the international financial institutions once it had reconciled its relationship with the West and its membership application gained the support of the United States. However, the Russian experience also demonstrates the dangers inherent in a rapid transition to a mar-

---

38. Steven H. Hanke, "IMF Money Will Buy Trouble for Russia," *The Wall Street Journal*, April 29, 1992.

39. Steven Greenhouse, "World's Lenders Offer Membership to Ex-Soviet Lands," *New York Times*, April 28, 1992.

40. *Assisting Russia's Transition*, 59.

41. *Assisting Russia's Transition*, ix.

42. *Assisting Russia's Transition*, xii.

ket-economy and in particular how the political imperative to rapidly provide financing can overtake the need for well thought-out institutional reforms. In particular, the IMF emerged as the key channel for the United States to channel aid to Russia, and this pattern remained in place for most of the 1990s. In retrospect, Russia's accession to the IFIs may have benefited from a more extended period of technical assistance and economic policy dialogue, as opposed to the disbursement of large sums on money during the volatile transition phase, during which Russia went through a major financial crisis.

VIETNAM AND THE IMF: THE LONG WAIT FOR REUNIFICATION

While both China and Russia joined the IMF and World Bank and sustained active participation after accession, Vietnam illustrates another model of membership "in name only" that did not consolidate into a normal working relationship for nearly four decades. This state of limbo was driven by the difficult bilateral relationship with the United States, which initiated with the Vietnam War but persisted until the early 1990s.

Vietnam was established as a single state under the Geneva Agreements of July 1954, and free general elections were to be held under international supervision in July 1956. Vietnam entered its original application for membership to the Fund on December 21, 1955 and the application was considered in the period from March to May 1956. But the application was submitted by the government of Vietnam that only controlled the southern half of the country. The country was eventually admitted as the "Republic of Vietnam," although one Executive Director abstained on the decision to forward the application to the Board of Governors on the ground that the country lacked full sovereignty and instead consisted of two provisional governments.[43]

In 1959, a Bank mission decided that Vietnam's high level of dependence on foreign aid made it unable to

qualify for an IBRD loan. Several years later, on May 7, 1964, the United States notified the Fund that it had placed restrictions on payments and transfers to North Vietnam, but the Fund took no subsequent action under the principle that North Vietnam was a non-member country.[44] Following the unification of Vietnam in 1976, the Socialist Republic of Vietnam assumed the membership previously held by the Republic of Vietnam. In 1978, IDA approved its first credit to Vietnam for rehabilitation of irrigation systems in the Mekong Delta. However, throughout most of the 1980s the Bank's interactions with Vietnam were limited to technical missions, due to the objections of the United States to a closer relationship. The policy prohibiting high level missions and the issuance of further credits lasted basically until 1993, when the IMF arrears were cleared and Vietnam reduced its spending on military activities in Cambodia.[45]

Perhaps more than any other country, Vietnam's relations with the IMF and World Bank were defined by its complex and difficult bilateral relationship with the United States. From the early 1960s to the mid 1970s, the United States and North Vietnam were locked in a long and bloody war intended to contain the spread of communism. On April 30, 1975, the United States withdrew its last batch of troops as the Viet Cong army successfully captured Saigon and unified the country under a socialist government. As a result, on April 30, 1975, the U.S. trade embargo in effect against North Vietnam since 1964 extended to the whole country. The broad U.S. sanctions included a prohibition on commercial, financial, and investment transactions. As a pivotal shareholder in the IMF, World Bank, and Asian Development Bank, the U.S. also blocked multilateral lending to Vietnam.

In 1977, the administration of U.S. President Jimmy Carter took steps to improve the bilateral relationship, agreeing to unconditional establishment of dip-

43. Gold, 50-51.

44. Gold, 51.

45. "Vietnam: Country Assistance Evaluation," Operations Evaluation Department, World Bank, November 21, 2001, p. 4, n. 6.

lomatic relations to be followed by the lifting of the embargo, renewed IFI support to Vietnam, and consideration of MFN status.[46] However, Vietnam refused this offer unless it included $3.25 billion in economic assistance that had been promised by President Richard Nixon as part of the 1973 Paris Accords. Washington rejected the claim to reparations, and the U.S. Congress passed legislation prohibiting aid to the North Vietnamese government that then controlled the country. Vietnam withdrew the demand in September 1978, but by that time the Carter administration was less inclined to opening with Hanoi because the attention had shifted to normalized relations with China.[47] The moment had passed.

The closing months of 1978 delivered the coup de grace to any détente between the United States and Vietnam. In October, the Soviet Union and Vietnam signed a mutual security treaty, and in December the government of Hanoi invaded neighboring Cambodia and breathed further life into the U.S. embargo. In 1979, the World Bank under Robert McNamara succumbed to pressure from congressional hard-liners and placed a one-year moratorium on loans to Vietnam during fiscal year 1980.[48] Vietnam's incursion into Cambodia in the 1980s produced the political rationale that strengthened the technical reasons that Vietnam had been blocked from borrowing from the IMF, namely a failure to pay arrears. The United States viewed the Vietnamese invasion of Cambodia as both an act of aggression and a proxy war between China and the Soviet Union. This situation persisted throughout the 1980s, freezing Vietnam's relations with the IFIs even while the country began a program of significant economic reform beginning in 1986 known as "doi-moi."

In February 1989, Vietnam received a bridge loan from France to pay off arrears of about U.S. $130 million.[49] However, in September 1989, the U.S. and Japan blocked Vietnam's reentry into the IFIs, despite a serious effort by Vietnam to achieve structural adjustment and economic stabilization. The withdrawal of troops in Cambodia had to be accompanied by a political settlement of the Cambodian crisis. This clash highlighted an underlying conflict between the technocrats that wanted to base their Vietnam lending decisions on the country's economic reform program, and the political rationale guiding some of the major shareholders. In March 1989, Vietnam had begun to implement an economic reform program after extensive consultations with the IMF, and the country was relying on a favorable consensus from the IMF board to receive a bridge loan from commercial banks that would allow the country to pay off its arrears and clear the way for an official IMF program. In the meeting with the Executive Directors, Managing Director Michel Camdessus elicited a positive response from most board members, including Britain, West Germany, and France—the second, third, and fourth largest quota holders.[50] Only the U.S. and Japan were opposed to moving ahead with a formal IMF program, and provided the economic rationale that the program had not been of sufficient duration and that was still burdened by "low-priority expenditures."[51]

In 1989, Vietnam withdrew troops from Cambodia only to discover that the goalposts had moved, with U.S. responding that it was unacceptable to leave Cambodia in a state of civil war.[52] Furthermore, the U.S. demanded progress on the full accounting of soldiers missing in action from the Vietnam conflict. At the time, the hold on lending to Vietnam caused

---

46. Frederick Z. Brown, "U.S.-Vietnam Normalization: Past, Present, Future" in James W. Morley and Masashi Nishihara, eds., *Vietnam Joins the World* (Armonk, New York: M.E. Sharpe, 1997), p. 204.

47. Brown, 204.

48. James Srodes, "An Enigma at the World Bank," *Far Eastern Economic Review*, November 16, 1979, p. 82.

49. Nayan Chanda, "Rewards of Retreat," *Far Eastern Economic Review*, July 6, 1989.

50. Susumu Awanohara, "Fiscal Interdiction," *Far Eastern Economic Review*, September 28, 1989, p. 22.

51. Awanohara, 1989, 22.

52. Charles P. Wallace, "15 Years After War's End, the U.S. Fights to Keep Vietnam Isolated," *Los Angeles Times*, April 29, 1990.

significant consternation within the IMF and World Bank, as summarized by one official quoted as saying that "the U.S. and Japan can do what they want with their bilateral aid, but they should not bring in their poorly disguised political agenda into multilateral institutions dedicated to solving economic problems."[53] In April 1991, the U.S. administration laid out a roadmap for normalization of relations with Vietnam, predicated on two main conditions: the satisfactory resolution of the Cambodian conflict and an effort to account for missing American servicemen in Vietnam. That October, four warring Cambodian factions signed a peace agreement in Paris, thereby ending the 12-year civil war. As a result, France, Sweden and Australia began lobbying for resources to help the country repay its debt of $150 million to the IMF. Vietnam had been in default of its IMF loans since 1985. In November 1991, China and Vietnam normalized relations

However, the issue of American prisoners of war in Vietnam was yet to be resolved. In April 1993, an unconfirmed report revealed that Vietnam had more POWs than it claimed publicly and failed to release 614 American POWs at the time of the 1973 Paris accords. This prompted the U.S. to delay granting Vietnam access to IFI loans that had been proposed at the annual meetings of the World Bank and IMF. That June, a Congressional delegation returned from Vietnam providing the impetus needed to break the deadlock, and President Bill Clinton announced that the U.S. had dropped its opposition to IFI loans to Vietnam.[54]

On July 2, 1993, President Clinton signaled that the United States would no longer block multilateral lending to Vietnam.[55] By ending the four years of opposition to lending, the U.S. allowed the "Friends of Vietnam" group to arrange for the clearance of Vietnam's arrears to the IMF and open the way for lending from the World Bank and Asian Development Bank. At the 1993 annual meeting, France and Japan were key players in clearing the arrears of both Vietnam and Cambodia—respectively $140 million and $51 million.[56] In September and October 1993, Vietnam cleared its $140 million in arrears with the IMF. Shortly thereafter, the World Bank and Asian Development Bank pledged loans valued at $800 million for infrastructure development, while the IMF provided an additional $223 million credit.[57] In November 1993, the first World Bank-chaired donors conference for Vietnam resulted in aid commitments of $1.86 billion in additional multilateral and bilateral aid.[58]

With the multilateral funds released, but the trade embargo maintained, the U.S. faced mounting pressure between two political constituencies: American business interests that wanted to invest and bid on IFI-financed projects, and veterans groups that resisted normalization without a full accounting of POWs and MIAs. However, by the end of 1993, the lifting of the trade embargo became increasingly inevitable. U.S. President Bill Clinton announced the lifting of the Vietnam trade embargo on February 3, 1994, several days after the Senate voted 62-38 to approve the move in a non-binding resolution. The support of Sen. John McCain (R-AZ), a former POW, and Sen. Bob Kerrey (D-NE), who was injured during the Vietnam War, was crucial to the bill's passing. On July 11, 1995, President Bill Clinton announced the attention to re-establish full diplomatic relations with Vietnam which was completed by August 5 of that year.

---

53. Awanohara, 1989, 23.

54. Brown, 210.

55. John Rogers, "Vietnam Getting Ready to Seek Infusion of Foreign Aid, Investment," *Journal of Commerce*, July 26, 1993, p. 5a.

56. Susumu Awanohara, "Open the Floodgates," *Far Eastern Economic Review*, October 7, 1993, p. 92.

57. Julie Marie Bunck, "Marxism and the Market: Vietnam and Cuba in Transition," *Cuba in Transition—Volume 6* (Washington: Association for the Study of the Cuban Economy, 1996), p. 237.

58. "Vietnam's Economic Options: Coping With Mounting Resources," *Transition*, Volume 5, No. 1, January 1994, p. 14.

Vietnam's subsequent relationship with the IFIs from 1994 on has garnered positive reviews, and the country's economic reform process has incorporated more market mechanisms. In retrospect, however, the period from 1989 to 1993 proved to be crucial for relations between Vietnam and the international financial institutions. Vietnam was forced to confront adjustment problems at a moment when political differences with major shareholders precluded any direct support from the IMF and World Bank. In the absence of lending, officials from the two institutions remained engaged in an economic policy dialogue with Vietnam's key policymakers, and also managed some of the technical assistance provided by the United Nations Development Programme. For example, in 1991, the World Bank and UNDP jointly organized a conference in Kuala Lampur where top Vietnamese economic officials met with ministers from Indonesia, South Korea, and Malaysia to discuss comparative reform processes.[59] This type of information sharing was complemented with the World Bank's provision of training courses and policy workshops with Vietnam. Due to the political obstacles to lending, this economic policy dialogue emerged as a key avenue to explore different ideas and reform mechanisms in the absence of conditionality. As a result, during the critical period from 1989 to 1993, the focus of Vietnam-IFI relations was on ideas instead of lending arrangements. While there is no way to value precisely the effect of this policy dialogue on Vietnam's economic reform process, there is a strong argument that the intensive time spent by World Bank and IMF staff made an important contribution to Vietnam's economic development.[60]

CUBA AND THE IFIs: A TALE INTERRUPTED

The experiences of China, Russia, and Vietnam demonstrate the benefits and pitfalls for socialist countries that wish to pursue accession to the IMF and World Bank at various stages of their economic transition. Despite the unique circumstances of each country, their membership processes share several features: the importance of normalizing relations with the United States and the West, the will to embrace at least limited market reform, and the importance of IFI membership as a step to opening up to the wider global economy. This insight will be important to the economic future of Cuba should the country choose to join the IFIs.

In fact, Cuba, and more specifically the Castro government, is no stranger to the international financial institutions, and the island was even one of the founding signatories of the Bretton Woods institutions in 1944. During the administration of Fulgencio Batista, Cuba criticized the "Wall Street" approach of the IFIs at the eleventh annual IMF-World Bank joint meetings in 1956. Joaquín A. Meyer, the alternate governor for Cuba, was quoted as saying "my government believes that the pressing needs of the less developed countries are so numerous and urgent that the bank ought to revise some of its present policies in order to make available its resources to its members on a much larger scale than it has done in the past or is doing now."[61] While the Cuban representative strongly criticized the policy of not granting loans to member countries in debt arrears, Meyer also noted that he was not speaking on behalf of Cuba, as the country had never tried to borrow from the Bank.

Beginning with Fidel Castro's ascension to power on January 1, 1959, relations between Cuba and the IFIs became increasingly strained. Initially, however, communication and exchange between Cuba and the IFIs actually represented an improvement over the end of Batista's term. Prior to Castro, the last IMF staff visit to Cuba occurred in March of 1957. By contrast, in the first few months of 1959, IMF staff traveled to Cuba twice—including a two-week mission to Havana—and three officers from the Cuban National Bank visited Washington. The initial IMF mission concluded that the new government inherit-

59. *Assessing Aid: What Works, What Doesn't and Why* (New York: Oxford University Press, 1998), p. 106.

60. *Assessing Aid*, p. 108.

61. Charles E. Egan, "Cuba and Jordan Charge Creditor Countries Run World Bank," *New York Times*, September 26, 1956.

ed a seriously weakened financial situation, with 13 percent unemployment at the end of 1958.[62] However, by 1960, communication between the IFIs and Cuba had almost completely broken down, with multiple pieces of IMF correspondence left unanswered. To further complicate matters, President Castro announced on several occasions that Cuba had withdrawn from the IFIs, sparking confusion among IMF and World Bank officials who had received no such notice through formal channels. On October 18, 1960, Cuba withdrew from the World Bank following a presidential decree stating that "the economic policy of that institution is far from being effective in regard to the development and expansion of the Cuban economy, which the Revolutionary Government is carrying out according to a definite plan."[63] The withdrawal became official on November 14, 1960, when the World Bank received written notification of the government's decision to withdraw.[64] At the time of withdrawal, Cuba's capital subscription to the Bank was equivalent to $70,000,000—with $700,000 paid in dollars, $6,700,000 available in pesos, and the remainder subject to call.[65]

Cuba's relationship with the IMF continued for three more years, until the country withdrew in 1964 and settled its remaining accounts over a five-year period ending in 1969. However, the voluntary withdrawal occurred merely days before an executive board meeting held to consider Cuba's failures to fulfill its obligations under the articles of agreement, including repurchasing IMF shares obtained by the previous government. Cuba had purchased $25 million from the Fund in 1958 and had negotiated a repurchasing agreement that was payable by September 12, 1963; thus five years had passed since the purchase without the complete repurchase completed by

Cuba. In addition, Cuba had agreed in an increase of its quota from $50 million to $100 million, but had not paid the subscription that had come due in the fall of 1959. Cuba had also lapsed in furnishing the necessary financial information to the Fund that was required for the calculation of repurchase obligations. Monetary, banking and balance of payments data had not been forthcoming since July 1961, and information on monetary reserves had not been furnished since the fiscal year ending in April 1960.[66]

As a result of these and other lapses, the Managing Director sent a notice to Cuba on October 11, 1963, detailing the concerns of the Executive Directors. However, no reply was received from Cuba, prompting the directors to arrange a meeting on April 15, 1964, to determine whether Cuba should be declared ineligible. However, once Cuba learned of these complaints and the plan for the forthcoming meeting, it responded by notifying the Fund of its withdrawal from membership, effective April 2, 1964. On May 1, the Executive Directors approved a letter to Cuba that generally accepted a previous Cuban proposal for the settlement of accounts. The basic elements of the proposal included: Cuba's redemption of the Fund's holding of Cuban pesos valued at $12.5 million; payments were to be made in gold or convertible currency in five annual installments; the Fund would return 50 million pesos to Cuba and pay the balance in gold to an account with the National Bank of Cuba.[67] Cuba formally accepted the terms of settlement on May 29, 1964, and completed the agreement accordingly, after receiving a six-month extension on the last installment of payment, which was made in January 1969.

Today, nearly forty years after Cuba's initial withdrawal from the international financial system, the

---

62. *Review of Cuba's Financial Position and Problems*, International Monetary Fund Archives, April 6, 1959.

63. "Cuba Withdraws from World Bank," *The New York Times*, October 19, 1960.

64. "Cuba Withdraws from Membership," Joint Press Release by International Finance Corporation and World Bank, November 15, 1960.

65. "Cuba Withdraws from World Bank."

66. Gold, 343-344.

67. Gold 380-381.

Cuban government remains committed to maintaining the socialist revolution and the centrally planned economic system that this implies. Furthermore, the relations between the United States and Cuba remain a long way from the period of rapprochement that presaged IFI membership for China, Russia, and Vietnam. Nevertheless, the country's need for external financing for development projects remains critical, and the IMF and World Bank are much better positioned to address the challenges of post-communist transition than they were during the collapse of the Soviet Union in the early 1990s. Given the importance of economic policy dialogue in shaping successful transitions in China and Vietnam, Cuba and the IFIs would be well advised to initiate a formal policy discussion prior to membership and lending—regardless of whether the process of IFI accession begins while Fidel Castro is in power or under a successor government.

The recent experience of socialist countries also demonstrates that the IMF and World Bank, with the support of the United States, has pursued two distinct strategies towards centrally planned economies. The first model, illustrated by the Russian experience, favors the elimination of the communist system and rapid transition towards free-market democracy. This entailed massive financial flows from the IFIs to Russia, in the midst of severe economic decline, considerable corruption and wasted resources, accompanied by a parallel process of rapidly expanding freedom to express political and civil liberties and engagement in the democratic process. The second model, used with China and Vietnam, encouraged more limited financial flows, an expanded private sector and some market reform. This formula has achieved considerable economic success and rising living standards, but has also consolidated the strength of the communist governments at the expense of democratic reform. These considerations will be central in shaping the potential relationship between the post-Castro regime and the international financial institutions.

THE CUBAN DIASPORA AND U.S. CUBA POLICY: WHO WANTS IT CHANGED?

Benigno Aguirre

For more than 40 years, longer than many people can remember, the U.S. and Cuban governments have not had diplomatic and trade relationships (for a chronology of the U.S. embargo see Kaufman Purcell and Rothkopf, 2000, Appendix A). During most of that time this anomalous state of affairs did not attract much controversy, for it was seen as an intrinsic part of the dominant Cold War rhetoric. The lack of relations with the U.S. did not pose an important challenge to the survival of the political regime in Cuba, for the continued break in relations was part of worldwide strains in international affairs. It allowed Cuba to profit handsomely from the financial support of the former USSR bloc of countries at the same time that it used a well-conceived and managed emigration policy of Cubans to the U.S. for the exit of surplus labor and discontented citizens (Kaplowitz, 1998). All of this changed soon after the miracle year of 1989, as Cuba now finds itself in the most serious and chronic economic crisis of its history.

What to do? From the perspective of the Cuban state the answer is obvious: bring in the dollar and the American investor, but do it in such a way that they do not challenge the political hegemony of the regime (Robinson, 2000; Pickel, 1998). Indeed, all the social engineering that is going on in Cuba today can be understood as trial and error efforts to find ways to successfully carry out this balancing act; the ongoing uncertainties and shifts and half steps indicate the inherent difficulties of carrying it out.

The prospect of change is at least as complex a problem from the traditional perspective of the Cuban Diaspora of opposition to the regime and its totalitarianism. Over the years, the Diaspora has become very diverse in experiences, professions, perceptions, political outlooks, and intimate life worlds (Dukes, 1999). Most members of the Diaspora cannot be oblivious to the suffering of the Cuban people and thus are attracted to a change in U.S. policy that will bring about change in the society and culture of the island and perhaps a rebirth in freedom. And yet, such a change will benefit their political enemy. Thus is the complex drama of passion and reason of the Cuban Dispora that fuels the so far intractable nature of the controversy over reestablishing relations between the two countries.

Fortunately, as is true with everything else, the stalemate is being gradually resolved by time. In the grand scale of things, Cuba has been a near non-entity for American foreign policy, particularly since the disappearance of the Soviet Union. The demise of the socialist world has brought about a radical transformation of the U.S. political elite's understanding of the prerogatives of superpower status of the American state (for a defense of the U.S. embargo law see Horowitz, 1998; Kaufman Purcell, 2000; Lopez, 2000; for the value of "engagement" as applied to Cuba see Haass and O'Sullivan, 2000). The old anticommunist rhetoric is no longer seen as relevant. In the new climate, what to do with/to Cuba is now increasingly open to the answers offered by the pecuniary interest of influential segments of the American capitalist class (Rosell, 2001; Taylor, 2002), particularly the agriculture and tourism industries (Jayawardena, 2003). What has stopped the normalization of relations is not Washington but Havana.

Time is also changing the Cuban Diaspora in myriad ways. Most inexorably, death transforms it. Moreover, as life passes outside Cuba, the exile or migrant changes in unexpected ways, and the all consuming memory of experiences in Cuba gives ways to other emotions and to other understandings. Even as important, over the course of decades different migratory cohorts have enjoined it. The aggregate result is that the Diaspora is now much more heterogeneous than ever before (Bonnin and Brown, 2002), much more attuned to the subtleties of life in the U.S. and the rest of the world, perhaps more sophisticated than before about what sort of future would be best for the homeland.

This is the setting for this paper, presenting an empirical analysis of Cubans' opinions on the matter of normalization of diplomatic and trade relations between the two countries.

METHODS

Data

The data comes from the 1999 Washington Post/ Henry Kaiser Family Foundation/Harvard University National Survey on Latinos in America.[1] The study included interviews with 818 Mexicans, 318 Puerto Ricans, 312 Cubans, and 593 Central or South Americans throughout the United States. The survey, part of a series, includes both citizens and non-citizens, native and foreign born Latinos. It provides a comprehensive look at Latinos and at their attitudes regarding values, politics, race relations and social policies, asking them about their perceptions of U.S. culture and their adoption of American customs.[2]

The analysis presented here uses un-weighted data and is based on all the Cuban-origin respondents (n=312) included in the survey. The dependent variable asks the respondents "Do you approve or disapprove of re-establishing diplomatic and trade relations with Cuba? It was scored 0 and 1 (yes). Twelve predictors were chosen to represent the dimensions of ideological conservatism, acculturation, immigration experiences, and demographics that are often assumed to be important determinants of attitudes of Cubans in the Diaspora towards the present day Cuban government.

Ideological conservatism

Abortion. Do you think abortion should be legal in all cases, legal in most cases, illegal in most cases, or illegal in all cases? Scored 0 through 3.

Political. Did you come to the United States to escape political persecution? Scored 0 and 1 (yes).

Republican. In politics today, do you consider yourself a Republican? Scored 0 and 1 (yes).

Traditionalism, a multi-item scale ranging from −14 to 18.

Acculturation

Attention to Politics. How much attention would you say you pay to politics and government? A lot, a fair amount, not much, none at all. Scored 1 through 4.

Citizen. Are you a legal citizen of the United States? Scored 0 and 1 (yes).

Language. What language do you usually speak at home? Only Spanish, more Spanish than English, both equally, more English than Spanish, or only English. Scored 1 through 5.

---

1. It was conducted by "telephone between June 30 and August 30, 1999. Fieldwork was conducted by International Communications Research. It used a representative sample of 4,614 adults, 18 years and older, including 2,417 Latinos and 2,197 non-Latinos. Among the non-Latinos were 1,802 non-Latino white adults and 285 non-Latino black adults. Respondents were selected at random. The margins of sampling error for each group are 2% for total respondents, 2% for Latinos, 2% for non-Latino whites, and 6% for non-Latino blacks. Individuals were identified as 'Latino' if they answered 'yes' to the question 'Are you, yourself of Hispanic or Latin origin or descent, such as Mexican, Puerto Rican, Cuban, or some other Latin background?' Latino adults were interviewed in their choice of English or Spanish. Fifty-three percent of the Latino interviews were conducted in Spanish."

2. *Washington Post* article reprints from the Latino survey and information about the survey can be obtained from the Kaiser Family Foundation publications request line at 1-800-656-4KFF; also at www.kff.org.

Immigration

Golden Immigrants scored 0 and 1 (for immigrants that came before 1969).

Send Money. Do you regularly send money back to your relatives in Cuba? Scored 0 and 1 (yes).

Demographics

Age. What is your age? Scored 18 through 89.

Education. What is the last grade or class that you completed in school? None or grade 1 through 8, High school incomplete, High school graduate, Business, technical or vocational school, some college, college graduate, post-graduate training. Scored 1 through 7.

Gender, scored 0 and 1 (for males).

We use binomial logistic regression (BLR)[3] on all categorical variables to model the respondents' attitudes towards reestablishing trade and diplomatic relations with Castro's government. We tested the model assumptions of BLR; in terms of its additivity, extensive exploratory analysis indicated that there were no statistically significant second-order interaction terms in the models presented. For example, interaction terms of Age with Golden, Republicanism with Golden, and Education with Traditionalism did not add to the analysis substantively or improve the statistical fit of the model. In term of its linearity, mathematical transformations of the continuous predictors (Age, Education, Traditionalism) did not strengthen the overall fit of the model. There is also the absence of multi-collinear relationships among the predictors in the model; all of their tolerances are above .60 (except for Language (.49)), as well as the absence of statistically significant residuals.

Results

Table 1 presents two BLR models. The first model includes all of the predictors. In the second BLR model, the Backward Stepwise (Likelihood Ratio) method of regression is used to identify a more parsimonious subset of statistically significant predictors.

In both models, the Hosmer and Lemeshow's goodness of fit test indicate that the models do not differ significantly from the observed data. There are a number of surprising findings in these results.

As model 2 indicates, respondents who considered themselves members of the Republican Party, if compared to respondents who were not Republicans, tended not to want rapprochement with Castro (B=-.55), the log odds are about one half that they would want to change the existing policy. More generally, it is the case that opposition to the change in policy is stronger among conservative, traditional respondents; a one-unit increase in the traditionalism scale decreased the desire to change the policy by B=-.04.

Table 1. Binary Logistic Regression Models of Normalization of Relations

	Model 1		Model 2	
	Exp (B)	Wald[a]	Exp (B)	Wald
Ideological Conservatism				
Abortion	1.03	.05 (ns)		
Political	.92	.31 (ns)		
Republican	.58	14.42	.58	15.3
Traditionalism	.96	4.5	.95	6.87
Acculturation				
Attention to Politics	1.25	2.34 (ns)	1.28	3.08
Citizen	1.32	3.11	1.29	3.4
Language	1.18	1.58 (ns)		
Immigration				
Golden Immigrants	.84	.94 (ns)		
Send Money	1.14	.51 (ns)		
Demographics				
Age	.99	1.51 (ns)	.98	5.94
Education	1.02	.04 (ns)		
Gender	1.35	5.20	1.36	5.78
-2 Log Likelihood	416.53		355.51	
Hosmer and Lemeshow				
Test Chi Square	4.97 (ns)		2.63 (ns)	
Nagelkerke R Square	.26		.25	

a. All coefficients significant at the p<.05 level except as indicated. Backward Stepwise (Likelihood Ratio) method of regression.

An interest in politics is associated with an increasing desire to change the policy; thus, the more the respondents put attention to politics the more they fa-

---

3. For a review of BLR see Field, 2000; another excellent discussion of BLR is found in http://www2.chass.ncsu.edu/garson/pa765/logistic.htm. BLR is appropriate for the present case, for it is designed to model a dichotomous dependent variable with categorical and continuous predictors.

vored a policy of rapprochement; the log odds go up .25 for every increase in reported attention to the political process. Moreover, naturalized respondents also favored it. They had a B=. 25 log odds to desire the change if compared to the non-naturalized.

Finally, two demographic variables, age and gender, also proved to be statistically significant predictors of the desire for a change in policy. A year's increase in the age of the respondents was associated with a negative effect; a B=-.02 log odds that they would disapprove of the change. Moreover, men were almost one third more likely than women to approve it (B=. 31).

Assumptions that are prevalent in some mass media and public discussions about the attitudes of the Cubans in the U.S. towards the policy of rapprochement (Grenier and Pérez, 2003) did not receive support from this research. For example, as shown in the models, the so-called Golden exiles, or respondents who came to the U.S. in the immigration cohort immediately after the post 1959 Castro exodus and are considered the quintessential political refugees, were not more likely than other Cubans to oppose the policy change. Other multivariate BLR analysis (not shown, available upon request) indicates that the reverse is also true, and that the so-called Red Worms, or those Cubans who came to the U.S. in the aftermath of Cuba's present day economic crisis and had personal association with the regime in power, were no more likely to support the policy change.

Similarly contradicting the opinion of some, respondents who had family in Cuba and regularly sent money to them were no more likely than other Cubans in the U.S. Diaspora to approve of the change. This is also true of respondents who stated that they came to the U.S. to escape political persecution; they are no more likely than other Cubans to disapprove of the policy change. It is also worthwhile to mention that the so-called second generation—Cuban-origin native born respondents—were not more likely than the foreign-born Cuban respondents to support the policy change (not shown, available upon request).

Given the contrary assumptions made by some observers of the Cuban Diaspora about the supposed important political differences among the generations towards the Castro regime (Grenier and Pérez, 2003, 93-95), these negative findings are extraordinary and unexpected. They contradict commonly expressed assumptions about the attitudes of the Cuban community in the United States towards the desirability of U.S. policy change towards Cuba, its assumed emotionalism, intolerance and irrationality (Grenier and Pérez, 2003, 92-93), instead documenting the high level of maturity in the thinking of Cubans about the issue. Their desire for a change in official policy towards Cuba is not a reflection of degree of support of the present day regime in power.

WHAT DOES IT ALL MEAN

The most statistically important predictor in the models was whether or not the respondents identified themselves with the Republican Party.[4] Opposition to the policy change is by now an article of faith among conservative Republicans in the Cuban Diaspora,[5] and it is not inappropriate to suggest that until now the Party's stand on the Cuba policy is an important reason for the vote of Cubans on behalf of Republican Party candidates. This happy coincidence is bound to change, however, as the search for profits by American corporations in a future Cuba helps jettison increasing number of national Republican Party officials from their traditional approach towards Cuba (Brenner, Haney, and Vanderbush, 2002).

In the meantime, the acculturation of Cubans into the society and culture of the United States, such as

---

4. Opinion polls (e.g., *Time*/CNN, January 7, 2000; CBS News/*New York Times*, October 25, 2000) indicate that both nationwide and in Florida, Republicans, if compared to Democrats and Independents, have a slightly greater tendency to oppose opening diplomatic relations with Cuba. They also show (e.g., ABC News, May 13, 2002) that the majority of respondents would like the U.S. government to lift travel restrictions.

5. Grenier and Pérez (2003, chapter 7) assume the presence of a conservative, anti Castro "exile ideology" among large segments of the Cuban-origin population in the U.S. However, our findings indicate that this ideology exists only among a small segment of this population.

obtaining citizenship, gaining command of the English language, and knowledge of political news, makes them, both those in the first and the second generation, more prone to want to abandon the present policy. Thus, when the shift in the national Republican Party's stand towards Cuba happens, as I believe it will, large segments of the Cuban community in the Diaspora will be ready and waiting, defusing the issue and its impact on voting behavior, and thus making it less painful for the Republican Party.

REFERENCES CITED

Brenner, Philip, Patrick J. Haney, and Walt Vanderbush. 2002. "The Confluence of Domestic and International Interests: U.S. Policy Toward Cuba, 1998-2001." *International Studies Perspectives*, vol. 3, 192-208.

Bonnin, Rodolfo and Chris Brown. 2002. "The Cuban Diaspora: A Comparative Analysis of the Search for Meaning Among Recent Cuban Exiles and Cuban Americans." *Hispanic Journal of Behavioral Sciences*, vol. 24, 465-478.

Dukes, Tamara R. 1999. "Beyond the Binary of Cuban Identity: Review Essay of Bridges to Cuba/Puentes a Cuba." *Cultural Studies*, vol. 13, 346-357.

Field, Andy. 2000. *Discovering Statistics Using SPSS for Windows*. London: Sage Publications.

Grenier, Guillermo and Lisandro Pérez. 2003. *The Legacy of Exile: Cubans in the United States*. Boston: Allyn and Bacon.

Haass, Richard N. and M. L. O'Sullivan. 2000. "Terms of Engagement: Alternatives to Punitive Policies." *Survival*, vol. 42: 113-135.

Horowitz, Irving L. 1998. "The Cuba Lobby Then and Now." *Orbis* (Fall), 553-564.

Jaramillo Edwards, Isabel. 2000. "Initiatives for Cooperative Regional Security: Reintegrating Cuba into Regional Projects." Pp. 151-157 in J. S. Tulchin and R. H. Espach, editors. *Security in the Caribbean Basin: The Challenge of Regional Integration*. Boulder, Colorado: Lynne Rienner Publishers.

Jayawardena, Chandana, 2003. "Revolution to Revolution: Why is Tourism Booming in Cuba?" *International Journal of Contemporary Hospitality Management*, vol. 15, 52-58.

Lopez, Juan J. 2000. "Sanctions on Cuba are Good, But Not Enough." *Orbis* (Summer), 345-361.

Kaplowitz, Donna Rich. 1998. *Anatomy of a Failed Embargo: U.S. Sanctions Against Cuba*. Boulder, Colorado: Lynne Rienner Publishers.

Kauffman Purcell, Susan. 2000. "Why the Cuban Embargo Makes Sense in a Post-Cold War World." Pp. 81-103 in Susan Kaufman Purcell and David Rothkopf, editors. *Cuba: The Contours of Change*. Boulder, Colorado: Lynne Rienner.

Pickel, Andreas. 1998. "Is Cuba Different? Regime Stability, Social Change, and the Problem of Reform Strategy." *Communist and Post Communist Studies*, vol. 31, 75-90.

Robinson, Linda. 2000. "Towards a Realistic Cuba Policy." *Survival*, vol. 42, 116-129.

Rosell, Andrew Jose. 2001. "The Future of U.S.-Cuba Relations, a Policy Shift from the Helms-Burton Act," *Law and Business Review of the Americas*, vol. 7, 235-264.

Taylor, J. Michael. 2002. "The United States's Prohibition on Foreign Direct Investment in Cuba—Enough Already?" *Law and Business Review of the Americas*, vol. 8, 111-139.

DEMOGRAPHIC AND SOCIOECONOMIC CHARACTERISTICS OF CUBAN-AMERICANS: A FIRST LOOK FROM THE U.S. 2000 POPULATION CENSUS

Daniel J. Perez-Lopez[1]

The 2000 U.S. Population Census, conducted between January and September 2000, was, according to the U.S. Census Bureau of the Department of Commerce, "the largest peacetime effort in the history of the United States" (U.S. Census Bureau 2001). The first bits of data – overall estimates of the resident population on April 1, 2000 – were released in December 2000 (U.S. Department of Commerce 2000). Since then, the Census Bureau has released several data sets that allow for analysis of the 2000 U.S. population by a variety of demographic and socioeconomic criteria. In particular, the recent release of some of the Public Use Microdata Sample (PUMS) files permits analysis of the demographic and socioeconomic characteristics of the Cuban-American population in the United States in 2000. This paper barely skims the surface and presents a preliminary look at some of the tabulations from the PUMS data. The author hopes that the paper will generate interest by others in analyzing the wealth of information on Cuban-Americans available from the 2000 Population Census.

THE U.S. 2000 POPULATION CENSUS: DATA AVAILABILITY

The Census Bureau used two different data collection instruments, a short form administered to all households, and a long form, administered to one in six households. The short form was focused on enumeration, although it did capture basic age, sex, race and ethnicity data. The longer questionnaire included all of the questions on the short form, plus detailed questions that expanded on the topics covered by the short form and covered other areas of interest.[2] The information collected in the long form is of great interest to researchers interested in the Cuban-American population of the United States, since it includes questions about income, employment, housing, year of arrival to the United States, country of origin, and English-language ability, among other areas. The Cuban-American population comprises both persons born in Cuba who migrated to the United States (immigrants) as well as those persons who were born in the United States of Cuban descent. Information is also available for each of these two subgroups.

Data released from the short and long forms was made available throughout 2002 and 2003 in publications and releases of the Census Bureau, and some of it still awaits release. All data released until recently, however, was based on geographic boundaries. This type of data allows for analysis of the characteristics of a given state, county, city, census tract, block

---

1. I would like to thank Jason Ost for assistance in preparing the statistical tabulations from the Census Bureau data and Lisandro Pérez for very helpful comments.

2. For detailed information on the questions in the short and long forms, see U.S. Census Bureau (1998).

group, and block, but only on the basis of a geographic unit. This data may be useful to city planners and community leaders. For example, it would enable a city or county to determine how many Cuban-Americans live within its borders and also how many immigrants have arrived since 1990. But it does not allow a researcher to determine how many Cuban-Americans have arrived since 1990, or since 1959, or any other year. Nor does it permit comparisons, for example, of auto ownership between Mexican-Americans and Cuban-Americans in a given city, even if the overall number of car owners and of Mexican-Americans and Cuban-Americans in that city are available.

These limitations inherent in the geographic area data are addressed by Census's release of PUMS, also known as the one- and five-percent samples. These data releases provide researchers with actual responses to census questionnaires that allow for customized cross-tabulations. Due to the specificity of the data, these releases widen the geographic areas to maintain confidentiality and avoid identifying any respondent. While the initial geography-based releases discussed above divide the country into 8.5 million blocks, with an average of 33 persons in each,[3] the one-percent sample provides information for population concentrations of 400,000 or more only. That is, over an area with population of 400,000 or more, the one-percent sample allows a comparison of Mexican-American and Cuban-American car-owners and many other comparisons. The one-percent national sample was released between April and June 2003, and is now available to researchers.

PRELIMINARY RESULTS

The rest of this paper presents some tabulations and some observations of the one-percent PUMS data as it pertains to Cuban-Americans. The tables update some of the tabulations regarding the demographic and socioeconomic characteristics of the Cuban-American population carried out by academic researchers (e.g., Pérez 1985 and 1986a; Pedraza 1996)

---

3. Author's calculation based on Census documentation.

Table 1. Population Censuses

	1990 Census	2000 Census
Population	1,053,197	1,254,439
Median Age	38.9	40.0
Education (25 years+)		
Less than High School	43.4%	36.9%
Labor Force Status (16 years+)		
In Labor Force	65.0%	55.5%
Employment Status (16 years+) (participating in labor force)	92.5%	93.9%
Number of Households	392,200	474,258
Household Income		
Less than $14,999	28.7%	24.7%
$15,000 to $24,999	16.7%	12.1%
$25,000 to $34,999	14.7%	10.3%
$35,000 to $49,999	16.8%	15.1%
$50,000 to $74,999	13.9%	16.7%
$75,000 and above	9.2%	21.3%
Poverty Status		
Below Poverty Level	11.4%	14.3%

Source: For 1990: U.S. Census Bureau, 1993, Persons of Hispanic Origin in the United States, 1990; for 2000, author's calculations from Census 2000, 1% Public Use Microdata Samples.

based on the 1980 and 1990 U.S. Population Census.

Table 1 presents summary demographic and socioeconomic characteristics of the Cuban-American population in the United States in 2000 compared to 1990. This tabulation includes both immigrants born in Cuba as well as persons born in the United States of Cuban descent.

• The number of Cubans in the United States in 2000 (1,254,439) was 19.1 percent higher than in 1990 (1,053,197).

• The 2000 Cuban-American population was older (median age 40.0 years v. 38.9 years in 1990), had higher educational attainment (36.9 percent of the population had less than a high school education in 2000, compared to 43.4 percent in 1990), had a lower labor force participation rate (55.5 percent in 2000 compared to 65.0 percent in 1990) and had a higher employment rate (93.9 percent compared to 92.5 percent).

- The number of Cuban households in 2000 was 474,258, 20.9 percent higher than in 1990.

- The income of Cuban households generally rose during the 1990s, with the share of households earning under $25,000 per annum declining from 45.4 percent in 1990 to 36.7 percent in 2000, while at the other extreme, the share of households earning more than $50,000 per annum rose from 23.1 percent in 1990 to 38.0 percent in 2000.

- Nevertheless, the share of Cuban families living below the poverty line rose in 2000 to 14.3 percent compared to 11.4 percent in 1990.

Table 2 presents selected demographic and socioeconomic characteristics of the Cuban-American population in the United States in 2000 distinguishing between those persons born in the United States and those who were born in Cuba and migrated to the United States.

- The U.S.-born Cuban population of the United States totaled 390,705 persons in 2000 (31.1 percent) while the immigrant population totaled 863,734 (68.9 percent).

- The U.S.-born Cuban population is much younger than the immigrant cohort, has a higher labor force participation rate, has a lower unemployment rate and has attained higher educational achievement.

- A lower share of the U.S.-born population lived in families under the poverty line compared to the immigrant cohort (12.6 percent v. 15.4 percent) and also a much higher share of U.S.-born group lived in families earning five times the poverty line income or higher (28.3 percent v. 19.9 percent).

- Finally, the U.S.-born population had significantly higher representation than the immigrant population in professional and office and administrative support occupations (white collar occupations) compared to the immigrant cohort.

Table 3 presents information on selected demographic and socioeconomic characteristics of the Cuban-American population in comparison with Mexican-Americans, Puerto Ricans, All Other Hispanics, and the U.S. population at large. Based on this table, it can be concluded that in 2000:

- Cuban-Americans were substantially older than the other Hispanic cohorts and the U.S. population at large.

- Cuban-Americans had a lower labor force participation rate than the other Hispanic groups and the U.S. population at large.

- Cuban-Americans had lower unemployment rates than other Hispanic groups, but higher than the U.S. population at large.

- Cuban-Americans had higher levels of educational achievement that other Hispanic groups other than Puerto Ricans; the level of educational achievement of Cuban-Americans was below that of the U.S. population at large.

- A far lower percentage of Cuban-Americans lived in families earning below the poverty line than other Hispanic groups, but this represented a higher share than for the population at large.

- The same seems to be the case for income. Income of Cuban-Americans in 1999 was higher than for other Hispanic groups, but lower than for the U.S. population at large.

FUTURE RESEARCH

This paper is a first effort to produce some tabulations from the U.S. 2000 Population Census for the Cuban-American population. We have made some observations regarding the characteristics of the Cuban-American population from comparisons with the 1990 Census and with other ethnic cohorts. Subsequent investigations should include, inter alia, isolating the different waves of Cuban migrants. In particular, developing additional tabulations for a range of indicators broken down by period of entry of Cuban immigrants would be extremely useful. The release of the PUMS five-percent sample, which is scheduled for the fall of 2003, will provide another rich source of data on the Cuban-American popula-

Table 2. Selected Demographic Characteristics of the Cuban-American Population in the U.S., by Place of Birth, 2000

	U.S.-born		Immigrants	
Number		390,705		863,734
Sex				
Share Female		48.7%		50.1%
Age				
25th %ile		8		37
50th %ile		18		50
75th %ile		31		65
Share Married with Spouse Present[a]		34.9%		55.4%
Labor Force Participation[b]				
Share in labor force		67.2%		52.4%
Employment status[c]				
Share unemployed, given participation in labor force		5.9%		6.2%
Education[d]				
less than ninth grade	7222	5.0%	173424	21.8%
9th to 12th, no diploma	14367	9.9%	151985	19.1%
HS grad or some college	71828	49.3%	322921	40.6%
4-year college degree or more	52278	35.9%	146361	18.4%
Share that speaks only English at home[e]		34.9%		5.6%
Poverty (omits college, military and institutionalized persons)				
Below Poverty Level	47603	12.6%	131156	15.4%
Above Poverty Level, Below 200% of poverty	61130	16.2%	188860	22.2%
200 up to 500 percent of poverty	161305	42.8%	361024	42.5%
500 percent of poverty or more	106715	28.3%	168973	19.9%
Citizenship status				
Born US citizen		100.0%	0	0.0%
Naturalized citizen		0.0%	523662	60.6%
Non-citizen		0.0%	340072	39.4%
Share living in linguistically isolated households		3.5%		7.6%
Occupation				
Management occupations:	16734	9.0%	46928	8.0%
Business and financial operations occupations	7340	4.0%	21640	3.7%
Professional and related occupations:	39370	21.2%	83103	14.2%
Service occupations:	30644	16.5%	92489	15.8%
Sales and related occupations:	26041	14.0%	70341	12.0%
Office and administrative support occupations	39597	21.4%	86979	14.9%
Farming, fishing, and forestry occupations	507	0.3%	4457	0.8%
Construction and extraction occupations	7087	3.8%	38986	6.7%
Installation, maintenance, and repair occupations	6157	3.3%	25692	4.4%
Production occupations	4380	2.4%	65804	11.3%
Transportation and material moving occupations	7541	4.1%	47709	8.2%

Source: U.S. Census, 1% Public Use Microdata Samples.

a. ages 15 and older
b. ages 16 and older
c. ages 25 and older
d. ages 5 and older
e. Restricted to workers (17 years and older) with positive 1999 total incomes.

tion, and will allow for even more precise national level analysis. Another area of potential research is comparisons of the characteristics of the Cuban-American population in Florida and South Florida

Table 3. Selected Characteristics of Cuban, Mexican, Puerto Rican, Other Hispanic, and U.S. Populations, 2000

	Cuban	Mexican	Puerto Rican	All Other Hispanics	All US
Number	1,254,439	20,957,540	3,390,399	9,646,760	281,510,519
Sex					
Share Female	49.7%	47.4%	51.4%	50.8%	51
Age					
25th %ile	24	11	13	13	17
50th %ile	40	24	27	27	35
75th %ile	60	37	42	41	51
Labor Force Participation[a]					
Share in labor force	55.5% 586567 / 1056324	62.2% 866325900.0% / 13927155	59.0% 139154500.0% / 2359250	61.3%	63.9%
Employment status[b]					
Share unemployed, given participation in labor force	6.1% 35907	9.2% 800,071	10.9% 151621	14.6% 38554300.0% / 2646857	5.7%
Education[b]					
less than ninth grade	19.2% 180646	33.5% 3409015	15.5% 283937	22.1% 116805500.0%	7.5% 13657814
9th to 12th, no diploma	17.7% 166352	20.7% 2112054	21.3% 390022	18.2% 96159700.0%	12.0% 21938300
HS grad or some college	42.0% 394749	38.2% 3893901	51.0% 934713	46.2% 24416900.0%	56.0% 1.02E+08
4-year college or beyond	21.1% 198639	7.6% 775347	12.2% 223707	13.6% 7171000.0%	24.4% 44529215
Poverty (omits college, military and institutionalized persons)					
Below Poverty Level	14.6% 178759	23.4% 4804353	25.0% 821734	20.3% 1912472	12.2% 33446872
Above Poverty Level, Below 200% of poverty	20.4% 249990	31.1% 6382569	22.9% 753602	27.3% 2567103	17.3% 47437378
200 up to 500 percent of poverty	42.6% 522329	37.2% 7631734	38.4% 1261679	40.1% 3779705	43.8% 1.20E+08
500 percent of poverty or more	22.5% 275688	8.4% 1716288	13.7% 449409	12.3% 1155397	26.7% 73102565
Total Income (1999)[c]					
25th %ile	$6,000	$2,000	$4,200	$3,000	$6,600
50th %ile	$14,100	$12,000	$13,000	$12,400	$19,000
75th %ile	$30,000	$22,600	$27,300	$25,000	$36,000

Source: U.S. Census, 1% Public Use Microdata Samples.

a. ages 16 and older
b. ages 25 and older
c. Restricted to workers (17 years and older) with positive 1999 total incomes

with Cuban-Americans elsewhere in the nation. There is much work to be done in preparing tabulations regarding income variables and conducting analyses on this important variable.

Further, while the focus of this paper has been on Cuban-Americans, the same techniques could be used to analyze Census Bureau data regarding other ethnic groups as well. Finally, I have left modeling of individuals' outcomes based on demographic characteristics for future exploration, but it is clear that this data set is well suited to modeling income based on race, education and other characteristics. Clearly, the U.S. 2000 Population Census data provides the basis for the analysis of many potentially interesting relationships.

BIBLIOGRAPHY

Díaz-Briquets, Sergio, and Jorge Pérez-Lopez. 2003. *The Role of the Cuban-American Community in the Cuban Transition*. Coral Gables: Cuba Transition Project, Institute for Cuban and Cuban-American Studies, University of Miami.

Pedraza, Silvia. 1996. "Cuba's Refugees: Manifold Migrations." In *Origins and Destinies: Immigration, Race, and Ethnicity in America*, eds. Silvia Pedraza and Rubén Rumbaut, 263-279. Belmont: Wadsworth Publishing Company.

Pérez, Lisandro. 1985. "The Cuban Population of the United States: The Results of the 1980 US Census of Population." *Cuban Studies/Estudios Cubanos* 15:1-18.

Pérez, Lisandro. 1986a. "Cubans in the United States." *The Annals of the American Academy of Political and Social Science* 487 (September), 126-137.

Pérez, Lisandro. 1986b. "Immigrant Economic Adjustment and Family Organization: The Cuban Success Story Reexamined," *International Migration Review*, Vol. 20, No. 1 (Spring), 4-20.

Pérez, Lisandro. 1992. "Cuban Miami." In *Miami Now! Immigration, Ethnicity, and Social Change*, eds. Guillermo Grenier and Alex Stepick, 83-108. Gainesville: University Press of Florida.

Portes, Alejandro. 1982. "Immigrants' Attainment: An Analysis of Occupation and Earnings among Cuban Exiles in the United States." In *Social Structure and Behavior: Essays in Honor of William Hamilton Sewell*, ed. R.M. Hauser et al., 91-111. New York: Academic Press.

Portes, Alejandro, and Stepick, Alex. 1993. *City on the Edge: The Transformation of Miami*. Berkeley: University of California Press.

Stepick, Alex, Grenier, Guillermo, Castro, Max, and Dunn, Marvin. 2003. *This Land is Our Land: Immigrants and Power in Miami*. Berkeley: University of California Press.

U.S. Census Bureau. 1998. "Uses for Questions on the Census 2000 Forms." March. http://www.census.gov/dmd/www/2000quest.html

U.S. Census Bureau. 2001. "Introduction to Census 2000 Data Products." MSO-01-ICDP. Washington, D.C. June. http://www.census.gov/prod/2001pubs/mso-01icdp.pdf

U.S. Department of Commerce. 2000. "Census 2000 Shows Resident Population of 281,421,906; Apportionment Counts Delivered to President." News Release CB00-CN.64, December 28. http://www.census.gov/Press-Release/www/2000/cb00cn64.html.

CUBA: THE NEXT RETIREMENT HAVEN?

Matias F. Travieso-Diaz and Armando A. Musa

A haven is defined, *inter alia,* as a "a place offering favorable opportunities or conditions."[1] A "retirement haven" is thus a location—city, state, country or other geographic entity—offering favorable living conditions for those wishing to withdraw from business life. Many countries (e.g., the Philippines, Costa Rica and Belize) and domestic political subdivisions (e.g., Florida) seek to be recognized as retirement havens. One incentive for attaining such recognition is the benefit to the local economy from retirees spending their income and, often, their remaining capital in the retirement haven.[2] Furthermore, retirees are likely to provide a stabilizing influence on society and their presence can confer social benefits, such as their contribution to volunteer projects and other beneficial activities.[3]

What constitutes a "retirement haven" is somewhat subjective. Whether living conditions in a particular locale are "favorable" depends on a retiree's values and perceptions. Nonetheless, The most often cited among them are the availability of affordable and high quality health care, a low cost of living, incentives to immigration, the possibility and ease of acquiring real estate, and the existence of recreational and cultural opportunities.[4] Benign climate, physical safety and social and political stability are also factors that influence whether a locale may be considered a "retirement haven."[5]

This paper addresses Cuba's potential for becoming a retirement haven at some point in the future and attracting retirees from developed countries, particularly the United States. The pursuit of "retirement haven" status should be attractive to Cuba given the deterioration of the country's economy. As is well known, Cuba has been for over a decade in a serious economic crisis due to the disappearance of the Socialist bloc, which previously provided the main source of trade and economic assistance for the coun-

---

1. Merriman-Webster Dictionary, *available online at* http://www.m-w.com/cgi-bin/dictionary.

2. See, *e.g.,* Retirement Incentives Update, Belize Report Vol. 6 No. 1, available online at http://www.belizereport.com/info/perpturist2.html.

3. See, e.g., Frank Jones, *Seniors who Volunteer, available online at* http://www.statcan.ca/english/indepth/75-001/archive/1999/pear1999011003s3a01.pdf [hereinafter "Seniors Volunteer"]; and see Gene Ruffenach, *Heed the Call to Volunteer and Discover a New Career,* July 19, 2003, *available online at* http://www.peacecorpsonline.org/messages/messages/2629/2015320.html. Some volunteer opportunities are available through special programs structured by non-profit organizations. For example, the Florida Association for Volunteer Action in the Caribbean and the Americas (FAVACA) sponsors a Seniors in Service Overseas Program. A description of the program is available online at http://www.favaca.org/ [hereinafter "FAVACA"].

4. *Id.*

5. *Id.*

180

try.[6] The stagnant Cuban economy and the decline in production of traditional industrial and agricultural commodities such as cane sugar suggest that Cuba will increasingly need to turn to activities in the services sector, such as tourism, to provide foreign currency revenue to the state and employment for some sectors of the population.[7]

Some have suggested that Cuba may already be an "ideal place to live" for a person considering retirement abroad.[8] As will be discussed below, that is clearly not the case at the present time. However, Cuba has the potential of becoming an attractive retirement haven, provided the island's government takes appropriate steps to foster the influx of retirees from other countries. Certain actions by the U.S. government will also be either necessary or highly desirable before Cuba could become a viable and attractive retirement destination for U.S. nationals and permanent residents.

This paper describes actions that a future Cuban government[9] might implement to make Cuba a desirable retirement haven for foreign nationals. We also identify some actions that the United States may take to assist Cuba in its economic reconstruction by making retirement in Cuba by U.S. residents and nationals a possible and attractive proposition.[10]

FACTORS THAT FAVOR CUBA'S FUTURE DEVELOPMENT AS A RETIREMENT HAVEN

Cuba enjoys several of the advantages that qualify a country for retirement haven status. As noted above, a retirement haven should meet criteria such as easy availability of real estate; ample recreational and cultural opportunities; a low cost of living; a safe and stable society; low cost, high quality health care; favorable climate; special benefits for immigrants; and an adequate infrastructure.[11] Obviously, Cuba already meets some of these criteria, such as favorable climate. The balance of the paper addresses the criteria Cuba meets and those that it does not, and suggests steps that Cuba could take to satisfy the latter.

Proximity to United States

Cuba's geographic location makes it a potentially favored destination for retirees. The territories of both Mexico and the United States are approximately 100 miles from Cuba. In addition, Cuba has infrastructure in place that is necessary to serve international passenger and cargo traffic. There are 21 airports on the island, 9 of which have international terminals.[12] Havana is three hours or less by plane from all major

---

6. Prior to 1990, Cuba depended on the Socialist bloc (mainly the Soviet Union) for over 80% of exports and imports, and for the financing of the economy through loans and subsidies. The demise of the Socialist bloc had a catastrophic impact on Cuba, which suddenly lost is markets, its sources of supply, and its credit and financing mechanisms. Banco Central de Cuba, Cuban Economy in the Special Period 1990-2000 (hereinafter "Special Period") at 7-8. The current deteriorating state of the Cuban economy is described in a number of recent papers. See, e.g., Carmelo Mesa-Lago, *The Cuban Economy in 1999-2001: Evaluation of Performance and Debate on the Future*, in CUBA IN TRANSITION—VOLUME 11 (Aug. 2001) ["hereinafter ASCE-11"]. The series of ASCE proceedings is available online at http://lanic.utexas.edu/project/asce/publications/proceedings/

7. See Sergio Díaz-Briquets, *Medicare: A Potential Income-Generating Activity for Cuba in the Future*, ASCE-11 at 185 (hereinafter "MEDICARE").

8. Christopher Howard, LIVING AND INVESTING IN THE NEW CUBA (Costa Rica Books, 2001) at 5 [hereinafter "HOWARD"].

9. The actions described in this paper include political, economic and social changes that the current socialist government is unlikely to be willing to undertake. Therefore, our implicit assumption is that a transition to a free-market, democratic society must be underway before Cuba can position itself as a competitive alternative to established retirement havens.

10. This paper focuses on the individual retiree who intends to live on a pension or on wealth accumulated during his work years. Some retirees may also be investors, that is, have sufficient capital to acquire productive assets in the country. The issues relating to foreign investment in Cuba are addressed elsewhere and will not be discussed here. See, e.g., Matias F. Travieso-Diaz and Charles P. Trumbull IV, *Foreign Investment In Cuba: Prospects and Perils*, in CUBA IN TRANSITION—VOLUME 12 (August 2002) [hereinafter "ASCE-12"]; see also, MATIAS F. TRAVIESO-DIAZ, THE LAWS AND LEGAL SYSTEM OF A FREE-MARKET CUBA—A PROSPECTUS FOR BUSINESS (1997), [hereinafter "LAWS AND LEGAL SYSTEM"], Chapter 5.

11. See INTERNATIONAL LIVING, *supra*.

12. Timothy Ashby, *IT in the Land of Salsa, Rum, and Fidel*, WORLD TRADE, July, 2001.

metropolitan areas on the eastern seaboard, as well as from Atlanta, New Orleans, Houston, and Dallas. Retirees of U.S. origin could easily travel back and forth to their former cities of residence. Of course, an air trip to Miami would take only a few minutes from most places in the island.

Relatively Low Cost of Living

Advocates of retirement in Cuba also tout the low cost of living on the island as a significant advantage.[13] In reality, the current cost of living in Cuba is lower in some respects than comparable costs in the United States, but not in others. For example, the cost of electric power, telephone service and other services subsidized by the government is low; on the other hand, most consumer goods are scarce and available only in "dollar stores" at prices that are often much higher than what the merchandise would cost in the United States.[14] While it is impossible to predict what economic conditions will prevail in Cuba after the country makes its transition to a market economy, it is likely that the overall cost of living to a retiree in Cuba will be lower than in the United States or other developed countries. This is a reasonable expectation because the price of goods and services will tend to reflect the salaries paid to the Cuban workforce, and average Cuban salaries are likely to remain below those in the United States.

Elderly people often list assistance with domestic chores as one of their most important needs.[15] At the current time, due to the low wages being paid to most Cuban workers and the existence of massive unemployment or underemployment, low-cost domestic help is potentially plentiful in Cuba.[16] Although this may not be the case after Cuba's economy has recovered, domestic service at low cost should be available to foreign retirees during and beyond the country's transition to a free-market economy.

High Level of Investment in Health Care

The Cuban government has made health care one of its top priorities, and has devoted considerable resources to improving selected aspects of the country's health care system.[17] The country has one of the highest physician-to-patient ratios in the world (58.2 per thousand persons), and equally high numbers of dentists (8.9 per thousand) and nurses (74.3 per thousand).[18] Physical facilities are also abundant (e.g., 5.2 hospital beds per thousand inhabitants).[19] And, although the quality of health care services delivered to the population has deteriorated significant-

---

13. See, e.g., HOWARD at 107-09.

14. As one of the measures taken to meet the economic crisis caused by the disintegration of the Soviet Bloc, Cuba allowed in 1993 the free circulation of U.S. dollars in the country. That measure was coupled with the establishment of "stores for the recovery of foreign exchange" (*Tiendas de Recuperación de Divisas*) where otherwise unavailable products are available at government-set prices, payable in dollars. It has been reported that the cost of goods at the dollar stores can be more than 200% over the cost of importing the goods. José Alvarez, *Rationed Products And Something Else: Food Availability And Distribution In 2000 Cuba*, ASCE-11 305, 310. Therefore, the cost of most basic staples to a hypothetical foreign retiree in today's Cuba would probably be at least as high as the cost of the same products in other countries.

15. See, e.g., http://www.co.dakota.mn.us/services/FinalGaps.pdf. "Domestic service is also on nearly every retiree's budget." Jenalia Moreno, *Paradise Found*, Houston Chronicle, October 6, 2002. The average cost of domestic help in a region is often cited in articles describing the desirability of potential locales for retirees, for example: Mary Beth Franklin, *Belize It or Not*, Kiplinger's Personal Finance Magazine, Vol. 56 No. 6, June 1, 2002, at 90 [hereinafter "FRANKLIN"]; Christopher Howard, *Retire to Costa Rica—An Expert Tells You How*, available online at http://www.escapeartist.com/efan/retire_in_costa_rica.htm; and, Cheryl Taylor, *International Living Conference in Dublin, Ireland*, available online at www.escapeartist.com/international/0600_readers.html.

16. The average monthly salary of Cuban workers in 2001 was 245 pesos, equivalent to U.S. $9 at the then current exchange rate. Oscar Espinosa Chepe, *Cuba: La Crisis Se Profundiza*, in ASCE-12 1, 5 [hereinafter "ESPINOSA"] The current rate of unemployment and underemployment has been conservatively estimated as 20%. *Id.* The average monthly salary of employees of state-owned and mixed-ownership entities in Cuba according to the National Office of Statistics is 234 pesos, or $11.70 according to unofficial exchange rates. See *Indicadores Generales*, available online at http://www.cubagob.cu/otras_info/one/indicadores_generales.htm.

17. Felipe Eduardo Sixto, *An Evaluation of Four Decades of Cuban Healthcare*, in ASCE-12, *supra*, 325, 340.

18. *Id.* at 332.

19. *Id.* at 341.

ly in recent years due to the unavailability of medicines, equipment, and medical supplies, the basic resources are still available to provide high quality health care services to foreign retirees.[20]

Other Factors

Cuba has a low crime rate. Although theft occurs, Cuba is virtually free of violent crime. Havana boasts one of the lowest murder rates per capita and the smallest number of unsolved murders of metropolitan cities in the world. The high degree of personal safety could provide an incentive for potential retirees, particularly in comparison to the situation in other Latin American countries.[21]

Other factors that are often mentioned among Cuba's selling points to potential retirees are the physical beauty of the country, the friendliness of its people, and the richness of the island's cultural and recreational opportunities.[22] These and other intangible factors (such as Cuba's mystique to many abroad, particularly in the United States) make Cuba a potentially favored place for many foreigners to call home.

CURRENT IMPEDIMENTS TO CUBA'S ABILITY TO BECOME A RETIREMENT HAVEN

Impediments that Apply to All Potential Retirees

Despite the above mentioned advantages, Cuba today is hardly a choice destination for foreign retirees. The reasons are multiple, but fall into three categories: (1) an inhospitable, repressive, and potentially unstable, political system; (2) a government-controlled economy that has remained in a state of crisis for at least the last twelve years and shows no signs of improvement; and (3) scarcities and other day-to-day difficulties that make residence in Cuba unappealing.[23] Because of these impediments, Cuba remains unattractive as a place to retire, and not even the current Cuban government appears to argue otherwise.

Impediments that Apply Particularly to U.S. Citizens and Permanent Residents

Some of the current impediments to Cuba's ability to become a viable retirement haven are of particular import to U.S. citizens and permanent residents. For instance, U.S. law grants retirees who possess U.S. citizenship the right to receive their social security benefit payments abroad in almost any country in the world.[24] However, U.S. Treasury regulations specifically list Cuba as one of a handful of countries to

---

20. Evidence of the continuing viability of Cuba's health care system is the fact that Cuba actively promotes "medical tourism," that is, the travel to Cuba of foreign visitors who seek medical care and are able to pay for medical services in hard currency. For example, Cuba's state-owned Centro Iberoamericano para la Tercera Edad ("CITED") advertises its ability to serve *"turismo de salud"* (health tourism), geared particularly to the elderly. Its website identifies Cuba as an ideal "tourist" destination for senior citizens on account of the variety of health services it provides to the elderly. See http://www.infomed.sld.cu/instituciones/gericuba/cited/tursalud/principal.htm. Cuba has historically promoted itself as a prime "medical tourism" destination for foreign nationals who seek Western-quality medical services at reduced prices. *See* Health Care in Cuba: Myth Versus Reality, *available online at* http://www.canf.org/Issues/medicalapartheid.htm. Cuba's success at attracting medical tourists suggests that the country remains capable of providing high quality medical services to those able to pay for them.

21. As further discussed below, there may be political unrest and social instability following a transition to a free-market society, with an attendant increase in crime. A future Cuban government must ensure that foreign retirees are protected to the greatest extent possible from personal safety risks.

22. HOWARD at 1-3.

23. For an insider's view of current conditions in Cuba see ESPINOSA, *supra*. Mr. Espinosa, an independent journalist, was incarcerated and sentenced in April 2003 to 20 years' imprisonment, for violation of articles 7 and 11 of Cuba's Law 88. He was accused of "activities against the integrity and sovereignty of the State" by allegedly receiving money from abroad, collecting press cuttings about meetings between representatives from the USA and dissidents and other activities. See Amnesty International Report No. AMR 25/016/2003, *available online* at http://web.amnesty.org/library/Index/ENGAMR250162003?open&of=ENG-CUB. The plight of Mr. Espinosa and many others exemplifies current political conditions in the island.

24. See Social Security—Your Payments While You Are Outside The United States (based on SSA Publication No. 05-10137, ICN 480085), *available online at* http://www.ssa.gov/international/your_ss.html (hereinafter "Your Payments Outside the U.S.")

which the U.S. Social Security Administration ("SSA") is prohibited from mailing social security benefits.[25]

In addition, U.S. law provides that absent an international social security agreement ("totalization agreement")[26] between the U.S. and the relevant foreign country, retirees who are U.S. permanent residents (as opposed to U.S. citizens) lose their right to have social security benefits mailed to them after being abroad for more than six (6) months.[27] So, even if the specific prohibition on sending social security payments into Cuba were repealed, the current absence of a U.S-Cuba totalization agreement will present an obstacle to U.S. permanent residents desiring to retire in Cuba.

A further hindrance to Cuba's successful development into a retirement haven for U.S. nationals and permanent residents is the current uncertainty surrounding the tax treatment by Cuba of various sources of retiree income. One important factor in the decision of U.S. nationals on where to retire will be the extent to which their retirement income will be subject to taxation by the host country. A tool regularly used by countries desiring to minimize the problem of dual taxation by overlapping taxing jurisdictions is the bilateral tax treaty.[28] Consequently, the absence of a tax treaty for the reduction of dual taxation be-tween Cuba and the U.S. is a further barrier to Cuba's ability to evolve as a retirement haven.

Also, to the extent that a U.S. individual's decision to retire in a particular foreign country is influenced by the presence of home country companies that are able to provide familiar products and services in the host country, Cuba would need to address potential deterrents to foreign investment by U.S. companies in Cuba. The single largest impediment for U.S. based persons wishing to retire in Cuba is the U.S. embargo on trade and economic transactions in and with Cuba. This topic is addressed below.

STEPS THAT CUBA COULD TAKE TO FOSTER THE INFLUX OF FOREIGN RETIREES

Immigration Policies

Facilitating Immigration: In its transition to a free-market system, Cuba will need to develop policies that promote the unimpeded movement of goods, ideas and people across its borders with minimum restriction. Once it becomes apparent that Cuba intends to liberalize its economy and to commit to a more democratic form of government, foreign investors and Cuban expatriates will want to visit Cuba in substantial numbers. During the transition, it is essential that Cuba encourage such visits by developing an open and efficient immigration policy.

---

25. *Id.* Some other countries to which the mailing of social security benefits is prohibited are Cambodia, North Korea, and Vietnam.

26. The terms "international social security agreement," "bi-national social security agreement," and "totalization agreement" are synonymous and are used interchangeably. They refer to a form of agreement entered into between two countries for the purposes of coordinating their respective social security coverage and taxation regimes. Totalization agreements aim to eliminate the problems of dual coverage, dual taxation, and gaps in benefit protection that are likely to arise when an employee divides his/her work between two or more countries. See generally JoAnne Chernov Adlerstein, *Concerns of the Global Employer*, Practicing Law Institute, September 2002; see also *Tax Guide for U.S. Citizens and Resident Aliens Abroad*, IRS Publication 54.

27. *Your Payments Outside the U.S., 2003 Edition;* see also, Jonathan Wiseman, *U.S. Social Security May Reach to Mexico*, Washington Post, December 19, 2002, at A01.

28. A tax treaty is an agreement between two countries that contract in order to coordinate the application of their respective—and often conflicting and/or overlapping—tax systems to cross-border transactions and investments. The aim is to ensure that only one country ends up taxing any one item of income. See Daniel M. Berman, *Tax Treaties—Fundamentals*, Practicing Law Institute, October-November 2002 (551 PLI/Tax 353). Negotiation of a tax treaty is often a complex, drawn out process.

The visa granting structure and procedures should be open and simple to administer. Cuba should eliminate all visa requirements for short-term pleasure or business trips originating in the United States and other developed countries.[29] Eliminating the need for visas avoids Cuba expending scarce resources in the administration of the immigration program, and allows foreign travelers easy access to the island. While Cuba should seek reciprocal arrangements with the United States and other countries, the importance of U.S. travel to Cuba is so significant that Cuba should unilaterally eliminate visa requirements for U.S. citizens and permanent residents, even if reciprocal treatment is not granted by the United States.[30]

In addition to opening its doors to travel by foreigners, Cuba should institute special measures to attract the potential retiree population from developed countries, particularly the United States. Such measures could include lowered immigration requirements, the ability to import personal property free of tax, and the ability to receive income from sources outside Cuba without paying local taxes.[31] A particularly useful immigration provision would be one that granted retirees permanent resident status in Cuba as long as they qualified for treatment as such, typically by maintaining a level of income from abroad.[32]

Clarifying the Legal Status of Cuban Expatriates: It is to be anticipated that a large number of Cuban expatriates who are now citizens or residents of the United States or other countries will wish to return to Cuba to spend their retirement years on the island.[33] However, one potential obstacle to the return of Cuban exiles is their legal status in Cuba. Presently, the Cuban Constitution provides that Cuban citizenship is lost by a person who becomes a citizen of a foreign country; dual citizenship is not allowed.[34] Thus, unless the new Constitution or other transition-period statute provides otherwise, those Cuban émigrés who have become naturalized citizens of other countries, including the United States, will have to renounce the other country's citizenship and apply for reinstatement of their Cuban citizenship if they

---

29. There are several countries in close proximity to Cuba having large impoverished populations. Unskilled migrants from those countries, under favorable conditions, may seek to relocate in Cuba. For that reason, some sort of visa structure must be retained to control the entry of immigrants who may become public charges.

30. See *Opening the Door for Business Travel to a Free-Market Cuba,* 1 FREE MARKET CUBA BUS. J. 8, Shaw, Pittman, Potts & Trowbridge (Spring/Summer 1992).

31. A package of such measures was, for example, enacted into law in 1999 by Belize. Retired Persons (Incentives) Act of 1999, Belize Gen. L. Vol. II, Ch. 62 (1999), *available online at* http://www.belizelaw.org/lawadmin/index2.html (hereinafter "BELIZE ACT").

32. For example, Belize allows a foreign retiree to retain its protected status as long as he or she deposits in a bank or other financial institution in Belize the sum of two thousand U.S. dollars (or its foreign currency equivalent) each month. BELIZE ACT, Section 3.-(1)(c).

33. In a survey conducted by a Spanish-language television station in Miami, "one in five Cubans in the metropolitan area said they would return home, although the results are regarded ... more as coming from the heart than the head." Laura Parker, *Radio Marti Director Ousted as Exiles Discuss Returning to Cuba,* WASHINGTON POST, Mar. 13, 1990, at A3. It is possible, but by no means certain, that the passage of time will result in a diminution of interest by Cubans abroad to return permanently to the island.

34. Under Cuba's Constitutions, both pre- and post-revolution, a Cuban citizen who becomes a citizen of another country loses his Cuban citizenship. CONSTITUCION DE LA REPUBLICA DE CUBA (1940) [CONSTITUTION], art. 15 (CUBA), reprinted in 1 CONSTITUTIONS OF NATIONS 610 (Amos J. Peaslee ed. & trans., 2d ed.), *also available online at* http://www.rose-hulman.edu/~delacova/constitution-1940.htm [hereinafter "1940 CONSTITUTION"]; see also, CONSTITUCION DE LA REPUBLICA DE CUBA (1992) art. 32 (Cuba), *published in* Gaceta Oficial (Aug. 1, 1992), *available online at* http://www.georgetown.edu/pdba/Constitutions/Cuba/cuba1992.html [hereinafter "1992 CONSTITUTION"]. See also *Reglamento de Ciudadanía* ("Citizenship Regulations"), Gaceta Oficial (Mar. 3, 1944), Art. 33 [hereinafter REGLAMENTO].

want to regain the rights of Cuban nationals.[35] Retired Cuban expatriates, who may feel more vulnerable on account of age and other factors to discriminatory treatment by the general population, will probably welcome their being placed on equal legal footing with Cuban nationals without losing their benefits as citizens of other countries.

Removing Obstacles to Bringing Property into Cuba: A number of countries, including Ireland, Costa Rica, and Belize allow foreign retirees to import cars and household goods free of taxes or import duties.[36] Cuba should do the same. The loss of tax revenues due to the free importation of these articles will likely be outweighed by the positive influence that such a measure would have on encouraging foreign retirees to settle in Cuba, bringing hard-currency with them.

Allowing the Purchase of Real Property in Cuba: Cuba places severe restrictions on the sale of residential property. Any proposed sale must be subject to the state's prior approval with the state reserving the right of first refusal at a state-set price.[37] Restrictions also exist on the ability to swap property, which is one of the favorite loopholes used by the population to get around the restriction on home sales.[38] Clearly, these restrictions must be eliminated in order for a housing market for foreign retirees to develop.

---

35. It has been argued, based on the presumed continued vitality of Cuba's 1940 Constitution (which in Art. 15(a) states that those Cubans who acquire another country's citizenship lose their status as Cubans) that the automatic loss of citizenship provided by Art. 15(a) should not apply to Cuban exiles that have opted to become citizens of their country of residence because to do so would bar the exiles from "participating in the Cuban political process." José D. Acosta, *El Marco Jurídico-Institucional de un Gobierno Provisional de Unidad Nacional en Cuba*, in CUBA IN TRANSITION—PAPERS AND PROCEEDINGS OF THE SECOND ANNUAL MEETING OF THE ASSOCIATION FOR THE STUDY OF THE CUBAN ECONOMY 61, 82 (August 1992). However, the opposite argument can also be made: it is precisely to protect the Cuban political process from undue influence by those who have sworn allegiance to a foreign country that the automatic loss of Cuban citizenship provision for those who opt to become citizens of another country should remain in effect. In this context, it is instructive to recall that the process for regaining Cuban citizenship that was in place before 1959 was anything but automatic. It required a formal re-application for citizenship, followed by one year of continuous residence in Cuba, followed by another formal appearance before a public official, in order for the reinstatement of citizenship to become effective. REGLAMENTO, *supra*, Art. 35. One of the issues that should be considered by a future Cuban Government is whether to follow the lead of certain countries, such as Israel, that allow their nationals to hold dual citizenship. The concern about protecting the Cuban political process against foreign influence could be addressed by means such as establishing relatively lengthy residence requirements before being eligible to vote, imposing limits on campaign contributions, and imposing restrictions on the ability of those holding dual citizenship to hold public office.

36. See Adam Starchild, *Finding Your Retirement Haven*, *available online at* http://www.familyhaven.com/retirement/chapt5.html [hereinafter "RETIREMENT HAVEN"]. Belize allows foreign retirees to bring into the country, free of taxes and duties, "new and approved means of transportation" for his personal use every five years after entry into the country, upon proof that he has properly disposed of the means of transportation he had previously imported into Belize. BELIZE ACT, Section 4.-(1)(c). The definition of "approved means of transportation" includes motor vehicles, boats, and light aircraft. *Id.*, Schedule A.

37. Ley No. 65, 23 de Diciembre de 1988, Ley General de la Vivienda, art. 70 (requiring government approval for the sale of homes, with right of first refusal by the state at a state-set price). Many Cubans have found ways of circumventing the laws restricting the transfer of residential properties. Two (illegal) methods in particular are worthy of note. First, many Cubans engage in unequal *permutas* (swaps), whereby two people exchange houses of unequal value. The party receiving the house of greater value augments her portion of the trade with an agreed amount of cash. A second means of circumventing the law is the creation of "phantom apartments" which then become the subject of a *permuta* for the purposes of transferring title. Eduardo M. Peñalver, *Redistributing Property: Natural Law, International Norms, and the Property Reforms of the Cuban Revolution*, 52 Fla. L. Rev. 107, 128 (2000) [hereinafter "PEÑALVER"]

38. Resolucion No. 381, September 25, 1989 (Instituto Nacional de la Vivienda) (requiring parties seeking to exchange houses to apply for permission to a local housing authority, which has the right to refuse permission if it suspects that the exchange is motivated by a desire for profit). Despite these restrictions, swapping of property for property appears to still flourish in Cuba. Douglass S. Norvell, *Cuban Real Estate: The Next Boom?*, Illinois Real Estate Letter (Summer 1999) at 12, *available online at* http://www.cba.uiuc.edu/orer/V13-3-4.pdf. [hereinafter "NORVELL"].

A number of countries prohibit or limit real estate ownership by aliens.[39] Cuba should avoid any such limitation, particularly with respect to residential property. In addition, buying real estate is made difficult in a number of countries due to the absence of licensed real estate agents.[40] While it may not be feasible to establish regulations for the licensing of real estate agents in the short-term, Cuba should seek (perhaps through a revitalized Chamber of Commerce) to create a listing of real estate agencies that can be relied upon by foreigners to assist with the purchase of property on the island.

Taxation Policies

Minimizing Taxation of Retirement Income: Unlike the United States, where the Internal Revenue Code aims to tax a broad range of income-generating activities,[41] Cuba lacked until relatively recently a system of direct income taxation.[42] In fact, some have noted that Cuba does not have a tax-paying culture.[43] Nevertheless, in 1994, Cuba introduced a system of direct income taxation.[44] The system was designed primarily to tap into the sources of revenue being generated at the time by newly legalized forms of self-employment.[45] However, it may also be applied to retirees' income, thus raising a disincentive to retire in Cuba. Cuba may therefore want to implement a tax policy that grants special benefits to foreign retirees. For example, Cuba might offer a combination of income tax exemptions, deductions, and credits to foreign retirees, as well as push aggressively for pro-retiree provisions when negotiating tax treaties with other countries that may assert tax jurisdiction over the retirees.[46] By taking into account the special

---

39. For example, Mexico's Constitution prohibits the acquisition of real estate by foreigners in the area within 100 kilometers (62 miles) of Mexico's borders and within 50 kilometers (31 miles) of the coastline. Constitucion Politica de los Estados Unidos Mexicanos, Art. 27 (2003), *available online at* http://info4.juridicas.unam.mx/ijure/fed/9/28.htm?s.

40. Many countries that seek to attract foreign retirees have yet to regulate real estate agents through licensing, including but not limited to Belize (FRANKLIN, *supra*, at 90), Mexico (*Buying Property in Mexico, available online at* www.mexonline.com/propmex.htm), and Costa Rica (*Costa Rica Real Estate Buying Tips, available online at* http://realestateguide.axnmls.com/buyingrealestate.php).

41. See I.R.C. § 61 defining gross income as "all income from whatever source derived, including (but not limited to) the following items: (1) compensation for services, including fees, commissions, fringe benefits, and similar items; (2) gross income derived from business; (3) gains derived from dealings in property; (4) interest; (5) rents; (6) royalties; (7) dividends; (8) alimony and separate maintenance payments; (9) annuities; (10) income from life insurance and endowment contracts; (11) pensions; (12) income from discharge of indebtedness; (13) distributive share of partnership gross income; (14) income in respect of a decedent; and (15) income from an interest in an estate or trust."

42. See United States International Trade Commission, *The Economic Impact of U.S. Sanctions With Respect To Cuba*, Investigation 332-413, Publication 3398 (February 2001), Ch. 3 at 3-16, *available online at* ftp://ftp.usitc.gov/pub/reports/studies/pub3398.pdf (visited February 14, 2003) (noting, inter alia, that Cuba basically lacked a taxation regime from 1967 to 1994).

43. See generally Archibald R. M. Ritter & J.A. Turvey, *The Tax Regime for Micro-Enterprise in Cuba*, Carleton University's Department of Economics' Carleton Paper Series number 99-04, February 2000, *available online at* http://www.carleton.ca/economics/cep/cep99-04.pdf (visited on February 12, 2003) (hereinafter "TAX REGIME").

44. *Id.* Cuba's basic taxation framework consists of Law 73—The Tax Systems Law, Gaceta Official (August 1994), and Decree-Law 169 (January 1997). Decree-Law 169 granted primary taxation authority to the Ministry of Finance, and created the National Office of Tax Administration (ONAT).

45. See TAX REGIME, *supra*, at 3. The legalized economic activities were primarily in the areas of transportation, housing services, and family and personal services. Furthermore, Decree-Law 141 limited self-employment to a subset of the population, namely retirees, housewives, and laid-off workers.

46. The United States is one of those countries. Whereas most other countries seek to tax only their residents, the United States imposes worldwide taxation on its citizens and residents, regardless of where they have their home. This might create special problems of dual taxation. In negotiating a bilateral tax treaty with the United States, Cuba might seek to have U.S. retirees taxed only by Cuba on their retirement income, although this may prove difficult to achieve.

Furthermore, when designing tax policy, the Cuban government must remain mindful not only of efficiency and effectiveness concerns, but also of the perceived fairness of the tax laws. The main concern here is that—to the extent that foreign retirees are given different, more favorable tax treatment than domestic retirees—there is a potential for the domestic taxpayers to feel that they are being unfairly discriminated against. Therefore, the government must be able to deploy credible arguments that the benefits afforded to foreign retirees provide, in the final analysis, a net benefit to the well-being of the country as a whole.

needs and concerns of retirees when formulating its revamped tax policies, Cuba could provide a stimulus to the influx of foreign retirees.

Entering into Tax Treaties to Avoid Double Taxation of Retirees' Income: As noted earlier, a U.S. citizen or resident[47] is subject to U.S. taxation on their worldwide income. At the same time, a U.S. person who retires in Cuba is likely to be treated by Cuba as a resident of Cuba. As such, assuming that Cuba will continue to impose an income tax on its residents and that the United States does not alter its long-standing policy of taxing the worldwide income of its citizens and residents, U.S. persons retiring in Cuba will likely face a risk of double taxation (i.e., both Cuba and the United States will seek to tax their income).[48]

By entering into a tax treaty with the U.S. and other countries from which retirees might hail, Cuba could achieve three objectives. First, it could reduce the incidence of double taxation of retirees' income. Second, Cuba could bring some certainty into retirees' calculations of how much tax liability they would face in Cuba, and thus assist retirees in their planning process. And third, Cuba could use tax treaties that include retiree-friendly provisions as a signaling device to foreign retirees that Cuba welcomes them within its borders.

Social Services Policies

Providing Adequate, Affordable Health Care: Cuba should seek in the future to build upon its accomplishment in the health care area and also strive to t remedy the current deficiencies in facilities, equipment, and other infrastructure caused by the economic crisis. It is essential that, as foreign retirees start considering Cuba as a potential destination, the country have the necessary health care services that would make it possible for the retirees to receive the services they require without having to travel outside the country.[49]

Establishing Retirement Communities: The economic crisis has also resulted in a housing crisis of unprecedented proportions. As is widely reported, the absence of adequate housing is perhaps the greatest urban problem that Cuba currently faces.[50] When a transition to a free-market economy occurs, the housing market could be very tight both due to the absence of housing on the market and the demand for it from returning Cuban émigrés as well as others seeking to establish residence in the country for business reasons. Indeed, some predict that a real estate "boom" will occur in Cuba comparable to those experienced in "Florida, California, the Colorado Highlands, and other 20th Century boom locations."[51]

---

47. The term "U.S. resident" includes not only permanent residents (i.e., green-card holders), but also any person who meets the "substantial presence test" of I.R.C. § 7701. Both U.S. citizens and residents are considered "U.S. persons"—and thus are subject to worldwide taxation—under I.R.C. § 7701.

48. The problem of double taxation is not limited to U.S. persons. Although the U.S. is one of the few countries in the world that impose tax on the basis of citizenship, most countries impose tax on the basis of residence. Given the multiplicity of tax systems with differing concepts and definitions, it is possible that an individual can be considered simultaneously a resident of more than one country. See Daniel M. Berman, *Tax Treaties—Fundamentals*, Practicing Law Institute, October-November 2002 (551 PLI/Tax 353), at 362, (noting that most tax treaties contain "tie-breaker" provisions to deal with the problem of dual residency).

49. Several countries, such as Mexico and Costa Rica, have established low-premium health insurance programs that are available to foreign retirees. See RETIREMENT HAVEN, *supra*; http://www.internationalliving.com/eletters.cfm?eid=1129.

50. See, *e.g.*, Ginger Thompson, *Cuban Housing a Tight Squeeze; Many Complain Prime Land Targeted for Tourists*, CHICAGO TRIBUNE, Aug. 16, 1998, *available online at* http://www.rose-hulman.edu/~delacova/cuba/housing-98.htm

51. See NORVELL, *supra*.

The combination of a limited supply of housing and significant, and probably speculative, demand might place housing out of reach for potential foreign retirees. For that reason, a future Cuban government may well need to develop housing communities, perhaps in partnership with foreign developers, for the use of retirees.[52] Such communities could integrate living and health care facilities and provide an attractive, yet affordable, environment for retirees, thereby increasing the attractiveness of the island as a potential retirement destination.

Economic and Social Policies

Ensuring Personal Safety of Retirees: One of the challenges of a transition government in Cuba will be to maintain order and assure public safety. The probability of unrest and violence during the transition makes it necessary that adequate numbers of trained internal order forces, particularly police, be available to ensure domestic tranquility. One of the great challenges of the transition government will be to retrain and enlarge the roster of internal order personnel, and ensure that they are capable of maintaining law and order while exercising proper respect for due process and individual rights.[53]

Additionally, the safety of foreign retirees in Cuba might be at particular risk. Individual criminals or organized criminal groups often target foreign retirees.[54] If adverse economic conditions worsen in Cuba during its free-market transition, foreigners may become the victims of common crime, politically motivated acts of terrorism, or other violence.

Instituting Economic Policies that Minimize Inflation: Countries experiencing a transition from a command-style economy to a more liberalized economy often experience inflation.[55] A prolonged, high level of inflation erodes savings, discourages investment, creates uncertainty, and may cause social unrest. Various researchers have set the threshold for high inflation at levels between 2.5% and 40%.[56]

In some transition economies, there may be an initial inflationary burst as prices rise from their state-set level to their market-determined level. In other cases, there is prolonged high inflation, even hyperinflation. Latin American countries in particular have experienced bouts of chronic inflation.[57]

Evaluating the techniques that Cuba could potentially use to control inflation is beyond the scope of this paper. Whatever mechanisms are utilized, their success will be an important factor in persuading foreign retirees, many of whom will be living on fixed incomes, to settle in the island. While the pensions or other income of foreign retirees would be in foreign currency and thus protected from fluctuations in the value of the local currency, the increase in the cost of

---

52. For a discussion of the status of current Cuban land development ventures and the regulatory improvements that would be valuable before commencement of further real estate development see W. Paul Rosenau, Paul Fenske, John Gilderbloom, *Flirting with Capitalism*, URBAN LAND 98 (October 2002). In addition to the US retirement village developers, there are developers with similar expertise who have been successful in Australia and the UK, and who are seeking new sites; see Andrew Heathcote, *Retirement Villages are as Good as Gold*, BUSINESS REVIEW WEEKLY, December 5, 2002 (Australia); Graham Norwood, *Cash-Property—A to Z*, THE OBSERVER, March 9, 2003 (UK).

53. See LAWS AND LEGAL SYSTEM, *supra*, Chapter 3.

54. For example, it has been widely reported that foreign nationals, including retirees, have been targeted for kidnapping and extortion by organized crime cartels in the Philippines. See, *e.g.*, Philippine Weekly Report (January 2002), *available online at* http://www.virtual-asia.com/newsletters/samples/020107ph.pdf. Similar incidents have been reported in other retirement havens, such as Costa Rica. See http://abcnews.go.com/sections/travel/DailyNews/costarica000609.html; http://travel.state.gov/costa_rica.html.

55. This has been the case in most Eastern European countries, where immediate price liberalization occurred. See Bryan W. Roberts, *Inflation and the Monetary Regime During the Cuban Economic Transition*, See CUBA IN TRANSITION—VOLUME 4 (1994).

56. Recent research suggests that the threshold is different for industrialized and developing countries, and places the threshold inflation level for developing countries in the range of 7-11%. Mohsin S. Khan and Abdelhak S. Senhadji, *Threshold Effects in the Relationship Between Inflation and Growth* 48 IMF STAFF PAPERS 1, 16 (December 2001).

57. Average inflation in Latin American is projected to be 11% this year, the highest of any region in the world. *Latin Inflation: Another Setback*, LATIN BUSINESS CHRONICLE, April 2003.

local goods and services due to inflation would be detrimental to the retirees' financial security.

Extending to Foreign Retirees the Equal Protection of Cuban Laws: The fair and equitable treatment of foreign nationals should be guaranteed expressly in the Constitution through a declaration that foreign nationals enjoy the full protection of the country's laws and are subject to the same treatment given to domestic individuals.[58] If there is a need to create any distinctions between foreigners and Cuban nationals (e.g., on health insurance and immigration matters) such distinctions should be justifiable and clearly set forth in the applicable legislation. Indeed, as discussed above, to the extent that disparate treatment of foreign retirees is warranted in some areas, the distinctions should be in the nature of favorable concessions to retirees intended to encourage their settlement in Cuba.

STEPS THE UNITED STATES COULD TAKE TO FACILITATE THE RETIREMENT IN CUBA OF U.S. NATIONALS AND PERMANENT U.S. RESIDENTS

Lifting the Trade Embargo Prohibitions

Clearly, the first and most important step necessary to make it possible for U.S. nationals and permanent residents to retire in Cuba is the lifting of the U.S.

trade embargo prohibitions.[59] U.S. law currently imposes restrictions on travel to Cuba by persons under the jurisdiction of the United States. The Cuban Assets Control Regulations ("Regulations"), promulgated by the Office of Foreign Assets Control ("OFAC") of the U.S. Department of the Treasury, implement the travel restrictions and other aspects of the U.S. trade embargo against Cuba.[60] With limited exceptions, U.S. citizens or permanent residents are prohibited under current U.S. law from incurring expenses related to their traveling to Cuba without first obtaining a license from OFAC.[61] Likewise, persons subject to the jurisdiction of the United States are prohibited from engaging in economic transactions in which Cuba or Cuban nationals have an interest.[62] Clearly, these and other aspects of the trade embargo would need to be removed before migration to Cuba of U.S. based retirees is possible. Lifting the trade embargo would require either a change in current U.S. policy toward Cuba, or dramatic political changes in the island.[63]

Allowing Payment of Social Security Benefits to U.S. Citizens and Permanent Residents in Cuba

As noted above, current U.S. law prohibits making cross-border payments of social security benefits to any person residing in Cuba. As a result, many U.S. based persons who would otherwise consider retiring

---

58. Art. 34 of the current Cuban Constitution declares that aliens residing in Cuba "are in parity with Cubans with respect to: the protection of their persons and property; the enjoyment of the rights and the fulfillment of the duties established in this Constitution, subject to the conditions and limitations established by law; in the duty to abide by the Constitution and the laws; in the obligation to finance public expenditures in the manner and amount established by law; and in the consent to the jurisdiction and decisions of the courts and the public officials of the Republic." 1992 CONSTITUTION, *supra*, Art. 34. Missing from this declaration is what was included in the counterpart provision of the pre-Revolution 1940 Constitution, which also contained the following language: "With regard to the enjoyment of civil rights, under the conditions and within the limitations prescribed by law." 1940 CONSTITUTION, *supra*, Art. 19. Indeed, civil right protections, including protection of the foreigners' assets against unlawful taking by the State, must be expressly protected by the Cuban laws in order for foreign nationals to feel that they can retire in Cuba without risk of adverse action against them by the Cuban State.

59. A detailed discussion of the U.S. trade embargo against Cuba is beyond the scope of this paper. For such a discussion see, *e.g.*, LAWS AND LEGAL SYSTEM, *supra*, Chapter 2.

60. 31 C.F.R. Part 515 contains most of the regulations that implement the U.S. trade embargo against Cuba.

61. 31 C.F.R. § 515.560.

62. 31 C.F.R. § 515.201.

63. The Cuban Liberty and Democratic Solidarity (LIBERTAD) Act of 1996," Pub. L. No. 104-114, 110 Stat. 785, *codified as 22 U.S.C. Chapter 69A*, also known as the "Helms-Burton Law," codified the trade embargo provisions that were in place as of March 1, 1996 and made the lifting of the embargo and the provision of aid to the Cuban people dependant, *inter alia*, on the establishment of a democratic government in the island. See generally, Jorge Pérez-López and Matias Travieso-Díaz, *The Helms-Burton Law and Its Antidotes: A Classic Standoff*, 7 SW J. L.& Trade Amer. 95 (2000).

in Cuba may decide not to do so for fear of losing their social security pensions. Therefore, once appropriate conditions arise in Cuba, one of the first steps the U.S. should take—should it desire to cooperate with Cuba's effort to transform itself into a retirement haven—is to repeal such restrictions on cross-border social security payments into Cuba.

Entering into a Totalization Agreement with Cuba

A problem related to, but independent of, the current U.S. restrictions on cross-border social security payments into Cuba, is the rule that cuts off the right of U.S. permanent residents to have their social security payments mailed to them outside the country once they have been abroad for a period longer than six months.[64] However, the six months rule does not apply if the U.S. permanent resident is present in a country with which the United States has a totalization agreement.[65]

It is unlikely, however, that the United States will base its decision to enter into a totalization agreement with Cuba solely out of a desire to allow U.S. permanent residents to continue receiving their social security payments while present in Cuba beyond the six month period.[66] Instead, the process that might

move the U.S. to consider signing a totalization agreement with Cuba will have to address the many issues that will arise with the increase of commercial ties and cross-border movement of people between the two countries.[67] Perhaps illustrative of the United States' measured approach to totalization agreements—and despite the vast number of countries with which the U.S. has commercial relations— is the fact that the U.S. to date has signed only twenty totalization agreements.[68]

Entering into Tax Treaty with Cuba

Unlike the rather limited number of totalization agreements to which it is a party, the United States is a signatory to over fifty international treaties for the elimination of double taxation.[69] As discussed earlier, one of the primary purposes of tax treaties is to coordinate the application of the parties' tax systems in order to avoid needless impediments to cross-border investments and transactions.[70] Tax treaties accomplish this result by allocating the right to tax between the country where the income arises (the source country) and the country where the income recipient resides (the residence country).[71] Typically, the country giving up the right to tax a given item of income

---

64. See 42 U.S.C. § 402(t); 20 C.F.R. 404.460.

65. *Id.*

66. After all, that a U.S-Cuba totalization agreement would ultimately vitiate the impact of the six months rule with respect to U.S. permanent residents retiring in Cuba is only a byproduct of what totalization agreements generally seek to accomplish.

67. Because the primary purpose of a totalization agreement is to ameliorate the inequities that result when a worker divides his/her working life between two or more countries, the United States will likely not perceive a need for a U.S.-Cuba totalization agreement until the countries have reached some critical mass of workers dividing their working life between the two countries.

68. See *The Social Security's Office of International Programs*, *available online at* http://www.ssa.gov/international/inter_intro.html#International_Agreements. The countries with which the United States has a totalization agreement are the following: Australia, Austria, Belgium, Canada, Chile, Finland, France, Germany, Greece, Ireland, Italy, South Korea, Luxembourg, Netherlands, Norway, Portugal, Spain, Sweden, Switzerland, and the United Kingdom. Additionally, the U.S. and Mexico are currently negotiating a totalization agreement. See Jonathan Wiseman, *U.S. Social Security May Reach to Mexico*, WASHINGTON POST, December 19, 2002, at A01.

69. Among the countries with which the U.S. has signed international tax treaties are: Australia, Austria, Barbados, Belgium, Canada, The People's Republic of China, Cyprus, Czech Republic, Denmark, Egypt, Estonia, Finland, France, Germany, Greece, Hungary, Iceland, India, Indonesia, Ireland, Israel, Italy, Jamaica, Japan, Kazakhstan, South Korea, Latvia, Lithuania, Luxembourg, Mexico, Morocco, Netherlands, New Zealand, Norway, Pakistan, Philippines, Poland, Portugal, Romania, Russia, Slovak Republic, South Africa, Spain, Sweden, Switzerland, Thailand, Trinidad & Tobago, Tunisia, Turkey, Ukraine, United Kingdom, and Venezuela.

70. See Daniel M. Berman, *Tax Treaties—Fundamentals*, Practicing Law Institute, October-November 2002 (551 PLI/Tax 353), 357-362.

71. Id.

will do so by granting the taxpayer a tax credit for the foreign taxes paid to the other country.

The decision of a country to forego taxation of revenue originating from abroad does not necessarily mean a net economic loss to that country. Such a decision is premised on the expectation that the tax revenues that are given up will be more than offset by the economic benefits resulting over time from the retiree's moving to the country, despite the immediate loss of revenue. The negotiation of a tax treaty between the United States and Cuba would benefit Cuba and the foreign retiree if either (1) the retiree's obligation to pay U.S. income taxes is waived and Cuba's income tax rate is lower than that of the United States, or (2) if the retiree's obligation to pay U.S. income taxes is retained and Cuba waives application of its own income tax to retirees out of an expectation that doing so will reap greater benefits in terms of a greater flow of retiree income into the country than the loss of revenues that results from waiving the Cuban income tax.

Most tax treaties contain provisions that address a wide range of sources of income, including personal services income, interest income, royalty and rental income, portfolio income, social security income, and more.[72] Although domestic tax laws provide the basic rules for the treatment of these items of income, tax treaties supplement the domestic source rules and delineate the allocation of taxing authority over given income items subject to competing jurisdictional claims.

Of the numerous treaty provisions, arguably the most important one for retirees is the one governing the treatment of social security benefit payments. Therefore, it is on this issue that a future Cuban government might want to focus its tax treaty negotiations with the U.S. Present U.S. tax treaty policy calls for exclusive source-based taxation of social security payments.[73] Because the Internal Revenue Code classifies social security payments as U.S.-source,[74] this means that the U.S. government retains the sole right to tax an individual's social security benefit payments even when mailed abroad.[75] Current U.S. law imposes a tax on 85% of an individual's social security benefit payments.[76] Thus, assuming that a U.S. person retires in Mexico[77] and continues receiving monthly U.S. social security benefit payments in the amount of $1,000, the U.S. will impose a tax on $850 of his monthly benefits.[78]

Although the vast majority of U.S. tax treaties retain the exclusive source-based taxation rule for cross-border social security payments, the treaties with Canada, Egypt, Germany, Italy, Japan, Britain, and Ireland provide for exclusive residence-based taxation.[79] This means that the U.S. has given up its right to tax social security payments sent to individuals residing

---

72. There are three major model treaties that are used as reference points during treaty negotiations. (1) The OECD Model Tax Treaty is relied upon heavily in negotiations between developed countries. (2) In 1996, the United States unveiled the U.S. Model Tax Treaty that is very similar to the OECD treaty but contains some additional provisions. Since 1996, the U.S. has relied heavily on the U.S. Model Treaty in conducting tax treaty negotiations. (3) The UN Model Tax Treaty was developed as a reference point for negotiations between developed and developing countries, and therefore some of its provisions are tilted toward higher levels of taxation by source countries. See Daniel M. Berman, *Tax Treaties—Fundamentals*, Practicing Law Institute, October-November 2002 (551 PLI/Tax 353), 379-380.

73. See Cynthia Blum, *Should The Government That Pays Social Security Benefits Across Borders Also Tax Such Benefits?*, 18 Va. Tax Rev. 621, 645-646 (1999) [hereinafter "BLUM"].

74. I.R.C. § 861(a)(8).

75. See BLUM, *supra* at 645-646.

76. *Id.* at 631-636.

77. *Id.* at 639-640.

78. If the person receiving U.S. social security benefits happens to be a non-resident alien, then a 30% withholding tax will be applied to 85% of the social security benefit, for an effective tax rate of 25.5%.

79. See BLUM, *supra*, note 39 at 641-644.

in one of these countries.[80] This arrangement effectively leaves it up to the residence jurisdiction to decide whether, and if so how much, to tax U.S. social security payments. Furthermore, some tax treaties—such as the U.S.-Israeli and U.S.-Romanian tax treaties—go one step further and bar taxation of social security benefits by either the source or residence country.[81]

Despite the United States' general tax treaty policy of retaining the right to tax cross-border social security benefit payments at their source, the treaties mentioned in the paragraph above are examples of foreign countries that succeeded in obtaining concessions from the United States with respect to its tax treatment of cross-border social security benefits paid to their residents and provide potentially useful precedents for Cuba.[82] Should the United States be interested in assisting Cuba in developing into a retirement haven, it would do well by granting Cuba exclusive, residence-based taxation authority over cross-border U.S. social security benefits mailed to retirees living in Cuba. That way, Cuba can control the level of tax, if any, imposed on such receipts, and thereby signal to retirees the island's favorable treatment of social security benefits.

Extending Medicare Benefits to U.S. Nationals and Permanent Residents who Retire in Cuba

The availability of affordable, high quality health care is a major concern of individuals reaching retirement age, but it is especially of concern to those contemplating retirement abroad.[83] Unfortunately, ever since its inception, and unlike the Social Security program, Medicare has linked eligibility for health care benefits to the beneficiary's physical presence in the United States.[84] Therefore, even though individuals have contributed to the Medicare fund through payroll taxes throughout their working lives, subject to a few very narrow exceptions, the Medicare program is forbidden by law from covering any health care expenses incurred while traveling or living overseas. This Medicare foreign exclusion rule could create an obstacle to Cuba's development into a retirement haven for U.S. persons.[85]

Americans of retirement age view Medicare as a form of entitlement. Even though some might also be covered by HMOs or Medigap policies, the coverage provided by Medicare is real. Many Americans—especially those of relatively limited means—might not be willing or able to forego Medicare coverage for the sake of retiring abroad, unless the host country is capable of meeting the health care needs of its retirees with quality, low cost services.

---

80. Although most tax treaties contain a savings clause that allow a country to reserve the right to tax all of its citizens and residents equally regardless of whether they happen to be residents of another country as well, the tax treaties with Egypt, Germany, Italy, Japan, Britain, and Ireland contain exceptions to the savings clause. In other words, a U.S. citizen who becomes a resident of one of these countries could effectively avoid U.S. taxation of their social security benefit payments.

81. BLUM, *supra*, at 641-643 (1999).

82. See BLUM, supra, at 655-656 and footnote 129 (1999) (noting that the favorable social security provision in the U.S.-Ireland Tax Treaty owed a great deal to the aggressive lobbying of Irish recipients of U.S. social security payments; since the U.S. "is a popular destination for Irish emigrants, but many return to Ireland on retirement and receive social security benefits.")

83. For an example, see the frequently asked questions (FAQ) section of the Association of Americans Resident Overseas' web site, *available online at* http://www.aaro.org/faq.html.

84. For an excellent detailed account of the Medicare foreign exclusion, please see James R. Whitman, *Venturing Out Beyond the Great Wall of Medicare: A Proposal to Provide Medicare Coverage Outside the United States*, 8 Elder L.J. 181 (2000).

85. Since Medicare coverage is based on the principle of territoriality, individuals who retire abroad would have to travel back to the United States to receive medical treatment that would be covered by Medicare. Although it is theoretically possible for retiree's to hop an a plane to Florida (the nearest U.S. state to Cuba) every time they want their medical treatment to be covered by Medicare, this may well prove impractical and outweigh other benefits of retiring in Cuba.

A post-transition Cuba could be particularly well suited to emerge as a high-quality and comparatively low-cost provider of medical services. [86] Assuming this observation holds true, it is unlikely that Cuba would want to bear single-handedly the added financial burden of providing medical care to foreign retirees despite the existence of sufficient medical infrastructure and trained personnel. [87]

Thus, although it is perhaps safe to assume that health care will remain more affordable in Cuba than in the United States, it is not at all clear that the cost-savings will mean much to foreign retirees if the lack of Medicare coverage for services received in Cuba forces them to incur substantial out-of-pocket expenses for their health care.

Foreign retirees might be able to purchase private health insurance with coverage in Cuba, but the attractiveness of Cuba in this regard as a retirement haven will then hinge on the specific economics of each prospective retiree's medical insurance situation. Thus, absent Medicare coverage, it is unlikely that foreign retirees unable to afford private health insurance would find Cuba an attractive retirement haven when they will have to pay out-of-pocket for medical care. In the alternative, if retirees were to contemplate returning to the United States to receive health care services that would be covered by Medicare, this would result in additional travel costs, also making Cuba economically less attractive. Therefore, a significant number of retirees from the United States who rely on Medicare coverage for their health-care needs—and who would otherwise consider retiring in Cuba—might quickly experience a change of heart once they discover that Medicare coverage stops at the border.

The most obvious solution to the problem would be to lobby Congress to amend the Medicare statute[88] by repealing the foreign exclusion vis-à-vis Cuba. However, absent a broader public policy goal, it is unlikely that Congress would repeal the Medicare foreign exclusion solely for Cuba's benefit, particularly since such a measure would elicit an adverse reaction from many other potential foreign retirement locations, such as Mexico and the Central American countries.

There is at least one potential policy argument for why Congress might eventually want to re-evaluate the Medicare foreign exclusion, at least with respect to Cuba.[89] By the year 2010, when U.S. baby boomers start entering retirement in large numbers, the number of workers per Medicare beneficiary in the U.S. is projected to start to decline from 3.8 in 1997 to 2.2 by 2030.[90] This projected decrease in payroll contributions, with a concomitant increase in Medicare outlays, is likely to place an enormous strain on the Medicare system. As a result, these events might very well lead Congress to devise alternative or supplemental funding sources or methods to address these problems.

One way to address the looming Medicare problem is to allow Medicare to reimburse health care providers in Cuba for medical services rendered to Medicare recipients on the island. Assuming that quality health-care in Cuba will be provided at a lower cost than in the United States, such a move could argu-

---

86. As noted earlier, Cuba has been for some time in the business of actively promoting "medical tourism," whereby foreign patients travel to Cuba to receive medical treatment at internationally competitive rates. See n. 22, *supra; see also* MEDICARE, *supra,* ASCE-11 at 186.

87. For an article discussing the tremendous financial burden imposed on Central and South Florida hospitals by uninsured foreign nationals, see Alfonso Chardy, *Foreign Visitors Burden Hospitals*, The Miami Herald, January 8, 2003 (quoting a Florida Hospital Association Survey that found that "among the many challenges facing hospitals, providing healthcare services to uninsured non-US citizens is placing an additional burden on already limited financial resources" . . . and that those hospitals who participated in the study reported spending over $40 million in treating uninsured foreign nationals).

88. Actually, the Medicare program was created through a series of amendments to the Social Security Act in 1965. See Social Security Amendments of 1965, Pub. L. No. 89-97.

89. See MEDICARE, *supra.*

90. *Id.* at 186.

ably result in reduced Medicare outlays for retirees who choose to retire and seek medical care in Cuba—thereby ameliorating the projected strain on the Medicare program.[91] Apart from potential political and legal challenges from U.S. health care providers and other foreign countries, the main difficulty with this approach is proving to Medicare that the quality of care available in Cuba meets U.S. standards.[92]

CONCLUSIONS

Cuba's long-term prospects of becoming a retirement haven appear to be high, provided that there is the political will to make the necessary legal changes and financial investments by the country.[93] Some of the changes will be relatively easy to implement, such as enacting retirement-friendly legislation. Others will be potentially costly (such as establishing retirement communities) and require a cost-benefit analysis given the competing claims for limited financial resources that will be available to a Cuban transition government. Still, other changes will require the co-operation of the governments of foreign countries, including but not limited to the United States.

Despite the difficulties, the potential benefits of having many thousands of foreign nationals settle in Cuba and bring their assets and retirement income into the country appear to make considerable economic sense. [94] In addition, foreign retiree settlement in Cuba may have incidental social stabilization benefits. Therefore, the authors recommend that once Cuba returns to a free-market economic system and political relations with the United States improve, a program be instituted along the lines suggested in this paper.

---

91. Id.

92. *Id.* at 190-93.

93. It can be argued that development of programs to foster foreign retirement in Cuba may be a misallocation of Cuba's scarce financial and human resources, and that encouraging foreigners to retire in the country may create domestic discontent due to the perceived inequality between the standard of living and facilities and services available to foreign retirees (e. g., adequate housing) and the inferior living conditions of the general population. However, any program that is implemented to draw upon foreign resources to promote economic development (such as promoting foreign investment) is likely to be subject to the same criticism, and yet foreign investment is courted by the Cuban Government today and is widely recognized as an indispensable ingredient in the economic reconstruction of the country. See generally, LAWS AND LEGAL SYSTEM, *supra*, Chapter 5.

94. While reported figures vary, as many as 50,000 Americans have retired in Costa Rica. See, http://www.time.com/time/archive/preview/from_redirect/0,10987,1101001211-90593,00.html; http://www.realtor.org/intlprof.nsf/469d23f47d4701f786256811004ee3cd/a1d22a3c4d6eeba0862568100067d03d

LOS DERECHOS HUMANOS EN CUBA

Ricardo Bofill

El Movimiento pro Democracia y Derechos Humanos de Cuba ha llegado a los veintisiete años de existencia. Durante todo este tiempo hemos estado bregando, a cara descubierta y a voz en cuello, a favor del respeto integral de las libertades ciudadanas. Este activismo también ha incluído la defensa del tránsito, de un orden estalinista, a un estado de derecho fundamentado en la herencia de la civilización occidental.

Como era de esperar, Fidel Castro ha respondido a nuestra labor de resistencia y, de desobediencia civil frente a la ignomia del totalitarismo, con todo un arsenal de armamentos diseñados para la guerra sucia y, para la extorsión criminal, llevadas hasta el paroxismo.

Desde las conspiraciones, como lo fueron las dirigidas al exterminio físico de varios opositores civiles, entre los que están los casos de Aramís Taboada, Sebastián Arcos Bergnes, Diosdado Amelo Rodríguez y Dámaso Aquino del Pino; incluyendo la organización de escenarios proclives al linchamiento de intelectuales contestarios por parte de turbas de gamberros, como ocurrió con la poetisa María Elena Cruz Varela; hasta el regodeo con la perversidad del encarcelamiento y, el sometimiento a condiciones de vida infrahumanas, contra cientos de librepensadores que, eran y son, inocentes de cometer el mas leve delito real.

Sin embargo, todas estas acciones, incubadas en la soberbia, el odio y la ira desenfrenadas de Fidel Castro contra los integrantes de las organizaciones oposicionistas, de derechos humanos y de la nueva sociedad civil independiente, han tenido que enfrentar la más humillante de las derrotas en el campo de la batalla de las ideas. Esta realidad ha sido posible, porque nuestra disidencia no solo no ha podido ser aniquilada, sino que se ha multiplicado por miles. Así lo demuestran , los adherentes a los proyectos Varela, de la Asamblea para una Sociedad Civil, el Movimiento Todos Unidos, el periodismo independiente, el sindicalismo emancipado y, a otras múltiples manifestaciones de que, el castrismo, ya se encuentra en el basurero de la historia.

Tampoco Fidel Castro escarmienta con las derrotas que ha debido enfrentar, al emplear la modalidad de las campañas de desinformación, difamación y pretendidos linchamientos morales, llevadas a cabo por las maquinarias de agitación y propaganda de los comisarios comunistas de La Habana, contra diversos sectores disidentes, como aconteció desde los años sesenta con la microfracción; se recrudeció con tintes fascistas en 1977 contra la Dra. Marta Frayde y, en 1988, contra el Comité Cubano Pro Derechos Humanos, y ahora pretenden reeditar con dos libelos, de puro estilo dirigido al burdo chantaje gangsteril.

Todas estas fascetas del padillerismo criminal de Fidel Castro, que pudieron ser relativamente efectivas en el terreno de la lucha armada, en estas esferas de las confrontaciones del pensamiento, inspirado en la defensa integral de los Derechos Humanos, que ha propiciado la oposición civilista cubana, se han convertido en un instrumento extraordinariamente efectivo para dejar al desnudo y así, reducir de manera muy considerable la impunidad de que en otras épocas disfrutó el castrismo, en relación a sus fechorías políticas . De manera particular en Europa y, ante los sectores de la izquierda ilustrada de Estados Unidos y de América Latina, en los que poseía no pocos adeptos.

El nuevo presidio político cubano de hoy es heredero directo de las tradiciones de resistencia infinita y, de la lucha constante por la democracia en Cuba que, a partir del año 1959, existió entre la vanguardia de los prisioneros políticos cubanos, en especial en aquellos sectores de entre los opositores encarcelados que, jamás, aceptaron los llamados "planes de rehabilitación" y, de manera muy especial, en el segmento de los defensores de la Cuba Republicana que adoptaron la postura de "Plantados Hasta la Libertad de Cuba."

El ejemplo de esta minoría selecta de entre el pueblo cubano representó a la parte de la sociedad que nunca pudo ser vencida por el terror estalinista del castrismo. Precisamente, de esos estamentos de avanzada que, a pesar del salvajismo pandillero y de las atrocidades de los sicarios de Castro, que asesinaron mediante los paredones de fusilamiento a una parte considerable de la flor y nata de esos luchadores por las libertades ciudadanas, sin embargo, de esos paradigmas del sentido de misión, aunque ello fuera, al decir de Armando Valladares, "Contra Toda Esperanza," de que el triunfo pudiera esta cercano, surgió dentro del presidio político cubano, la iniacitiva principe para la organización del movimiento pro derechos humanos y democracia de Cuba, que se fundó en 1976.

La promoción de los valores relacionados con el ideal de los derechos humanos y, las denuncias de las atrocidades sistemáticas que Fidel Castro lleva a cabo contra estos fueros inalienables a todo ser humano, se convirtieron para nosotros en una vía civilista para coadyuvar al desmantelamiento total del modelo de tiranía totalitaria, impuesto por los comisarios de La Habana.

Cuando, junto a la Dra. Marta Frayde, concebimos los primeros proyectos de acción del Comité Cubano Pro Derechos Humanos, en momento alguno de nuestras proyecciones estuvo la del "adecentamiento," mediante las reformas de algunos de los peores aspectos del castrismo, para intentar la búsqueda de la continuidad de los patrones marxistas, en ninguna de sus variantes.

Nosotros teníamos la convicción en aquellos momentos iniciales, como la proseguimos teniendo de manera reforzada en la actualidad, de que el marxismo-leninismo, el marxismo, el castrismo y, los demás engendros diseñados para camuflar las ansías frenéticas de control absoluto y de perpetuación en los poderes públicos de los tiranos y, de los aspirantes a serlo, representan la negación total de las esencias fundamentales de la Declaración Universal de Derechos Humanos y, de todos los tratados complementarios que, en nuestro tiempo, conforman las nuevas reglas del "Derecho Humanitario Internacional."

Sabemos que existen diversas agrupaciones de la actual disidencia cubana que poseen múltiples interpretaciones en torno a estas ideas. En tal sentido, somos respetuosos de la libertad de opinión de todo individuo y de los programas de cada una de las entidades políticas y sociales del país. No obstante, también siempre estamos dispuestos para el debate lúcido, que esté inspirado en la apertura de nuevos rumbos hacia la luz.

DEALING WITH THE PAST: THE ROLE OF TRUTH IN NATIONAL RECONCILIATION

Armando M. Lago and María C. Werlau[1]

The three key components of a national reconciliation process are truth, justice, and reconciliation. History has shown that *all three* should be properly addressed for a transition from a repressive regime to take place successfully, that is, in a way that allows society to heal and integrate a painful past in a productive manner.

The Cuban process, we believe, is inevitable and will hopefully begin sooner rather than later. Whether it's tomorrow, next year, or 5-10 years from now, the Cuban people will, in an open society, no doubt have to confront the violence, loss, and trauma of the last half-century. Cuba is not there yet. Until the time for a transition process begins, we can only lay foundations to undertake then each of these three challenges responsibly.

In the last 25 years, there have been at least twenty processes worldwide generally known as Truth and Justice or Truth and Reconciliation Commissions. This trend began in the early 1980s in Argentina after the end of its military rule and extended to Uruguay, Chad, Brazil, Chile, El Salvador, Guatemala, Germany, South Africa, and so on. There is a definitive movement of growing international awareness of the value, need, and use of this tool to face the challenges of transition from violent dictatorships to democracy, which is also a worldwide trend. This has

generated a wealth of experience in facing the past, ample and lively intellectual debate regarding all its aspects—intellectual, psychological and practical—and vivid awareness of the huge individual and collective challenges that this process implies. This lets us draw from a vast literature and practical know-how that will one day help us face our unique history and develop our own path to overcoming what many believe to be the darkest chapter of our national history.

On this occasion, we will deal briefly with the issue of truth. Due to a series of events we cannot relate here, in 1998 the authors embarked on a partnership of common purpose with this project, which we came to call *Truth Recovery Archive on Cuba* (T.R.A.C.). Over time, a handful of supporters have believed in this work, but our resources are minimal and the work is entirely voluntary. What really sustains this project is the conviction that uncovering the truth is not only necessary, but, importantly, constitutes a debt with those who've lost their lives and their loved ones. In addition it is essential to present and future generations.

Despite tremendous challenges, for six years one of the authors (Armando Lago) has worked line by line, page by page, composing a volume of over 1,000 pages drawn from a massive bibliography that cross-

---

1. The presentation of the paper was made by María C. Werlau. The paper borrows heavily from remarks delivered at the conference "The State, Justice and the Rule of Law in Cuba on the Centennial of the First Republican Constitution," hosted by St. Thomas University, Miami, May 11-12, 2001.

references and pulls together thousands of sources to give a name and a story to the victims of the political process we know as the Cuban Revolution. This work is to be published in a forthcoming volume titled *The Human Cost of Social Revolution: The Black Book of Cuban Communism*. His research is the starting point for the other aspects of this project, which: 1) seeks to organize the assembled information in a database and other useful ways in order to disseminate it through a website, reports, documentaries, and other forms; and 2) attempts to create an archive to expand on each documented case by gathering evidence, pictures, testimonies, etc., to tell each story as fully as possible.

The scope of the project is the loss of life attributed to political-military causes from Batista's March 10, 1952 coup d'etat onwards. It encompasses actions taking place inside or outside the island and affecting Cubans and non-Cubans alike. Abundant sources have been used for this research: existing lists, press reports, prison memoirs, personal testimonies, and others. Each name is documented with the source of the information.

Tables 1 and 2 provide a few snapshots into this groundbreaking work. In addition to the 102,794 victims of the Castro Regime (Table 1), we have documentation of 191 extra-judicial assassinations committed by anti-Castro groups or individuals and 2,739 losses by Castro forces in combat at Escambray and Bay of Pigs and in infiltration raids. These numbers, however, do not include work that has not been done yet—deaths of foreign nationals resulting from international incursions, sabotage, or support for subversion outside of Cuba, sponsored and/or funded by Cuba or with Cuban participation. If we are ever able to embark on documenting this, numbers will total in the thousands in Central and South America alone, not to mention Africa.

In addition, we have documented 2,741 reported deaths for the Batista period (from Batista's March 10, 1952 coup d'etat to Castro's takeover on January 1, 1959). Of these, 1,807 deaths were caused by Batista's forces and 912 deaths by revolutionary elements. The Appendix provides more detail on these

Table 1. Victims of the Castro Regime (post-1958 period) Documented to Date (figures as of August 2003)

Firing squad executions	5,519
Extra-judicial assassinations	1,149
Deaths in prison	1,178
Missing and disappeared	189
Assassinated in exit attempts	172
Sub-total	**8,207**
Combat deaths (Escambray & Bay of Pigs)	2,707
Combat deaths (infiltration raids)	35
Cuban soldiers killed in internationalist wars	14,031
Sub-total	16,773
"Balseros" (high end of estimated range)	77,814
Total	**102,794**

Table 2. Victims of the Batista period (1952-58)

	Deaths caused by Batista forces	Deaths caused by Revolutionaries
1952	7	3
1953	113	34
1954	6	5
1955	19	4
1956	152	25
1957	216	146
1958	1303	708
	1816	**925**

summary figures. Actually, each case is substantiated with the name and circumstances of death.

It is important to take into account, however, that this is work in progress, and therefore the numbers change as names are added and errors corrected. Because the criteria for inclusion are quite strict and we lack access to the island for field research, we believe these numbers do not reflect the true dimension of loss of life. Just to give one example: several persons in Cuba or who have left Cuba in recent years and are familiar with the situation inside some prisons have given anecdotal accounts of prisoners who have died for lack of medical attention or have committed suicide as a result of the awful conditions they faced. Most of these victims cannot be accounted for yet for lack of adequate information. There are many other challenges with respect to the research and classification of deaths, which we cannot detail here. The reality is that until Cuba is free and this work can be done inside the island—hopefully as part of a state-sponsored effort—many of these deficiencies will not be properly addressed and corrected. And even then, the work will never be flawless, as has been seen in other countries. Although the forthcoming book by Lago is quite comprehensive, we intend to continue documenting cases as they happen or as reports and evidence of past victims surface.

WHAT ARE THE REASONS FOR OUR EFFORT?

There are several motives behind this project. First, to raise awareness—both inside Cuba and around the world—of individual and collective human suffering and of the magnitude of the Cuban tragedy, hoping to generate international pressure to help put a stop to the continued loss of life and to other human rights abuses, all with the purpose of helping bring about the end of the Castro regime. This compelling motivating factor exists independently from the desire to establish truth with the eventual goal of national reconciliation. To us, it seems logical that the path to reconciliation means that, first, we must work to end the cause of violence.

To put these numbers in the context of an experience close in time and space, the Pinochet regime in Chile has been documented officially as having killed or disappeared 3,197 people (2,095 extra-judicial executions and deaths under torture and 1,102 disappearances). Think about the worldwide condemnation of the Pinochet regime and imagine the impact the facts about the magnitude of the Cuban tragedy could have if they were better known, in particular ways—through testimony about its victims—and in a general way—by presenting information about its scale. Fidel Castro and the Cuban leadership have traveled the world with impunity, and wined and dined with figures of international prominence without shame or fear. We believe they must be held accountable. The record of their crimes is the first step to making that possible.

Second, to help, in a way, to make sense of the countless stories of loss and sacrifice and, in a small way, honor the memory of those who died seeking or defending freedom.

Third, to sensitize the Cuban people about the huge cost of this national tragedy and the importance of

resolving conflicts peacefully and democratically, so historic mistakes and injustices are not repeated. We believe that truth is the most solid foundation to embrace forgiveness and achieve true reconciliation. We count all victims—regardless of race, social or economic status, nationality or political affiliations or ideological belief. Our duty is to the facts.

LESSONS FROM OTHER EXPERIENCES

Let us very briefly address several key issues we have learned from truth and reconciliation processes worldwide. This cursory selection summarizes some of the challenges ahead of us.

Should we know and remember or should we move on?

This debate takes place in every country. There are always those who call for burying the past and focusing on building the present and the future; they regard processes to document the truth of the past as uncovering psychological wounds that are best left to heal on their own. They argue that investigating and documenting the truth brings us closer to the mindset of abuse we would rather distance ourselves from, and could even derail peace initiatives. We, of course, do not agree with this position. In fact, there seems to be a universal trend that indicates that:

> Tuth is healing—at an individual and collective level, it is psychologically restoring to victims, survivors, and society as a whole.

Knowledge and official acknowledgement of some sort are required for the healing to begin. Mental health professionals can well attest to the fact that mourning without knowledge of the facts is more painful and prolonged. Closure eases the burden of grief and helps us move forward.

Constructive remembering helps a society control the future, thus promoting reconciliation. There appears to be no solid foundation for reconciliation without a search for the facts or "the truth." (We confess, however, that to us "the truth" seems elusive, and it is particularly so in this context. We prefer to see it as "searching for, achieving and/or understanding 'as much truth' as possible." This seems to be an important distinction to keep in mind.)

Whatever the arguments, let us keep in mind that forgetting cannot be decreed.

If it is established that we ought to embark on a process that includes remembering, how do we do that?

The strategies adopted to deal with the past are necessarily shaped by the existing political and social context and should be creative while carefully thought out. Informal processes, such as the one conducted in Guatemala through the Catholic Church, have taken place, but there is growing consensus of the imperative of remembering "officially," that is, through some official body created by the government for this purpose that will create an official record.

The implications and pragmatic realities that will need to be resolved are enormous. Societies must deal not only with the practical aspects of compensating victims, but also with moral questions of whether to trade justice for truth and how to deal with informers, accomplices, and even neighbors who remained silent.

The following are just some examples of what must be dealt with:

- What defines a victim? For example, overemphasizing victims who lost their lives may underemphasize the high cost paid by their surviving family members, including violence they may have suffered directly of indirectly. Should emotional suffering be taken as a basis for compensation?

- What abuses should be taken into account? For example, South Africa's Truth and Reconciliation Commission dealt with a broad category of "gross human rights violations," while the Chilean commission dealt only with deaths and disappearances.

- Who should be appointed to carry out the process? What powers shall they have? Will they be seen as credible and impartial? If seen as biased, how will that affect the process?

All of these questions raise issues of methodology, delivery of justice, forgiveness, the successful managing of legitimate rage, addressing demands for justice and desire for revenge, political implications, role of institutions society (for example, should the Catholic Church play a role?), and so on.

How do we deal with the abusers, those who committed the crimes or gave the orders?

This involves considering remedies from blanket amnesties to trials and actual convictions of perpetrators. In order to get perpetrators to provide information, should justice be exchanged for truth?

Who gets blamed or punished—from foot soldiers to commanders—must be addressed. In East Germany, for example, the trials of border guards have provoked huge debates regarding what responsibility individuals following orders have and how should they be punished vis-à-vis the officials who directed the very system that stopped people from leaving. In Chile, after several years of amnesties granted during the transition to democracy, deals made with the Pinochet government have been overturned and perpetrators sentenced.

In the Cuban case, the length of time of some of the crimes could potentially impact how certain decisions are taken. For example, many of the executions took place up to 43 years ago. Many of the perpetrators, if still alive, are in their seventies. A sentence would mean that they would spend the rest of their lives in prison. Should a minimum sentence be applied? Should elderly or infirm people be amnestied? All of these questions will need to be addressed.

It is important to point out that there is a definite trend in world conscience, in international law—both customary and written—as well as in the actual practice of the delivery of justice worldwide, to address past wrongs, provide reparation, and bring perpetrators to justice. This permeates across a wide spectrum, from the billion-dollar settlement of German companies to compensate victims of slave labor, to the freezing and return of funds stolen by government leaders and stashed away in Swiss banks, and to the restoration to their rightful owners of art work stolen during World War II.

How do we legitimize the remembering process? How do we provide reparation?

This brings up such issues as acknowledgement, apology, compensation, expectation on the victims and survivors to cooperate and to forgive or, rather, to demand justice, sensitivity to victims and survivors from the commission members, the media, and society in general. The psychological, economic, and political implications are obvious.

How do we shape the future?

It is important for these processes to include recommendations to protect human rights and ensure political and social reform that will provide assurance that past crimes will be avoided in the future and that society will be transformed. This can be done through education programs, human rights awareness campaigns, victim support systems, and the creation of forward-looking structures.

CONCLUSION

There is considerable evidence to suggest that it is through taking control of "memory and history" that societies can develop a constructive collective memory to deal positively and successfully with periods that follow trauma and violence. It is crucial for society as a whole participate in an extensive preparation and consultative process to determine what strategy is best and carefully define the process to be undertaken. We firmly believe that only when Cuba is a free country and when Cuban society can, as a whole, participate fully in an entirely informed and open manner, that all of these questions can be resolved with fairness and over time to allow true societal healing.

The work ahead is enormous. We can begin by setting the tone for when circumstances are right, but we must recognize that this will be an imperfect process, fraught with limitations, dissatisfactions, disagreements, mishaps, and imperfections. No society has escaped that.

Finally, we believe that for this process to be healing and allow us to move forward successfully, we should prepare to courageously confront its challenges head on and address its full complexities with great attention to fairness, integrity, and, ideally, with great doses of compassion.

Appendix A. Resumen de Muertes por Causas Políticas del Período Insurreccional de la Revolución Cubana (1952-1958)[a]

	Muertes causadas por fuerzas de Batista
448	Guerrilleros muertos en combate en las campañas de las sierras (4/1956, 35/1957, 409/1958)
37	Revolucionarios y civiles muertos en bombardeos de la Fuerza Aérea (1958)
15	Guerrilleros asesinados luego de rendirse en combates, Central Macareno y otros (1958)
21	Guerrilleros prisioneros de guerra asesinados en Alegría del Pío (en 1958)
20	Prisioneros de guerra de la Expedición Corinthia asesinados por Fermín Cowley (1957)
105	Fusilamientos de campesinos colaboradores de la guerrilla (40/1956, 14/1957, 51/1958)
8	Revolucionarios muertos en combate en el Asalto al Moncada (1953)
10	Revolucionarios muertos en combate en el asalto al Cuartel Céspedes de Bayamo (1953)
60	Marineros y revolucionarios muertos en combate en la insurrección naval de Cienfuegos (1957)
25	Revolucionarios muertos en combate en el asalto a Palacio Presidencial (en 1957)
16	Revolucionarios muertos en combate en el asalto al Cuartel Goicuría (1956)
1	Asesinato de prisioneros de guerra en el cuartel Goicuría (Reynold García, 1956)
56	Asesinato de prisioneros de guerra del Moncada (1953)
15	Asesinato de prisioneros de guerra del Cuartel Céspedes de Bayamo (1953)
9	Civiles asesinados en Santiago en represalia por el asalto al Moncada (1953)
664	Asesinatos extra-judiciales (6/1952, 7/1953, 6/1954, 14/1955, 38/1956, 23/1957, 570/1958)
1	Soldados leales a Prío muertos en tiroteos en el Palacio Presidencial (1952)
12	Desapariciones de revolucionarios arrestados (2/1955, 4/1957, 6/1958)
147	Revolucionarios muertos en tiroteos urbanos durante la Huelga General (1958)
125	Revolucionarios muertos en otros tiroteos urbanos (7/1953, 2/1955, 24/1956, 33/1957, 59/1958)
12	Presos políticos asesinados en prisión (1/1954, 7/1956, 1/1957, 3/1958)
1	Muertes en prisión de revolucionarios por negligencia médica (1957)
8	Suicidios de revolucionarios bajo arresto (1/1956, 1/1957, 6/1958)
1,816	**Sub-total**
	Muertes causadas por fuerzas revolucionarias anti-Batistianas
487	Soldados muertos en combates en áreas rurales y sierras (2/1956, 33/1957, 452/1958)
96	Campesinos fusilados o ahorcados en sierras y áreas rurales (1/1956, 46/1957, 49/1958)
3	Guerrilleros muertos en accidentes de jeep en las sierras (1958)
9	Guerrilleros muertos accidentalmente por tiros escapados o tiros al aire (1958)
3	Desertores revolucionarios ejecutados en México (1956)
22	Soldados muertos en combate en el Cuartel Moncada (1953)
3	Asesinatos de soldados y enfermeros en el Hospital Saturnino Lora del Cuartel Moncada (1953)
12	Soldados y policías muertos en combates durante la Insurrección Naval de Cienfuegos (1957)
191	Asesinatos extrajudiciales (1/1952, 2/1953, 4/1954, 2/1955, 10/1956, 36/1957, 136/1958)
2	Policías muertos en tiroteo en Palacio Presidencial durante el golpe de estado (1952)
28	Muertos en bombardeos terroristas (3/1953, 1/1954, 1/1955, 1/1956, 11/1957, 11/1958)
52	Muertos en otros tiroteos urbanos (4/1953, 1/1955, 7/1956, 5/1957, 35/1958)
1	Soldados muertos en fugas de prisión (1956)
2	Desapariciones de oficiales del gobierno de Batista (1958)
11	Secuestradores y civiles muertos en actos de piratería aérea (1958)
3	Civiles muertos accidentalmente en tiroteos de fuerzas revolucionarias (Cienfuegos, 1957)
925	**Sub-total**
2,741	**Total**

a. La mayoría de las víctimas a las cuales se refiere este resumen están catalogadas por nombre y demás datos circunstanciales. El menor número que no está identificada por nombre fue reportado en informes de prensa de la época.

NUNCA MÁS: PROPUESTA PARA ESTABLECER LA COMISIÓN CUBANA DE LA VERDAD Y LA RECONCILIACIÓN NACIONAL

Rolando H. Castañeda y George Plinio Montalván[1]

La patria es dicha de todos, y dolor de todos, y cielo para todos, y no feudo o capellanía de nadie.

— José Martí

Cuba: Colón la llamó "la tierra más bella que ojos humanos han visto," para Juan Bosch era "la isla fascinante," generalmente es conocida como "la perla de las Antillas," la patria de Martí, el apóstol venerado por todos los cubanos dentro y fuera de la isla, quien soñó con una "patria de todos y para el bien de todos."

A lo largo de su historia, cubanas y cubanos han escrito páginas gloriosas por sus brillantes contribuciones e innumerables logros reconocidos mundialmente en las artes, las letras, las ciencias, la música, los deportes, en cantidad desproporcionada, considerando que se trata de un país pequeño.

La lucha con España por la independencia fue por mucho la más cruenta de todos los países latinoamericanos. Se estima que entre 300.000 y 400.000—20 por ciento de la población—perdieron la vida en una colonia cuya población era de menos de 2 millones a finales del Siglo XIX; el país y su gente fueron devastados a consecuencia de las "reconcentraciones" del capitán-general Valeriano Weyler y la "guerra total" dispuesta por Máximo Gómez. No hubo esfuerzo alguno por siquiera reconocer los crímenes ni las víctimas de ese período, sino que se consideró que "borrón y cuenta nueva" sería la mejor manera de cumplir el sueño martiano.

No hay duda que el violento nacimiento de la Cuba republicana tuvo serias consecuencias, porque—a partir de su "independencia" el 20 de mayo de 1902, pero particularmente los dos regímenes que han ejercido el poder en los últimos 50 años, el primero autoritario y el segundo totalitario—el Estado cubano ha aportado a la historia de Cuba muchas páginas de infamia, vergüenza, crímenes de lesa humanidad, torturas, terror, fusilamientos, prisión, exilio, ruptura familiar y dolor. No se trata de alegatos pérfidos ni de fantasmas, sino de un capítulo auténtico y extenso de la historia de la Cuba republicana, cuando se ha considerado enemigos a los opositores, se utiliza la violencia para eliminar las disensiones y no hay instituciones para dirimir pacíficamente las discrepancias y los desencuentros políticos, como lo demuestra el trato dado al Proyecto Varela en 2002 y 2003.

Cuba es el país latinoamericano con mayor número de prisioneros de conciencia según el Informe de Amnistía Internacional (AI) de 2003, "Cuba: ¿Medidas esenciales? Violación de derechos humanos en nombre de la seguridad." El Informe otorgó esa con-

---

1. Las opiniones expresadas son de las exclusivas responsabilidades de los autores y no reflejan sus vínculos institucionales presentes ni pasados. Una versión anterior de este trabajo, consultado con opositores residentes en Cuba, tiene fecha 21-06-02. Esta segunda versión ha sido actualizada con algunos acontecimientos recientes para ser presentada en ASCE en agosto de 2003. Como economistas consideramos que no puede haber desarrollo económico si no prevalece un clima de libertades y derechos fundamentales, tal como lo ha manifestado elocuentemente Amartya Sen (2000), el premio Nóbel de Economía de 1998.

dición a los 75 opositores pacíficos condenados en marzo de 2003, muchos de los cuales fueron sancionados a largas penas de prisión por practicar el periodismo independiente o por conceder entrevistas a medios de prensa extranjeros mediante juicios sumarísimos que se basaron en adjetivos más que en cargos legales al amparo de la Ley No. 88 de 1999, denominada "Ley de Protección de la Economía Nacional y la Independencia de Cuba" y que no se atuvieron a los estándares internacionales establecidos del debido proceso.

Igualmente, AI lamentó el fusilamiento de tres jóvenes el 11 de abril de 2003, quienes secuestraron una lancha de pasajeros que intentaron desviar hacia los Estados Unidos sin realizar actos de violencia y que se entregaron pacíficamente. Las autoridades cubanas declararon que las ejecuciones fueron en previsión de nuevos secuestros que condujeran a un éxodo masivo que hubiera provocado una confrontación militar con los Estados Unidos.

Desdichadamente, éstos no son hechos aislados, ya que en julio de 1994 se produjo el hundimiento deliberado del remolcador 13 de marzo donde murieron 41 personas, 10 de ellos menores de edad y en febrero de 1996 dos avionetas civiles fueron derribadas por aviones militares cubanos en aguas internacionales.

La transición a la democracia es inevitable en Cuba. En vista de la cruenta historia republicana del país hasta el presente, el objetivo de este ensayo es proponer el establecimiento de una Comisión Cubana de la Verdad y la Reconciliación Nacional (CCVRN), la cual facilite esa transición a la democracia, transforme la cultura política del país hacia el respeto de los derechos humanos y laborales, y siente las bases para la reconciliación y la paz social. Esto se acentúa porque con la ola de represión desatada por el régimen en 2003, la probabilidad de una transición violenta es mucho mayor (Bond, 2003, p. 129).

Algunos opinarán, con indudable razón, que conocer la verdad no es suficiente para producir reconciliación, porque es necesario hacer justicia. Pero ante la magnitud de los crímenes cometidos por el Estado, junto con el hecho de que el sistema judicial cubano es y será sumamente débil y estará politizado por va-

rios años, no será posible aplicar la justicia a todos los casos. Consideramos que conocer la verdad de lo sucedido, con base en un proceso de gran transparencia pública, es un primer paso hacia la reconciliación. De ninguna manera se excluye el proceso judicial para tratar los casos de mayor gravedad. El futuro de Cuba dependerá en gran medida de las respuestas que el Estado y la sociedad sepan dar a la tragedia vivida por todos los cubanos en carne propia.

Con base en el estudio de una serie de Comisiones de la Verdad (CV) en aproximadamente 20 países, incluyendo América Latina, Sudáfrica y Europa oriental, se presenta la justificación, los objetivos, los términos de referencia, los recursos que requiere y los costos de la CCVRN. En síntesis, se plantea lo siguiente:

- El derecho fundamental prima sobre el principio legal de la no-retroactividad. Los delitos de lesa humanidad y crímenes contra la humanidad no prescriben y no pueden, en ningún caso, ser objeto de amnistía. En consecuencia, leyes de "amnistía," "prescripción," "punto final," "obediencia debida," etc., con la pretensión del olvido y de impunidad, son actos ilegítimos de gobierno que no tienen validez alguna y además han fallado sistemática y marcadamente en los países que lo han intentado, pues una parte importante de la población no ha cerrado el capítulo del pasado.

- El derecho internacional ha decidido reiteradamente que no son admisibles las justificaciones de los gobiernos para violar generalizada y sistemáticamente los derechos humanos, incluso amenazas externas. El fin no justifica cualquier medio, y no existen valores que estén por encima de la existencia y el bienestar de la sociedad.

- La CCVRN debe investigar los crímenes de lesa humanidad cometidas por el Estado cubano, incluyendo ejecuciones, torturas y maltratos crueles y degradantes que resultaron en muerte o incapacidad permanente, uso indebido de la fuerza que haya ocasionado la muerte o incapacidad permanente, desapariciones, detención arbitraria prolongada y exilio forzado. Sus objetivos principales deben ser:

- Identificar, clarificar y reconocer públicamente los crímenes, la represión, las violaciones de los derechos humanos y los abusos del pasado (*Verdad*);

- Recomendar sanciones y condenar moralmente los hechos ocurridos y a los responsables principales y directos de las violaciones y abusos a los derechos humanos (*Justicia*);

- Promover la reconciliación nacional y reducir las tensiones y conflictos sobre el pasado que faciliten el desarrollo social futuro (*Reconciliación Nacional y Paz Social*); y

- Establecer las responsabilidades institucionales, recomendar reformas para impedir repeticiones futuras y para asegurar un orden público de seguridad, democrático y de tolerancia que garantice los derechos fundamentales de los ciudadanos y permita un desarrollo integral del país (*Cultura e instituciones políticas*).

- La CCVRN debe cubrir el período 1952 hasta el presente, es decir, las violaciones de derechos humanos y laborales cometidas en los últimos 50 años por el Estado cubano. Debe realizar una investigación especial sobre violaciones de derechos laborales cometidas en Cuba y a ciudadanos cubanos por empresas mixtas con capital extranjero.

- La CCVRN debe hacer un esfuerzo especial por establecer la "cadena de mando," es decir, identificar a los autores intelectuales y las autoridades responsables hasta el nivel más alto posible, especialmente los altos funcionarios civiles, militares y policiales; en este sentido debe recomendar a quiénes aplicar las leyes de "lustración" (depuración) para impedir la participación política de las personas estrechamente vinculadas al antiguo régimen durante determinado tiempo.

- La CCVRN debe establecerse inmediatamente al comienzo de la transición, preferiblemente por acción legislativa a fin de darle mayor representatividad o, alternativamente, por decreto ejecutivo, por un período de 15 meses, 12 para realizar la investigación detallada y 3 meses para preparar y presentar su informe, el cual debe incluir una lista de los nombres de todas y cada una de las personas halladas responsables de violaciones de derechos humanos.

- Existe abundante información pormenorizada sobre crímenes de lesa humanidad y otras violaciones de derechos humanos en poder de entidades que no son parte ni dependen del Estado cubano. Por consiguiente, los esfuerzos por destruir o hacer desaparecer la información no impedirán la investigación ni las sanciones eventuales.

- La CCVRN debe incluir un total de siete comisionados, tres de los cuales serían profesionales internacionales de gran prestigio nombrados por la Comisión Interamericana de Derechos Humanos o el Alto Comisionado de las Naciones Unidas para los Derechos Humanos.

- Todas las sesiones de la CCVRN deben ser transmitidas por radio y televisión y ser cubiertas por la prensa, a fin de imprimirle transparencia a su trabajo y que el inmenso desafío de la reconciliación a través de la verdad sea enfrentado con éxito.

- La comunidad internacional ya está dando los primeros pasos para llevar la justicia al caso de Cuba por medio de procesos judiciales, tales como los relacionados con el asesinato de los pilotos civiles de Hermanos al Rescate en 1998, la ejecución del empresario norteamericano Howard Anderson en 1961, las torturas de presos políticos por el antiguo enfermero Eriberto Mederos en el Hospital Psiquiátrico de La Habana, quien fue residente en Miami,[2] así como el recurso interpuesto en una corte de Bélgica contra el propio Fidel Castro.

El ensayo tiene tres secciones adicionales. La primera señala algunos antecedentes históricos sobre los derechos humanos y la situación actual de éstos en Cuba La segunda resume algunas consideraciones básicas sobre el establecimiento de una Comisión de la Verdad. La tercera presenta una propuesta concreta para los términos de referencia y otros aspectos importantes de la CCVRN.

ANTECEDENTES

El Siglo XX probablemente fue el más sangriento de la historia de la humanidad. Las muertes por combate en la Primera y Segunda Guerras Mundiales, las purgas en la Unión Soviética en los años 20 y 30, el "holocausto," la revolución cultural en China, las matanzas en países africanos (Ruanda) y asiáticos (Camboya), junto con las violaciones sistemáticas de los derechos humanos por parte, o con el beneplácito de estados totalitarios y autoritarios, aparentemente excedieron las de cualquier otro siglo de la historia.

Tal vez por ello, hacia finales del Siglo XX, el progresivo aislamiento internacional por las violaciones a los derechos humanos y a los convenios de la Organización de las Naciones Unidas, la lucha permanente de los activistas y de las organizaciones de derechos humanos, el desgaste generalizado por la corrupción de las instituciones y la creciente aceptación de la democracia representativa; entre otros hechos, determinaron el alejamiento político de los militares y la devolución del poder a los civiles en América Latina y Europa oriental. Así, luego de convulsionados períodos de dictaduras militares, terrorismo y represión del Estado, y de violación masiva y sistemática a los derechos humanos, las dictaduras comunistas totalitarias de Europa oriental se transformaron en democracias y estados de derecho en la década de los noventa, al igual que antes lo habían hecho los regímenes militares autoritarios de América Latina en la década de los ochenta.

Paralelamente se consideró que una mejor manera de promover una cultura sociopolítica de respeto a los derechos humanos sería a través de la constitución de "comisiones de la verdad" a fin de dar reconocimiento oficial tanto a las víctimas como a los victimarios, como un primer paso hacia la reconciliación nacional tan añorada en muchos casos. Particularmente en la

década de los noventa, se establecieron CV en más de 20 países, muchas de ellas en América Latina y el Caribe, desde Argentina, Chile y Uruguay, hasta El Salvador, Guatemala y Haití. Pero la necesidad de reconocer delitos por parte del Estado incluso alcanzó también a países como los Estados Unidos, donde si bien no se estableció una comisión como tal, se reconocieron oficialmente los abusos cometidos contra personas de origen japonés durante la Segunda Guerra Mundial, e incluso se pagaron reparaciones a algunas de las víctimas. En junio de 2001 se estableció una CV en Perú, que estuvo sesionando durante dos años, para identificar las violaciones de derechos humanos ocurridas en las décadas de los 80 y los 90, que el Estado trató de justificar por la amenaza que las acciones del Partido Comunista de Perú-Sendero Luminoso y del Movimiento Revolucionario Túpac Amaru (MRTA) representaban. Como se verá más adelante, de acuerdo con el derecho internacional, amenazas al Estado, incluso guerras y amenazas externas, no justifican la violación de derechos humanos por el Estado.

Antecedentes sobre la situación de derechos humanos en Cuba[3]

La historia de Cuba republicana, es decir, mayormente del Siglo XX, se caracteriza por períodos largos y cortos de violencia y violaciones de derechos humanos y laborales por parte del Estado, así como por grupos que actúan con impunidad, frecuentemente dirigidos por o con el beneplácito del Estado. Probablemente esta trágica historia ha sido resultado de una larga y cruenta guerra de independencia, caracterizada al final del Siglo XIX por las reconcentraciones implantadas por el último gobernador español, Valeriano Weyler, por un lado, y la "guerra total" liderada por Máximo Gómez, por el otro. Se estima que entre 1870 y 1900, la población de Cuba se redujo en alrededor de un 20%.[4] No hubo esfuerzo alguno por siquiera reconocer los crímenes ni las víctimas de ese período, sino que se consideró que "borrón y cuenta

---

2. En agosto de 2002, Eriberto Mederos fue condenado por obtener ilegalmente la ciudadanía estadounidense al ocultar su participación en lo que los fiscales calificaron como una década de tortura con electrochoques en un hospital psiquiátrico cercano a La Habana. Menos de un mes después, Mederos murió de cáncer y su condena fue anulada porque no pudo apelarla.

3. Parte de esta sección se basa en el Informe de Human Rights Watch/Américas, 1999.

nueva" sería la mejor manera de cumplir el sueño martiano de una patria "de todos y para el bien de todos." El resultado fue que la violencia perpetrada por el Estado cubano—asesinatos, ejecuciones, torturas y otros crímenes de lesa humanidad—se convirtió en elemento característico de la cultura política de Cuba, con particular severidad durante los regímenes autoritarios y totalitario encabezados por Gerardo Machado (1925-1932), Fulgencio Batista (1952-1958) y Fidel Castro (1959-presente), respectivamente. Una lógica de fines partidarios absolutos se apoderó de la política y utilizó sistemáticamente la violencia para excluir a los que disentían.

Las guerras y revoluciones parecen llevar consigo y mantienen a grupos de activistas que, al llegar la paz, persisten en vivir por la violencia en la que habían vivido durante el período de lucha. Así, el historiador inglés Hugh Thomas indica que en los primeros 30 años de la vida republicana de Cuba, bajo gobiernos liderados por ex-generales de la guerra de independencia de 1895-1898,[5] no se había creado un sistema político "creíble," dado el alto nivel de corrupción, junto con la violencia patrocinada por el Estado. Herminio Portell-Vilá se refiere al "gangsterismo político" producto de la revolución de 1933, apadrinado por Fulgencio Batista, Ramón Grau San Martín y Carlos Prío-Socarrás,[6] lo cual nos lleva precisamente hasta el año 1952 cuando Batista tomó el poder nuevamente mediante golpe de estado. Inmediatamente comenzaron actividades de resistencia y arrestos casi constantes de opositores políticos; la violencia comenzó con el asesinato del estudiante Rubén Batista (no emparentado con el dictador) en enero de 1953. La represión brutal comenzó en julio de dicho año, cuando ocurrió el asalto al Cuartel Moncada; a partir de ese momento, el Estado cubano liderado por Fulgencio Batista se constituyó en un régimen de crimi-

nales caracterizado por asesinatos y torturas bajo las órdenes de altos y notorios oficiales del ejército y del Servicio de Inteligencia Militar—SIM (por ejemplo, Alberto del Rio Chaviano, Andrés Pérez Chaumont, Manuel Lavastida, Julio Laurent y otros) y de la policía (por ejemplo, Esteban Ventura, Pilar García, Carratalá y otros). Thomas y Armando Lago estiman que hubo entre 1,800 y 2,000 muertes por violencia política entre 1952 y 1958 (Thomas, 1998, edición actualizada, p. 1044, nota #21; Lago, 2003).

Con la caída de Batista el 31 de diciembre de 1958, comenzó la era castrista. A partir de 1959, Cuba ha experimentado 43 años de permanentes abusos, situaciones de violencia y represión contra los hombres y mujeres que se han opuesto pacíficamente o han denunciado las numerosas atrocidades y violaciones a los derechos humanos, debido a la naturaleza de la dictadura totalitaria que se instaló para establecer un orden político-económico socialista en la isla.

En los años sesenta hubo una guerra civil en Cuba en la cual hubo una fuerte represión del Estado en forma de fusilamientos, traslados masivos de poblaciones campesinas, prisiones preventivas, etc.; éste es un período que requiere ser investigado en detalle para establecer lo sucedido y evitar las violaciones masivas y sistemáticas de los derechos civiles y políticos por el Estado en el futuro. En 1976 se constituyó el Comité Cubano Pro Derechos Humanos que formalizó la oposición pacífica a las violaciones a los derechos civiles y políticos por el régimen cubano.

Ello ha sido documentado con frecuencia a partir de los años sesenta por varios organismos y ONGs internacionales: además de secciones sobre Cuba en sus informes anuales, a partir del año 1961 ha habido 8 informes especiales sobre Cuba de la Comisión Interamericana de Derechos Humanos (CIDH)[7] y 6 de

---

4. El historiador Hugh Thomas indica que las muertes en Cuba "se pueden comparar con las de la Unión Soviética en la Segunda Guerra Mundial, con las de Serbia en la Primera Guerra Mundial y representan, proporcionalmente, el doble de las muertes de las guerras civiles de España y de Estados Unidos." Hugh Thomas, 1998, p. 423 (nota #36).

5. Hasta 1933 Alfredo Zayas fue el único presidente que no había sido general del ejército libertador. Véase Hugh Thomas, 1998, p. 599.

6. Herminio Portell-Vilá, 1986, pp. 617-620.

7. El primer informe especial sobre Cuba de la CIDH es el documento OEA/SER. L/VII.4, doc. 30, del 7 de noviembre de 1961.

las Naciones Unidas, así como varios de Human Rights Watch, de Amnistía Internacional, de la Organización Internacional del Trabajo, de Pax Christi y otros. A partir de 1992, la Comisión de Derechos Humanos de Naciones Unidas ha aprobado resoluciones condenatorias de Cuba todos los años, excepto 1998. Todos estos informes han sido enviados oficialmente al gobierno de Cuba. Asimismo, Cuba es el único país de América Latina que no tiene un acuerdo de cooperación con la Unión Europea, ya que la "posición común" de la UE condiciona la cooperación económica a la liberación de los presos políticos, y reformas para la promoción de la democracia y la protección de los derechos civiles y políticos.[8]

El párrafo introductorio del informe de Human Rights Watch, *La Maquinaria Represiva de Cuba*, publicado en 1999, describe en forma sucinta el Estado cubano encabezado por Fidel Castro, de la manera siguiente:

> Durante los últimos 40 años, el Gobierno de Cuba ha desarrollado una maquinaria represiva muy eficaz. La negación de los derechos civiles y políticos básicos está contemplada en la legislación cubana. En nombre de la legalidad, las fuerzas de seguridad, con ayuda de las organizaciones de masas controladas por el Estado, silencian la disidencia con duras penas de prisión, amenazas de enjuiciamiento, hostigamiento o exilio. El Gobierno cubano emplea estos instrumentos para limitar gravemente el ejercicio de los derechos humanos fundamentales a la libertad de expresión, asociación y reunión. Las condiciones en las prisiones cubanas son inhumanas y los presos políticos padecen el trato degradante y la tortura. En los últimos años, el Gobierno cubano ha añadido nuevas leyes represivas y continuado los procesamientos de disidentes no violentos mientras hace caso omiso a los llamamientos internacionales de verdadera reforma y apacigua a los dignatarios que visitan el país con la puesta en libertad ocasional de presos políticos.[9]

A diferencia del *Estado de criminales* encabezado por Batista, los informes sobre el régimen liderado por Fidel Castro muestran las características de un *Estado criminal.*

Así, mientras la legislación cubana cuenta con amplias declaraciones de derechos fundamentales, otras disposiciones otorgan al estado el poder de sancionar a las personas que intentan ejercer sus derechos civiles y políticos a la libertad de expresión, opinión, prensa, asociación y reunión. En los últimos años, en lugar de modificar la legislación para ajustarla a las normas internacionales de derechos humanos,[10] el Estado cubano ha aprobado leyes que limitan aún más los derechos fundamentales; la única excepción destacable es la restauración parcial de la libertad de culto. Elementos oficiales del Estado se han manifestado en el sentido de que toda actividad relativa a la defensa de los derechos humanos tiene como fin destruir el sistema político vigente y favorecer intereses foráneos. De ahí que estos grupos no solamente sean hostigados sistemáticamente, sino que también se les minimiza tildándolos de "contrarrevolucionarios" y "grupúsculos."

En el contexto de la "Guerra Fría" entre la Unión Soviética y los Estados Unidos, todo el que se oponía pacíficamente o era crítico de la construcción del rígido y dogmático proyecto político-económico socialista, que reñía y menospreciaba valores humanitarios fundamentales, era considerado como "enemigo de la patria." Por lo tanto, debería ser reprimido, excluido, encarcelado o desterrado sin disponer de instrumentos jurídicos para defender sus derechos, protestar, criticar, proponer y ejercer la soberanía popular. Para ello, fue preciso dividir al país de manera maniquea entre los que están con el régimen y los que no están con él ("Con la revolución todo, contra la revolución nada"). A estos últimos se les equiparó a subversivos o cómplices en "delitos de sedición," y en la larga lis-

---

8. En 1996 la UE solicitó al Estado cubano realizar la reforma de la legislación nacional en lo referente a los derechos civiles y políticos, incluido el Código Penal, la ratificación del pacto Internacional de Derechos Civiles y Políticos y poner fin al presidio político y al hostigamiento y las medidas represivas contra los opositores.

9. Human Rights Watch, 1999, p. 1.

10. Cuba suscribió la Declaración de la Cumbre Iberoamericana de Viña del Mar de 1996 donde se comprometió con la democracia, el Estado de derecho y el pluralismo político, así como con las libertades de expresión, asociación y reunión.

ta de sospechosos quedaron inscritos, automáticamente, intelectuales que tenían reservas sobre el paradigma escogido y los métodos para construirlo, así como los activistas de derechos humanos acusados de actos contra la seguridad del estado—delitos tipificados en los artículos 99 y 124 del Código Penal cubano.

La cárcel, la exclusión, la represión y el destierro, se convirtieron en una realidad diaria en Cuba que ha afectado a miles de personas en el contexto de una sociedad controlada por medio de la represión del estado. Las autoridades continúan calificando como delitos penales actividades no violentas tales como las reuniones para debatir las elecciones o la economía, las cartas al Gobierno, las informaciones periodísticas sobre acontecimientos políticos o económicos, hablar con reporteros internacionales o defender la puesta en libertad de presos políticos. La prensa oficial es sometida a una estricta censura. La Policía Nacional Revolucionaria y la Seguridad del Estado son órganos del Ministerio del Interior y las Brigadas de Acción Rápida son funcionarios vestidos de civil utilizados por el Estado para reprimir a la oposición pacífica. Estos y otros agentes del departamento de seguridad del estado se han convertido en una casta de poder con un privilegiado sistema de seguridad social (Mesa-Lago, 2003).

Las Brigadas fueron creadas por la Fiscalía General de la República en junio de 1991 con la misión de controlar cualquier signo de "manifestación contrarrevolucionaria" o descontento público. Según informaciones proporcionadas a la CIDH, sus actuaciones quedan impunes especialmente cuando violan los derechos civiles y políticos de las personas que se dedican a la promoción y protección de los derechos humanos. La modalidad más utilizada por las Brigadas son los llamados "actos de repudio", que consisten en turbas que se reúnen frente a los domicilios de los activistas de derechos humanos para lanzarles todo tipo de improperios y lemas a favor de la revolución y el gobierno.[11]

Las prácticas represivas de derechos humanos del régimen se ven reforzadas por la estructura legal e institucional del país, establecida después de 1959. El Artículo 62 de la Constitución Política de 1976 señala que: "Ninguna de las libertades reconocidas a los ciudadanos puede ser ejercida contra lo establecido en la Constitución y las leyes, ni contra la existencia y fines del Estado socialista, ni contra la decisión del pueblo cubano de construir el socialismo y el comunismo. *La infracción de este principio es punible.*" Esta última frase del artículo 62 es aplicada por las autoridades en concordancia con el Código Penal cubano, para reprimir cualquier tipo de oposición pacífica al régimen. Así el Código Penal es el fundamento de la maquinaria represiva, que criminaliza sin ningún reparo la disidencia no violenta. Está concebido para aplastar la disidencia y mantener en el poder al gobierno actual por medio de la restricción rigurosa de las libertades fundamentales.

Varias disposiciones penales castigan expresamente el ejercicio de las libertades de expresión, asociación, asamblea, movimiento y prensa, mientras que otras tienen tal imprecisión y subjetividad que ofrecen amplia discrecionalidad a los agentes de seguridad del estado para reprimir todo disentimiento de la política oficial. Así, los delitos contra la seguridad del estado que aparecen tipificados en el Código Penal y bajo los cuales son procesados y luego condenados la mayoría de activistas de derechos humanos, sindicalistas, periodistas independientes, y opositores pacíficos al régimen son: *"propaganda enemiga," "peligrosidad social," "rebelión," "desacato," "asociación ilícita," "desorden público," "sedición," "clandestinidad de impresos," "actos contra la seguridad del Estado," "difamación contra héroes y mártires," "advertencia oficial," "medidas de seguridad pre-delictivas y post-delictivas," "vínculos o relaciones con personas potencialmente peligrosas para la sociedad," "legalidad socialista," "incitación a delinquir,"* entre otras, las cuales son incompatibles con principios universales de protección de los derechos humanos.

---

11. Comisión Interamericana de Derechos Humanos, *Informe Anual 1993*, Situación de los Derechos Humanos en Cuba, Capítulo IV, OEA/Ser.L/V/II.85, Doc. 8 rev., 11 de febrero de 1994, página 415, nota 2.

Por ejemplo, el delito de "*propaganda enemiga*" está previsto en el artículo 103 del Código Penal y castiga directamente el ejercicio de la libertad de expresión y asociación al establecer una pena de uno a ocho años al que "(a) Incite contra el orden social, la solidaridad internacional o el Estado socialista, mediante la propaganda oral o escrita o en cualquier otra forma; (b) confeccione, distribuya o posea propaganda del carácter mencionado en el inciso anterior." Este mismo artículo eleva la pena al "que difunda noticias falsas o predicciones maliciosas tendientes a causar alarma o descontento en la población, o desorden público, incurre en privación de libertad de siete a quince años."

La Constitución declara explícitamente que los tribunales están "subordinados jerárquicamente a la Asamblea Nacional del Poder Popular y al Consejo de Estado," un órgano supremo del Poder Ejecutivo, y que el Consejo de Estado puede dar instrucciones a los tribunales. Esta estructura institucional compromete gravemente la independencia e imparcialidad de los tribunales En ocasiones, los jueces deciden juzgar a puerta cerrada a opositóres no violentos al Gobierno, violando el derecho a un juicio público. Además, el Gobierno permite el juicio de civiles en tribunales militares, cuya independencia e imparcialidad también están en entredicho.

La legislación cubana no sólo limita el derecho a un juicio justo, permitiendo que las más altas autoridades controlen a los tribunales y los fiscales, sino que concede amplios poderes para que los cuerpos represivos realicen arrestos sin órdenes judiciales y detenciones arbitrarias, y restringen el derecho a un abogado. Según la ley, las autoridades pueden realizar arrestos sin órdenes judiciales de cualquier persona acusada de un delito contra la seguridad del estado, tienen que mantener al acusado en detención preventiva y juzgar al sospechoso a puerta cerrada en un tribunal especial de seguridad del estado. El procedimiento penal permite a la policía y los fiscales retener e incomunicar a un sospechoso durante una semana antes de que un tribunal revise la legalidad de la detención. Esto viola claramente las normas internacionales que exigen que un tribunal revise toda detención sin dilación. De manera a aumentar las probabilidades de que los funcionarios adopten medidas contra los delitos de rebelión y sedición, que incluyen actos no violentos según la definición del Código Penal, los funcionarios que no lo hagan incurrirán en condenas de prisión de tres a ocho años por infracción de los deberes de resistencia.

Lamentablemente, los tribunales ni siquiera observan los escasos derechos al debido proceso de los acusados contenidos en la legislación. Las estrechas relaciones entre jueces, fiscales, abogados nombrados o aprobados por el estado y los órganos policiales hacen que muchos acusados tengan muy pocas esperanzas en que sus abogados puedan o vayan a hacer algo más que pedir una condena menor. Las graves deficiencias procesales del sistema legal cubano y la falta de independencia judicial violan los derechos de todos los acusados y aumentan en la práctica la posibilidad de constantes injusticias.

La situación actual de los derechos humanos en Cuba[12]

Las prácticas de derechos humanos del gobierno cubano continúan siendo arbitrarias y represivas. Cientos de opositores pacíficos siguen presos, y muchos más son sometidos a detenciones breves, arrestos domiciliarios, vigilancia, simulacros de ejecución, registros arbitrarios, expulsiones, restricción de movimientos, despidos laborales por razones políticas, amenazas y otras formas de hostigamiento. Además, las autoridades continúan encarcelando u ordenando la vigilancia de personas que no han cometido delitos, recurriendo a las leyes que penalizan el "estado peligroso" y disponen la "advertencia oficial."

Los numerosos presos políticos están sometidos a condiciones penitenciarias abusivas y sufren con frecuencia insalubridad y desnutrición, languidecen en celdas hacinadas con la conformidad de los guardias, o durante largos períodos en celdas de aislamiento, y

---

12. Esta sección se basa principalmente en el Informe Anual 2001 de Human Rights Watch/Américas sobre los derechos humanos en Cuba. También utiliza material del Informe Anual del 2000 de Reporteros sin Fronteras, versión digital, y de Amnesty International, Annual Report 2000, versión digital.

se enfrentan al abuso físico y sexual. Las autoridades penitenciarias insisten en que todos los detenidos participen en sesiones de "reeducación" política o se enfrenten a castigos. Los presos políticos que denuncian las malas condiciones carcelarias son castigados con el encierro en solitario, la restricción de las visitas o la negación de tratamiento médico. La insistencia de las autoridades en que los presos políticos trabajen sin salario y en malas condiciones viola las normas internacionales del trabajo. Las prácticas penitenciarias cubanas no se ajustan en muchos aspectos a las Reglas Mínimas de las Naciones Unidas para el Tratamiento de los Reclusos, que ofrecen las directrices más autorizadas sobre el tratamiento de presos.

Las condiciones inhumanas y las medidas punitivas adoptadas contra los presos en varios casos investigados por Human Rights Watch son tan crueles que alcanzan el grado de tortura. El tratamiento que el Estado cubano da a los presos políticos es una violación de sus obligaciones de conformidad con la Convención contra la Tortura y otros Tratos o Penas Crueles, Inhumanos o Degradantes, que Cuba ratificó el 17 de mayo de 1995. Según la Convención, los períodos prolongados de detención incomunicada de presos preventivos o condenados, las palizas y los procesamientos de presos políticos previamente juzgados cuando esas prácticas resultan en dolor o sufrimiento grave, constituyen tortura. Es más, la Convención contra la Tortura prohíbe expresamente las represalias contra las personas que denuncian las torturas.

El régimen mantiene una firme postura en contra del periodismo independiente y detiene a los reporteros periódicamente, a los que a veces procesa por "insultar" al Presidente Fidel Castro. En una declaración insólita en junio de 1998, el Ministro de Justicia Roberto Díaz Sotolongo justificó las restricciones a la disidencia, explicando que, al igual que España ha promulgado leyes para proteger de las críticas al monarca, Cuba tiene motivos para proteger a Fidel Castro de las críticas, dado que cumplía una función similar, la de "rey" de Cuba.

Cuba es actualmente el único país de la región que, al decretar que la libertad de prensa debe ser "conforme a los fines de la sociedad socialista," ejerce un control total sobre la información que llega a la población. También es el único país de la región donde se encarcela a periodistas. Para mantener este estado de hecho, las autoridades cuentan no sólo con la represión sino también con el aislamiento social de los periodistas independientes. El instrumental represivo de que dispone el gobierno varía: desde los decomisos de material y otras trabas al trabajo de los periodistas independientes, hasta su detención y condena a largas penas de prisión. El departamento de la seguridad del estado es el principal ejecutor de esta política que tiene la finalidad de "dejar" a los periodistas independientes la posibilidad de escoger entre la prisión o el destierro. Adicionalmente, se destacan el arresto y la expulsión de corresponsales extranjeros de paso en la isla y una evidente intensificación del uso de los medios oficiales como mecanismo de propaganda política.

El Estado cubano continúa su hostigamiento sistemático y la represión de los defensores de los derechos humanos. Las autoridades utilizan habitualmente la vigilancia, la intervención telefónica y la intimidación para limitar la observación independiente de las prácticas gubernamentales de derechos humanos. En algunos casos, emplean los registros arbitrarios, las expulsiones, las restricciones de movimientos, los despidos laborales por razones políticas, las amenazas y otras formas de hostigamiento contra los activistas locales.

El Estado niega el acceso al país a los observadores de derechos humanos y humanitarios internacionales. El Comité Internacional de la Cruz Roja (CICR) no ha sido autorizado a realizar visitas a las cárceles desde 1989, lo que convierte a Cuba en el único país de la región que le niega el acceso. Igual sucede con el Relator para Derechos Humanos de Naciones Unidas y desde 1995 tampoco ha permitido a Human Rights Watch enviar a ningún representante a observar las condiciones de derechos humanos en Cuba.

El 18 de marzo de 2003, el gobierno arrestó y juzgó a 75 disidentes, periodistas independientes, defensores de los derechos humanos y miembros de sindicatos independientes. Los acusados recibieron sentencias de hasta 28 años de cárcel. Como respuesta al duro golpe represivo, el más intenso sufrido por la oposición pacífica cubana en toda su historia, Human Rights Watch hizo un llamado para que se debatiera el historial de derechos humanos de Cuba en la Comisión de Derechos Humanos de las Naciones Unidas. Asimismo, el 13 de abril de 2003 el gobierno de Cuba ejecutó a tres alegados secuestradores después de juicios sumarios. Si bien los crímenes que se alega cometieron los acusados son serios y podrían ameritar un severo castigo, repugna la naturaleza sumaria de los juicios sin semblanza alguna de debido proceso y que fueron ejecutados inmediatamente después de que se les negara el proceso de apelaciones. "El ejecutar a estos hombres es, por sí, una violación a los derechos humanos y el hacerlo a menos de dos semanas de sus supuestos crímenes muestra un flagrante menosprecio del derecho a la defensa," señaló José Miguel Vivanco, Director Ejecutivo de la División de las Américas de Human Rights Watch.

CONSIDERACIONES GENERALES PARA EL ESTABLECIMIENTO DE LA CCVRN

> ¿Cuál es el camino que conduce al pleno restablecimiento del orden moral y social, violado tan bárbaramente? La convicción a la que he llegado, razonando y confrontándome … es que no se restablece completamente el orden quebrantado, si no es conjugando entre sí la justicia y el perdón. Los pilares de la paz verdadera son la justicia y esa forma particular del amor que es el perdón.

> — Su Santidad Juan Pablo II, *Mensaje para la Celebración de la Jornada Mundial de la Paz*, 1º de enero de 2002

El propósito de este ensayo es presentar un instrumento, la Comisión de la Verdad y la Reconciliación Nacional, que ha sido utilizado prácticamente en todos los continentes después de regímenes autoritarios o totalitarios, para facilitar la consolidación de la paz social y la transición, con base en la verdad y sentar las bases para la reconciliación nacional. Estas comisiones pueden tener consecuencias significativas, no sólo a corto y mediano plazo en el proceso de transición, sino también de largo plazo. Nosotros considera-

ramos que es necesario que se establezca una tan pronto comience la transición en Cuba.

¿Borrón y Cuenta Nueva? o No a la Impunidad

Con el retorno de los civiles a la conducción del estado y el establecimiento de un estado de derecho, surge el crucial debate sobre qué hacer con los responsables de las violaciones masivas y sistemáticas a los derechos civiles y políticos y de la represión. ¿Cómo reconstruir la sociedad ultrajada, cómo hacer justicia, cómo lograr la paz social y la reconciliación nacional, cómo facilitar la transición, cómo sentar las bases para un desarrollo económico integral?[13]

En primer lugar, el poder judicial que emerge de una situación totalitaria está manejado por individuos ligados al antiguo régimen y no goza de la independencia ni de los instrumentos legales necesarios para conducir investigaciones eficaces. Por ello hay que enfrentarse a la realidad de un sistema judicial que es técnicamente incapaz de llevar a cabo las investigaciones y procesos de establecimiento y divulgación de las violaciones a los derechos humanos fundamentales.

Por otra parte, generalmente los propios regímenes totalitarios y dictatoriales, antes de dejar el poder, tratan de cerrar la etapa de la historia que dirigieron y procuran bloquear o neutralizar cualquier enjuiciamiento posterior de sus actos ilegítimos de gobierno y de sus violaciones a los derechos humanos. Con la ilusión de borrar el horror de sus acciones, y con la pretensión del olvido y de la impunidad, dichos regímenes al final de sus mandatos o los gobiernos que les suceden, dictan leyes de *"Amnistía," "Prescripción," "Punto Final," "Obediencia Debida,"* etc. De esa forma pretenden ignorar que el derecho a la justicia es un derecho humano, anterior y superior a la autoridad del estado y leyes dictadas, de carácter universal, del cual depende la seguridad jurídica de las personas, el orden y la paz social. Pretenden desconocer que los delitos de lesa humanidad y crímenes contra la humanidad no prescriben y que no pueden, en ningún caso, ser objeto de amnistía.

---

13. Siguiendo al Premio Nóbel de Economía de 1998 Amartya Sen (2000), consideramos indispensable la vigencia de libertades políticas y económicas fundamentales para que pueda realizarse un verdadero proceso de desarrollo económico en Cuba.

La amnistía, con su carga moral de olvido e impunidad, no debe aplicarse a las atrocidades como desapariciones, ejecuciones y torturas. No se puede solicitar a las víctimas que renuncien a su derecho, sin exigir de los que violaron sus derechos ninguna conducta especial.

Los crímenes de lesa humanidad cometidos de manera masiva, generalizada y sistemática son violaciones de los derechos a la vida, a la integridad física y a la libertad. La tortura y la detención arbitraria prolongada, también son crímenes de lesa humanidad. Si bien toda violación de una obligación internacional hace surgir una obligación de parte del estado responsable de reparar el daño causado, cuando se trata de crímenes de lesa humanidad la obligación del estado es más amplia. No puede considerarse integral la reparación si no incluye la investigación y revelación de los hechos, un esfuerzo para procesar y castigar penal y disciplinariamente a quienes resultaren responsables, y la obligación de extirpar de los cuerpos de seguridad a quienes han cometido, ordenado o tolerado estos crímenes.

En algunos casos, el no realizar juicio a los que detentaron el poder es parte de la oferta de los movimientos políticos que pretenden suceder a los regímenes totalitarios en la conducción del país. En la práctica, "para salvar la democracia, lograr la reconciliación nacional y la paz social, facilitar la transición," se renunciaría a esta obligación. Con ello no resulta fácil eliminar las estructuras de seguridad del estado, judiciales y políticas que apoyaron a dichos regímenes, y que aún permanecen fuertes e intactas en los nuevos períodos democráticos.

No obstante, el clamor de justicia de las víctimas, sus familiares y amigos, así como la lucha de algunos periodistas, religiosos, abogados, magistrados, políticos y organizaciones de derechos humanos, han conducido a la creación de comisiones investigadoras de la verdad. Adicionalmente, está el interesante dictamen alemán.

El dictamen jurídico alemán
Durante la era comunista de la República Democrática Alemana (RDA), muchas personas recibieron la muerte por intentar salir del país, "fugarse del paraí-

so," al cruzar la frontera o saltar el infame muro. Murieron tan sólo porque querían realizar su derecho humano a salir del país. El artículo 12 de la Declaración de los Derechos Humanos en el párrafo 2 señala: "Toda persona tendrá derecho a salir libremente de cualquier país, incluso del propio." Y el párrafo 4 afirma: "Nadie podrá ser arbitrariamente privado del derecho a entrar en su propio país." La RDA consideró a su pueblo como su propiedad y lo privó de su libertad personal e inalienable.

Cayó el muro, llegó la reunificación de Alemania y con ésta el problema de cómo tratar a los autores de tales "crímenes." Ponemos la palabra crímenes entre comillas, puesto que hay debates sobre este punto. Unos dicen que los soldados sólo obedecieron órdenes y que por la ley de fuga de la RDA y por la ley de la frontera, tenían la obligación de disparar contra los que pretendían huir del país. Por esta legislación los soldados podían confiar en que sus actos eran conformes a la ley. Otros argumentaron que los soldados siempre tenían la posibilidad personal de disparar lejos de las personas, sin hacerles daño. Además, se trata de crímenes, puesto que los derechos humanos están sobre las leyes estatales.

En 1991 comenzaron los primeros procesos judiciales contra varios soldados que mataron a personas que querían refugiarse en la Alemania Federal. Desde el principio estos procesos tenían muchas dificultades jurídicas en su contra. En el Tratado de Unificación de las dos Alemanias hay un párrafo que establece que los delitos solamente se pueden procesar según las leyes de la RDA. Además, estaba el principio jurídico de la no-retroactividad, *nulla poena sine lege*. No obstante esas dos objeciones importantes y que había recursos pendientes ante la Corte Constitucional, las cortes iniciaron los procesos judiciales que tenían importancia, no sólo para sancionar a los autores, sino también como un modo de establecer lo que había pasado en los años anteriores.

Simultáneamente a los procesos contra los autores materiales e intelectuales de tales crímenes, comenzó un fuerte debate público sobre los hechos criminales, debate que aún continúa en la actualidad. Entre los procesados no solamente estaban los autores materiales directos de esos crímenes, los soldados, sino también sus oficiales, entre ellos el jefe de las tropas fronterizas, el ex ministro de defensa y su viceministro. También se realizó un proceso contra el último jefe de estado y del partido y contra otros funcionarios del partido socialista por su responsabilidad en los asesinatos del muro y de las fronteras. Los procesados apelaron a la Corte Suprema con el argumento que un principio de ley importante (la no-retroactividad) excluía estos procesos.

La Corte Constitucional en su dictamen afirmó que los asesinatos en la frontera atentaron contra el principio de la justicia y los derechos humanos; por ello se justifica el castigo a los autores de tales crímenes. El principio de la no-retroactividad de la ley no vale en este caso, puesto que existe un derecho fundamental por encima de un principio legal. Con este dictamen la Corte Constitucional adoptó una postura similar a la que prevaleció después de la Segunda Guerra Mundial en lo referente a los crímenes nazis. O sea, se puede castigar a los responsables de esos crímenes descuidando el principio de la no-retroactividad cuando la ley vigente o principios de derecho están en oposición fundamental a la justicia y a violaciones a derechos civiles y políticos primordiales.

Lo importante de esta decisión de la Corte Constitucional es que se dio una nueva interpretación al principio de la no-retroactividad: Ya no se ve ésta de manera positivista como un principio intocable y aislado, sino desde su función dentro del sistema jurídico como tal. Los jueces constitucionales afirmaron que cuando el Estado socialista, mediante algunas leyes, excluyó la punibilidad para crímenes graves, también eliminó la aplicación del principio de la no-retroactividad. Los magistrados consideraron este principio desde su función en un estado de derecho y desde una definición superior de servir a la justicia y a los derechos fundamentales del hombre.

En casos de crímenes de lesa humanidad ningún estado tiene el derecho de promulgar leyes que sirvan para violar los derechos humanos y que por el principio de la no-retroactividad garantizarían la impunidad. Un estado de derecho no es justificable dentro de sí mismo, sino solamente desde su fundamentación en el respeto de los derechos civiles y políticos y las libertades básicas. El dictamen y su fundamenta-

ción teórica también tienen un significado universal. Según este dictamen, no puede haber "leyes" que atenten contra el principio de la justicia y contra los derechos humanos. Además, las diferentes acciones jurídicas de prometer y promover la impunidad de los crímenes de lesa humanidad no se pueden justificar y hay que descalificarlas como lo que son: un atentado contra los principios fundamentales de la convivencia humana, la justicia y los derechos humanos. El derecho no debe ser un instrumento discrecional en las manos de alguna línea política. Por eso es un gran aporte a la jurisprudencia internacional, en lo que concierne a la discusión de la impunidad en Cuba.

Algunas de las leyes de "lustración" (depuración) de los países de Europa oriental, aunque tienden a poner en conocimiento de la sociedad la verdad de lo acontecido durante los regímenes comunistas, son criticables porque impusieron sanciones como la inhabilitación para ciertos puestos a los que resultaron nombrados en las listas de los antiguos servicios de inteligencia, sin darles a los sancionados oportunidad alguna para hacer sus descargos. Esto está contra del principio del debido proceso.

¿Qué es una Comisión de la Verdad (CV)?

Una CV es una entidad de investigación constituida para ayudar a una sociedad que ha enfrentado graves situaciones de represión y violación sistemática a los derechos humanos, a enfrentarse críticamente con su pasado, a fin de superar las profundas crisis y traumas generados por ellos y evitar que tales hechos se repitan en el futuro.

A través de las CV se busca investigar los hechos más graves de violaciones y abusos a los derechos humanos, establecer las responsabilidades correspondientes, proponer reparaciones a las víctimas y sus familiares, conocer las causas de la violencia, identificar a los elementos en conflicto, y sentar las bases para la reconciliación nacional, la paz social y la transición.

El trabajo de una CV permite identificar las estructuras del terror, sus ramificaciones en las diversas instancias de la sociedad (fuerzas de seguridad y paramilitares, policía política, fuerzas armadas y poder judicial), entre otros factores inmersos en la problemática. Esta investigación abre la posibilidad de reivindicar la memoria de las víctimas, proponer una política de reparación de los daños, impedir que las prácticas utilizadas en las violaciones de los derechos civiles y políticos continúen y que los que participaron sigan ejerciendo funciones públicas, ridiculizando el estado de derecho. Asimismo, la CV deberá hacer recomendaciones para establecer una nueva institucional jurídica y sus leyes fundamentales que aseguren el ejercicio de los derechos políticos y económicos básicos.

Los principales objetivos de una CV

Los principales objetivos de una CV son: (1) identificar, clarificar y reconocer públicamente los crímenes, la represión, las violaciones a los derechos humanos y los abusos del pasado; (2) contribuir a la justicia y a la responsabilidad social, identificando las prácticas y los responsables, así como proponiendo reparaciones a las víctimas y sus familiares para atender los daños infligidos; (3) promover la reconciliación nacional y reducir las tensiones y conflictos sobre el pasado que faciliten el desarrollo social futuro y el logro de la paz social; y (4) establecer las responsabilidades institucionales y legales, y recomendar reformas para impedir repeticiones futuras.

1. Identificar, clarificar y reconocer públicamente los crímenes, la represión, las violaciones a los derechos humanos y los abusos del pasado (objetivo de la Verdad).

   El Estado cubano ha negado y ocultado regularmente las violaciones masivas, generalizadas y sistemáticas de los derechos humanos (crímenes, torturas, detención de opositores, destierro forzoso, etc.), tanto nacional como internacionalmente e incluso ha pretendido legalizar algunas de estas prácticas. Es necesario establecer claramente lo sucedido. Al establecer los hechos de manera solemne y oficial, la sociedad le manifiesta a las víctimas y sus familiares que su padecimiento no ha pasado desapercibido, que se lo conoce y se lo reconoce con la intención de contribuir a evitar que se repita en el futuro.

   La reconciliación no es posible sin que al menos haya un esfuerzo importante por reconocer la verdad en cuanto al abuso de los derechos humanos y de las libertades fundamentales, cuyo castigo legal es imprescriptible.

2. Contribuir a la justicia y a la responsabilidad social (objetivo de la Justicia: Sanciones y Reparaciones).

   Si bien la justicia como tal corresponde a los tribunales y las cortes, es necesario hacer recomendaciones para sancionar y condenar moralmente los hechos ocurridos y a los responsables principales y directos de las violaciones y abusos a los derechos humanos, (tal como ser separados e inhabilitados temporal o permanentemente para ocupar cargos públicos), y hacer reparaciones a las víctimas y sus familiares. Las víctimas y sus familiares están en una situación de indefensión jurídica; y es necesario dignificarlas, restaurarle los derechos conculcados y compensarlas (repararlas) por los daños sufridos, mediante pensiones, becas a los hijos, diversas medidas de bienestar social, pensión única de reparación, atención especializada en salud, educación, vivienda, condonación de deudas y hacerles un monumento nacional conmemorativo u otras medidas simbólicas.

3. Promover la reconciliación nacional y reducir las tensiones y conflictos sobre el pasado que faciliten el desarrollo social futuro (objetivo de la Reconciliación Nacional y la Paz Social).

   La reconciliación nacional es un objetivo prioritario para cerrar un ciclo de enfrentamientos, especialmente en momentos en que un país procura encontrar soluciones negociadas. Las amnistías y otros actos de perdón y olvido por hechos menores para facilitar y promover la reconciliación nacional, la paz social y la transición son necesarios para mirar al futuro. Sin embargo, deben basarse en el reconocimiento público de los errores y el arrepentimiento por lo sucedido para tener bases sólidas.

   Dado que la responsabilidad penal es siempre personal, la reconciliación es ante todo una iniciativa de cada individuo respecto a sus semejantes. Sin embargo, la persona tiene una dimensión esencialmente social, por la cual establece una red de relaciones sociales en las que se manifiesta a sí misma. Consecuencia de ello es que la reconciliación es necesaria también en el ámbito social. Las familias, los grupos, los estados, la misma comunidad internacional, necesitan abrirse a la reconciliación para remediar las relaciones interrumpidas. La capacidad de reconciliación es básica en cualquier proyecto de una sociedad futura más justa y solidaria.

4. Establecer las responsabilidades institucionales y recomendar reformas para impedir repeticiones futuras (Objetivo de la Transición).

Las fuerzas de seguridad del estado (particularmente los funcionarios de los cuerpos de seguridad del MININT, las brigadas y los comités de barrio) deberán ser eliminadas, el sistema judicial y las leyes que deberían proteger a los ciudadanos y que fueron y siguen siendo utilizadas para reprimir, atemorizar y propiciar una cultura de desconfianza en la población, necesitan modificarse sustancialmente, a la vez que se establece un sistema de democracia representativa. Por ello, la Comisión deberá hacer recomendaciones para dificultar e impedir las violaciones y abusos sistemáticos a los derechos humanos en el futuro, así como para reconstituir y consolidar un nuevo orden moral y legal incluyente, un verdadero estado de derecho y su sistema de fiscalización, que permita la convivencia, el desarrollo social y el derecho ciudadano a disentir sin sufrir represalias por ello y las instituciones para dirimirlas.

Armonías y conflictos entre los objetivos fundamentales de una CV

Los responsables de las violaciones a los derechos humanos, así como los sectores no afectados por la violencia oficial, generalmente proponen un acuerdo político para llegar pronto a la reconciliación nacional, para reconstruir el país y facilitar la transición y la paz social. No les preocupa tanto saber la verdad de los hechos, mucho menos que se haga justicia. Desconocen que la Comisión Interamericana de Derechos Humanos en 1985, estableció que "Toda sociedad tiene el irrenunciable derecho de conocer la verdad de lo ocurrido, así como las razones y circunstancias en las que aberrantes delitos llegaron a cometerse, a fin de evitar que esos hechos vuelvan a ocurrir en el futuro."

En cambio, las víctimas, los familiares y amigos de las víctimas, los grupos de derechos humanos, y algunos sectores de la sociedad reclaman el conocimiento de la verdad y la aplicación de la justicia como pasos previos a la reconciliación nacional, la paz social y la transición. Como señaló Luis Pérez Aguirre, "Se ha dicho que hurgar en estos acontecimientos del pasado es abrir nuevamente las heridas del pasado. Nosotros nos preguntamos, por quién y cuándo se cerraron esas heridas. Ellas están abiertas y la única manera de cerrarlas será logrando una verdadera reconciliación nacional que se asiente sobre la verdad y la justicia respecto de lo sucedido. La reconciliación tiene esas mínimas y básicas condiciones."[14]

El jurista peruano Carlos Chipoco precisa que el derecho a la verdad tiene fundamentos doctrinarios jurídicos y prácticos, así como que la verdad debe ser completa, oficial, pública e imparcial. Añade que la búsqueda de la verdad es importante, por ser un deber moral hacia las víctimas, los familiares y los deudos, para descubrir y sancionar a los responsables, para afirmar la democracia y el control ciudadano de las instituciones públicas, y para evitar que las violaciones se repitan en el futuro. Chipoco sostiene que el respeto del derecho a la verdad es importante para abrir la posibilidad del perdón y la reconciliación, y para cumplir con el Derecho Internacional.[15]

El derecho a la verdad es parte de la reparación del daño ocasionado por los agentes del Estado, reparación que también debe incluir medidas de carácter

---

14. Luis Pérez Aguirre, "El Uruguay impune y la memoria social," Tribunal Permanente de los Pueblos. Sesión Uruguay, abril de 1990. Montevideo, Uruguay, pág. 31.

15. Carlos Chipoco, "El derecho a la verdad." En *Paz*, N 28, págs. 83-106, Lima, marzo de 1994. Chipoco comenta el desarrollo de esta teoría en los casos de Argentina, Chile y El Salvador.

económico, social, médico y jurídico, para reivindicar la memoria de las víctimas y aliviar en parte la tragedia ocasionada a los familiares afectados. Las reparaciones tienen profundas implicaciones éticas y políticas pues revierten el estado de indiferencia hacia las víctimas con actos públicos de solidaridad hacia ellas.

Con base de su experiencia en Chile, el médico psiquiatra Carlos Madariaga señaló que existe una confusión conceptual respecto a lo que se entiende por reparación y que generalmente las instancias gubernamentales han considerado la reparación de manera reduccionista, privilegiando las soluciones económicas, en desmedro de los aspectos jurídicos, éticos, sociopolíticos y psicosociales, hecho que ha generado fuertes sentimientos de frustración y desencanto en las víctimas y sus familiares, estados psicoemocionales que han hecho abortar en gran medida los esfuerzos de reparación.[16] Cuando se trata de violaciones que tienen carácter de crímenes de lesa humanidad, el derecho de las víctimas frente al estado no se agota en la obtención de una compensación pecuniaria, sino que requiere una *reparación integral* que incluye el derecho a la justicia y al conocimiento de la verdad.

La negociación y los acuerdos políticos condicionan a que los gobiernos de transición atiendan, en cierta medida, las exigencias de justicia y de reconciliación, prefiriendo esta última, para facilitar la reconciliación nacional, la paz social y la transición. Por eso ponen mayor énfasis en favorecer la amnistía de los violadores de los derechos humanos, volviendo a agredir así a las víctimas y sus familiares, en nombre de la reconciliación nacional, la paz social y la transición.

Las posibilidades tanto de armonía como de conflicto entre los cuatro objetivos señalados están siempre presentes y dependen en buena medida de la capacidad de acción e ingenio de los principales agentes involucrados (políticos, víctimas y sus familiares, activistas y organizaciones de derechos humanos).

En Chile después de la transición pactada hacia la democracia a fines de los años 1980 ha habido significativos acuerdos entre las coaliciones democrática y la que apoyó al gobierno militar, que han permitido al país progresar económica y políticamente en forma sostenida. Por ejemplo, en enero del 2003 se llegó a un acuerdo histórico para realizar una reforma del Estado encaminada a hacerlo más eficiente, controlar la corrupción y expandir la carrera administrativa, reduciendo sustancialmente las posiciones de designación política. Sin embargo, aún después de muchos acuerdos y casi 14 años de transición, no se ha llegado a acuerdos sobre temas que envuelven la compensación apropiada a las víctimas, concluir los procesos de verdad y justicia, etc.

¿Cómo se constituye una CV?

En algunos casos las CV surgen como un proceso legal, o formal, por designación de los gobiernos, bajo la presión de los grupos defensores de los derechos humanos, de un grupo de expertos; tal como se hizo en Argentina, Chile, El Salvador y Guatemala. En estos países, las CV se establecieron, tras exigencias masivas, por mandato legal, después de negociaciones y acuerdos políticos.

Generalmente las Comisiones surgen en vista de la probada ineficacia del poder judicial existente para sancionar las violaciones sistemáticas y los abusos a los derechos humanos. En los países sometidos a regímenes totalitarios, generalmente el poder judicial se convirtió en un apéndice del poder ejecutivo y no tenía capacidad para juzgar independientemente los crímenes de los agentes del Estado. Quienes debían velar por la justicia se hicieron cómplices del terror oficial. En varios países de la región son diversos los casos de abdicación del poder judicial ante el predominio de los gobiernos y de las fuerzas de seguridad. Por esta causa, violaciones evidentes a los derechos humanos quedaron en la más absoluta impunidad. No obstante, ahora la Corte Internacional Criminal de la Haya puede juzgar delitos de lesa humanidad cometidos después del 1 de julio del 2002.

En otros casos, las Comisiones se han establecido como producto del trabajo solidario de las organiza-

---

16. Carlos Madariaga, "La reparación por parte del Estado hacia las víctimas de la tortura." En *Reflexión*, año 7, N° 22, diciembre de 1994, págs. 9-11.

ciones de derechos humanos, que desarrollaron un esfuerzo autónomo para investigar los graves hechos de violencia oficial. Así ocurrió con el trabajo de la Archidiócesis de Sao Paulo en Brasil, que elaboró el informe *Brasil Nunca Más* bajo la dirección del Cardenal Evaristo Arns. El Comité de Iglesias para Ayudas de Emergencias en Paraguay publicó una serie de investigaciones sobre la dictadura de Stroessner en el documento *Paraguay Nunca Más*. Igualmente se ubican los esfuerzos del Servicio de Paz y Justicia de Uruguay, con su informe *Uruguay Nunca Más* y del grupo de organizaciones colombianas y extranjeras que publicaron el informe *El terrorismo de Estado en Colombia*.

Con auspicio de Naciones Unidas se crearon CV en El Salvador, Guatemala y Haití, y se financió un esfuerzo de esclarecimiento parecido en Honduras, emprendido por el Comisionado Nacional para los Derechos Humanos de ese país. Sin embargo, la CV auspiciada por Naciones Unidas en Haití no produjo ninguna información importante que no se conociera de antemano, y cometió además el grave error de mantener su propio informe en secreto durante varios meses.

Ha habido casos en donde las CV se crearon con fines encubridores, para procurar darle un respaldo a la "verdad" oficial. Así pasó con la "Comisión Uchuraccay" en el Perú en 1983, que investigó la masacre de ocho periodistas y un guía campesino que los acompañó.

Información básica para una CV

Buscar la verdad de las violaciones a los derechos humanos, cuando los acontecimientos están aún muy cercanos, implica muchos riesgos, tanto para los comisionados e investigadores, como para las víctimas, los familiares y los testigos. La sospecha injustificada de que los activistas de derechos humanos apoyan la subversión, así como el temor de que sus organizaciones cuentan con archivos con materiales relacionados con la historia de la violencia y represión policial, muchas veces llevó a las autoridades paramilitares a allanamientos de las sedes de estas organizaciones y a la detención, o "desaparición" de los activistas de derechos humanos. Esta agresión directa contra las or-

ganizaciones de derechos humanos fue una norma de casi todos los gobiernos militares en América Latina.

En Argentina, las autoridades militares, con apoyo judicial, allanaron las sedes de la Liga Argentina por los Derechos del Hombre, la Asamblea Permanente de Derechos Humanos, el Movimiento Ecuménico de Derechos Humanos, y el Centro de Estudios Legales y Sociales y detuvieron a varios de sus miembros. Las Fuerzas Armadas y policiales, en los años de las dictaduras, allanaron los locales de la Vicaría de Solidaridad de Chile, el Servicio de Paz y Justicia de Uruguay, así como de la Comisión Nacional de Derechos Humanos y Defensa de la Democracia, y la Asamblea Permanente de Derechos Humanos de Bolivia. Igualmente allanaron las sedes de la Comisión de Derechos Humanos de El Salvador, el Servicio de Paz y Justicia de Ayacucho, Perú, entre otras organizaciones. La historia de la lucha por los derechos humanos enseña que cada organización debe estar prevenida para que cuando las ataquen, sus daños se reduzcan al mínimo. Hay que mantener normas básicas de seguridad para proteger a los colaboradores y también la documentación testimonial y los archivos, conservando duplicados del material y ubicándolos en lugares en donde no sea posible que los cuerpos de seguridad los encuentren fácilmente.

En muchos casos, por el lado de las víctimas, existe abundante material documental, en forma de denuncias legales, recursos jurídicos, certificados de defunción y autopsia, testimonios ante jueces y fiscales, que también deben ser archivados por las organizaciones de derechos humanos.

El testimonio de sobrevivientes de operaciones de detención y represión, así como los informes de los testigos y familiares de las víctimas, son algunos de los recursos más valiosos para avanzar en la obtención de la verdad. Estas personas requieren una protección especial, hasta que la paz social, la reconciliación nacional y la transición se hayan consolidado. En el Perú y El Salvador, fueron numerosos los casos de testigos de violaciones de los derechos humanos que desaparecieron o fueron asesinados poco tiempo después de haber informado a la prensa o a las comisiones investigadoras oficiales.

Durante el proceso de investigación y elaboración del informe *Brasil Nunca Más*, el grupo de trabajo adoptó muchas medidas de seguridad para no dejar huellas de lo que estaban haciendo. Además de usar casas fuera de la capital del país, y de tener duplicados de los documentos, emplearon un lenguaje cifrado, codificado, en sus comunicaciones orales y escritas sólo entendible por ellos. La documentación fue microfilmada y procesada dos veces, para que una copia fuese guardada, sin riesgos, fuera del país. Se aprovechó el viaje al extranjero de personas con rango diplomático para transportar las copias microfilmadas y los recursos para el financiamiento de la investigación.

La ONUSAL apoyó a la CV en El Salvador, facilitando equipos electrónicos para la distorsión de la voz y el aislamiento de las ondas sonoras. De esa manera se protegió la identidad de los declarantes y sus testimonios. Asimismo, ante el temor de intimidación policial a los declarantes, las entrevistas se realizaron muchas veces en sedes diplomáticas o en lugares reservados, lejos de los ojos y los oídos militares.

En el ámbito oficial, las organizaciones de derechos humanos o las CV han logrado algunas veces la cooperación de los jueces y fiscales de las diversas regiones fuera de la capital, para elaborar un diagnóstico más exacto del número de víctimas de violaciones de los derechos humanos. En el Perú, por ejemplo, una Fiscalía Provincial registró documentadamente una cantidad de casos de violaciones a los derechos humanos en 1993, que casi duplicó el balance anual nacional establecido por los grupos de derechos humanos.

Aunque resulta difícil, también es posible obtener documentos confidenciales que circulan al interior de la seguridad del estado y las fuerzas armadas y policiales, en forma de órdenes, planes de acción, estrategias, doctrina y filosofía de represión interna, etc. Sus propias publicaciones (revistas, boletines, libros) son una fuente que no hay que desechar. Su vanidad les lleva a exponer allí sus puntos de vista, justificando las violaciones a los derechos humanos, e informes de los ascensos otorgados por "servicios especiales a la patria" para premiar a los ejecutores. Aunque son raros, en diversos países ha habido casos de efectivos militares y policiales que discrepan con la guerra sucia, o que tienen remordimientos de conciencia, o se

sienten traicionados por sus jefes, y que han aportado información valiosa sobre las estructuras oficiales de la represión y el terror. Sin embargo, aquí debe actuarse con suma cautela, por los riesgos de infiltración de la seguridad del estado, policial o militar en el trabajo de los grupos de derechos humanos.

A pesar de los problemas de censura, los medios de prensa diaria pueden ser una valiosa fuente de información para las investigaciones de la CV, pues ahí se registraron los partes de guerra, los casos de detenciones, las denuncias, etc. Igualmente se han encontrado valiosos datos en publicaciones gremiales de los sindicatos, las universidades, los grupos religiosos, entre otros.

También las organizaciones internacionales de reconocido prestigio, como Amnistía Internacional, Human Rights Watch y la Comisión Interamericana de Derechos Humanos, pueden aportar muy valiosa información sobre las víctimas de los abusos y los presuntos responsables, ya que los han denunciado y documentado por años. En algunos países las CV obtuvieron abundante material sobre las violaciones de los derechos humanos de las delegaciones diplomáticas. Por ejemplo, los documentos suministrados por la Embajada de Estados Unidos en San Salvador, dieron bastantes evidencias sobre los escuadrones de la muerte que actuaban con apoyo de la Agencia Central de Inteligencia (CIA) y del ejército salvadoreño en los años 80.

Las comunidades de exiliados y las organizaciones de derechos humanos dispersas por todo el mundo también conservan un importante caudal de información, en forma de cartas, boletines, recursos jurídicos y otros documentos sobre casos de violaciones a los derechos humanos que se conocen muy poco dentro del país.

Principales lecciones aprendidas, resultados y debilidades de las CV en América Latina[17]

Es necesario aprender de las experiencias y resultados de más de 20 comisiones establecidas desde 1974, incluyendo las de varios países latinoamericanos, así como de aquellas que están en proceso de establecerse en varios países. Muchos de los problemas que estas comisiones han tenido ya se habían experimentado y se deben mayormente a que las experiencias anteriores no se analizaron con suficiente detenimiento. Las principales lecciones aprendidas de las CV son:

1. La incapacidad e ineficacia del Poder Judicial existente, después de largas dictaduras, especialmente de regímenes totalitarios, requiere el establecimiento y la existencia de una CV para revelar la verdad y aplicar la justicia ante las violaciones masivas, generalizadas y sistemáticas a los derechos humanos.

2. Las CV muestran diferentes procesos de constitución, desarrollo y aporte a la sociedad. En general sus aportes han sido mayores que sus debilidades. Parte de los problemas es que no han tenido términos de referencia claros y se les ha dejado a la discreción de las comisiones determinarlos, lo cual ha influido decisivamente en sus alcances y resultados.

3. El éxito de una CV requiere, además de la participación activa de las organizaciones de derechos humanos, de un amplio apoyo popular, el cual incorpore y una los esfuerzos de las organizaciones políticas, académicas, sindicales, campesinas, religiosas, etc. La búsqueda de la verdad tiene mayores posibilidades restauradoras en la sociedad cuando forma parte de un esfuerzo común y franco de reconciliación nacional, paz social y transición que comprometa a la mayoría de la población.

4. Al revelar la historia oculta de la represión y la violación generalizada y sistemática a los derechos humanos, las CV abren la posibilidad de compensar a las víctimas, sancionar a los responsables y establecer un nuevo orden institucional con base a un estado de derecho, que contribuyan decididamente a la reconciliación nacional, la paz social y la transición.

5. Cuando las CV no establecen lo ocurrido ni sancionan a los violadores de los derechos humanos ni reparan a las víctimas, se convierten en un me-canismo de impunidad, un recurso oficial para superar el pasado sin sanar las heridas, lo que dificulta los procesos de reconciliación nacional, paz social y transición como lo muestran las experiencias recientes de Argentina, Chile y Uruguay.

6. Las investigaciones realizadas durante el proceso de violencia y represión, tienden a ser parciales e incompletas, por el peligro que conlleva identificar y señalar públicamente los hechos y los responsables de las violaciones y abusos a los derechos humanos.

7. Las CV tienen mayores probabilidades de llegar al pleno conocimiento de la verdad cuando actúan en el período inmediatamente posterior a la finalización de la represión y la violación a los derechos humanos. Hay una especie de regla de lo antes, lo mejor.

8. Las CV independientes tienen mayores probabilidades de llegar al conocimiento de la verdad y a la reconciliación nacional que las integradas por personas que forman parte de los gobiernos acusados de violar los derechos humanos.

9. Las investigaciones globales de los sucesos de la etapa de represión y violencia y las medidas de reparación correspondientes, tienen un impacto restaurador mayor de la paz social que las investigaciones y las soluciones parciales.

Entre los aportes importantes de las CV que han existido en América Latina se destacan:

1. La revelación, divulgación y reconocimiento de una realidad ignorada, oculta.

2. La identificación de los hechos y los sectores involucrados en el desarrollo de las violaciones a los derechos humanos.

3. La personalización y humanización de las víctimas y sus familiares.

4. La reparación parcial del daño causado.

---

17. Esta sección se basa en las conclusiones de los ensayos de Esteban Cuya, *Las Comisiones de la Verdad en América Latina y El Impacto de las Comisiones de la Verdad en América Latina*, versiones digitales.

5. Aportes, mediante recomendaciones, a la reconciliación nacional a través de la verdad y la justicia.

6. Aportes, mediante recomendaciones, a la prevención de futuras violaciones a los derechos humanos, a la transición y al establecimiento de un orden donde prevalezcan las libertades y derechos políticos y económicos fundamentales.

Las principales deficiencias de las CV de América Latina son:

1. La reserva en la identificación y divulgación de la información acerca de los responsables de las violaciones a los derechos humanos. Ello favorece la impunidad para los violadores de los derechos humanos y dificulta la reconciliación nacional, ya que las víctimas y sus familiares están en un permanente proceso de pedir justicia. Así han sido las experiencias argentina y chilena.

2. La imposibilidad práctica de reconstruir la historia global de las violaciones a los derechos humanos, abarcando, además de las violaciones a los derechos civiles y políticos fundamentales, los cometidos en contra de los derechos económicos, sociales y culturales. A veces las comisiones se han limitado a investigar casos emblemáticos dejando fuera la investigación de otros muchos casos a los que sólo hay referencias que también constituyeron violaciones a los derechos humanos.

3. Incapacidad de lograr la restitución a sus legítimos dueños de las expropiaciones a los desaparecidos o asesinados en el período de violencia. No se ha logrado que los represores devuelvan los bienes que les quitaron a los familiares de sus víctimas. Por ejemplo, en Argentina y Nicaragua algunos represores viven en las propiedades de sus víctimas y administran las empresas que les quitaron.

4. Ineptitud de divulgar la información obtenida, a la población afectada por la violencia, en lenguaje sencillo, claro, y a través de métodos modernos de comunicación.

5. Imposibilidad de controlar y asegurar la ejecución cabal de sus recomendaciones en las diversas áreas para la superación de la impunidad, la prevención de nuevas violaciones a los derechos humanos y las acciones de reparación a las víctimas o a sus familiares, después del final de su mandato. Riesgos de politización de sus conclusiones y recomendaciones.

PROPUESTA DE TÉRMINOS DE REFERENCIA PARA LA CCVRN

La CCVRN deberá atenerse a elevadas reglas morales y jurídicas, tanto en la elección de sus miembros, sus objetivos y los medios que utilice en su trabajo. La identificación de los delitos y de los responsables deberá ser sustentada apropiadamente, para superar situaciones de estéril condena mutua, para vencer la tentación de excluir a los transgresores, sin concederles posibilidad alguna de apelación o el debido proceso.

Las normas internacionales de los derechos humanos, así como las leyes de guerra y del derecho internacional humanitario, deberían formar parte del marco conceptual y jurídico con el cual la Comisión trabajará al analizar los distintos crímenes y hechos de violencia.

Establecimiento de la Comisión

Una de las lecciones del caso de la Comisión de Sudáfrica, una de las más amplias y minuciosas, fue el establecimiento de la Comisión por el poder legislativo, lo que le representó apoyo de las diferentes corrientes de pensamiento en el país, y así dicha Comisión tuvo mayor credibilidad en general. Por lo tanto, se considera recomendable que la CCVRN sea establecida inmediatamente al comienzo de la transición por decisión legislativa, puesta en conocimiento del Poder Ejecutivo y monitoreada por las Naciones Unidas u otro organismo internacional con capacidad y experiencia en el tema. Alternativamente, si las circunstancias impiden que el poder legislativo tome tal decisión, un decreto ejecutivo podrá establecer la CCVRN. Un aspecto importante a considerar es que un alto grado de apoyo popular que reciba la Comisión sería un fuerte paliativo a la oposición de los perpetradores de las violaciones de derechos humanos, aún si algunos se mantienen en puestos importantes al principio del período de transición.

Areas principales que la Comisión debe investigar

La Comisión deberá concentrarse principalmente en determinados tipos de violaciones especialmente graves en sí mismas, o representativas de un patrón generalizado o sistemático de conducta criminal, o que han tenido un efecto particularmente traumático en la conciencia pública. La pregunta evidente es cómo justificar la posible selección que es necesaria sobre la base del respeto a los principios legales y a las obligaciones del país respecto a los instrumentos más importantes del derecho internacional de los derechos humanos y del derecho internacional humanitario.

La Comisión deberá esclarecer con suma objetividad, uniformidad e imparcialidad un cuadro, lo más completo posible, sobre los hechos y circunstancias de las violaciones a los derechos civiles y políticos más fundamentales (a la vida, a la integridad física de las personas, al debido proceso y a un juicio justo), y los actos de violencia flagrantes por razones políticas cuyo impacto en la sociedad demandan de manera inmediata que el pueblo los conozca, tales como:

- Ejecuciones efectuadas por agentes del gobierno;

- Torturas y maltratos crueles y degradantes que resultaron en muerte o incapacidad permanente;

- Uso indebido de la fuerza que haya ocasionado la muerte o incapacidad permanente;

- Desapariciones; y

- Exilio forzado

También la Comisión deberá investigar las prácticas que deberán desaparecer y que requieren cambios institucionales y jurídicos de importancia en la sociedad, con el fin de colaborar a la reconciliación de todos los cubanos y la paz social, tales como:

- Negación de libertades fundamentales como libertad de credo, de prensa, y de asociación;

- Detenciones arbitrarias y abuso de poderes de detención por agentes del gobierno;

- Negación a un juicio público y justo con el debido proceso;

- Torturas y maltratos crueles y degradantes no resultando en muerte o incapacidad permanente; y

- Actos de violencia económica, social y cultural ejercidos por el Estado.

Simultáneamente a las investigaciones contra los autores materiales directos de los crímenes y las violaciones a los derechos humanos, debe incluirse a las autoridades responsables y autores intelectuales de tales crímenes. O sea, los oficiales y supervisores de los criminales por su responsabilidad en los niveles de decisión o encubrimiento en esos procesos o por no ponerles coto desde su posición de autoridad.

A fin de evitar unas de las debilidades de las CV (véase sección anterior), la Comisión deberá identificar y nombrar en su informe a los culpables de los crímenes y las violaciones a los derechos humanos en los casos que tenga suficiente evidencia y después de haber llamado a declarar y oído a los mismos.

Incluir la investigación de las empresas mixtas con capital extranjero asociadas al Estado cubano

En 1995, a raíz de la severa crisis económica resultante de la desaparición del bloque socialista y de la masiva ayuda soviética, el Estado cubano puso en vigor la ley No. 77 que permite la inversión privada extranjera en forma de empresas mixtas, con participación de capital foráneo. Dicho Decreto-Ley constituye un régimen explotador del trabajador cubano por razones ampliamente cubiertos en los informes de derechos humanos de organismos internacionales citados anteriormente, así como los Convenios No. 111 (discriminación del trabajador por diversos motivos), No. 87 (libertad de formar organizaciones sindicales) y No. 29 (proscripción de trabajos que no se derivan de la libre contratación entre trabajadores y empleadores). La CCVRN debe abrir una investigación especial sobre los sueldos y salarios no percibidos por los trabajadores cubanos que han trabajado en las empresas de capital mixto, así como otros daños causados por discriminación en la contratación y despido de trabajadores y recomendar las sanciones correspondientes a dichas empresas.

Areas principales sobre las cuales la Comisión deberá hacer recomendaciones

La Comisión deberá hacer recomendaciones fundamentales para restablecer el estado de derecho, de libertades básicas y la democracia representativa, para la administración efectiva de la justicia y la reforma del poder judicial, la adecuación del ordenamiento jurídico nacional al derecho internacional de los derechos humanos y la ratificación de tratados internacionales sobre derechos humanos, la reforma de las fuerzas de seguridad pública y la policía nacional, la compensación moral y reparación material a las víctimas y sus familiares, sanciones morales, penales y lustración (depuración) para los perpetradores de los crímenes, medidas para promover la reconciliación nacional, la paz social y facilitar la transición.

Ventajas y desventajas de incluir la reconciliación

La Comisión debería denominarse de la Verdad y de la Reconciliación Nacional para hacer claro que no sólo contempla los temas de la verdad y justicia sino también un primer paso hacia la reconciliación nacional, la paz social y facilitar la transición a un estado de derecho, de libertades y derechos fundamentales, y convivencia social pacífica. Es decir, si bien el objetivo principal de la CCVRN no debiera ser lograr la reconciliación entre víctimas y victimarios, uno de sus objetivos importantes es establecer las bases para una futura reconciliación nacional.

Período a ser cubierto

La Comisión debería cubrir el periodo de la violencia y la violación masiva, generalizada y sistemática a los derechos civiles, políticos y laborales que comenzó en Cuba con el golpe de estado del 10 de marzo de 1952.

La Comisión deberá tener poderes de citar a comparecer, buscar, y proteger a los testigos debido a lo muy débil y comprometido que está el poder judicial en Cuba, el cual requiere profundas reformas estructurales, institucionales y jurídicas.

Los integrantes de la Comisión

Los comisionados serían unas 7 personas, 4 nacionales y 3 internacionales de gran prestigio y reconocimiento público. Los tres internacionales podrían ser nombrados por la Comisión Interamericana de Derechos Humanos o el Alto Comisionado de las Naciones Unidas para los Derechos Humanos. Los cuatro nacionales deben poseer antecedentes intachables en lo que a derechos humanos se refiere; al menos uno de ellos debe haber pertenecido a una de las organizaciones nacionales de derechos humanos o haber sido activista de derechos humanos. El presidente de la Comisión debe ser una persona ejecutiva, ya que deberá desempeñar el liderazgo de supervisar la recopilación, organización, análisis e investigación de los casos; reclutar y supervisar el personal variado y multidisciplinario requerido (aproximadamente unas 50 personas); determinar los procedimientos operativos y metodológicos (tipos de evidencia); administrar los recursos de la Comisión; y preparar y publicar el informe final con sus hallazgos y recomendaciones. El personal profesional de la Comisión debe incluir profesionales en las áreas de derecho, médicos forenses, investigadores, psicólogos, informática y sistemas, seguridad y administración.

Fecha límite para la Comisión

La Comisión deberá tener la fecha límite de 15 meses, unos 12 meses para hacer la investigación detallada y 3 meses para hacer y presentar su informe a las autoridades nacionales y al pueblo de Cuba. Este período se considera razonable y suficiente con base en las experiencias de las comisiones de Chile y El Salvador.

Alcance del poder/mandato de la Comisión

El tema de amnistía es de vital importancia para una CV. Ciertamente una amnistía general desvirtuaría el trabajo de la CCVRN, por lo cual la amnistía sería utilizada selectivamente, limitada solamente a ciertos tipos de violaciones y perpetradores, así como condicional, es decir, a cambio de la solicitud escrita y el testimonio por parte de los perpetradores.

La cobertura por los medios masivos, prensa, radio y televisión, nacional e internacional, también será necesaria, tanto de las sesiones públicas de la Comisión, así como para la divulgación y análisis del Informe Final, a fin de que el pueblo quede interiorizado de los detalles de las violaciones, así como para dar transparencia al proceso. Asimismo, se recomienda la distribución masiva de un informe resumido.

Recursos y costo

El esfuerzo sostenido y sistemático de identificación, recopilación, investigación y acumulación de evidencias, y realizar las recomendaciones para facilitar la transición y consolidar el estado de derecho y la democracia representativa demandarán atención y recursos humanos y materiales de envergadura.

1. Recursos necesarios para la operación de la Comisión

Se estima el costo total de la CCVRN en US$5.500.000. Para un personal nacional de unas 54 personas por 15 meses (4 comisionados x US$60.000 y 50 profesionales y paraprofesionales x US$45.000) con unas tres personas prominentes del exterior por 15 meses (3 x US$150.000) se calcula un costo en salarios de aproximadamente US$2.490.000. Además, estarían los costos de viajes, oficinas, materiales, personal de apoyo e imprevistos (US$3.010.000). Este personal y presupuesto es comparable al utilizado en las Comisiones de Chile y El Salvador.

2. Pagos e indemnizaciones

Como los pagos e indemnizaciones cubrirían pagos iniciales, así como pagos periódicos por más de un año, la Comisión sólo haría recomendaciones de pagos e indemnizaciones a las víctimas y sus familiares que el Estado debería cubrir dentro de su presupuesto anual.

3. Presupuesto y financiamiento

El presupuesto de la Comisión sería cubierto principalmente con recursos nacionales, pero se podría solicitar recursos de gobiernos (Canadá, Dinamarca, Noruega) o entidades no gubernamentales (Instituto de la Paz, de Washington, D.C.) que suelen colaborar en este tipo de actividades, así como de las Naciones Unidas, que ha financiado parcialmente las Comisiones de El Salvador, Guatemala y Haití.

REFERENCIAS PRINCIPALES

Bond, Theresa. "The Crackdown in Cuba." *Foreign Affairs*, Vol. 82, No. 5 (September/October 2003), pp. 118-130.

Comisión Interamericana de Derechos Humanos. *Informe sobre la situación de los derechos humanos en la República de Cuba.* Washington, DC: CIDH, 1962 (OEA/Ser. L/V/II.4 doc. 2).

Comisión Interamericana de Derechos Humanos. *Informe anual de la Comisión Interamericana de Derechos Humanos 2001.* Washington, DC: CIDH, 2001 (OEA/Ser. L/V/II.114 doc. 5 rev, Capítulo IV).

Grupo de Trabajo Memoria, Verdad y Justicia. *Cuba la reconciliación nacional.* Miami, Florida versión digital (http://memoria.fiu.edu).

Hayner, Priscilla. *Unspeakable Truths: Confronting State Terror and Atrocity.* Nueva York y Londres: Routledge, 2001.

Human Rights Watch. *La Maquinaria Represiva de Cuba: Los derechos humanos cuarenta años después de la revolución.* Nueva York, Washington, Londres, Bruselas: Human Rights Watch, 1999.

Kritz, Neil J. *"The Dilemmas of Transitional Justice."* Instituto de la Paz de Estados Unidos, versión digital (http://www.usip.org/research/rol/tjintro.html).

Lago, Armando M. *Cuba: The Human Costs of Social Revolutions.* Versión preliminar (a ser publicado en 2003).

Lago, Armando M. y Charles J. Brown. *The Politics of Psychiatry in Revolutionary Cuba.* Nueva Jersey: Transaction Publishers, 1991.

Mesa-Lago, Carmelo. *Crecientes disparidades económicas y sociales en Cuba: Impacto y recomendaciones para el cambio.* Miami, FL: Instituto de Estudios Cubanos y Cubano-Americanos de la Universidad de Miami, 2003.

Portell-Vilá, Herminio. *Nueva historia de la República de Cuba, 1898-1979.* Miami, FL: La Moderna Poesía, 1986.

Rotberg, Robert I. y Dennis Thompson. *Truth v. Justice: The Morality of Truth Commissions.* Princeton, NJ: Princeton University Press, 2000.

Sen, Amartya. *Development as Freedom.* NY: Anchor Books, 2000.

Thomas, Hugh. *Cuba or The Pursuit of Freedom.* Nueva York: Da Capo Press, 1998 (versión actualizada).

Teitel, Ruti. *Transitional Justice.* Nueva York y Londres: Oxford University Press, 2000.

Universidad de Harvard, Facultad de Derecho; Search for Common Ground (ONG internacional con sede en Washington, DC); y European Center for Common Ground (ONG europea con sede en Bruselas). *Strategic Choices in the Design of Truth Commissions.* Sitio en el Internet, http://www.truthcommission.org.

Universidad de Harvard, Facultad de Derecho y Fundación Mundial para la Paz. *Truth Commissions: A Comparative Assessment.* Boston, MA, 1996, versión digital (http://www.law.harvard.edu/programs/HRP/Publications/truth1.html).

NATURAL DISASTERS AND CUBA'S AGRICULTURAL PERFORMANCE: IS THERE A CORRELATION?

José Alvarez[1]

Almost since the beginning of the revolution in 1959, the Cuban leadership and some foreign scholars have blamed mother nature for the failures or inefficiencies of the agricultural sector.[2] I could easily fill many pages with quotes from Cuban officials, especially from President Castro, that illustrate my point. I think that the quotes in Box 1 are sufficient. They speak of both droughts and hurricanes. The abundance of such quotes challenged me to research the topic. Several questions came to mind: Can we really say that nature has been especially devastating during the current Cuban regime? Have there been more natural disasters during the socialist period than during similar prior periods? Is it easier to prepare for, and recover from, natural disasters after the revolution? If yes, Why? Finally, and a *sine qua non*, could I find data on droughts, flooding from excessive rains, hurricanes, and cold fronts? With those questions in mind, I looked for the definition of the events that encompassed natural disasters that apply to Cuba, and then I began my search of the literature to see what data were available. My objective was to compare the period 1959-2002 with 1915-1958; that is, 43 years before and after the revolution took power.

DEFINITION OF TERMS

Although there are several natural disasters, I chose those applicable to Cuba. They are: cold fronts, flooding, drought, and hurricanes.

Cold fronts are not specifically defined in Cuba's official statistics since they do not consider the temperature of the events. Rather, they are classified in terms of wind velocity during the cold front: weak (winds from 20 to 35 km/hour); moderate (winds from 35 to 55 km/hour), and strong (winds of 55 or more km/hour). The official cold front season is from September to June (*Anuario*, various issues).

Flooding occurs when a body of water rises and overflows onto normally dry land. The Grade 7 Natural Disasters Project[3] classifies flooding according to its origin into: coastal flooding of lakes and oceans, and river flooding. In the case of Cuba, our concern would be coastal flooding from hurricanes, and river flooding from excessive rains. The *Anuario Estadístico de Cuba* does not contain a specific definition.

Drought is a period of abnormally dry weather that causes serious hydrological imbalance in an area. There are three types of drought: meteorological (lack of rain over a long period of time); hydrological (critically low ground tables and reduced river and stream flow); and agricultural (extended dry periods

---

1. The author would like to thank Jorge Pérez-López for his comments and suggestions on an earlier draft.

2. It is interesting to note that "extreme climatic conditions" also have been used to justify other revolutionary agricultural failures. For example, Utting (1992) uses the excuse for the Sandinista experiment in Nicaragua.

3. http://www.germantown.k12.il.us/html/floods.html.

227

Box 1.   Selected Statements by Cuban Officials on Natural Disasters

And what was that forced us to pay attention to the hydraulic problem?...It was the drought phenomenon, the tremendous drought that took place in the years 1961 and 1962.

> — Fidel Castro (1990, p. 282).

Our farmers can not continue at the mercy of hurricanes, of floodings, of droughts. Our work can not depend on whether or not it rains.

> — Fidel Castro (1990, p. 284).

Unless we conquer nature, nature will conquer us.

> — Fidel Castro (1992, p. 71).

First all of, Cuban agriculture performed more poorly during 1985 and 1986. This was principally attributable to two factors: (1) there was an intensifying drought from 1983 through 1986; by 1986 rainfall was 35 percent below the historical average; and (2) in November 1985 Cuba experienced its most devastating hurricane since the revolution.

> — Zimbalist and Brundenius (1991, pp. 250, 258).

We have heavy damage from the drought to our sugarcane... We have pushed back the [2000-2001] harvest start a bit to allow the cane to benefit a little more from the rain.

> — Ulises Rosales del Toro ("Current Developments," 2000, p. 18).

Given the reduction in cane yield caused by the drought, the [2000-2001] harvest, which is about to begin, will result in lower production than the last one.

> — Vice-President Carlos Lage ("Current Developments," 2000, p. 18).

Due to the embargo, and to adverse climatological conditions, production of vegetables and of meat from cattle, pigs and fowl decreased [in 1999-2000].

> — Alfredo Jordán (Zúñiga, 2000, p. 1).

We know that the imperialists sometimes have been trying to deflect hurricanes. And I suspect that on certain occasions to deflect them to where they are interested; even against us with counter-revolutionary purposes. We know—and it has been published—that the Pentagon was conducting experiments to see if they could make the clouds discharge their water on the sea without reaching Cuba.

> — Fidel Castro (1990, p. 441).

and general lack of rainfall resulting in a lack of moisture in the root zone of the soil, which severely damages the plants in the area). The "Palmer Drought Severity Index" is used to indicate areas of the country that are more susceptible to drought. The agricultural and economic impacts are the most damaging events.[4] The *Anuario* does not contain a specific definition.

Hurricanes are warm-core tropical cyclones in which the minimum sustained surface winds is 74 mph (119 km/hr) or more. The Saffir-Simpson Hurricane Scale classifies hurricanes as: category 1 (winds 74-95 mph or 119-153 km/hr); category 2 (winds 96-110 mph or 154-177 km/hr); category 3 (winds 111-130 mph or 178-209 km/hr); category 4 (winds 131-155 mph or 210-249 km/hr); and category 5 (winds greater than 155 mph or 249 km/hr. This classification also considers differences in the size of storm surge and resulting damages.[5] The *Anuario*'s classification, according to their intensity, differs slightly from the previous one. The three categories are: low intensity (winds 115-150 km/hr); moderate intensity (winds 151-200 km/hr); and high intensity (winds

---

4. http://www.germantown.k12.il.us/html/droughts1.html

5. http://www.nhc.noaa.gov/aboutsshs.html.

over 200 km/hr). The official hurricane season is from June to November (*Anuario*, various issues).

SOURCES OF INFORMATION AND THEIR USEFULNESS

Data were needed to quantify the previous four types of natural disasters. My first place to search was the *Anuario Estadístico de Cuba*. I found that the official statistics had not changed in recent years. The *Anuario* still reports, with more or less degree of sophistication, several climatic parameters in different tables. However, not all data were useful for this type of analysis:

- cold front information, and related data, are provided in several tables. They include: (a) the median temperature by province and selected weather stations by year and month, for the current and several preceding years, but the comparisons are an average that includes only a few years; and (b) the absolute maximum and minimum temperatures registered in two selected weather stations by province, but there are few observations for the period preceding 1959;

- flooding information is not provided. A number of variables that could be used as proxies appear in several tables: (a) the median for total rainfall by province and selected weather stations by year and month, for the current and several preceding years, but none is provided before 1959; and (b) the median for total annual rainfall by province for a few preceding years, compared with an average for previous decades, but the latter could not be broken down by the periods under study;

- drought data are not provided *per se*. The discussion of the preceding information is also applicable to droughts; and

- hurricane data are provided. They include: (a) total number of hurricanes by intensity, by month, and for the current year and an average of previous years sometimes starting in the nine-

teenth century; these data can not be broken down by the periods under study, however; (b) number of times that each region (western, central, and eastern) has been hit, by intensity, for the current year and an average of previous years sometimes starting in the nineteenth century, but can not be broken down by the study periods.

All in all, despite the abundant information provided by the *Anuarios*, none could be used because, either some data were not reported, or those reported did not correspond to the periods considered in this study. A search of other Cuban official publications, on hard copies or on the world wide web, did not provide better results. For example, the web site of the Institute of Meteorology (INSMET), part of the Ministry of Science, Technology and Environment,[6] only contains a summary of the history of the national weather service but provides no comprehensive statistical information.

During my search on the web, I came across the web site of the U.S. National Oceanographic and Atmospheric Administration.[7] One of the documents related to hurricanes contains more or less appropriate data to assess if there are any differences between the two periods under study. A very comprehensive and voluminous publication by Rappaport and Fernández-Partagás covers the period 1492 to 1997. More information was found in another site.[8] Both were used in an attempt to elucidate the questions posed at the beginning of this article.

THE INCIDENCE AND SEVERITY OF HURRICANES IN CUBA, 1915-1958 AND 1959-2002

Atlantic tropical hurricanes[9] from 1492 to date have been compiled from historical documents and current weather data by Rappaport and Fernandez-Partagas. They list a total of 467 hurricanes. The first list contains the deadliest 259, those hurricanes causing at least 25 deaths. The second list contains 208 hurri-

---

6. http://www.met.inf.cu/historia/breve.htm.

7. http://www.nhc.noaa.gov/.

8. http://www.hurricanecity.com/.

Table 1. Ranking of 259 Atlantic Tropical Hurricanes Causing at Least 25 Deaths, Cuba, 1915-1997[a]

Rank (by number of deaths)	Name of Hurricane[b]	Dates active
5	Flora	9/30 - 10/8, 1963
10	—	11/4 - 11/10, 1932
43	—	10/20, 1926
50	—	9/9 - 9/14, 1919
54	Fox	10/23 - 10/25, 1952
78	—	10/12 - 10/18, 1944
79	Hilda	9/11 - 9/16, 1955
115	—	8/30 - 9/5, 1933
155	Alma	6/4 - 6/8, 1966
165	—	9/22 - 9/29, 1917
168	—	9/23 - 9/29, 1935
253	—	8/25 - 8/31, 1950

Source: http://www.nhc.noaa.gov/pastdeadlya1.html.

a. Atlantic refers to the North Atlantic Ocean, Caribbean Sea, and the Gulf of Mexico.
b. Hurricanes did not start receiving names until after 1950.

Table 2. Areas or Cities Most Likely to be Affected by Hurricanes, How Often Area or City is Affected, Frequency of a Hurricane Brushing Within 60 Miles, and Frequency of Actual Hits, Cuba, 1915-1958 and 1959-2002.

Area or city	How often area is affected	Frequency within 60 miles		Frequency area hit	
		1915-58	1959-02	1915-58	1959-02
Isle of Youth	2.64 yr.	19	10	4	7
Cabo Corrientes, Pinar del Río	2.93 yr.	8	14	3	5
Havana	3.14 yr.	13	13	5	10
Cienfuegos	4.26 yr.	12	6	2	2
Manzanillo	4.55 yr.	12	5	1	1
Baracoa	4.71 yr.	10	8	0	4
Nuevitas	6.28 yr.	9	4	1	3
Total	—	83	60	16	32

Source: http://www.hurricanecity.com/cities.htm.

canes that may have caused at least 25 deaths. Twelve of the hurricanes in the first list (the deadliest hurricanes) affected Cuba and none in the second list. Ten of the 12 hurricanes hit Cuba during the 1915-58 period, while only two did so after 1959 (Table 1). That would give an incidence of one hurricane every 4.2 years for the first period versus one hurricane every 21.5 years for the second period. That, however, does not seem reasonable and is only part of the story.

More detailed data are provided in Table 2. The seven Cuban cities or areas most likely to be hit by a hurricane or having one passing within 60 miles, based on 1915-2002 data, are: Isle of Youth (every 2.64 years), Cabo Corrientes in the province of Pinar del Río (every 2.93 years), Havana (every 3.14 years), Cienfuegos (every 4.26 years), Manzanillo (every 4.55 years), Baracoa (every 4.71 years), and Nuevitas (every 6.28 years). The Isle of Youth, Cabo Corrientes and Havana rank 6, 26, and 42, respectively, among the 51 areas or cities hit or brushed the most by hurricanes or tropical storms in the United States, Mexico and all Caribbean islands during 1871-2002. For comparison sake, Grand Cayman is ranked 1 (every 2.24 years), Morehead City, North Carolina, is 51 (every 3.38 years), and Miami is 16 (every 2.75 years).[10]

Table 2 also contains the number of times that each of the seven areas in Cuba has been brushed within 60 miles and the number of times it has experienced a direct hit. During the 1915-1958 period, these seven areas or cities were brushed within 60 miles more often (83 times) than during the 1959-2002 period (60 times). The opposite is the case with respect to the frequency of actual hits; there were 16 during the first period and 32 during the second period. It is very difficult to arrive at a definite conclusion.

9. They include those in the North Atlantic Ocean, the Caribbean Sea, and the Gulf of Mexico.

10. The frequencies, of course, are based on averages. Some countries, and even regions within a country, can experience wide deviations from those averages. Cuba is a case in point for the last years. Hurricane Georges swept the eastern part of Cuba in September 1998. One year later, in October 1999, Irene hit the western and central provinces. Michelle did the same to 45% of the island in November, 2001, resulting in the most devastating hurricane of the last 50 years. Then came Isidore and Lili, in October and November, 2002, respectively, which affected the Isle of Youth and the province of Pinar del Río within days of each other. These five hurricanes proved devastating to Cuban agriculture.

To check for the significance of these differences, I conducted a Student's t-test for both events. This tool tests the means of two small samples to determine whether differences between them are significant. The results (at %=0.05) show that, concerning hurricanes brushing the island or passing within 60 miles, the differences between the sample means of the two periods are statistical significant at $P < 0.07$. Therefore, the greater number of events during the first period is in fact significant. Concerning direct hits, the results show that the differences between the two periods are statistically significant at $P < 0.01$. It is safe to assume with 99% confidence that Cuba has been hit by hurricanes more times during 1959-2002 than during 1915-1958. It is safe to state, then, that the data in Table 2 convey a statistical significance: there were more brushes of hurricanes within 60 miles during 1915-1958, but more direct hits during 1959-2002.

The frequency numbers, however, do not tell the whole story. For example, and since we are discussing the impact of natural disasters on agriculture, a hurricane classified as Category 2 may be worse for agriculture than one classified as Category 3. It depends on whether or not its path followed an important agricultural area. Using the classification based on the number of deaths may also be misleading in terms of impact of agriculture. First, because the casualties may have occurred in the cities, with little damage to agriculture. Second, because a certain level of deaths may not be reached because of precautionary measures to minimize the hurricane's impact.

The latter may be particularly relevant for contemporary Cuba. Cuba has developed an impressive Civil Defense System (*Defensa Civil*), established by Law 1194 of 1966 and placed under the Ministry of the Armed Forces. During the process of institutionalization of the revolution in the mid-1970s, the Civil Defense System (CDS) was associated more closely,

with the Committees for the Defense of the Revolution (CDR), becoming an integral part of the system, as dictated by Law 1316 of the same year (Lezcano, 1995, p. 401).[11] As mentioned above, Cuba also has a good national meteorological service. When a hurricane is approaching, the CDS evacuates residents from the coastal and low areas, moving them to shelters until the storm has passed. This action changes the number of casualties and affects the perception that one obtains by looking only at the classification of the hurricane based on number of deaths since the loss of many lives typically is prevented by timely evacuation.

SUMMARY AND CONCLUSIONS

A definitive answer to the questions posed at the beginning of this paper can not be stated. Lack of data hindered the analysis of cold fronts, floods, and droughts. In the case of the latter, there are abundant descriptions and quantifications on the more damaging droughts in the 1959-2001 period. But there is no consistent reporting, and data for the pre-1959 period are completely lacking.

This is not the case with hurricanes. Detailed data are available on the number of hurricanes affecting the archipelago, although not on the agricultural or economic damage they might have caused.[12] With the caveats stated above, the empirical results show:

- data on the 12 hurricanes causing at least 25 deaths from 1916-1999 show that 10 occurred during 1915-58 and only two during the most recent period;

- data on the number of times hurricanes that have passed within 60 miles of Cuba's coasts also show a huge difference between the two periods: 83 times during the 1915-1958 period and 60 during the 1959-2002 period. The analysis using a simple t-test confirms the statistical significance of that difference. The variable analyzed

---

11. Interested readers can consult Lezcano (1995), who has a detailed description of the essential features of the system to address natural disasters in Cuba.

12. The Economic Commission for Latin America and the Caribbean (ECLAC) has developed a disaster assessment methodology for the Caribbean region. It identifies the long term social and economic effects of a natural disaster. Interested readers can consult http://community.wow.net/eclac/CARLINKS/DISMETH.HTM.

here, however, does not reflect the agricultural or economic damage those hurricanes might have caused to Cuba;

- data on the number of times a hurricane hit the archipelago indicate that 16 did so during the 1915-1958 period, and 32 during the 1959-2002 period. The analysis using a simple t-test confirms the statistical significance of that difference. This variable appears to be a better indicator of agricultural and/or economic damage since the storms actually entered Cuba. The difference in the level of damage between the two periods, however, can not be determined;

- data on the strength of hurricanes given by its category and/or wind velocity are also misleading because information on both the agricultural and/or economic damage, and on the path of the storms, is not available;

- information about the process of preparing for, and recovering from, the damage inflicted by hurricanes is incomplete during the 1959-2002 period and almost unavailable during the preceding period. This fact impeded the analysis of this important aspect of the impact of natural disasters. However, the existence of a very effective system of civil defense in socialist Cuba, which did not exist to the same extent in the previous period, leads me to conclude that the process of prevention and recovery from damages is better now than in the past.

To conclude, let us summarize the tentative answers to the questions posed at the beginning of this article:

- Can we really say that nature has been especially devastating during the current Cuban regime? No, we can not, but we can not give an affirmative answer about the 1915-1958 period either.

- Have there been more natural disasters during the socialist period than during a similar period prior to the revolution? In terms of hurricanes, the answer is "no" and "yes." The answer is "no" because the period 1915-1958 experienced more brushes or passing of hurricanes than the 1959-2002 period. However, the answer is "yes" for the frequency with which Cuba has been actually hit by hurricanes. Both answers convey highly statistical significance.

- Is it easier to prepare for, and recover from, those disasters after the revolution? If yes, why? It seems that the answer is "yes." The current civil defense system may be the reason. However, I did not even explore the recovery from the loss of financial resources. Therefore the answer would appear to be a qualified "yes."

REFERENCES

Anuario Estadístico de Cuba. La Habana: Comité Estatal de Estadísticas, Editorial Estadística, annual issues.

Castro, Fidel. *Ciencia, Tecnología y Sociedad 1959-1989*. La Habana: Editorial Política, 1990.

Castro, Fidel. *Ecología y Desarrollo: Selección Temática 1963-1992*. La Habana: Editorial Política, 1992.

"Current Developments in the Cuban Sugar Industry." *Sugar y Azúcar* 95:11 (2000), pp. 18-19, 22-23.

Lezcano, José Carlos. "Aspectos Esenciales Sobre la Mitigación de los Desastres Naturales en Cuba." *Cuba in Transition—Volume 5*. Washington: Association for the Study of the Cuban Economy, 1995, pp. 399-406.

Rappaport, Edward N. and José Fernández Partagás. "The Deadliest Atlantic Tropical Cyclones, 1492 - Present." http://www.nhc.noaa.gov.

Utting, Peter. *Economic Reform and Third World Socialism—A Political Economy of Food Policy in Post-Revolutionary Societies.* London: The Macmillan Press, 1992.

Zimbalist, Andrew and Claes Brundenius. "The Organization and Performance of Cuban Agriculture." In Michael J. Twomey and Ann Helwege (Eds.) *Modernization and Stagnation—Latin American Agriculture Into the 1990s.* New York: Greenwood Press, 1991, pp. 233-260.

Zúñiga, Jesús. "Cuban Minister of Agriculture Blames Embargo for Deficiencies." CubaNet (http://www.cubanet.org/CNews/y00/jul00/20e7.htm).

FAMILY FARMS: THE CORNERSTONE OF THE AGRICULTURAL SECTOR IN THE CUBA OF THE FUTURE

José M. Ricardo[1]

Cultivators of the earth are the most valuable citizens. They are the most vigorous, the most independent, the most virtuous, and they are tied to their country, and wedded to its liberty by the most lasting bonds.

— Thomas Jefferson

This paper presents some thoughts regarding the role of small farmers and family farms in the restructuring of the agricultural sector in Cuba after the demise of the communist regime. One of the challenges of the new government will be to foster rural transformation by eliminating rural poverty, improving the livelihood of smallholders, especially those living in adverse-conditioned lands in remote areas thus hindering rural migration to urban areas, intensifying agricultural production and sustainability, and managing land and water resources to feed a growing population. Peter Rosset (1999) has stated that:

> ... small farms have multiple functions which benefit both society and the biosphere, and which contribute far more than just a particular commodity—there is ample evidence that a small farm model for agricultural development could produce far more food than a large farm pattern ever could.

This paper address some issues and options in the operation and organization of small and family farms, including their natural resources, enterprises, farming methods and techniques, rural development policies, family labor use, new organic practices, latest farm-related innovations, comparison of large farm versus small farm operations, family farm definitions, garden tools and farm machinery, and other farming-related practices.

The two main objectives of this paper are: (1) to emphasize the important role that operators of small farms and family farms will have during Cuba's transition and the future economic, social and political development of rural areas and their participation in modeling civil society in the countryside and in rural communities, and (2) the importance of developing a nation-wide agricultural network integrated by operators (owners and non-owners) of small farms. Basically, we are referring to members of the National Association of Small Farmers (ANAP), non-ANAP members who presently are members of the Cooperatives of Agricultural Production (CPA) and of the Cooperatives of Credit and Services (CCS), and independent small farmers.

To facilitate the design and implementation of agricultural policies we suggest that the agricultural sector be divided into several interrelated sub-sectors with dynamic and strong backward and forward linkages. Of course, there is some overlapping and intertwining of these sub-sectors, which together constitute one of the most important segments of the economies of most Less Developed Countries (LDCs). In this paper, family farms, small farms and campesino farms (peasants units) are considered to-

---

1. I would like to express my gratitude to Antonio Gayoso for comments and for the presentation of this paper.

gether as part of the small/traditional production sub-sector.

FAMILY FARMS, SMALL FARMS, FARM SIZE, ECONOMIC SIZE

Typology in the United States

Small farms are defined by Steel (1997) as farms with sales under $20,000 per year, consistent with the definition in the Food and Agricultural Act of 1977. They represent 60% of all farms, 4% of all U.S. sales, and 20% of hay and tobacco sales. Small farm operators purchased 11% of non-capital goods and 22% of capital goods within the farm sector. They held 39% of farm assets and 18% of farm debt in 1994. In addition, smallholders payed 24 % of real estate and property taxes within the farm sector, thus adding to local government revenue, and owned 29% of U.S. agricultural land held by farmers. Trends suggest that small farms will continue to produce nontraditional crops, also called specialty crops.

The Economic Research Service (ERS) classification defines "family farms" as farms organized as proprietorship, partnership, and family corporations, excluding farms organized as non-family corporations or cooperatives, as well as farms with hired managers. Such farms with sales up to $250,000 are still called small family farms, while family farms with sales between $250,000 and $499,999 are called large family farm, and those with sales over $500,000 are called very large family farms.

Gross value of farm sales is an indicator of economic size. It measures what the farm sold during the year, including sales from inventories, regardless of whether the proceeds were received by the operators, landlord(s), or contractor(s). It includes any and all cash sales of all farm products. For purposes of U.S. Census statistics, farms with gross value of sales under $50,000 are referred to as noncommercial-size farm businesses, while farms with sales over $50,000 are called commercial-size operations. Other farm-size measuring sticks, besides total farm area in hectares (ha.) used commonly in the literature and in this paper are: the total value of farm assets and the annual farm net income.

Family farms are those run by the farmer and his family without hired help. The ideal family farm operators are those who were raised on the farm, learned of what they know from their ancestors and willingly have self-committed to improve the way of living in the farm and use the latest technological advances and innovations in crop and livestock raising. In general, family farms should be self-sufficient, except for specialized farms (e.g., tobacco farms in Cuba).

Small and Large Farms: Perceptions and Realities

In most LDCs small farms are central to the production of staple foods (this is also the case in Cuba). Small farms have been described as technically-backward, unproductive and less efficient than large farms, which are technically advanced and heavily mechanized for large-scale operations, accounting for higher crop yields per unit of land and total farm output. Peter Rosset, an international expert in small farm operations, claims that small farms have multiple functions that benefit both society and the biosphere and contribute far more than just a particular commodity. Cuba is a good example where thousands of *campesinos* vigorously resisted the land socialization drive of the Castro regime and used traditional cultural practices that reduced soil erosion and degradation of the Cuban ecosystem.

Writing about Cuba, Jiménez (1992) notes the following advantages of small farms:

- Promote agricultural diversification;
- Keep cost of food products low;
- Avoid the creation of a rural proletariat;
- Consolidate the system of private property.

Jiménez (1992) also notes the following disadvantages of small farms:

- Scarcity of economic resources to purchase machinery for crop mechanization;
- Use of deficient techniques;
- Low enterprise profitability.

Rosset (1999) has identified the following advantages of small farms in the United States:

- Diversity: Small farms embody a diversity of ownership, of cropping systems, of landscapes, of biological organization and biodiversity.

- Environmental benefits: Responsible management of the natural resources of soil, water and wild life.

- Empowerment and community responsibility: Decentralized land ownership.

- Places for families: Family farms can be nurturing places for children.

John Ikerd (2000) has noted the following perceptions and realities regarding small farms:

- **Perception:** Small farms are not really a significant part of American agriculture. Government farm programs for many decades have been exclusively concern of increasing production rather than people. **Reality:** Small farms make up about 60 percent of all farms, according to the 1992 Agriculture Census.

- **Perception:** Small farmers are not real farmers; they are just part-time or hobby farmers. **Reality:** More than half of these farmers spent most of their time at the farm, which is considered his or her residence, and farming is their main occupation as reported in the agricultural censuses.

- **Perception:** A family cannot depend on a small farm for a significant part of their living. There is not way that a farm with gross sales of less than $50,000 a year can be a serious commercial operation. **Reality:** A small farm can support a family. Successful small farmers pursue a fundamentally different approach to farming than do big business.

- **Perception:** Technologies are scale neutral; the only way small farmer can succeed is for it to grow larger. **Reality:** Technologies are not scale-neutral. Industrial technologies were developed for larger commercial farming operations are not appropriate for small farms.

Measuring Small Farm Productivity and Efficiency

In economic analysis, efficiency provides a "measuring stick" for evaluating choices. Efficiency refers to the ratio of valuable output to valuable input. One technique or a package of resources is said to be more efficient than another when it produces a greater valuable output per unit of valuable input used. From an economic standpoint, efficiency is desirable (Bishop and Toussaint, 1996, p. 26).

Rosset (1999, pp. 4-6) argues that as long as we use crop yield as the measuring stick for productivity, larger farms will have an unfair advantage. Table 1, compiled from a national survey taken by ERS in 1995, shows that all acreage classes show an inverse relationship between acreage size and the value of sales and cash farm income. The smallest farm class (49 or fewer acres) shows about ten times greater productivity than the larger class (1,000 or more acres). This is largely so because smaller farms grow high-value specialized crops compared to the crops grown by larger farms, and also reflects relatively more labor and inputs applied per unit area, as well as the use of diverse farming systems. Other important factors and techniques used by small farmers are (Rosset, 1999, pp. 5,6):

- Multiple cropping, probably multiple planting times per year, and more likely inter-cropping various crops on the same field, while large farms almost always use monoculture.

- Intensive land use, using their entire parcel, while larger farmer leave some of their land idle.

- Emphasis on resource-intensive use of land.

- Family labor personally committed to the success of the farm.

- More input per unit area, particularly of non-purchased inputs like manure and compost.

Cuban Agricultural Productivity: State and Non-State Sectors

Puerta and Alvarez compared productivity in Cuba of state farms (very large farms) versus non-state farms (small dispersed private farms and relatively small farms organized as pseudo-cooperatives by the state, namely in Cooperatives of Agricultural Production (CPA) and Cooperatives of Credit and Services (CCS)). They used yields as the measuring stick to determine productivity. They also took into consideration the degree of access to agricultural inputs and farm-related services and credit by the two sectors

Table 1. Economic Statistics on U.S. Farms, 1995

Farm Acreage Class	Farms	Mean Acres Operated	Mean gross cash farm income ($)	Income $/acre	Mean gross value of sales ($)	Sales $/acre
Totals	2,068,000	434	73,474	169	80,621	186
49 or fewer acres (20ha)	578,127	23	21,441	932	29,168	1268
50 - 179 acres (20 - 73ha)	670,378	104	29,326	282	34,217	379
180 - 499 acres (73 - 202ha)	439,630	308	74,413	242	82,190	269
500 - 999 acres (202 - 405ha)	196,752	680	170,176	250	191,222	281
1,000 or more acres (>405 ha)	183,113	2,979	293,222	98	290,353	98

Source: USDA, *Structural and Financial Characteristics of U.S. Farms, 1995.*

(Puerta and Alvarez, 1993). They selected four major groups of crops: *viandas* (roots and tuber crops), vegetables (tomatoes, peppers and onions), grains (rice, corn, beans) and the main Cuban exports crops, sugar cane and tobacco. They tested their hypothesis and, even with the lack of complete data, concluded that the non-state sector produced more, with better quality, than the state sector when given the right incentives (Puerta and Alvarez, 1993, p. 117).

Alvarez (2000) repeated the same comparison between state and non-state producers using additional data for the same crop groups. He concluded that:

- For vegetables (called more-perishable commodities in the new study), non-state growers of onions and peppers outperformed state farms; however average yield of tomatoes for the non-state farm sector were below those of state farms. Tomatoes are a very popular vegetable in Cuba and are easily swapped with other farmers and sold directly to final consumers. Hence it is likely that the figures reported by non-state producers to *Acopio* (she state purchasing agency) understate actual production.

- For *viandas* (called less-perishable commodities in the new study), the results were mixed, with yields from non-state producers were slightly higher for potatoes, which probably require refrigerated storage before distribution, and lower for sweet potatoes than state producers. A large difference in yields was observed in *malanga*, were yields for state producers were 40 percent higher than for non-state producers. As explained by Alvarez (2000, p. 103), *viandas* do not spoil soon after harvest, thus farmers can hide them from *Acopio*.

- For grains, since rice is grown in large farms using heavy modern mechanization and advanced technology, it was expected that yields from state farms would be higher than those obtained from small farms and this was the case. Also, yields were higher in the production of corn and beans in the larger state farms than in small farms of the non-state sector.

- For export crops sugar cane and tobacco: Non-state farmers growing sugar cane out-produced state farms in all seasons and tobacco growers did the same, except in one season when their yield were slightly lower.

My personal explanation for these differences, in addition to those explanations given by Alvarez, is that the majority of small farmers not only in Cuba but also in most LDCs, use intercropping practices growing a variety of other crops between the furrows of planted corn and beans. This practice involves the sowing or planting of a second crop between the rows of the first crop before it is harvested. Thus the crops' cycles may overlap for a short period of time, says a few weeks (Dalrymple, 1977, p. 3). When crop yields are used as the only measuring stick to determine farm productivity, large farms in developed countries show to be more productive than small farm, because the yields in their monoculture practices without competing with others planted crops are higher than the yield of the same crop in small farms. However, small farms produce a larger value of output per unit of land even if their yield of the principal crop is lower because of their labor intensive practices and better utilization of the land resource by planting a variety of cash-earning crops. Alvarez (2000) concludes that the new study corroborates results obtained in a previous study made by Puerta and Alvarez (1993) that "as State intervention decreases over agricultural production units, the quantity and quality of output increases despite a decreasing access to factors of production and other resources" (Alvarez, 2000 p. 106).

Overview of Small Farms in Selected Countries—1997

In most industrialized countries, trends of increasing large mechanized farms, producing higher yields per unit, have been observed in the last three decades of the twentieth century. There is also a favorable sentiment toward small farms, whose cultural practices protect the ecosystems and the rural landscape of the country, thus pleasing the increasing tourist industry of all these countries.

- In the United States, small farms with less than 20 ha, still accounted for 30 percent of the total number of farms.

- Japan, with only 10.6 percent of arable land, the lowest percentage in the industrialized countries, had 59 percents of its agricultural units in very small farms, with 86 percent having less than 20 acres. In addition, Japan had 769,000 noncommercial farm households (those with annual sales of less than five thousand yens) not included in their statistics. Rice production represented 26 percent of agricultural gross income, and vegetables 23 percent.

- Swiss agriculture is characterized by small holdings that should be able to supply the nation's food needs in case of an emergency and should protect the landscape. As a result of tourism, the Swiss have discovered their own landscape and the farmers have thus become landscape gardeners.

- Denmark's agricultural land accounted for about 60 percent of its total area of approximately 4.3 millions ha. The average farm was around 45 ha. with 67 percent of the farm holdings between 5 and 50 ha. About 91 percent of Danish farm holdings are operated by owners. Most of the farms are mixed operation growing grains, forage and vegetables, mixed with raising poultry (meat and eggs), hogs and cattle (both beef and dairy cows). Organic farming in Denmark has increased considerably during the last few years, from 677 organic holdings in 1994 to 2,228 in 1998 (Danish, 1999 p. 74).

- France is the largest producer of agricultural products within the European Union and the largest exporter of processed food products. Farm operators and their families accounted for 90 percent of the active agricultural population. Small farms between 5 and 20 ha. accounted for 37 % of all farms. Mechanization, land re-allotment and industrialization have lowered the number of farms in the last few years.

- Rough estimates of the number of small farms in Cuba for year 1997 by the author put it at about 275,000 agricultural units[2] operated by small farmers, members of the National Association of Small Farmers (ANAP), private dispersed farmers, and farmers who are members of CPAs and CCS. This represents an increase of almost 250 percent from the 111,278 farms of less than 25 ha reported in the 1946 Agricultural Census. This increase in the number of small farms is explained by the subsequent division and fragmentation of larger farms into smaller ones that were distributed among relatives and extended family members of the original owners of larger farms (Puerta and Alvarez, 1993 p. 93), and by the im-

---

2. Author's estimates derived from information provided in Puerta and Alvarez (1993, p. 93) quoted from government agencies as follows: National Planning Board showed 165,866 private producers in 1961 in a total area of 4.0 million hectares showing and average of 24.1 ha. per farm. However, figures from the July 1965 Census shows 197,207 "private" producers with a total area of 2.69 million ha., or an average of 13.5 ha. per farm. There is a difference of 1.31 million ha. that have not been accounted for. If we assume that the average area remained as it was in 1961 (that is, 24.1 ha. per unit) we obtain 253,790 producers presumably not counted. If the average area per unit established for the 1965 Census of 13.5 ha. per unit is used, then we get and increase of up to 296,234 producers. The mid-point of both figures is 275,012 "private" producers, rounded to 275,000 producers with less than 20 ha. per farm (24.1 + 13.5 = 37.6/2 = 18.8 ha.).

plementation of the agrarian reform acts enacted by the communist regime.

CONVENTIONAL AGRICULTURE VERSUS ORGANIC FARMING

Conventional agriculture, or industrial farming, relies upon the proper application of synthetic chemicals in the production of agricultural products, both crops and livestock. When combined with the use of modern methods of irrigation and large farm machinery, conventional agriculture increases crop yields, reduces labor utilization and decreases crop cost per unit of output produced (economies of scale).

There are several major classes of chemical inputs in conventional agriculture: (1) pesticides—these are basically: insecticides, fungicides, and herbicides; (2) chemical drugs used in the treatment and control of livestock diseases and parasites; (3) antiseptics and disinfectants used in general sanitation control and regular household and farm buildings cleaning; and (4) chemical synthetics used in both plant food and livestock feed.

Meanwhile, organic farming uses natural systems to enhance productivity. Organic food usually costs more due to labor-intensive practices and limited availability. Some of the advantages of this system are ("Organic Farming," 2000):

- Improves soils by adding compost and mulch, which feeds a system of naturally occurring bacteria, fungi, earthworms and other organisms that make nutrients available to crops. Loose organic soils promote root growth, and holds more water.

- Plants grown organically may be healthier and therefore more resistant to diseases and pests. Pests outbreaks are controlled by mechanical and biological methods.

- Weeds are controlled with mulch, mechanical tilling or cover crops, which hold and fertilize soils and provide habitat for beneficial insects.

- Animals have access to outdoors and are fed organically-grown feed.

Organic cropland in the United States doubled between 1992 and 1997, to 1.3 million acres. During the 1990s, organic farming was the most rapidly growing segment of agriculture, with sales up over 500 percent between 1994 and 1999 (Dimitri and Greene, 2002).

Sustainable Agriculture

Sustainable agriculture is defined in the U.S. Food, Agriculture, Conservation, and Trade Act of 1990 as an integrated system of plant and animal production practices that over the long term, satisfy human food and fiber needs; enhance environmental qualities and the natural resource base upon which the agriculture and the economy depends; make the most efficient use of nonrenewable resources of farm resources; integrate where appropriate, natural biological cycles and controls; sustain the economic viability of farm operations; and enhance the quality of life for farmers and the society as a whole (Steel 1997). Sustainable land use is an opportunity to improve the quality of the environment, increase soil fertility, better quality air and water. Sustainable farms must be environmentally sound and socially acceptable. For instance, plowing up and down a hill that causes your soil to wash out into public roads, is not environmentally sound, and losing a lot of healthy soil is neither economically sound nor is it socially acceptable because every body must pay for the cost of cleaning (external diseconomies).

USDA Organic Standards include: (a) some pesticides and fertilizers are prohibited at least three years before harvest; (b) crop rotation required to avoid pest and disease outbreaks; (c) sewage sludge and genetically engineered products prohibited; (d) soil managed through tillage and supplemented manage with plant waste, composted, animal waste and permitted synthetic materials; (e) organic seeds preferred, but some non-organic seeds and planting stock allowed; (f) pests, weeds, and diseases controlled with physical, mechanical, and biological controls; some synthetic substances allowed; (g) animals for slaughter are raise organically from birth, eat organic feeds and allowed access to outdoors, including access to pastures for ruminants; (h) hormones and antibiotics prohibited; vaccines allowed; (i) poultry must be raised under organic management from no later than the second day of life.

PROPOSED " IDEAL" FAMILY FARM FOR CUBA

Our proposed "ideal" family farm for Cuba would be a general mixed farm of around two *caballerías*[3] (27 ha.). This is based on historical facts—such as that about 70 percent of the total number of farms in the 1946 Census were 25 ha. or less, and all farms expropriated in 1959 (those over 30 *caballerías*), were to be distributed to peasant farmers on the basis of a "vital minimum" of two *caballerías* (27 ha.) per family. The size of a family farm could vary depending on location of the farm and the quality of the natural resources, such as abundant source of quality water, amount of cultivable land, relative fertility of soils, and other important farm characteristics.

A family farm should comprise mixed enterprises—both crops and livestock raising—in order to minimize risk and generate a weekly or monthly steady cash flow to pay for purchased inputs and the household necessities. Profit, however, should not be the principal goal of the farm. It should be to reach a high level of living and the maximum satisfaction of each family's values.

The first task of a small farmer should be to prepare an inventory of all his natural resources and assets. The farmer should draw a simple map dividing his farm in fields according to type of soil (slope and color), if possible taking two or three samples of each type and have them tested either by the government or using a laboratory kit. The farmer should begin to develop a budget for the next season or calendar year, based on last year's activities and new ones he may want to start as new business. It is important not to forget to account for the use of family labor, for the utilization of agricultural inputs by crop and animal enterprises, and their respective crops yield and product outputs and sales. The farmer should also check for water availability for animals, household use, vegetables gardens, and irrigation.

Let's visualize our "ideal" family farm as follows:

- Main enterprise—cash earner—is chicken for meat. One thousand birds every eight weeks. This includes time for cleaning and preparing poultry houses for the next batch of baby chicks.

- The farmer needs a detailed plan for planting field corn to provided about 50 percent of the total feed needed to grow 6,000 birds per year. (You actually can grow eight flocks per years, if chicks and feed is available.) In addition the farmer will need to grow more corn to feed other livestock, like a dairy cow, a sow, layers and other animals for farm income and for self-consumption. Open-pollinated corn is desirable, because it usually has more nutrients than hybrid corn and seed can be saved for replanting; the new genetically modified seeds will save a lot of money on unnecessary purchased pesticides. Intercropping with corn could be beans, peanuts, or other legumes.

- Some hectares should be planted to permanent crops, such as tropical fruit trees (mangos, avocados, sour sops, cashew nuts, tamarind, guavas and citrus fruits like oranges, lime, grapefruit).

- Several hectares should be planted to root crops and tubers, like *malanga*, cassava, sweet-potatoes and some potatoes, and one or two hectares dedicated to plantains and bananas and perhaps planted with fruits in great demand for export, like papayas and pineapples.

- In an area around the farm house, the farmer and family members should prepare raised beds to grow vegetables including, tomatoes and strawberries for selling fresh to the tourist industry, special consumer stores or local markets. Some of the vegetables and fruits may be canned in jars and some fruits processed into jams and marmalades.

- A portion of the land should be dedicated to pastures and others to fallow or planted to grass, according to a predetermined rotation plan.

---

3. One caballería equals 13.42 hectareas.

- If desired, a section of the farm of few hectares could be set aside, dedicated exclusively to the production of organic crops and livestock. Proper certification from the Department of Agriculture of the United States would be required if exports to that country are planned.

- Water supplies should be constantly checked for availability, especially during the driest months of the year.

All the above activities should be included in a budget plan to be presented to the credit institution that will finance farm input expenses, feed, veterinarian services, custom machinery services, and handling and transport of harvested products. The farmer might also need financing for buying a small tractor (usually 30 to 35 H.P for a small farm) or draft animals (that return to the soil over 60 percent of their ration and forage). For the preparation and maintenance of the raised beds and other manual-tilling operations, a roto-tiller is commonly used. There is nothing wrong with using draft animals: the Amish, for example, is a successful agrarian society that uses draft-horses in the United States. Draft-oxen can be very useful in small farms and may be more economic for some jobs than tractors. The Amish succeed by having low input costs, minimal needs and a strong support network of family, friend and neighbors.

A family farm is expected to generate revenues almost every year sufficient to sustain the farmer's business and household expenses and pay contracted debts. Any revenue left after all expenditures are met should be used for the family recreation and education of the children and young teens, and to invest in farm improvements such as better sanitation (including water supplies for the house and farm, if is not currently available), purchase of manual tools and farm implements and machinery, draft animals or a small tractor that can be used 12 months of the year, or purchasing young animal stock to increase the number of animals for milk or meat on the farm.

Why raise animals? Diversification spreads risk. Chickens and cows provide food for the household; additional dairy cows or layers for egg production can generate products for sale. Multi-species grazing—cattle, goats and sheep all together grazing in the same lots—increases land carrying capacity; parasites that affect one species usually do not affect the others. All small family farm operators should consider some value added activities such as: canning fruits and vegetables, preparing jam and marmalades, packaging selected fruits and vegetables with stickers pasted on them with the farm's name (product differentiation), packing eggs in boxes, making white farmers' cheese, etc.

Constraints to the Development of Family Farms in Cuba

There are several constraints to the development of family farms in Cuba:

- Fragmentation of land, indicating very small farm size, sometimes very close to marginal, borderline size; farmers operating three-hectare farms do not have enough land to plan for expanding farm enterprises;

- The number of independent small farmers has increased substantially, making more difficult for agricultural programs to reach them at remote areas;

- Transportation of farm products to local markets and consumers become a critical bottleneck for many isolated family farms;

- Scarcity of credit for buying farm machinery and hand tools to increase farmers' productivity and farm output;

- Small farmers' concerns about government policies such as imposing socialization drives under communism or lack of adequate concern for the real importance to the nation what agricultural production from campesinos farming represents;

Small farmers in Cuba have excellent experience and skills in growing crops, but it seems that some of them lack both qualifications in operating livestock enterprises.

Small Farmers: Summaries of Four Case Studies in Cuba After 1959

Municipality of Santo Domingo, Province of Villa Clara: The farmer, 65 years old with 30 years of farming experience, was a beneficiary of the first

Agrarian Reform Act. He operates a 7.5 ha farm, producing peppers, tomatoes, corn, cucumbers, and different varieties of squash. He practices multi-cropping production, reducing the sensitivity to pests and increasing the soil fertility. Crop variety spreads his risk of crop failure. He owns fowl and two oxen. His farming skills improved by reading a self-study book on soil and farming. His four-inch turbine pumps underground water he uses to irrigate all of his land. He is very careful, irrigating slowly to maximize water absorption and at the same time minimize run off and thus erosion. He constantly rotates his crops, uses nitrogen-fixating crops serving as green manure. His rotation and intercropping patterns are closely associated with his fertilizer and pest control needs. He has used urea and chicken manure as fertilizer. Apparently the application of chicken manure requires a very labor intensive process of soil preparation. Fields treated with chicken manure are left idle for two years; the farmer believes that fields treated with chicken manure do not need fertilizer for up to five years. He also fertilizes his field with *cachaza* (a sugar by-product), crop residues, and tree debris (Sáez, 1997, p. 478).

Municipality of Santo Domingo, Province of Villa Clara: Another *campesino* in the same geographic area specializes in the production of fruits. This farmer started as a producer of mangos and oranges. However, because after planting there is an eight-year wait for the trees to start producing fruit commercially, the farmer's father started grafting locally-improved varieties of mangos, orange, and avocados and sold young trees locally. The farmer has a variety of fruit trees such as cashews, custard apple, papaya, mamey, sweetsop, guavas, grapefruits and other tropical fruit and trees. There are 12 family members living on a 27-hectare farm. He has a 6-inch oil-powered turbine that is not in use because of lack of fuel. He uses his tractor for cultivating between mangos trees and for mixing the soil with organic debris, improving its moisture and fertility (Sáez, 1997, p. 479).

Municipality of Santo Domingo, Province of Villa Clara: This is a farmer who uses organic fertilizers. He lives in a 3-ha. farm inherited from his father, who was a beneficiary of the first Agrarian Reform Act. His brother's family, daughters, sons-in-law and grandchildren live in two other houses at the edge of the farm. He produces more than forty products in this little farm. His rotation sequence is based upon planting a nitrogen-fixing crop (e.g., beans) or one that leaves large amounts of residues (e.g., rice), before planting a demanding crop (e.g., corn). He uses an alley distribution with crops in between lines of planted trees, and also a mosaic pattern, with fruit trees on one quadrant, livestock on another, annual crops on another, and variety of vegetables in another. A dirt road divides the farm into two halves with fences made of cacti (Sáez, 1997, p. 478).

Güira de Melena, Province of La Habana: Small farmer owns a 7 ha. farm. He grows mainly grapes for the tourist sector combined with many other crops sold to the state procurement agency. He has an area devoted to growing food crops destined to self-consumption and that of his eight permanent workers, to whom he pays 15 pesos per day, in addition to their food crops' share. He also makes wine at the farm. He belongs to the local CCS in order to gain access to agricultural inputs; otherwise he would not be a member. He stated that he likes the concept of a free market but without eliminating the price guarantee offered by the State. In that way, he would not be completely exposed to the vagaries of the market (Alvarez, 2000, pp. 162-163).

Observations About Family Farms in Cuba

• Small farms are more productive than large farms in most countries, including the United States. The value of total output per unit area composed of several crops and various animal products is greater than the value of the output per unit of large monoculture farms producing a single commodity.

• The small/traditional production sub-sector, is a reality, with over 250,000 small producers operating over 25% of the total agricultural land in Cuba and constituting a powerful and dynamic force to exert great influence in the economic development of the Cuba of the future.

- There is ample evidence that the non-state sector, particularly the small independent farmers, have substantially demonstrated their farming skills and capacity in producing larger output per hectare of food crops than their counterparts in the state sector.

- There is also evidence to affirm that small farmers in Cuba, using traditional cultural practices, had substantially contributed to the preservation of national resources, in contrast to the degradation caused by large state farms that used poor management and poor farming practices of mono-cropping, combined in many cases with excessive irrigation leading to water logging and increase in the salinity of soils.

- Small farmers will be able to make important contribution to solve some future critical national economic issues such as:

  - In the transition from state to market economy, by quickly increasing production of food commodities;

  - Increasing exports by increasing production of quality tobacco, fruits and winter vegetables for future exports to the United States; and

  - Keeping inflation as low as possible by responding quickly to credit incentives and increasing production of food crops at reasonable prices.

- They will also make contributions to local economic activities in rural communities by buying farming and construction materials, garden tools and agricultural inputs from local merchants.

- They will slow down the rural migration to large cities by staying in their farms and in this way mitigating the critical scarcity of urban houses.

- They will also strength the feasibility of rural development programs, initiated at the national or regional level, with their vigorous active participation in these social and economic programs.

RECOMMENDATIONS FOR THE NEAR FUTURE AND THE TRANSITION PERIOD

Our principal recommendation is the development of a nation-wide network—integrated by all small farm operators, independent private producers, and members of ANAP, CCS and CPAs—for the purpose of maintaining them constantly informed about market activities and policies enacted primarily to foster farm businesses, providing technical assistance, and promoting in rural communities economic, social an cultural developments. The organization and operation on a Small Farmer Network (SFN) is discussed in an Annex.

A second recommendation relates to the provision of agricultural credit to stimulate a rapid increase of food production from the small farmer sub-sector. This is almost a universal recommendation: Arturo Pino, an experienced credit specialist, believes that the prompt granting of credit requested by small farmers is the right way to quickly increase the availability of all types of food crops in the nation. He proposes a simple credit application form, together with the farmer's personal signed promissory note, to accelerate the credit process (Pino, 1995). I absolutely agree with the above recommendation, but I believe it is imperative that the credit applications should indicate approximately the expected transportation costs and proposed schedule of deliveries to specific markets.

A third recommendation relates to agricultural processing facilities. We recommend taking immediately a nation-wide inventory of all agricultural processing plants to determine their present production capacity and structural conditions, determine needed repairs, possibilities of plant expansion and estimated total costs. In Cuba, the following actions regarding processing industries are of utmost importance:

- Expand current poultry processing capacity and build new plants.

- Increase table oil extracting capacity by building new plants, in addition to the one in Santiago de Cuba, to extract oil from peanuts and imported soybeans. If we have to import vegetable oil, it is a better economic decision to import the raw material, soybeans, process it locally and use the main byproduct, soybean cake, for poultry and other livestock feed.

- Other processing plants that need capacity expansion are feed mixing plants and storages facilities with refrigeration for perishable vegetables. Other storage facilities for non-perishable agricultural products probably need to be reconstructed or new ones built. Rice, and other grains are harvested when their moisture content is relatively high; for safe storage, they must be dried artificially and then stored. This is done at the farm level in large rice farms, but commercial facilities for storage of small volumes produced in small farms probably would be needed.

Fourth, promote organic agriculture among small farmers to diversify their annual income. The provisional government or the SFN should conduct a survey among hotels and restaurants serving the tourist industry to determine the demand for organic products. The results should be made available to interested farmers, and they should be provided with proper training and education in some practical techniques and farming practices specific for organic production of crop and livestock products.

Fifth, stimulate small farmers to produce more livestock products. Livestock turn grasses into high-quality protein for human consumption. By covering more soil with long-term grasses for livestock, the livestock feed themselves and at the same time the grasses improve the environment by reducing soil erosion. Some incentives, like better credit terms or special sales of breeding stock to small farmers just starting livestock enterprises would be positive steps.

Sixth, creation of an autonomous institution for stabilizing the rural property market. France created SAFER, a rural property development and settlement company for the purpose of safeguarding the family nature of farms by preventing rural property speculation. SAFER buys land or farms for sale and resells them after having outfitted them, if needed. It also handles regrouping plots or parcels belonging to the same owner to increase farm size. A similar institution in Cuba could administer the creation of a "Land Bank" composed of land donations from former owners or cash from donors, unclaimed land located within state farms, and farms under litigation provided the litigating parties agree to give up their legal rights in exchange for other state property or compensation.

REFERENCES

Alonso, José F. "The Free Farmers Market: A Rejected Approach but a Possible Solution." *Cuba in Transition—Volume 2*. Washington: Association for the Study of the Cuban Economy, 1992, pp. 173-181.

Alvarez, José. "Differences in Agricultural Productivity in Cuba's State and Non-State Sectors: Further Evidence." *Cuba in Transition—Volume 10*. Washington: Association for the Study of the Cuban Economy, 2000, pp. 98-120.

Anderson, Joan. *The American Family Farm*. Harcourt Brace Jovanovich Publisher, New York, 1989.

Bishop, C. and Toussaint, W. *Introduction to Agricultural Analysis*. New York, John Wiley & Sons, 1966.

Burchardt, Hans-Jurgen. "La Decentralización de las Granjas Estatales en Cuba: ¿Gérmen para una Reforma Empresarial Pendiente?" *Cuba in Transition—Volume 10*. Washington: Association for the Study of the Cuban Economy, 2000, pp. 64-66.

Dalrymple, Dana. *Survey of Multiple Cropping in Less Developed Countries*. U.S. Department of Agriculture, Washington D.C., October, 1977.

Danish Farmers Union. *Agriculture in Denmark 1999*. Copenhagen, Denmark, 1999.

Dimitri, Carolyn and Greene, Catherine. *Recent Growth Pattern in the U.S. Organic Food Market.* U.S. Department of Agriculture, Bulletin # 777, Washington D.C.

Economic Research Service. "ERS Farm Typology: Classifying a Diverse Agricultural Sector." U.S. Department of Agriculture, *USDA Outlook*, November 1999.

France. Ministry of Agriculture and Fisheries. *A Comprehensive Survey of Agriculture and Agribusiness.* ADEPTA, Paris, February, 1998.

Ikerd, John. *Small Farm: Perceptions versus Realities.* University of Missouri, October 2000.

Japan. Ministry of Agriculture and Fisheries. *Abstract of Statistics on Agriculture, Forestry, and Fisheries in Japan.* Government of Japan 1998.

Jiménez, Francisco, M. "Regimen de Estructura Agraria: Tenencia de la Tierra y Tamaño de las Fincas en la Cuba del Futuro." In *Desarrollo Agrícola de Cuba*, Vol. I, Miami, Florida, 1992.

Kansas City Wind Power. *Independent Power Systems: Energy Efficient Products.* Kansas, 2002.

Lele, Uma. *The Design of Rural Development.* World Bank, Washington D.C., 1975.

"Organic Farming Growth." *Washington Post* (April 3, 2000).

Pino, Arturo. "La Agricultura en la Cuba Post-Castro." Conference at the Rotarios Club, Miami, Florida, May 1995.

Puerta, Ricardo and Alvarez, José. "Organization and Performance of Cuban Agriculture at Different Levels of State Intervention." *Cuba in Transition—Volume 3.* Washington: Association for the Study of the Cuban Economy, 1993.

Rosset, Peter M. *The Multiple Functions and Benefits of Small Farm Agriculture.* The Institute for Food and Development Policy, Oakland, CA, 1999.

Saez, Héctor. "Property Rights, Technology, and Land Degradation: A Case Study of Santo Domingo, Cuba." *Cuba in Transition—Volume 7.* Washington: Association for the Study of the Cuban Economy 1997, pp. 475-484.

Shell International Renewable. *Shell Solar- Photovoltaic Products 2002.* Catalog, 2002.

Steel, Cheryl J. "Why U.S. Agriculture and Rural Area Have Stake in Small Farms." *Rural Development Perspectives*, Vol. 12, No. 2, 1997.

Switzerland. "Welcome to the Best of Switzerland." Web Page: www.blw.admin.ch, statistics, 2000.

"Tweaking Genes Helps Plants Survive Elements." *Washington Post* (March 18, 2002).

ANNEX
DEVELOPING AN SMALL FARMERS NETWORKS (SFN) REGISTRY

This nation-wide register of all potential interested independent small farmers and those associated with pseudo-cooperatives, is estimated to include over 250,000 producers operating over 25% of the total agricultural land in Cuba. There are several components in the organization, functioning and implementation plan of the SFN that should be considered after the transition government has established its initial political, economic and social preliminary programs, including addressing the nation's immediate critical priorities. Hopefully, one of these priorities will be the preparation of a short-term plan to quick-

ly increase the supply of staples and other food products to feed the deprived Cuban population.

The SFN should be a computerized national data base system. The system should be designed by an experienced and credible international software company with the highest technical expertise and willing to do the job at a reasonable cost.

It should register, beginning with ANAP members, each small farm in the country, by municipality and province, assigning each farm an specific geographical code, the name and address of the farm, and the name of the head of the family owner or operator.

All information registered in the SFN should be available to the public, probably for the payment of a nominal fee, except for small farmers who will be able to access it without charge. Small farmers will register all crops grown, their yields, area planted and number of animals raised by species, family laborers by age and time availability, and any other information they would like to provide. Data from the SFN may assist small farmers in preparing their annual farm budget, in calculating cash expenses, yields, and income from cash sales, etc, and more generally in determining their approximate credit requirements, including household expenses.

Technical input into the system should be provided by professionals from the Ministry of Agriculture, credit specialists, commercial providers of inputs, processing industries, local agricultural authorities, marketing specialists, and officers from the Planning Board, the National Bank and the Armed Forces.

The farm data contained in the SFN will represent nearly a complete enumeration of all small farms in the nation. It will be relatively easy for statisticians to draw samples with a high degree of confidence for specific analyses. Large farms also could be registered in a separate data bank under the umbrella of the SFN to complete the national agricultural data needed to conduct national sample surveys, whenever they are needed, as well as a data source for microstudies such as specific commodity cases studies.

In addition to the farm data, the SFN may register, for a fee, all interested national and foreign companies, partnerships and individuals supplying agricultural inputs and services, agricultural processing industries buying raw agricultural products, and enterprises involved in exports and imports and other related businesses to the agricultural sector. The SFN will keep constant communication with local membership (*campesinado*) to inform them about prices, new markets for value-added products, demand from the tourist industry, etc.

There are several components of the SFN implementation plan:

1. Agricultural data from farmers credit applications made at government and private banks would be transferred, after being authorized by farmers, to the local SFN office in order to update already-registered farms or register new ones. This important component should be monitored by the National Bank or the Agricultural Credit Agency.

2. The technical research and technical farming guidelines will be developed by agricultural engineers, veterinarians, and other professionals of the Ministry of Agriculture as well as consultants from international organizations and technical experts from developed countries. The representative of the SFN at the local level will deliver technical assistance directly to farmers through regular and special meetings, distribution of farm publications, showing of farm movies, presentations and lectures about specific farming techniques by agricultural experts. The local SFN representative generally will be a graduate from an agricultural technical schools (Maestro Agrícola) or a qualified retired volunteer from government or international organizations.

3. The Armed Forces will provide the manpower to run the computerized network at both local and national level. Work Youth Army (EJT) members could be designated to assist the local SFN representatives in attending to farmers' inquires, input data into the system, prepare the SFN local offices for technical meetings, showing movies, etc.

4. The SFN will educate farmers about shifting to organic methods, explaining the ecological advantages of this type of farming and the premium prices for both vegetables and animals products. The SFN could assist the Ministry of Agriculture in sponsoring small farmers interested in experimenting with new crops or varieties from other countries until agricultural experiment stations are established.

LA RECONSTRUCCIÓN DE LA INDUSTRIA AZUCARERA CUBANA

Juan Tomás Sánchez[1]

INTRODUCCIÓN Y CONCLUSIONES

La reconstrucción de la industria azucarera que se plantea en este estudio es un mapa concreto y completo para estabilizar la sociedad creando trabajo durante los primeros meses del cambio. Primero, debemos entender que hay que salirse del círculo vicioso que crearía la falta de estabilidad política, la falta de un estado de derecho, y la falta de los derechos de libertad de expresión, asociación y propiedad por un lado; y por el otro lado, la necesidad de mantener fuentes de trabajo y un mínimo de inversión para poder empezar a andar el camino de la reconstrucción plena. En el caso de la industria azucarera, es viable mantener las estructuras de producción para comenzar sobre una base estable.

a. Se asume incorrectamente que Cuba no puede reinsertarse como exportador de azúcar de importancia. Cuba tiene todas las condiciones físicas y humanas para producir a bajos costos y alto rendimiento agrícola. No se trata de destronar a Brasil. Se trata de empezar a sobrevivir y reconstruir con los recursos que se encuentren y los que se puedan obtener.

b. Se puede argumentar que la reconstrucción de la industria azucarera cubana como la mayor y mejor perspectiva de crear cientos de miles de empleos y oportunidades de negocios pequeños y grandes en manos de cubanos. Cuba puede producir azúcar a menos de 6 centavos la libra. Ver Tabla 1.

c. La industria azucarera cubana, históricamente crea 57 horas-hombre[2] por tonelada de azúcar producida. Si la inversión promedio para restaurar toda la industria azucarera cubana fuese de $2,500[3] por tonelada de capacidad de caña de molienda diaria, por 0.13 toneladas de azúcar por tonelada de caña diarias, en zafras de 100 días efectivos, 13 toneladas de azúcar. A 57 horas-hombre por tonelada de azúcar, serían 741 horas hombre con una inversión de $2,500 dólares, equivalente a $3.50 por empleo permanente. Por cada 100 empleos, 87 son agrícolas en zafra y 13 son permanentes en el central azucarero.

d. Existe todo un andamiaje constitucional y legal, antes de 1959, que garantiza al obrero y al agricultor una protección y una participación justa del ingreso azucarero a precios del mercado de exportación. Algo que no puede sustituirse por modelos no probados en Cuba.

e. El obrero y el campesino cubano tenían garantías constitucionales y legales, antes de 1959, que implantadas crean la estabilidad laboral necesaria

---

1. Dedicado a los hombres y mujeres que han hecho, hacen y harán azúcar en Cuba. Para recibir un costo detallado de operaciones agrícolas e industriales, favor de dirigirse a Juantsanchez@Asociaciondecolonosdecuba.org.

2. *Anuario Azucarero de Cuba 1959* para la zafra de 1958, página 160.

3. Puede variar de $10-12 mil por tonelada de caña a muy poco, dependiendo de las condiciones actuales.

Tabla 1. Costos de Producción por Libra de Azúcar

Contrato No. 11, NY. Base 96 Polarización, Ctvs. / Lb.	10.00		6.55		5.00	
Por libra a 98 Pol. Ctvs./lb.	10.28		6.73		5.14	
Por Tonelada Métrica de Azúcar 98 Pol.	$ 226.52		$ 148.37		$ 113.26	
CAPITAL (depreciación e intereses)	$ 0.0129	11.88%	$ 0.0129	18.04%	$ 0.0129	24.00%
COSTO DE OPERACION						
Compra de caña, 80% independientes; 10% vinculados .; 10% de administración (propia).	$ 0.0494	45.56%	$ 0.0330	46.14%	$ 0.0256	47.64%
Transporte de caña al ingenio[a]	$ 0.0071	6.53%	$ 0.0071	9.92%	$ 0.0071	13.20%
Químicos [b]	$ 0.0064	5.94%	$ 0.0064	9.02%	$ 0.0064	12.00%
Combustible [c]	$ 0.0001	0.12%	$ 0.0001	0.19%	$ 0.0001	0.25%
Mantenimiento [d]	$ 0.0001	0.12%	$ 0.0001	0.19%	$ 0.0001	0.25%
Mano de Obra [e]	$ 0.0080	7.38%	$ 0.0052	7.34%	$ 0.0040	7.45%
Costo Total de Operación por Libra de Azúcar	$ 0.0712	65.67%	$ 0.0520	72.79%	$ 0.0434	80.80%
TOTAL COSTOS, POR: LIBRA DE AZÚCAR	$ 0.0841	77.55%	$ 0.0649	90.83%	$ 0.0562	104.80%
INGRESOS, POR:						
Azúcar	$ 0.1028		$ 0.0673		$ 0.0514	
Mieles Finales. 6.478lb/GAL. Azúcar Total. New Orleans 79.5 Brix, 43% AT. FOB Cuba.	$ 0.0057		$ 0.0041		$ 0.0023	
Total de Ingresos	$ 0.1084	100.00%	$ 0.0714	100.00%	$ 0.0537	100.00%
TOTAL UTILIDAD BRUTA, POR LIBRA DE AZÚCAR	$ 0.0243	22.45%	$ 0.0066	9.17%	$ (0.0026)	-4.80%
UTILIDAD BRUTA, ANUAL	$1,889,579		$ 508,620		$ (200,090)	
Producción Anual Lb. Az.	77,639,398		77,639,398		77,639,398	

a. Precio contratado: $2 tonelada de caña por hora de transporte (ida y vuelta). Con equipo propio se puede calcular a $0.76/tonelada de caña por hora de transporte.

b. *Cane Sugar. The small-scale processing option.* Raphael Kaplinsky. Intermediate Technology Development Group. 1989. Economic viability of large-scale vacuum pan technology, by Edward Mallory, with a capacity of 3,600 tcd. Págs. 84-93

c. Op. cit.

d. Op. cit.

e. Costo promedio en Cuba (1952) base 4.8 Ctvs./lb. entre $0.60-$1,50 por saco de 250 lbs. para centrales automatizados y centrales poco automatizados. Resultados de la "Comisión Técnica Azucarera" en 1953.

para las grandes inversiones, y no que quitándolas se logran grandes inversiones.

f. No se considera el acceso a la cuota azucarera americana de importación por encontrarla muy impredecible en términos políticos.

g. Los sindicatos y asociaciones democráticas que representen coherentemente los sentimientos y ambiciones de los sectores de la producción azucarera, van a ser aquellos que mayor oposición presenten a una transición disfrazada y al extremismo político y económico. La reconstrucción de la industria azucarera tiene una fuerza inigualable para hacerle frente a la apatía, la división, y para generar estabilidad social.

h. Para los EE.UU., la mayor preocupación es, sin duda, una Cuba inestable política y económicamente. Cualquier ayuda (aunque la intención no sea el bienestar de los cubanos) para poder producir y para la compra de productos cubanos se-

ría de las más eficientes inversiones en que pudiera pensar Washington, para crear estabilidad social en Cuba. Todas las zonas azucareras de Cuba tienen un "derecho inviolable" de mantener y evitar su desaparición. Sería absurdo pensar que la solución para que la industria azucarera sea más rentable está en que Cuba termine con 40 mega centrales porque se asume que "mientras más grande más económico." ¿Y del resto del país, qué?

i. El mercado de exportacion de azúcar es este año 2003 un mercado de 39 millones de toneladas, a un precio promedio a la fecha (septiembre) de 7.32 centavos de US dólar la libra, $161.38 por ton. métrica, unos $6,300 millones de dólares. Es un mercado grande, estable (no va a desaparecer), y libre sin que nadie lo controle, en el que crece el consumo anual al 2 por ciento (casi un millón de toneladas de azúcar por año).

j. El cambio de empresas controladas por el estado seria por la vía judicial. Todas las empresas azucareras en Cuba están en quiebra. Las Leyes de Quiebra protegen la propiedad y le dan garantías a la nueva inversión. Se elimina la participación del gobierno en la restitución, y las soluciones son con derechos a todos de ser escuchados por un juez imparcial y de poder apelar.

k. Las reclamaciones por la expropiación ilegal a empresas y ciudadanos norteamericanos caerían en las siguientes categorías:

   * La restitución (la más factible y moral para la reconstrucción de Cuba empobrecida).

   * El que no acepta la restitución escogería: (i) que Washington lo represente ante La Habana en La Haya; (ii) representarse a sí mismo en los tribunales en Cuba; (iii) rechazarla por lo que implica en impuestos al IRS, a lo que Washington pasaría a vender la propiedad.[4] Caso que puede llegar a ser muy generalizado y que abriría la Caja de Pandora de quien y como subasta/vende y quien y como puede comprar. Ejemplo: Los centrales Preston y el Boston, con una capacidad combinada de 16 mil toneladas de caña por día (tcd), pueden valer hoy mucho más de $160 millones, y en tierras de 2,500 caballerias de caña (75 mil acres, 33,500 ha.) al precio de 1959 de $3 mil la caballería ($90/acre, $224/ha.) parecería un regalo.

Las siguientes aclaraciones son pertinentes. Primero, la estrategia que posiblemente sigan la mayoría de los empresarios agrícolas de caña de azúcar, colonos y hacendados, será la de mantener bajo los costos, aunque el rendimiento por unidad de área sea relativamente bajo, para garantizarse su supervivencia en los relativamente bajos precios del mercado de los últimos años. Segundo, la transición a manos privadas seria a través del *secuestro* (embargo judicial) de bienes de manos del estado a manos del Poder Judicial bajo la legislación de Quiebras y Derecho Mercantil, mientras tanto se dilucida el derecho de propiedad y administración. El juez daría un Mandato con Facultades de Administración al mejor calificado de los solicitantes. Esta estrategia asegura que todos tengamos derechos a ser oídos ante un juez imparcial y a la apelación. Los desafíos por los que se plantea la solución judicial estriban en: propiedades habidas ilegalmente (antes y durante la transición), propiedades que podían ser transadas en procesos extra-judiciales por las multinacionales expropiadas ilegalmente después de 1959 y que sus dueños originales renuncian a la propiedad (como puede ser para no asumir una deuda con Hacienda en EE.UU. (Internal Revenue Service, IRS) americano, al recibir un bien que ya se había declarado como pérdida, están en conflicto los propietarios, no aparecen, y otros tipos de incertidumbres que se pudieran anticipar.

Cuba no es un país rico en el que se plantea una nueva estrategia para conquistar un nuevo mercado. Cuba es un país depauperado que sabe hacer azúcar, que tiene una población ansiosa de trabajar libre y productivamente, un clima, una tierra, una cantidad de sol y de lluvia que hace que sea un productor de altos rendimientos y bajo costo. Los cubanos sabemos cosechar caña de azúcar y hacer azúcar en grandes cantidades y en las peores circunstancias. Nuestra isla es estrecha y larga, los puertos listos para embarcar azúcar son buenos y muchos, nuestros centrales están cerca de los puertos y nuestros puertos están más cerca de los más grandes importadores que los otros exportadores de azúcar.

El propósito de este trabajo no es una lección de historia. Nada más lejos de eso. Este es un trabajo sobre la ejecución de un Plan para rescatar la industria azucarera cubana. Cualquier plan de ejecución puede fallar, por muy buenas intenciones que tenga, si no está basado en principios valiosos y en un análisis profundo de la situación.

Aquellos proyectos que presenten las mayores posibilidades de atraer a los cubanos hacia el verdadero Es-

---

4. Ejemplo: La United Fruit Company, $85 millones en deducción de impuestos. Si acepta la propiedad en restitución, puede adquirir una responsabilidad de $42.5 millones, al 50 por ciento de impuestos en efecto en 1969. Decision CU-3824 de la FCSC.

tado de Derecho y a la representación democrática dentro de sus asociaciones y sindicatos, van a ser aquellos que presenten la oposición más fuerte al extremismo político y la transición disfrazada.

No se puede asumir que el cambio vendrá fácil, sobre las protecciones a los derechos humanos y democráticos que una generación quisiera pasarle a la siguiente generación. El cambio debe influenciarse por aquellas agrupaciones de la sociedad civil cubana que representan coherentemente los sentimientos e intereses de los sectores laboral, agrícola e industrial de la industria azucarera cubana. Estos tres sectores subsisten hoy en día dentro de la sociedad cubana, unas de una forma clandestina en Cuba y las otras exiladas.

LOS PRINCIPIOS ÉTICOS Y LEGALES DE LA RECONSTRUCCIÓN

La propuesta para la reconstrucción de la industria azucarera debe ser un Plan que pueda sostenerse en cualquier foro, y hacer que cualquier otro plan sea efímero. El Plan está basado en los más altos principios, y en una moral y legalidad conforme a la tradición moral y legal en Cuba. Como también esta fundado en un modelo exitoso, y no en modelos especulativos.

El Plan se presenta bajo el régimen de Derecho Constitucional que protege los logros laborales y de los agricultores, como sus obligaciones, establecidos a partir de 1937 con la Ley de Coordinación Azucarera y después ratificados por la Constitución de 1940, y los Decretos, Leyes y Sentencias del Tribunal Supremo que la suplementaron.

El Plan reconoce como doctrina social y legal el "Derecho Inviolable de Todas las Zonas Azucareras," de mantener y de evitar la desaparición de ingenios y las zonas agrícolas, en detener el proceso de concentración en los ingenios que sobrevivan la crisis actual, colocando el interés nacional por encima de los intereses privados, proclamado así: [5]

Descansa sobre el principio fundamental de reconocer y respetar como inviolables los intereses que existen en tales zonas, a saber: el de la unidad industrial, el ingenio; el del colono, que ha invertido allí su dinero y su trabajo; el del propietario de la tierra, que sin caña perdería su valor de renta; el de los obreros, tanto industriales como agrícolas, que allí tienen su fuente de trabajo; el del..."

No tiene las más mínimas posibilidades de éxito un plan que esté basado en los deseos de "privatizar,"[6] lo que sería la venta pública de la actual industria azucarera, por noble que fuese la intención. Un plan con esas características carece de moralidad, carece de legalidad, carece de un modelo exitoso, y solamente beneficiaria al comprador astuto y al político corrupto.

El objetivo del Plan es crear estabilidad política creando empleos y produciendo en libertad. Este estudio presenta el Plan para comenzar a rescatar la industria azucarera cubana sobre los más altos principios morales y legales. Compartir ideas y soluciones para ir mejorando el plan, y un análisis profundo de las condiciones que la rodean. Comenzar por determinar cuales serían los costos y beneficios de la industria azucarera cubana en un ambiente que se sabe fue exitoso. Desarrollar y explicar las bases de un funcionamiento justo y legal para todos los factores que la integran. Proyectar los beneficios y esfuerzos que serian necesarios para la implementación del Plan.

La meta sería devolver a Cuba la posibilidad de poder ser algún día un productor y exportador de azúcar y sus sub-productos de acuerdo a su potencial. El éxito lo veríamos si la industria y la agricultura son rentables como la base para la creación de empleos y divisas para la nación, con la reconstrucción de todos los ingenios demolidos.

Tomamos como base para este estudio el caso más difícil: el de los centrales demolidos, debido a la importancia en la reconstrucción de la sociedad cubana a lo

---

5. José Antonio Guerra, Apéndice 5, *Azúcar y Población en las Antillas*, 1942.

6. Las encuestas en Rusia hoy dan que el 75 por ciento desea que se anulen las privatizaciones de los años 90 que creó una oligarquía sin límites que amenaza el lento proceso democrático. "Privatizar," como concepto de reconocer que todo lo incautado es legítima propiedad del estado cubano y no de sus legítimos dueños, para sacarlo a subasta pública, sería intercambiable por "piratizar" la propiedad ajena.

largo y ancho de Cuba. No se considera en el estudio económico acceso a la cuota azucarera americana de alto precio y grandes complicaciones, para hacer el estudio más realista. Como tampoco se toman en consideración financiamientos fuera de lo que normalmente se puede esperar para un productor de azúcar (un *commodity* que se cotiza en la Bolsa de New York), ni subsidio a bases de altos precios al consumo nacional, como sucede en la inmensa mayoría de los países del mundo. Estudiamos la reconstrucción de la industria azucarera cubana sobre las bases de ventas en el mercado mundial.

La fortaleza de la industria azucarera cubana dependerá de que no se encuentre comprometida en nada con nada que pueda impedir su desarrollo. Como tampoco debe ser objeto de negociaciones de gobierno a gobierno, a espaldas de los trabajadores y empresarios azucareros.

La industria azucarera cubana, con su indiscutible capacidad excepcional de producir azúcar con alto rendimiento y bajos costos, tiene mucho que ofrecer en un cambio doloroso, como el que nos espera. Mucho que ofrecer en la calidad y la cantidad de empleo y recursos; mostrando un ejemplo para obreros, empresarios y gobierno, de cooperación entre sus factores: trabajadores, colonos y hacendados, y la estructura democrática de sus respectivas agrupaciones, basadas en elecciones democráticas a nivel local y provincial, para la selección de la representación a nivel nacional.

Tratamos en este trabajo de estudiar el caso más crítico: cuando el central ha sido prácticamente demolido y las tierras con un ínfimo rendimiento en azúcar, para así poder servir en algo a los "hombres en Cuba que hacen el azúcar" a labrarse un futuro de acuerdo con sus posibilidades.

EL MODELO CUBANO DE PRODUCIR AZÚCAR EN LIBERTAD

Los que comentan sobre la imposibilidad de Cuba recuperarse participando en el mercado azucarero mundial ignoran la realidad del empresario azucarero en Cuba y las condiciones del mercado actual:

1. Cuba casi nunca fue de altos rendimientos en el campo, pero siempre de bajos costos debido a ahorros en fertilización y regadío. Las condiciones existentes de acuerdos internacionales y bajos precios no permitían otra alternativa para poder subsistir. Así se protegía de perdidas en los años de bajos precios (la mayoría de los años), aunque no realizaba el máximo de utilidad en los años excepcionales (unos pocos en la primera mitad del siglo XX, muchos a partir de 1964). Un agricultor puede ser optimista o puede ser realista (conservador), de ahí parte la política agrícola azucarera ayer y mañana en Cuba. No se puede comparar a Cuba con los otros productores como Brasil. La estrategia económica del agricultor en ambos países es muy diferente. Primeramente, el agricultor en Cuba no tuvo ni espera recibir subsidios. Menos de una sociedad empobrecida como está Cuba, ni tampoco ser una carga a un gobierno en situación muy difícil. La industria azucarera debe estar para ayudar. La mayoría de los ingenios en Cuba tienen grandes extensiones de tierra propias cultivables para caña de azúcar, lo que abarata grandemente el costo de producción industrial de azúcar para el central al no tener que pagar por esas cañas el 50 por ciento del rendimiento industrial al *colono*.

2. La ecuación costo-ingreso en Cuba futura es la siguiente: Preparar y sembrar una hectárea para que produzca 43 ton. o 85 ton. de caña por año, cuesta $75 o $600 por ha. de inversión, una vez cada 10 años. Cada ha. produciría 5 o 10 ton. de azúcar. El *colono* recibiría el 50 por ciento, el equivalente de 2.5 o 5 ton. de azúcar por ha. de caña recolectada y entregada. Los ingresos serian entre $330 a $510 para uno, $660 a $1,020 para el otro, a precios del mercado mundial de 6 ctvs. o 10 ctvs. la libra, rendimiento industrial del 13 por ciento, participación del colono del 50 por ciento del azúcar producido. Todos los otros costos son iguales por tonelada de caña. Lo que demuestra que es una decisión basada en riesgo-oportunidad de financiamiento, y numero de hectáreas. Aquí se trata de demostrar que la baja inversión garantiza la supervivencia, y la alta, con financiamientos razonables, sería extremadamente beneficiosa y creadora de empleos.

3. Cuando se evalúa el caso cubano no se puede medir por el modelo del mercado mundial que existía con restricciones a la producción en Cuba. Eso ya no existe, cada país puede producir y vender lo que le parezca bien. Cuba, llegando a exportar 2, 3 o 4 millones de toneladas de azúcar crudo, solamente participa en menos del 10 por ciento de un mercado que hoy es de 39 millones de toneladas.

4. Cuba siempre tuvo y puede aspirar a altos rendimientos industriales a bajo costo debido a una continua renovación y modernización de la planta industrial, que nada tiene que ver con el año de su fundación. Y en muchos casos con una gran inversión en vías férreas, todavía existente en alguna proporción, que es el menor costo de transporte, para algo voluminoso y pesado como la caña, conocido hasta hoy.

El Modelo del Ingenio Demolido

Para llevar la Reconstrucción a todo el territorio, hay que rehacer toda la industria y la agricultura. Existe un gran potencial en hombres y mujeres, tierras y algo de planta industrial que quede donde quiera que una vez hubo un ingenio y una zona azucarera. No hay una fórmula para determinar en cuanto es rentable una inversión en la reconstrucción de una zona azucarera. Pero sí se puede señalar que según la disponibilidad de caña, medios de transporte, áreas para caña propia del central, y lo que quede de un central azucarero demolido, van a determinar cuanto y en que condiciones de pago hace falta en inversión para la Reconstrucción.

Primeramente señalamos en está estudio que el ofrecer cantidades exactas de cuanto es que cuesta un central azucarero hoy en día, no aplica al caso de la reconstrucción de la industria azucarera de Cuba. Basar una conclusión de que cuesta hoy en día $10 mil dólares por tonelada de caña de molienda diaria, ignora las condiciones físicas en las que se puede encontrar un central desmantelado, y mucho menos la rentabilidad de la inversión.

La rentabilidad de la inversión necesaria está íntimamente ligada a las condiciones de amortización, depreciación e intereses, por un lado. Por el otro, cuanto costaría reponer la planta a una producción deseada y con qué suministro de caña (la materia prima) puede contar. Mientras más caña propia, mayor las posibilidades de rentabilidad. El costo de operación de un central azucarero es casi el mismo en cualquier parte del mundo, pero el costo de producción de caña de azúcar y el contenido en azúcar extraíble es muy variable.

La situación estudiada ha sido el siguiente ejemplo:

¿Es viable invertir $7.5 millones de dólares para lograr una capacidad de molienda de 3,500 tcd un diez por ciento de "caña de administración,"[7] 10 por ciento de colonos vinculados al central (en tierras del central), y el 80 por ciento de colonos libres (en tierra propia o de terceros) para hacer zafras con ingreso promedio de $8.4 millones de dólares (3,150 toneladas efectivas de caña diaria) cuando el precio en mercado mundial es de 10 Ctvs. por lb.?

¡Si! El costo total de operación puede ser de 5.5 centavos la libra de azúcar. Una nueva inversión promedio de $2,143 por tonelada de caña diaria de molienda puede cubrir todos los costos hasta cuando los precios caigan a 5 ½ centavos la libra.

Si la inversión necesaria fuese mayor, las condiciones de financiamiento deben mejorarse. Cada caso lo ve cada empresario a su manera, aunque hay unas bases comunes de riesgo que se pueden predecir. La función de los interesados en que se realice la inversión para crear un centro de producción y empleos, es la de presentar y respaldar el beneficio social que representa una fuente de empleo que beneficia a toda una comunidad, a los posibles proveedores de condiciones de financiamiento aceptables para la inversión.

La Solución Legal a la Restitución de la Propiedad Privada

Todas las empresas azucareras en Cuba son empresas en quiebra. Las leyes de Quiebras y los códigos de Derecho Mercantil y Derecho Civil establecen las ba-

---

7. "Caña propia" es aquella que se produce en tierras de terceros en la que el central paga el 50 por ciento del rendimiento industrial al colono independiente. La "caña de administración" es en la que produce el dueño o el operador del central.

ses para la protección de los activos y la plusvalía de una empresa en vías de recuperación, y de otras en vías de desaparición. La transición de empresas controladas por el estado sería por la vía judicial. Jueces Municipales decidirán según los meritos, a quien puede otorgar un Mandato con Facultades de Administración. Las leyes de quiebra ofrecen plenas garantías a los nuevos acreedores que harían posible es funcionamiento de la empresa con debida protección preferencial a los nuevos acreedores, y a la propiedad, hasta que la propiedad y la capacidad de administrarla se establezca ante el mismo juez. Otro beneficio es que saca de la ecuación la corrupción administrativa por parte del estado.

El Margen de Costos y Utilidades de una Nueva Inversión

La nueva inversión económica estimada para reconstruir la capacidad de molienda y producción de un central demolido se calcula sobre las bases siguientes, para establecer un modelo económico:

Productos: Azucar y molazas.
Capacidad: 3,500 tcd.
Duración de la zafra: 106 días el primer año.
Días efectivos de zafra: 86.
Utilización de la capacidad el primer año: 79 por ciento.
Suministro de caña, por ciento: 80-10-10, colonos independientes, colonos vinculados, y "caña de administración."
Nueva inversión industrial en maquinaria (y vehículos y gastos): $7.5 millones de dólares garantizada en azúcar y propiedades del ingenio.
Maquinaria y equipos: $ 7 millones, depreciación en 20 años. 50 por ciento en dólares, 50 por ciento en Cuba por mano de obra y algunos equipos de fabricación en Cuba. Interés al 7 por ciento annual.
Vehículos y gastos: $500,000, depreciación en 4 años. 100 por ciento en dólares. Intereses al 7 por ciento.

Por ejemplo, para restaurar la capacidad industrial por cada millón de toneladas de azúcar haría falta una inversión de $213 millones de dólares. Cada tonelada

de azúcar históricamente crea en Cuba 57 horas-hombre. En $213 millones de dólares se crean 57 millones de horas-hombre. Una inversión de capital de $3.75 crean una hora-hombre permanente. Se puede estimar que debería de restaurarse un millón de toneladas adicionales cada año por tres años consecutivos para lograr una capacidad adicional a cualquiera que fuese la actual al momento del cambio, de 6 millones de toneladas de azúcar.

La nueva inversión en maquinaria (tractores, arados y sistema de regadío) e insumos agrícolas (abono) es toda en dólares. Se calculó una inversión original de $7 mil dólares por caballería el primer año, para lograr un rendimiento de 100,000 arrobas por caballería (85 ton por ha.) financiada en 5 años, por el ingenio o por la banca nacional o extranjera en Cuba, al 7 por ciento de interés. Garantizada en azúcar. Se entiende que cada central es un caso diferente ya que seria según la inversión que fuese necesaria para lograr la capacidad de producción deseada, y el ingreso neto, después del pago de las cañas a los colonos, que varía según la proporción de caña propia-caña de otros-tierra propia.

Para aumentar la producción anual en un millón de toneladas de azucar, harían falta aumentar la producción de caña en 7.7 millones de toneladas cada año. A una inversión de $8.25 por tonelada de caña,[8] se necesita en la agricultura una inversión aproximada de $63.5 millones por año durante 5 años para lograr una producción azucarera adicional de 5 a 6 millones de toneladas de azúcar.

No se contemplan en este estudio, para hacerlo más estricto, el acceso a la Cuota Americana de importación de azúcar, por considerarlo altamente especulativo el ingreso a dicho mercado. Tampoco se consideran financiamientos altamente favorables como pudieran estar disponibles a través de las instituciones financieras mundiales. Solo se consideraron lo que se puede esperar de experimentados azucareros cubanos e inversionistas en medios de producción de azúcar.

---

8. La *FNP Consultaría & Agroinformativos* de Brasil, reporta un costo total de siembra para un rendimiento promedio de 95 toneladas por ha., con resiembra cada 6 años, de US$ 6.84 por tonelada de caña.

La Función Social de la Industria Azucarera

La función social y económica de la industria azucarera en Cuba, quedó firmemente y legalmente establecida en la Ley de Coordinación Azucarera de 1937 y el Derecho de Permanencia que comenzó prácticamente con el Decreto-Ley de 15 de mayo de 1934.[9] Luego ratificada y ampliada por la Constitución de 1940 y por Leyes y Decretos posteriores. "Posiblemente ninguna otra actividad económica en Cuba ofrece un grado tan alto de distribución de sus ingresos."[10]

El Costo Actual en Cuba

Los que han reportado sobre el tema han concluído que el costo de producción de azúcar es de 15 centavos la libra de azúcar. Nunca aparece una separación entre los factores de costo en dólares, y en pesos cubanos sin valor. No se puede determinar el costo de producción futuro en Cuba basado en lo que cuesta hoy en día. Los métodos y los objetivos que plantea una producción en manos de gobernantes son muy diferentes a los objetivos que tiene un agricultor independiente y el industrial independiente. Tratar de rebatir las estadísticas publicadas por Cuba sería inútil ya que no son fiables. Es el resultado que tenía que esperarse cuando la propiedad estatal de hombres y plantas es absoluta.

¿Cuánto se Puede Recobrar en Divisas?

No necesita mucho estudio el determinar que la industria azucarera favorece la recuperación de divisas como posiblemente ninguna otra actividad importante. ¿Cuál sería el promedio que se recobraría en divisas? Sería alta la recuperación en divisas. Podemos asumir debido a la naturaleza de los costos: las grandes inversiones en materia de importación, en maquinarias y equipos son financiables y depreciables a largo plazo; los costos recurrentes año tras año de importación son mínimos bajo el sistema de corte manual que requiere poca maquinaria.

Costos de Producción y Costo y Utilidades del Modelo Industrial

Si tomamos como base un precio promedio de 10 centavos la libra Contrato No. 11, rendimiento industrial del 13% a 98° de polarización, los costos industriales que representan los por cientos del precio de venta serían los dados en la Tabla 1. Nótese que el pago por depreciación e intereses oscila entre el 11.88 y el 24 por ciento, según el precio de venta sea de 10 a 5 centavos la libra. El costo por depreciación e intereses está basado en maquinaria depreciada a 20 y equipos a 4 años. Interés al 7 por ciento anual.

El Empleo Agrícola Azucarero

El empleo directo que genera la industria azucarera se pudiera calcular a base del reporte del *Anuario Azucarero de Cuba 1959* para la zafra de 1958, página 160: 364 millones de Horas-Hombre por año (6.375 millones x 57.06 Hombre/tonelada de azúcar). Los salarios e ingresos de los trabajadores agrícolas serían los indicados en la Tabla 2 para diferentes alternativas de precio del azúcar en el mercado mundial.

El desarrollo del salario agrícola azucarero en Cuba a partir de la Ley de Coordinación Azucarera de 1937 está indicado en la Tabla 3. Podemos concluir que para un obrero agrícola de 1940 y hasta la fecha, los principios legales que protegen al trabajador azucarero cubano, casi totalmente representados por poderosos organismos sindicales independientes, son protecciones que se deben defender, por todos dentro y fuera de la industria azucarera, en una recuperación democrática en Cuba.

Es de notarse el que desde 1947 se legisló que el precio mínimo para determina el salario diario seria el de 4.82 centavos la libra, aunque en años posteriores el mercado no alcanzo ese nivel.

El Empleo Industrial Azucarero

El empleo azucarero industrial es estable y bastante consistente en los días y horas de trabajo durante el

9. *Gaceta Oficial* de mayo 17 de 1934 prorrogó por dos años los contratos de colonato, arrendamiento, subarrendamiento y aparcería de fincas rústicas dedicadas principalmente al cultivo de la caña, hasta que entró en vigor la Ley de Coordinación Azucarera.

10. José Antonio Guerra, "La Industria Azucarera en Cuba," *Diario de La Marina*, Número Extraordinario. SIGLO Y CUARTO. 1957

Tabla 2. Salarios e Ingresos

Al trabajador agrícola:	Contrato No. 11	10	6.50	5.00
Por otras labores, mínimo diario, 65.45 más beneficios	65.45	$ 6.72	$ 4.40	$ 3.36
Importe por Corte, Alza y Tiro. Libras por 100 arrobas = 2,500 lbs.	61.06	$ 6.27	$ 4.11	$ 3.14
Por Corte, Alza y Tiro, por tonelada de caña, libras de azúcar	53.85	$ 5.53	$ 3.62	$ 2.77
Corte y Alza, 62.5%, por tonelada de caña.	38.16	$ 3.92	$ 2.57	$ 1.96
Tiro, 37.5%, por tonelada de caña.	33.65	$ 3.46	$ 2.26	$ 1.73

Tabla 3. Desarrollo del Salario Agrícola Azucarero en Cuba a Partir de 1937[a]

Año	Ley / decreto	Corte y Alza	Tiro	Otros trabajos en Zafra Diario, min.	Trabajos de Tiempo Muerto, Diario, min.
1937	Ley de Coordinación Azucarera, 2 de septiembre de 1937 Art. XXXV, lbs. de azúcar por 100 @ de cana	62.5% de 50 lbs. de azúcar por 100 @ de cana	37.5% de 50 lbs. de azúcar por 100 @ de cana		
		50.5 a 52.5 lbs. de azúcar		50 lbs./ día	50 lbs. /día
	Basado en rendimiento industrial	11.50% < a >13.25%			
Constitución de 1940	Art. 67. Días de fiesta y de duelo nacional, descanso anual, y retiro incluído, equivalente al 9.09%	+ 9.09%		+ 9.09%	+ 9.09%
1943	Decreto 3383 de Noviembre 16 de 1943	Aportación patronal para el Retiro Azucarero			
1944	Decreto 903 de 5 de Abril de 1944	Disponiendo que por los colonos se pagara a sus trabajadores, por concepto "bonificación circunstancial agrícola," un 10% de aumento sobre lo que estos recibían por el corte, alza y tiro de la cañas + 10%			
1945	Decreto 117 de 17 de Enero de 1945	Ratificó el Decreto 903 para la zafra de 1945			
1945	Decreto 4164 de 31 de Diciembre de 1945	Se convirtió en aumento permanente, no solo para las labores del Decreto 903 sino para todas las demás labores agrícolas azucareras		+ 10%	+ 10%
TOTAL A LA FECHA, lbs. de azúcar por 100 @ de cana.		**58.70—61.06**		60	60
1948	Decreto 4602 de 30 de Diciembre. Se implantó como mínimo el precio máximo de 1947.	Precio teórico máximo de 1947: 4.824940 cts. / lb. (de aquí en adelante)			
1948	Decreto 1568 de 6 de Mayo de 1948. Se implantó para tiempo muerto, la jornada de 44 horas de trabajo semanal por 48 horas de sueldo,			+ 9.09% para labores	
TOTAL A LA FECHA, lbs. de azúcar por día, mínimo		**58.70—61.06**		**65.45 lbs. por día**	
1952	Decreto 2693 de 5 de Julio de 1952	Aportación patronal a la Maternidad Obrera			
1953	Decreto 456 de 20 Febrero de 1953	Participación mínima del 50% del rendimiento en azúcar a los colonos.			

a. Fuente: Asociación de Colonos de Cuba. Comité Ejecutivo Nacional. Análisis global de la situación del Colonato desde 1937 a la fecha. Marzo de 1959. 1 arroba = 25 libras año. El único caso en que se nos ha confiado información confidencial de un central azucarero promedio en Cuba, coincide plenamente con el promedio obtenido de un estudio de centrales venezolanos. al que hacemos referencia:[11] Por cada 1,000 toneladas de caña de molienda diaria se crean 1,000 empleos, 130 empleos industriales, y 870 empleos agrícolas mayormente durante tiempo de zafra.

LOS MERCADOS PARA EL AZÚCAR CUBANO DE EXPORTACION

¿Cuáles Son las Expectativas a Largo Plazo?

Este estudio no es para proyecciones largo plazo; solo se contempla lo que es factible lograr en poco tiempo cuando comience el cambio en Cuba, con la industria azucarera como fuerza estabilizadora para los primeros meses y tal vez uno o dos años hasta que el país se estabilice. Pero no hay razones para temer al largo plazo. El azúcar crudo es un producto que tiene su mercado, sus suministradores y sus consumidores. El mercado de importación de azúcar crudo en 2003 es de más de 39 millones de toneladas, valor crudo, equivalente a un promedio de 6.5 centavos la libra, US$ 143.30 tonelada métrica, un mercado de $5,645 millones de dólares este año. Para el 2004 la International Sugar Organization (ISO), pronostica un crecimiento del consumo del 2.4 por ciento, según su publicación *Perspectiva Trimestral de Mercado*, Septiembre, 2003.

El consumo de azúcar crece como crece el Producto Interno Bruto mundial. Las liberalizaciones en el comercio mundial y el desplome de la Unión Soviética han resultado en un aumento del mercado mayor al aumento en consumo. Dentro del por ciento de producción, el mercado mundial del azúcar ha aumentado del 18 por ciento en 1991 al 28 por ciento en 1999.

La Caída en Producción de Azúcar de Remolacha

La caída se debe a que se estima que el costo de refinar azúcar de remolacha es en promedio un 35 por ciento mayor que el de la de caña de azúcar. A medida que han ido desapareciendo los subsidios en la Europa del Este, la producción mundial de azúcar de remolacha ha continuado bajando del 36 por ciento en 1990 al 28 por ciento en 1999, al 25 por ciento en el 2003.[12]

Cada vez hay una mayor concentración en el número de países exportadores y un aumento en el número de países importadores. Esto significa que las fluctuaciones de precio están concentrada en las condiciones en los 3 o 4 mayores países exportadores. Y, a mayor número de compradores, menor es la fluctuación en precio.

Australia

De todos los grandes exportadores, Australia es probablemente el más susceptible a una entrada de Cuba reconstruida como exportadora de azúcar y a los precios bajos por sus altos costos de producción. Australia tiene que cubrir sus costos de producción en el mercado mundial, ya que apenas tiene acceso a la cuota Americana y con muy poca flexibilidad en su costo por estar totalmente mecanizada. La producción para el 2003 caerá por debajo de los 5 millones de toneladas, de un nivel de 5.35 millones en el 2002. La presión de bajos precios y las sequías tienen a los productores australianos en una crisis tras otra. Los niveles de producción futura dependen de cuan bien o mal se recupere Australia de las crisis que la han azotado durante los últimos años.

Alternativas de Acceso al Mercado Americano

Cuba sería un país de mucho más bajo costo de producción y mejores posibilidades de acceso a los mercados preferenciales de los EE.UU. y Rusia. Al de los EE.UU. por muchos factores, entre ellos legales: los tratados bilaterales; morales: la crítica situación social imperante en Cuba en comparación con la de los otros países exportadores de azúcar al mercado americano; ambientales: trasplante de la zona azucarera de los Everglades en la Florida a los productores para que muevan sus inversiones a Cuba a cambio de be-

---

11. *Estudio de las condiciones de trabajo y vida de los trabajadores en la industria azucarera en Venezuela.* Capítulo II, Análisis Socio-Económico. Unión de Productores de Azúcar de Venezuela (UPAVE), 1977.

12. ISO International Sugar Organization. May 2003.

neficios tributarios como la seccion 939;[13] la defensa de las fronteras de la Florida con lacreación de empleos estables a todos los niveles educacionales; influencia política para lograr acceso preferencial—de productos americanos—a un potencialmente lucrativo mercado cubano de productos y equipos agrícolas y bienes de consumo, a cambio de concesiones al azúcar cubano.

El Azúcar Artificial

Los azucares artificial es no parece que sean gran peligro; como también pueden aparecer oportunidades otra vez en competencia con el JMAF (Jarabe de Maíz en Alta Fructosa, HFCS) en el mercado de los refrescos. Todavía hoy no hay un consenso sobre el beneficio de sustituir el azúcar artificial por sucrosa para obtener un mejor control del peso. El JMAF tiene un altísimo costo de producción, solo subsiste basado en los altos aranceles de los países protectores del producto.

Brasil

Indiscutiblemente, a largo plazo, Brasil es nuestro gran adversario en el mercado de exportación. Pero hay otros más susceptibles a la presencia de Cuba en el mercado internacional del azúcar. Brasil exporta una tercera parte de su producción, pero su exportación depende de los precios del petróleo y del éxito que logren en sus programas de alcohol. A mayor precio del petróleo, menos exportación, y viceversa. Tiene buenas relaciones con los EE.UU. y ha tenido algo éxito en sus negociaciones de la naranja a costa de la industria del cítrico de la Florida. No creo que pueda ganarle otra batalla a la Florida en el azúcar.

Brasil se prepara para exportar 19 millones de toneladas de azúcar crudo en el 2013/2014, de un nivel de 14.5 millones de toneladas en el 2003/2004, según los Consultores FNP en *Agrianual 2004*, Mercados y Perspectivas, Cuadro 3, página 215. Equivale a un aumento de casi 5 millones de toneladas en 10 años.

Esto nos indica que hay planes de expansión para un exportador eficiente.

Cuba presenta las siguientes ventajas sobre Brasil en costos de producción y transporte:

a. *En flete marítimo*, varios días de ahorro a la gran mayoría de los importadores. Un barco con 45 mil toneladas de capacidad, cuesta el flete US $25 mil diario.

b. *El transporte de azúcar interno* en Brasil, de los centrales a los puertos, está a distancias promedio de varios cientos de kilómetros. En Cuba, por su formación larga y estrecha, y su gran cantidad de buenos puertos, todos los centrales están a unos pocos kilómetros de los puertos.

c. *El costo de oportunidad de la tierra* en Brasil es muchísimo más elevado que en Cuba. Ejemplo, en el centro de gravedad del Estado de Sao Paulo, en San José de Río Prieto, tierra agrícola con caña de azúcar, con rendimiento de 85 toneladas por hectárea, se cotiza a R$8,426 en Julio-Agosto de 2003, equivalente a US$2,926 por hectárea, US$1,200 el acre, US$40,000 la caballería.[14] En Cuba, la tierra se cotiza al 5 por ciento del rendimiento industrial, un 10 por ciento del ingreso del agricultor. Una buena solución para los años de bajos precios.

d. *La legislación azucarera en Cuba* hasta 1958 daba garantías al trabajador, al colono y al hacendado para invertir a largo plazo que no existen en Brasil.

México y el NAFTA

México logró un milagro en concesiones bajo el NAFTA, especialmente en el azúcar. México pudiera exportar azúcar, crudo o refino, sin límite de cantidades, y sin arbitrios, fuera de la cuota TRQ americana, después del 2008.[15] Pero parece que la pelea con los productores y los cabilderos americanos no está ganada. A la fecha de este trabajo México, debido a la ventaja fiscal que favorece el azúcar doméstico para los

---

13. Beneficio otorgado a Puerto Rico entre el ex Gobernador Luis Muñoz Marín y el Presidente Franklin D. Roosevelt, en el que las utilidades generadas por exportación estaban exentas de contribuciones al IRS (Hacienda).

14. FNP, obra citada, página 77.

15. USDA Baseline Projections, February 2002, Página 44.

refrescos sobre el JMAF, parece que antes de fin de año importará azúcar refino. Para tener acceso al TLC, tiene que ser un exportador neto, es una condición previa del Tratado con los EE.UU.[16]

Los Tratados y la Cuenca del Lago Okeechobee

El acceso del azúcar importado al mercado americano está en tal estado de confusión que nadie sabe como va a terminar. Entre el NAFTA, el WTO, los TLC, el impostergable combate a muerte entre ambientalistas y políticos por un lado, cabilderos y productores de azúcar en la cuenca del lago Okeechobee en la Florida por el otro lado, y el lobby de los productores de azúcar americano y el lobby de los exportadores, no se sabe donde va terminar la cuota Americana de importación de azúcar (TRQ). Una cosa es cierta: sin una apertura razonable a los productos agrícolas de los países sub-desarrollados, no hay tal libre comercio.

El Acceso al Mercado Americano

Por primera vez desde que se le quitó la cuota azucarera a Cuba en 1962 y se le repartió a 40 países hace 40 años, no ha habido un mejor momento para insertarnos en las negociaciones. Un buen momento para empezar a reclamar concesiones equitativas a cambio de un potencialmente lucrativo mercado para cuando Cuba no esté bajo sanciones económicas. Un tema que hemos perseguido, pero parece que hasta ahora "nadie escucha" en la administración del Presidente George W. Bush, pero seguiremos tratando.

Podemos estar seguros de que un gobierno independiente en Cuba no perdería la oportunidad de negociar acceso al mercado azucarero a cambio de beneficios arancelarios a los productos americanos para competir con otros potenciales exportadores a Cuba. Hay muchos ejemplos que estudiar, en Cuba, a partir de 1902.

Rusia y EE.UU.

Cuba nunca tendrá un mercado interno con la proporción que lo tiene Brasil, mucho más razón para encontrar socios en los EE.UU. y Rusia. Y aparecen,

por las razones expresadas anteriormente, y porque Cuba puede ser un suministrador confiable en calidad, costo y de buen crédito.

LA ESTRUCTURA DE PRODUCCIÓN ESTABLECIDA EN CUBA

Modelos de Producción Agrícola

La estructura de producción de azúcar en Cuba no ha cambiado mucho en los últimos 100 años: mayormente pequeños y medianos ingenios (promedio de 2,500 tcd) en las provincias centrales y occidentales, con casi una casi absoluta producción cañera en manos de pequeños y medianos colonos, antes de 1959; en las áreas de las provincias orientales, un menor numero de centrales (promedio de 5,000 tcd) con una mayor proporción de caña propia y a la vez el predominio de colonias de mayor tamaño.[17] Las excepciones son en las provincias de Camagüey y Oriente las zonas históricas productoras de azúcar desde el siglo XIX como Santiago de Cuba, Manzanillo y Guantánamo, que se asemejan a la zona occidental. En la situación que enfrentará la industria azucarera para su restablecimiento, cada una de las dos zonas identificadas presenta ventajas y desventajas. Todos con la gran ventaja sobre Brasil en que en Cuba los centrales están muy cerca de los puertos de embarque, a un promedio de solo unos kilómetros.[18]

Las áreas productoras de las provincias occidentales por su tamaño les resultará más rápido lograr niveles de alta producción cerca del 95% de capacidad, debido a las pequeñas distancias entre las colonias y el central, el abundancia en recursos humanos y materiales, y el gran anhelo de los pequeños agricultores de integrarse a una actividad confiable y predecible en costos e ingresos. Los ingenios relativamente pequeños probablemente tendrían un mayor costo de producción, pero una mayor flexibilidad en resolver situaciones inesperadas por estar el control de la dirección en una familia. Los ingenios mayores pueden tener un acceso más fácil a recursos de financiamiento de nuevas inversiones.

---

16. Organización Internacional del Azúcar, *Reporte Mensual*, Septiembre 2003, página 6.

17. *Anuario Azucarero de Cuba 1959*, página 79.

18. *Anuario Azucarero de Cuba 1959*, páginas 145-149.

En las provincias orientales en los grandes ingenios tomará más tiempo el lograr niveles de producción y eficiencia altos, debido a la complejidad y el costo en la reconstrucción de las vías y equipos para el transporte y la recolección de la caña, como serían los ferrocarriles.

Los Costos de Producción Agrícola

Los grandes factores que rigen la supervivencia del agricultor deben citarse aquí, con respecto al *colono* en Cuba, hasta 1958, y en un futuro estado de derecho. Factores que permiten un gran sentido de seguridad contra todas las otras inseguridades de la naturaleza.

No es fácil conseguir información imparcial y bien documentada de cuales fueron los costos de producción en Cuba antes de 1959. Sin embargo, existe la información de los archivos de la Guantánamo Sugar Company, que era una compañía de Wall Street, NY, con documentación enviada desde Cuba a los auditores en New York, que se encuentra en Miami, gracias a los buenos oficios de sus dueños. La Guantánamo Sugar Co. tenía de su propiedad 3 ingenios y 607 caballerias (8,152 ha, 20,000 acres) con una producción de 247,223 toneladas de caña en 1958, unas 33.32 toneladas por ha., y un rendimiento industrial del 13.77 por ciento en 1958. La empresa agrícola de la Guantánamo Sugar Company, la Compañía Agrícola del Valle, reportó en sus estados financieros de Agosto de 1958 un costo total de producción de caña para 1958 de $6.815, en 1957, $6.808, y en 1956, $6.597 por tonelada de caña. No aparecen gastos de importancia en regadío y ninguno en fertilizantes, pero si aparecen todos los gastos indirectos.

También existe la documentación certificada de la United Fruit Company para los centrales Boston y Preston para el U.S. Foreign Settlement Comisión. El Central Boston certifica un rendimiento promedio de 66,569 arrobas por caballería (56.25 ton/ha.) en 1,116 caballerias (15,000 ha., 37,000 acres) a un rendimiento industrial del 12.13 por ciento, un precio promedio oficial para el año 1959 de 3.891 centavos

la libra, una utilidad neta de $810.82 por caballería ($60.42 por ha., $24.50 por acre), a un costo de producción de $4.56 por 100 arrobas de caña ($5.17 por tonelada de caña). No aparecen especificados los gastos indirectos en la reclamación. Los costos agrícolas, según los detalles:

Guantánamo Sugar Company: $49.49 por tonelada de azúcar.
United Fruit Company (Central Boston): $42.62 por tonelada de azúcar.

Conclusión: No hay gran diferencia en los costos de hoy con los de hace 50 años. Los costos en Cuba promediaban $6.00 por tonelada de caña, $46 por tonelada de azúcar. [19] ¿Qué ha cambiado los costos para el futuro? Muy poco. El gran costo es la nueva siembra que se hace cada 10 años, lo que resulta en un costo amortizado anualmente casi insignificante. La *FNP Consultaría y Agroinformativos* de Brasil, reporta en el *Agriannual 2004*, costos de producción en Brasil de $7.00 por tonelada de caña, a lo que otros reportes añaden un costo de arrendamiento de tierra de $0.68 la tonelada, más $1.81 por tonelada, un 12 por ciento, por uso de la tierra. Se puede asumir conservadoramente que los costos de producción de caña de azúcar se han mantenido constantes debido a la eficiencia ganada en los costos.

Se puede destacar que una siembra nueva de caña requiere unos 10 días máximos de tractor-día, unas 80 horas. Hoy en día, por el método de la Extensión Agrícola de la Universidad de Iowa, la hora tractor con todos los costos, y el combustible a $1.50 el galón, para equipos de 125 caballos de fuerza (HP), es de $17 por hora. ¿Cuál es el costo anual de equipo amortizado a 10 años? $17 x 80 / 10 años = $136 / año, en 700 toneladas por caballería, es 20 centavos de dólar por tonelada de caña, $1.54 por tonelada de azúcar.

Los otros factores que afectarían la seguridad en la inversión en la agricultura cañera en Cuba:

a. Mercado libre. El mercado azucarero mundial esta muy lejos de poder ser controlado por nada

---

19. El precio para liquidación final para 1959 fue de 3.891 la libra, $85.78 la tonelada de azúcar. El colono recibe el 50 por ciento, $42.89. El mayor y casi único costo de importancia es Corte, Carga y Transporte, de $21.36 por ton de azúcar.

ni por nadie. Si bien tiene fluctuaciones debido a la oferta y la demanda, sabemos por experiencia que nadie la pudo salvar en los 1930 de la *Depresión Mundial*, ni de los precios de *"Vacas Gordas"* en los 1970 y 1990, sobre los 10 centavos la libra.

b.   El derecho a moler sus cañas. El derecho del colono a que se le muelan sus cañas sin necesidad de renovar contratos con el central, y en proporción al volumen fijado para la producción general del país. Ley de Coordinación Azucarera de 1937 (LCA) y Ley de Propiedad de la Cepa del Colono, 2da Ley de marzo de 1925.

c.   El pago según el mercado. Que se le pague de acuerdo al rendimiento industrial el 50 por ciento del azúcar que se produzca (LCA).

d.   El pago por las tierras. Si no está en tierra propia, se le limita el pago al 5 por ciento del rendimiento industrial (LCA).

e.   El Derecho de Permanencia. No puede ser desalojado. Solamente tiene que cumplir una producción mínima. Ley de Moratoria Hipotecaria, 4 de abril de 1934.

f.   El Salario Mínimo. La Ley determinó cual es la proporción en azúcar que debe pagarse por las distintas labores agrícolas, y las industriales (LCA).

g.   El pago quincenal, en efectivo, sin demoras, y sin juegos.

h.   El derecho a que no se le obligue a entregar sus cañas más lejos de lo que la tradición estableció. Ley-Decreto posterior a 1940.

i.   No se podía embargar la liquidación por las cañas del colono. Se consideraba como un sueldo inembargable (LCA).

La Protección Legal al Colono-Agricultor de Caña de Azúcar[20]

La transformación de la distribución del ingreso azucarero a partir del 4 de abril de 1934 con la Ley de Moratoria Hipotecaria y luego con la Ley de Coordinación Azucarera del 2 de septiembre de 1937, fueron en el pasado las bases de la eficiencia, y en el futuro la base de la reconstrucción y las oportunidades para el desarrollo. La Ley de Moratoria Hipotecaria acabó con los juicios de remate hipotecario por falta de pago de arrendamiento o de hipoteca. En virtud de la Ley, el colono se asegura la posesión de sus cañas independientemente de la posesión de la tierra del terrateniente—lo que le asegura al colono la posesión de la colonia de caña; el derecho a moler sus cañas; un pago por sus cañas equivalente al 50 por ciento del rendimiento industrial en azúcar al precio de venta en el mercado internacional; la fijación legal de una renta módica por las tierras, equivalente al 5% del rendimiento industrial, con muy pocas obligaciones por parte del colono. No se conoce de un solo caso de desahucio de un colono por falta de pago, a partir de 1937. A su vez el colono se comprometió y nunca falló en cubrir su compromiso de molienda con el central.

La Presencia del Estado en la Industria Azucarera Cubana

Una de las primeras actividades a realizarse es la formación de los organismos encargados de dirigir la política azucarera de Cuba.

Cada país tiene su propia estructura azucarera que define la relación entre los participantes. La situación ejemplar que existía en Cuba se diferenciaba de casi todas las demás naciones en que el estado no estaba entre los productores, aunque participaba, a partes iguales, en los organismos que regulaban la industria azucarera, como fueron:

- El Instituto Cubano de Estabilización del Azúcar (ICEA),

- La Comisión de Arbitraje Azucarero,

- La Comisión Fiscalizadora de Promedios, y

- La Comisión para la Investigación de Gastos de Puertos y Transportes.

---

20. *Un Estudio Sobre Cuba.* op. cit., Pág. 452. "La Ley del 2 de marzo de 1922, modificando los preceptos de la Ley Hipotecaria vigente, fue la disposición legal de mayor importancia, constituyendo un paso de trascendencia indudable en el terreno de la intervención del Estado en defensa del campesino cubano." Se separó la propiedad de la planta de la propiedad del suelo, a beneficio del agricultor. Esta es la base legal en el Derecho Civil de la Ley de Coordinación Azucarera de 1937.

OUT OF COMMUNISM: AN ETHICAL ROAD MAP—THE DIGNITY OF THE HUMAN PERSON AS THE FOUNDATION OF THE TRANSITION FROM COMMUNISM

Alejandro A. Chafuen

Transitions from communism created many new and important ethical concerns. Some countries have yet to start this transition or are on its very early stages. Cuba is one example. The major concern is that the transition will maintain the worse at the top. Such a result might bring internal discontent, create new negative moral incentives and build the conditions for instability.

The paper addresses the issue of the ethics of the transition from a Judeo-Christian perspective. It will emphasize economic ethics and recommend policies that are more consistent with the dignity of the human person. After cautioning about the danger of current fashionable new ethical foundations I offer recommendations for action from inside and outside Cuba that might enhance the chances for minimizing moral hazards during the transition.

The paper makes no effort to thoroughly explain or justify the superiority of Judeo-Christian moral philosophy. It will only describe in more detail the notion of *distributive justice* as it is essential for the topic of the paper and very poorly understood by moralists, economists, and legal experts.

In conducting research for this paper and interviewing people who have lived during transitions from Communism, it soon became apparent that the task at hand deserves a book more than a paper. But even a book would have to reach very few conclusions as "the jury is still out," and will be out for a long time, on the impact that different transition policies have

on some of the most important ethical questions. The many different methods of privatization, the difference that exists between the size, history, and productivity of the company to be privatized, all pose different moral dilemmas. Much research needs to be done to have empirical proof of some of the tentative conclusions that I will offer in this paper.

THE ETHICAL FOUNDATION

For those who believe in a single Creator, its essence, or nature, is the ultimate source of morality. The proximate norm is man's nature, created in the image of God. This is not the place for a complete explanation of the foundations of ethics from a Judeo-Christian perspective. It will suffice to say that my approach to the question of this paper will be based on traditional ethics or, at least, in a view of the human person that is largely consistent with the above.

Social ethics distinguishes the reciprocal ties between persons in relation to the end that has to be achieved in common (the common good). The social moralist questions if a particular institution is fulfilling its natural function in civil society. It also asks how should we, in order to seek the common good, distribute rights and duties among the members of that institution. (Utz 1964, pp. 361-362).

Ethics is the science of the morality of human acts. Although ethics and morality (or moral philosophy) have the same object, their means for discovering truth are different: "Moral theology relies on revealed religion for its conclusions, whereas ethics depends on human reason alone" (Noonan 1947, p. 3). "Ethics is essentially practical. Its object is to direct human action toward morally good ends," and "morality is the goodness or the badness, the rightness or the wrongness, of human acts" (Noonan 1947, p. 1). "The act of the will, then, is right (and also good) when the object of the act is the morally good; contrariwise, it is wrong (and also bad) when its object is morally evil." "Moral good is a quality of the human act by which it tends to its proper purposes or end." It is always necessary to distinguish between real and apparent good.

In ethics, we are only concerned with free or voluntary acts. These are acts where the will is in control. One can choose not to do them. These acts can be directly voluntary or indirectly voluntary, as when "the will chooses another object from which it can be foreseen that the second result will follow" (Noonan 1947, p. 7). When one channels funds to the accounts of an evil dictator or his cronies, for example, one is *directly* supporting an evil. When one invests or provides resources for an activity that will end up providing jobs and services to human beings in a dictatorial state, one might be *indirectly* providing support for a dictator.

Human beings are accountable for their moral acts. Such accountability requires "knowledge of what we are doing and freedom of choice." One is more or less accountable for human acts in relationship to the degree of knowledge and freedom about the act. Concupiscence, fear and violence, also influence the imputability of the act.

The dignity of the human person will be the guiding principle of this paper. The Catechism of the Roman Catholic Church provides a good summary: "Respect for the human person entails respect for the rights that flow from his dignity as a creature. These rights are prior to society and must be recognized by it. They are the basis of the moral legitimacy of every authority: by flouting them, or refusing to recognize them in its positive legislation, a society undermines its own moral legitimacy. If it does not respect them, authority can rely only on force or violence to obtain obedience from its subjects" (Catechism, point 1930).

In addition, "respect for the human person proceeds by way of respect for the principle that 'everyone should look upon his neighbor (without any exception) as another self, above all bearing in mind his life and the means necessary for living it with dignity.'" "No legislation could by itself do away with the fears, prejudices, and attitudes of pride and selfishness which obstruct the establishment of truly fraternal societies" (Catechism, point 1931). While human persons have equal dignity, their "talents" are not distributed equally: "These differences encourage and often oblige persons to practice generosity, kindness, and sharing of goods; they foster the mutual enrichment of cultures" (Catechism, point 1937).

Apart from natural inequalities there are unjust *inequalities* that affect millions of men and women. "Their equal dignity as persons demands that we strive for fairer and more humane conditions. Excessive economic and social disparity between individuals and peoples of the one human race is a source of scandal and militates against social justice, equity, human dignity, as well as social and international peace" (Catechism, point 1938).

Some of the problems that arise in a free society can only be overcome with Solidarity: "Solidarity is manifested in the first place by the distribution of goods and remuneration for work. It also presupposes the effort for a more just social order where tensions are better able to be reduced and conflicts more readily settled by negotiation. Socio-economic problems can be resolved only with the help of all the forms of solidarity: solidarity of the poor among themselves, between rich and poor, of workers among themselves, between employers and employees in a business, solidarity among nations and peoples. International solidarity is a requirement of the moral order; world peace depends in part upon this" (Catechism points 1940-1941).

One should not confuse true solidarity with the attitude of being a willing or passive actor in government led efforts to "help" the poor. Even Pope John Paul II was aware of this when he wrote *The Acting Person*. Quoting Karol Wojtyla: "opposition is not inconsistent with solidarity. The one who voices his opposition to the general or particular regulations of the community does not thereby reject his membership; he does not withdraw his readiness to act and to work for the common good." And he adds: "It would be too easy to quote endless examples of people who contest—and thus adopt the attitude of opposition—because of their deep concern for the common good (e.g., parents may disagree with the educational system or its methods because their views concerning the education of their children differ from those of the educational authorities)" (Wojtyla [1969] 1979, p. 286).

Although I am not going to focus on the issue, as human capital is essential in today's economy, intellectual property rights (IPR) might play a very important role in the Cuban economy. IPRs are important both to attract foreign direct investment, and also to enable the most creative Cubans, to put their talents to good use and letting the person, rather than the state, receive the rewards. This fact was recognized more than half a century ago, "Modern wealth is due in no small part to the talent and genius of gifted men. To deny them a just return for these talents is to undermine all justice in the social order, and therefore society itself" (Noonan 1947, p. 190).

In addition to the dignity of the human person, the concept of "just law" is also key for recommending policies conducive for more ethical transitions from communism. As it will become apparent in the pages that follow, the many conflicting claims, and material possibilities, will make the transition far from perfect from an ethical perspective. But a law, and a legal framework, need not be perfect or required to produce perfect results in order to be just. This principle is not only recognized in Thomistic ethics but also by individualist philosophers such as Herbert Spencer: "it is impossible during stages of transition which necessitate ever-changing compromises, to fulfill the dictates of absolute equity; and nothing beyond empirical judgments can be formed of the extent to which they may be, at any given time, fulfilled. While war continues, and injustice is done between societies, there cannot be anything like complete justice within each society" (Spencer, pp. 331-332). Yet, it is only by knowing or having an approximate knowledge of the requirements of absolute equity

that one can begin to act and promote policies that take us to a better ethical outcome.

There might be an attempt to apply another ethical principle, *catastrophic emergency*, to the transition. For centuries, a similar principle, that of *extreme need*, was common doctrine among Western moral philosophers. One should be extremely careful before using it as a justification to violate justice. "In a catastrophic emergency, survival may 'trump' justice" (Silver 1989, p. 174). In old moral philosophy, a typical example given was that of a lady who in order to escape from a bunch of potential rapists, takes the horse of the neighbor (Chafuen 2003, pp. 42-45). In recent times, we can recall that after an anthrax scare following the terrorist attacks of 2001 in the United States, the Secretary of Health and Human Services stated that the emergency was justification enough to tell a pharmaceutical company that if they did not lower the price of their drug, the government would violate the patent.

In traditional moral philosophy, moralists distinguished between *grave need*, which did not justify violations, and *extreme need*, which did. Silver argues that "an individual who steals in 'bad-but-not-so-disastrous' circumstances will be blamed—that is, his action will trigger moral indignation and a desire for punishment" (Silver 1989, p. 165).

I chose to ground my definitions on Roman Catholic ethics due to their wider acceptance (at least in theory) in Latin America. Classical Liberal and libertarian authors might reach similar conclusions. Two valuable attempts to build an ethical foundation of an economic system based on private property and without having recourse to God are *The Right to Private Property* by Tibor Machan (2002) and *The Foundations of Economic Justice* by Morris Silver (1989).

Machan bases his views on "the basic notion held that the kind of being we are, namely, human (and this possessed of personal authority or sovereignty), has the right to private property as a basic principle of our social existence" (Machan 2002, pp. 3-4).

In his work, Silver presents Durkheim's view that "Property is property only if it is respected." That is to say, the feelings of other members of society must also be taken into account" (Silver 1989, p. 14). While I do not endorse Silver's view that feelings are the foundations of private property, I do agree that they are essential for their exercise.

Silver is correct to add that "The gaps in our *evolved* property feelings exposed by the occurrence of the truly novel must be filled by legal rule or social convention" (Silver 1989, p. 169). He concluded that "The implications of the psychology of property for public policy are monumental" (Silver 1989, p. 170).

I do believe that to be successful in helping create the right ethical incentives one needs to have the right values. It was F.A. Hayek, the noted free-market Nobel Laureate who wrote "It should also be obvious that the results of freedom must depend on the values which free individuals pursue. It would be impossible to assert that a free society will always and necessarily develop values of which we would approve, or even, as we shall see, that it will maintain values which are compatible with the preservation of freedom. All that we can say is that the values we hold are the product of freedom, that in particular the Christian values had to assert themselves through men who successfully resisted coercion by government, and that it is to the desire to be able to follow one's own moral convictions that we owe the modern safeguards of individual freedom. Perhaps we can add to this that only societies which hold moral values essentially similar to our own have survived as free societies, while in others freedom has perished. (Hayek 1962, p. 45-46).

Policies that Encourage Virtue

To speak about ethics, and professional ethics, without dealing with moral virtues is similar to speaking about physics without mentioning the law of gravity (Termes 1992, p. 186). When one speaks of solidarity without focusing on it as a virtue, one is speaking more about the *spirit* of solidarity. The confusion between virtue and feelings is a type of moral suicide, as much as in the individual as in the social sphere.

While the feeling of solidarity leads to the welfare state, with all its weaknesses, the virtue of solidarity moves people to help others with concrete acts, with personal sacrifice. It is almost impossible to find *vir-tue* discussed in today's world: "Without moral virtues one can't have rational behavior, as rationality, which is not rationalism, consists in the right use of reason. It does not exclude sentiment, or feelings, but it excludes sentimentalism, as a guide for personal action; and it is the virtues that determine the capacity of a subject to use reason in the right way" (Termes 1992, p. 210).

What is more important for the economic process, is that as virtues are a good habit, they are acquired by learning. It is in that learning that a process of change takes place in the person, giving ethical value to his acts. Although it has not been immune to abuse, the advantage of privatization through vouchers, or any other scheme of distribution of shares, has a bigger chance to produce a learning process by dissemination of property and the opening of a space for market in vouchers.

The reforms, in an ideal transition, need to engage the person, the individual, more than the "collective" (which usually means the bureaucrat or those anointed by the dictator). This is especially important, from the learning process perspective, during a transition from communism. From the short-term perspective of pure economic expediency, it might be easier, for example, to "privatize" a company and give it to the former communist bosses. Such privatization would have almost no positive effect on the learning process needed to acquire the virtues that are needed for the free society. On the contrary, it might teach people that the bad always win.

The more people participate in markets, in small trade, in stock exchanges, the more used they will get to the virtues of the market place. As James Bryce wrote "the more the citizens acquire capital and themselves enter on commercial undertakings, and form business habits, and get to look at things with a practical eye, the stronger and more general will grow the public sentiment that insists on replacing the reign of force by the reign of law" (Bryce 1912, p. 573).

When the government of Cuba began the experiment to allow "personal" small businesses, thousands took advantage of the opportunity. Despite new taxes and restrictions to their operations, these truly micro-enterprises continue to create wealth. When liberated, they could serve as the fountainhead of Cuban reform. This, coupled with the many small and large investments of expatriates and returning Cubans would have a much more salutary ethical impact than a top down, IMF, IADB, or World Bank led reform that would mostly benefit the bureaucrats (both in Washington and Havana).

True Versus False Prudence

Another fundamental virtue that needs to play a role in the transition process is prudence. If solidarity is interpreted more as a feeling than as a virtue, prudence today is presented as the ability to escape responsibility or avoiding tough choices. Its true meaning, however, requires that the will and the action conform to truth, to objective reality (Termes 1992, p. 212).

The fact that I mention the importance of virtues does not mean that only virtuous people can be given freedoms. F. A. Hayek warned us that: "it is most important that a free society be based on strong moral convictions and why if we want to preserve freedom and morals, we should do all in our power to spread the appropriate moral convictions. But what I am mainly concerned with is the error that men must first be good before they can be granted freedom" (Hayek 1962, p. 46).

Human works have two aspects, the doing (*facere* in Latin) and the action (*agere*). The art, the technique, the knowledge of the market process, are important for the doing. The virtue of prudence, is important for the action. It is in acting that a person discovers value. And doing so he discovers the most important value: the self, the person.

When prudent and rational people decide to sacrifice their personal interest when they see that those interests can go against the true interests of others and the development of virtue, they can maximize the development of moral virtues. Perhaps some of my libertarian allies think that I have turned into a moralizer, and advocate something that seems that goes against economic theory: self-sacrifice. Yet it was Ludwig von Mises who wrote: "Mankind would never have

reached the present state of civilization without heroism and self-sacrifice on the part of the elite. Every step forward on the way toward an improvement of moral conditions has been an achievement of men who were ready to sacrifice their own well-being, their health, and their lives for the sake of a cause that they considered just and beneficial. They did what they considered their duty without bothering whether they themselves would not be victimized. These people did not work for the sake of reward, they served their cause unto death" (Mises 1974, p. 78).

Communism and the Transition from Communism

I will work with the definition of communism as the economic system based on state ownership of the means of production. During the last century, communist leaders have interpreted this as including the laborer thus infringing on his rights to emigrate and even to move internally from job to job or from region to region. This is a clear affront to the dignity of the human person.

It is proper to speak of a *transition* from Communism when a continuous process of weakening of the state apparatus of coercion begins, both in the economic and political arena. This process can start in either field, but it only becomes certain and almost irreversible when it encompasses both.

Transitions can take several forms. There are three typical scenarios. That of a "liberal" revolution (LR), such as the one that took place in several Central and Eastern European countries; that of a controlled transition (CT) such as the one taking place in China and Vietnam; and a mixture of both, where liberal and "conservative" forces alternate in power without achieving ultimate victory. A more thorough analysis should take into consideration that each of these scenarios might create a different set of ethical issues.

Applying the Principles of Distributive Justice

All different species of justice are relevant for the issues brought up by transitions from communism. Restitution of property to its rightful owners should be determined by the principles of *commutative justice*. The right to be taxed or have access to the goods, services and jobs provided by authority should be ruled by *distributive justice*. *Legal justice*, is responsible for the principles of the concrete order, limited by time and space. These transitions also bring up issues relevant for *international justice*, such as the principle of abiding by all past treatises between states.

The traditional notion of Distributive Justice is an essential guide for the distribution of taxes, government jobs, subsidies, and all other issue involving the distribution, allocation and maintenance, of goods held by the state. The traditional definition follows the teachings of Aristotle and St. Thomas Aquinas. As did Aristotle, St. Thomas postulated two forms of justice:

> In the first place there is the order of one part to another, to which corresponds the order of one private individual to another. This order is directed by commutative justice, which is concerned about the mutual dealings between two persons. In the second place there is the order of the whole toward the parts, to which corresponds the order of that which belongs to the community in relation to each single person. This order is directed by distributive justice, which distributes common goods proportionately. Hence there are two species of justice, distributive and commutative (Aquinas, II-II, qu. 61. art. 1).

Noting that this definition of distributive justice is consistent with the principle of justice in general, i.e., "to render to each one his right," he continued:

> Even as part and whole are somewhat the same, so too that what pertains to the whole, pertains somewhat to the part also: so that when the goods of the community are distributed among a number of individuals each one receives that which, in a way, is his own (Aquinas, II-II, qu. 61. art. 2-3).

It is important to note that in the Thomist tradition, distributive justice refers only to common goods. Furthermore, St. Thomas distinguished between public common goods and common goods belonging to a family or to other groups of people. Since "the act of distributing the goods of the community belongs to none but those who exercise authority over those goods" (Aquinas, II-II, qu. 61. art. 2-3), he indicated that the charge of distributing public common goods falls to governmental authorities, bureaucrats or anyone charged with their care or provision. The "subjects" are also responsible for distributive justice "in so far as they are contented by a just distribution" (Aquinas, II-II, qu. 61. art. 2-3).

Aristotelian, Thomist and Scholastic thought provided that just distribution of common goods involves proportionate allocation. St. Thomas noted that

> In distributive justice something is given to a private individual, in so far as what belongs to the whole is due to the part, and in a quantity that is proportionate to the importance of the position of that part in respect of the whole. Consequently, in distributive justice a person receives all the more of the common goods, according as he holds a more prominent position in the community. This prominence in an aristocratic community is gauged according to virtue, in an oligarchy according to wealth, in a *democracy according to liberty*, and in various ways according to various forms of government (Aquinas, II-II, qu. 61. art. 3, Italics mine.).

The Jesuit Luis de Molina (1535-1600) reasoned similarly:

> Distributive justice refers precisely to what is owed to someone because he belongs to a community, in which case common goods must be divided among the members (something that seldom occurs). And since a republic is a collection of members, it is evident that its goods belong to its members, who own them in common. If they come to be overabundant, they should be distributed and divided among the members of the republic, and each should receive a share (Molina 1614, bk. 1. col, 24).

Some lines later, he defined this kind of justice as that which "gives each member of the republic what belongs to him when the common goods are divided according to geometric proportion." It appears that, for Molina, it was rare for common goods or the surplus of a common good to be divided among the citizens ("something that seldom occurs"). In his experience the opposite is the norm: the citizens are obliged to maintain common goods.

While distributive justice takes place in the context of the relationship between the state and the people, "*commutative* justice directs *commutations* that can take place between two persons" (Aquinas, II-II, qu. 61. art. 3).

Late Scholastic theory analyzed profits, wages and rent as matters of commutative justice and applied rules similar to those used to analyze the prices of goods. The Schoolmen determined that wages, profits and rents are not for the government to decide. Since they are beyond the sphere of distributive justice, they should be determined through common estimation in the market.[1]

For the sake of this paper the principles of distributive justice need to be applied to each of the matters that were handled by authority as being part of the "common good." The principles of *commutative justice* need to be applied with all the property and contracts that were not respected by the communists and are in need of restitution. As part of the costs of restitution fall on a large segment of society, there is a difficult area of overlap where elements of distributive and commutative justice need to be taken into account.

Transferring and Returning Productive Assets from the State to the Private Sector

Privatization has been accompanied by unethical behavior and accusations of corruption in most transitions from communism. As one analyst wrote: "In Russia, following privatization of the oil industry, the controlling shareholder of Yukos Oil 'skimmed over 30 cents per dollar of revenue, while stiffing his workers on wages, defaulting on the payments by claiming that Yukos couldn't afford them, destroying the value of minority shares in both Yukos and the production companies that Yukos controlled but only partly owned, and *not* reinvesting in Russia's run-down oil fields, which badly needed new investment'" (Black, Kraakmanm and Tarassova (1999:1737). In the Czech Republic, firms were "tunneled out," that is, stripped of their assets and left with debt, disenchanted workers and investors, and little hope of raising capital to fund future investment projects. As one foreign investor warned in

a full-page ad in the *New York Times*, "Think twice before you invest in the Czech Republic. Otherwise, you could be left to 'twist in the wind'" (*New York Times*, November 8, 1999) (Dick 2001, pp. 59-84).

Alexander Dyck recommends strengthening the governance chains in order to achieve more just solutions. One needs to "find a way to protect public and private investors by providing information and accountability." A good method, which is applicable only to the largest companies to be privatized,[2] is to list the company in the New York Stock Exchange (NYSE), or one of the few other Stock Exchanges that has very strict requirements for listing. As the Enron, and other scandals proved, including the governing of the NYSE, this is not a foolproof method, but it goes a long way to reduce unethical practices.

During revolutions, as it happened in Romania, the losers have less time to protect their power or their lives. But after a period of time, it is likely that some of them will find their way to positions of power. Under controlled transitions, leaders will carve for themselves an important slice of all major sources of wealth. Although friends and foes alike deny that there is a transition in Cuba, partial "privatizations" have been taking place. In order to increase its power base, some of the pie is given to "new" entrepreneurs.

Land Restitution

Restitution to the victims of communism should be one of the most important guiding principles during a transition from communism. The late Murray Rothbard correctly stated that "The idea of primacy for restitution to the victimy...has been allowed to wither away as the State has aggrandized and monopolized the institutions of justice...in the Middle Ages generally, restitution to the victim was the dominant concept of punishment" (Rothbard 1983, p. 87). As the State grew more powerful "emphasis shifted from restitution to the victim, from compensation by the criminal to his victim, to punishment for alleged crimes committed 'against the State'" (Rothbard 1983, p. 87).

---

1. For a more detailed analysis see Chafuen (1985).

2. At least on this regard, the privatization of the Argentine oil company YPF is a good example to follow.

There are many ethical questions surrounding the restitution of land that continue to create barriers for faster economic development in former communist countries. One of the typical concerns, such as the fear that foreigners will crowd out the locals and therefore create a social backlash, end up putting in place a vicious circle. Valentin Braikov, referred to as one of the most prominent lawyers in Bulgaria, explained "New owners cannot afford the necessary farming equipment to make land efficient, prices of farming land are ridiculously low due to almost no demand . . .[The] government is afraid to allow foreign purchasing power to buy the cheap land because it will cause a social earthquake. ... As a result of low land prices farmers cannot use a part of their land as collateral for bank loans, which is a vicious circle." (Rhett Miller 2003, p. 81).

The problems with land restitution in Bulgaria can serve as warning for when the time comes to restitute land in Cuba. A partial list of problems affecting other transitions include: short application periods to apply for restitution (which can create a flood of requests that no bureaucracy can handle); property boundaries that "had been obliterated with the formation of state farms"(Rhett Miller 2003, p. 81); land records that have been destroyed; "privatised plots [that] are illicitly handed-out to associates" (which makes restitution very difficult since "in most cases the participants are now *former* party cadres who have become businessmen with a proficiency in stockpiling former state assets."); requirements that the old owners compensate the state for "improvements" done since expropriation; conflicting rights between current tenants and old owners; and a weak history of judicial independence.

According to Rhett Miller, one of the most un-ethical aspects of land restitution in Bulgaria is that land that was seized by the state by force (without an order of expropriation) was determined by legislators to fall "under the so-called '10 years possession rule'...Thus even though seizure represented an illegal act, the state nevertheless legally acquired owner-ship of the seized properties through adverse possession once 10 years had gone by. Landowners were afforded no legal remedy" (Rhett Miller 2003, p. 79). It is these properties that are in a legal limbo which have largely failed to be maintained or returned to full productivity.

Despite these problems, Bulgarian reforms and restitutions are seen and presented as being highly successful. Going back to one of our guiding ethical principles, what we seek are legal institutions that will maximize respect for the human person, and provide the right, although not perfect incentives. The experience in Bulgaria provides useful lessons for further transitions.

Monetary System

Money is the most commonly used medium of exchange. Reducing its value arbitrarily reduces the wealth of any person holding money. One of the major lessons that I remember from my years at the Argentine Catholic University is the analysis by our professor of economic ethics, that "monetary emission is lying knowing that you are lying and stealing knowing that you are stealing."[3]

The late William Hutt, one of the leading market oriented economists of the twentieth century, is one of the few English speaking economists who, although sparingly, used the concept of distributive justice in a correct manner, especially in the area of inflation:

> Nor can we be blind to the **distributive injustices associated with inflation**; its merciless treatment of the politically weak; its tendency to reward those responsible for the discoordinations which it so crudely rectifies; its penalization of those whose actions have in no sense been responsible (those classes which loathe the idea of striking or threatening to strike-the salaried middle classes, the thrifty rentiers, the learned and charitable institutions which have relied upon interest on endowments, the pensioners, and so forth); its encouragement of a sordid scramble on the part of each organized group to get more for itself out of the common pool; its destruction of the motive to give of

---

3. Prof. Cayetano Licciardo in 1976-7, former minister of economics.

one's best in the common social task, particularly at the entrepreneurial level; its weakening of the rewards for ingenuity, enterprise and effort; its sapping of the incentive to thrift and growth; its discouragement of individual responsibility toward one's own future and that of one's dependents; its creation of resignation toward a taxation system which robs the community of capital for the financing of innovations; its encouragement of acquiescence in the squandering of the community's capital; its need, in practice, for a multitude of officials and controllers with delegated judicial and legislative powers, able to make or destroy fortunes and subject therefore to the temptations of corruption; and the tendency it serves toward the degeneration of representative government into a system of vote buying (Hutt 1979, bold mine, p. 179).

Our guiding principle is that inflation is akin to theft and if the country chooses to have a local monetary system it should be handled by and independent but strongly accountable monetary authority. This has been the case in New Zealand, where if the central bank cannot meet its inflation goal, the president has to resign.

In addition to the litany of evil results mentioned by Hutt, another example of unethical acts in monetary policy is the dissemination of information regarding Central Bank actions to privileged parties.

As a means to reduced unethical practices, currency boards are even better than rule-constrained Central Banks: "A currency board is a monetary institution that issues notes and coins (and in some cases, deposits) fully backed by a foreign 'reserve' currency and fully convertible into the reserve currency at a fixed rate on demand. The reserve currency is a convertible foreign currency or a commodity chosen for its expected stability. The country that issues the reserve currency is called the reserve country. (If the reserve currency is a commodity, the country that has the currency board is considered a reserve country)" (Hanke, Jonung, Schuler, p. 5).

Dollarization, especially if is accompanied by a law authorizing the freedom to use any currency, is another easy way for a country to minimize the temptation to conduct unethical monetary policies. Although dollarization seems the easiest road for Cuba,

in order to increase the political feasibility of the reform one could explore establishing a currency board requiring half of the reserves be constituted in dollars and half in Euros. A similar reform failed in Argentina but, as the great champions of currency boards, Hanke and Schuler, had been warning since the early 1990s, Argentina did not have a currency board. It had a Central Bank pretending to act as a currency board. As in other pretentious experiments, it was only time until the public realized that the emperor had no clothes.

A currency board backed by dollars and euros might, by its symbolism, encourage a climate of cooperation between Europe and America.

Price Dislocations

The artificial prices that exist for most products and services during the period of communist control create another set of special ethical issues.

During the reform period that preceded the collapse of the Soviet Empire, several communist leaders implemented mild reforms that created very different categories of prices. In Hungary, for example, prices were "divided into four categories: centrally fixed, maximum, limited (both as to a maximum and minimum), and free" (Ureña 1988, p. 172).

Whenever these mild reforms were tried, while centralized power continued, when they failed to produce rapid results, bureaucrats used the opportunity to increase controls rather than to further liberalize. When partial reforms are tried within a totalitarian framework several results create problems in a society brainwashed by socialist propaganda including: "a broadening of the wage scale, contrary to the socialist distributive ideal (arousing numerous protests); a weakening of the job security that prevailed in the centralized models (except for ideological reasons), arousing discontent in broad sectors" (Ureña 1988, p. 174).

According to Ureña, the resistance of old time party leaders "is not, then, merely the fruit of a selfish fear of loss of privilege, but has an objective basis as well: the fear of an economic, and consequently a political, decentralization and liberation that would go beyond limits tolerated by socialism" (Ureña 1988, p. 175).

As I believe that no one should play God and try to know what the market prices should be, I believe that the most ethical path is to liberate all prices. Very much like Ludwig Earhard did in Germany breaking with the recommendations of U.S. bureaucrats and experts. Whenever the price of commodities which are deemed essential for daily life are very different from the prices in comparable economies, one could explore policies to mitigate the suffering by providing vouchers and subsidies rather than by maintaining artificial prices. If a price jumps too high, one should allow these "extraordinary profits" to encourage entry in the trade or business. When prices were artificially high and are reduced drastically by open markets, one could consider a temporary subsidy to the seller or producer.

Personally, I would not favor such subsidies. They would require a large bureaucracy to implement and they would have the incentives to continue, rather than eliminate, the controls, and therefore their government jobs.

CAN THE WEST HELP?

If we judge by past experience, the role of the so-called West in providing the right incentives for an ethical transition from communism, is dubious at best. Analysts, such as Brian Mitchell, have argued that in Central and Eastern Europe, U.S. administrations have favored returning the power to the former communists and collaborators because they have been more willing to engage in economic and financial dealings, from sale of assets to purchase of weapons, than the center-right and "anti-communists."

There could be a right motive in this. The dissemination of ownership, even when it goes to a few large foreign owners with ties to local elites, might create new incentives, which can alter the political landscape forever. Foreign governments and investors, understand that the goal of some of the former communist or current totalitarian regimes is to sell assets and contracts to obtain resources to maintain and consolidate power and wealth. But they might also

be thinking that they will outlive the current regime and that it is better for them to make a fast deal now than to lay their hope on weak center-right coalitions.

This has not only happened in Central and Eastern Europe but might be happening also with Venezuela. The argument goes as follows: "Let us make deals with Chávez and get some contracts, we will make some money, one day he will not be there and the opposition is so ineffectual that there is little cost to us for working with the regime." Stories in *The Wall Street Journal* and other important newspapers have described the role played by "free-market" advocates, such as former Vice Presidential Candidate Jack Kemp, acting if not as agents, at least as friendly ambassadors for the Chávez regime.[4]

Several of the ethical questions relevant for a transition from communism, have also been difficult for transitions from economies with a high degree of government ownership and intervention in the economy. Accusations of corruption have accompanied not only the privatization processes in Russia, Poland and the Czech Lands, but also in non-communist, highly interventionist economies such as Argentina, Peru, and Mexico.

Differential exchange rates, and official exchange rates that diverge from the free-market rates have been a formidable incentive for corruption. They are easily fooled, they can make bureaucrats and accomplices rich and, from the point of view of natural law, differential exchange rates are seen as so artificial that parties feel justified in their attempt to elude them. A trader who undervalues the cost of his export load, might be violating a regulation and lying, but the foreigner who buys it, sees nothing wrong when asked to pay full value to a foreign account or subsidiary of the trader.

Locals and foreigners know that most Latin American governments have acted as predators rather than protectors of economic human rights. During the

---

4. It is always possible that Jack Kemp is collaborating with Chavez to infiltrate the regime. That would be a redeeming factor, but I do not have any information to confirm or deny that possibility.

last decades, governments from Argentina, Brazil, Ecuador, to name a few, have prevented nationals from having access to their own deposits.

I will stop here because I think that there is a growing consensus about the need for having a uniform exchange rate that does not differ much from market rates. This is important from the economic aspect but much more important from the ethical point of view.

A Special Clash of Cultures

Perhaps, as in no other case, when the signs of transition are certain, we can expect a massive flow of foreign direct investment by expatriates. We might also expect "half-year" migrations, from Cuban-Americans.[5] Some of the ethical questions that such an influx might create have more to do with *personal morality* (such as the feeling of envy that it might incite), and *social ethics* (large groups of local residents, and also returning expatriates reacting to this clash of wealth and culture), than with economic ethics.

The attraction of the "pearl of the Caribbean" will be hard to resist, not only for Cuban-Americans, but for citizens of most western countries.

Three Special Challenges

During the transition process actors need to be aware of three challenges faced by most developing countries: inequality, environmental degradation and corruption. I choose these three problems as current fashionable approaches to deal with them might make them worse.

Inequality: Unequal distribution of economic freedom is exacerbating natural inequalities. Those who are involved in the transition will need to become champions in the battle against the unequal distribution of economic freedom. Studies show that inequality in Latin America is not the result of wealth inequality but of income inequality. In an open economy, income is determined by workers productivity, which is, in turn, highly correlated with levels of education and capital accumulation in the economy. In lower levels of the scale, the poor have little

access to useful education. Studies conducted in Chile, even after more than two decades of reform, show that public schools contribute very little to increase the ability to earn an adequate income. Other Latin American countries also show very poor scores. Only the wealthier, and a few lucky ones, can escape the bad schools.

In closed economies, wealth depends more on accepting an education useful to promote the system. Cuba has the best scores of educational achievement in several areas but has never been compared on the issues relevant to prosperous civil societies. One might need strong verbal comprehension skills to understand the interminable speeches uttered by dictators, and strong imaginative mathematical skills to justify their numbers, but unless one is educated on the value of respect for human dignity, there is little profit to be had from such high educational scores. Fidel Castro might take pride that in his Cuba, "even the prostitutes" have university degrees. But educated people would be more proud if they could use their talents with the freedom required by their personal dignity.

What we say here about education can be generalized to other areas of the economy. In many countries, only those in better position in society can afford adequate pensions, legal access, security, and other services where the government plays a key role. Only the well off can exercise economic freedom because local authorities have closed the doors to private solutions to many public problems that could benefit the poor. To the natural inequality based on productivity that would exist in a free economy is added an unequal access to economic freedoms.

Pension reform: Public and semi-public pension systems, if not structured properly, might also generate more inequalities. A pension reform needs to take into account the interest of current and future generations. Need and history are important but should not override all other considerations especially the possibilities of the economy. One of the first steps is to establish the starting point and use it as a bench-

---

5. Given what has taken place in other transitions, I doubt that most Cuban-Americans will "jump ship" and move full time to Cuba.

mark. Given the dislocations in the economy, the benchmark should be set in purchasing power more than in monetary units.

In addition to the typical problems faced by any society willing to reform a pension system, in most communist countries, civil society will have to face the additional problem of a very fragile family structure. Communist regimes had an active policy of attacking and dividing the family, helping sever family bonds and therefore making it less likely that younger generations will take care of the old.

In a recent unpublished paper, "Paying for the Transition to Private Market Provision of Elderly Entitlements," Thomas Saving shows how "future generations are unambiguously better off when a generation transfer system of providing retirement benefits is replaced with a prepaid system" (Saving 2003). He concludes that in order that the old generation is not made worse off during the transition, the young and the new entrants to the labor force will have to pay more in taxes.

One could try to establish a scheme where the companies that have been dealing and profiting with a communist regime, when the tide changes would be allowed to continue doing business only if they would pay an extra contribution to the pension system. As several countries in Central and Eastern Europe have implemented or are implementing pension reforms, those involved in the Cuban transition should study those cases in great detail. In Poland, for example, payments do not go directly from the contributor to the private companies but go first to the government that then distributes them to the pension fund. What the government retains is open to political and economic mischief. An old saying in Spanish is that "el que parte y reparte se queda con la mejor parte" (he who cuts and distributes the parts, keeps the best parts).

There is no room to analyze in detail the process of reform of the pension, health and educational system

in order to maximize the proper ethical incentives. I will refer the reader to the records of the Vatican on a meeting held in Vatican City from March 6 to March 9, 1996, on "The Family and the Economy in the Future of Society."[6] The guiding principle of the reforms proposed in that meeting focused on empowering the person and the family rather than bureaucratic institutions. Educational vouchers, transferable medical savings accounts, and individual retirement accounts were the recommended process.

Development and environmental degradation: Compare the scenery around Niagara Falls and Iguazú Falls, on the Northern limit of Argentina and Brazil. One borders the two most powerful countries of North America, the other one, those of South America. Judging by surrounding flora and fauna, Iguazú wins hand-down. If we judge by income and health of the surrounding population, Niagara is far ahead. Does development and wealth always have to be at the expense of nature?

Increased economic freedom, when it is real and not fiction, is bringing increased development to small and large countries alike. Once the storms of the war against terrorism settle, we will again see most nations return to a path to prosperity. People agree that most wars are devastating for the environment but what about prosperity? In its earlier stages economic development might produce an increase in environmental degradation. Yet as incomes rise, economic development becomes the best ally of the environment and poverty its main enemy. Analysts from the right and left of the ideological spectrum recognize this. Even the main Cuban environmental official center has blamed Latin American environmental degradation on poverty.

The human person needs to be at the center of any environmental policy. Increasing life expectancy by improving access to clean water, adequate medicines, nutritious food, and adequate housing is essential for human ecology. During this last decade, child mortality rates have decreased significantly in most Latin

---

6. The proceedings were published in the *Osservatore Romano* and were also published in *La Società: Studi, Ricerche, Documentazione, Sulla Dottrina Sociale Della Chiesa*, Anno VII, N. 1/97, Verona.

American countries. For the process to continue, the region and Cuba, need more respect of private property not less. That is the only path to prosperity. Just titles to property are "the only safeguard of freedom. If ownership of all these resources is turned over to the state there perish the dignity and liberty of men" (Noonan 1947, p. 190).

There is no need to repeat mistaken policies which we know carry environmental costs much higher than the economic benefits. But it makes less sense to ignore the dynamic relationship between wealth and the environment and put barriers on any policy potentially harmful to the environment. By some definitions of sustainable development, mining for fossil fuels is unsustainable. A push by NGOs and rich nations to absolutize the environment will condemn resource-rich nations into poverty. Bolivian environmental challenges also provide good examples. The population is still subject to malaria and other infectious diseases, which could be eradicated by the responsible use of DDT. Worldwide bans on the manufacturing and trade of some of these useful chemicals can prove devastating for humans. Bolivia is the poorest country in South America, and a land-locked country, it could also reap great benefits with a planned hydro-way connecting its southern region with the Paraná River. Yet many environmental lobbies have been blocking the project.

Think tanks in Chile, Argentina, Bolivia, Venezuela, Guatemala, Spain and France, to name a few, have been addressing the issue of environmental degradation with much less funds than the environmental lobbies. Their analysis shows that secure property titles and prosperity are the best allies of the environment and that following paths of extreme environmentalism will condemn poor countries to permanent stagnation.

One of the most important issues that might be affected by environmental disputes, for its potential impact not only in Cuba but in neighboring islands and Florida, is off-shore drilling. Again I would recommend an economic policy that prioritizes human needs. If one can have off-shore drilling off the coasts of the British Isles, or of California, the possibility of such methods used in the Cuban waters should be an alternative.

Corruption

In other academic settings I have shown the high correlation that exists between the lack of free-markets, free trade and corruption (Chafuen and Guzmán, 1999). As economic freedom rises, corruption tends to fall. This is not an automatic process and people in countries undergoing radical changes take time to adapt. In addition, the same complex regulatory frameworks that have evolved in several developed nations, might not show a large increase in the perception of corruption in those countries (e.g., Scandinavia, Western Europe, and even the U.S. and Canada). This is possible because countries in that region have a long tradition of public service and equality before the law. Governments have earned a better reputation than in less developed countries. Unless one can import those institutions, as when countries join a trading block that has lower corruption levels, corruption will likely increase in less developed countries that try to copy complex Western regulatory schemes.

Apart from hyper-regulation, high taxation is another incentive for corruption. Of all the international financial organizations, the International Monetary Fund is on a class of its own when recommending high levels of taxation. In country after country of Latin America, the IMF has been pushing for governments to tax as much as they can. Value added taxes of over 20% might not be uncommon in European countries where institutions have evolved over centuries. Attempts to impose such level of taxation in Latin America, and the same would happen in Cuba, always led to huge evasion, justified a large informal economy, and undermined overall respect for the rule of law. Amongst post-communist economies, Russia and Slovakia have already implemented tax reforms based on a flax-tax imposed at levels much lower than western countries. These reforms have been led by local economists, not by Washington based technocrats, and often, against the advice of the IMF.

CHECKLISTS FOR REFORM

As a summary for what will continue to be a "working paper" I offer checklists for government policy during a reform process away from Communism. As a starting point let us use the list of government activities deemed legitimate by the late Lord Peter Bauer, another renowned figure in the world of liberal economists. He lists:

- public security (protection of life and property, including the definition of property rights)

- maintenance of the value of money

- management of external relations in the interests of the population

- provision or oversight of basic education, public health, and transport

- assistance to those in need who cannot help themselves and are not helped by others (Bauer 1998, pp. 243-244).

I addressed the first two, but similar principles to those listed below should be applied to the others. Such analysis calls for a much larger paper and multi-disciplinary collaboration.

Apart from being careful that the transition policies are conducive to economic development, to establish the foundation for long term growth policy makers need to be concerned about the effects of the policies on:

- The dignity of the human person;

- The short and long term efforts to build a rule of law;

- The incentives to acts of solidarity;

- The respect of past contracts and just titles to property;

- The victims who suffered more from communism;

- Those who profited from dealing with the regime or who committed the worse type of human rights abuses; and

- The learning process of market virtues

I could add more items to the list, but the above seven elements need to be complemented with an overall preferential option for the poor. After so many years of communism, many poor will find themselves ill-equipped to deal in an open and free society and policies need to take that into account.

Our major challenge to help in the transition from communism is to try to create incentives that will increase the chances of:

1. seeking and building the right moral foundations for the free society;

2. creating structures, institutions that will make it easier to reward good and punish evil; and

3. preventing the initial reforms from becoming a "shooting star" or to have a boomerang effect.

All the efforts to produce the above are relevant for those who are preparing the ground for the transition from inside and outside Cuba.

As final words, let me conclude quoting again F. A. Hayek:

> It is also an old insight that a free society will work well only where free action is guided by strong moral beliefs, and, therefore, that we shall enjoy all the benefits of freedom only where freedom is already well established. To this I want to add that freedom, if it is to work well, requires not only strong moral standards but moral standards of a particular kind, and that it is possible in a free society for moral standards to grow up which, if they become general, will destroy freedom and with it the basis of all moral values (Hayek 1962, p. 45).

It is up for each of us to promote, with our actions and words, moral standards that will help us move away from the tragedy of communism.

REFERENCES

Aquinas, St. Thomas, 1975, *Summa Theologica*, London: Blackfriars.

Bauer, P.T., 1998, "Western Subsidies and Eastern Reform," in *The Revolution in Development Economics*, Dorn, Hanke and Walters, eds., Washington, D.C.: Cato Institute.

Bryce, James 1912, *South America: Observations and Impressions*, New York: The McMillan Company.

Catechism of the Catholic Church, 1994, United States Catholic Conference, Inc. Libreria Editrice Vaticana.

Chafuen, Alejandro A., 2003, *Faith and Liberty*, Lanham: Lexington Books.

Chafuen, Alejandro A., 1985, "Justicia Distributiva en La Escolástica Tardía," *Estudios Públicos*, Santiago, Chile: 18 (1985).

Chafuen, Alejandro, and Guzmán, E., 1999, "Economic Freedom and Corruption," in O'Driscoll, Holmes and Kirkpatrick, eds., *2000 Index of Economic Freedom*, Washington, DC: The Heritage Foundation-Wall Street Journal. Spanish version: http://www.atlas.org.ar/economia/chafuen_guzman.asp.

Dick, Alexander, 2001, "Privatization and Corporate Governance: Principles, Evidence, and Future Challenges," *The World Bank Research Observer*, vol. 16, no. 1. Pp, 59-84

Hanke, Steve H., Jonung, L., Schuler, K., 1993, *Russian Currency and Finance: A Currency Board Approach To Reform*, London and New York: Routledge.

Hayek, Friedrich A. von, [1961] 1962, "The Moral Element in Free Enterprise," *The Freeman*, 12, July 1962, pp. 44-52.

Hutt, William H, 1979, *The Keynesian Episode: A Reassessment*, Indianapolis: Liberty Press.

Machan, Tibor R., 2002, *The Right to Private Property*, Stanford, California: Hoover Institution Press.

Mises, Ludwig von, 1944, *Bureaucracy*, New Haven: Yale University Press.

Noonan, John P. 1947, *General and Special Ethics*, Chicago: Loyola University Press.

Rhett Miller, Leland, 2003, "Land Restitution in Post-Communist Bulgaria," *Post-Communist Economies*, Vol. 15, No. 1.

Rothbard, Murray N., 1983, *The Ethics of Liberty*, Atlantic Highlands, N.J.: Humanities Press.

Saving, Thomas R., 2003, "Paying for the Transition to Private Market Provision of Elderly Entitlements," Paper presented at the Mont Pèlerin Society meeting, September 19, 2003.

Silver, Morris, 1989, *Foundations of Economic Justice*, New York-Oxford: Basil Blackwell.

Spencer, Herbert [1879] (ND), *The Data of Ethics*, New York: American Publishers Corporation.

Termes, Rafael, 1992, *Antropología del Capitalismo*, Barcelona: Plaza & Janes, Cambio 16.

Ureña, Enrique M. [1981] 1988, *Capitalism or Socialism: An Economic Critique for Christians*, Chicago: Franciscan Herald Press.

Utz, Arthur Fridolin [1958], 1964, *Etica Social*, Barcelona: Editorial Herder.

Wojtyla, Karol, [1969] 1979, *The Acting Person*, trans. Andrzej Potocki, Dordrecht: D. Reidel Publishing Company.

ETHICS AND THE CUBAN TRANSITION

Armando P. Ribas

Morality is a subject that interests us above all others: We fancy the peace of society to be at stake in every decision concerning it.

— David Hume, *A Treatise of Human Nature*

PASSIONS AND REASON

My main concern with respect to the so-called Cuban transition is "transition to what?" It seems to me that all the discussions with respect to this theme appear to refer only about the way for transition to occur, while the final outcome seems to be taken for granted. That final outcome, of course, is democracy and liberty but nobody takes the time to define the meaning of these two over-politically correct words. It was Abraham Lincoln who once said: "we all declare for liberty; but in using the same word we do not mean the same thing... Here are two, not only different but incompatible things called by the same name, liberty." I may say that the same semantic problem arises with respect to democracy and I may add that this confusion has had a long history in Western civilization.

Coming back to Cuba, it seems to me that there is a conviction that as soon as Fidel Castro fades away, we may expect a return to paradise. Well, maybe this is an exaggeration, but certainly it is obvious that with Castro there is no possible solution. But his disappearance at best is just the beginning of the road. However Seneca said, "for those that don't know where they are going, there is no favorable wind." And when we have a glimpse of the panorama presented by the democratic processes in Latin America, it is apparent that there is no favorable wind.

These skeptical words should not be construed as a despair or dismal pessimism. Pessimism is a determinant for the lack of action and that attitude is far away from my present disposition. But following Seneca, I am trying to find out where are we trying to go in order to find favorable winds. Cuba, as I have always said, is not different from the rest of Latin America, but an extreme case of the historical democratic failures in the region.

Allow me another quotation, in this case from James Madison, the American thinker who under the influence of David Hume most influenced the framing of American democracy. In letter 10 of the *Federalist Papers*, Madison wrote:

> A common passion or interest will, in almost every case, be felt by a majority of the whole; a communication and concert result from the form of government itself; and there is nothing to check the inducements to sacrifice the weaker party or an obnoxious individual. Hence it is that such democracies have ever been spectacles of turbulence and contention; have ever been found incompatible with personal security or the rights of property; and have in general been as short in their lives as they have been violent in their death. Theoretic politicians, who have patronized this species of government have erroneously supposed that by reducing mankind to a perfect equality in their political rights, they would, at the same time, be perfectly equalized and assimilated in their possessions, their opinions, and their passions.[1]

Forgive me for the length of this brilliant quotation, but it seems to me that once we share this view, it is possible to start being optimistic, not only with the Cuban transition but with the necessary transition of the rest of the continent. And we may be optimistic because then it is not nature but a system that condemns us to the chains of oppression and poverty. Once we accept this spirit, we can start the cultural process of developing our virtues in the same way the Americans did.

Most unfortunately our perceptions of ourselves have gone from one extreme to the other. We have thought that we were superior souls endowed with generous feelings, not contaminated by the materialism that appears to affect the Americans. That was the approach of the Uruguayan Rodó in his *Ariel*, where he associated us to Ariel and the Americans to Calibán. None other than our José Martí had previously thought in those romantic terms, and so we learned to compensate our social failures with the conviction that that was the cost of our spiritual superiority. If that were the case, there would not be a solution to our maladies, because that would imply the selling of our soul to the devil. And talking about the devil, there is another explanation for our failures that was proposed by Max Webber concerning the apparent material superiority of Protestantism over Catholicism. If religion were the cause of differences in economic and political success, I would say that there is no hope for any successful transition.

My contention is that there is hope precisely because neither one of the above explanations is valid. On the one hand, there is no conflict between spirituality as such and material well-being, and it is not true that we are more spiritual than the Americans. On the other hand, the Webberean explanation clashes with European history, since capitalism was developed in England and not in Luther's Germany. Allow me to say that Argentina was during the second part of the 19th Century the main contradiction to Webber's theory. Without changing its religion, Argentina was ahead of other Anglo-Saxon and Protestant countries like Canada and Australia.

Where, then, lies the reason for the different results in the United States and Latin America? Before answering this key question, let me cross the Atlantic and remind you about European history. It was only after the Glorious Revolution in 1688 that the British started to liberate themselves from the oppression of the Tudors and the Stuarts, as David Hume showed in his *History of England*. Moreover, we should remember that in the Second World War, the Europeans offered the world to be Nazis or Communists, and democracy got there with the Sherman tanks.

After these historical reflections, I may answer the question about the reasons for the different performances. The origin of these different historical developments is found in the realm of ethics and its foundations. We should therefore start with what may be considered the foundations of ethics, Plato's *Phaedrus*. There, Plato states that the soul[2] is divided in three parts: a white horse, a black horse and a charioteer. The white horse is supposed to represent goodness in the sense of reason, whereas the black horse is madness as a result of passions. This dichotomy of good and evil is a tergiversation of human nature that most unfortunately has come to our days through the influence of Kantian moral philosophy as expressed in the categorical imperative.

It was Aristotle, however, the first philosopher, who challenged the Platonic approach to moral rationalism. In his *Nicomachean Ethics* he admits that judgement "is distinguished by its falsity or truth not by it badness or goodness."[3] Then, it is most important to distinguish morality from reason, as Hume clearly explained when he wrote:

Since morals, therefore, have an influence on the actions and affections, it follows that they cannot be derived from reason and that because reason alone, as we have already proved, can never have any such influence. Morals excite passions, and produce or prevent actions. Reason is utterly impotent in this partic-

---

1. James Madison, *The Federalist Papers: Letter 10*.

2. Plato, *Phaedrus*. This expression is in the words of Socrates.

3. Aristotle, *Nichomachean Ethics*.

ular. The rules of morality therefore are not the conclusions of our reason.[4]

In this approach—that coincides with Aristotle's—Hume recognizes the complexity of human nature, where passions (or feelings) are parts of humanity as much as reason and not its base animal side. Hume repeats Aristotle's words when he says: "Reason is the discovery of truth or falsehood…. Moral distinctions, therefore, are not the offspring of reason." It is in this sense that Alfonse de Lamartine in his *The History of the Girondins* wrote with respect to the crimes during the French Revolution: "The theories which revolt the consciousness are just spiritual paradoxes in service of the aberrations of the heart... Everything that curtails part of man's sensibility, deprives him of a part of his true greatness."[5]

Here we have what we may consider the ethical *divortium aquarium* that arose from the enlightenment, which in Kant's words, "was man's emergence from his self- incurred immaturity. Immaturity is the inability to use one's own understanding without the guidance of another."[6] In this definition we have the origin of what Karl Popper called epistemological optimism, which was the starting point of the development of knowledge and science. Unfortunately, from Descartes onward, there was rationalism, which meant the absolutization of reason as the substitute for truth. The main offspring of this absolutization of reason was the rationalization of morality in the hands of Kant, that brought us back to the principles of Plato *Phaedrus* and to what we consider a denaturalization of humanity.

In his *Fundamental Principles of the Metaphysics of Morals*, Kant states:

> From what has been said, it is clear that all moral conceptions have their seat and origin completely a priori in the reason, and that, moreover, in the commonest

reason just as truly as in that which is in the highest degree speculative; that they cannot be obtained by abstraction from any empirical, and therefore mainly contingent, knowledge.[7]

From this premise Kant concluded that principles dictated by reason "must have their source wholly a priori and thence their commanding authority, expecting everything from the supremacy of the law and the due respect for it, nothing from inclination, or else condemning the man to self-contempt and inward abhorrence."[8] It is with respect to this conclusion, according to which man becomes an authomat of pure reason, without feelings, that Ayn Rand wisely condemned it by saying that "what Kant propounded was full, total abject selflessness: he held that action is moral only if you perform it out of a sense of duty and derive no benefit from it of any kind, neither material nor spiritual: if you derive any benefit, your action is not moral any longer. This is the ultimate form of demanding that man turn himself into a shmoo."[9] And then she concluded that an unpracticable morality becomes an excuse for any practice. I am not going to insist on Ayn Rand's analysis of Kant's moral philosophy, but it should be acknowledged that it is the antithesis of the one that is at the heart of the ethical recognition of individual rights.

UNIVERSALS AND POLITICS

The second divergence in the so-called Western civilization relates to universals. This is a major issue that started in Greece and has lasted to our days. It has been ignored as a consequence of the apparent difficulty in understanding the meaning of universals and its necessary political implications.

Let us start by explaining the nature of the universals issue. It is not my purpose to delve into the ontological question as such, but only about its implications

---

4. David Hume, *A Treatise on Human Nature*, Book III of Morals.

5. Alfonse de Lamartine, *The History of the Girondins*.

6. Enmanuel Kant, *What is the Enlightenment?*

7. Enmanuel Kant, *Fundamental Principles of the Metaphysics of Morals*.

8. Enmanuel Kant, *The Metaphysics of Morals*.

9. Ayn Rand, *Philosophy—Who needs it. Faith and Force.*

in politics. Notwithstanding, it is necessary to know the nature of the argument in order to understand its political implications. Since Plato, some argued that universals, or so-called essences, were real and a condition for the existence of particulars. That was the position maintained by the realists. On the other side of the argument was the nominalist position, which maintained that universals were only nominal abstractions to better understand the real nature of the particulars. But as Tocqueville once said: "general ideas are not a proof of the strength of human intelligence, but its weakness, because there are no equal beings in nature, no identical facts."[10]

There are profound political implications resulting from these two different approaches to the nature of the universals. What we may call the Franco-Germanic political philosophy, after Rousseau, believes in universal realism whereas the Anglo-American political philosophy is based on the nominalist approach. It was John Locke who in his *Second Treatise of Civil Government* challenged what may be considered the assumed perfection of the universals.

In his *First Treatise of Government* Locke had already denied the divine right of monarchs, but in this case he apparently was arguing against the Leviathan theory of Thomas Hobbes. Hobbes had tried to justify the necessity of absolute power of the monarchs in order to control man's unsocial nature. So he insisted in the abstract reality of the Leviathan, which in my view he associated with Elizabeth I's pattern of behavior and defined it as the mortal god inspired by the immortal one. It is obvious that Locke argument in this case was more related to Hobbes' contention and he said:

> But I shall desire those who make this objection to remember that absolute monarchs are but men; and if government is to be the remedy of those evils which necessarily follows from men being judges in their own cases, and the state of nature is therefore not to be endured, I desire to know what kind of govern-

ment that is and how much better it is than the state of nature, when one man commanding a multitude has the liberty to be judged in his own case, and may do to all his subjects whatever he pleases without the least question or control of those who execute his pleasure... As if when men, quitting the state of nature entered into society, they agreed that all of them but one should be under the restraint of laws; but that he should still retain all the liberty of the state of nature, increased with power, and made licentious by impunity. This is to think that men are so foolish that they take care to avoid what mischiefs may be done them by polecats or foxes, but are content, nay, think it safety, to be devoured by lions.[11]

In the above contention Locke gives the major reasons for the need to limit political power, such as by the law, which would guarantee freedom through the limitation of powers. About 80 years later, Jean Jacques Rousseau overcoming in some sense what I consider his romantic period of the *Discourse on Inequality* and his love for the "noble savage," entered the rationalist school and published *The Social Contract*. Coming from the antipodes of Hobbes' views respecting human nature, Rousseau arrives at similar conclusions in his concept of sovereignty and the general will. So he says: "Just as nature gives each man absolute power over the parts of his body, the social pact gives the body politic absolute power over its members, and it is this same power which under this direction of the general will, bears the name of sovereignty..."[12]

Sovereignty is the new name of the Leviathan, and through it we return to the obvious realism of the universals as it is well expressed by Rousseau in his anthropomorphism of the sovereignty. We perceive there that rational approach which gives to the body politic the nature of the real men who compose it, and in so doing men become just a part of the universal that is the sovereignty. Hence Rosseau comes to the conclusion that the very idea of the distribution of power is a fallacy of composition that leads to

---

10. Alexis de Tocqueville, *Democracy in America*.

11. John Locke, *The Second Tratise of Civil Government*.

12. Jean Jacques Rousseau, *The Social Contract* .

nowhere and so he says: "The sovereign, being formed only by the individuals who compose it, neither has nor can have any interest contrary to theirs; consequently there is no need for the sovereign power to give guarantees to the subjects, because it is impossible for the body to want to harm all its members..."[13] According to the above principle, he rejects the necessity to divide sovereignty, against the best judgements of Locke and Monstesquieu. Then as sovereignty is indivisible, he says that those authors "make the sovereign a fantastic being put together from various bits and pieces; it is as if they composed man of several bodies, each one with eyes, arms or feet and nothing more... After having dismembered the social body by a sleigh of hand trick worthy of a fair, they reassemble the pieces in a manner known only to themselves."[14]

The above quotations give the essence of what has been called "reason of state" (*raison d'état*), which is evidently the source of the tyranny, since the sovereignty is provided with impunity and the false assumption that it cannot do wrong to the individuals and has no interest but the common one. Following Rousseau came Kant, who considered Rousseau the Newton of Moral Sciences. So in his *Theory of Right*, which is part of *The Metaphysics of Morals*, Kant expands on the impunity of sovereignty following Rousseau. So he says: "The legislative power can belong only to the united will of the people. For since all right is supposed to emanate from this power, the laws it gives must be absolutely incapable of doing anyone an injustice."[15] We can see that Kant has now included another universal as the source of political power: the people. So we have gone three hundred and sixty degrees back—from the divine right of the monarchs we have fallen into the hands of the divine rights of the people.

Notwithstanding Kant's apparent acceptance of the division of power, that does not diminish his decisive acknowledgement of the prerogatives of the supreme power. Forgive me for this long quotation but I think that Kant's words on political realm are the source of the rational absolutism that was the philosophical foundation of the totalitarian systems which became the Atilas of the 20th Century. Kant says:

> For since the people must clearly be considered as united under a general legislative will before they can pass rightful judgement upon the highest power within the state, they cannot pass any judgement other than that which is willed by the current head of state. A law which is so sacred that it is practically a crime even to cast doubt upon it and thus to suspend its effectiveness for even an instant, cannot be thought of as coming from human beings, but from some infallible supreme legislator. That is what is meant by the saying that "all authority comes from God," which is not a historical derivation of the civil constitution but an idea expressed as a practical principle of reason. ... From this follows the proposition that the sovereign of a state has only rights in relation to the subject, and no (coercive) duties... Indeed even the actual constitution cannot contain any article which might make it possible for some power within the state to resist or hold in check the supreme executive in cases where he violates the constitutional laws.[16]

It is obvious that the above principles are the fundamental basis of the absolutism that finally through Hegel and Marx gave rise to the totalitarian regimes of the Nazis and the Communists as the successors of the Jacobins who were entitled to the supreme power under the aegis of the goddess reason. Evidently this philosophy is the antithesis of the principles that are at the base of the liberal or open society as expressed most notably by Locke and Hume. Coming back to the *Second Treatise of Civil Government* one can read there the following: "This freedom from absolute, arbitrary power is so necessary to, and closely joined with a man's preservation, that he cannot part with it

---

13. Jean Jacques Rousseau, *The Social Contract.*

14. Jean Jacques Rousseau, *The Social Contract.*

15. Enmanuel Kant, *The Metaphysics of Morals; The Theory of Right.*

16. Enmanuel Kant, *The Metaphysics of Morals; The Theory of Right.*

but by what forfeits his preservation and his life together."[17] Locke, then, with full consciousness of the human character of governments and legislations, completely disagrees with the idea of a supreme and arbitrary power and he defends the rights of the subjects against the arbitrariness of governments. So he says: "the legislative or supreme authority cannot assume to itself a power to rule by extemporary arbitrary decrees, but is bound to dispense justice and decide the right of the subjects by promulgated standing laws and known authorized judges. ... Whereas by supposing they have given up themselves to the absolute arbitrary power and will of a legislator, they have disarmed themselves and armed him to make a prey of them when he pleases."[18]

We can see that this approach is the opposite of the conceptual Leviathan arising from the political theories of Hobbes, Rousseau and Kant. Locke is even more specific in favor of the rights of the subjects when he wrote: "The supreme power cannot take from any man any part of his property without his own consent... Hence, it is a mistake to think, that the supreme or legislative power of any commonwealth can do what it will, and dispose of the estates of the subject arbitrarily or take any part of them at pleasure."[19] The very idea that the nature of government is sustained on the necessity to avoid the possibility that anyone could be judged in his own case, means that rights exist as such before government. Then it is the obligation of governments to protect those rights, which are life, liberty, property and the right of men to the pursuance of their own happiness. These rights, as Ayn Rand said, have been ignored by the Europeans who believe in the reason of state.

PRIVATE AND GENERAL INTEREST

The other basic question defining the difference between the open society and the totalitarian system is the moral nature of the private interest. In the previous section we explained the political implications of the arguments with respect to the real or nominal nature of the universals. Here we will analyze the political implications of the moral qualifications of the private interests with respect to the general interest.

This issue is deeply related to the controversy about the universals since the realism position is based on the assumption that governments are free from man's frailty, which appears to be present only in private interests. It is obvious that Locke's appreciation of individual rights as a precondition for freedom necessarily recognizes the *juris tantum* morality of private interest. We may say that the mere idea of individual rights is the juridical expression of the moral qualification of private interest.

Starting with Hobbes, the assumption that man is a wolf-man, is actually recognition that there is no rationality or moral content in private interest. This is so even though Hobbes considered that absolute power was a necessary condition for the defense of private rights. At the same time, his apparent adherence to nominalism is disqualified as such by his Leviathan, which ignores the private interest that prevails in absolute power. On the other side of the channel, Jean Jacques Rousseau, based on the opposite assumption of human nature, arrived at similar conclusions with respect to the antagonism between private and general interest. Rousseau had previously arrived at the conclusion that man's nature had been corrupted by society as he explained in his *Discourse*, "Has the Revolution of the arts and sciences been conducive to the purification of morals?" and his response in the negative. Later, in his *Discourse on Inequality Among Men*, he blamed private property for that. Founded on these two assumptions, he wrote the *Social Contract*, where he clearly established the necessary antagonism between private and general interests. He wrote: "For an individual will by its na-

---

17. John Locke, *Second Treatise of Civil Government*.

18. John Locke, *Second Treatise of Civil Government*.

19. John Locke, *Second Treatise of Civil Government*.

ture tends to partiality, and the general will tends toward equality."[20]

Hence Rousseau contends that the "social pact requires each individual to relinquish only that part of his power, possessions and freedom which is important for the community to control; but it must also be acknowledged that the sovereign is the sole judge of that importance." [21] Based on his contention, he asserts that through the absolutism of the sovereignty, the individual will exchange independence for security. This is the opposite of Locke's conclusion with respect to the necessary limits to political power in order to retain individual freedom.

But more than that, Rousseau is the originator of the idea that for society to survive, it is necessary to change human nature, or what later was proclaimed by the Marxists as the necessity to create a new man. Rousseau wrote: "Anyone who dares to undertake the task of instituting a nation must feel himself capable of changing human nature, so to speak; of transforming each individual who by himself is a complete and solitary whole into a part of a greater whole from which he in a sense receives his life and his being."[22] So Rousseau, by rejecting human nature as such, not only denies the morality of private interest, but transfers the very reason to exist to a universal which may be denominated the state or the nation. Hence, the individual has no rights per se but only privileges granted by the sovereignty.

As Kant later contended, Rousseau thinks that "the forces that move the state are then simple and vigorous: its principles are clear and illuminating; there are no tangled, conflicting interests; the common good is always so obvious that it can be seen by anyone with common sense." Here we find the origin of Kant's moral philosophy and hence the categorical impera-

tive. Again, Rousseau considers that in this assumed antagonism between private and general interests: "The better the state is constituted, the more public affairs take precedence over private business in the minds of citizens."[23] This is certainly the starting point for the deification of the state that through Kant reaches its ultimate height in Hegel's mind. And for that very reason Rousseau also thought that "the supreme authority can no more be modified than alienated; to limit it is to destroy it. It is absurd and contradictory that the sovereign should give itself a superior."[24] In this assumption, Rousseau gave up any role for the rule of law and, of course, there is no role for a Supreme Court as a guardian of individual rights.

Standing on the shoulders of Rousseau and Kant, Hegel developed further the absolutism of power through the final deification of the state. According to Karl Popper, Hegel's radical collectivism where the state is everything and the individual nothing comes from Plato, but I think that he owes even more to Rousseau's and Kant's ideas on rationality and morality. It was Kant in his *Idea for a Universal History with a Cosmopolitan Purpose* who first developed the idea of reason in history and the antagonism as the dialectical dynamics of history. He wrote there: "The only way out for the philosopher, since he cannot assume that mankind follows any rational purpose of its own in its collective actions, is for him to attempt to discover a purpose in nature behind the senseless course of human events, and decide whether it is after all possible to formulated in terms of a definite plan of nature a history of creatures who act without a plan of their own,"[25] and in his fourth proposition he writes: "the means which nature employs to bring about the development of innate capacities is that of antagonism within society in so far

---

20. Jean Jacques Rousseau, *The Social Contract*.

21. Jean Jacques Rousseau, *The* Social Contract.

22. Jean Jacques Rousseau, *The Social Contract*.

23. Jean Jacques Rousseau, *The Social Contract*.

24. Jean Jacques Rousseau, *The Social Contract*.

25. Enmanuel Kant, *Idea for Universal History with a Cosmopolitan Purpose*.

as this antagonism becomes in the long run the cause of a law governed social order."[26]

There is no doubt that it was from Rousseau's and Kant's thinking that Hegel developed his philosophy of history as well as his philosophy of state, which are decidedly intermingled through the dialectical reason. He wrote: "The universal is to be found in the state; the state is the Divine Idea as it exists on earth ... the State is the march of God through the world."[27] Hegel established the absolutism of reason and rationalized collectivism through the state and the assumed morality of bureaucracies as representatives of the general interest against what he called the concupiscence of the corporations. That is the State is the very idea of ethics, and in his philosophy of right he says: "The State is the actuality of the ethical Idea." Following this statement, he disqualifies private interest and says: "If the state is confused with civil society and if its specific end is laid down as the security and protection of property and personal freedom, then the interest of the individuals as such becomes the ultimate end of their association and it follows that membership of the state is something optional."[28]

That is why only those who care for the general interest are moral, and that is the case of the bureaucracy that he calls the universal class. He wrote: "The universal class, as more precisely the class of civil servants, must purely in virtue of its character as universal, have the universal as the end of its essential activity."[29] It is not the purpose of this paper to analyze all Hegel's philosophy, but only those aspects that relate to the idea of the morality of private interest and the consequent rights of individuals. For that purpose it is important to remember his theory of alienation according to which existence is perceived as self-conscience: "This conscience implies the dual-

ism of men between the finite and the infinite, between the particular and the universal. So the individual finds a tension between his own being and he as part of a totality which is his nature as a citizen."[30] That means that he faces a world in which he is the other, so he is objectified and he feels alienated in society.

Among other considerations concerning what Hegel calls the negation of the negation by accepting the phenomenological character of the world, he sustains that the state is that rationality which represents the absolute spirit and subsumes the individual in the dialectical designs of the Idea. We can see in this philosophy the rejection of individual rights and in particular the right of men to the pursuance of their own happiness. It also ignores the real human nature in favor of the rationalization that depriving man of his right to the pursuance of happiness actually destroys the possibility of freedom and then of the creation of wealth.

This moral philosophy is exactly the opposite of Hume's approach, according to which reason has nothing to do with morality that is in the realm of passions. So he contends that: "For whether the passion of self-interest be esteemed vicious or virtuous, it is all a case; since itself alone restrains it. So that if it be virtuous, men become social by their virtue; if vicious, their vice has the same effect."[31] Given this realism of human nature, Hume distinguishes between morality and justice and so he sustains that the stability of society depends on the stability of possession, the transference by consent and the fulfillment of promises.

Moreover, Hume realizes that if men were benevolent and nature generous, the very idea of justice would disappear, because it would become useless. That is why he also states very clearly that "in gener-

26. Enmanuel Kant, *Idea for Universal History with a Cosmopolitan Purpose.*
27. Wilhem Hegel, *The Theory of the State.*
28. Wilhem Hegel, *The Theory of the State.*
29. Wilhem Hegel, *The Theory of the State.*
30. Wilhem Hegel, *The Phenomenology of the Spirit.*
31. David Hume, *A Treatise on Human Nature.*

al, it may be affirmed that there is no such a passion in human minds, as the love of a mankind merely as such, independent of personal qualities of services or of relations to ourselves. It is true that there is no human and indeed no sensible creature whose happiness or misery does not in some measure affect us when brought near to us and represented in lively colors."[32] To pretend otherwise is to universalize particular feelings that actually exist in human nature. That is a rationalization as a sort of political romanticism that has been the source of much demagoguery in the struggle for power.

THE MARXIAN APPROACH

It was Karl Marx who, using Hegel's dialectics, arrived at opposite philosophical conclusions that in practice developed into another totalitarian system. It was Engels who said that since Hegel had reached the ultimate heights of German philosophy, the only choice was to discuss him from within his system. Hence Marx tried and succeeded in placing Hegel's philosophy upside down. As Von Mises once wrote, Marx believed that he knew better than Hegel the wishes of the Geist. So accepting Hegel's and Kant's antagonism as the driving force of history, Marx contended that actually world history was not the war among the states but the class struggle.

Hegel took to the logical conclusion Kant's theory of antagonism and forecasted a never-ending dialectical process of war among states and the winner was the one who better read God's wishes. Marx, on the other hand, decided that history has nothing to do with God, and the dialectical process of antagonism between classes will ultimately reach a synthesis in which the proletariat will be the real universal. That was the final stage of communism, in which freedom had been reached overcoming scarcity, which was not a natural fact but the result of a particular way of production established by the bourgeoisie. That was the theory of exploitation of man by man, according to which the workers were deprived of the value of their product by the capitalist.

For Marx, then, Hegel's theory of State was another philosophical rationalization that tried to explain and justify the actual phenomenological situation. In his *Critique of Hegel's Philosophy of the State*, Marx argues that the state is the proof of the antagonism of classes and it represents the machinery to impose the freedom of the bourgeoisie at the expense of the exploitation of the labor class. At the same time, Marx criticizes the assumed ethics of the bureaucracy as representative of the general interest. He wrote: "Transcendence of bureaucracy can mean only that the universal interest becomes the particular interest in actuality and not as with Hegel merely thought and abstraction. This is possible only when the particular interest becomes universal. ... For the individual bureaucrat, the state purpose becomes his private purpose of hunting for a higher position and making a career for himself."[33] Thus, Marx's philosophy is not only anarchical, but actually it is dictatorial, as was showed in theory and practice by Lenin.

The fundamental aspect of Marxism is its polylogism and its false theory of exploitation as the basis of private property. So it comes out to be another kind of collectivism that incorporates all the ethical assumptions respecting to which men nature should be superseded by the new man who will overcome scarcity in a world of true freedom. This kind of heaven on earth was to come after the dictatorship of the proletariat had expropriated the expropriators. As Karl Popper said, Marx philosophy was the worst kind of historicism or historical determinism. It still prevails in the world in spite of the implosion of the Soviet empire and the crumbling of the Berlin wall.

Social democracy, as presented by Eduard Bernstein, has been the successor of the original revolutionary Marxism. After been saved by the Americans of Nazism and Communism in the Second World War and during the so called Cold War, universal suffrage as had been forecasted by Bernstein in the *The Revolutions of Socialism* has succeeded and social democracy prevails in Europe, even with governments that

---

32. David Hume, *A Treatise on Human Nature*.

33. Karl Marx, *Criticism of Hegel: Civil Society and Bureaucracy*.

are supposed to be of the right. So we cannot be surprised by the present antagonism between Europe and the United States, which is just a reflection of the actual profound differences in political philosophies.

CONSTITUTIONALISM VS. MAJORITY RULE

In the previous sections, we have explained the two opposite political and moral philosophies which arose from the enlightenment and which may be called collectivism and individualism. Here we are going to analyze the important contribution of American political philosophy, which made the United States the greatest society in history in only two hundred years. We may say that it was in the United States where the fundamental principles of constitutionalism were developed. In *The Federalist Papers* we find the fundamental tenets of a Republic subject to the rule of law. Those principles, which are the basis of American society, are mainly ignored or even worse despised and hated in the rest of the world, including Latin America.

The actual meaning of the Rule of Law is the change in the relationship of the government with the governed, that is, the citizens. Thus, the Rule of Law is the antithesis of the Reason of State and according to it, there is a major change with respect to the role governments and the limits of political power. As Madison said: "In Europe charters of liberty have been granted by power. America has set out the example ... on charters of power granted by liberty."

The most important character of the American Republic is the Bill of Rights, which is based on the assumption that the and of governments is justice, which is the protection of individual rights. The most distinguished characteristic of the American democratic process is the consciousness of human frailty. So in Letter 2 of the *Federalist Papers*, Alexander Hamilton wrote: "... a dangerous ambition more often lurks behind the specious mask of zeal for the rights of the people."[34] Regarding this perception of human nature, Jack N. Raskove in his *Original*

Meanings says with respect to Madison: "It took a decade of experience under the state constitution to expose the triple danger that so alarmed Madison in 1787: first, that the abuse of legislative power was more ominous than arbitrary acts of the executive; second, that the true problem of rights was less to protect the ruled from their rulers than to defend minorities and individuals against factious popular majorities acting through government; and third, that agencies of central government were less dangerous than state and local despotism."[35]

We can see then that the major concern of the Founding Fathers was the protection of individual rights, which were life, liberty, property and the right of men to the pursuance of their own happiness. This last right, which has been ignored or disqualified in the rest of the world (Europe and Latin America included) is of major moral importance, because this is the ethical admission of private interests. Never in the minds of the Founding Fathers was the idea that they were creating an economic system denominated capitalism, but a new political organization in which the major contribution was the consciousness of human frailty, as had been acknowledged by Christianity.

This principle was certainly derived from Hume's moral philosophy, who wrote: "But it is evident, that the only cause why the extensive generosity of man, and the perfect abundance of everything, would destroy the very idea of justice is because they render it useless."[36] On the basis of this analysis, as well as Locke's "discovery" of the human nature of monarchs, Madison wrote in Letter 51 of *The Federalist Papers*:

> But what is government itself but the greatest of all reflections on human nature? If men were angels no government would be necessary. If angels were to govern men, neither external nor internal controls on government would be necessary. In framing a government which is to be administrated by men over men

34. Alexander Hamilton, *The Federalist Papers: Letter 2*.

35. Jack N. Raskove, *Original Meanings*.

36. David Hume, *A Treatise on Justice*.

the great difficulty lies in this: you must first enable government to control the governed; and in the next place oblige it to control itself. A dependence on the people is no doubt the primary control on the government; but experience has taught mankind the necessity of auxiliary precautions.[37]

In the above quotation we may find the evident difference between the American and the Franco-German political and moral philosophy, as expressed by Montesquieu, Rousseau, Kant, Hegel and finally Marx. Here we find the fundamentals of such philosophy. In the first place, the recognition of the human frailty in both the governors and the governed. That is why governments are needed in the first instance, because as Locke said, without law there is no freedom, because the very idea of justice is freedom under the law. But at the same time—and this is the Anglo-American contribution to political philosophy—there is self-controlof the government through the role of the Supreme Court as the guarantor of individual rights. That is, the essence of the rule of law is that it is applicable also to the government, which is not an entelechy but an administration of men over men.

Another important aspect is the relative importance given to universal suffrage as a means to control the government and so Madison also says: "In a society under the form of which the stronger faction can readily unite and oppress the weaker, anarchy may as truly be said to reign as in a state of nature, where the weaker individual is not secured against the violence of the stronger."[38] It is evident, then, that the system is based on the assumption that majorities cannot violate individual rights, as Locke had postulated, and so the very idea of constitutional rights is the limit of the power of the majority. When majorities rule, there is no right and in fact there is no constitution.

Moreover, Madison had expressed the need for additional precaution to limit political power. He said: "In a free government, the security for civil rights must be the same as for religious rights. It consists in the one case in the multiplicity of interest and in the other, in the multiplicity of sects."[39] We can see in this citation the different approach with respect to private interest that is not contrary to the general interest. That is, the morality implied in private interest becomes the rationale for the protection of civil rights, against the arbitrariness of majorities acting through governments.

At the same time, religious liberty was accepted on similar basis. This was the first time that a country went from religious tolerance to liberty, as it accepted the wisdom of Adam Smith who in his *The Wealth of Nations* had established the principle that religious freedom depends on the multiplicity of sects. This was also a major achievement in the road to the open society because religion had been the source of dictatorial governments. In that sense, Adam Smith had said in his *Theory of Moral Sentiments*:

> The administration of the great system of the universe, however, the care of the universal happiness of all rational and sensible beings, is the business of God and not of man. To man is allotted a much humbler department, but one much more suitable to the weakness of his powers, and to the narrowness of his comprehension; the care of his own happiness.[40]

Again, the right of man to the pursuance of happiness is a moral principle, and it is the obligation of the government to protect that right. This is the opposite of the unlimited rights of the majorities, which has been the main character of the democratic processes in Latin America, and that is why Madison also said: "An elective despotism is not the government we fought for."[41]

---

37. James Madison, *The Federalist Papers: Letter 51*.
38. James Madison, *The Federalist Papers: Letter 51*.
39. James Madison, *The Federalist Papers: Letter 51*.
40. Adam Smith, *The Theory of Moral Sentiments*.
41. James Madison, The Federalist Papers: Letter 48.

We see, then, that the Constitution or even the Bill of Rights are the limits of political power. And we can say that freedom is no more than the limitation of political power. Hence, as Locke had already said in his *Second Treatise of Civil Government*, the legislative could not be arbitrary with respect to the lives and fortunes of the people. Any law that violates the principles established in the Bill of Rights is necessarily unconstitutional. In that sense, Alexander Hamilton in Letter 78 of *The Federalist Paper* says: "No legislative act therefore contrary to the Constitution can be valid. To deny this would be to affirm that the deputy is greater than his principal; that the servant is above his master; that the representatives of the people are superior to the people themselves."[42] And Hamilton continues: "A constitution is in fact, and must be, regarded by judges as a fundamental law." This is the principle that actually decided the viability of democratic governments, and it was decided as such in 1803 by John Marshall in the famous case Marbury v. Madison. There he established:

> ... all those who have framed written constitutions contemplate them as forming the fundamental and paramount law of the nation, and consequently the theory of every such government must be that an act of the Legislature, repugnant to the Constitution, is void. ... It is, emphatically, the province and duty of the Judicial Department to say what the law is. Those who apply the rule to particular cases must, of necessity, expound and interpret that rule. If two laws conflict with each other, the courts must decide on the operation of each. ... If, then, the courts are to regard the Constitution, and the Constitution is superior to any ordinary act of the legislature, the Constitution, and not such ordinary act, must govern the case to which they both apply.[43]

THE ROAD TO LIBERATE LATIN AMERICA FROM ITS LIBERATORS

In 1910 Luis Alberto de Herrera wrote a book, *La Revolución Francesa y Sudamérica*, and there he said: "The inflexible dogmas of the French Revolution commanded to collide against reality.[44] On its behalf, and in order, every South American society has fallen and continues falling in the abyss of institutional fraud, which leads to civil war." *Mutatis mutandi* this observation more than explains the continuing failures of democratic processes in Latin America during the twentieth century, which appear to continue in the third millennium.

Evidently, as Herrera had discovered, our historical failures result from the original error of confusing the American Revolution with the French Revolution, which were actually antithetical. More than that, we also ignored the so-called Glorious Revolution of 1688 in Great Britain, led by the sound principles of John Locke, as expressed in his *Second Treatise of Civil Government* as well as the *Letter Concerning Toleration*. Hence, democracy in Latin America—under the aegis of the *Social Contract*—was the realm of majority rule, ignoring the major achievement of civilization which was the recognition of individual rights: "life, liberty, property and the pursuance of happiness."

The alternative to the *Social Contract*, which through the *Communist Manifesto* led to communism, was the *Leviathan* which was represented as expressed by Thomas Hobbes by the state which was the "mortal god as inspired by the immortal God." Latin America then changed, through its independence, from the divine rights of monarchs to the divine rights of the people. No one realized the important finding of Locke regarding the apparently historically-ignored fact that monarchs were also men.

That was the confusion that so wisely explained Juan Bautista Alberdi in his *Conferencia de Luz del Día* between external freedom (independence) and domestic freedom as individual freedom. So he said: "What is the condition of the Latin liberty? Is the liberty of all refunded and consolidated in one single collective and solidary liberty, that is exclusively exercised by an emperor or a liberator czar? It is the liberty of the

---

42. Alexander Hamilton, *The Federalist Papers: Letter 78.*

43. John Marshall, *Marbury vs. Madison.*

44. Luis Alberto de Herrera, *La Revolución Francesa y Sudamérica.*

country personalized in the government and the entire government personalized in one man."[45] And Alberdi suggested: "South America will be free when it becomes free from its liberators." This distinction between external freedom or independence from foreign governments and internal freedom as individual rights is of major importance to understand the causes of domestic failures in Latin America. As an example we should realize that Puerto Rico is not independent, but the Puerto Ricans are free, whereas Cuba is independent but the Cubans are not free.

Evidently, the father of the Argentine Constitution of 1853 had realized the difference between Franco-German and Anglo-American political philosophies, which as Balint Vazonyi argued, are as different as day and night. Unfortunately, not even at this stage of history have we realized this obvious opposition and we insist in the fallacy of shared values in the history of Western Civilization. Argentina in 1853 chose the Anglo-American political philosophy and in only fifty years—at the beginning of the 20th century—developed as the eighth richest country of the world. That was not the case with the rest of the Latin American countries, which continued torn between the *Leviathan* and the *Social Contract*.

My major concern is that not only Latin America ignores the opposition between these philosophies, but that the whole world appears to have this philosophical confusion, as the so-called globalization becomes the new philosophy of history, which according to Fukuyama has led to the end of history. But we should remember that it was Emmanuel Kant who in his essay "What is Enlightenment?" said: "Enlightenment is man's emergence from his self incurred immaturity. Immaturity is the inability to use one's own understanding without the guidance of another. The motto of Enlightenment is therefore 'Sapere Aude.' Have courage to use your own understanding." Unfortunately, from that very motto surged what I have called the obscurantism of reason. That is, Cartesian rationalism, which postulated that at the end

reason was the unfailing way to truth. Then came the Kantian reason in history aside from reason in men's minds and this was followed by the Hegelian dialectical process in which reason per se closed the gap between reality and rationality.

On the other side of the British Channel a different approach to the validity of reason, gave rise to a completely different and opposing view of human nature. Reason was another imperfect instrument to the difficult road to knowledge, which is always contingent. As Hume had said: "It is from the non-rational elements of our minds that men are saved from total skepticism."[46] From the very source of superseding immaturity surged a different approach whose motto could be "non sapere aude." That is, to acknowledge that we live in a world of uncertainty and that men's frailty is a fact of nature and not the lack of courage to know.

Recent history throughout the 20th Century showed how these two opposing views of the world developed into the final antagonism between freedom and servitude. The Franco-German political philosophy, arising from "sapere aude" or what I have called the obscurantism of reason, gave arise to the oppressive ideologies of Nazism, Fascism and Marxism (Communism). Meanwhile, liberal democracy prevailed through the Anglo-American political philosophy under the consciousness of men's fallibility.

Unfortunately, the demise of Communism in the Soviet Empire in no way determined the disappearance of Marxism. Social democracy is Marxism through Bernstein rather than Lenin. Hence we can see that in Europe, now including Great Britain through the Labour Party, social democracy and not liberal democracy is the new name of the game. Eduard Bernstein, who should be included as a "master thinker," as la nouvelle droite called the German philosophers, wrote the main tenets of social democracy. In his *The Preconditions of Socialism*, Bernstein wrote: "Socialism was the legitimate heir of liberalism… there is no really liberal thought which does not also belong to

---

45. Juan Bautista Alberdi, *Conferencia de Luz del Día*.

46. David Hume, *A Treatise on Human Nature*.

the elements of the ideas of socialism." This is the greatest mistake of social democracy, because socialism is not the heir of liberalism but its antithesis, as Marx very well explained.

Liberalism in the Anglo-American philosophy is an ethical approach to society based on the awareness of the fallibility of human nature. It is for that very reason that liberalism proposes the limits to political power as a safeguard of individual rights. In that sense, civilization is a learning process of controlling the base passions of humanity through justice and property. It is not the reason in history as a fateful process of liberty based on the improvement of human nature. In contrast, Socialism is conceived as the historical process of liberation in order to overcome scarcity. This is the Marxian approach and it was later admitted by Bernstein himself.

That is what I have called the syncretism of Western philosophy that has politically developed in the so-called human rights. This divinization of humanity as such ignores man's fallibility as recognized by the gospel. In this process, private interests are anathematized and the state as the representative of general interest becomes, in Hegelian terms, the "Divine idea as it exists on earth." This concept, according to which the state monopolized morality, means that all idea of limited political power is actually precluded. By the same token, this monopolization of social morality by the state means the actual power of bureaucracy to violate individual rights in order to achieve equality through social rights. Hence, philosophical syncretism was politically transformed into the intermingling of individual rights and its opposite, the social rights or social privileges granted by political power.

The striving for equality through the manipulation of social rights, has produced the worst political mistake, which in the end means the legitimation of violence in the name of income equalization. As Karl Popper had said: "Utopianism is self defeating and it leads to violence."[47] In my view, this political utopianism comes out of three different sources. The first

one is religious fanatism; the second one is rationalism, which is what I have called the obscurantism of reason. This is the pretension that reason *per se* equals truth. And the third one is political romanticism, which ignores the Hume dictum respecting the fact that there is not such a thing as the love to humankind. Love is a particular feeling and political romanticism is the universalization of such feeling, as a categorical imperative. I may add a fourth source, which is the ignorance of the people, and the natural tendency to envy. That is why I have argued that the so-called globalization can hardly tend to a unified system of common interest, because what people learn through communications is precisely the huge differences in wealth and not its determinants. Little by little, the original European confusion between democracy and socialism, as developed since Monstesquieu, degenerated into the political mess that has affected democracy in Latin America.

As had been brilliantly perceived by Herrera, French philosophical and political muddle as rationalized by the "Master Thinkers" has produced the ongoing civil war, whose worst result was the Cuban Revolution. An illuminating book by the Venezuelan Carlos Rangel, *From the Good Savage to the Good Revolutionary*, describes the political mythology that García Márquez defines as magic realism. But Rangel knows that we did not invent the myths, but inherited them from Europe, and so he says: "the fundamental myths of America are not American. They are myths created by the European imagination or they even came from afar, from the Judeo-Greek antiquity..."[48]

Cuba, in my opinion, was not an exception in Latin America, but the final outcome of this political mythology confronted with reality, which ended in civil war. The difference is that in Cuba the guerrillas defeated the army, that was the exceptional circumstance. But actually it was not. In my view, there are two main reasons that explain why Cuba fell under communism.

---

47. Karl Popper, *Conjectures and Refutations.*

48. Carlos Rangel, *Del Buen Salvaje al Buen Revolucionario.*

First, Cuba had enjoyed a very special economic relationship with the United States, which saved her from the poverty that other Latin American countries experienced and continue to experience on account of their own ignorance with respect to the main tenets of a Republic, which are individual rights. The stupidity was the same but, thanks to the Americans, we did not pay for it. So the main reason of our support of Castro's anti-Americanism was the gap between our relative wealth and the lack of knowledge about the reasons that created it. We believed ourselves to be above the other Latin Americans and of course we assumed that we could challenge the greatest civilization ever achieved in the history of mankind with no cost.

The second determinant of this fatal destiny was the fact that the Sergeant Fulgencio Batista and Saldivar had decapitated the Cuban army in 1933. The sergeants became generals and got power with the support of the revolutionaries. In 1959, the sergeants turned the power back to the revolutionaries thinking that they were going to share it, but actually they lost their heads. The United States had two opportunities to revert this setback to Western civilization, but the New Frontier—with Mr. John Fitzgerald Kennedy at the helm—decided to exchange crocodiles for missiles in what Paul Johnson defined as "America's suicide attempt."

The lesson was learned in the rest of the continent, where the military, not withstanding their political weaknesses, had been the one and only safeguard against the communist assault. At the same time that the guerrillas lost the war against the Army in Latin America, the left, under the umbrella of the European social democracy, is winning the peace and the so-called populism appears to be the alternative to the economic failure of the pejorative misnomer of neoliberalism. The latter is the democratic attempt to liberalize and stabilize the economy and privatize state enterprises.

Apparently no one even tries to recognize that the only Latin American exception to this democratic failure has been the Chilean case. While Castro remains the very symbol of anti-imperialism, General Pinochet barely overcame the Europeans attempts to imprison him while forgetting their own historical sins. His main fault was that he succeeded while all the other military governments failed. His success was so great that he changed the course of history of a country where, for the first time in the world, communism won a presidential election. Today Chile has become an example for the rest of the Latin American countries. But the left once again has succeeded in confusing the mind of the people, associating the militaries with the right and the right with capitalism in collusion with imperialism. In Europe they succeeded in confusing aristocracy with capitalism, when actually it was through capitalism that aristocracy lost power. Commerce and labor, which are the determinants of wealth, replaced war as the main object of the state.

We insist, however, in ignoring that the aristocratic character rests on the assumption that distribution, and not wealth creation, is the foundation of ethics. So we go back to square one, and private interests are a priori considered to be contrary to the so called common good and efficient production is pure materialism while distribution through political power is spiritualism. Thus, Hegel is back and the increase in government expenditures is the economic outcome of that ethical approach.

The irruption of the military into the Latin American political arena and uncontrolled inflation were considered the political and economic maladies that destroyed the natural well-being the Latin Americans deserved. The recovery of democracy and the economic stabilization that occurred during the 1990s while Latin America collapsed under political upheavals and deep recession has shown the fallacy of such assumption.

The political problem was not the rise of the military as such, just as inflation was not the economic problem. The rise of the military and inflation were the consequence of a deeper political and ethical problem, the lack of juridical security. That is, the ignorance of the rule of law, which is the respect of individual rights. Unfortunately the European example is more and more the main problem faced by the world, and in particular the Latin American countries, which tend to be a farse of the European tragedy. While the European economies, including France, Italy and Germany, collapse under the burden of an overwhelming welfare state, protectionism is again the main threat to the world economy. Socialism is a very expensive way of organizing production, and protectionism appears to be the only wise and ethical political solution. If the developed economies are fumbling under social democracy, it is not difficult to imagine that such a recipe is a great stumbling block to development.

The failure of the so-called neoliberalism was not the opening of the economy, or the privatization process as the left argues, but the impossibility to control government expenditures coupled with the inflexibility of the labor system. As long as we continue believing that distribution is ethical whereas the creation of wealth and profit is materialism, the producers of poverty will always get the votes to be in power. The very appeal of the distribution of wealth is the main cause of the unequal distribution of wealth as well as of the pauperization which comes about as a consequence not of capitalism, but of the corruption implied in socialism. As Marx brilliantly explained in his criticism to Hegel's *Theory of the State*, the bureaucrats convert their own private interest into general interests. Unfortunately, the so-called globalization is a fallacy, while communications have globalized information but not formation. The very system that produces the wealth that is known through the communication system is not only ignored, but resented, by the majority of the countries of the world and not least by the European Union, where social democracy prevails.

It is very important, then, to understand the real nature of the failure of the so-called neoliberalism, because otherwise the left will succeed in reverting to populism and violence. This lesson has to be learned more than anyone else by the International Monetary Fund, whose dogmatic approach to adjustment and monetary and fiscal equilibrium has been unable to solve the recent financial crisis in the world. I may say, then, that, as George Gilder explained in his

Wealth and Poverty, government expenditures are not part of the product, but a factor of production, in other words part of the cost of producing. Coming back to basics, macroeconomic theory has forgotten the fundamental source of wealth, which is microeconomic, and so Gilder says:

> Sooner or later, the American liberals like the British Laborites are going to discover that monetary restrictions are a wonderful way to destroy the private sector while leaving government intact and offering pretexts for nationalizing industry. Since government has become a factor of production, the only way to diminish its impact on prices is to economize on it—just as one would economize on the use of land, labor or capital—by reducing its size or increasing its productivity.[49]

And he continued: "It is not principally the federal deficit that causes inflation. If the deficit were closed by higher tax rates—and the money supply were held constant—the price level would likely rise in the orthodox way of the law of cost." I would add that interest rates would also rise and a fundamental disequilibrium would be created as market interest rates are above the profitability of the business sector, or what Keynes called the marginal efficiency of capital.

In Argentina, we have experienced once and again the deleterious results of the attempts to compensate for the increase in government expenditures by higher taxes, monetary controls, and a fixed nominal exchange rate. The last experience of the so-called convertibility was worse than others because it lasted longer and while inflation is an equilibrating process of disequilibrium, real interest rates above the rate of return creates cumulative disequilibrium, which finally explodes and the economy collapses and ends up in a banking crisis. The problem is that utopianism determines the expansion of government expenditures, and monetary orthodoxy is the dogmatic rationalism that is tantamount to what I have called the obscurantism of reason. This lethal symbiosis of "solidarity" and "dogmatic rationalism" has been at the center of all of the recent financial crisis. We have acknowledge that once you cannot control govern-

---

49. George Gilder, *Wealth and Poverty*.

ment expenditures, you cannot control the nominal exchange rate or the money supply.

CONCLUSIONS AND RECOMMENDATIONS

From what I have set out in previous sections, it is evident that the Cuban problem is not Castro but the final result of a rationalist ethic that necessarily leads to tyranny. That is, as Tocqueville had said: "It was believed that there was a love for freedom but it was discovered that only the master was hated." I think that this phrase summarizes the confusion that reigns in the world, and in particular among intellectuals, and not least the economists.

The fall of the Berlin Wall and the implosion of the Soviet Empire has added to the reigning confusion about the new historical determinism contained in the so called globalization. This new historicism was presented by Francis Fukuyama in his *The End of History*, where misreading Hegel, he forecasted the end of history as a result of the final triumph of liberal democracy over socialism. According to Fukuyama, the ideological antagonism had ended in the opposite way than foreseen by Marx, and the so-called socialist synthesis had reverted to the capitalist antithesis. The history of our time shows that actually the crumbling of the Berlin Wall has been far from the final triumph of liberal democracy in the world. Even in Europe, the prevailing political system is social democracy, which is Marxism without revolution through universal suffrage. Another recent book which has certainly contributed to the confusion respecting globalization is Samuel Huntington's *The Clash of Civilizations*. His theory is a reductionism which ignores the clash within the so-called Western civilization and to some extent confuses culture with civilization, reducing terrorism to religious causes.

The truth of the matter is that communications have globalized information, but ignore the formation required to reach the heights of civilization, which is the recognition of individual rights. Regardless of the universal ignorance about Marx's fundamental ideas, the rationalist ethics of the West intermingles with the religious fanatism of the East. Latin America is evidently the realm of rational obscurantism, where individual rights are ignored in favor of so-called human rights, which include social rights that are actu-

ally privileges granted by governments ignoring the rule of law.

Widespread information regarding the wealth differentials globalizes the feeling of envy that leads to the justification of violence and terrorism. Castro will finally die, no doubt, but the problem that leads to tyranny will remain as long as we do not learn and teach the fundamental principles of the rule of law as the basis of a viable democracy, and not what Madison called an "elective despotism." As long as democracy in Latin America continues ignoring the rule of law in favor of majority rule, we will fail in our purpose of attaining freedom and well being. The Cuban experience in Florida should be an example of what can be achieved by Latin America provided that we accept the "rule of law." And the problems that Cuba will encounter after Castro will not be very different from those that Latin America as a whole, with the possible exception of Chile, is presently facing.

Majority rule based on fallacious rationalist ethics according to which there is an a priori contradiction between general and private interest, is the reason of the impunity of governments and the insecurity of rights. As increasing poverty will affect our economies, increasing envy will lead more and more to violence and terrorism. We have to acknowledge that poverty is not an economic problem, but a moral one, and unless we fight socialism in moral terms, proponents of socialism will keep the moral edge that leads to unlimited power and limited rights. That is, it will lead to oppression and actual inmiserization not because of neoliberalism, but for the lack of it.

Sovereignty and solidarity have been the main political instruments to achieve political power in the name of the nation and the people. To defeat them, it is of utmost importance to learn and preach the moral philosophy that sustains the rule of law. As long as we remain in this continent thinking that universal suffrage is the landmark of democracy, forgetting Madison's advice respecting auxiliary precautions to control the government, we should not be surprised by democratic failures. And let us not forget that socialism is not, as Eduard Bernstein pretended, the heir of liberalism (conservatism) but its ethical antithesis.

TARGETING CASTRO, NOT CUBA: CONSIDERING A SMART SANCTIONS APPROACH TOWARD CUBA

Brian Alexander

Through writing, public advocacy, and other personal and professional endeavors, I have demonstrated my firm belief that greater engagement with Cuba would advance America's national interest and at long last bring economic and democratic reform to the island. As former executive director of the Cuba Policy Foundation (CPF), I had the fortunate experience of participating in one of the most successful initiatives to date to ease sanctions against Cuba. Our economic impact studies demonstrated billions of dollars in economic opportunity in Cuba, including over $1 billion for the Miami economy alone. However, on April 23, 2003, I walked away from this project following one of the worst human rights crackdowns in the Western Hemisphere in over a decade, when the CPF board of directors and I resigned in collective protest.

The round up by the Castro government was unconscionable. Over 75 of Cuba's leading human rights activists, following summary trials lasting in many cases less than a day each, were sentenced to a total of more than 1,400 years in Cuba's prisons—all for their crimes of seeking greater freedom of speech and participation in their government.

Moreover, it was the conclusion of the CPF Board of Directors and me that the political outcome in the United States of these events in Cuba would be the effective shutdown of any hope that legislative efforts to ease sanctions against Cuba would succeed. Even though we remain firm in our view that engaging Cuba would advance both America's national interest and peaceful political and economic change in

Cuba, we also recognized that the great strides that we had taken forward toward these goals were wiped from the board.

We were faced with a choice: continue onward in what we were certain would be a futile enterprise, or take the opportunity to make a principled statement of protest against the Castro government. We chose the latter. This is a decision that I am proud of, and one I stand behind today.

All of us continue to face the challenging question of what to do about Castro's Cuba? How, at last, to help bring about economic and political reform to the island, reverse decades of human rights abuses, and help set Cuba and its people on a productive path toward a positive future? How to unlock billions of dollars in lost economic opportunity? We have seen that four decades of economic sanctions have not produced reform on the island; efforts to ease sanctions and try a new approach toward Cuba will eventually be shot down by Castro at every turn; while efforts by the U.S. Government to promote civil society on the island have been used by Castro as bogus justification to undertake what leading Cuban dissident Elizardo Sánchez has called the "decapitation" of Cuba's dissident movement. At a time of the greatest humanitarian crisis we have faced in Cuba in many years, and while America's national and economic interests remain not served by current U.S.-Cuban relations, our options for moving on a successful path forward seem few, if not simply not known.

Is it possible that the period we have now entered in U.S.-Cuba relations is best described as a death-watch? That is, until Fidel Castro passes from the scene, are there any good policy options available to the United States regarding Cuba? But to call this period a "deathwatch" would indeed be a cynical conclusion, one that would suggest that the international community and Cubans themselves ought simply to throw-up their hands and wait for biology to take care of our problems. This, obviously, is not a desirable course of action.

One area of possible promise, a glimmer of hope, that has emerged following the Havana Spring, is increased international recognition of Cuba's human rights abuses, the difficulties of applying a constructive engagement model with the Castro government, and, as this paper will focus on, the prospect of stepped-up multilateral efforts to promote freedom and prosperity in Cuba. This new context provides a unique opportunity to marshal international support behind creative approaches to promoting a rapid, peaceful transition in Cuba. Such a transition would bring obvious benefits to the Cuban people, but is also an essential step toward achieving the full potential of the Cuban economy and of Cuba as a U.S. trading partner.

Numerous proposals regarding multilateral approach toward Cuba have been discussed and foundered over the years. International opposition to the U.S. embargo has tended undercut productive multilateral discussions about Cuba. But, at last, with the crackdown, hope has been ignited that this discussion might shift away from the United States and finally focus on Castro. Indeed, in recent months the international landscape has shifted dramatically. Formal and informal discussions about cooperating on Cuba between the United States and foreign partners have increased; the European Union, Canada, Mexico and others, incensed by what has happened in Cuba, have increased their focus on human rights abuses in Cuba, including following upon the U.S. model of greater outreach to Cuba's dissidents; the trouble of fully realizing the trade potential of Cuba under Castro has been reinforced, in particular, as illustrated by the fall-out over the Cotonou Agreement and the

way the crackdown will impede efforts in the United States to open trade with the Island; Cuba itself, under Castro's direction, has soured relations and ratcheted up hostile rhetoric against the EU and others.

So, if the international context has presented a unique and perhaps unprecedented opportunity for multilateral cooperation on an approach toward Cuba, what options for multilateralism exist?

THE SMART SANCTIONS MODEL

One possible option is a policy of "smart sanctions." Smart sanctions or "targeted" sanctions, are limited coercive measures intended to focus pressure or leverage on decision-making elites and other culpable parties for unacceptable behavior. Differing in significant ways from comprehensive sanctions, a smart sanctions approach is meant to limit the impact of a sanctions regime to specific individuals or entities, while minimizing the impact or negative fallout on third parties. Smart or targeted sanctions may include such devices as: targeted financial sanctions, arms embargoes, travel bans, commodity embargos, and diplomatic restrictions. Applied effectively, a multilateral smart sanctions can focus attention on unacceptable actions of targeted individuals and entities, pressure such individuals or entities to modify their behavior, and serve as a valuable component of a broader strategy at promoting political or economic reform in a target country. Smart sanctions, while not a panacea, can serve a strategy of bringing about reform.

Notably, unlike comprehensive sanctions, a multilateral smart sanctions policy is less likely to exclude other policy tools, including expanding limited engagement. For example, smart sanctions would not necessarily be mutually exclusive to lifting the U.S. travel ban, or broadening U.S. commercial engagement with the island. Proposals to expand U.S. exports to Cuba, floated among Washington policy circles during the months prior to the crackdown, could still proceed under a targeted sanctions program and immediate, limited economic gains potential of Cuba could be achieved in the short-term, coinciding with a multilateral targeted sanctions program.

Since the latter part of the 1990s, smart sanctions have become an increasingly used tool in international affairs, but to date this approach has not been given serious consideration regarding the case of Cuba. To the author's knowledge, no literature exists on the topic of applying smart sanctions toward Cuba, and this paper is the first attempt at spelling out such an approach.[1]

A smart sanctions policy toward Cuba would not be a perfect solution. As the discussion in the next section will illustrate, the verdict is still out on how best to apply smart sanctions. However, smart sanctions offer the promise and opportunity for a strong, effective multilateral policy approach toward Cuba, for no fewer than the following reasons:

- The international climate is more favorable toward a multilateral approach than at other times in recent memory.

- Smart sanctions offer a viable "third way," toward Cuba that bridges the gap between the constructive engagement of America's allies and the comprehensive sanctions of the United States. Unilateral U.S. comprehensive sanctions have not been successful in achieving goals of political and economic reform in Cuba. Meanwhile, America's comprehensive sanctions are internationally disdained and viewed as ineffective. Comprehensive sanctions have caused unintended consequences that unnecessarily harm third parties and, according to some, they have provided Castro justification for Cuba's shortcomings. Moreover, neither is constructive engagement viewed, in itself, as a perfect solution or panacea for promoting political and economic reforms. Smart sanctions, because they are targeted would also minimize unintended or unnecessary harm to the political and economic interests of international allies.

- A multilateral smart sanctions policy would minimize unnecessary hardship to potential allies on the island who oppose the unacceptable behavior of the Castro government while sending a symbolic support to their cause.

- Smart sanctions would direct attention of the Cuba debate to the Castro government, its human rights abuses, and its failure to adopt or adhere to meaningful political and economic reforms, and its responsibility for Cuba's faltering economy. Targeted sanctions would help direct pressure on the Castro government to respond to the demands behind the sanctions policy or to undertake broader reform.

- Smart sanctions do not preclude some forms of economic, political and cultural engagement that international actors may find favorable, and they do not necessarily exclude application of other approaches for addressing Cuba.

THE SMART SANCTIONS MODEL AND CUBA

The favorability of the current international context toward multilateral approach to Castro's Cuba warrants investigation into a targeted sanctions policy. This section is a preliminary look into some of the major concepts and issues surrounding smart sanctions, including the merits and challenges of applying this tool in international affairs, and in particular how smart sanctions may be applied toward Cuba.

Defining "Smart Sanctions"

"Smart sanctions," as used in this report, follows the definition of David Cortright and George Lopez, whose groundbreaking work on the application of inducements and incentives in international affairs has been influential on the conceptual background for this report.[2] According to Cortright and Lopez: "A smart sanctions policy is one that imposes coercive pressures on specific individuals and entities and that

---

1. The author is taking the opportunity of presenting this paper at the Association for the Study of the Cuban Economy's 2003 annual conference to generate discussion and feedback on a smart sanctions approach toward Cuba. Insights gained during the conference will inform a longer research study, which will elaborate on points neglected or only touched upon lightly in this report. Feedback to the author is most welcome at alex@giraldilla.com.

2. The author worked for David Cortright, President of the Fourth Freedom Forum, while serving as Research Analyst at the Forum in 2001.

restricts selective products or activities, while minimizing unintended economic and social consequences for vulnerable populations and innocent bystanders."[3]

Examples of smart sanctions may include targeted financial sanctions, arms embargoes, travel bans, commodity embargoes, and diplomatic restrictions. Smart sanctions are intended to be a less blunt instrument than comprehensive embargoes, and are intended to maximize pressure on decision making elites or perpetrators of unacceptable behavior, while minimizing the negative impacts that comprehensive sanctions often have on civilian populations, possible domestic reformers or allies in the target countries, nontargeted third parties and other innocent bystanders both in the target country and abroad. A more exhaustive list of examples of smart sanctions, which may be considered in the case of Cuba, appears later in this report. As "smart sanctions" are, by definition, targeted sanctions, the terms "smart sanctions" and "targeted sanctions" will be used interchangeably throughout.

Smart sanctions emerged as a tool of coercion over the course of the 1990s, when the application of sanctions policies grew in frequency and greater understanding evolved of how to use sanctions to achieve intended goals while minimizing unintended or unwanted consequences. Beginning in the early 1990s, the frequency of multilateral application of coercive economic sanctions as tools of international diplomacy increased, principally, but not exclusively, through the United Nations.

Despite their increased application, the track record of the success of sanctions is at best mixed (like most tools in international affairs, they do not provide a perfect solution), and attempts at measuring what is meant by success are fraught with analytic problems. Nonetheless, in some instances, sanctions, when combined with other tools of diplomacy and persuasion, have yielded intended results (Libya, Haiti and South Africa are possible examples) and sanctions, regardless of their track record, appear to be a permanent component of international diplomacy.[4] By mid-decade, as the sometimes negative, unintended impacts of comprehensive sanctions became increasingly apparent—either in humanitarian consequences on civilian populations or harm to nontargeted individuals or entities[5]—a more nuanced approach toward applying sanctions became dominant. For example, except in the cases of Iraq, Haiti (1993-1994), and Yugoslavia (1992-1995), each of the fourteen cases of UN imposed sanctions during 1990 through 2001 were limited or targeted.[6]

Measuring the Success of Smart Sanctions

Qualitative and quantitative analyses of smart sanctions policies applied during the 1990s suggest that targeted sanction have yielded only limited success.[7] Cortright and Lopez determined that with regard to the application of targeted sanctions by the United Nations in the period 1990-2001, "only two of the ten… cases of more limited sanctions… were partially successful." Meanwhile, comprehensive sanctions appear to have a better track record of effectiveness, with three of four comprehensive sanctions policies yielding political effects.[8][8] However, despite the

---

3. Cortright, David and George Lopez, "Introduction: Assessing Smart Sanctions: Lessons from the 1990s," in Cortright and Lopez (eds.), *Smart Sanctions: Targeting Economic Statecraft*, Lanham, Maryland: Rowman & Littlefield Publishers, Inc., 2002, p. 2.

4. Cortright, David and George Lopez, *The Sanctions Decade: Assessing UN Strategies in the 1990s*, Boulder: Lynne Rienner Publishers, 2000, Chapter 2.

5. The case of UN sanctions against Iraq was a particularly compelling factor in the evolution of smart sanctions policies. The humanitarian consequences of the embargo, particularly the oil-for-food program, and the negative impact sanctions had on international commercial interests to engage Iraq, were two negative side-effects that were attempted to be corrected as Iraq sanctions were revised as the decade moved on.

6. Cortright and Lopez, *Smart Sanctions*, p. 1.

7. Determining the effectiveness of sanctions programs is subject to methodological and other analytic challenges. The fact that there are a relatively small number of cases to analyze, combined with problems of determining which variables may or may not be contributing to particular outcomes, challenge the integrity of any assessment of the effectiveness of sanctions policies—whether comprehensive or targeted. These are fairly standard problems in any academic exercise to assess outcomes in international affairs and should not preclude determining a positive role for smart sanctions.

8. Cortright and Lopez, *Smart Sanctions*, pp. 7-8.

appearance that targeted sanctions are only minimally successful, and perhaps less successful than comprehensive sanctions, smart sanctions hold promise as a tool of international diplomacy and measures can be taken to improve their effectiveness.

Cortright and Lopez have adopted three "pragmatic, modest criteria" for evaluating the effectiveness of sanctions, which are also instructive in formulating specific goals that smart sanctions are determined to achieve:

- Did sanctions help to convince the targeted regime to comply at least partially with the senders' demands?

- Did sanctions contribute to an enduring, successful bargaining process leading to a negotiated settlement?

- Did sanctions help to isolate or weaken the military power of an abusive regime?[9]

As can be inferred from these criteria, smart sanctions should not be intended as ends in and of themselves, nor should they be expected to be the only component of a successful strategy of achieving desired behavior out of the target country. As number two suggests, a smart sanctions policy should be a component of a greater negotiating or bargaining process if they are intended to produce results. Regarding Cuba, this may pose a particular stumbling block in the international community, as some will oppose negotiating with Castro, or at the very least be skeptical that any such negotiation would yield a desired outcome. However, in as much as smart sanctions limit their effect to the regime, they focus their pressure on particular individuals. If these individuals do not comply with demands or participate in productive negotiations, then they will bear the primary brunt of the targeted sanction.

An additional consideration raising the promise of success in a smart sanctions policy is that it may be easier to muster the international political will to apply them, given their intrinsic safeguards against un-

intended humanitarian harm or negative impact on third parties. In the case of Cuba, this is a key consideration, given historic international opposition to the U.S. approach of comprehensive sanctions against the island. Narrowing the target of the sanctions and limiting the potential for unwanted effects may increase the international will to apply a sanctions program. That smart sanctions may be easier to apply does not necessarily mean that they will succeed—this must be addressed in the nature of the smart sanctions policy itself; but the greater ease of acquiring international consensus behind a multilateral measure has a positive value that should not be overlooked.

Other factors to consider in measuring the success of smart sanctions policies are the symbolic and deterrent value. Simply employing measures that target specific entities sends a signal of condemnation, which may erode the authority of perpetrators of unacceptable behavior and draw international and domestic attention to their transgressions that led to such condemnation. In the case of Cuba, a multilateral program of condemning Castro could have significant symbolic value in undermining his authority and encouraging greater outspokenness among those holding divergent views on the island. A deterrent value may emerge from usage of smart sanctions as well, wherein international actors may be hesitant to undertake certain reprehensible acts if there is credible reason to believe that they may be subject to targeted sanctions.

CRITERIA FOR APPLYING A POLICY OF SMART SANCTIONS

The apparent limited track record of success for targeted sanctions does not mean that they do not work. Indeed, the experience of applying smart sanctions throughout the 1990s is instructive on how to improve their effectiveness. The following guidelines, which should be applied in a smart sanctions policy toward Cuba, will improve the likelihood that such a policy will achieve its intended result.

---

9. Cortright and Lopez, *Smart Sanctions*, pp. 6-7.

Smart Sanctions Must Have Specific Policy Goals

Targeted sanctions will be "only as effective as the overall policy they are designed to serve."[10] The application of a smart sanctions policy must identify specific behaviors that have led to the imposition of sanctions, which will serve as well to inform the preconditions that must be met in order for the targeted sanctions to be lifted.

The character of behavior targeted by the sanctions policy may also impact the probability of whether the sanctions will serve to promote reform of behavior in the targeted individuals or entities, or will simply serve to punish them. Ideally, sanctions will encourage reform and the prospect of sanctions being lifted will serve as an inducement to comply with demands. However, one can imagine demands that, if met, would so undermine the power of those targeted that they would never be met, and the punishment of targeted sanctions would be opted for in favor of compliance. This has particular bearing in the case of Castro's Cuba. Tying targeted sanctions to a demand for the release of political prisoners or greater civil liberties or economic freedoms for the Cuban people would be much less significant for regime longevity than tying sanctions to free and fair elections or a government in which the Castro brothers play no role. The former would lend targeted sanctions a greater role in a bargaining or negotiation process, whereas the latter would effectively undermine the prospect of bargaining or negotiating at all.

However, simply because a demand might be unlikely to be met does not mean that it should not be a goal of smart sanctions. First, by denying individuals or entities access to resources or activities, their capacity to undertake objectionable behavior can be diminished, which is a positive outcome in itself. For example, UN the embargoes on the sale of diamonds from Angola (1998), Sierra Leone (2000) and Liberia (2001) were intended to deny warring factions cash resources that enabled them to fund hostilities.

Secondly, targeted sanctions that hold little prospect to contribute to a bargaining process may encourage reform by symbolically or literally weakening the perpetrators of objectionable behavior, and thus encourage domestic opposition to engage in activities to promote reform from within the targeted country. For example, a ban on international travel by Cuban officials would publicly undermine Castro's projection of invulnerability on the island, and may encourage dissenters within and outside of the government to press for reforms similar to those demanded as part of the smart sanctions policy. This raises the issue that smart sanctions should not be the only component of overall policy toward a target country, but part of a broader strategy that could include, in the example of Cuba, greater outreach and coordination with dissidents and civil society actors. This is elaborated below.

Targeting

A smart sanctions policy must weigh the impact on the target, versus humanitarian impact or impact on non-targeted persons or entities. Such an approach will first identify decision-making elites most responsible for objectionable behavior and then identify activities, assets or resources most valuable to these individuals that should be denied under targeted sanctions.[11]

Cortright and Lopez list three possible categories for identifying the targets of sanctions: specific individuals engaged in objectionable behavior; a "functional definition of those to be sanctioned," which would be anyone serving in a particular capacity in a regime which would enable them to engage in or facilitate objectionable behavior; or "by casting a broad net over the economy of a society and then rolling back coercive pressures to signal support and encouragement for reformers and to protect innocent or vul-

---

10. Cortright and Lopez, *Smart Sanctions*, p. 15.

11. Cortright and Lopez, *Smart Sanctions*, p. 16.

nerable populations… [selectively] lifting pressures on key social groups and constituencies."[12]

Combine Sanctions with Incentives

Targeted sanctions do not need to be thought of only as a policy of punishment. When combined with offers of other cooperation or benefits upon meeting of conditions demanded by the smart sanctions policy—such as, for example, increased aid or trade—targeted sanctions can be part of a broader package of carrots and sticks meant to bring individuals or entities into compliance with acceptable behavior. Sometimes the promise of having the sanctions lifted may in itself be an incentive in itself. In the case of Cuba, for example, compliance with demands of a targeted sanctions program could be combined with the promise of efforts at greater integration into regional trading organizations (e.g. FTAA or Cotonou), or the promise of other efforts to address issues of concern.

Smart Sanctions Not the Only Policy Tool Employed

The historic track record of sanctions policies suggests that on their own, they are less likely to produce intended results than when combined with other policy tools. Targeted sanctions may be more effective when combined with incentives, as outlined above, or as part of a broader strategy of bargaining and negotiation, or in combination with tools of limited engagement, such as, for example, increased humanitarian assistance, expanded commercial relations in areas of non-targeted economic activities.

Compliance

The success of sanctions policies—whether smart or targeted—is determined by how effectively they are enforced. A policy of multilateral targeted sanctions, in order to achieve its intended political effect, would need to be realistically enforceable and vigorously enforced. Cortright and Lopez, in their quantitative analysis of the effectiveness of targeted and comprehensive sanctions, conclude that: "The most important ingredient of success is not whether sanctions are

comprehensive or targeted but whether they are seriously enforced."[13]

A CATALOGUE OF SMART SANCTIONS: OPTIONS FOR ADDRESSING CASTRO'S CUBA

A smart sanctions strategy toward Cuba would bring with it several benefits: (1) symbolic; (2) deterrent; and (3) focus international attention on Castro. Where applied effectively, taking into account the pros and cons of the preceding discussion of smart sanctions, a strategy of smart sanctions could yield specific intended results, and provide a viable policy alternative in the face of few good options.

As stated previously, a key component of any sanctions program is a clear policy behind it. That is, what are the goals hoped to be achieved, what are the demands being made, as a condition for lifting targeted sanctions?

What might be the policy goals of a multilateral targeted sanctions policy toward Cuba? In selecting goals of a multilateral smart sanctions policy, controversial items, such as settlement of U.S. property claims or action based on U.S. allegations of Cuban development of bioweapons, would be more divisive and less prone to result in agreement than matters o greater consensus such as Cuban political prisoners or lack of adherence to internationally accepted standards of civil liberties. A non-exhaustive list of considerations that could be candidates for multilateral agreement might include:

- Release of the political prisoners incarcerated in the Spring of 2003;
- Release of all political prisoners;
- Allow UN Special Rapporteur on Human Rights;
- Permit internationally-monitored elections;
- Greater commitment to economic reforms begun in the 1990s;
- Demonstrated effort to respond to the June 2002 EU letter on foreign investment in Cuba;

---

12. Cortright and Lopez, *Smart Sanctions*, pp. 17-18.

13. Cortright and Lopez, *Smart Sanctions*, p. 9.

- Commitment to settlement of all outstanding property claims;
- Adherence to some or all of the five proposals of the Varela Project: (1) the right to freedom of speech; (2) the right to free enterprise; (3) amnesty for all political prisoners; (4) the right of Cubans to create enterprises; and (5) a new electoral law.[14]

Though not necessarily comprehensive, the following "catalogue" of smart sanctions options provides a useful starting point of proposals for multilateral targeted sanctions that could be employed against the Castro government. These options for multilateral smart sanctions include:

- International travel ban on the Cuban leadership: Castro and a handful of the Cuban leadership would be prohibited from international travel. This also serves to identify the real target of the multilateral sanctions.
- Suspend commercial credits and international loans to Cuba: This move may be largely symbolic, given Cuba's poor credit rating and the fact that many may not be interested in lending to Cuba, and therefore perhaps easier to gain consensus around.
- Diplomatic measures/Recall of Ambassadors: Adherent countries would downgrade diplomatic relations.
- Total ban on commercial air travel: Making coming and going from Cuba very difficult would yield immediate reduction of tourism. Charter flights might remain in order that families could continue to visit. Similar measure applied with success against Libya. Downsides are that the Cuban population gets hit the hardest in economic terms, and key allied states, Canada and Spain, would feel strong direct economic impact as well. An exception for "humanitarian" flights could be included, which would allow family visits.
- Targeted financial assets freeze: Freeze assets held abroad by the Cuban regime, perhaps seeking Swiss and other aid in tracking foreign accounts of the Cuban leadership.
- Commodity embargo: Adherent countries would agree to ban imports of selected Cuban commodities such as sugar, nickel, tobacco—a ban on Cuban cigars would be easy to implement. A downside is that key allied countries have commercial stakes in such trade and the U.S. does not.

Note that none of these measures preclude the U.S. from unilaterally lifting its travel ban or export restrictions; in fact, it might be more palatable for these multilateral steps to be taken, from the point of view of U.S. supporters of the embargo, as an international sanctions regime would be in place to address unacceptable behaviors by the Castro government.

COMPARATIVE CASE STUDIES

A comparative analysis was not completed in time for presentation of this report. However, case studies of the application of targeted sanctions that could be instructive for a multilateral smart sanctions policy toward Cuba would include the following: EU sanctions against Zimbabwe (2001-present), joint EU-U.S. sanctions against former Yugoslavia (1998-2000); UN targeted travel sanctions against Libya.

CONCLUSION

A smart sanctions approach is a promising policy option in answer to the question, what to do about Castro's Cuba? But mustering domestic and international political will for adopting a multilateral smart sanctions program poses unique challenges, left unexplored by this report. The domestic battle over U.S. policy toward Cuba in the United States is vexing territory for anyone wishing to propose new policy approaches or to alter the status quo. Internationally, even if domestic will in the United States could be achieved, a smart sanctions policy would face the predictable challenges of any U.S. proposals on Cuba, wherein foreign leaders are motivated both by their own domestic political constituencies (among whom it remains harder to paint Castro as a problem), historic animosity toward U.S. policy toward

---

14. Source: http://www.puenteinfocubamiami.org/varela_project_003.htm.

Cuba (the recent events at the OAS and UN human rights committees are evidence suggesting that this phenomenon lingers), as well as competing trade and security interests that each country may have vis-à-vis Cuba.

However, a smart sanctions approach would sidestep many of the traditional hurdles both domestically and internationally. By limiting negative humanitarian and unintended economic impacts on both non-targeted Cubans and international actors, smart sanctions would cut a middle ground that minimizes commercial and political objections.

Finally, a smart sanctions approach toward Cuba would build upon the unique and perhaps unprecedented climate of international condemnation that has followed Havana Spring. This is an opportunity that should not be squandered. Given that our current options are few, smart sanctions could be a winning prospect, well worth committing the energy, strategy and political capital necessary for success.

THE LEGACIES OF SOCIALISM:
SOME ISSUES FOR CUBA'S TRANSITION

Jorge F. Pérez-López[1]

For the last 40-odd years, Cuba's ruling government has actively sought to eliminate the institutions that prevailed in Republican Cuba and to replace them with institutions that support a socialist, centrally-directed economy. The Cuban socialist regime undermined the institutions it inherited: eliminated private property, disassembled the legal framework that enabled private enterprise and decentralized economic decision making to operate, disabled the banking and credit system that supported economic activity, shackled the free press, and repressed civil society. That it has not fully succeeded in obliterating all of the Republican institutions is a tribute to the latter's resilience and to the fact that institutional change is a process that takes time. Nevertheless, it is fair to say that sufficient change has occurred since 1959 that the architects of Cuba's transition will be faced with a legacy of socialist institutions that will complicate creating the framework for a modern economic system in which enterprises and individuals can freely operate.

Notwithstanding the governments's efforts to make socialism a permanent feature of the Cuban nation,[2] it is clear that significant changes will occur when Castro departs from the scene or even before then. When change toward a free market and multi-party democracy does occur, certain legacies of socialism

will need to be overcome. Experiences of other former socialist countries have shown that it is indeed possible for successful transitions to occur, but for the most part transitions have turned out to be far more difficult, and to take longer, than reformers initially envisioned. Indeed, at the beginning of the 1990s, some optimistic reformers thought that the very act of removal of the ruling socialist party and its leadership and the dismantling of formal socialist institutions—primarily state ownership over the means of production and central planning—would be sufficient to start a process that would quickly result in free markets and multi-party democracies. This has not turned out to be the case.

During the initial stages of the transition, the focus of Cuban policymakers is likely to be on macroeconomic stabilization and microeconomic restructuring. Once these processes are advanced, the construction of institutions that support the market can commence, among them a market-oriented legal system, a viable commercial banking sector and the appropriate regulatory infrastructure; labor market regulations; and creation or modification of institutions related to public unemployment and retirement systems. The record of a decade of reforms in the former socialist countries of Eastern and Central Europe indicates that the leading countries in terms of growth

---

1. This paper expresses only the personal views of the author. It is a revised version of a paper prepared for the Rand Corporation, July 2002.

2. The reference is to the campaign launched by Fidel Castro in June 2002 to reform the Cuban Constitution to declare the "irrevocable" nature of its socialist political and social system.

Table 1.   State and Non-State Employment (in thousands)

	1981		1995		1998		1999		2000		2001	
	Level	%	Level	%	Level	%	Level	%	Level	%	Level	%
Total Employment	2867.6	100.0	3591.0	100.0	3753.6	100.0	3821.3	100.0	3843.0	100.0	3968.9	100.0
State Sector	2632.8	91.8	2902.8	80.8	2985.7	79.5	2979.0	78.0	2978.2	77.5	3039.0	76.6
Of which Sociedades anónimas	—	—	71.6	2.0	130.9	3.5	140.2	3.7	160.3	4.2	168.3	4.2
Non-State Sector	234.8	8.2	688.2	19.2	767.9	20.5	842.3	22.0	864.8	22.5	929.9	23.4
Joint Ventures	—	—	13.8	0.4	21.0	0.6	26.0	0.7	26.8	0.7	26.6	0.7
Cooperatives	30.7	1.1	348.6	9.7	328.8	8.8	324.9	8.5	323.4	8.4	318.5	8.0
Private Domestic	204.1	7.1	325.8	9.1	418.1	11.1	491.4	12.9	514.6	13.4	584.8	14.7
Of which Self- Employed	46.5	1.6	138.1	3.8	112.9	3.0	156.6	4.1	153.3	4.0	152.3	3.8

Source: ONE (2002, p. 118).

in gross domestic product (GDP) have been those that pursued a relatively complete set of reforms, including maintaining relatively clear property rights, a functioning legal framework and corporate governance rules (Svejnar 2002, p. 10).

This paper deals with some of the legacies of socialism that will complicate Cuba's transition. The set of issues examined is not exhaustive. Moreover, they are not discussed in this paper in order of priority or importance. They are: (1) a highly educated and low productivity labor force; (2) a small and deformed private sector; (3) high vulnerability to corruption; (4) unaffordable social services and pensions; and (5) lack of transparency. These challenges are by no means insurmountable, but presage a difficult transition for the Cuban nation.

HIGHLY EDUCATED, LOW PRODUCTIVITY LABOR FORCE

Despite the structural changes in the 1990s that promoted employment outside of the state sector (e.g., the liberalization of self-employment and the break-up of state farms and the creation of cooperatives), the state continues to be by far the largest employer in the nation. In 2001, the state employed 76.6 percent of all workers, a sizable drop from over 90 percent in the early 1980s, but still an overwhelming share of the nation's workforce (Table 1).

Human capital theory posits that education enhances worker productivity and thus leads to higher wages. In socialist Cuba, however, educational achievement bears little correlation with labor productivity or with wages. One of the many paradoxes of today's Cuba is a nation with a very highly educated work force with

abysmally low worker productivity. In fact, Cuba may have one of the most highly educated tourism sector workforces in the world—trained physicians, lawyers and technicians leave jobs in the profession for which they were trained and take instead low-skill jobs as taxi drivers or tour guides because these occupations carry the possibility of earning tips or payments in dollars or other freely convertible currencies.

Cuba's pursuit of full employment has increased the government's payroll and kept open unemployment very low; meanwhile, underemployment has been rampant. Mesa-Lago (2000, pp. 192-193) has noted that the sharp reduction in open unemployment in the early 1960s, early in the Castro regime, was achieved by transforming most of the open unemployment into underemployment, a policy decision that had the effect of alleviating the short-term unemployment problem but spreading the economic costs to the entire population and negatively affecting long-term labor productivity and economic growth. Mesa-Lago states (2000, p. 193): "In 1963 employees of state farms worked an average of 4.5 to 5 hours per day but were paid for 8. Industrial mergers and shut downs should have generated unemployment, but unneeded workers remained on the enterprise payrolls. The tertiary sector became hypertrophied with the expansion of the bureaucracy, social services, the armed forces, and internal security."

Underemployment became an even more serious problem in the 1990s under the explicit government policy of preserving state sector jobs despite extensive plant closings and work interruptions brought about by the economic crisis and the associated shortages of raw materials and spare parts. According to CEPAL (1997, p. 187), Cuba's open unemployment rate hovered in the 6-7 percent rate in 1990-96, while "equivalent unemployment"[3]—an estimate of underemployment—climbed as high as 35.2 percent in 1993. Combining open unemployment and underemployment, over 40 percent of the labor force was not fully productively employed in 1993. In 1996, the most recent year for which the open unemployment rate (6.8 percent) and CEPAL's estimated equivalent unemployment (27.3 percent)[4] are available, over one-third of workers (34.1 percent) were not fully productively employed.

There are no systematic and reliable time series on labor productivity in socialist Cuba. This results in part from problems with the methodology used by Cuba to calculate its national income and product during the first three decades of socialist rule.[5] Fragmentary information suggests that despite national campaigns and exhortations by the official workers organization, the government-controlled *Central de Trabajadores de Cuba* (Cuban Workers Central, CTC), labor productivity has been very low.

Based on fragmentary information, Mesa-Lago (2000, p. 260) concludes that average labor productivity growth rate during the period 1971-85— arguably the period of strongest economic growth by socialist Cuba—was low and well below planned targets; in fact, Mesa-Lago argues that if the exceptionally high economic growth rate of 1981 is excluded,[6]

average labor productivity growth for the entire period 1971-85 was actually negative. Low productivity growth during this period is consistent with other information on underutilization of labor across several sectors of the economy (Mesa-Lago 2000, p. 260). For the second half of the 1980s, average labor productivity declined at an annual average rate of 2.6 percent, compared to a planned annual increase of 3.5 percent per annum (Mesa-Lago 2000, p. 286). There are no official statistics on labor productivity in the 1990s but the CEPAL estimates mentioned above suggest that it declined severely in this period.

Although there are many reasons for Cuba's low and declining labor productivity—among them the abominable state of the capital stock and the lack of steady supplies of raw materials—it is clear that absenteeism and labor indiscipline are also important factors. The full employment policy that guarantees a job regardless of work effort, the meager wages that workers receive, and the generous health and education services that are available to the population at large, breed limited on-the-job effort. The popular saying attributed to Soviet workers—"We pretend to work and they pretend to pay us"—is applicable to Cuban workers as well.

Table 2 reproduces official data on average monthly salaries of workers in state enterprises and joint ventures during the period 1995-2001. The average monthly salary rose from 202 pesos to 245 pesos, or by 21.3 percent, over this period. These statistics re-

---

3. CEPAL (1997, p. 165) estimates "equivalent unemployment" for a given year with reference to 1989 as the product of the underutilization of the labor force (i.e., the gap between average productivity in a given year compared to 1989) times the labor for the given year.

4. Although CEPAL updated its study of the Cuban economy through the end of the 1990s (CEPAL 2000), it did not update the "equivalent unemployment" estimates, which end with 1996.

5. At least through 1990-91, socialist Cuba based its national income and product accounts on the Material Product System (MPS), the system used by the Soviet Union and other socialist countries. Nearly all other countries (developed and developing) used the System of National Accounts (SNA). There are numerous differences in the two systems, but perhaps the most significant is that the MPS excludes the contribution of "nonmaterial services" (e.g., social services, national defense, education, government administration) but includes the value of intermediate outputs (i.e., it is affected by double counting of some outputs). For a fuller discussion of these methodological differences, see Mesa-Lago and Pérez-López (1985). Around 1990-91, Cuba seems to have abandoned the MPS and adopted the SNA.

6. Mesa-Lago suspects that the exceptionally high growth rate for 1981—a growth of 16 percent in the global social product— overstates actual performance in that year and may have been the result of a change in the price base for the series and other methodological changes. See Mesa-Lago (2000, p. 251).

Table 2.   Average Monthly Salary of Employees in State Enterprises and Joint Ventures (pesos)

	1995	1996	1997	1998	1999	2000	2001
Total	194	202	206	207	222	234	245
Agriculture, hunting, forestry and fishing	184	207	205	203	212	218	233
Mining	235	241	246	251	254	264	270
Manufacturing	211	211	212	214	225	234	245
Electricity, gas and water services	207	211	221	219	230	244	268
Construction	212	229	246	252	262	284	301
Commerce, restaurants and hotels	162	164	172	175	180	182	190
Transportation, warehousing and communications	197	197	217	213	212	227	242
Banking, insurance, real estate and business services	206	213	223	222	234	239	323
Community, social and personal services	190	191	203	203	233	249	259

Source: ONE (2002, p. 121).

fer to salaries in current pesos, however, and therefore they do not reflect purchasing power since they are not adjusted for inflation. Cuba does not publish statistics on inflation, but based on official household consumption statistics a rough estimate can be made that inflation during 1996-2001 was 19.9 percent, so that the purchasing power of the salaries earned by Cuban workers in 2001 was actually virtually unchanged from 1996 (21.3 percent rise in money wages compared to 19.9 percent inflation).[7] Add to this the fact that many of the basic household consumer products are not available in peso-denominated stores and must be purchased in dollar-denominated outlets, at prices that approximate those in world markets. Considering that the peso to dollar exchange rate recently has hovered around 25 pesos for one U.S. dollar, in 2001 the 245 pesos per month average salary of a Cuban worker was equivalent to under 10 U.S. dollars per month.

The severe shortage of consumer goods that the Cuban population has endured during the special period and the possibility of being able to obtain such goods from dollar stores means that time away from a job that pays in pesos to engage in wheeling and dealing to earn dollars is preferable as a family survival strategy than going to work in a job that pays in pesos or working overtime for pesos. This explains in part the lack of on-the-job effort and the poor work habits of the workforce, particularly in state-owned enterprises.

During the transition, workers will expect that the purchasing power of their salaries will rise and they would at last be able to enjoy levels of consumption similar to those enjoyed by workers in other free market countries. Educated workers will have high expectations of material reward. Particularly those workers who have endured the socialist system longer will show little patience with a system that does not reward them immediately. The lessons from Central and Eastern Europe in this regard are not encouraging for a Cuban transition: "Decades of stifling bureaucracy, incessant propaganda, and an extreme nanny state destroyed people's will to work. Entitlements became a way of life. No one expected to get fired, and the government was viewed as the solution to all problems. As a result, most people over the age of 40 were lost, and it will be left to the youth to forge a future" (Aslund and Hewko 2002).

SMALL AND DEFORMED PRIVATE SECTOR

Although the state owns most of the factors of production, it has not been able to eradicate entrepreneurship in Cuba. The booming black market of the 1990s, and the enthusiasm with which the population initially accepted the liberalization of self-employment in 1993, suggest that the Cuban popula-

---

7. According to official statistics (ONE 2002, p. 89), between 1996 and 2001 household consumption at current prices rose by 35.8 percent while consumption at constant prices did the same by 15.9 percent. It follows, then, that prices of articles consumed by households rose by 19.9 percent during this period.

tion has unbounded ingenuity and is capable of making ends meet under very unfavorable economic conditions.

What 40-odd years of socialism has done, however, is to wipe out the market-oriented skills of the cadre of managers, accountants, auditors, etc., that were responsible for running the Cuban economy in the 1950s. Several generations of Cubans who have grown up under socialism have meager market-oriented skills and their exposure to private sector activities has been through deformed practices such as black markets and underground (illegal) economic activities. Murrell and Wang (1993, pp. 390-1) identified this problem in the context of the reforming Eastern European economies:

> The ability to function effectively within a particular set of market institutions comes about as a result of market activity rather than being endowed or learned quickly through formal education. Therefore the lack of market institutions under communism leads to a dearth of both market-oriented human skills and organizations that can function in the market environment. Moreover, the market experiences of most individuals have been with largely unsophisticated market institutions, often with those of the black market. The market skills that do exist are ones geared to markets with simple institutional prerequisites rather than those fit for the types of markets in which large organizations would prosper.

Cuba's private sector is very small. According to official statistics (Table 1), total private domestic employment in 2001 amounted to 584,800 workers, or 14.7 percent of total employment. Reportedly, the majority of these private sector workers are small agricultural operators. Self-employed workers accounted for about 26 percent of private sector employment in 2001. It is interesting to note that when self-employment was liberalized in the summer of 1993, there was a strong response in the form of a rush of workers to register as self-employed. By December 1993, only a few months after the new self-employment regime had been in place, 70,000 persons had gone through the necessary steps to be registered as self-employed workers; by the end of 1995, approximately 208,000 workers had registered (Jatar-Hausmann 1999, p. 97). Since then, the number of regis-

tered self-employed workers has fallen off as the government increased fees and taxes, issued more restrictive regulations, and stepped up oversight, reducing the space that these private workers needed to operate. According to Table 1, the number of self-employed workers in 2001 was about 152,300.

It is also a precarious and deformed private sector. Because there are no factor markets for the self-employed and other private sector workers to obtain the raw materials that they need to ply their trade, they must resort to the black market or some other illegal source of goods and services. That is, private sector workers almost by necessity must operate outside of the law, finding ways to survive outside of the legal framework. Cuban self-employed workers generally obtain their raw materials and equipment from the black market, which in turn is fed by theft (euphemistically called *desvíos*) from the state sector. As an analyst that has interviewed self-employed workers describes it (Jatar-Hausmann 1999, pp. 108-9):

> Cuba has no wholesale distributors. The Cuban government has not opened supply markets. Intermediaries are not only illegal, but unwanted. ... When Jorge [a self-employed shoe maker] is asked about where he has been buying the little equipment he uses to work, he answers coyly, "little by little I have been collecting it," but his smile seems to say "Why are you asking such a dumb question?" And it is, in fact, a silly question. Everybody knows that there are no free markets for any of the instruments used by Jorge; nor are there supplies for most of the products the artisans make. They either take them from their workplaces (in other words, steal them) or they buy them in the black market. Where do the products in the black market come from? From other workers who do the same thing. Everyone has to steal in Cuba for survival.

The existence of a private sector in some former socialist countries has been a positive factor in their transitions. For example, Poland and Hungary, two socialist countries that for historical reasons had well established private sectors prior to the transition (recall that Poland's agricultural sector remained largely outside of state control and reforms in Hungary that began in the 1960s promoted limited consumerism and market forces earned that country's system the label of "Goulash Socialism") saw the existing private sector as the basis for the expansion and multiplication of private enterprises once the shackles of the socialist system were removed.

The experiences of Poland and Hungary suggest that where there is an existing private sector, it is relatively easy to create conditions that allow entrepreneurs who have created small businesses to expand their activities and multiply, creating new businesses and generating employment opportunities. Barely two years after the transition in Poland, retail trade was almost completely in private hands, as was 55 percent of the construction industry and 24 percent of transportation services. By the end of 1992, 56 percent of the labor force worked in the private sector, generating almost half of the country's gross national product (Nagorski 1993, p. 175). In Hungary, there was an explosion in the creation of small businesses immediately after the transition. The number of enterprises grew six-fold between 1989 and March 1992, from 10,811 units to 58,951 units. Nearly all of the new enterprises created were small companies. While in 1989, 53 percent of Hungarian enterprises employed more than 50 workers, by 1990 that share had fallen to 36 percent, with about one half of the latter employing fewer than 20 workers. The major sources of the emerging class of new private entrepreneurs in Hungary were reportedly the state sector (it was customary in Hungary for state workers to hold legal secondary jobs), small businesses, industrial or agricultural cooperatives, and operators of agricultural household plots (Kiss 1992, pp. 1027-1028).

VULNERABILITY TO CORRUPTION

Corruption, the misuse of public property for private gain, is as old as government itself. The potential for corruption exits whenever a public official has discretionary power over distribution to the private sector of a benefit or a cost (Rose-Ackerman 1997, p. 31). Private individuals or firms are willing to pay bribes to obtain these benefits or avoid costs. All other things being equal, the size and structure of the state determine the demand for corrupt services, that is, the supply of bribes. Klitgaard (1988, p. 75) has summarized the "basic ingredients of corruption" as follows:

Corruption = Monopoly + Discretion – Accountability

That is, the level of corruption depends on the degree of monopoly exercised by the state over the supply of a given good or service, of discretion enjoyed by a government agency in making resource allocation decisions, and of accountability of the government (or its agents) to others.

Socialist systems present a complex interplay of governmental and economic institutions, ideologies and traditional political cultures that make them particularly prone to corruption (Heidenheimer et al 1989, pp. 443-444):

- The overwhelming size of the public sector means that the state employs an inordinately large number of workers. Therefore the potential for corruption is very large.

- Central planning of thousands or even millions of production enterprises, and an even larger number of retail outlets and individual products and services requires a huge bureaucratic apparatus. At every turn, production and distribution decisions are regulated by inflexible plans and allocation procedures; enterprise managers often have little choice but to use illicit influence to get around planning strictures to obtain labor or raw materials.

- The ruling party itself is often the locus of corruption, as the top leadership is normally immune to exposés and reprisals from below, and can engage in self-serving behavior. The ruling class or political elite has been referred to as the "new class" (Djilas 1957) or the *nomenklatura* (e.g., Voslensky 1984). It was typically able to draw on the resources of the state and to treat socialist property as its own: salary supplements, the best housing; special food allocations; access to restaurants, stores and other facilities; vacation country villas or *dachas*. It also participated heavily in the system of taking bribes in return for doing favors such as appointing persons to prestigious posts, protection, promoting people up the bureaucratic ladder, and using influence to stop the government from taking actions.

While there is little official information on the breadth and depth of corruption in Cuba, it stands to reason that it would follow closely patterns in other socialist, centrally-planned economies whose ideology and political systems Cuba emulated. Illegal economic activities associated with corruption in the island for which there is concrete evidence are black market operations, misuse of office, and special perquisites extracted by the Cuban *nomenklatura*. To be sure, other forms of corrupt behavior—e.g., bribes to influence government decisions such as installing a telephone or exchanging homes (*permutas*)—are probably also rampant, but they are more difficult to document:

- The Cuban state's overwhelming control over the economy translates into black markets in nearly all areas of economic activity. Thus, not only are there black markets for food and consumer goods—goods ostensibly covered by the rationing system—but also for construction materials for home repairs and spare parts for appliances and motor vehicles. Misappropriation of government resources (via theft, diversion of goods, short-changing of customers) has traditionally been one of the main sources of goods entering black markets.

- The extremely high concentration of resources in the state, and the centralized nature of decision making, place a great deal of power in the hands of government officials and hence create ample opportunities for corruption. In addition to corrupt behavior in return for bribes, corruption in socialist Cuba takes the form of using power to obtain access to other things, degenerating into a generalized "I'll scratch your back if you'll scratch mine" system that rewards those who are friendly with government officials and is referred to as *sociolismo*, a take-off on *socio* (buddy) and *socialismo*.

- As in the former Soviet Union and other socialist countries, Cuba has a system of special perqui-

sites for the *nomenklatura*, whose members are referred to in the island as *pinchos*, *pinchos grandes* or *mayimbes*. These perquisites include: total or partial exemption from the commodity rationing system; the ability to obtain imported foods and other consumer goods; good housing (including vacation homes); use of government vehicles; access to special hospitals and imported medications; admission to special schools for their children (the so-called *hijos de papá*); and the ability to travel abroad, to name a few.[8]

- A new and troubling form of corruption is what has been called in other socialist countries "spontaneous privatization." This refers to the appropriation of state property by members of the *nomenklatura* through the paper reorganization of state-owned enterprises into "private" corporations of which the *nomenklatura* members are owners or directors. This activity "is the very essence of corruption, being the outright theft of public assets by politicians and/or enterprise directors associated with the *nomenklatura*" (Kaufmann and Siegelbaum 1997, p. 439). By the end of 1992, reportedly 63 of these privatized entities, called *sociedades anónimas* or just S.A. were operating in Cuba, and many others have been created since then (see Table 3 for information on selected Cuban S.A.). The "owners" of these corporations have not purchased their assets from the state nor have they contributed intellectual property, invested any savings or incurred any risks. Instead they are individuals loyal to the Cuban government who have been given control over state assets illegally in a manner reminiscent of the systemic theft of private property in Nicaragua by the Sandinista regime in Nicaragua known as *la piñata*. The S.A. tend to operate in the more dynamic sectors of the economy that generate hard currency and are capable of attracting foreign investment: tourism, electronics and telecommunications, biotechnology, commercial real estate, financial services.

---

8. See Clark (1990 and 1999) for a thorough treatment of this subject, including through surveys of emigrés.

Table 3. Selected Cuban *Sociedades Anónimas* and Their Principal Economic Activities

Grupo Gaviota S.A.
- International tourism
- Hotels, villas, marinas, automobile rentals, hunting preserves and retail stores

Corporación Cubanacán S.A.
- International tourism
- Hotels, retail stores, a broad range of tourism services

Habaguanex S.A.
- International tourism, focused in the city of La Habana
- Hotels, hostels, restaurants, cafeterias, retail stores, open air markets, museums

Grupo Cimex S.A.
- Export-import and retail trade, financial services
- 550 retail stores throughout the island (using hard currency only)
- Warehousing facilities, cargo ships, domestic transportation equipment

Corporación Cubalse
- Holding company with 17 S.A. subsidiaries
- Among subsidiaries are Lares Inmobiliaria S.A. (real estate), Meridiano S.A. (operation of dollar stores) and Automotriz S.A. (car rentals)

- Other subsidiaries involved in data processing, legal services, land and water transportation, advertising, photo and video services, and employment services.

Grupo de la Electrónica
- Production and sale of consumer electronics products and computer equipment and provider of computer services
- Also involved in telecommunications, informatics and automatics
- Composed of several companies, including Copextel, S.A., which manufactures and sells computer and electronic equipment, and Centersoft, which provides computer software and consulting services.

Heber Biotec S.A.
- Biotechnology products
- Commercializes products manufactured by the Centro de Ingeniería Genética y Biotecnología

Real Inmobiliaria S.A.
- Real estate (commercial and residential)

Havana Asset Management Limited
- Investment management

Bravo S.A.
- Processed meat products (ham, sausages, etc.) for sale to customers with hard currency

Source: Alfonso (1999), "Cubalse Reorganized" (1999) and webpages of individual S.A.

As Naím (1995, p. 251) points out, a corollary to Klitgaard's stylized corruption equation is that the deepening of democratization should have corruption-curbing effects. Why, then, is there a perception that corruption has been rampant in countries transitioning from authoritarian, centrally-planned regimes to democratic, market economies?

One explanation for this phenomenon is that in the absence of strong institutions, democracy and free markets provide more—and more visible—opportunities for corruption than under authoritarian rule. Under the latter, corruption can be more in-

stitutionalized, controlled and predictable. Naím argues that a well organized dictatorship can provide "one-stop" shopping for corruption services, where the right amount of money given to the right official will take care of all needed interventions. Under this system, bribe takers under the control of an authority (either the authoritarian leader or a political party) collude and keep their actions out of the public's view. Under a democratic system, in contrast, the central government's control over the providers of bribery services is diluted and corrupt officials compete for bribes, resulting in a process that is more visible to the public than under authoritarianism.

Particularly during the early stages of the transition, as the "old" national institutions of authoritarianism are being torn down and decentralization, privatization and the opening of the economy to international participation are taking place, while new institutions promoting good governance have not yet taken hold, there are opportunities for corruption to explode. As Glynn et al. have put it (1997, p. 10):

> Corruption in these emerging markets is doubly pernicious. First, it compromises the efficacy and efficiency of economic activity, making the transition to free market democracy more difficult. Second, and equally important, corruption distorts public perceptions of how—and how well—a proper market economy works. Under such circumstances it becomes all too easy for economically beleaguered publics to confuse democratization with the corruption and criminalization of the economy—creating fertile soil for an authoritarian backlash and engendering potentially hostile international behavior by these states in turn.

It is probably fair to argue, however, that democratic regimes, over the long run, engender more powerful antibodies against corruption than authoritarian systems under which political liberties are stifled (Glynn et al 1997, p. 11).

UNAFFORDABLE SOCIAL SERVICES AND PENSIONS

Cuba has had a long history of providing social services and pensions to its citizenry. A public elementary school system was in place since the early days of the Republic as was also a system of public health services. Although there were serious differentials in availability of social services between rural and urban areas, Republican Cuba performed quite well in comparison with other countries in the region.[9] In 1957-58, Cuba's performance in providing education, sanitation, health care, and social security to its citizens was among the three highest in Latin America, but social service facilities were concentrated in La Habana and in urban areas, and availability and qual-

ity of services dropped off significantly in rural areas (Mesa-Lago 2000, p. 172).

Cuba introduced a pension scheme in the 1920s, one of the first countries to do so, and pensions expanded significantly in the following decades. Before the 1959 revolution, Cuba had one of the most developed pension systems among countries with a similar level of income. However, the pension system was fragmented in more than 50 autonomous programs that covered certain groups of workers in urban areas and were subject to their own regulations and financing. An estimated 55 to 63 percent of the population was covered by the pension systems although not the poorest segments of the population such as rural workers, the self-employed, domestic servants and the unemployed (Pérez 1998, pp. 520-521).

After the 1959 revolution, the Cuban government undertook a deliberate policy of expanding social services and reducing urban-rural differentials in the delivery of such services. Private schools, hospitals and other health facilities were nationalized and taken over by the state. In 1961, the Cuban government launched a national campaign to eradicate illiteracy and began a drive to build schools and educational facilities in rural areas. By 1962, the Cuban government had unified the different pension programs and in 1963 a new law broadened the coverage of the pension system to all of the salaried workforce and made the financing of the system the direct responsibility of the state.

In the 1970s and 1980s, the Cuban government devoted a large share of the nation's resources to creating an infrastructure to provide social services to the population and expanded the delivery of such services. These investments resulted in dramatic improvements in social indicators such as: increase in literary and in school enrollment; increase in life expectancy; decline in infant mortality; and increase in the availability of physicians, dentists and hospital beds. At the same time, the coverage of the pension system was expanded to agricultural cooperative members and retirement requirements eased (the retirement

---

9. See Smith and Llorens (1998) for international comparisons of socioeconomic indicators for pre-socialist Cuba.

age was lowered to 60 years of age for men and 55 years of age for women), contributing to a tremendous increase in the number of pensioners. The ratio of active workers per pensioner, which was 14.7 in 1958, dropped to 7.2 in 1970, 5.2 in 1979 and 4.2 in 1990 (Mesa-Lago 2000, p. 396).

As social services and pensions expanded, so did the cost to the state of providing them. Government expenditures on social services (education and health; social security, welfare and culture; and housing and community services) ranged from 33 to 36 percent of the national budget in the 1960s and 1970s. It climbed to 41 percent in 1982 and remained at above 40 percent for the 1980s, peaking at nearly 46 percent in 1988 (Mesa-Lago 2000, pp. 352-353). Arguably, Cuba could afford this very extensive safety net because of the huge financial assistance it received from the former Soviet Union.

The economic crisis of the 1990s exposed the frays in Cuba's social safety net after the loss of Soviet assistance (Mesa-Lago 2001, pp. 10-11):

- Morbidity rates for 6 contagious diseases (chicken pox, hepatitis, syphilis, gonorrhea, tuberculosis and typhoid) increased in 1994-99;

- Daily supply of calories fell by 6 percent, of protein almost 24 percent, and of fat almost 28 percent between 1970 and 1997;

- The real average pension declined by 48 percent in 1989-98; and

- The average pension in 2000 of 104 pesos per month was equivalent to 5 U.S. dollars.

The cost of social security (pensions, health care and social assistance) has been climbing as a result of several factors: nearly universal coverage, very low retirement ages, the maturity of the pension scheme, and the aging of the population.[10] Social security expenditures as a percent of GDP rose from 10 percent in 1989 to 13 percent 1999-2000 and is expected to continue to rise in the future. The state is covering the expanding deficit of the pension system out of current revenues (Mesa-Lago 2001, p. 10).

To complicate matters for the architects of a Cuban transition, when asked, Cubans opine that while they want to change their current system of government and have freedom, democracy, and free markets, they want to keep the achievements (*logros*) of the revolution in the social services area.

The Cuban government does not permit private research organizations to conduct surveys to study the attitudes and behavior of the population. As a second best alternative, in 1998-99, U.S. researchers interviewed 1,023 Cuban emigrés who had been in the United States less than three months and asked them a host of questions to learn their opinions on a range of political and social issues. For purposes of this paper, the most relevant findings of the survey are:

- 67 percent of respondents agreed with the proposition that the revolution had improved education and, of these, 93 percent saw free education as a desirable feature of a Cuba of the future;

- 53 percent of respondents had a favorable view of the health care offered to the population, while 90 percent opined that the greatest accomplishment was that health care was free; and

- 55 percent favored retaining some of the policies of the revolution after the transition to a democratic, free market Cuba. In fact, 90 percent of the respondents who had a favorable reaction to the educational system favored its continuation beyond the transition. On health services, while 98 percent of the respondents thought that a free market would lead to better quality health care, 71 percent felt that the free health care should be maintained.

How to reconcile the reality of an unaffordable social services system with the desire of the population to continue to receive the free social services they have grown accustomed to receiving? Developing a na-

---

10. It is estimated that by 2025, Cuba will have the oldest population of the region and there will be two persons of productive age for every person of retirement age (Mesa-Lago 2001, p. 10).

tional consensus on a reasonable, affordable level of social services targeted at those that need them the most and identifying ways for those who can afford to pay for their own in the marketplace will be a major challenge of the government of a Cuba in transition.

LACK OF TRANSPARENCY

Nobel Laureate Joseph Stiglitz, in the Oxford Amnesty Lecture he delivered in 1999, argued that "there is, in democratic societies, a basic right to know, to be informed about what the government is doing and why." He further argued that there should be a strong presumption in favor of transparency and openness in government. Secrecy gives those in government exclusive control over certain areas of knowledge, and thereby increases their power, making it more difficult for even a free press to check that power. In short, Stiglitz argued, a free press is necessary for a democratic society to work effectively; without access to information, a democratic society's ability to perform its central role is gutted (Stiglitz 1999).

Transparency, openness, the right to know, free speech and a free press provide checks on the power of the government and prevent it from abusing power. Secrecy, their antithesis, shelters bad government, misallocation of resources, illegal behavior and corruption. Amartya Sen, also a Nobel Laureate, has observed that famines do not occur in societies in which there is a free press—it is not the lack of food that gives rise to famines, but the lack of access to food by the poor in famine-stricken regions. A free press exposes these problems; once exposed, the failure to act is absolutely intolerable (Stiglitz 1999).

Socialist societies are notorious for their secrecy and for the lack of accountability of their leaders and governments. The population in socialist societies is subservient to the Communist Party and the government. Since there are no free elections, whatever legislative bodies might exist are merely instruments of the leadership. Government decisions are made behind closed doors. There is no public right to know. The press, and more broadly all forms of media, express the official views of the state in their reporting and editorial opinions. Civil society is very

weak: the main mass organizations are controlled by the state and independent civil society institutions are rare and those that exist have very little space to operate.

Socialist Cuba scores very high in secrecy and opaqueness. The primacy of the Cuban Communist Party is well established in Article 5 of the 1976 Constitution which states that "the Cuban Communist Party, *martiano* and marxist-leninist, organized vanguard of the Cuban nation, is the supreme leading force of society and of the state…" The Communist Party is unchallenged—and unchallengeable—in its decision making. It reaches decisions behind closed doors and announces them through the voice of government officials, often through Fidel Castro who is at once Chief of State and Head of Government (President of the Council of State and President of the Council of Ministers), leader of the only political party in the country (First Secretary of the Cuban Communist Party), and commander-in-chief of the Armed Forces. As Damián Fernández (1992, p. 53) has written, "the decision-making process of the Cuban state is one of the blackest of the black boxes, mysterious and impenetrable."

All Cuban mass media are owned and operated by the Cuban government, the Cuban Communist Party, or affiliated organizations. The Cuban government took over most newspaper and broadcast stations in 1959. In February 1961, only six daily newspapers were being published in La Habana compared to 16 in 1959. After 1963, *Granma*, the organ of the Central Committee of the Cuban Communist Party patterned after the Soviet Union's *Pravda*, became the only newspaper in the country. Other government-operated newspapers were created in the 1970s and 1980s to address special groups (workers, farmers, youth, military personnel) or geographic areas; most of these were shut down or their frequency of publication scaled back during the 1990s as a result of shortages of newsprint. The government also owns and operates all broadcast stations. According to the international organization Reporters Without Borders (2002), the Cuban media "is subtly and effectively repressed so as to maintain the state's monopoly over information." A U.S. journalist who visited the island in 2002 said about his Cuban counterparts: "These are not journalists. ... These are government public relations agents. ... Regardless of how they try to spin it, they work for the state-owned media—TV, radio and newspapers—and they spew the official line of Fidel Castro" (Curry 2002).

In the 1990s, independent journalists began to challenge the government's monopoly over information at significant personal risk. Although they were unable to disseminate their dispatches within the island—since all media outlets are controlled by the government—these independent journalists filed their reports via telephone through collaborators in foreign countries and from there made available to the public through the internet by the organization CubaNet (www.cubanet.org). The foreign press carried many of the stories filed by independent journalists from the island.[11]

In mid-March 2003, the Cuban government cracked down on nonviolent dissidents, independent journalists, human rights advocates, independent librarians and other dissidents, arresting dozens of people, searching their homes, and, in many cases, confiscating fax machines, computers, books, typewriters and personal papers. They were accused of working with U.S. diplomats to undermine the Cuban government and damage the country's national interests. In April, 75 the defendants were tried using "facilitated" procedures and sentenced to jail terms ranging from 6 to 28 years of imprisonment, with an average sentence of more than 19 years ("Crackdown" 2003). Clearly, the crackdown dealt a severe blow to independent journalism within the island.

Finally, the Cuban state does not permit—more accurately, it actively prevents—the creation and oper-

ation of independent organizations. Although the Associations Law (*Ley de Asociaciones*) purportedly guarantees the right of Cuban citizens to associate freely and form independent associations, in practice,

the law effectively bars the legalization of genuinely independent organization. The law requires organizations to "coordinate" and "collaborate" with a state counterpart entity. Fulfilling this condition necessitates the group's subjugation to the government organization, by allowing a representative of the state entity to attend and speak at any planned or unplanned meetings; requiring the group to notify the government entity in advance of any publications; coordinating with the government entity regarding participation in any national or international event; regularly reporting to the government entity on its activities; and providing prior notice of the date and hour of any meetings or any other activities (Human Rights Watch 1999).

The Cuban state uses the registration process to thwart the creation of independent organizations. Only those organizations that are authorized by the state can operate legally.

However, the state encourages citizen participation in officially-sanctioned mass organizations such as the Committees for the Defense of the Revolution (CDR), the Federation of Cuban Women (FMC), the Cuban Workers Central (CTC) and the Union of Communist Youth (UJC).[12] Participation in these organizations or their activities

should not be equated either with individual or group autonomy or with genuine mass spontaneity. Participation .... means discussing local affairs, doing volunteer work, receiving "guidance" from party officials, marching in the street against fellow citizens who choose to emigrate, attending mass rallies, and engag-

11. Among other press outlets in the United States, *El Nuevo Herald* often carries news reports filed by independent journalists residing in the island.

12. In fact, the Cuban Socialist Constitution of 1976 in its Article 7 stated that: "The Cuban socialist state recognizes, protects and supports social mass organizations, such as the Cuban Workers Central, which includes in its ranks the fundamental class of our society, the Committees for the Defense of the Revolution, the Federation of Cuban Women, the National Association of Small Farmers, the Federation of University Students, the Federation of Mid-Level Students, and the Union of Cuban Pioneers, as well as others that originated from the historical class struggle process of our people and that represent specific interests of our citizens and incorporate them in the tasks of building, consolidating and defending socialist society." The revisions to the Constitution in 1992 maintained the same article, but dropped the listing of the specific mass organizations.

ing in other revolutionary duties (del Aguila 1988, p. 181).

In contrast with the organizations sanctioned by the state, there are myriad truly independent civic organizations seeking recognition to be able to operate legally in the island. Common threads running through these organizations are that they are very small, command very few resources and operate illegally since they have not sought the required registration from the state or, if they have sought such registration, have not received it. Thus, members risk the possibility of being harassed, fined, arrested, or imprisoned at any time for breaking the law, and many were in the March 2003 crackdown on dissidents. The fact that these organizations are illegal also hinders their ability to receive resources from abroad.

CONCLUDING REMARKS

Over the last four decades, Cuba has made remarkable strides in adopting the key institutions and practices that characterized socialist societies. Cuba's diligence in becoming a socialist nation, eagerness in embracing socialist institutions, and rigidity in applying orthodox socialist policies and practices, do not augur well for an easy transition in the island. Transition planners would do well to recognize the many legacies of Cuban socialism so that they can counteract them effectively in the transition policies they design.

Two experts with extensive familiarity with transitions in Central and Eastern Europe have some advice for the architects of the Cuban transition that is worth heeding. Aslund and Hewko (2002) worry about the lack of understanding on the part of emigrés and potential foreign investors about the nature of Cuban society and the life experiences of those who stayed. They worry about the potential for painful misunderstandings and clashes. Based on their experience in Central and Eastern Europe, they write:

> Emigrés and foreign advisers arriving with a can-do swagger and the confidence that they "know it all" often failed to understand how society functioned. Under communism people may have forgotten how to work and never learned to use a credit card, but they were bright and had pride. The combination of local pride and emigré arrogance excluded all but a handful of emigrés from prominent government positions. Without genuine humility, returning emigrés are not likely to succeed. An awareness of these problems helps to harness them.

Let us hope that the architects of the Cuban transition consider explicitly the legacies of socialism as they design long-term strategies that lead to freedom, democracy and prosperity for the Cuban people.

BIBLIOGRAPHY

Alfonso, Pablo. 1999. "La piñata castrista." *El Nuevo Herald* (13 June), pp. 1A, 2A, 13A.

Aslund, Anders, and John Hewko. 2002. "Lessons for Cuba after communism." *The Christian Science Monitor* (24 June), p. 11.

Betancourt, Ernesto, and Guillermo Grenier. 1999. "Measuring Cuban Public Opinion: Economic, Social and Political Issues." Pp. 251-269 in *Cuba in Transition—Volume 9*. Washington: Association for the Study of the Cuban Economy.

Clark, Juan. 1990. *Cuba: Mito y Realidad*. Miami: Saeta Ediciones.

Clark, Juan. 1999. "Igualdad y privilegio en la revolución de Castro." Pp. 219-252 in Efrén Córdova, editor, *40 años de revolución: El legado de Castro*. Miami: Ediciones Universal.

Comisión Económica para América Latina y el Caribe. 1997. *La economía cubana: Reformas estructurales y desempeño en los noventa*. Mexico: Fondo de Cultura Económica.

Comisión Económica para América Latina y el Caribe. 2000. *La economía cubana: Reformas estructurales y desempeño en los noventa*. Mexico: Fondo de Cultura Económica.

"Crackdown Against Dissidents in Cuba." (2003). Human Rights News (April 16) at http://www.hrw.org/press/2003/04/hcirtestimony041603.htm#Anatomy%20of%20a%20Crackdown

"Cubalse Reorganized." 1999. *Economic Eye on Cuba* (26 April-2 May 1999).

Curry, George E. 2002. "Reporting on Cuba's 'Reporters.'" (June 14). http://www.blackpressusa.com/op-ed/Speaker.asp?NewsID=2371

del Aguila, Juan M. 1988. *Cuba: Dilemmas of a Revolution*. Revised Edition. Boulder: Westview.

Djilas, Milovan. 1957. *The New Class*. New York: Praeger Publishers.

Fernández, Damián. 1992. "Opening the Blackest of Black Boxes: Theory and Practice of Decision Making in Cuba's Foreign Policy." *Cuban Studies* 22, pp. 53-78.

Glynn, Patrick, Stephen J. Kobrin, and Moisés Naím. 1997. "The Globalization of Corruption." Pp. 7-30 in Kimberly Ann Elliott, editor, *Corruption and the Global Economy*. Washington: Institute for International Economics.

Heidenheimer, Arnold J., Michael Johnston and Victor J. Levine. 1989. *Political Corruption: A Handbook*. New Brunswick: Transaction Publishers.

Human Rights Watch. 1999. *Cuba's Repressive Machinery: Human Rights Forty Years After the Revolution*. http://www.hrw.org/reports/1999/cuba/.

International Monetary Fund (IMF). 1997. "IMF Adopts Guidelines Regarding Governance Issues." *IMF Survey* 26:15 (5 August) 233-238.

Jatar-Hausmann, Ana Julia. 1999. *The Cuban Way: Capitalism, Communism and Confrontation*. West Hartford, Connecticut: Kumarian Press.

Kaufmann, Daniel, and Paul Siegelbaum. 1997. "Privatization and Corruption in Transition Economies." *Journal of International Affairs* 50:2 (Winter), pp. 80-94.

Kiss, Yudit. 1992. "Privatization in Hungary: Two Years Later." *Soviet Studies* 44:6, pp. 1015-1038.

Klitgaard, Robert. 1988. *Controlling Corruption*. Berkeley: University of California Press.

Mesa-Lago, Carmelo. 1993. "The Social Safety Net in the Two Cuban Transitions." Pp. 601-670 in *Transition in Cuba: New Challenges for U.S. Policy*. Miami: Florida International University.

Mesa-Lago, Carmelo. 2000. *Market, Socialist and Mixed Economies: Comparative Policy and Performance—Chile, Cuba and Costa Rica*. Baltimore: The Johns Hopkins University Press.

Mesa-Lago, Carmelo. 2001. "The Cuban Economy in 1999-2001: Evaluation of Performance and Debate on the Future." Pp. 1-17 in *Cuba in Transition—Volume 11*. Washington: Association for the Study of the Cuban Economy.

Mesa-Lago, Carmelo, and Jorge Pérez-López. 1985. *A Study of Cuba's National Product System, Its Conversion to the System of National Accounts, and Estimation of GDP Per Capita and Growth Rates*. Washington: World Bank.

Murrell, Peter, and Yijiang Wang. 1993. "When Privatization Should be Delayed: The Effect of Communist Legacies on Organizational and Institutional Reform." *Journal of Comparative Economics* 71:2 (June), pp. 385-406.

Nagorski, Andrew. 1993. *The Birth of Freedom*. New York: Simon and Schuster.

Naím, Moisés. "The Corruption Eruption." *The Brown Journal of World Affairs* 2:2 (Summer), pp. 31-60.

Oficina Nacional de Estadísticas (ONE). 2002. *Anuario Estadístico de Cuba 2001*. La Habana.

Pérez, Lorenzo L. 1998. "The Pension System of Cuba: The Current Situation and Implications of International Pension Reform Experiencs for

Addressing Cuba's Problems." Pp. 520-534 in *Cuba in Transition—Volume 8*. Washington: Association for the Study of the Cuban Economy.

Pérez-López, Jorge F. 1995. *Cuba's Second Economy: From Behind the Scenes to Center Stage*. New Brunswick: Transaction Publishers.

Pérez-López, Jorge F. 1999. "Corruption and the Cuban Transition." Pp. 453-468 in *Cuba in Transition—Volume 9*. Washington: Association for the Study of the Cuban Economy.

Reporters Without Borders. 2002. *Freedom of the Press Throughout the World—Report 2002*. Paris. http//:www.rsf.org/article.php3?id_article=1388

Rose-Ackerman, Susan. 1997. "The Political Economy of Corruption." Pp. 31-60 in Kimberly Ann Elliott, editor, *Corruption and the Global Economy*. Washington: Institute for International Economics.

Smith, Kirby and Hugo Llorens. 1998. "Renaissance and Decay: A Comparison of Socioeconomic Indicators in Pre-Castro and Current-Day Cuba." Pp. 247-259 in *Cuba in Transition—Volume 8*. Washington: Association for the Study of the Cuban Economy.

Stiglitz, Joseph. 1999. *On Liberty, the Right to Know, and Public Discourse: The Role of Transparency in Public Life*. Oxford Amnesty Lecture. Oxford, U.K. (January 27). http://www.worldbank.org/html/extdr/extme/jssp012799.htm.

Voslensky, Michael. 1984. *Nomenklatura: The Soviet Ruling Class*. New York: Doubleday.

LECCIONES DE IRAK: UN CONTRAPUNTO

Alberto Luzárraga

Cuba e Irak son sociedades muy disímiles en cultura, historia, religión y costumbres. Pero comparten una desgracia: arribaron al siglo XXI en manos de un dictador sin escrúpulos experto en la simulación que no paró mientes en destruir a un país en aras de lograr sus objetivos personales.

Comparten también una lista de problemas. La lista que sigue es la base de nuestro contrapunto:

- Jefe de estado dictador de edición original. Se rodea de adeptos incondicionales cuyas vidas ha comprometido a la suya en forma inexorable.

- Como consecuencia crea una casta privilegiada vinculada al dictador por privilegios especiales que incluyen puestos, viajes, remuneraciones, educación, vivienda, salud y el poder presumir de amigo del "jefe."

- Economía y moneda sujeta al capricho personal del dictador y su camarilla. Se toman decisiones en función de la permanencia en el poder y no del bien común. El estado es el aparente dueño de los medios de producción pero en realidad están a la disposición de los gobernantes y sus allegados. Los privilegiados acumulan riquezas.

- Contratación internacional de bienes y servicios sujeta a la premisa anterior. La inversión extranjera es vista primariamente como un medio de mantener al régimen y no de desarrollo del país.

- Deuda externa impagable y en mora, unida a infraestructura seriamente deteriorada y deficiente.

- Ejército y fuerzas de seguridad hipertrofiadas y consumidoras de grandes recursos incluyendo los dedicados a programas de armamento.

- Fuerzas de seguridad interna comprometidas con el régimen y detestadas por el pueblo. Abusos y crímenes ampliamente documentados.

- Medios de comunicación y escuelas utilizados para adoctrinar, intimidar y manipular a la población.

- Relaciones internacionales intensas, conflictivas y enfocadas a la propaganda.

- Ausencia de partidos políticos y de criterios ponderados para arreglar el país, consecuencia de la existencia de un partido único dedicado a mantener la dictadura.

Cuba e Irak difieren en algunas cosas. En Cuba no hay fanatismo ni odio religioso, exceptuado el que puedan sentir los adeptos al ateísmo marxista extremo, que detestan todo sentimiento religioso. Cuba, a pesar de los marxistas, es parte del mundo cristiano/occidental por historia y geografía. Su cercanía a la democracia americana y la influencia del gran número de cubanos que han tenido éxito en dicha sociedad es un factor de gran peso que no puede soslayarse.

Otra diferencia importante: Irak ha sido derrotado en una guerra y es un país ocupado.

En cuanto a Cuba, no se sabe a ciencia cierta cuál será el desenlace final del régimen castrista. No parece probable una ocupación militar ni una intervención por fuerzas internacionales a no ser que Cuba se suma en el caos.

Lo más probable es que los problemas de salir del castrismo los tengan que enfrentar los propios cubanos y resolver ellos mismos con mayor o menor ayuda extranjera que no es lo mismo que ocupación o intervención.

No obstante los problemas apuntados son comunes. La experiencia de Irak es útil a fin de examinar lo que se está haciendo en un país y lo que podría ocurrir en otro.

Una de las constantes de todo proceso de rescate de un país que sale de una dictadura es que en vísperas del desenlace las posiciones se polarizan en función de intereses y experiencias. Los que detentaron el poder pretenden explotar su posicionamiento y "vender" la conveniencia de no caer en un desorden que lleve al caos. Defienden su interés. Los que han sufrido mucho reclaman justicia y un país nuevo pues no están dispuestos a repetir la experiencia. En el caso cubano las posiciones son:

- Los castristas incondicionales deliran con un "continuismo revolucionario" extendido a algunas partes de América Latina que les sirva de coro y apoyo.

- Otros menos absurdos sueñan con una "transición pacífica" que los deje en posesión parcial o total de sus prebendas mientras cambian de camiseta y todo se diluye en borrón y cuenta nueva. Estiman que sus contactos y negocios con los inversionistas internacionales los protegerán. Se sienten además en capacidad de controlar las fuerzas armadas y de vender "estabilidad."

Las posiciones del exilio son:

- Los que quieren un cambio a fondo, definen la revolución castrista como un desastre nacional que requiere castigar a los autores principales y hacer una limpieza a fondo, para restaurar el estado de derecho.

- Los que piensan que se puede hacer una transición pacífica con el gobierno castrista, pero sin Castro, dejando en sus puestos al aparato administrativo del régimen con cambios más o menos cosméticos.

El objeto de este trabajo es examinar, con los pies puestos sólidamente en tierra, olvidando por un momento las posiciones ideológicas si es posible o no un resurgimiento cubano sin un cambio a fondo de las estructuras actuales.

CONTRATACIÓN, DEUDA Y MONEDA
Contratación y Deuda

Por formación profesional estoy de acuerdo con que los contratos deben respetarse y cumplirse. Pero hay diferentes contratos y circunstancias que hacen que la frase no sea máxima absoluta. El caso de Irak es fuente de importantes lecciones para los cubanos. Terminada la guerra se debate si los contratos firmados por el régimen tiránico de Hussein son o no son válidos y obligatorios para el gobierno sucesor. Este mismo tema va a tener que ser considerado a fondo por el futuro gobierno de una Cuba libre.

Según el Center for Strategic and International Studies,[1] existen deudas Iraquíes por $127 billones, en buena parte para compra de armas, y contratos pendientes por $57 billones. Rusia y Francia tienen posiciones importantes por ambos conceptos incluyendo contratos para desarrollo y explotación petrolera. Y además Irak podría deber casi $200 billones por concepto de indemnizaciones de guerra reconocidas o posibles. Buena parte nunca serán pagadas porque $20 billones al año de exportaciones petroleras no dan para mantener 24 millones de personas y hacer esos pagos.

Cuba no tiene esa magnitud de deudas en números gruesos, pero debe $12 billones al mundo occidental y por lo menos $20 billones a Rusia, en buena parte proveniente de compras de armas. Y además ha firmado contratos de co-inversión enfocados principalmente a la explotación turística (es nuestro petróleo) en condiciones de verdadero abuso para el trabajador cubano.

En concepto de indemnizaciones, los Estados Unidos han certificado 1 billón de dólares por propiedades confiscadas a empresas americanas hace 44 años. Hoy día con intereses al 6% esa suma alcanzaría 10 billo-

---

1. http://www.csis.org/isp/wiserpeace_I.pdf.

nes. Lo debido a todos los afectados por confiscaciones, que sepamos, no ha sido calculado con precisión no sólo por la dificultad de asignar valores sino tal vez por la certeza de que será de imposible pagarlo.

Cuarenta billones más indemnizaciones es suma impensable para 11 millones de cubanos empobrecidos y sin el recurso petrolero. Es un hecho innegable que Cuba e Irak son países altamente endeudados y empobrecidos por la casta gobernante. Ambos enfrentan obligaciones al menos parcialmente indeterminadas por concepto de indemnización.

En el caso cubano ni los Estados Unidos ni los exiliados harán de esta cuestión tema de imposible solución. Quieren que Cuba prospere. Pero hay otros acreedores con miras puramente comerciales que pretenden pago y sería irónico que la generosidad de unos premiase la falta de ética o prudencia de otros.

Y aquí viene el argumento que será esgrimido por dichos terceros. Bajo la teoría tradicional de la contratación entre estados, supuestamente los estados perduran, asumen las obligaciones de los malos gobiernos, y los pueblos las pagan. De lo contrario se alega que se daría al traste con la seguridad jurídica indispensable para el desarrollo comercial porque supuestamente los extranjeros no deben ser jueces del comportamiento interno. Contratan con quien detente el poder.

No es necesario explicar que esta teoría beneficia a los que pretenden continuar en el gobierno cubano pero sin Castro. Son aliados naturales de dicha posición pues les permite consolidar apoyos a base de hacer concesiones, que mal pueden negar, ya que en buena parte lo pactado es obra suya.

Pero decimos: Un momento, los vendedores y acreedores no son menores de edad. Por lo común, saben con quien contratan y en muchas ocasiones se avienen a exigencias de dinero por gobernantes corruptos. Para lograr vender conceden créditos y a veces lo hacen a países notoriamente insolventes. A menudo venden con precios exagerados, condiciones abusivas y objetivos contrarios a los intereses de la nación receptora. Ejemplo: ¿Qué interés nacional cubano fue servido al gastar el país enormes sumas a fin de convertirse en una mini potencia militar?

Para que exista una obligación válida que afecte a una nación tiene que haber representación válida de esa nación o por lo menos contratar algo que beneficie a la comunidad. Y aquí es donde hay que considerar las características del mandato que tiene un gobierno, de su desempeño y del objeto de los créditos que contrata. Un gobierno, sea cual fuere su origen, debe gobernar en beneficio de la colectividad. Cuando su origen es legítimo, o sea por el consentimiento de los gobernados a través de una elección, hay cierta lógica en decir que los errores los debe pagar el pueblo porque erró en la elección de sus gobernantes.

Supongamos otro caso. Un gobierno que no es transparente y democráticamente electo pero gobierna en beneficio de la colectividad (aunque sea esporádicamente), y sin corrupción contrata bienes o servicios útiles a dicha colectividad, como por ejemplo una central eléctrica. Podría en ese caso reconocerse la legitimidad de dicha deuda porque de lo contrario habría un enriquecimiento injusto a favor de esa nación y en contra del vendedor.

Pero cuando un gobierno tiránico degenera en pandilla aferrada a mantenerse en el poder a toda costa y por décadas hace caso omiso de la nación (caso de Irak y de Cuba), las cosas se complican porque hay demasiadas evidencias de que se contrata no con un gobierno sino con una pandilla que sólo se representa a sí misma y que la mayor parte el tiempo sólo busca su propio beneficio.

Esos "gobiernos" son verdaderas empresas criminales que toleran transacciones serias sólo cuando les ayuden a mantener una buena cara o cuando carecen de alternativa viable pues ni los criminales empedernidos pueden serlo el 100% del tiempo.

Mantener el principio de la santidad de todos los contratos frente a evidencias espeluznantes de asesinato, tortura, robo, y abusos contra la nación perpetrados por el gobierno contratante, va contra la razón. Especialmente cuando el objeto del contrato es fortalecer a la pandilla y su usurpación del poder con armamentos o con estructuras comerciales diseñadas especialmente para mantenerlos en ese disfrute abusivo y explotador.

Cargar esas deudas y obligaciones sobre las generaciones futuras es asegurar la inestabilidad social. No obstante hay quien clama parcial o totalmente por esa solución en el caso de Irak. Y no son sólo los acreedores. Hay quienes, aún en este país y en aras de las llamadas "buenas relaciones internacionales," están dispuestos a reconocer toda clase de depredaciones comerciales. Para los cubanos el asunto está clarísimo, pero para algunos sectores del mundo financiero internacional el tema es preocupante pues se temen las consecuencias. Se preguntan: ¿Qué pasaría si esa teoría de repudio de las deudas de tiranías execrables se extiende? ¿Y quién, se preguntan además, traza la línea divisoria entre los regímenes dictatoriales y los que además son execrables?

Hay que proveer una solución moralmente sana, jurídicamente defendible, y aún comercialmente razonable pues no es sensato declararle la guerra al mundo. La conclusión en el caso cubano es ésta: Todos los contratos no nacieron iguales. Hay contratos que tienen una causa viciada de origen y no pueden ser reconocidos como válidos, porque son producto de una estructura discriminadora diseñada para la rapiña del salario y el control de la población. Ejemplo clásico: el sistema de co-inversión con sustracción del salario del trabajador cubano que percibe el 5% de lo pagado.[2]

Hay contratos que crearon enormes deudas en contra del interés esencial de la nación y esas no pueden ser asumidas por las generaciones venideras porque sería un suicidio social.

Ejemplo: Las contraídas con Rusia por armamentos para lanzarnos en aventuras militares "internacionalistas" en las que no teníamos que mezclarnos porque eran extrañas a los intereses a largo plazo de la nación. Igualmente contrarios a esos intereses fueron los costos y deudas provenientes de los intentos de integración en el absurdo sistema de la economía soviética que nos relegó a simple proveedor azucarero sujetos a un monocultivo destructivo que en definitiva terminó con la ruina de esa misma industria. Son deudas contraídas para apoyar el sistema del marxismo internacional y no para desarrollar el país. Rusia, la "heredera" de ese "activo," nunca pagó la deuda zarista y dado el precedente mal puede pretender cobrarle a Cuba los créditos del difunto sistema soviético.

Y hay en fin contratos y deudas en que tal vez pueda probarse que el objeto y el bien contratado fueron útiles a la nación (equipos médicos por ejemplo), que el precio y las condiciones fueron justos y que por ello probablemente no hubo corrupción. Esas deudas podrían ser reconocidas.

En resumen las deudas y contratos castristas tienen que ser revisadas en función de su origen, condiciones y propósito.

Esta tesis ha ganado virtualidad vista la reciente resolución 1443 de 23 de Mayo 2003 de la ONU[3] que entre otras cosas establece (nuestra traducción) que se debe revisar la "relativa utilidad de cada contrato a fin de determinar si dichos contratos proveen bienes necesarios para hacer frente a las necesidades del pueblo de Irak ahora y durante la reconstrucción y a posponer aquéllos que sean de dudosa utilidad, así como las correspondientes cartas de crédito hasta que un gobierno Iraquí representativo e internacionalmente reconocido pueda determinar si dichos contratos deben ser cumplidos."

---

2. Ver una discusión del tema en la red: http://www.futurodecuba.org/default.htm y pulsar en Estado de Derecho, "La Nulidad de los Contratos de Inversión Extranjera por Causa Ilícita: Defraudar al Trabajador Cubano," o http://lanic.utexas.edu/project/asce/pdfs/volume11/luzarraga.pdf.

3. El texto de dicha resolución en su original en inglés dice que establece, entre otras cosas, "to review, in light of changed circumstances, in coordination with the Authority and the Iraqi interim administration, the relative utility of each approved and funded contract with a view to determining whether such contracts contain items required to meet the needs of the people of Iraq both now and during reconstruction, and to postpone action on those contracts determined to be of questionable utility and the respective letters of credit until an internationally recognized, representative government of Iraq is in a position to make its own determination as to whether such contracts shall be fulfilled."

Es un precedente importante que no sólo pone en tela de juicio la contratación entre el régimen y sus proveedores sino que también entra a cuestionar la contratación con terceros pues eso significa afectar las cartas de crédito que propiamente son contratos entre un banco y un comprador en beneficio de un tercero.

Es también un precedente moderno que en el caso de Cuba remacha uno antiguo. Después de la guerra hispano/cubano/americana los Estados Unidos, como poder ocupante, aplicaron la doctrina de las deudas odiosas y no se pagaron las deudas con las que España había gravado a Cuba para pagar los gastos de guerra. Esa doctrina está basada en los mismos principios que apuntábamos antes: los oprimidos no deben pagar los gastos en que incurrió el opresor para mantener esa situación.

Conclusión: el tránsito de Cuba hacia una transición pacífica y feliz en la cual la burocracia que creó éstos problemas pueda mantenerse incólume es bastante improbable.

Si Cuba pretende incorporarse al mundo civilizado y vivir ajustada a reglas de conducta y a un estado de derecho va a tener que hacer frente a muchas reclamaciones internas y externas y los que crearon los problemas mal pueden ser jueces imparciales sobre cuáles contratos son legítimos y cuáles no lo son. Su gestión de gobierno va a quedar inexorablemente ligada a los resultados desastrosos.

Los continuistas internos y externos pecan en este caso de optimismo iluso. El mundo es mucho más complicado de lo que piensan. Los cubanos que hoy en día sufren en silencio sus malos manejos no lo harán en un clima de libertad. Imponer otra dictadura no es viable. El cambio a fondo de estructuras inoperantes y corruptas será exigido y es inevitable.

Queda pendiente el problema del monto de lo que pueda pagar Cuba de aquellas deudas que reconozca. Es otro asunto porque al fin y al cabo por mucho tiempo ha sido país notoriamente moroso y quebrado a quien se extendió crédito imprudentemente. Sin embargo la reestructuración de esas deudas y cuales rebajas proceden es un segundo paso y tema para otro momento. Pero basta decir que el monto de la deuda legítima a reconocer y pagar deberá ser función de la capacidad de endeudamiento y servicio de deuda del país, definida así: La capacidad de deuda de un país quebrado y en proceso de reconstrucción es aquélla que pueda servir sin crear condiciones sociales peores que las que pretende remediar.

Quiere decir que hay que dar entrada en la ecuación a un concepto de flujo de fondos libre en el que se incluya primero a las obligaciones nuevas que haya que servir para reconstruir el país, y su servicio de principal e intereses así como remunerar al nuevo capital extranjero de inversión que tanto necesitaremos, lo cual implica remesas de utilidades. El remanente será lo que esté disponible para pagar deudas antiguas. Es justo y equitativo. Las deudas antiguas pierden valor con el transcurso del tiempo y los créditos concedidos a Cuba por muchos países fueron notoriamente imprudentes dada la historia financiera de Castro. Querer cargar esa imprudencia sobre generaciones futuras no es viable.

Moneda

Este es un tema cuya dificultad inicial estriba en los legados desastrosos de las tiranías. En Irak el problema es que muchas personas no se ganaban la vida produciendo, sino sirviendo al régimen para mantenerse en el poder. Los que no servían al régimen con frecuencia vivían de empleos marginales. Cesados los incondicionales o supernumerarios del régimen en sus cargos, piden un estipendio hasta que se ubiquen en la economía. Como el estado Iraquí en situación de post guerra no tenía recursos para pagar, las fuerzas de ocupación efectuaron los pagos en dólares y en dinares. Se utilizaron también grandes cantidades de divisas sustraídas por los gobernantes y luego recobradas. También se emitieron grandes sumas en billetes de los de antiguo diseño. Las fluctuaciones cambiarias fueron enormes con la consiguiente inflación. Mientras esto ocurre se estudia el lanzamiento de una nueva moneda.

En Cuba el problema es similar. Los salarios míseros encubren una inflación reprimida pues si el gobierno fuera a pagar lo que debiera sería a base de emitir. Sin tiranía el clamor popular por mejores remuneraciones será ensordecedor. El dólar ya circula abundantemente y post Castro aumentará notablemente el volumen pero no llegará a la mayoría de los trabajadores que no están en el sector turístico. Surgirán los mismos problemas de emisión que enfrenta Irak.

¿Qué hacer? ¿El gobierno único empleador inicial, dolariza y paga todos los salarios en dólares? ¿Tiene ingresos con que hacerlo? ¿O emite y crea una inflación? ¿Mantiene dos monedas circulando con los problemas que ello acarrea? ¿Crea un nuevo peso adecuadamente respaldado? ¿Va a un sistema de junta monetaria (monetary board) a lo Hong Kong?

Hay respuestas y soluciones a todas esas difíciles preguntas y no corresponde analizarlas aquí. Basta decir que las soluciones no fructifican sino con mucho trabajo, ingenio y sobre todo confianza internacional (cualquier solución va a requerir gran apoyo externo) en un equipo honrado, hábil y con buena trayectoria profesional.

Seguramente existirán en Cuba personas capacitadas. Hay que encontrarlas, darles oportunidad y suplir la falta de experiencia que tengan. Otra razón más para pronosticar que la transición con el equipo castrista "mejorado cosméticamente" no parece factible.

CASTA PRIVILEGIADA Y PRIVATIZACIÓN

Con anterioridad hemos tocado el tema de la privatización desde el punto de vista técnico examinando los aspectos jurídicos y económicos y sociales.[4] Es preciso considerarlo también como una necesidad social encaminada a crear libertad y eficiencia. Es requisito en cuanto a libertad, porque la concentración de la riqueza en manos de los otrora allegados al régimen no puede producirla. Utilizarían su riqueza para perpetuar su influencia y además generarían enormes resentimientos sociales.

Es requisito en cuanto a eficiencia porque el estado cubano administrado por dicha casta ha demostrado que sólo pudo producir pobreza en 44 años. Sin embargo, cómo llevar a buen término una privatización es el quid de este difícil asunto pues tiene aristas jurídicas, económicas y sociales de gran importancia. En

el trabajo citado, conscientes de que el capital de riesgo en un principio será mayormente extranjero, mostrábamos preocupación por no producir una situación de cuasi-monopolio del capital extranjero y por dar al cubano oportunidad de crear empresas.

Decíamos entonces: Cuba está descapitalizada y por tanto lo están la inmensa mayoría de los cubanos. Proteger la creación de empresas controladas por nacionales de Cuba y la acumulación de la propiedad en manos de cubanos sería un objetivo razonable. Lograrlo, "sin caer en demagogias ni restricciones inoperantes no es sencillo, pero puede hacerse pues existen múltiples esquemas de estímulo fiscal y administrativo aptos para lograr ese resultado."

Favorecer la participación de la empleomanía en la empresa a base de paquetes accionarios, representación en las directivas, etc. pudiera hacer surgir empresas muy ágiles y creativas capaces de competir con cualquiera. ¿Créditos suaves para comprar acciones? Seguramente que sí, pero hay que pagarlas y mientras tanto están dadas en garantía. Y naturalmente remuneraciones adicionales en forma de acciones, u opciones de compra por un trabajo bien hecho sería una muy buena política.

Privatizar no es sino redistribuir el poder económico de un país con las consecuencias sociales que ello implica. Disyuntiva: ¿Se privatiza concentrando la propiedad y creando un ejército de asalariados no interesados en las empresas; o se crea un ejército de pequeños empresarios y de empleados accionistas en las grandes empresas que son necesarias en ciertos giros?

Lo más razonable sería hacer ambas cosas. El arte del diseño consistirá en estimular la participación obrera en las grandes empresas y dejar campo a la legítima libertad de acción que la gerencia requiere. Y al mismo tiempo estimular y dar facilidades a la creación de las pequeñas empresas que emplean gran número de per-

---

4. "Privatización en Cuba: ¿Factor de Unión y Desarrollo o de Conflicto Social? http://www.futurodecuba.org/Privatizacion.htm; *Cuba in Transition—Volume 7,* http://lanic.utexas.edu/la/cb/cuba/asce/cuba7/luzarrag.pdf.

sonas en actividades que no suelen acometer las grandes.

En las empresas grandes, las diferencias en las aportaciones de capital y de riesgo a correr tienen que ser reconocidas, acordándoles las protecciones pertinentes. No se llegará a nada práctico con un esquema ilusorio, repleto de derechos para los trabajadores y ninguna protección para el capital de riesgo porque nadie lo aceptará como base para hacer nada importante. La esencia del diseño es la libertad. No se puede forzar a nadie a ser socio de nadie. Lo que sí puede hacerse es dar estímulo a esas asociaciones y aquí hay mucho campo para la política económica y fiscal. El empresario que quiera ser dueño 100% y que pague muy buenos salarios tal vez tenga tanto éxito como el que de participación en acciones. En buena parte dependerá de las características de cada industria, de las cualidades que deben tener las personas empleadas en ella y de lo necesario para motivarlas.

El reto para Cuba será este: producir diversidad de artículos y servicios de buena calidad a precios competitivos, pero sin que este resultado se base en la creación de una isla factoría con exclusión del capital nacional. Lo anterior es una aspiración elevada y difícil. Pero el tema es el siguiente: ¿Entramos en 20 años de conflictos sociales agudos o intentamos algo nuevo y más sensato?

Nuestra preocupación parece ser compartida por la intervención americana en Irak. Mr. L. Paul Bremer III, máxima autoridad de la misma, en comentario publicado por el New York Times,[5] expresó la necesidad (nuestra traducción) "de privatizar las empresas del estado y distribuir parte de los ingresos por concepto de exportaciones petroleras como un dividendo a la población o bien crear un fideicomiso nacional que financiase ciertos servicios sociales. Cada individuo entendería así que comparte el éxito económico del país."

El esquema petrolero no es aplicable al caso cubano y aún falta mucho camino por andar en Irak pero lo importante es lo siguiente: el aserto de que en un país que surge de una dictadura personal y de un estado absorbente, hay que involucrar a la población en la creación de su destino económico.

Conclusión: El esquema de un grupo reducido de altos ex-funcionarios castristas enriquecidos, que de inicio controlen la economía, asociados al capital extranjero no es viable aunque sea acariciado por elementos internos y externos.

Enfrentan un problema. La idea ronda como un fantasma horrible en la mente de los cubanos. Los tiempos de dejar el feudo en herencia a lo "Papa Doc-Baby Doc" ya pasaron. El capital extranjero serio no se va a considerar seguro ni bien visto con esa clase de asociación. Sin él los comienzos de la recuperación serían muy difíciles. La repulsa interna y externa de los cubanos sería constante y enfática y nada asusta más al capital que el pronóstico de acusaciones y luchas constantes.

Lo que sí ocurrirá es que muchos ex-funcionarios de nivel medio descubrirán a Adam Smith, se harán empresarios y buscarán socios. Y aquí viene a cuento el siguiente tema.

LUSTRACIÓN, TRIBUNALES, JUSTICIA, FUERZAS ARMADAS

Las poblaciones de los países que sufren dictaduras muy largas requieren un período de desintoxicación durante el cual la población vuelva a la normalidad, recapacite y compare. Existe un denominador común: el deseo de que no vuelva a ocurrir un desastre similar. Es por eso que se hace preciso desmantelar el aparato administrativo y de terror que sostenía cada régimen. Se ha hecho en Alemania y Japón y recientemente en Europa Oriental. Hablar de pasar la página y simular que no ha pasado nada no sólo es injus-

---

5. *New York Times*, June 23, 2003. "L. Paul Bremer III, the chief United States administrator in Iraq, vowed today to dismantle that country's state-run economy by selling off government-owned companies and writing new laws to encourage foreign investment. Recognizing that a rapid shift would cause pain to many in the short term, Mr. Bremer also raised the possibilities of distributing part of Iraq's oil revenues as "dividends" to citizens or creating a national trust fund that would help finance a "social safety net." "Every individual Iraqi would come to understand his or her stake in the country's economic success," he told business and political leaders gathered here for a meeting of the World Economic Forum.

to, es inoperante porque desconoce la historia, la naturaleza humana y los requisitos esenciales para progresar.

No hay progreso con resentimiento social, venganzas por cuenta propia, tribunales poblados de jueces que fueron servidores disfrazados del poder ejecutivo, delincuentes que deambulan libremente haciendo gala de sus riquezas mal habidas, y fuerzas armadas y de seguridad compuestas de los mismos individuos que abusaron de la población. Sin embargo, es preciso ayudar a la sociedad a producir el resultado apetecido porque ordinariamente las personas están tan preocupadas por sobrevivir que no pueden reflexionar en forma equilibrada y profunda.

La lustración (término usado en Europa que etimológicamente significa purificar) tiene dos vertientes. La administrativa y la criminal.

- En el caso administrativo se separan de sus cargos a funcionarios del régimen o se les inhabilita para el ejercicio de ciertos cargos públicos bien sean administrativos o por elección. También, se eliminan entidades y cargos que no son necesarios incluyendo el disminuir las hipertrofiadas fuerzas armadas.

- En el supuesto criminal aparte de las sanciones civiles se responde por delitos mayormente contra las personas y con frecuencia también por malversación.

En Irak, Mr. Bremer ha hecho lo siguiente:

- Desbandar el ejército de Hussein compuesto de 400 mil hombres sustituyéndolo por uno nuevo de 40 mil hombres que será reclutado y entrenado con un enfoque democrático. Se les pagará un estipendio a los cesantes por un tiempo reconociendo que la mayor parte de los soldados no tienen de momento otra fuente de ingresos que su sueldo.[6]

- Crear dos nuevas entidades, la Comisión de Revisión Judicial y el Tribunal Criminal Central.[7] La Comisión consistirá de seis miembros, tres iraquíes y tres miembros de las fuerzas de ocupación que examinarán el desempeño de los jueces y fiscales a fin de efectuar los cambios pertinentes. Tendrán un plazo de cuatro meses para realizar esta labor. El Tribunal Criminal Central encausará a los criminales culpables de delitos comunes. El gobierno interino iraquí, recientemente instalado por el Sr. Bremer, ha anunciado además su intención de crear un tribunal especial para juzgar a los miembros del gobierno de Hussein acusados de crímenes de guerra.

- Eliminar de los puestos civiles los cuatro primeros niveles de miembros del partido Baath que mantenía a Hussein en el poder y no admitir excepciones basadas en la eficiencia. Veamos las palabras de un militar norteamericano a quien se le enfatizó la necesidad de mantener en sus cargos a ciertos elementos de la policía. Respuesta: "Entre la eficiencia y la limpieza, la orden es limpieza."[8]

Siguió así los precedentes de Alemania donde se exigió a los residentes de la zona americana llenar un formulario declarando su afiliación al partido nazi. Se dividió a los nazis en cuatro grupos que iban desde funcionarios importantes con un grado alto de responsabilidad hasta los simples "compañeros de viaje." 9,000 fueron condenados a penas de cárcel, 25,000 a confiscación de sus propiedades, 22,000 a exclusión de cargos públicos y 500,000 fueron multados. En la zona británica 350,000 fueron separados de sus cargos. En cuanto a delitos graves, 481 fueron condenados a la pena máxima tras los procesos de Nurenberg.

---

6. Patrick E. Tyler, "U.S. to Form New Iraqi Army and Pay Soldiers of Old One," *New York Times*, June 23 2003; Richard A. Oppel, Jr., "Banking Overhaul and New Currency Planned for Iraq, *New York Times*, July 8, 2003.

7. Jim Krane and Donna Abu-Nasr, "Iraq Gets Court Reform; U.S. Soldier Dies," Associated Press, June 17, 2003; Richard A. Oppel, Jr. and Patrick E. Tyler, "Iraqis Plan War-Crime Court; G.I.'s to Stay Until Elections, *New York Times*, July 15, 2003.

8. Yaroslav Trofimov, "Odd Couple Rebuilds Iraqi Town; U.S. Odd Couple Rebuilds Iraqi Town; U.S. Officer Backs Former Baathist," *Wall Street Journal*, June 26, 2003; Amy Waldman, "U.S. Struggles to Transform a Tainted Iraq Police Force," *New York Times,* June 30, 2003.

Enfrentar la realidad produjo resultados. Muchos ex nazis colaboraron para restablecer la democracia y fueron rehabilitados. Konrad Adenauer hombre de impecables credenciales anti-nazis ascendió a algunos. La magnanimidad con los que la merecen también fue positiva. Dos décadas después, la normalidad había vuelto y un ex nazi, Kurt-Georg Kiesinger fue elegido canciller.[9]

En el caso de Europa Oriental la lustración ha seguido un camino más enfocado a las sanciones civiles. Los delitos de naturaleza criminal, aunque importantes y dolorosos, eran de menor envergadura que los cometidos por los nazis. Se hicieron precisiones entre los delincuentes y los políticos. Algunos de los principales funcionarios de los gobiernos comunistas mostraron flexibilidad y sentido patriótico para propiciar un cambio como por ejemplo Jaruzelzki en Polonia lo cual le valió escapar relativamente incólume y pasearse hoy en plena libertad por su país. En buena parte el comunismo en esos países era visto como una imposición soviética mantenida por un ejército de ocupación y no como un deseo de la nación.

Así la ley Checa[10] de lustración, se enfocó en la inhabilitación de los funcionarios colaboracionistas a los que se les prohibió continuar en altos cargos administrativos del estado, cargos de jueces, altos grados en el ejército (a partir de coronel) cargos administrativos de gerencia en empresas del estado incluyendo las educacionales, cargos en las fuerzas de seguridad, en las academias de ciencias, medios de comunicación social y en fin en todas las palancas del poder.

Para poder aspirar a los cargos más importantes los ciudadanos tenían que presentar una prueba negativa: un certificado del Ministerio del Interior estableciendo que la persona no fue oficial de la seguridad del estado o informante o colaborador consciente de los servicios de seguridad. Otra prueba negativa era la de no haber pertenecido a los niveles superiores o de mandos medios del partido.

Para cargos menos importantes el sistema funcionaba mediante la presentación de una declaración por la persona que ocupa o aspira al cargo de que no se encuentra afectado por ninguna inhabilitación. Esa declaración podía ser impugnada como falsa por cualquier ciudadano sometiéndose el caso a una comisión que emitía juicio sobre la cuestión. En caso de decisión adversa debía renunciar en un período de quince días.

Como proceder en Cuba es asunto complicado en el cual los métodos de Irak y otros países pueden ser o no aplicables. Un hecho si es consistente: Hasta ahora ningún país que se ha puesto en el camino del progreso ha hecho caso omiso del pasado.

Los que pretenden ignorar el pasado, como Rusia, aún se debaten en una sociedad plagada de injusticias y violencia o enfrentan reclamaciones y protestas como en la Argentina. España es un caso citado a menudo pero se hace a un lado el hecho de que más que olvido hubo agotamiento y cambio de guardia. Horrible guerra civil, un millón de muertos y una nueva generación que estaba menos traumatizada aunque consciente de los costos de la guerra civil.

El problema de Cuba es que Castro y comparsa son el producto original y continúan arrastrando a otros jóvenes y viejos en sus desmanes. Es el totalitarismo en permanente renuevo que a diario crea nuevas víctimas.

Conclusión: con esas credenciales el pretendido borrón y cuenta nueva no está basado en ninguna apreciación de la realidad cubana e histórica. Más que una postura seria es un lema a repetir.

Ello no significa que lo que se haga tiene que ser tremendista. En materia penal hemos dicho en otras ocasiones[11] que no somos partidarios de penas de muerte. Ya basta de sangre en Cuba. Lo esencial con los procesos que se sigan es informar y crear ejemplos. Es preciso que se conozcan los abusos en detalle

9. Daniel Johnson, "De-Baathification," *Wall Street Journal*, April 24 2003; Paul Gigot, "This Was a Good Thing to Do," *Wall Street Journal*, July 28 2003.

10. Act No. 451/1991 SB. of 4th October 1991.

11. Alberto Luzárraga, "Impunidad y Libertad: ¿Son Compatibles?," http://www.futurodecuba.org y pulsar Sociedad y Educación.

y que se haga en un marco legal con todas las garantías procesales para los acusados de modo que se les pruebe, a satisfacción del más exigente jurista, su culpabilidad.

Y si escapa alguno por falta de pruebas esto aunque lamentable moralmente tiene un buen efecto: se habría probado que el estado de derecho ha vuelto a regir en Cuba y que los acusados son inocentes hasta que se les pruebe lo contrario. Entonces, ya seríamos un país civilizado apto para recibir inversiones de todas partes.

Lo cual nos lleva a otro espinoso problema, como efectuar la lustración de jueces y tribunales. El sistema castrista es una burla en materia judicial. No hay incompatibilidades entre cargos ya que entre otras cosas se puede ser juez y legislador y el partido está dentro de la judicatura con el sistema de incluir jueces legos. Es necesaria una comisión, como la impuesta en Irak, que examine el sistema y lo reforme. Es un tema muy extenso que abarca no sólo jueces sino leyes de organización del Poder Judicial, leyes de procedimiento, códigos a aplicar y formación de jueces. Aparte de que el Poder Judicial en Cuba, no es sino un brazo más del Poder Ejecutivo, es un hecho cierto que Cuba carece de jueces experimentados en materia civil y comercial. Crearlos no es obra de un día. Hay que ir a crear una escuela de jueces. Existe en otras partes. Hemos intentado señalar criterios prácticos a seguir en otro trabajo[12] y no es este el momento para reproducirlos pero basta la conclusión:

En materia judicial el cambio tiene forzosamente que ser a fondo por razones tanto políticas como técnicas. Tanto daño hace un juez politizado como uno incompetente.

Sin tribunales justos y competentes no hay estado de derecho, ni seguridad jurídica, ni banca que conceda créditos con garantías que los respalden, ni desarrollo

comercial e industrial. No vale solamente la buena intención hay que ser competente.

En materia administrativa no judicial nos parece obvio que un sistema similar al checo tiene sentido. Hay que abrirle campo a otra generación.

Queda el tema militar que en Irak se resolvió a base de desbandar el ejército y crear uno nuevo que será entrenado para que opere dentro de un marco democrático.[13] Mientras tanto se abonará un estipendio a los licenciados.

En Cuba algo parecido será necesario pero sin ejército. No vamos a ser invadidos por nadie ni invadiremos a nadie. Cuba necesita una buena policía urbana y rural, cuerpos técnicos de investigación, una policía judicial y un buen servicio de guardacostas para que su extenso litoral no sea utilizado por los contrabandistas de estupefacientes. No necesitamos ni un ejército ni una fuerza aérea, excepto en cuanto sea necesario para guardar las costas.

Castro ha corrompido parte de la oficialidad con diversas prebendas en empresas administradas por el ejército. Los oficiales de carrera no comprometidos podrán encontrar empleo remunerativo en el sector privado como es común en muchos países, utilizando su educación y hábitos de disciplina en otros menesteres. Mientras lo encuentran es justo que se les abone un estipendio.

Los que quieran mantenerse en las fuerzas que existan deberán ser re-entrenados en el concepto esencial de defender y servir a la sociedad y no a un régimen.

ELECCIONES Y CONSTITUCIONALISMO

Irak surgió como nación tras la Primera Guerra Mundial a partir de la desmembración del Imperio Otomano. Inglaterra recibió un mandato de la Liga de las Naciones para administrar el país. Eventualmente se retiró dejando establecida una monarquía constitucional que fue derrocada por un golpe militar

---

12. Alberto Luzárraga, "Reflexiones sobre un Futuro Poder Judicial en Cuba," http://www.futurodecuba.org y pulsar Estado de Derecho. In English: "Reflections on a Future Judicial Power in Cuba," http://www.futurodecuba.org/ and click Articles in English, scroll to Law Section.

13. "U.S. Agrees to Pay Salaries of Former Iraqi Soldiers, Pentagon will also Hire American Firm to Train a New, Smaller Iraqi Infrantry," *Wall Street Journal*, June 24, 2003.

en 1958 que abrogó la constitución anterior. Quiere decir que ambos países, Irak y Cuba, sufren de gobiernos totalitarios desde aproximadamente la misma fecha.

Llegar a un acuerdo social cuando se emerge de una tiranía es muy difícil. En Irak se complica aún más por el sectarismo religioso y el remanente de adeptos a Hussein que entorpecen todo lo posible incluyendo la violencia en todas sus formas. Las autoridades de ocupación han prometido un referéndum constitucional seguido de elecciones. Para prepararlas se ha seleccionado un gobierno interino compuesto de iraquíes de los principales sectores sociales. Es lógico pensar que buena parte de los miembros del partido Baath serán inhabilitados para ejercer el voto pues las autoridades lo han declarado disuelto y la oposición democrática reclama se extirpe al partido de la vida civil.[14] Sin duda, una cosa es el partido Baath como entidad política y otra cosa cada individuo y sus circunstancias. En estos casos parece probable que los principales dirigentes y ciertos niveles intermedios sean inhabilitados para ejercer cargos públicos, y los advenedizos, y los jóvenes que militaban en el partido para obtener mejoras materiales no lo sean, siempre y cuando no hayan sido miembros o coadyuvantes de los cuerpos represivos.

En Cuba el proceso será tal vez menos traumático. No hay sectarismo religioso que complique el proceso aunque si existe el político y gran división de opiniones en cuanto al camino a seguir. Las diferencias tendrán que ser zanjadas en las urnas tras la organización de partidos políticos. Esto plantea un problema que ha sido enfrentado antes por países que han emergido de sistemas totalitarios.

Una sociedad que aspire a la libertad tiene derecho a vivir en paz sin que se vea constantemente asediada por agitadores bajo diversos disfraces. Como hacerlo sin menoscabar la libertad personal es un problema a resolver pero una formulación útil es la de la consti-

tución alemana que enfrentada con el mismo problema, lo resolvió así: (mi subrayado)

> Art. 21.2 Son inconstitucionales los partidos que por *sus fines o la conducta de sus seguidores* se propongan menoscabar o destruir el orden fundamental libre y democrático y poner en peligro la existencia de la República Federal de Alemania. Corresponde al Tribunal Constitucional declarar dicha inconstitucionalidad.

Este precepto mejora el contenido del Art. 37 de la constitución del 40 que enfrentada a la doble amenaza del fascismo y el comunismo también consideró el problema al expresar: "Es ilícita la formación y existencia de organizaciones políticas contrarias al régimen del gobierno representativo democrático de la República, o que atenten contra la plenitud de la soberanía nacional."

Lo mejora porque se entra a considerar los fines o la conducta de los afiliados al partido y refiere la resolución del asunto al Tribunal Constitucional con lo cual convierte el problema en tema de relevancia fundamental para la sociedad en vez de lo que pudiera ser considerado como asunto meramente partidista.

De esta forma, se va al fondo sin entrar a perseguir al individuo por sus ideas pues bien puede tener todas las ideas totalitarias que quiera y aun expresarlas por todos los medios (para eso está la libertad de expresión personal) pero organizarse políticamente para imponerlas es un evento al que una sociedad como la alemana pone coto porque el precedente fue funesto. Y en la Cuba post Castro vamos a tener que pensar estas cosas muy a fondo a fin de crear una sociedad libre y dinámica que no pierda tiempo en defenderse de minorías fanatizadas.

Queda en fin el tema constitucional. A nadie en Irak se le ha ocurrido reformar la constitución de Saddam Hussein. Sin embargo en el exilio hay quien propone hacer esto con la de Castro que es de origen netamente estalinista.[15] No es un aserto peyorativo. Es un he-

---

14. Robert Pollock. "Politics for Lunch," *Wall Street Journal,* May 6 2003; Patrick E. Tyler, "In First Step, New Iraq Council Abolishes Hussein's Holidays," *New York Times,* July 14, 2003.

15. Alberto Luzárraga, "Derecho Constitucional Cuba: Un Analisis de losCambios Necesarios para Restaurar el Estado de Derecho," http://www.futurodecuba.org y pulsar Constitucional.

cho que fue copiada de la estalinista de 1936 que luego desecharon los reformadores de la perestroika, dándose una nueva que también fue desechada en su momento. Después de la "reforma" castrista del 2002, eliminando la facultad de modificar la constitución del 76 en nada que fuera contrario al socialismo, pensar en reformar ese adefesio jurídico es perder el tiempo.[16]

Cuba debe darse una nueva constitución o reformar la del 40 y en el ínterin dictar una ley de garantías ciudadanas.[17] En el trabajo citado decíamos:

- el gobierno provisional debe dictar un "bill of rights" o sea, unas garantías fundamentales que bien puede extraer del título IV de la Constitución del 40 tal vez con pequeños retoques para dar aún más protección al ciudadano y funcionar con ello durante la transición. Si se garantiza la libertad de expresión, asociación, educación, empresa, derecho de propiedad, habeas corpus, inviolabilidad del domicilio y correspondencia y todas las demás que constituyen las limitaciones clásicas al poder, entonces estaremos en el verdadero camino de la libertad.

- Pero no basta. Un documento en sí no da garantías. Es preciso crear un Tribunal Provisional que proteja esas garantías. En España se resolvió el problema por la Ley 62/78 que creó una Sala Especial de lo Constitucional en tanto se organizaba el nuevo estado y se creaba un Tribunal Constitucional. Funcionó por dos años, del 78 al 80. En Cuba desafortunadamente no contamos con la tradición judicial que sí tenía la España de Franco. Los regímenes autoritarios respetan usualmente la propiedad y el derecho privado y solo son autoritarios en lo político. Pero los totalitarios consumen toda la sociedad incluyendo el Poder Judicial en todas sus manifestaciones.

- Sin embargo, encontrar cinco o siete juristas decentes, justos y entendidos podrá hacerse y es la clave para mantener la transición dentro de cauces democráticos en los cuales se ponga coto al poder del estado. Se irá acostumbrando entonces el pueblo al hecho de que un decreto de la autoridad no es la palabra final. Y esa es la base de la democracia y la convivencia civilizada. Qué es conveniente hacer después, modificar la Constitución del 40, o dictar una nueva es tema para discutir a fondo en un clima de libertad.

CONCLUSIÓN

El desenlace del proceso de Irak y el de Cuba tiene mucho por andar. Habrá sorpresas en el camino. Los iraquíes tienen la desventaja de una sociedad más violenta y dividida que la cubana paliada por la ventaja de que tienen un árbitro. Los cubanos no tendrán otro árbitro más que ellos mismos a no ser que creen un caos.

En Cuba, como en Irak, se ve clara la necesidad de ir a cambios de fondo, de reformar las estructuras administrativas y cambiar los funcionarios principales del castrismo y sus allegados. Ya es hora que los talentos no politizados, que sin duda existen en Cuba, tengan su oportunidad. Es un problema tan político como administrativo. Un equipo fracasado no es un buen reformador. Emplea mucho tiempo en defender su gestión. Cuba no tiene el tiempo. Es a veces asombroso como los partidarios del borrón y cuenta nueva no reparan en un hecho elemental: se trata de entregar la plana a alguien que no la emborrone de nuevo.

16. "Reforma Constitucional Castrista Junio 2002," http://www.futurodecuba.org y pulsar Base de Referencia.

17. Alberto Luzarraga, "Confusión para Cuba: Anatomía de un Pensamiento y sus Consecuencias," http://www.futurodecuba.org y pulsar Constitucional.

LOOKING TO THE FUTURE FROM THE PAST: GENERATIONAL ROLES

Sergio Díaz-Briquets

Most attempts to reflect on Cuba's future have relied on the assessments of political scientist and others who, while examining a broad spectrum of political, economic and social variables, place emphasis on the role of leadership figures in the transition (for selected representative views see Horowitz and Suchlicki 2001, 533-660). Another alternative, suggested by Strauss and Howe (1991), based on their study of the American historical experience, gives pride of place to the examination of generational change, and how the juxtaposition of various generational segments at any given point in time can help assess the future course of history.

The foundation of this latter analytical approach rests on the assumption that generational worldviews are shaped by defining events, that these events differentially impact each generation according to the stage of the life cycle at which they are located when the defining events occur, and that, on the bases of their own generational experiences, each generation helps mold the generation to which it gives rise. Strauss and Howe's approach, while sophisticated and innovative, draws on a long scholarly tradition of generational analysis, dating back to the Ancient Greeks (citations to this literature may be found in Strauss and Howe 1991, particularly pages 518 and 519).

A preliminary assessment of how historical events may have shaped the worldviews of different Cuban generations, and what these worldviews suggests about the future, is presented in this paper. It draws heavily from, and applies to Cuba, a simplified ver-

sion of the framework developed by Strauss and Howe. In doing so, it considers seven distinctive Cuban cohort-groups (or generations) from 1850 to the present. A brief presentation of the analytical approach, and of its theoretical premises, is followed by its application to the Cuban case.

It goes without saying that this is a highly speculative, inexact and preliminary exercise intended to illustrate possible analytical paths that could be partially utilized to consider the significance of generational interactions in anticipating the future. Forecasting the future through the development of analytical models, as economists and other social scientists are well aware of, is a rather difficult and challenging endeavor. The model developed by Strauss and Howe is a systematic attempt to apply and contrast some conceptual constructs developed on the basis of the analysis of a wealth of historical information pertaining to American generations that led the authors to the conclusion that specific outcomes were preordained by given events and how different generations were influenced by them. Despite some obvious shortcomings—including critiques that it may simplify far too much complex social, political and economic realities, selectively highlighting some dimensions while minimizing or glossing over others—the approach provides a useful starting point to reflect on how different generations are impacted by common historical experiences and how generational interactions may help shape the future course of developments in Cuba. In this sense, the approach is similar to that followed in disciplines

Table 1. Phase of Life Generations and Central Roles

Elderhood (age 66-87). Central role: Stewardship (supervising, mentoring, channeling endowments, passing on values)	**Rising Adulthood** (age 22-43). Central role: Activity (working, starting families and livelihoods, serving institutions, testing values)
Midlife (age 44-65). Central role: Leadership (parenting, teaching, directing institutions, using values)	**Youth** (age 0-21) Central role: Dependence (growing, learning, accepting protection and nurture, avoiding harm, acquiring values)

Source: Strauss and Howe (1991, 60-61.)

that attempt to forecast the future by abstracting from a complex world some specific features worthy of study.

ANALYTICAL MODEL

While it is impossible to do justice to the model here, it is opportune to provide a definition of its most relevant concepts. They include what constitutes a "generation" and what is meant by "peer personality." The former is said to be a "cohort-group whose length approximates the span of a phase of life and whose boundaries are fixed by peer personality" (Strauss and Howe 1991, 60). Rather than utilizing the term cohort in the conventional way (technically, a set of people identified by a common event as they move through live, a birth cohort being the best example), "generational cohort-groups" are represented in terms of the length of a phase of life, each phase been roughly about 22 years in length (although the variation around the mean could be substantial). The four phases and the central roles within each are presented in Table 1.

Crucial to the model is the assumption that significant events occurring at a moment in history will impact differently each generational cohort-group according to the central roles they are playing, reinforcing separate identities and creating new ones. A good example is provided by a revolution that affects very differently those who live through it according to age and accumulated life experiences, the effects being determined in part by what people at each age can and cannot do, their station, etc. The end result is four age distinct cohort-groups encompassing everyone alive, although of course the relative position (in terms of age) of each individual within a given cohort will determine how s/he is influenced

by a defining event. In Strauss and Howe's (1991, 61) words:

> The decisive event, therefore, creates four distinct cohort-groups—each about twenty-two years in length and each possessing a special collective personality that will later distinguish it from its age-bracket neighbors as it ages in place. If future decisive events arrive when all of these cohort-groups are well positioned in older life phases, then those events will reinforce the separate identities of older cohort-groups and create new and distinct twenty-two year cohort-groups among the children born since the last event.

Peer personality, in turn, is a broad construct that transcends other categorizations, such as sex or ethnicity, but that links all member of a generation in terms of how they are shaped by defining events. As Strauss and Howe (1991, 64) define it, "a peer personality is a generational persona recognized and determined by (1) common age location; (2) common beliefs and behavior; and (3) perceived membership in a common generation." Not all individuals, of course, internalize experiences or react to events similarly on the bases of experiences, but these experiences influence many generational attributes. Moreover, each generation reinterprets its experiences over time as a result of the occurrence of new defining events at different phases of the life cycle.

Another important element of the model is what Strauss and Howe (1991, 71) call a "social moment." The relevance of this concept is particularly appropriate for the interpretation of Cuba's past, as the country has undergone several profound political and socio-economic transformations over the course of a century. And, if the model is robust enough, appreciating the significance of particular social moments may be helpful in narrowing down what may happen

Table 2. Generational Types; Characteristics by Life Cycle Stage

Idealistic	Reactive
Youth—Dominant, inner fixated, indulged, following a Secular Crisis	**Youth**—Recessive, under-protected and criticized during a Spiritual Awakening
Rising—Inspires a spiritual awakening	**Rising**—Risk taking, alienated
Midlife—Moralistic, cultivates principles	**Midlife**—Pragmatic leaders during a secular crisis
Elder—Visionary guiding next secular crisis	**Elder**—Maintains respect but less influence
Civic	**Adaptive**
Youth—Dominant, increasingly protected during a Spiritual Awakening	**Youth**—Overprotected and suffocated during a Secular Crisis
Rising—Come of age overcoming a secular crisis, heroic and achieving	**Rising**—Matures into risk averse, conformist
Midlife—Sustains image while building institutions	**Midlife**—Indecisive arbitrator leaders during Spiritual Awakening
Elder—Busy elders attacked by next spiritual awakening	**Elder**—Maintains influence but less respect

Source: Strauss and Howe (1991, 74.)

in the future. A social moment is purported to be "an era, typically lasting about a decade, when people perceived that historic events are radically altering their social environment…history is moving swiftly … the familiar world is disappearing and a new world is emerging." Moreover, two types of social moment can be identified: "secular crises, when society focuses on reordering the outer world of institutions and public behavior; and spiritual awakening, when society focuses on changing the inner world of values and private behavior."

Strauss and Howe postulate that social moments alternate in type and are generally separated by two life phases (40 to 45 years). The alternation comes about as "the growing incongruity between peer personality and age must induce a new social moment and realign social roles back into their original life phases" (Strauss and Howe 1991, 72). A cornerstone notion is that "each generation tries to redefine the social role of older phases of life as it matures through them" (Strauss and Howe, 1991, 72). This means that cohort-groups that internalize a given behavior pattern as children or youth (Youth Phase of Life) would be prone to act accordingly as they enter into Rising Adulthood. Cohort-groups, for example, induced by the mother generation to assume a discrete or not overtly outgoing modal behavior, are prone to become more passive than would otherwise be the case. The opposite is true for more outgoing cohort-groups. The U.S. historical experience suggests, in

fact, that a dominant generation tends to follow a recessive one, and so on.

The alternation of social moments gives rise, finally, to four generational types, "Idealist," "Reactive," "Civic," and "Adaptive," whose main characteristics are presented in Table 2. These four types recur in the same sequence, caution Strauss and Howe (74), as long as "society resolves with reasonable success each secular crisis that it encounters," a condition that may or may not apply to Cuba.

"Generational awareness," in short, "applies not only to where a cohort-group finds itself today, but also to where it is expected to go tomorrow…A generation, like an individual, merges many different qualities, no one of which is definite standing alone" (Strauss and Howe 1991, 68). And awareness of these shared perspectives is what gives the model the ability to present some educated speculations as to what the shared worldviews of the various cohort-groups of Cuba's population today may portend for the future.

THE CUBA COHORT-GROUPS DEFINED

Table 3 presents a schematic overview of a preliminary attempt to identify Cuba's cohort-groups according to the Strauss and Howe criteria and encompassing crucial historical periods with well-identified defining events. Each cohort-group is assigned a one-word label to encapsulate those developments that broadly impacted generational worldviews at different stages of the life cycle. Defining events for each historical period, organized primarily by the stage at

Table 3. **Schematic Representation of Seven Cuban Cohorts with Defining Events Indicated During the Rising Adulthood Years, 1876 to Present**

Cohort-Group	Born	Defining Events	Age in 2003
Colonial	1850-1875	Relations with Spain Role of slavery U.S. Civil War	(not alive)
War	1876-1898	Wars of independence Economic devastation Spanish-American War	(not alive)
Republic	1899-1919	Economic reconstruction Political instability High immigration levels American hegemony	84-104
Crisis	1920-1940	1933 revolution Economic Depression End of Platt Amendment 1940 Constitution	63-83
Transition	1941-1962	1952 Batista Military Coup 1959 Revolution 1961 Bay of Pigs Invasion 1962 Missile Crisis	41-64
Revolution	1963-1985	Radicalization 1970 sugar harvest Cuban internationalism	18-40
Survival	1986-present	General Ochoa execution Soviet collapse Social and economic crisis 2002 U.S. opening	0-17

which each cohort-group was in its Rising Adulthood stage, are shown in Table 4. For purposes of this discussion, seven cohort-groups are roughly identified: Colonial, War, Republic, Crisis, Transition, Revolution, and Survival.

To set the context for the social, economic and political events that shaped these cohort-groups, it is convenient to briefly review some of the historical events that left an indelible mark in the Cuban ethos and that in many ways defined the character of each cohort-group as well as relationships among them.

Colonial Cohort-Group

The first, labeled the Colonial cohort-group (born 1850-1875), came into being during a period in which competing visions of Cuba's future were being debated with eventual outcomes foreshadowed by developments beyond the confines of the then Spanish overseas colony. As Spain's "most faithful" colo-ny, Cuba remained tightly in the hands of the Iberian metropolis, as most nations formerly included in its American empire gained independence (other than Puerto Rico).

Why Cuba remained a Spanish colony responded to many causes, including among others, its insular character and the fear of many *criollos* (Cuban-born whites) and *peninsulares* (Spanish born Cuban residents) of what would happen to an independent Cuba. Haiti's experience, in particular, was a source of concern for the dominant White elite worried that independence would lead to the establishment of another Black republic. Although by the time this cohort-group was born, the slave trade had been abolished, slavery was not.

Cuba was also regarded as a potential pawn in the resolution of the slavery question in the United States; for the South, an annexed slaveholding Cuba

Table 4. Defining Events during Rising Adulthood Years by Cohort-Groups

Colonial	Dominated by debate about the nature of relations with Spain. Options considered included autonomy, independence or annexation by the United States. Several minor armed upheavals (slave revolts, invasion by annexionist forces) occurred during this period. Victory of the North in the U.S. Civil War weakened the annexation camp.
War	Two major wars for independence (1868-78 and 1895-98) were fought during this period. The country lay in ruins by the time of the Spanish- American War in 1898, followed by a four-year occupation (1898-1902) by American forces.
Republic	Cuba attained independence in 1902, but under widely resented American tutelage (Platt Amendment). Due to return of peace, sanitary campaigns and immigration, a significant increase in population size occurred. Foreign investment in the sugar industry, mainly from the United States, led to rapid economic growth, fueled by the end of the period of high global demand during and following the First World War. Immigration, primarily from Spain (and to a lesser extent from other European origins) and the West Indies (Jamaica and Haiti) had a major impact on the country's ethnic composition. Under the Platt Amendment, U.S intervened in Cuba twice (1909 and 1919).
Crisis	The impact of the Great Depression devastated the Cuban economy. In combination with nationalism, the economic crisis gave rise to Cuba's first major political upheaval during the Twentieth Century: the populist and nationalist 1933 Revolution. During the first term of office of President Franklin Delano Roosevelt, the Platt Amendment is abrogated. Fulgencio Batista first becomes Cuba's strongman. A national convention drafts the 1940 Constitution, a landmark achievement of the Republic.
Transition	Cuba enjoys twelve years (three presidential terms) of constitutional rule with democratically elected presidents and legislatures. Cycle is broken with Batista's military coup in 1952. Fidel Castro attains national prominence in 1953 when he leads an armed attack on the Moncada barracks in Eastern Cuba. His guerrilla forces assumed power in early 1959, to popular acclaim, when Batista fled the country. Between 1959 and 1962 Castro's government radicalizes and seeks support from the Soviet Union. Upper and middle classes break with the regime and seek exile abroad. Eighteen months after the U.S.-supported Bay of Pigs invasion in April 1961, the world comes to the brink of nuclear annihilation with the 1962 October Missile crisis.
Revolution	Close ties with the Soviet bloc ensure the survival of the Revolution despite disastrous economic policies (e.g., rapid industrialization, attempt to produce ten million tons of sugar in 1970) as the social fabric of Cuban society is radically changed. Deep political cleavages lead to large-scale emigration, as the revolutionary government embarks on the creation of the New Man. During the 1970s and early 1980s, revolutionary Cuba attains its zenith of international political influence, with military interventions in Ethiopia, Angola and Nicaragua, after many failures in promoting revolution in Latin America. The 1980 Mariel boatlift, coming on the heels of visits by exiles in the late 1970s, becomes a very visible manifestation of domestic discontent among some sectors of Cuban society. By the mid-1980s, the economy entered into a crisis with winds of change blowing from the East as a consequence of Glasnost and Perestroika.
Survival	The execution of General Arnaldo Ochoa and three of his subordinates (associates) in 1989 was a major domestic political shock. The end of the Soviet Union and the disintegration of the Communist world brought to Cuba a severe economic crisis (Special Period in Time of Peace) eroding the socialist safety net. The United States strengthens economic pressures (Torricelli and Helms-Burton Laws). Internal opposition, although weak, begins to gain some strength and international recognition. By 2002, signs of a weakening of the consensus in the United States to maintaining the U.S. economic embargo on Cuba.

strengthened its standing within the Union. The Civil War and the North's victory put to rest the annexation issue, but did not quench U.S. interest in a Cuba that provided a potentially rich export market and a profitable destination for investment in the sugar industry. This period saw the beginning of Cuba's first war of independence (the Ten Years War) that lasted from 1868 to 1878.

The colonial cohort-group provided much of the leadership (e.g., José Martí, born 1853) and many of the troops that battled Spanish colonial forces during Cuba's War of Independence (1895-1898), a bitterly fought and bloody conflict that came to an abrupt end after the battleship Maine's explosion in Havana harbor and the U.S. declaration of war on Spain. The end of the Spanish-American War left a troubled legacy in U.S.-Cuban relations. While grateful the conflict had come to an end, and pleased that Cuba managed to sever its colonial link to Spain, many Cubans felt bitter about the U.S. imposition of the Platt Amendment on Cuba's constitution as a condition for eventual independence in 1902.

This generation, whose life experiences were shaped by a spiritual awakening (seeds of independence), entered Rising Adulthood during a crisis (Independence wars), and later during their Midlife laid the bases for and ruled the Republic, corresponds quite nicely with Strauss and Howe's description of a Civic generation.

War Cohort-Group

The relatively small War cohort-group born between 1876 and 1898, reduced in size by the low fertility and high mortality of the war years, but whose relative size was later augmented by Cuba's largest ever immigrant influx, entered adulthood in the midst of war, or during the first twenty years of the Twentieth Century. The 1902-1919 period was tumultuous in Cuban history. Independence marked a major social moment as Cuba severed its colonial ties to Spain. The country's politics were dominated by contesting and corrupt political parties led by former insurrectional heroes drawn primarily from the Colonial (e.g. President José Miguel Gómez, b. 1858), and some of the oldest members of the War, cohorts. During this period, American economic and political hegemony was decisive, most domestic disagreements being resolved through American influence under the threat of or actual U.S. intervention.

The period also saw occasional violence. The United States formally intervened in Cuba under the Platt Amendment in 1909 and 1919, whereas a brief racial war erupted in 1916 that caused the death of more than 10,000. Thanks to substantial foreign investment—mostly from the United States—the economy grew rapidly during the first two decades of the century, particularly during and immediately after the First World War.

Cuba's early prosperity began to unravel by the mid-1920s, as the end of the First World War and declining sugar prices gradually unleashed a period of decline that anteceded by several years the Great Depression. It assumed catastrophic proportions by the 1930s. Republican Cuba's first great political upheaval, the 1933 Revolution—associated with what in Cuban history is known as the "1933 Generation"—was intensely nationalistic, some political factions being deeply influenced by radical notions in vogue at the time.

In terms of the cohort-groups being used here, the 1933 Revolution was led by members of the War cohort (e.g., Ramón Grau San Martín), signifying a leadership generational transfer from the Colonial cohort-group, but most of all by the Republic cohort's university students and non-commissioned officers. Defining moments for the latter cohort-group were the early years of independence, ensuing political instability and American oversight over the country's destiny, coupled with the promise of economic prosperity, major social transformations associated with foreign ownership of the national patrimony, and high immigration rates. The 1933 Revolution, led by the Republic cohort-group youth, saw the nation's leadership gradually begin to shift away from the Colonial and War cohorts. The Republic cohort-group would be very much entrusted with Cuba's destiny for the next twenty-five years.

This generation fits relatively well the Adaptive categorization, as it entered Rising Adulthood at a convoluted period of Cuban history dominated by members of the Colonial generation. In their older years, and after the travails of the 1930s, this generation failed to have the influence of the generations preceding and following it.

Crisis Cohort-Group

The dominant experiences of the Crisis cohort-group (born roughly between 1920 and 1940) were political turmoil and economic uncertainty. Members of this cohort-group grew up in a highly volatile political environment brought about by the institutional end economic failures that prevented the realization of the early hopes of the Republic. The fate of this cohort-group was ordained by the nationalistic impulses of the 1930s. This cohort-group witnessed revolution, but also the abrogation of the Platt Amendment and the democratic renaissance that in

1940 led to the participatory constitutional development process, to be followed by a dozen years of democratically elected governments. The Crisis cohort-group was to dominate Cuba's political and economic destiny for the latter half of the century, cutting short the preeminence the Republic cohort-group would normally have achieved had the 1959 Cuban Revolution not ensued. Fidel Castro Ruz (b. 1926), Cuba's unchallenged ruler for the last 44 years, is the leading personality of the Crisis cohort-group.

If anything describes the events that shaped the political evolution of the Crisis cohort-group during its youth, were the aftermath of the 1933 Revolution in the 1940s and the upheaval that followed Fulgencio Batista's 1952 military coup. The 1950s decade was notorious for its violence, although the country's economy performed relatively well. This cohort-group bore the brunt of the fighting between Batista's forces and the many groups that opposed them. Later, following Castro's rise to power, members of this cohort-group were pitted against each other, on one side the Revolutionary army and popular militias, and on the other, guerrilla bands, the urban resistance, and the invading Bay of Pigs landing force. Large-scale emigration and the separation of countless families also impacted this cohort-group. At a later point in life, the leadership for Cuba's internationalist missions between the 1960s and 1980s was largely drawn from the ranks of this cohort.

If any generation fits the Strauss and Howe characterization, it is this one. Members of this generation have dominated the country's political life following a Secular Crisis (the 1950s) since their Rising Adulthood years, and well into their Midlife and Elder years. To the extent that the fervor of the early years of the Revolution can be denoted as reflecting a Spiritual Awakening—the proposed transformation of values and private behavior (e.g., the rejection by many of Republican values, the embrace of Marxism-Leninism and attempts to create a "new man")—this generation was moralistic. Through its actions, it even set the eventual stage for a Secular Crisis.

Transition Cohort-Group

Beyond doubt, the three most significant defining events for the Transition cohort-group (born roughly between 1941 and 1962) were Batista's 1952 military coup, the 1959 revolutionary victory, the 1961 Bay of Pigs invasion, and the October 1962 Missile Crisis. These events, and Cuba's momentous social, economic and political transformation between 1959 and 1962, indelibly marked this cohort-group, a true "social moment" when the structures of Cuban society were radically modified. Politics and the creation of the revolutionary social order of selfless new men and women were the driving forces in their lives, although many retained childhood memories of pre-revolutionary Cuba. This generation was imbued with a historical sense of mission and provided the bulk of the foot soldiers for most revolutionary projects, ranging from the 1961 alphabetization campaign and the 1970 ten million ton sugar harvest, to the rank and file of the armed forces that saw action in Angola, Ethiopia and Nicaragua, among many other countries.

In some respects, this generation, although an active participant in Cuba's Revolutionary transformation and its "heroic" domestic and international missions, has in fact been quite passive and reactive since it has not had a decision-making role; in the totalitarian state, the leadership of the Crisis generation largely determined the course of their lives. Thus, the Transition cohort-group can be characterized as a Reactive, alienated generation. The longevity of the leadership has preempted this generation from achieving the leadership positions it should have occupied as it entered Midlife. Strauss and Howe's model predicts, interestingly, that during their Midlife, leaders of this generation are likely to be pragmatic, but that they will lose influence in their Elder years.

Revolution Cohort-Group

While marked by the many upheavals that characterized the first decades of the Cuban Revolution, the Revolution cohort-group (born between 1963 and 1985) inherited the world created by its elders, with only its older members participating in the "epic struggles" portrayed by the official media. During the 1970s and early 1980s, they were the main beneficiaries of the economic largess of the Soviet Union, growing up under an institutionalized political and economic regime and sheltered by the safety net provided by Cuba's "cradle to grave" social welfare system. This cohort will be Cuba's largest ever since its ranks were swelled by a short-lived baby boom in the years immediately following the Revolution.

Although most members of the Revolution cohort-group were too young to serve in the country's foreign ventures, the most significant defining events for the Revolution cohort included Cuba's long military involvements in Africa, the 1980 Sandinista victory in Nicaragua, the Mariel emigration outflow that same year, and the U.S. invasion of Grenada during President's Reagan Administration. Coming on the heels of the first large-scale authorized émigré visits since Castro had assumed power in 1959, the Mariel incident, a likely social moment for the older members of the cohort-group, was a dramatic demonstration of the impact the visits (by bringing outside perspectives) had on some sectors of Cuba's closed society.

Despite this development, during their childhood and adolescence, the members of the Revolution cohort-group grew up in a relatively stable environment where nothing seemed to challenge the prevailing political order. The complacency of this cohort-group was rudely shaken in 1989 by the trial and execution of General Arnaldo Ochoa, a Hero of the Revolution, Gorbachev's reforms in the Soviet Union, and the eventual collapse of the Socialist world after 1991—dramatic social moments certain to have deeply influenced this cohort-group's worldview.

If the cycle predicted by Strauss and Howe is to recur, the Revolution cohort should assume a Civic role and inspire a Spiritual Reawakening. It is interesting that about half of this generation was growing up as Cuba was entering into the economic and political crisis of the late 1980s, produced by the collapse of the Socialist bloc and the beginning of the endless Special Period. Interestingly too is that members of this generation are the ones displaying more displeasure about the penuries of the system. They appear to be at the forefront of those hoping for change, as reflected in the Balsero outflow, emigra-

tion to other destinations, increasing signs of dissatisfaction (reflected, for example, in high rates of school desertion), and by seeking non-conventional employment options, whether legally or illegally.

Survival Cohort-Group

The same experiences of the Revolution cohort-group, magnified by Cuba's opening to the outside world in the form of Western tourists, should have a major impact on the evolution of the Survival cohort-group (born after 1986) worldview. Many observers have commented, in fact, of a major cleavage between those cohort-groups that embraced the Revolution's values in their youth and their children and grandchildren, many of whom have rejected them (see, for example, Rojas 2002; Collazo 2003; Díaz de Villegas 2003).

IMPLICATIONS FOR CUBA'S FUTURE

Figure 1, following Strauss and Howe, shows the generational diagonal for Cuba's five surviving cohorts at the beginning of the current century. The figure should be read according to the designed grid but following the arrows' direction. By 2015, but perhaps much earlier, most members of the Crisis cohort-group that ruled Cuba for nearly half a century will be quite old or dead, and thus no longer governing the country. On the basis of age alone, their places will be taken over by members of the Transition cohort-group that up to now have been largely relegated to secondary leadership positions due to the political longevity of the revolutionary leadership in power since they were in their late 20s or early 30s.

A tantalizing possibility is that the Transition cohort-group may only rule Cuba briefly, and mostly during a transition period, since by 2015 even their younger members will be approaching retirement age. Carlos Lage, one of Cuba's most visible and influential current politicians, considered by some a relative moderate, even if a Castro loyalist, is one of the better known representatives of this cohort-group. Better educated than their predecessors, and with a less extreme peer personality, members of this cohort-group include many of the technocrats gradually easing Cuba into the global market by managing military-run enterprises and joint ventures with foreign partners.

Figure 1. Cuba's Generational Diagonal in the Twentieth and Early Twenty First Century

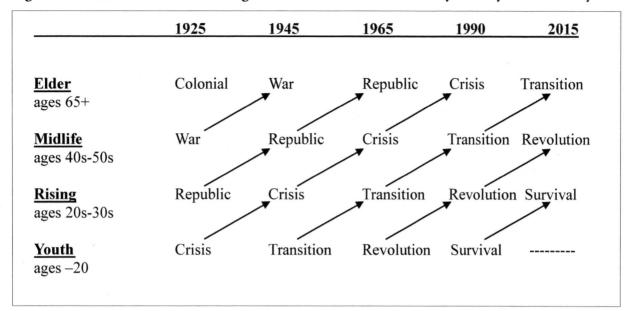

	1925	1945	1965	1990	2015
Elder ages 65+	Colonial	War	Republic	Crisis	Transition
Midlife ages 40s-50s	War	Republic	Crisis	Transition	Revolution
Rising ages 20s-30s	Republic	Crisis	Transition	Revolution	Survival
Youth ages –20	Crisis	Transition	Revolution	Survival	---------

Economic failure and the evaporation of a political world in which they may have once believed, has instilled in members of the Transition cohort-group a healthy dose of skepticism. After a life spent under a state of perpetual political mobilization and having experienced the collapse of the formerly subsidized Cuban economy, this cohort-group lacks the revolutionary zeal that drove so many Crisis cohort-group Cubans during the early decades of Castro's rule. Among members of the Transition cohort-group there appears to be a yearning for more pragmatic and less confrontational policies and a desire to end Cuba's political isolation. They are fed up with the struggles of daily life in Cuba's economy of scarcity and there are indications (suggested, for example, by focus group discussions among recent emigrants, in-depth interviews conducted in the island, the weakening of the totalitarian mass control organizations, and the eruption of illicit activities) that this cohort has already turned away from politics and ideology.

At the peak of their intellectual ability, they were rattled by the major social moment of the Socialist world collapse. For them, economic motivations are likely to take preeminence over politics; on the basis of generational peer personality alone, it can be posited that once Castro's generation is a memory, younger generations, and hence future governments, will be more accommodating, as the Cuban people will be more prone to embrace values contrary to those preached by the leaders of the 1959 Revolution. In all likelihood, they will be receptive to more politically open and tolerant political system and a market economy.

It seems predictable that as the Revolution cohort-group assumes the reins of power in the not too distant future, that the political cycle will turn around full circle. Note was already made of the general disenchantment with radical politics within this generation, but socioeconomic circumstances will also force future Cuban leaders to be more pragmatic and to reach an accommodation, if not close linkages, with the United States. Not least among these is the aging of Cuba's population, as the baby boom cohorts of the 1960s and early 1970s begin to retire in droves. With few workers to support the elderly and still reeling from the economic devastation induced by more than 40 years of economic mismanagement, Cuba's future rulers need to be pragmatic.

This generation will be obsessed with the necessity of finding workable solutions to the nation's problems. Closer trade and economic ties with the United States will advance this goal, a trend likely to be accelerated by the regional thrust toward North American and Caribbean Basin economic integration. Cuba's growing median age will also contribute to the coming conservative wave. Also promoting closer and friendly relations with the United States, once the Castro era is over, will be the Cuban-American community, a natural bridge between the two nations.

CONCLUDING REMARKS

Some elements of the Strauss and Howe model seem to fit quite nicely Cuba's historical experience, even though Cuba can hardly be said to have successfully resolved its secular crises. If past concurrence with the model's predicted phases are a good indicator of things to come, then the model suggests that in the next few years, once the chaos of the transition is sorted out, the nature of Cuban politics will be transformed. This will come about, in part, from the exhaustion of more than four decades of revolutionary politics and associated economic difficulties, and partly from the mortal ideological blow caused by the collapse of the Socialist world, and the impact these developments have had in shaping generational worldviews. Cuba will respond to global challenges just as any other nation. These challenges are making national governments the world over more open and responsive to citizens' concerns.

It appears, as the model predicts, that a process of generational change will be easing this evolution. The differences in formative experiences of Cuba's several cohort-groups over the last century and a half, and particularly during the last 80 years or so, resulted in diverse outlooks and expectations. The proclivities of those coming of age or born since the 1960s—currently in their Rising Adulthood and Midlife life cycle stages that will assume power in Cuba in the next few years—appear to be more consistent with the routine of daily life than with the challenges of revolutionary strife preferred by Fidel Castro and his generational peers.

REFERENCES

Collazo, Enrique. 2003. "Para el día después." *Encuentro en la Red*. 4:534, January 15.

Díaz de Villegas, Néstor. 2003. "Siempre es 10 de Marzo." *Encuentro en la Red*. 4:534, January 15.

Horowitz, Irving Louis and Jaime Suchlicki. 2001. *Cuban Communism*. 10th Edition. New Brunswick: Transaction Publishers.

Rojas, Rafael. 2002. "El postcomunismo y el hombre en Cuba." *Encuentro en la Red*. 3:499, November 22.

Strauss, William and Neil Howe. 1991. *Generations: The History of America's Future*. New York: Quill William Morrow.

LA DISCRIMINACIÓN RACIAL EN EL CAMPO CUBANO

Dominga González Suárez

DINÁMICA DEL CAMBIO EN LA TENENCIA DE LA TIERRA

En un país cuya actividad económica fundamental es la agricultura, resulta necesario estudiar, en la medida de lo posible, como se ha manifestado el prejuicio en las zonas rurales. Una de las más sutiles formas de discriminación racista que se practicó en Cuba contra la población negra del país es el relativo a la casi absoluta imposibilidad de acceder a la propiedad de la tierra por parte de los miembros de esta raza.

En los primeros años de la República existía una norma social informal que consistía en no vender las tierras a los negros o mulatos. Como veremos, esta se cumplía estrictamente.

A través del estudio de la dinámica de la estructura de la tenencia de la tierra veremos como los grupos raciales muestran importantes desigualdades (asimetría), lo que determinará las posiciones que ocuparán cada uno de ellos en el entramado de la estructura social.

Cuadro 1. Distribución Territorial de las Razas (1899)

| Territorio | Total | De ellos | |
		De color	Blanca
Urbano	480 191	160 922	318 967
Rural	1 092 654	359 178	733 478
Cuba	1 572 845	520 400	1 052 445

Fuente: Tabla elaborada por la autora con datos de U.S.A. War Department, *Report on the Census of Cuba, 1899.*

Si analizamos la estructura racial del país por zonas rurales y urbanas, encontramos que en 1899 el 33,1 por ciento del total correspondían a la población de color (negros, mulatos y chinos). La población rural era de 359 178 negros y 733 478 blancos que representaban respectivamente, un 32,9 y un 67,1 por ciento del total. Es muy pequeña la diferencia, en cuanto a estructura racial, de ambos territorios.

Cuadro 2. Distribución de las Razas en Zonas Rurales por Provincias (1899)

| Provincias | Raza | |
	De color	Blanca
Matanzas	64 831	79 299
Pinar del Río	44 492	119 692
Puerto Príncipe	10 533	52 599
Santa Clara	82 297	193 894
Santiago de Cuba	117 001	153 160
Habana	40 024	134 834
Cuba	359 178	733 478

Fuente: U.S.A. War Department, *Report on the Census of Cuba, 1899*, p. 554.

En cuanto a su distribución por provincias, observamos que la de Santiago de Cuba era la que más población de color tenía con un total de 117 001 personas, le seguía Santa Clara con 82 297 y en tercer lugar se encontraba Matanzas con 64.831 (Gráfica No. 1).

Los asentamientos de las futuras migraciones de raza negra incrementarán, como es lógico, esta proporción. Esta será una de las causas por las que aumentará el prejuicio y la discriminación en Cuba. Una de las manifestaciones fundamentales de estas conductas racistas va a tener su base en los cambios ocurridos, a través de más de 30 años, en la propiedad de la tierra.

En 1899 existían un total de 14.339 fincas cuyos propietarios eran personas de color. Estas fincas abar-

Gráfica 1. Distribución Territorial de las Razas

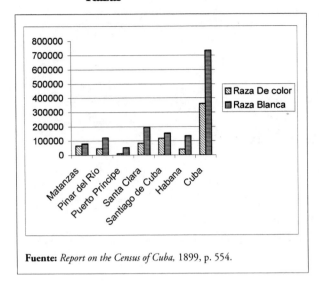

Fuente: *Report on the Census of Cuba*, 1899, p. 554.

caban un total de 2.935,17 caballerías.[1] El tamaño promedio de las fincas era de 0,2 caballerías, correspondiéndole a cada habitante de color de las zonas rurales 0,008 caballerías.

Mientras, había un total de 43.635 fincas de propietarios blancos, con un área total de 23.007,47 caballerías. El tamaño medio de las fincas era de 0,53 caballerías, lo que representaba más del doble que el de los de color. A cada habitante blanco de las zonas rurales le correspondía 0,031 caballerías, que es cuatro veces más que lo correspondiente a los de color.

Dentro de los campesinos pobres, los negros, evidentemente, eran los más pobres. El minifundio no posibilitaba el mantenimiento de los numerosos miembros de la familia. Muchos de ellos, al no encontrar trabajos, tenían que migrar a las ciudades en busca de una forma de ganarse la vida.

A esto hay que añadir que la población negra de las provincias de Camagüey y Oriente aumentó aceleradamente en el primer cuarto de este siglo como consecuencia de las inmigraciones haitianas y jamaicanas. Los negros cubanos que permanecieron en el campo se vieron obligados a compartir el mismo segmento del mercado de trabajo que estos inmigrantes,

quienes, por lo general, eran peor remunerados que los negros nativos.

En el Cuadro 3 podemos observar las formas de usufructo de la tierra según la extensión de las fincas y el color de la piel.

Vemos que el por ciento general de fincas de menos de 1/4 de caballería se elevaba al 63,4% del total. Es interesante observar que en la misma medida que aumenta la extensión de las fincas, disminuye el por ciento de negros y mulatos usufructuarios, hasta llegar a las fincas de tamaño entre 3 y 5 caballerías, segmento en el cual no existían propietarios de color, y solamente el 0,2% de los arrendatarios de color usufructuaban fincas de este tamaño. Nótese también que ningún negro era dueño o usufructuaba fincas mayores de 5 caballerías.

Si analizamos con más detalle la situación de la posesión y usufructo de la tierra por parte de blancos y de color, vemos que en el año 1899 el total de propietarios blancos de fincas menores de ½ caballería ascendía a 34.768, y poseían un área total de 5.512,5 caballerías, por lo que sus fincas tenían un tamaño promedio de 0,159 caballerías. Contrasta con estos números los referidos a la población de color: los propietarios de color de fincas menores de ½ caballería eran 13.120 personas, y poseían un total de 1.803,25 caballerías, por lo que sus fincas tenían un tamaño promedio de 0,05 caballerías, es decir, la tercera parte de las de los blancos.

Tales cifras son una muestra de la extrema inferioridad de los campesinos negros con relación a los campesinos blancos al inicio de la República. Durante estos años esta desigualdad en el reparto de recursos, en un país con una estratificación social racista, fue percibida por el grupo negro como algo natural y aceptado socialmente, por lo que atribuía la responsabilidad de esta desventaja a las características inherentes de su propio grupo.

Las relaciones intergrupales discriminatorias que tuvieron lugar en situaciones de desigualdad y de dominación-dependencia facilitaron, en gran medida, la

---

1. Una caballería es igual a 13,2 hectáreas.

Cuadro 3. Proporción del Tamaño de las Fincas Según Forma de Posesión y Razas (1899)

	Tamaño de finca (caballerías)							
	<0,25	0,25-0,5	0,5-0,75	0,75-1	1-3	3-5	5-10	>10
Propietarios blancos	56,0	20,3	9,2	2,4	7,9	1,6	1,2	1,4
Arrendatarios blancos	60,0	21,1	9,1	2,4	5,6	0,9	0,6	0,3
Propietarios negros	75,6	14,3	6,0	1,0	2,6	0	0	0
Arrendatarios negros	77,0	15,0	5,2	0,8	1,8	0,2	0	0
Ocupación mixta	70,8	16,0	6,0	1,5	3,8	0,8	0,5	0,5
Total	63,4	19,2	8,1	2,1	5,1	0,9	0,7	0,5

Fuente: *Informe sobre el Censo de Cuba, 1899*, p. 557.

Cuadro 4. Comparación de la Distribución de la Tierra por Raza y Tipo de Usufructo en por Ciento (Años 1899 y 1931)

	Propietarios				Arrendatarios			
	1899		1931		1899		1931	
Provincias	Blancos	Negros	Blancos	Negros	Blancos	Negros	Blancos	Negros
Pinar del Río	91,63	8,36	92,3	7,69	89,57	10,42	89,04	10,95
La Habana	97,63	2,26	97,69	2,31	92,38	7,61	95,61	4,38
Matanzas	93,4	6,59	96,22	3,77	80,11	19,88	93,49	6,5
Santa Clara	92,25	7,74	94,48	5,51	78,68	21,31	93,62	6,37
Camagüey	95,59	4,41	96,37	3,52	87,11	13,89	94,14	5,85
Oriente	61,52	38,47	77,46	22,35	54,5	45,49	71,47	28,52
Cuba	81,8	18,19	87,83	12,16	72,55	27,44	88,82	11,17

Fuente: Cuadro elaborado por la autora basado en los datos de los siguientes censos:- *Informe sobre el Censo de Cuba, 1899*, p. 556. *Censo de Población* (1931), Tabla 37.

tendencia hacia el empeoramiento de la situación socioeconómica de los negros y mulatos en el campo cubano, como se desprende de las cifras del Cuadro 3, donde se muestra el régimen de tenencia de la tierra de blancos y negros.

Esta situación fue empeorando año tras año. Durante las tres primeras décadas del siglo XX, como se ve en la Gráfica 2, se produce un empeoramiento en la posición de los negros y mulatos en relación con el usufructo de la tierra.

Es evidente el aumento del número de propietarios blancos mientras que el de los negros disminuye. Este mismo movimiento se produce con los arrendamientos. Los propietarios negros de tierras disminuyeron del 18,19 al 12,16 por ciento, y en esos mismos años los arrendatarios negros descendieron del 27,44 al 11,17 por ciento. En ambas formas de usufructo se refleja un notable deterioro de la situación de los negros y mulatos en la estructura de la propiedad de la tierra.

Es importante observar que este fenómeno es significativo en las provincias orientales, sobre todo en la provincia de Oriente, a pesar de ser la que más población negra tenía en el país.

Cuadro 5. Ritmos de Crecimientos de la Población de Color

	Población de color total del país	% Población de color total del país	Población de color urbana	% Población de color urbana	Población de color rural	% Población de color rural	% Población urbana de color	% Población rural de color
1907	620.602	29,6%	195.158	31,5%	425.410	68,5%	31,9%	29,6%
1943	1.225.271	25,6%	507.775	41,4%	717.684	58,6%	28,8%	23,8%
Ritmo medio anual de crecimiento	1,9%		2,7%		1,5%			

Fuente: Cuadro elaborado por la autora con datos del *Censo de la República de Cuba de 1943*, pp. 733-755.

Cuadro 6. Extensión Media de la Familia de Color

	Jefes de familia de color	Total de personas de color	Tamaño promedio de la familia de color
Urbana	104072	511460	4,91
Rural	125245	713811	5,69
Cuba	229317	1225271	5,34

Fuente: República de Cuba, Censo de 1943, p. 997-1003.

Gráfica 2. Estructura Racial de la Propiedad de la Tierra

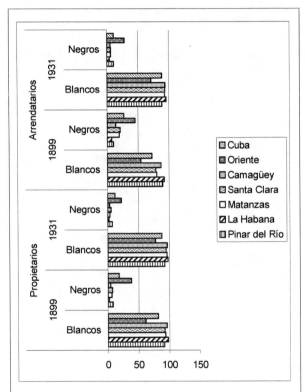

Source: Elaborada por la Autora con datos de los siguientes Censos: E.U.A. Informe sobre el Censo de Cuba, 1899, p.556; Censo de Población (1931), Tabla 37.

LAS MIGRACIONES INTERNAS

Uno de los factores que coadyuvaron a la expropiación de la tierra de los negros y mulatos, fundamentalmente en la región oriental, fue la Orden Militar No.62, o Ley de Deslinde de las Haciendas Comuneras, que tuvo como finalidad darle a la tierra carácter de mercancía, o sea, posibilitar la compra-venta de la misma. En los procedimientos de deslinde, se exigían pruebas de tener participación en los pesos de posesión, forma de propiedad indivisible de carácter feudal, que existían en la región oriental de la isla. Al verse imposibilitados de presentar las pruebas exigidas, numerosos campesinos pobres fueron despojados de sus pequeñas parcelas.

Por otra parte, debemos señalar que esa provincia fue protagonista en 1912, de los conflictos racistas más serios de toda la república: el levantamiento armado de los Independientes de Color, donde fueron asesinados más de 3000 negros y mulatos que eran, en su inmensa mayoría, indefensos campesinos pobres cuyas familias quedaron sin tierras.

El empeoramiento de la situación del grupo negro en lo relativo a la propiedad y usufructo de la tierra deviene en factor de incremento del flujo migratorio de negros y mulatos de las zonas rurales a las urbanas. En correspondencia con esta hipótesis vemos en el Cuadro anterior que mientras que la población negra del país creció, en el período de 1907 a 1943, a una tasa promedio anual del 1,9%, la población urbana de color lo hizo en ese mismo período al 2,7%, y la población negra rural creció, en ese mismo período, a una tasa anual promedio de 1,5%.

Como los factores de crecimiento de la población son dos, el migratorio y el vegetativo, a los fines de demostrar que el crecimiento menor de la población de color rural se debe al primero (es decir, a la migración de esta población hacia zonas urbanas) tomamos el tamaño promedio de las familias de color en las zonas urbanas y en las rurales. En estas últimas, según el Censo de la República de Cuba del año 1943 (ver Cuadro 6), las familias de color tenían, como promedio, una extensión de 5,69 personas, mientras que las de las zonas urbanas[2] las formaban, como promedio, 4,91 personas. Este dato nos indica que el crecimiento vegetativo de la población de color en las zonas rurales es mayor que en las zonas urbanas, sin embargo, el ritmo promedio anual del crecimiento en las zonas urbanas es de 2,7%, mientras que en la rural es de sólo 1,5% por lo que resulta prácticamente incuestio-

---

2. Tomando como criterio de zona urbana a aquellos núcleos de población con más de 5 mil habitantes.

nable que este crecimiento más acelerado de la población de color urbana en relación con la población rural de color es el resultado, en gran medida, del flujo migratorio de este segmento de la población del campo hacia las ciudades.

Al analizar el problema de la mayor concentración de población negra en las zonas urbanas, el propio Censo de 1943 reconoce:

> Esta mayor concentración de la población en las ciudades obedece, probablemente, a varias causas. Por una parte, para las personas que no poseen medios de fortuna o propiedades, el campo ofrece menos posibilidades de desenvolvimiento económico que las ciudades donde las oportunidades de trabajo siempre son mayores. Como la población de color, en sentido general, tiene un nivel económico inferior al de la población blanca, por causas históricas que no es el caso analizar aquí, es probable que esa motivación económica juegue algún papel en la mayor concentración urbana de esa raza (República de Cuba 1945, p.743).

Es harto conocido que una de las principales consecuencias de las migraciones del campo a las ciudades es el surgimiento de los llamados cinturones de miseria en los cuales se concentran dichos flujos y que pasan a engrosar las huestes de marginados sociales. Las migraciones de personas de color del campo cubano a las ciudades no fue una excepción de dicha regla.

LAS MIGRACIONES ANTILLANAS

Otro factor a considerar en el agravamiento del prejuicio y la discriminación hacia la población negra en el campo cubano fue el surgimiento de asentamientos de inmigrantes haitianos, con un idioma y costumbres diferentes, y que eran percibidos como una amenaza por la población autóctona.

Muchas veces la conducta de este grupo de inmigrantes provocaba un profundo malestar entre los guajiros que derivó, a la postre, en conductas discriminatorias. Esta situación repercutió desfavorablemente en el negro cubano puesto que el grupo blanco mayoritario no suele establecer diferenciación étnica entre negros cubanos, haitianos y jamaicanos, como resultado del proceso de homogeneización que se produce durante la comparación con el exogrupo. El rasgo saliente en el exogrupo es la raza (el color de la piel), y

en el proceso de categorización los miembros del grupo mayoritario, automáticamente, acuden al estereotipo racial, por lo que la percepción de las conductas de los antillanos, en muchas ocasiones, ayudaron a empeorar el estereotipo del negro e incrementar el racismo.

Este grupo de individuos era vilmente explotado, pues algunos empresarios no sólo se aprovechaban de su desconocimiento del idioma, de su desarraigo, y también, de su indefensión, para pagarles menos que a los nativos, sino también se aprovechaban de estas desventajas para manipularlos en provecho propio.

En el trabajo de campo de la investigación realizada por la autora en 1986 para la confección del *Atlas Etnográfico de la República de Cuba*, en la provincia de Holguín, en el pueblo de Mayarí, el campesino Rafael Calzadilla, protagonista de la rebelión campesina de esa zona durante la década de 1930, nos relató que cuando la Compañía Hato del Medio S.A. intentó hacer el deslinde de la Hacienda Caballería de Barajagua utilizó a los haitianos.

> La compañía empezó a pasarle desalojos a muchos campesinos. Logró desalojar a algunos como a Enriqueta López y Antolín Torres a quienes les tiraron todas sus cosas para la guardarraya, les tumbaron las casas y a las latas de manteca le metieron cuchillos. Más tarde pasaron a la finca de José (Pepe) Hernández pero allí encontraron un grupo de campesinos que se habían reunido armados con machetes y escopetas para evitar el desalojo. Ellos pelearon contra los guardajurados, los guardias rurales, y contra un grupo de haitianos que la compañía había llevado para que les tumbaran los platanales. La pelea comenzó cuando los campesinos defendían sus plantaciones de los haitianos que venían con la guardia rural. En la riña murieron varios haitianos y varias personas resultaron heridas. En esos años la compañía no pudo realizar más desalojos (González, 1987, p. 54).

En Mayarí, el recuerdo de los haitianos quedó asociado a un tipo de conducta repudiada por los valores morales vigentes en la sociedad.

La transmisión oral de padres a hijos, de este hecho, lamentablemente, reforzaría la imagen negativa del grupo negro. Durante esta investigación pudimos observar que existía entre los guajiros un alto grado de prejuicio racial. Un poco en broma, un poco en serio, muchos me comentaban que cuando veían pasar a un negro por sus tierras, tenían rápidamente que contar a sus gallinas.

En esta misma investigación, cuando me encontraba estudiando el mismo fenómeno, la discriminación del negro en el campo cubano, ahora en la provincia de Camagüey, visité en una zona azucarera dos poblados donde predominaban los haitianos: Macuto I y Macuto II. Para sorpresa mía, me sentí trasladada a principios del siglo XX. Allí nada, o muy poco, había cambiado. Después de dos generaciones, el idioma que hablaban entre ellos era el "patuá" o "creole" (dialecto hablado en Haití derivado del francés). Como manifestación de la conservación de su identidad nacional los haitianos mantenían las prácticas religiosas del Vudú, y cuando los visitaba en sus casas (bohíos) para entrevistarlos, muchos de los ancianos se escondían pensando que era de la policía y había ido allí para repatriarlos.

Vivían aislados, en sus bohíos prácticamente no había muebles, no les llegaba la prensa, el transporte era muy deficitario, y la pobreza era significativamente mayor que en el resto de las poblaciones del campo cubano. El único progreso social que observé fue que los hijos de los llamados "pichones de haitianos" (segunda generación de los inmigrantes asentados en el país) estudiaban (en los momentos en que era obligatoria la enseñanza, primero hasta el sexto y luego hasta el noveno grado) al igual que todos los niños campesinos cubanos.

Los factores psicológicos de defensa del yo y de auto conservación de las agresiones, o pretendidas agresiones del exogrupo, provocaban, a su vez, en los haitianos el etnocentrismo que a la vez los llevaba a su auto-marginación, con el consecuente incremento del racismo. Así, una de las cuestiones psicológicas que obstaculizaba la integración de estas personas, se observa en la reacción de los ancianos donde salieron a relucir los sentimientos de indefensión, de inseguridad, y de desconfianza y recelo hacia miembros del exogrupo.

Con mucha probabilidad, estos sentimientos, desfavorables para el desarrollo de niveles de autoestima

satisfactorios, han sido transmitidos a aquellas personas que han permanecido en esos asentamientos, constituyendo uno de los factores más importante para el estancamiento sociocultural de este grupo, y que a la postre, le ha hecho más difícil el proceso de integración.

Esto no es un fenómeno aislado en las provincias orientales donde existen asentamientos de haitianos. Aquí se puede observar el resultado de una de las prácticas de discriminación más fuerte que puede aplicar el grupo mayoritario blanco: la de ignorar.

La integración de los inmigrantes es un proceso intergrupal de interacción social donde los factores psicológicos individuales juegan un papel de primer orden. Por lo tanto, si una de las partes no ofrece la debida atención a la otra, pudiera ocurrir que el factor reciprocidad dejara de funcionar y esto pudiera redundar en el aislamiento del grupo más desfavorecido.

En las zonas azucareras la discriminación hacia el negro era patente. El testimonio de un antiguo vecino del central Hershey (hoy "Camilo Cienfuegos") en la provincia de La Habana, describe la estratificación racial en el campo cubano: "En el ingenio existían cinco zonas, en una vivían los norteamericanos, a ella era imposible entrar sin el correspondiente pase; en una segunda, habitaban los empleados blancos de confianza; en la tercera, los cubanos blancos de capas humildes, chinos y algunos mestizos; en la cuarta los negros cubanos; y en la quinta los haitianos, situados como la última escala social, a los que se les regulaba la entrada en los almacenes de víveres y en sitios de recreo"(Serviat, 1986, p. 84).

Este tipo de estratificación social establecido sobre bases racistas existía en numerosos centrales azucareros propiedad de norteamericanos. Obviamente, las relaciones intergrupales se desarrollaban en situaciones de desigualdad y de dominación-dependencia lo que posibilitaba a los grupos más poderosos mantener y justificar la discriminación racial. Esto pudo ser visto por los miembros de la sociedad de aquella época como una práctica normal porque como dicen Doland y cols.(1991), "El racista es el individuo normal en una sociedad racista."

En plena crisis económica y política, durante la Primera Conferencia Nacional de Obreros de la Industria Azucarera, celebrada clandestinamente en Santa Clara en los días 26 y 27 de diciembre de 1932, se aprobó un manifiesto que revelaba las condiciones en que se encontraban los trabajadores azucareros, incluidos los negros, haitianos y jamaicanos:

> De zafra en zafra nuestras condiciones de vida y de trabajo se empeoran más y más. En la pasada zafra fueron rebajados los jornales a un nivel de 20, 15 y hasta 10 centavos, para los macheteros y carreteros, por el corte y tiro de cien arrobas de caña, bajo el "componente" (obligarlos a tomar purgante: aceite de resino, si se negaban a trabajar) y "plan de machete" (la guardia rural o el capataz golpeaba con el canto del machete a quienes se rebelaran) nos hicieron trabajar 12, 14 y 16 horas diarias, pagándonos en vales y fichas (que sólo tenían valor en las tiendas del central azucarero); los precios de las tiendas de los centrales fueron altísimos y en muchos casos dejaron de pagarnos los jornales, como en el central "Almeida," cuyo propietario, el banquero y dirigente de la oposición burguesa latifundista Pedroso, explota terriblemente a los obreros; vivimos en barracones inmundos, sin luz, sin aire, llenos de piojos, chinches y pulgas, amontonados como esclavos, con el cuerpo muerto por el trabajo (Instituto de historia del movimiento, 1977, p.307).

Y más adelante se pronunciaron:

> Contra toda discriminación, en el salario y en el trato, a los negros, jamaicanos y haitianos. Salario igual por trabajo igual y derecho a ocupar cualquier empleo, para los negros, jamaicanos y haitianos (Instituto de historia del movimiento, 1977, p.307).

En el campo, los trabajadores negros cubanos, los haitianos y los jamaicanos constituían los núcleos más ferozmente explotados de los trabajadores azucareros, por lo que sus condiciones de vida eran lamentables, y una gran mayoría de los obreros blancos estaba consciente de esta situación.

El Sindicato Nacional de Obreros de la Industria Azucarera (SNOIA), al denunciar la brutal discriminación ejercida por los empresarios hacia esos sectores de trabajadores, exponía lo que creía era el propósito que perseguían las compañías azucareras con estos jornaleros: reducir el costo de producción, y mantener una masa de desempleados que presiona a la baja el precio de la fuerza de trabajo de forma que se deprimieran los salarios y empeoraran las condiciones de vida del trabajador en el campo.

El problema de la discriminación del negro se planteaba desde varios niveles. Entre ellos merece destacar el adoptado por la organización sindical, que se ajustaba a los valores sociales predominantes: igualdad en el acceso a las oportunidades, fraternidad entre los seres humanos, y solidaridad con los más infortunados. En este sentido, el sindicato planteaba, entre sus demandas, lo que consideraba sería la solución del problema de los negros cubanos y de los inmigrantes, exigiendo igualdad de salarios y de trato para negros, jamaicanos y haitianos, también se pronunciaban contra toda discriminación.

El otro nivel no institucional es el de la vida cotidiana, adoptado por los guajiros, muchos de ellos, en esos momentos de aguda crisis, jornaleros agrícolas en tiempo de zafra que compartían el mismo segmento del mercado laboral con negros e inmigrantes, que se ajustaba a la sociedad racista donde vivían.

La complejidad de las relaciones intergrupales e interpersonales se hacía evidente. Se podía ser prejuicioso y a la vez tener buenos amigos negros. Se podía defender los intereses de los negros y mantener la distancia social con el grupo. Se podía ser tolerante y no tener problemas en las relaciones interpersonales. Se podía ser racista y tener problemas con el grupo negro. Infinidad de ejemplos lo encontramos en la vida del pueblo cubano.

Pudimos constatar, cincuenta años más tarde, durante la investigación de campo realizada en 1986, que los diferentes niveles de discriminación concordaban con los diferentes niveles de integración de los grupos minoritarios (negros cubanos, haitianos y jamaicanos) en las zonas rurales.

Utilizando el método etnográfico, donde la observación, y las entrevistas juegan un papel muy importante, se pudo percibir que en la vida material y espiritual existían diferencias sustanciales entre ellos.

El grupo negro cubano estaba completamente integrado a la sociedad, aunque era discriminado, y su vida material—las casas, sus mobiliarios, vestuarios, comidas—eran similares a la de los blancos. La vida espiritual, las costumbres y tradiciones africanas se mezclaban con las cubanas (españolas) como en la música; lo más saliente era el sincretismo religioso (mezcla de la religión católica con la africana) practicado por el grupo.

En relación con los jamaicanos encontramos que vivían en los mismos lugares que los campesinos cubanos y sus niveles de integración eran mayores que el de los haitianos. En las casas que pudimos visitar, se observaba una diferencia sustancial con relación a la de los haitianos. La vida material del grupo: casas, mobiliarios, hábitos alimentarios (utilizaban condimentos no comunes para en el país), el vestuario (dentro de sus posibilidades todos los domingos se vestían elegantemente, con sombreros, para asistir a la iglesia), y los olores, también eran diferentes. Estaban, lógicamente, muy influenciados por la cultura anglosajona.

En la vida espiritual del grupo también se observaban diferencias sustanciales en relación con los haitianos. La religión que practicaban los jamaicanos era la protestante, y siempre, aún los más pobres, eran asiduos asistentes a sus iglesias, que ellos mismos constvruían con los pocos recursos que disponían. Casi todos sabían leer y escribir en su lengua materna, el inglés, y era difícil encontrar una casa donde no hubiera una Biblia.

Era destacable el alto nivel cultural,[3] incluso con relación a la media de los campesinos cubanos, y generalmente, era preocupación de la familia jamaicana proporcionarles estudios a sus hijos, por lo que muchos llegaron a ser profesionales y artesanos. Los hombres se casaban con sus compatriotas o con mujeres cubanas, la mayoría, mulatas.

Otra ventaja de gran importancia que gozaron para el desarrollo positivo de la autoestima, fue que siempre se sintieron protegidos por el Consulado inglés ya que eran considerados súbditos ingleses.

Una muestra de ello ocurrió durante la revuelta política conocida como "la Guerrita de Febrero de 1917" cuando fueron asesinados cobardemente varios jamaicanos. La Legación Británica exigió al gobierno cubano indemnización en metálico por la vida de los súbditos ingleses, y además, que se hiciese un consejo de guerra a los oficiales cubanos acusados de este asesinato (González, 1987).

Esta protección institucional los ayudó a superar, en cierto sentido, la situación de indefensión e inseguridad tan arraigada en los inmigrantes recién llegados, lo que repercutió en la elevación de su autoestima, y esto le posibilitó no percibirse en situación de marcada de inferioridad con relación a la población nativa.

El interés por integrarse a la sociedad y sus ansias de superación, sumado al hecho de haber recibido instrucción, les ayudó a aprender, con cierta facilidad, el idioma español. Por otro lado, el idioma que hablaban al llegar, el inglés, aunque diferente al nativo, también se hablaba en el país como consecuencia de la cercanía geográfica y de las relaciones directas con los Estados Unidos. Este grupo llegó a integrarse a la sociedad cubana.

En esta investigación de campo pudimos observar que el grupo más discriminado, y en donde se practicaba la segregación, era el de los haitianos.

Estos inmigrantes procedían de uno de los países más pobres del mundo, sin instrucción, habituados a vivir en extrema miseria, sus formas de vida eran lamentablemente pobres.

---

3. En las estadísticas publicadas por la Dirección de Estadística de la Secretaría de Hacienda en los folletos anuales titulados *Inmigración y movimiento de pasajeros* quedó reflejada esta superioridad. Al analizar la ocupación declarada por los inmigrantes de Jamaica y Haití durante los años 1916 y 1918 encontramos que en 1916 de un total de 7 133 jamaicanos entrados, el 0,32% eran profesionales, el 10,7% artesanos, y el 80,8% trabajadores agrícolas. En el caso de los haitianos, de los 4 922 llegados al país el 0,02% eran profesionales, el 0,02% artesanos, y un 97,62% trabajadores agrícolas. En el año 1918 los datos eran los siguientes: de un total de 9 184 jamaicanos, el 0,49% eran profesionales, el 26,76% artesanos, y el 66,37% trabajadores agrícolas. Por último, de 10 640 haitianos entrados ese año, el 0,05% eran profesionales, el 0,24% artesanos, y el 98,20% trabajadores agrícolas.

Según nos han relatado testigos de esa época, vivían en caseríos aislados habitados por 20 o 30 personas. Construían sus casas con yaguas y cogollos de caña; sus muebles se limitaban a unos cuantos palos para armar las hamacas, algunas banquetas pequeñas, una mesa y ocasionalmente taburetes.

A veces tenían una o dos mujeres comunes para veinte o más hombres para que los atendieran y satisficieran sus necesidades. Casi nunca se casaban y cuando lo hacían era con sus compatriotas. Excepcionalmente se unían con cubanas.

En la vida espiritual del grupo, lo saliente era la práctica del Vudú. Esta religión de procedencia africana no se mezcló con la católica. Su ritual, celebrado al aire libre, llamaba mucho la atención de los campesinos cubanos. Y, lógicamente, no era bien vista por los demás grupos minoritarios.

Por sus propias limitaciones culturales y socioeconómica, y por los jornales tan bajos que recibían, no podían tener otra preocupación que la de sobrevivir. El interés por integrarse a la sociedad era, por lo tanto, muy poco, dadas las relaciones discriminatorias con el grupo mayoritario.

En resumen, el deterioro de la tenencia de la tierra entre los campesinos negros y mulatos, la pobreza, generada esta última, en gran medida, por la discriminación (ejercida muchas veces a través de normas sociales informales), y agravada por la inmigración masiva de antillanos, fueron los factores básicos para que, gradualmente, el campo cubano fuese despoblándose de negros y mulatos, que migraban a las ciudades en busca de nuevas oportunidades.

BIBLIOGRAFÍA CITADA

Allport, G.W. (1977). *La naturaleza del prejuicio.* Buenos Aires: Eudeba.

Censo de Población (1931). Estadística industrial y agrícola de Cuba, La Habana.

Doland, B., Polley, K., Alle, R., and Norton, K. (1991). "Addressing racism in psychiatry: is the therapeutic model applicable?" *International Journal of Social Psychiatry*, 37 (2), pp. 71-91.

González Suárez, D. (1987). "La inmigración antillana en Cuba." *Economía y desarrollo*, 100, pp. 51-61.

González Suárez, D. (1988). "La inmigración negra y la situación socioeconómica de negros y mulatos en el campo." *Economía y Desarrollo*, 88, 3, pp. 104-115.

Ibarra, Jorge (1994). *Un análisis psicosocial del cubano:1898-1925.* La Habana: Editorial Ciencias Sociales.

Instituto de Historia del Movimiento Comunista y la Revolución Socialista (1977). *El movimiento obrero cubano. Documentos y artículos.* La Habana: Ciencias Sociales.

República de Cuba (1945). *Informe general del censo del año 1943.* La Habana: P. Fernández y Cia.

Secretaría de Hacienda (1916 y 1918). *Inmigración y movimiento de pasajeros.* La Habana: Rambla y Bouza.

Serviat, Pedro (1986). *El problema negro en Cuba y su solución definitiva.* La Habana: Editora Política.

USA War Department (1900). *Census of Cuba. Report of the Census of Cuba 1899.* Washington: Government Printing Office.

SANTIAGO VS. HAVANA: CUBA'S UNDERGROUND ECONOMY IN COMPARATIVE PERSPECTIVE

Ted Henken

El socialismo además de justicia, es eficiencia y es calidad.[1]

This celebratory motto can be found plastered on the walls and storefront windows in dollar-enterprises all across today's Cuba. Whether in retail dollar-stores, cafes and restaurants that cater to a dollar-paying clientele, or in the many newly-built or renovated tourist hotels, the declaration is intended to reassure foreigners and nationals alike that Cuba's development of tourism and acceptance of the *yanqui* dollar as legal tender do not contradict its presumably "irrevocable" socialist character. In fact, it would seem that socialism is just a synonym for "better business practices." However, the above motto takes on a surreal aspect given the fact that both *eficiencia* and *calidad*, not to mention *justicia* and even *socialismo* itself are in surprisingly short supply in the country today.

Of course, declaring over and over again that socialism equals justice, efficiency, and quality does not bring these laudable goals spontaneously into existence, despite the old totalitarian claim that a lie repeated often enough becomes the truth. Thus, in spite of trumpeted claims about the increasing health and wealth of Cuban socialism (especially during the recent 50th anniversary celebrations of the Moncada attack on July 26, 2003), Cuba's emperor continues

to wear a tattered cloak. What's more, given the depth and breath of Cuba's underground economy, perhaps it would be more appropriate to declare: "*El socio-lismo además de justo, es eficiente, inteligente y rentable.*"[2]

This paper focuses on the current state of Cuba's underground economy. In previous work, I have analyzed the origin and development of Cuba's underground economy over the last decade, with a focus on Cuba's experiments with self-employment (*trabajo por cuenta propia*) in the housing, transportation, and food service sectors. Here, I update my previous findings from Havana by giving attention to the current state of the city's *paladares* (private restaurants) and comparing them with new research carried out on these speak-easy eateries in Santiago, Cuba's second city.

In July, 2003, while in Santiago de Cuba for Carnival, a motley group of 12 Americans, including myself, caught three cabs into the city center in search of *La Azotea Tropical*, a clandestine *paladar*. Given the confusion of the carnival streets and because the address of the place was not public knowledge, we managed to get separated from the group and searched in vain for the restaurant for more than half-an-hour. Finally, we decided to give up on the quirky and un-

---

1. "Socialism, in addition to justice, is efficiency and is quality."

2. "Socio-lism, in addition to just, is efficient, intelligent, and profitable." In Cuban Spanish, the term "socio" is often used to refer to a close friend or associate. The term *socio-lismo* is a playful combination of "socio" with "*socialismo*." Fernández (2000: 53, 110) has defined *socio-lismo* as, "the system of access to goods and social standing based on who you know and who you love."

reliable private sector and eat at the large, state-run Casa Granda hotel on the central Plaza de Céspedes.

As we were about to go in, however, we were approached on the sidewalk by a pair of street hustlers who quietly dropped the name *La Azotea Tropical* before we could rebuff them. With our sense of adventure still intact, we decided to follow these two well-dressed, Afro-Cuban touts down a side street to the elusive *paladar*.

Having trouble keeping pace with our young guides, I asked them to slow down. However, one of the pair indicated with deft body language that we should keep our distance since a police officer on the corner had taken note of us. We soon found ourselves ushered through a doorway and up a steep, extremely narrow flight of stairs. Before we could catch our breath, we were then pushed out onto what turned out to be one of three elegant rooftop dining areas complete with six tables, over 25 chairs, and a well-dressed English-speaking waiter armed with silverware, menus, and a healthy sense of humor.

William, our enterprising waiter, apologized for the manner in which we were welcomed to *La Azotea*. "I know it seems like drug trafficking," he said with a smile, informing us that the rest of our party had arrived earlier, but were unceremoniously turned away since they had arrived in the midst of a surprise visit from the police. Luckily, the police did not actually go upstairs, but if they had, they would have found a group of nearly 30 French tourists crouching in the darkness, ready to hurry out the back through a secret escape door. "We had to turn off all the lights and music," said William. "But the cops just wanted to scare the owner into paying higher bribes. If they really want to get rid of us, it would be easy for them to do it. However, it is getting worse. It started with threats, then came the bribes, now it is just plain blackmail."

As I began to translate the Spanish menu to my American companions, William's eyes lit up. Hearing, "sparkling water, root vegetables, shredded pork, etc.," he quickly pulled up a chair and began taking notes, asking me to spell each translation and repeat its proper pronunciation. Despite the fact that few of

their guests are American, English is the language of international business and he was eager to improve his skills. He explained that he had originally started as a part-time waiter during the holidays from his state job as an elementary English teacher in the Sierra Maestra mountains nearby.

However, when he realized that he could earn the equivalent of his $12 monthly teaching salary in less than a week as a waiter, he quit his teaching position and began working full-time at *La Azotea*. "The thing is that the restaurant pays real money. I can be sure of making at least $2 each night. That's $2 today and $2 tomorrow, and with $2, I can eat."

Beyond the personal benefits that William sees from his position at the restaurant, he indicated that if given the chance he would make major reforms in the laws that severely restrict private enterprise. However, he does not have much hope that the government will voluntary choose more reforms. "The government knows that when you have money, you have time. It fears those who have money, because they will try to change the system. This is why it always tries to finish you [off] before you finish [off] the system."

LESSONS

What lessons about the future prospects for Cuba's small private sector can be drawn from this illustrative experience? First, the anecdote indicates that the costs of informality are high. For example, while no *paladar* is allowed to advertise, clandestine ones are especially vulnerable given the fact that the more well-known they become among potential clientele, the more likely it is that their unlawful operation will be detected by authorities—bringing on more and higher bribes, blackmail, or outright closure.

Second, all manner of illegalities, low-level corruption, and bribery are commonplace within the private, self-employed sector.

Third, despite its clandestine character, these operations provide employment and a substantial dollar income to a fairly wide range of people who would otherwise be employed in low-paying state jobs. For example, this operation employed three waiters, one bartender, two cooks, two doormen, at least two street hustlers, an *almacenero* (shopper), and the owner: a total of twelve people, not counting others employed through backward linkages and supply chains.

Fourth, while some operations, such as *La Azotea Tropical*, have become lucrative, long-established, and relatively advanced in terms of infrastructure, these private businesses are fundamentally unstable given the fact that much of their success is based on a tenuous, shifting, and often unreliable relationship with inspectors and police.

UNDERGROUND SANTIAGO

When compared with Havana's extensive self-employed sector, the private sector and underground economy are much less developed in Santiago. This is due first of all to the relative small size of the city's population (600,000 vs. 2.2 million) and the much less developed tourism infrastructure. Furthermore, given the fact that Santiago's housing and automobile stock is quite modest compared to that of Havana, there is much less space for potential entrepreneurs to operate.

While private lodging seems relatively inexpensive and ubiquitous, Santiago's stock of private restaurants has suffered from a series of crackdowns in recent years. For example, on a visit to the city over two years ago in March, 2001, I had to visit four *paladares* before finding one that was still in business.

During my more recent visit in July 2003, I conducted interviews with waiters from two different *paladares* (one legal, the other clandestine). Both agreed that while there had been as many as 115 legal operations in 1996, there were now only two legal ones remaining. Furthermore, while both the legal and the many clandestine operations seemed to flout the 12-chair limitation, the legal operations were more careful about following laws concerning menu limitations, the origin of foodstuffs, and family employees. The waiter at the legal *paladar* shared that his restaurant paid $675 each month in licensing fees.

PRIVATE FOOD SERVICE, LODGING AND TRANSPORTATION

In Santiago and Havana alike, the three areas of self-employment that are the most numerous and lucra-tive of all legal occupations are food-service, lodging, and transportation. Private services have proliferated in these areas first of all because it is precisely the constant demand for food, housing, and transportation that the state has been unable to meet since the start of the special period. They have also concentrated in these areas due to the fact that all three occupations provide their services in both the domestic peso market (mainly for Cubans) and the international dollar market (mainly for foreign tourists), even if they are not always licensed to operate in both currencies.

It is my contention that the differences in the government's approach toward each of these activities is largely determined by whether they constitute a competitive or complementary force vis-à-vis state services. In other words, as long as private operators provide niche services to their fellow Cubans and avoid challenging the state monopoly in the tourist market, they will be tolerated. Therefore, the harsh repression against *paladares* can be explained by the fact that they compete directly with state restaurants.

The relative tolerance toward private lodging operations is understandable given that a majority of them, much like private cabbies, provide necessary services to their fellow Cubans. Furthermore, allowing for the proliferation of private rentals may be the government's way of permitting cross-cultural sexual encounters to take place in private, while simultaneously cracking down against such activities in its more public hotels.

However, this tolerance seems to be coming to an end. Preliminary reports in August 2003, indicate that a new Housing Law (which regulates private rentals) has been approved and will take effect in January 2004. Changes to the current law include: an increase in monthly tax rates, extra charges imposed for the common areas used by house-guests, a limit of two rooms to be legally rented, requiring all renters to pay an extra 30% for the right to offer food service to guests, revoking the right to rent out an entire apartment, and requiring that someone must always be home.

Furthermore, it is not just the Cuban state that is behind this new law. While the state has always had an antagonistic relationship with the private sector, it seems that investors in foreign hotel chains who see private home rentals (*casas particulares*) as unfair and unwanted competition have lobbied insistently. By making deals with the state they can secure a monopoly over the hotel industry and have the state make laws that will effectively enforce that monopoly. Such an odd example of communist and capitalist bedfellows indicates one of the possible lamentable paths future Cuban development could take.

An antagonistic dynamism characterizes the peculiar relationships that sometimes form among operators in these three different sectors. On the one hand, the relationship is mutually beneficial with private cabbies acting as unofficial recruiters of new customers for *paladares* and bed and breakfasts. In turn, operators of these businesses will sometimes call on their cabbie associates when their clients need transportation. In these cases, the unwritten rule is for *paladares* and bed and breakfasts to provide a $5 commission. These commissions can quickly add up to a significant portion of the revenue earned on meals that rarely cost more than $15.

As a result of these rising costs, many operators have attempted to avoid using and paying the referring middlemen, relying solely on their established clientele. However, given the legal prohibition against most kinds of advertising, combined with the rising fixed minimum monthly taxes (that must be paid regardless of revenue), few *paladares* or home-stays can survive without the informal advertising and recruitment services provided by cabbies and other middlemen. Only the few well-known (and sometimes well-connected and well-protected) *paladares* and bed and breakfasts can survive without resorting to middlemen, further distancing these "untouchable" operations from their more modest and numerous counterparts in the private food service and housing sector.

THE COSTS OF INFORMALITY

As in much of the Third World and in many former communist countries, in Cuba there are many hidden costs (for both the individual and society) associ-

ated with the existence of an extensive "extralegal" (informal) sector. For example, underground enterprises waste many resources in their efforts to hide their activities from authorities. As a result, they lose income, produce fewer goods and services, and employ fewer people. Most of the self-employed are forced to operate in a small scale and often find that they end up paying more in bribes and commissions than what they would normally pay in taxes.

Furthermore, the extreme restrictions placed on their size and access to resources force most microenterprises to rely heavily on unskilled labor, low-technology production, and unreliable black market inputs. Moreover, with limited legal protection, they have little incentive to invest and can easily lose the small amount they have already invested through closure and/or confiscation of goods and equipment. Finally, Cuba's archaic housing laws deny most owners the right to transfer investments and or ownership to others, further discouraging investment in one's business. Thus, the "costs of informality" include declining productivity, reduced investment, and limits on technical progress (De Soto 1989).

Similarly, the government wastes its own precious resources in its increasing attempts at patrolling and inspecting the self-employed sector. As is abundantly clear from the articles in the official press, Cuban officials have consistently attempted, as Peruvian economist Hernando de Soto has put it, to "blame legislative failures not on bad laws but on inadequate enforcement" (De Soto 2000: 100). However, official law makes no sense if a sizable part of the population lives outside it. Furthermore, the "lawlessness" that is commonly denounced in the official Cuban media is not so much about crime, as it is a clash between rules made at the top and the survival strategies developed by those condemned to live without open protest by those rules, while they must maneuver around them, in silence, to keep their businesses up and running (De Soto 2000: 105-108).

Cubans commonly complain that they have attempted to "formalize" their businesses but have found legalization too costly or they discovered that new self-employed licenses are simply unavailable. However, as De Soto puts it, "most people do not resort to the extralegal sector because it is a tax haven but because existing law, however elegantly written, does not address their needs or aspirations" (De Soto 2000: 154). Therefore, it is an error to see clandestine work as motivated by a desire to avoid taxes. The government may achieve more success in eradicating the informal sector if its goal were making the costs of operating formally/legally lower than those associated with remaining underground. In the end, the fact is that the self-employed, microenterprise sector is taxed both inside (legal) and outside (clandestine) the legal enterprise system. The real question that must be confronted by Cuban policy-makers is: What is the relative cost of being legal?

In its current state, Cuba's self-employed, microenterprise sector suffers from what Cuban sociologist Fernández Peláez (2000) has called a "key problem of dysfunctionality": this nascent private business sector remains disarticulated from the larger restructuring of the Cuban economy. In other words, the existing regulatory and tributary framework for the private sector treats self-employed workers as second-class citizens, refusing to integrate them and their informal survival strategies into a coherent recovery plan for the Cuban economy. Though the Cuban state has by no means declared its intention to embrace capitalism, De Soto has rightly called the kind of restrictive policies in place in Cuba, "capitalist apartheid" (2000).

Intentionally or not, antagonistic state policies turn Cuba's experiments with capitalism into a "private club" for the government and its foreign partners, leaving the great majority of private capital "dead" in the hands of its holders who are in turn excluded from any legal participation in the national economy. The possibility that these small-scale, private enterprises could be a source of jobs and an aid in the provision of goods and services for both the island's population and the still-growing tourism sector is largely ignored by the Cuban leadership. As a result, local communities are denied a direct, participatory role in economic recovery.

CONCLUSION

In summary, we can draw six basic conclusions from this update and comparison of the underground economy in Cuba's two largest cities, Havana and Santiago.

First, despite an enormous difference in the size, development, and general reach of the underground sectors in the two cities, the underlying structural basis for its existence and persistence is the same in both places. In other words, the differences in the manifestation of informality between the two cities are more a matter of degree than of kind. In Cuba, the underground economy exists as an oppositional survival strategy in the face of the extensive restrictions, inefficiencies, and overall scarcity that characterize the state socialist economy.

Second, the state has been successful at lowering its prices and generally increasing the quality and number of services in its tourism infrastructure. As a result, many private operations are no longer a bargain vis-à-vis state offerings. This is especially the case in the food service and transportation areas. For example, the state has deployed a new fleet of state taxis, "Lada panataxis," and has cashed in on foreigners' fascination with classic American cars by transforming these normally 10-peso taxis into convertible state-dollar taxis.

Third, there is a pronounced polarization in the offerings of the second economy. In other words, the big fish have grown bigger, stronger, faster, and more competitive while smaller fish have died off or been eaten. A small number of very successful and presumably well-connected *paladares* thrive, while most others barely survive. Examples of the strategies utilized by some of the most successful operations include: having websites and e-mail addresses for information and reservations, making underground agreements with large tour groups, making major investments and infrastructure renovations, having a diversity of offerings in services and menu, combining with room rental, employing an army of workers, and using two sets of menus based on commissions.

Within Cuba, there is a debate over true nature of many of these very successful *paladares*. Some believe that they are private only in name, having been secretly taken over by state security (in part to gain profits, in part to spy, and in part to find out how these operations work). Others simply reason that the few very successful operations that openly violate the law with impunity have made semi-official accommodations (commissions and profit sharing in exchange for protection and public relations) with state food service providers and tour operators (beyond low-level corruption) to formalized (if secret) agreements with Palmares, the state-run food service enterprise. Others contend that their success derives from their ability to corrupt low-level police officers and inspectors. Still others argue that they survive due to economies of scale and entrepreneurial skills.

Fourth, most private sector operations (legal and underground) continue to exhibit an amazing inventiveness in the face of harsh laws, repression, and economic conditions. For example, many *paladares* have transformed themselves into bed and breakfasts (B&Bs) in order to avoid harsher requirements. However, the state is not far behind in its efforts at imposing new and harsher regulations on Cuba's B&Bs.

Fifth, many young people continue to be attracted to informal employment as hustlers as the only feasible way to make ends meet. Young people can be found lounging on street corners at all times of the day and night and concentrating around the exits to tourist hotels. There seems to be little incentive for them to work in a state job since they can earn much more as tourist hustlers. As one hustler exclaimed to me, "The only thing left here for us is contraband tobacco, *paladares*, and gypsy cabs."

Thus, there is an antagonistic dynamism that characterizes relations between some private operations and these street hustlers. On the one hand, many licensed operations must rely on hustlers since they cannot legally advertise. Also, clandestine operations must rely on hustlers as their only means of public relations. Thus, there is a very well developed (if informal) system of commissions. On the other hand, there is a group of *paladares* that totally refuse to pay commissions and have thus alienated many hustlers who will lie to potential guests telling them that the food is bad and/or expensive, or that the *paladar* is closed or has moved to another place. There are also *paladares* that willingly pay commissions but do so only to selected individuals, wanting to avoid the random street hustler.

Sixth and finally, the informal, underground economy has thoroughly penetrated virtually every area of the official, state economy. By and large, Cubans do not go to work in state jobs out of a sense of revolutionary obligation or loyalty (*conciencia*, or moral incentives), and much less for any material incentives. They work in state jobs because such a job provides them with access to state goods that can be "liberated" and resold on the black market.

For example, a routine visit to the state-run Corona cigar factory ends with two visits to the "company store." The first has low, black market prices, is located in a back room, and the profits go directly to the workers, while the second is in the air-conditioned *Habanos* outlet which provides cigars in boxes at market prices with the lion's share of the profits going to the state. While this kind of small-scale, systematic criminality is probably best seen as a form of resistance to the Cuban state's economic "embargo" against the Cuban people, it poses many difficult dilemmas for the building of any kind of transparent, civil society in Cuba in the future.

BIBLIOGRAPHY

De Soto, Hernando. *The Other Path*. New York: Harper and Row. 1989.

De Soto, Hernando. *The Mystery of Capital*. New York: Basic Books. 2000.

Fernández, Damián. *Cuba and the Politics of Passion*. Austin: University of Texas Press. 2000.

Fernández Peláez, Neili. *Trabajo por cuenta propia en Cuba*. Senior Thesis in Sociology, University of Havana. 2000.

FRANCISCO FRANCO AND FIDEL CASTRO: LOYALIST VS. REVOLUTIONARY? A PRELIMINARY EXPLORATION

Alfred G. Cuzán

In *Loyalists & Revolutionaries: Political Leaders Compared*, Mostafa Rejai and Kay Phillips develop and test a two-stage model of leadership.[1] According to Rejai and Phillips, individual psychology, acquired skills, and situational or environmental characteristics converge and interact in the making of leaders and, at the same time, channel them into either of two opposing paths at a time of political crisis. One is that of the loyalist, or defender of the status quo; the other is that of the revolutionary, or agent in the violent overthrow of the reigning regime.

This paper relies on Rejai and Phillips' framework in an effort to understand two Spanish-speaking dictators separated by a generation in time and the Atlantic Ocean in space but whose reigns in power overlapped: Francisco Franco and Fidel Castro. Selected facts from the biographies of these men (Preston 1994; Quirk 1993) will be analyzed in order to evaluate Rejai and Phillips' hypotheses about political leadership on as many variables as information has been collected, as well as to give a tentative answer to the question posed in the title of this paper.[2]

LOYALIST VS. REVOLUTIONARY: HYPOTHESES AND FINDINGS

Drawing from the existing literature and their own previous work, Rejai and Phillips started with a set of hypotheses about leadership and about differences between loyalists and revolutionaries. Most of the hypotheses did not withstand encounter with data obtained from a "a nonrandom purposive sample" of 100 political leaders representing several continents and three centuries (Rejai and Phillips 1988: xxi). Nevertheless, in this paper *all* their initial hypotheses will be evaluated in light of the evidence available on Franco and Castro. In this section, the original hypotheses are laid out; in the following section the hypotheses are applied to the study of Franco and Castro, with special attention paid to those that survived Rejai and Phillips' quantitative tests.

Although noting that "leadership is a timeless and universal phenomenon, and that all societies at all times have leaders," Rejai and Phillips never define political leadership explicitly. Instead, they say that "wherever we use 'leaders,' 'leadership' or 'political leadership' we refer only to the two populations of loyalists and revolutionaries we have studied" (Rejai and Phillips 1988: xxi). However, the authors convey an implicit understanding of the term, made manifest in the following sentences: "[L]eaders are in a position to internalize, articulate, and respond to the needs, wishes, desires, and aspirations of their people. Failure to maintain vital ties with the followers will

---

1. Many thanks to Professors Rejai and Philips and to Carlos Alberto Montaner for their kind words and encouragement on an earlier draft.

2. I have found no systematic, comprehensive comparisons of Francisco Franco and Fidel Castro, although Montaner (2002) draws several important parallels between the two *caudillos* in an essay on the politics of 20th century Cuba and Spain. Anyone who knows of other studies matching the two rulers is hereby asked to call it to the author's attention at acuzan@uwf.edu.

impede or block reaching high office…" "Situations of crises—whether political, military, social, economic, or psychological—catapult the leaders into prominence and provide them with ready and willing groups of followers" (Rejai and Phillips 1988: 9-10). Thus, for the purpose of this paper, where the subject of study are two men who conquered the pinnacle of power at a time of crisis, becoming absolute dictators for life, political leadership is understood to mean the exercise of control over the population of a country, made possible by the acquisition of a following of loyal supporters, be they elite or mass or a combination thereof.

Rejai and Phillips do define the two types of leaders they study, those who occupy opposing positions at a time of political crisis brought about by, among other things, such events as "coups d'etat, riots or rebellions, mass violence and civil strife" (Rejai and Phillips 1988: 10). One is the "revolutionary," "a person who risks his life by playing a prominent, active, and continuing role throughout the revolutionary process." By revolution is meant "the mass violent overthrow of a political regime in the interest of broad societal change." The other leadership type is the "loyalist," "the counterpart of a revolutionary in a key political (elective) or governmental (appointive) position" (Rejai and Phillips 1988: xiv). Juxtaposing the two leaders: "Loyalists extol the established order; revolutionaries denounce it, articulating an alternative vision embodying, in their view, a superior (perhaps even utopian) society" (Rejai and Phillips 1988: 12).

Be it noted that the characterization of loyalist or revolutionary is applicable only to the individual's behavior leading up to "a revolutionary *power seizure* or a loyalist's *assuming highest office*," not what he does afterward (Rejai and Phillips 1988: xvi). Also, it is possible for a loyalist to turn revolutionary and vice-versa. Rejai and Phillips cite the example of Fidel Castro himself: Loyalists-turned-revolutionaries participate in the legal political processes of their societies, find the system unresponsive, and turn to revolutionary politics. In other words, had it not been for the unresponsiveness of the system, these men might have become members of the establishment elite. To

use a single illustration, Castro was an active candidate in the Cuban parliamentary elections of 1952, when Batista's coup suspended the constitution and halted the electoral process, catapulting Castro toward a revolutionary course (Rejai and Phillips 1988: xix).

Three constellations of factors are hypothesized to converge in the making of a political leader. One is situational, operating at either or both the social and individual level. The political crisis that creates opportunities for leadership operates at the national or historical level. At the individual or family level are found "personal traits or characteristics that are 'external' to political leaders and over which they have, as individuals, no control. These include: birthplace, number of siblings, age ranking among siblings, ethnicity, and religious background" (Rejai and Phillips 1988: 10). Rejai and Phillips hypothesize that political leaders who emerge at a moment of national crisis are disproportionately to be found among men exhibiting the following characteristics: a first, only, or youngest son, born into a middle- or upper-class family belonging to the society's mainstream ethnic and religious group, who experienced city life from an early age.

Rejai and Phillips expected two other sets of factors to go into the making of a leader. One, applicable to both types, involves the individual's "mental set or psychology that propels him toward political action." Although they did not anticipate an "invariant mix of psychological dynamics [to be] universally applicable," Rejai and Phillips proposed a number of motivations. These included characteristics deep within the individual's psyche, such as vanity, egotism, and narcissism: "A degree of vanity appears to be an indispensable condition of rising to leadership roles." An oedipus complex, or father-son conflict, was expected to play a part, too. So was a feeling of deprivation, of "discrepancy between aspiration and achievement," and an awareness of "status inconsistency," or of marginalization. These internal conflicts were supposed to be particularly acute in the case of revolutionaries, driving them to displace their personal dramas onto the larger political stage. Less self-centered motivations include nationalism and patriotism, which were expected to characterize both types of leaders. Additionally, revolutionaries were assumed to be motivated by a sense of justice to "right the wrongs" of their societies, while loyalists to be driven more by an interest in "'national development' or 'modernization'" (Rejai and Phillips 1988: 11-12).

The final set of factors going into the making of a political leader was hypothesized to be "a set of skills—particularly verbal and organizational—that enables him to perform his tasks." Both loyalists and revolutionaries have to communicate a compelling vision to their followers, to the larger society, and even to foreign audiences. Also, they have "to fashion organizations of various kinds—political, military, and paramilitary. Loyalists, needless to say, by definition control the organizations of their societies. Revolutionaries, on the other hand, must build organizations from the ground up." "Without organization, there can be no leadership, whether of a loyalist or revolutionary nature" (Rejai and Phillips 1988: 12).

Rejai and Phillips found that statistical analysis of their "sample" of loyalists and revolutionaries yielded more socio-economic similarities than differences. Typically, a political leader, whether loyalist or revolutionary, was the only, first, or last son of a legally married couple belonging to the mainstream ethnic and religious group of the country. He was born in a city or gained urban exposure early in life, had a "tranquil, peaceful" family life, was exposed to politics no later than in his teens, was "highly educated, frequently at exclusive schools," traveled widely, was a published author, and had a "dualistic" attitude toward the international community, "distinguishing friends and foes" (Rejai and Phillips 1988: 18).

The differences that turned up between loyalists and revolutionaries were "largely situational in nature," having to do with differential access to political power (Rejai and Phillips 1988: 33). Specifically, they had to do with the father's occupation and, relatedly, age at which the leader "developed ideological orientations" and engaged in political activity. Many a loyalist was groomed for a career in government since childhood, learning about politics at his father's knee, who himself was a government official. In other cases the father's occupation was "the military,

banking or industry, the professions, the landed gentry" (Rejai and Phillips 1988: 40). In other words, loyalists were members of their country's establishment. Revolutionaries, on the other hand, were by and large outsiders who forced their way into power at a moment of crisis. As Rejai and Phillips put it:

> In short, we have, on the one hand, a group of men that begins very early to set the stage, stage, to prepare the way, and construct the building blocks of the political roles they come to play in later life: they are loyalist leaders who are, by and large, *career* oriented. On the other hand, we have a group that bursts upon the scene to claim political roles for which they have no particular preparation: they are revolutionary leaders who are propelled, by and large, by *crisis* situations. Returning to our idea of differential access, loyalist or career leaders grow to adulthood and maturity in close proximity to sources of power and prestige in societies. Lacking such proximity, revolutionary or crisis leaders spend their lives in pursuit of access to influence and authority, seizing upon such opportunities as may come their way (Rejai and Phillips 1988: 36).

Two other sets of differences discriminated between loyalists and revolutionaries, all having to do with the leader himself. One had to do with attitudes, the other with his occupation and age at which he reached the highest office. "A significant number of loyalists are likely to have careers in government service while not a single revolutionary had such an occupation as his *primary* line of activity. Loyalists tend to be older when assuming highest office; revolutionaries are younger at the time of power seizure" (Rejai and Phillips 1988: 40). Regarding attitudes, loyalists usually remained steadfast in their religious beliefs while revolutionaries frequently abandoned them, becoming atheists; loyalists were usually pessimistic about human nature but optimistic about their country, whereas revolutionaries were more sanguine about human nature but their feelings about their country were contingent "on the regime in power" (Rejai and Phillips 1988: 40).

Reviewing the variables that allowed them to discriminate between loyalists and revolutionaries, Rejai and Phillips summarize their findings thus:

[I]f a leader remains steadfast in religious beliefs, if his father is a government official or in such other occupations as the military, banking and industry, the professions, or landed gentry; if the leader himself is in government service; if he holds a pessimistic view of human nature but a uniformly optimistic view of his own country—under this set of circumstances, the leader is likely to become a loyalist rather than a revolutionary. By contrast, if a leader abandons his religion to become an atheist, if his father has an occupation not included above, if the leader is not in government service, if he has an optimistic view of human nature but a fluctuating attitude toward his own country depending on the regime in power—under this set of circumstances the leader is likely to become a revolutionary rather than a loyalist. (Father's occupation as government official and religious orientation, it will be recalled, have the greatest predictive value.) Once again, in other words, access to political power becomes the cutting edge separating the loyalists from the revolutionaries (Rejai and Phillips 1988: 109-110).

FRANCO AND CASTRO: LOYALIST VS. REVOLUTIONARY?

Tables 1-3 present evidence on Francisco Franco and Fidel Castro on all the traits that Rejai and Phillips considered, whether or not they passed their empirical tests or turned up as "critical" variables in predicting leadership or leadership type. Starting with the first table, which collects leadership traits considered by Rejai and Phillips, be it noted that both dictators unambiguously exhibit most of the seven "critical" characteristics of a leader, 86 percent in Franco's case and 71 percent in Castro's. The one exception they share is birth order, as neither was the only or first or last son.

The other miss in Castro's case has to do with his class background, which is ambiguous. His father, Angel Castro, was a Spanish immigrant from Galicia (Franco's own region). A former laborer, he was rich but uncouth. Lina, his mother, was once a maid in Angel's household. Castro himself was born out of wedlock, the issue of an illicit union between Angel and Lina. After his first wife died Castro's father married the mother. Lacking social respectability, the Castro's were hardly middle-, let alone upper-class. Thus, Castro came from a *nouveau riche* family not

easily classified. Recall that awareness of "status inconsistency" or "marginalization" is one of the variables initially considered by Rejai and Phillips as providing a motivation to make a bid for political leadership, although the evidence on the 100 leaders they studied did not support their expectation. However, in Castro's case this characteristic may have played a part in his political ambition not only to make himself a leader but to revolutionize Cuban society "from one end to the other," as he wrote from prison he "would sincerely love" to do (Quirk 1993: 66).

Regarding other traits, both Franco and Castro belong to the country's mainstream ethnic group and (in the case of Castro, at least initially) the mainstream religion; both acquired exposure to city life early on, and both were patriotic and nationalistic. Additionally, in contrast to Franco (who before seizing power had been out of Spain only once, on a brief visit to Germany for professional reasons), Castro traveled and resided abroad as a young man (Colombia, the United States, Mexico), was educated in exclusive schools, and had early involvement in national politics in Havana, the country's capital. All in all, out of a total of 17 leadership traits considered in Table 1, Franco unambiguously exhibits 12 (71 percent) and Castro 14 (82 percent).

Table 2 compares Franco and Castro on the traits typical of a loyalist. At a time of national crisis, a political leader exhibiting these characteristics is more likely than not to be found manning the barricades in defense of the status quo. Conversely, a leader lacking in these traits would in all probability be observed storming those same barricades in a revolution. Note that the only loyalist attribute that Castro unambiguously exhibits is politicization in school. This calls into question Rejai and Phillips' characterization of him, quoted earlier, as "a loyalist turned revolutionary."

The fact is that Castro embarked on a revolutionary path long before Batista's 1952 *coup* against the constitutional government, which derailed Castro's hope of winning a legislative seat. He plunged into quasi-revolutionary politics at the University of Havana, where he packed a pistol and twice was suspected of

Table 1. Rejai and Phillips' Hypothesized Characteristics of Political Leaders

Trait	Franco	Castro
MALE?	Yes	Yes
OLDEST, YOUNGEST, OR ONLY CHILD?	No	No
BORN INTO MIDDLE OR UPPER-CLASS FAMILY?	Yes	No#
VAIN, NARCISSISTIC, EGOTISTICAL?	Yes	Yes
VERBAL SKILLS?	Yes	YES
ORGANIZATIONAL SKILLS?	YES	Yes
DID LEADER EMERGE AT A TIME OF CRISIS?	Yes	Yes
Issue of legal marriage?	Yes	No#
Belongs to mainstream ethnic and religious group?	Yes	Yes
Born in a city? Or, if born and raised in rural environment, did he acquire early and sustained exposure to urban culture?	Yes	YES
Early involvement in national politics in urban area?	No#	Yes
Foreign travel?	No	YES
Cosmopolitan background?	No	Yes
Patriotic and nationalistic?	Yes	Yes
Feeling of deprivation?	Yes	Yes
Feeling of marginalization?	Yes	YES
Highly educated in exclusive schools?	No	Yes

Notation:

Row in capital letters: trait considered by Rejai and Phillips to be a "critical variable."

Row in italics: trait for which Rejai and Phillips found some evidence.

Row in normal type: trait for which Rejai and Phillips found no evidence.

YES in caps: relative to the other, this leader exhibits the trait more strongly or vividly.

Trait not unambiguously held. See text.

Table 2. Rejai and Phillips' Hypothesized Loyalist Traits

Loyalist Trait	Franco	Castro
STABLE RELIGIOUS BELIEFS?	Yes	No
EARLY POLITICIZATION: AT HOME?	No	No
EARLY POLITICIZATION: AT SCHOOL?	Yes	Yes
PESSIMISTIC VIEW OF HUMAN NATURE?	Yes	?
UNCONCERNED ABOUT SOCIAL JUSTICE?	Yes	No
IS FATHER IN GOVERNMENT, MILITARY, BANKING OR INDUSTRY, OTHER PROFESSIONS, LANDED GENTRY?	Yes	No#
LEADER EMPLOYED IN PUBLIC OFFICE?	Yes#	No
Upper class background?	No	No
Middle-class background?	Yes	#
Travel reinforced politicization?	Yes	No
High-status father in upper or middle class pursuits?	No#	No
Grew up in close proximity to power?	No	No
Middle age when reaching highest office?	Yes: 44	No
Internalized ideology of forefathers?	Yes	No
Warm relation with father?	No	No
Free of harassment from authorities?	Yes#	No
Cosmopolitanism more limited by local or national perspective?	Yes	No
Stable and tranquil family life?	Yes#	No
Uniformly optimistic about his own country?	No	No

Notation:

Row in capital letters: trait considered by Rejai and Phillips to be a "critical variable."

Row in italics: trait for which Rejai and Phillips found some evidence.

Row in normal type: trait for which Rejai and Phillips found no evidence.

Trait not unambiguously held. See text.

? Evidence lacking, insufficient, or unclear.

murdering members of a rival political gang. In 1947, at age 20, he joined the aborted Cayo Confites expedition to overthrow the dictatorship of Rafael Trujillo in the neighboring Dominican Republic. The following year found him in Bogotá, Colombia, where he participated in an attack on a police station during the days of frenzied violence known as the *Bogotazo*. When the leader of the opposition Ortodoxo Party to which Castro belonged, Eduardo Chibás, died of a self-inflicted wound, Castro tried to convince José Pardo Llada, a leading Ortodoxo who was in charge of the funeral, to exploit the outpouring of popular grief in order to seize power by diverting the procession from the cemetery to the presidential palace, taking over the building, and overthrowing the elected president.[3] In short, Castro fits the profile of the revolutionary almost perfectly, as is evident in Table 3. One suspects, then, that he was meant for a revolutionary life from the beginning. It was not Batista's 1952 *coup* which turned Castro from a loyalist into a revolutionary, as Rejai and Phillips allege. He was a revolutionary all along, for whom Batista's *coup* opened an enviable opportunity to employ violence as a means to conquer political power.

By contrast, Franco's profile is that of a loyalist, although less so than Castro's is that of a revolutionary. Franco unambiguously fits five of the seven "critical" loyalist variables, but only another four of the remaining seven for which Rejai and Phillips found some evidence. The two "critical" loyalist variables missing in Franco's profile are arguably the most important of all, father's occupation and early politicization at home, since they define what Rejai and Philips call proximity to power. Recall that father's occupation was one of the two (the other being religion) most important variables in predicting leadership type. Loyalists tend to be born into a family of the establishment by virtue of some combination of political power, wealth, professional prestige, and social connections. Franco was born into a family that for generations had served in the Navy. The father

was employed in government, but he was not powerful or influential. Moreover, he was a gambler and a womanizer who deserted the family when Franco was 15 years of age. Thus, he was of no help to Franco's career. In fact, Franco had wanted to follow the family's tradition of service in the Navy, even nurturing the hope of being admitted to the prestigious naval cadet ship. But admission restrictions closed this avenue to him. Presumably, his family lacked the pull to get him in, so he joined the infantry school in Toledo, instead.

Thus, Franco did not grow up in close proximity to power. It was his exploits as a military officer in Spanish Morocco, where he distinguished himself for valor combating the insurgents, that through successive combat promotions made him the youngest general in Europe. Unlike the typical loyalist, then, Franco did not have power served to him on a silver platter. Rather, like a revolutionary, he spent decades in pursuit of it. Like Castro, Franco was a self-made ruler.

Table 3 displays Rejai and Philips' hypothesized revolutionary traits. Only one, access to power, is a critical variable. Neither man was born inside or even close to the circles of economic or political power or social prestige. As for the other traits, note that Castro unambiguously exhibits all but two of them, father's occupation and class background, which have already been discussed. As for Franco, he fits 5 out of 12, or almost half. These include the Oedipus complex, an eclectic ideology that combines indigenous and domestic elements, a view of the country that is contingent on the regime, and, most importantly, lack of access to power early in life and the concomitant pursuit of it as an adult. His relation to his father has already been discussed. Franco's ideology evolved into a veritable *olla podrida* (stew of several meats, starches, and vegetables) of ideas: elements of Catholicism, Spanish traditionalism, corporatism, fascism, anti-communism, and anti-liberalism, with anti-English, anti-American, and anti-Masonic prejudices

---

3. The foregoing account tracks closely passages from my previous essay on Castro (Cuzán 1999: 27-28). On Castro's suggestion to Pardo Llada, see the latter's book (1989: 70-73).

Table 3. Rejai and Phillips' Hypothesized Revolutionary Traits

Revolutionary Trait	Franco	Castro
DISADVANTAGED RELATIVE TO ACCESS TO POWER?	Yes	Yes
Oedipus complex?	Yes	Yes
Professional revolutionary, self-taught in military affairs?	No	Yes
Lower status father in middle or working class occupation?	No	No#
History of illegality, arrest, imprisonment?	No	Yes
Foreign travel, exposure to other societies and cultures?	No	Yes
Eclectic ideology, combining foreign and indigenous elements?	Yes	Yes
View toward country contingent on regime?	Yes	Yes
Lower-class background?	No	No#
Stormy and conflict-riddled childhood?	No	Yes
Spent life in pursuit of access to influence and authority?	Yes	Yes
Reached highest office at relatively young age?	No	Yes: 33

Notation:

Row in capital letters: trait considered by Rejai and Phillips to be a "critical variable."

Row in italics: trait for which Rejai and Phillips found some evidence.

Row in normal type: trait for which Rejai and Phillips found no evidence.

Trait not unambiguously held. See text.

thrown into the mix. At times Franco said things that sounded like Fidel Castro, as in the following comment to one his intimates, made as late as 1967, after three decades in power and only eight years before his death: "I believe that all the activities which have been carried out in the western world against us have been carried out by organizations which receive funds from the CIA above all with the intention of establishing . . . an American-style political system on the day that I cease to be around" (Preston 1994: 733).

Ironically, Franco, who had most of the marks of the loyalist, who for the first two decades of adult life had faithfully served the existing order, paying homage to country and king, and who had even played a key role in 1934, under a conservative government, in repressing an insurrection against the Second Republic on the part of anarcho-communists and regionalists, was reluctantly drawn into a military conspiracy to overthrow the government after the Popular Front won the 1936 election. Franco abhorred the socialists' anti-monarchist, anti-military, and anti-clerical sentiments and policies, and felt that during their first administration, in 1931-1933, they had treated him shabbily, in a manner that was not in keeping

with his merits. Once he crossed the Rubicon to join the rebels in 1936, Franco cunningly maneuvered himself into a central position on the Nationalist side, using his contacts with Nazi Germany and fascist Italy to elbow the original organizers of the uprising out of the way. The fortuitous death of several of his rivals clinched his conquest of power even before the Nationalists emerged victorious in the Spanish Civil War. Upon defeating the Republicans, Franco did not immediately recall and restore to the throne the exiled King Alfonso XIII. On the contrary, he treated the exiled monarch coldly, even insinuating that the Spanish crisis had been his own fault.[4] Once triumphant, Franco embarked on a project to remake Spain according to some hybrid blueprint of ancient and modern models, a mixture of Catholic Medievalism and Italian fascism whose underlying ideology was anti-liberal and anti-bourgeois.

CONCLUSION

What we have in Francisco Franco and Fidel Castro, then, are two men who fit the political leadership profile about equally well. Furthermore, both are self-made rulers who, starting out far from the political center socially, economically, and geographically, forced their way into the palace of power. Both ac-

---

4. According to Preston (1994: 325), "The exiled King allegedly said before he died, 'I picked Franco out when he was a nobody. He has double-crossed and deceived me at every turn.'"

quired absolute mastery over their countries by violent means at a moment of political crisis. Once in charge both Franco and Castro set about remaking their countries according to an anti-liberal vision, one of the "right," the other of the "left." Castro's revolutionary project within and without Cuba needs no elaboration. What needs pointing out, though, is that Franco was, in his own way, something of a revolutionary himself, even if his "revolution" looked both backward, toward Spain's heroic age, as well as what in the 1930s and 1940s appeared to him to be forward, toward fascism. Franco did not return Spain to the *status quo ante*, as a loyalist would supposedly have done. Instead, he attempted to reverse something like a half-a-century of intermittent Spanish evolution in the direction of Western-style parliamentarism while looking to Mussolini's Italy and Hitler's Germany's for state-directed economic models. This was, in effect, a reactionary/revolutionary project.

However, unlike Castro, who fits the revolutionary profile perfectly, Franco had most of the characteristics of the loyalist. He was not born a *bona fide* member of the establishment, but from an early age he, like his ancestors, became its faithful servant. Had Spain's Second Republic not come into being, or even if only the conservatives had controlled the government or the socialists pursued a moderate course, in all likelihood Franco would have reached normal retirement age after an illustrious military career capped by a term as High Commissioner for Morocco, the post he had aspired to as a young Army officer. By contrast, Castro's profile is that of a man who was meant for revolution from the beginning. Had Batista not overthrown Cuba's constitutional government, it is all too probable that Castro would either have attempted the job himself, as he tried to get Pardo Llada to do at the time of Chibás' funeral procession. Or perhaps, like Ernesto (Ché) Guevara, he might have joined a revolutionary organization elsewhere in Latin America, e.g., in Colombia, the Dominican Republic, Nicaragua, or Venezuela.

Thus, with Rejai and Phillips, I conclude that in both cases the situation was critical in the making of these two dictators. However, circumstances played contrasting roles in the political fortunes of Franco and Castro. Spain's political crisis displaced Franco from the normal course of his career, turning him from a loyalist into something of a "revolutionary." In the case of Castro, however, Cuba's crisis simply enabled him to fulfill the role that he was meant to play from the beginning, that of the consummate revolutionary, a wrecker of regimes and countries.

REFERENCES

Cuzán, Alfred G. 1999. *Is Fidel Castro A Machiavellian Prince?* Miami, FL: The Endowment for Cuban-American Studies.

Montaner, Carlos Alberto. 2002. "La Transición Española y el Caso Cubano." Paper prepared for the Cuban Transition Project, University of Miami, Summer 2002.

Pardo Llada, José. 1989. *Fidel y el "Ché."* Barcelona: Plaza y Janés, S.A.

Preston, Paul. 1994. *Franco. A Biography*. New York: Basic Books.

Quirk, Robert E. 1993. *Fidel Castro*. New York: Norton.

Rejai, Mostafa and Phillips, Kay. 1988. *Loyalists & Revolutionaries: Political Leaders Compared*. New York: Praeger.

PROCESOS ELECTORALES Y ÉLITES POLÍTICAS EN LA CUBA DEL TERCER MILENIO

Domingo Amuchástegui

El régimen que encabeza Fidel Castro desde hace ya 44 años, plantea como objeto de estudio, entre muchas otras dimensiones, las del examen cuidadoso de procesos electorales y élites políticas. Un planteamiento usual es el que afirma que en Cuba no hay elecciones o elecciones competitivas y, subsecuentemente, la ausencia de democracia; el otro planteamiento—no menos usual y repetido—es el de percibir y proyectar la imagen del poder en Cuba centrada absolutamente en la figura de Fidel Castro, sin que nada más ni nadie más sea relevante o importante. A esto último, ha seguido un cierto, y más reciente, corolario que otorga a la desaparición física de Fidel Castro poderes mágicos en cuanto a condicionar lo que podrá o no podrá suceder después en términos de cambio de régimen, transición, sucesión o continuidad. Y de aquí la especial atención obsesiva a su estado de salud, desmayos, incoherencias, y el mal funcionamiento de otros signos vitales.

El presente análisis se propone examinar estas dos dimensiones—elecciones y élites políticas—con el objetivo, primero, de pasar revista a ambas desde una óptica crítica y que resuma sus rasgos más sobresalientes en las cuatro primeras décadas del régimen cubano, esto es, de los rasgos que el autor considera que marcaron hitos importantes para la proyección actual de esas dos dimensiones. En segundo lugar, y mediante la discusión del último proceso electoral celebrado en Cuba entre octubre del 2002 y febrero del 2003, analizar el comportamiento de ambas dimensiones en los albores de este tercer milenio.

ANTECEDENTES

En marzo de 1959, ante un multitudinario acto frente al antiguo Palacio Presidencial, Fidel Castro, al referirse a la celebración de elecciones en un futuro próximo, recibió un atronador rechazo a semejante idea de parte de los centenares de miles de asistentes. Como testigo personal y participante de aquello, nunca pareció cosa orquestada o manipulada, sino una reacción acumulada a la que Fidel Castro apostó con toda seguridad de obtener dicho resultado. Los términos políticos o legales de aquel rechazo nunca fueron delimitados y así aquel "No" a las elecciones proclamado en plaza pública sirvió como uno—otros muchos que desbordan los marcos de este análisis también sirvieron a ese fin—de los componentes públicos legitimadores a la conformación del régimen revolucionario tal cual se conoció de 1959 a 1976, fecha en que culmina el proceso de formación e implantación del así llamado Poder Popular.

De 1976 hasta 1992, con la adopción de una constitución aprobada—de acuerdo a cifras oficiales—mediante casi el 100% de los electores, se han venido celebrado comicios o elecciones generales cada seis años. En la primera de ellas, el Partido Comunista de Cuba (PCC) orientó a sus militantes a votar por uno de los varios candidatos, hasta seis en total, que aparecían en los boletas con sus biografías para conocimiento de los electores. Por un lado, el número de precandidatos ha ido disminuyendo hasta reducirse a dos. En cuanto al procedimiento del PCC indicando a sus militantes por quien votar de manera directa, éste fue desestimado para las siguientes. Si bien el

PCC no proponía ni lanzaba formal o públicamente los nombres de los candidatos, todos los electores o votantes en las asambleas de vecinos por circunscripción sabían que en la abrumadora mayoría de los casos los nombres surgidos como candidatos tenían el beneplácito del Partido, aunque no necesariamente fueran militantes del mismo.

La llamada Asamblea Nacional del Poder Popular (ANPP), o parlamento cubano, se constituyó por dos grupos. Uno, designado mediante deliberación o ratificación del Buró Político en representación de cargos y posiciones de Partido y Gobierno que se consideraban, por su importancia para el funcionamiento del país, debían estar representados en la ANPP (poco más del 50%). Estos designados, generalmente, aparecían también como elegidos o votados en diferentes circunscripciones, las que en su mayoría abrumadora no coincidían con sus áreas reales o verdaderas de residencia. El segundo grupo, estaba integrado por delegados de las asambleas provinciales, escogidos usualmente entre nóminas previamente preparadas o santificadas por las instancias provinciales y nacionales del Partido. Y como diputados nacionales no tenían que ser votados pues ya lo habían sido por sus circunscripciones o —como se argumentó entonces— por elección indirecta en tanto que el Buró Político, por un lado, y las asambleas provinciales, por el otro, devenían en una suerte de Electoral College o Gran Elector con poderes supremos.

Para julio de 1992, y bajo el impacto de la crisis interna que sobreviene luego de los acontecimientos externos de 1989-1991, entre las limitadas reformas que se acometieron entonces, estuvo la adopción de una nueva ley electoral (Ley Electoral Reformada Núm. 78, 10/29/92), que introdujo variaciones significativas. El cambio más importante, consistió en que todos los propuestos para diputados a la ANPP (609 integrantes en la actualidad) debían ser electos o votados individualmente y por más del 50% de los votos. En otras palabras, aunque se conservaba el mecanismo de la designación de los candidatos para representar a ambos grupos (50-50) en la Asamblea Nacional, con la particularidad de que ambos grupos ahora, y sobre bases individuales, tenían que ser electos o votados, con lo que se ponía término a los procedimientos de elección indirecta y se quebraba la imagen monolítica al individualizarse la elección y exigir como requisito no menos del 50% de los votos. Ello abría una diversidad de espacios para formas de voto negativo o de castigo, y en torno a éste las más diversas formas de movilización política y transmisión de mensajes y desafíos al régimen. Para este último, tales espacios y desafíos no pasaban inadvertidos, formaban parte de los riesgos previsibles y formaban parte de las limitadas reformas por entonces acometidas.

En el transcurso de esas décadas, las élites políticas históricas —el núcleo gestor y conductor de la gesta insurreccional y del régimen revolucionario posterior a 1959— se agotaban por diversas vías (fracasos repetidos, abusos de poder, incapacidad reiterada, corrupción, burocratización, intolerancia desmedida, conflictos sectoriales, choques de personalidades, pérdida de carisma y otros) hasta ver reducido su número a la mínima expresión que hoy son.

Sin embargo, en ese proceso de agotamiento, la dirigencia cubana supo advertir y recrear con no poco éxito el dilema del relevo generacional, esto es, el proceso de una promoción sistemática de jóvenes a lo largo y ancho de la totalidad de la estructura de poder y de toda la sociedad civil sobre la que dicho poder descansa.

A esta altura, afloraban públicamente tendencias nunca antes vistas. Primero, el V Congreso de la Unión de Jóvenes Comunistas (UJC), en 1988, y bajo la dirección de Roberto Robaina, daba cabida a planteamientos críticos a políticas y viejos dirigentes que se resumían en el planteo más aplaudido de todos: A la generación responsable de todos y tantos errores, no le era posible asumir y resolver con la capacidad crítica necesaria los errores del pasado. Esto sólo era posible por parte de una nueva generación.

Con tonos más conciliadores, pero con una igual carga demoledora de críticas, en 1990, aparece la discusión del documento conocido como Llamamiento del Partido al IV Congreso, cuya redacción y debate fueran promovidos por el entonces binomio Raúl Castro-Carlos Aldana. En éste, se reconocía plenamente la existencia del dilema generacional, aunque no en los términos críticos del V Congreso de la UJC. En cambio, razonaba la existencia de tres grupos pertenecientes a tres generaciones diferentes: la que hizo y defendió la revolución en sus inicios o generación histórica; la generación intermedia en sus 40 por entonces (hoy bordeando los 50) y la tercera o generación más joven, y de donde fluían los cuadros y figuras dirigentes—entiéndase bien, las nuevas élites políticas—de un presente y futuro relevo de la élite histórica. Esta última, con muy contadas excepciones todavía, ya ha dejado de ser la fuente principal de donde emergen figuras para nuevos cargos o recambios.

Estas tendencias comenzaron a ser advertidas en el exilio, con el debido rigor científico, en los comienzos de la última década del siglo XX por el equipo multidisciplinario de Florida International University (FIU) en su primer estudio sobre transición en Cuba. Los cambios operados en la dirigencia cubana en el transcurso de esa misma década, fueron confirmando más ampliamente la documentada constatación preliminar aportada por el equipo de FIU.

La segunda mitad de esa misma década aportó nuevas evidencias. En 1996, durante el único desfile militar conmemorativo de estos últimos 20 años, el general de brigada que lo encabezó nada tenía que ver con las élites históricas, ni por edad, ni por nexos familiares o de otro tipo. Estábamos ante una nueva generación de jefes militares, un componente clave de las nuevas élites. Un año más tarde, la celebración del V Congreso del PCC servía para aportar más evidencia a la tendencia que confirmaba una profunda transformación en la composición de las élites políticas del régimen cubano.

ELECCIONES

Después de 26 años de procesos electorales, entre octubre del 2002 y febrero del 2003 tuvieron lugar los últimos comicios. Son sabidas, consabidas y reiteradas las objeciones que se les hacen, pero hasta hoy el resultado último ha continuado siendo el mismo: el votante o electorado ha refrendado abrumadoramente, la opción ante ellos presentada por el régimen. Algunas lecturas y propuestas nuevas deberían producirse para refrescar la aproximación a y el análisis de este fenómeno. Nuestra contribución de hoy apunta

en esta dirección y las últimas elecciones son para ello una excelente oportunidad.

Comencemos por constatar que luego de 10 años de una ley electoral reformada—como ha sido descrita más arriba—ninguna corriente política de la disidencia u oposición interna ha podido estructurar la movilización efectiva de un voto negativo o de castigo; tampoco el exilio y mucho menos una concertación entre ambas fuerzas. Se puede diferir en la interpretación, pero el hecho es uno: tal cosa no se ha logrado, nadie se la propone coherentemente y para casi todos parecería como si ello no fuera importante.

Al régimen cubano, le interesa el proceso electoral tal cual lo ha reestructurado pues en ello tiene un importante instrumento de legitimación interna y externa. Ha exhibido y divulgado con creces las cifras obtenidas porque ellas mostraban un apoyo abrumador gracias a los múltiples mecanismos utilizados en promover una asistencia casi total a las urnas. Pero no olvidemos lo siguiente: Lo que pasa dentro del local donde el votante ejerce su derecho ante la urna, sin fiscalización ninguna, con la boleta en sus manos, es algo que hasta hoy no se ha transformado en un recurso de descontento, mucho menos de oposición. Y en cuanto al argumento de cifras alteradas o pucherazos mayúsculos, la observación directa muestra que, simplemente, no le ha sido necesario y de ahí el recurrente despliegue publicitario en torno a las cifras

Votar, aunque sea con mil restricciones, es importante. Tan sólo recordemos cuando en el seno del IV Congreso del PCC se instituyó el voto individual y secreto hubo delegados que no apoyaron las candidaturas de Fidel y Raúl Castro; pocos, pero los hubo, y hubo varios miembros del Buró Político que sacaron cantidades risibles en tanto miembros del Comité Central sacaban más votos que varios miembros del Buró Político. Y esto envió un claro mensaje, con múltiples implicaciones.

Y lo más curioso del caso es que esta vez, en el curso de las últimas elecciones, sin ser convocados ni orientados, un sector importante de la población, de una manera o de otra, decidió no refrendar la candidatura única del régimen. Veamos las cifras correspondientes a las municipales, que son las más importantes y representativas en alguna medida.

El término representativa no debe promover debates innecesarios; se aplica porque en las municipales los votantes o electores conocen perfectamente a los candidatos; es su vecino, comparten los mismos problemas, interactúan, compran en la misma bodega o compran por debajo de la mesa al mismo vendedor, van al mismo médico o policlínico y, por tanto, se le conoce perfectamente y esto influye en condicionar la manera en que muchos emiten su voto y que de ahí se califique como más representativa en oposición a la mayoría de los designados, donde no concurren semejantes circunstancias de conocimiento directo e interacción.

Pasemos ahora al examen cuidadoso de las cifras de las últimas elecciones municipales:

* Electores en el registro: 8 352 948

* No votaron: 4.25%

* Boletas en blanco: 2.78%

* Anuladas: 2.54%

El por ciento total de voto negativo (o de opositores o algo parecido para describir las tres categorías) era de un 9.57%. Redondeando, casi 850 000 personas, lo que puede sugerir que la cifra no anduvo lejos del millón.

En este punto, habría que recordar otros dos componentes que influyen en la configuración de las cifras finales de voto negativo o voto de castigo. Una es estimar o suponer que en esos 850 000 se incluyen de alguna manera aquellos que de manera explícita han solicitado participar del sistema de visas para marchar a los EE.UU. y que suman casi medio millón de solicitantes.

Lo otro es recordar que la ley electoral no incluye a la emigración que aún conserva su ciudadanía cubana y recordar también—cuestión ésta no menos importante—que en el seno de la ANPP hubo diputados que se pronunciaron a favor de adoptar la doble ciudadanía, con obvias implicaciones directas para el mecanismo electoral, moción ésta que fue desestimada.

De las cifras más arriba expuestas, es necesario proponernos el examen de varias hipótesis bien importantes.

* La primera de ellas es que la cifra de voto negativo o de castigo no ha sido producto de una estrategia o táctica de la oposición organizada; mucho menos del exilio también llamado por algunos históricos.

* Una segunda, es que los documentos más importantes promovidos por la oposición—los de Payá Sardiñas y Cuesta Morúa—luego de largos meses de proselitismo alcanzaron apenas, respectivamente, poco más de unas decenas de miles respectivamente. Esta hipótesis, es sólo con el propósito de hacer ver el abismo enorme que existe ente las muy modestas cifras obtenidas por ambos proyectos y el casi millón de voto negativo o de castigo de estas últimas elecciones; este abismo nos muestra cuán lejos está la oposición organizada o disidencia y el exilio de ser capaz de orientar, movilizar y captar coherentemente esos centenares de miles.

* Una tercera hipótesis, es que ese casi millón de votos puede estar reflejando también el voto de ese medio millón que busca irse del país. Si esto es así, la importancia o trascendencia del casi millón se relativiza y pierde potencialidad. Esto además ratificaría que una de las causas primordiales en explicar las debilidades del exilio y de la oposición interna, ha sido y sigue siendo lo que puede caracterizarse como patrón de evasión, esto es, que la mayor parte de los descontentos más agudos no se orientan ni se vertebran en términos contestatarios ni alimentan a las fuerzas de oposición, sino que se limitan a procurar la salida del país y, una vez fuera, su desactivación política es abrumadora.

* La última hipótesis con respecto a estas cifras, es contemplar la posibilidad de que el régimen mismo pueda o no acometer las políticas de cambios y mejoras locales y territoriales que les permita, eventualmente, detener y revertir la tendencia de tales cifras.

Para ambos—régimen cubano y oposición—tales hipótesis habrán de configurar, en buena medida, sus potenciales protagónicos a corto y mediano plazo.

Cuando el 19 de enero del 2003 los candidatos a diputados—designados entre la masa de delegados votados en las municipales—fueron sometidos a votación popular en elección general o nacional o de ratificación de los designados, casi un 9% rechazaba, de una forma o de otra, validar las candidaturas a diputados. La variación entre las municipales y las nacionales era apenas de un 1%. A diferencia de todos los anteriores procesos electorales, donde el gobierno pudo exhibir cifras entre el 95% y más del 98%, en esta ocasión las cifras oscilaban entre un 90% y un 91%.

Tales cifras jamás se habían producido anteriormente y su admisión pública era no menos inusual. Una simple progresión aritmética—y esta es otra importante hipótesis—pudiera crear en un plazo de seis años proporciones numéricas que echarían por tierra completa y definitivamente la imagen monolítica del pasado, consolidaría la imagen de un sector lo suficientemente numeroso y amplio que resulte imposible ocultarlo, desmeritarlo y continuar desconociéndolo política y legalmente, aún en los términos de su propio marco constitucional y jurídico.

Y todo esto que puede parecer poco importante para muchos acá y que otros ignoran o silencian, tuvo un impacto político enorme dentro de la estructura de poder en Cuba. Mientras que muchos dirigentes del PCC y del gobierno estimaban que los resultados eran—considerando las extremas tensiones económicas y sociales del período—muy satisfactorios, para Fidel Castro los resultados eran punto menos que inadmisibles. De inmediato, convocó sesiones de examen pormenorizado de las cifras y abundantes críticas y advertencias recayeron sobre los dirigentes de provincias con las cifras más altas de aquello que podía ser claramente identificado como voto negativo o de castigo. Cambios ulteriores entre estos dirigentes sugieren una clara conexión entre estos últimos y las cifras de dichas elecciones.

Curiosamente, varias de las provincias con las cifras más alarmantes eran aquellas más expuestas a la inversión extranjera y el turismo como Ciudad de La Habana (13.45%), Matanzas (10.20%) y Holguín (9.31%), en tanto que territorios como las provincias de La Habana, Pinar del Río, Cienfuegos y varias de las orientales se distinguían por sus bajos índices de voto negativo o de castigo pese a encontrarse en peores circunstancias económico-sociales que las primeras. Este fenómeno, nos recuerda una vez más la imperiosa necesidad de territorializar los estudios sociopolíticos de la realidad cubana pues se hace cada vez más evidente que no es posible una lectura lineal de los patrones de conducta social y política ni hablar del pueblo ni reclamar su representación en términos absolutos y lineales.

Las cifras, nuevamente, sugieren la necesidad de prestar más atención a dos cuestiones de especial importancia. Son ellas, primero la necesidad de constatar y analizar que los patrones de votación ofrecen algunas significativas variaciones territoriales por provincias y, segundo, que en la mayoría de los casos más importantes señalados hay una clara coincidencia entre los más altos índices de voto de castigo con los tres territorios (provincias) de más alto grado de inversión extranjera y de turistas, cuestión esta que puede servir de importante referencia para el interminable debate en torno a los pro y los contra del embargo y el turismo.

También vale la pena observar como otro importante resquicio de castigo tampoco era utilizado en esta ocasión: No hubo votaciones individualizadas en ningún caso significativo y se votó a favor o en contra en bloque, con lo que la consigna gubernamental del voto unido o votar por toda la lista completa de candidatos, de una manera o de otra prevaleció en lugar de ejercerse votaciones masivas selectivas para individualizar y penalizar los casos más conspicuos.

Debe recordarse que la consigna del Voto Unido o Votar por Todos surgió después de la reforma de la ley electoral y su objetivo era, y sigue siendo, que la fragmentación del voto o votar individualmente por unos y no votar por otros podía traducirse en que muchos candidatos quedaran sin votos suficientes, sobre todo entre los candidatos designados del poder central. Podía ser no ya un problema de segunda vuelta, sino otro mecanismo de castigo que podía emplearse de muy diferentes maneras y que hasta hoy no ha sido propuesto ni empleado de esta manera. El régimen se preocupó con creces cuando advirtió, mediante encuestas realizadas con posterioridad a la reforma electoral, cómo muchos encuestados se inclinaban por votar por unos y no por otros, esto es, de manera diferenciada o selectiva en el caso de los designados. La solución—mantenida hasta ahora—fue la de estructurar una muy fuerte propaganda a favor del Voto Unido. Muchas experiencias útiles pudieran experimentarse por esta vía con resultados bien interesantes, cosa esta hasta ahora desestimada por completo por la oposición interna y el exilio.

LAS ÉLITES

Los primeros estudios de una década atrás ya indicaban claramente un importante ascenso social y político entre las generaciones intermedia y más joven. La tendencia en esta última década continuó ganando terreno y expandiéndose hacia nuevas categorías de actividades y rangos hacia los que estas nuevas élites crecían de manera significativa.

Esto empezó abarcando varios sectores del espectro de la sociedad civil, el PCC y el gobierno; hoy abarca su totalidad. Veamos algunas de esas categorías y rangos:

- A nivel de Buró Político, se promovían jóvenes de la llamada generación intermedia como Carlos Lage, Abel Prieto, Yadira García, Roberto Robaina, Juan C. Robinson, Pedro Sáez y Jorge L. Sierra, hoy situados entre los 43 y los 53, esto es, nacidos entre 1951 y 1961.

- A nivel de primeros secretarios del PCC en la totalidad de las provincias la edad oscila entre los 43 y 50.

- A nivel de Consejo de Ministros, los cambios han sido mayores. Los ministerios de Relaciones Exteriores, Comercio Exterior, Finanzas y Precios, Auditoría, Transporte, SIME, Salud Pública, y Ayudantía del Presidente, se encuentran en manos de figuras por debajo de los 40 años, mientras Justicia, Fiscalía General, Cultura, Agricultura, Industria Pesquera, y el Equipo de Coordinación y Apoyo del Comandante en Jefe,

se encuentran en manos de figuras de la generación intermedia entre los 45 y los 53.

- Las elecciones 2002-2003 fueron igualmente ilustrativas y marcan notables ascensos con respecto a 1992-1993. De los 14 946 delegados votados a nivel de circunscripción, un total de 6 652 están por debajo de los 40 años de edad y 4 847 entre 41 y 50 años, cifra que sobrepasa por amplio margen los dos tercios de los mismos. Igualmente notable fue el ascenso femenino con un total de 3 493 para un 35.96%, lo que representó un 8% de aumento en comparación con el anterior proceso electoral.

- Otra variación significativa con respecto a los primeros 12 años de las elecciones, es la actual proporción de diputados con grados universitarios e instrucción media superior que alcanza ya un 99.1%. Entre los dirigentes de la llamada generación intermedia y la más joven, el perfil profesional predominante es el de los ingenieros.

- En la configuración de las nuevas élites, un componente no menos notable y singularmente sensible a la realidad cubana, lo es el factor racial. El tema comenzaría a debatirse con fuerza desde comienzos de la década de 1980 y, en particular, desde la celebración del III Congreso del PCC, donde una prolongada discusión del tema tuvo lugar. En la década pasada, y en lo que va de la actual, el componente negro y mestizo ha registrado un ascenso importante. Este controversial tema encuentra al interior de la dirigencia cubana dos posiciones. Una, es la de Fidel Castro, que públicamente, ha abordado la cuestión sólo un par de veces en 44 años, siendo su argumentación—retomando la parte del enfoque martiano—de que la definición de ser humano lo abarca todo y que este, blanco, negro o mujer, se reconoce y progresa por sus méritos en una sociedad que le abre todas las oportunidades. La posición de su hermano Raúl Castro, en repetidas ocasiones, ha sido la de hacer explícito la existencia del problema, llamarlo por su nombre, en cuanto a oportunidades, movilidad social y progreso y la necesidad de hacer más presente, estable y numerosa la representación de negros y mestizos en toda la estructura de poder y de lo cual las FAR son hoy el mejor ejemplo. La promoción a oficiales superiores de mayor, coronel y general de brigada ha sido la mayor de todos los tiempos en estos últimos 10 años. En la actual ANPP, con sus 609 diputados, el 67.16 por ciento de sus integrantes son blancos, mientras que un 32.8 por ciento son negros y mestizos, cifra ésta que representó un aumento del 4.55 por ciento.

- El relevo generacional en el ámbito de las FAR es, por razones más que obvias, de importancia crítica. En primer lugar, debe recordarse que los oficiales superiores con experiencia de combate habrán de prevalecer hasta el 2015, incluyendo un nutrido grupo de generales de brigada ascendidos en la pasada década y que representan la generación intermedia. Y los que representan la generación más joven como mayores y coroneles provienen ya de las filas de los camilitos, es decir, de las escuelas militares, iniciadas a fines de la década de 1960, donde se forma la masa de pre-cadetes que integrarán las academias militares de las FAR. Los camilitos pasan a dichas instituciones entre los 16 y 17.

Al respecto de la formación de estas nuevas élites, su papel actual y futuro en las FAR, y el resto de la estructura de poder del país, decía Raúl Castro a fines del 2001: "Los hombres y mujeres que en los años futuros ocuparán las principales responsabilidades en la defensa, al igual que en el resto de las esferas del país, incluida la máxima dirección de la nación, no están por llegar, ya se encuentran entre nosotros... En el caso de las FAR, ya hay camilitos que son generales o coroneles al frente de importantes unidades de combate y en la mayoría de los cargos claves de los estados mayores."

De esta manera, la vieja generación en proceso de agotamiento y extinción, los así llamados históricos, no sólo ha preparado un amplio proceso de relevo generacional en el poder, sino que al hacerlo han propiciado la configuración de una nueva élite.

CONCLUSIONES

Los resultados electorales del 2002-2003 muestran claramente cómo el mecanismo electoral cubano podía ser, desde la reforma de 1992, un importante instrumento para reflejar diversos descontentos nacionales, territoriales y locales.

La oposición o disidencia en Cuba ni el exilio—so pretexto de que se le hace el juego al régimen o que este manipula las cifras—se han propuesto o formulado estudios serios en este terreno. Desde tales maximalismos, resulta imposible experimentar y probar las potencialidades de semejante mecanismo para la lucha política.

Las cifras del 2002-2003 parecen ofrecer un enorme caudal para un activismo diferente y potencialmente más efectivo que todo lo probado hasta ahora y su mensaje sí impacta tremendamente a la estructura de poder, como quedó probado en esta ocasión. Oposición y exilio se encuentran a distancias enormes de poder capitalizar y movilizar semejante recurso.

La obsesión enfermiza de continuar absolutizando aún hoy la estructura de poder en Cuba en torno a Fidel y Raúl, desnaturaliza, impide ver y entender, las tremendas transformaciones que se han operado al interior de ella en términos de figuras que representan una élite enteramente nueva, cuyos componentes sociales, culturales, tecnológicos, psicológicos y políticos son también enteramente nuevos y con los que oposición y exilio tendrán que lidiar en las próximas décadas.

Y digo las próximas décadas no por desliz, sino porque a la postura subjetiva que percibe un desplome ipso facto a la desaparición o muerte de Fidel—para no mencionar la magia verbal del señor Otto Reich que promete en Madrid y Roma que el régimen de Fidel castro "caerá pronto"—les invito a releer las palabras de Raúl Castro: las nuevas generaciones o élites ya son parte importante del poder; mañana controlarán la totalidad del poder y a ellas corresponderá el reestructurarlo, rediseñarlo y reorientarlo. Serán estas nuevas élites, de acuerdo a sus experiencias e intereses vitales, las que habrán de repensar sus propias fórmulas de continuidad y cambio. Sería bastante ingenuo imaginar que porque se les convide o intimide a abandonar el poder lo vayan a hacer mansamente. No es esta la manera en que va a terminar el juego. Al menos, éste es el escenario que los hechos, y no los deseos, parecen prefigurar con más fuerza.

Entre tanto, el exilio perece biológica y políticamente. Jóvenes, negros y mestizos salidos de la isla y activos políticamente en años recientes, son excepciones muy contadas, mientras que los jóvenes de segunda generación del exilio se desconectan, en su abrumadora mayoría, de un activismo efectivo. Un relevo generacional y de élites como el que se ha producido en Cuba, y continúa produciéndose, no tiene su equivalente o contraparte ni del lado de acá ni entre la oposición o disidencia cubana.

CUBA'S DOLLAR FOOD MARKET AND U.S. EXPORTS

James E. Ross and María Antonia Fernández Mayo

Cuban visitors and residents have the option of buying certain types of food with either pesos or dollars. They may use one of four different currencies and have access to more than eight different types of official food markets. Cuban pesos are used in the ration stores, and various agricultural markets. U.S. dollars and, to a lesser extent, convertible pesos and euros are used to purchase food in retail stores authorized to recover foreign exchange (*divisas*).[1]

Currencies are not interchangeable at point of purchase. Cuban pesos are not accepted in tourist facilities and dollars cannot be used in ration stores. Dollars and pesos, however, may be exchanged before the sale. For purposes of this paper, food that can be purchased only with U.S. dollars, Cuba's convertible peso or euros is referred to as "dollar food." The thesis of the paper is that the hard currency cost of Cuba's imported food is offset by sales in Cuba of food for dollars. That is, the amount of dollars spent by Cubans and foreign visitors in Cuba for food at the consumer level is equal to, or greater than, the amount of dollars spent by the government to import food.

CUBA'S FOOD MARKETS

There are two general categories of food markets in Cuba, the peso food market and the dollar food market.[2] Peso food markets are not meant to compete with food being sold in dollar stores; however, the same or similar products may be available in both markets. Of Cuba's official food markets, only the dollar stores (*tiendas en divisas*, also referred to as TRDs—*tiendas de recuperacion de divisas* and "*la chopin*") trade in dollars.

Other internal food markets include: ration stores (*Mercado de Alimentos Racionados*); free agricultural markets (*Mercados Libres Agropecuarios*—MLA); Ministry of Agriculture markets selling food at fixed prices (*Mercados Agrícolas a Precios Topados*); agricultural "fairs" held on the last Sunday of each month (*Ferias Agropecuarias*); urban garden markets (*ventas en los huertos y organopónicos*); places of sale direct to the consumer by the Cooperatives of Agricultural Production (*Cooperativas de Producción Agropecuaria* —CPA) and the EJT (Youth Work Army); and the *Cadena de Tiendas Imágenes*—stores selling processed foods under the jurisdiction of the Ministry of Internal Trade (*Ministerio de Comercio Interior*— MINCIN). Other food outlets include fish shops, bread stores, and the unofficial *mercado subterráneo* or the black market.[3]

---

1. Euros are being accepted in dollar stores, tourist hotels and restaurants in Varadero, but currently not in Havana or other tourist areas.

2. As used in this paper, the term "dollar food market" refers to the buying and selling in Cuba of food and beverage products, whether imported or produced domestically, for dollars.

3. For detailed information on the internal markets, including price comparisons and an explanation of why consumers buy at dollar stores when the same product can be purchased for less at other markets, see José Alvarez, "Rationed Products and Something Else: Food Availability and Distribution in 2000 Cuba," *Cuba in Transition—Volume 11* (Washington: Association for the Study of the Cuban Economy, 2001), p. 305. See also Armando Nova González, "El Mercado Interno de los Alimentos," in *Cuba—Reflexiones Sobre Su Economía*, La Habana, 2002, p. 193.

SOURCES OF DOLLARS

Cubans who do not have dollars, or adequate pesos to exchange for convertible pesos, do not participate in the government's dollar food market. Reportedly, this applies to about one-third of the population. Another one-third has access to dollars from time to time. The remaining one-third has access to dollars on a continuing basis. Those Cubans living in Havana, about 20% of the 11.2 million, account for the highest percentage of the people with access to dollars.

Cubans who do not have direct access to dollars may purchase convertible pesos. One convertible peso is equal in value to one U.S. dollar. Convertible pesos may be purchased at government operated *Casas de Cambio, S.A.* (CADECA). During 2002, and until the present, *Casas de Cambio* have sold the convertible peso for 27 pesos and purchased U.S. dollars for 26 pesos. The peso and the dollar circulate freely in Cuba.[4]

There are three major sources for Cuban consumers to gain access to dollars: remittances, tourism and foreign businesses. Cuban nationals obtain dollars primarily through remittances, funds sent to them by family members living abroad. While the flow of remittances to Cuba is less than to many other Latin American or Caribbean countries, the amount is growing. Data from the Inter-American Bank show a 22% increase in 2002. Dollars sent to family members by the one million Cubans in the United States, and the thousands living in other countries, totaled $1.138 billion in 2002.

In addition to remittances, Cubans providing services for tourists may receive tips in dollars. Cubans working for foreign businesses operating in Cuba sometimes receive bonuses in dollars. Some mixed enterprises supplement workers' income with dollars, either through negotiated arrangements with the Cuban government or through other means. Private enterprises, such as in-home restaurants and home room-rentals, also earn dollars for Cuban families.[5]

CUBA'S DOLLAR FOOD SUPPLY POLICY

Cuba's purchasing and distribution system supplying the dollar food market is decentralized and complex. It is an intricate network of organizations authorized to purchase from domestic production and importation, and distribute food products in Cuba for dollars and/or pesos. Organizations include government agencies, state-owned companies, mixed enterprises, associated foreign firms and licensed private restaurants.

All of the following buy and/or sell food in Cuba for dollars:

- retail stores trading only with dollars, and the holding companies supplying those market outlets;

- government-owned and foreign-associated hotels and restaurants catering to tourists for dollars, and the companies servicing those establishments;

- food processing companies purchasing both domestic and imported products and selling a portion of their production within Cuba for dollars;

- government agencies and mixed enterprises supplying the system and/or purchasing for their own account, or for other companies, and wholesale and retail for either dollars or pesos;

- small in-home restaurants servicing customers for dollars; and

- the underground (black) market.

Dollar foods purchased and sold in Cuba are both produced domestically and imported.

The government's priority for supplying the dollar food market is to buy and sell fresh produce, pro-

---

4. The government of Cuba maintains a fixed exchange rate for its international dealings and a more flexible exchange rate for domestic use. Cuba's government does not vary the value of the peso for commercial transactions regardless of any fluctuation with the value of the U.S. dollar or other currencies on the international market. *Economic Eye on Cuba*, U.S.-Cuba Trade and Economic Council, Inc.

5. For detailed information on main sources of hard currency and possible uses by the Cuban population, see Paolo Spadoni, "The Role of the United States in the Cuban Economy," in this volume.

cessed foods and other food products that are of national origin. The second priority is to purchase production from mixed enterprises. When products are not available through national production or from mixed enterprises, the government will import products to supply the dollar food market.

Much of the food imported from the United States, Canada and the European Union is sold in Cuba for dollars. In addition, some fresh produce and manufactured foods originating in Cuba earn hard currency through sales in Cuba's dollar stores, the tourist industry and via other market outlets.

NATIONAL ORIGIN PRODUCTION

State production units include state farms, state-controlled agricultural cooperatives, and national food manufacturers. State farms and the Basic Units of Cooperative Production (UBPC) are the main national sources of fresh produce for the dollar market. They operate under the authority of the Ministry of Agriculture (*Ministerio de Agricultura*—MINAGRI). Processed products of national origin are provided by manufacturers operating under the jurisdiction of the Ministry of Food Industries (*Ministerio de la Industria Alimenticia*—MINAL).

Fresh Produce: Fresh fruit and vegetables of national origin are supplied by state-owned companies such as *Frutas Selectas S.A.* This semi-autonomous company, within the Ministry of Agriculture, selects the best fruits and vegetables produced by state-owned farms and state-controlled cooperatives. *Frutas Selectas* then markets the products to tourist hotels and restaurants.

Several other companies, under the jurisdiction of the Ministry of Agriculture, supply food and agricultural products for sale to the tourist trade. Companies include: *Cítricos Ceiba, Cítricos Ciego de Avila, Cítricos Caribe, CAN, La Cuba, Apicultura, Empresas Porcino, Empresa de Tabacos y Cigarros, Hortícolas, OROCA, CAI Arrocero, Empresas Pecuarias, Cuba Café* and *Suministros Agropecuarios.*

Processed Foods: All food manufacturers in Cuba are under the jurisdiction of the Ministry of Food Industries, created in 1965. MINAL oversees industries manufacturing milk and meat products, cereals, confections, bread, biscuits and crackers, pastries, fruit and vegetable products, alcoholic beverages, water, soft drinks, beer and other products. Industries milling bulk commodities, such as wheat and rice, also are under the jurisdiction of MINAL.

At the time of the establishment of the Ministry of Food Industries, Cuba was importing most of the processed food consumed in the country. In addition, most of the primary material used by the existing national food manufacturing industry was imported. There was little growth in food processing until food research centers were introduced. Between 1970 and 1975, the Food and Agricultural Organization of the United Nations and the governments of Sweden and the Netherlands provided financing for pilot plants devoted to applied research in the lactic, meat-processing, and vegetable and fruit-preserving branches.[6]

International assistance from 1975 to 1990 for research and development in Cuba's food industry led to substantial growth in food manufacturing. Production increases during this period included: canned meats, 157%; canned fruits and vegetables, 66%; cheeses, 143%; and wheat flour, 126%. The number of production lines had grown from 57 in 1975 to more than one thousand by 1989.

With the loss of Soviet and Eastern Bloc trade preferences in 1989 and 1990, there was a progressive decline in Cuban production in general until the mid-1990s. Food industry executives were forced to introduce products that made it possible to raise production volumes through increased use of extenders and substitutes in products destined for the domestic market. The imperative was to maintain nutritional values despite a reduction in agricultural production, especially of meat products.

---

6. *Business Tips on Cuba*, August 1996, p. 20.

Between 1990 and 1994, the worst period for the Cuban economy, the food processing industry registered a dramatic decline of 42% in the value of its output, along with a reduction of 74% in national raw-material supplies from the agricultural sector, and a 34% drop in imported raw materials.[7]

In 1994, Cuba's production of manufactured food products was 45% of the output in 1989. The output of beverages was 56%. By 2001, beverage production had increased to 83% of the 1989 level. Food manufacturing increased more slowly, reaching only 52%. While the food industry has had significant growth since 1994, production remains substantially less than the output level of more than a decade earlier.[8]

Production lines that are growing the most include: beer, soft drinks, mineral water, alcoholic beverages for export, powdered milk, pastas, flour, soft cheese, ice cream, and yogurt. Wheat flour production also showed some increase, while milled rice production decreased substantially.

MIXED ENTERPRISE PRODUCTION

A mixed enterprise generating dollar sales of food products may include a food manufacturer or an agricultural production unit. Enterprises producing dollar foods may take the form of a joint-venture investment, an international economic association, or a cooperative production agreement. There are no totally foreign owned food production or manufacturing operations in Cuba.

Mixed enterprises, the second highest priority, include foreign-associated companies such as Sherritt Green. The joint venture company, formed with Sherritt International of Canada, produces fruit and vegetables for sale to tourist hotels and restaurants. Mixed enterprises producing for the tourist trade, in addition to Sherritt Green, include Agro King of Canada, Grupo BM of Israel, and others.

Sixteen of Cuba's food-manufacturing companies are joint ventures and 12 are Cooperative Production Agreements.[9] Each of the 16 mixed enterprises are associated with Coralsa (*La Corporacion Alimentaria—CORAL S.A.*), a holding company constituted within MINAL in 1996. The Ministry restructured in the mid-1990s to promote increased support for food industry firms operating with foreign capital. Participation of Coralsa in the 16 enterprises ranges from 40% to 50%. Fixed assets of the companies at the time of restructuring were placed at $36 million. They had $4 million in working capital and $25.5 million in the process of investment.

Enterprises associated with Coralsa produce and market sausages, candies and confections, products derived from wheat, instant beverages, wines, beers, soft drinks and mineral waters, as well as technological and refrigeration equipment for the food industry. In 1994 the mixed enterprises had a combined value of production of $20 million. By 2000 the value of production of the mixed enterprises had reached $140 million, representing 6% of national production.[10]

Another area of activity in the Cuban food industries sector has been the overseas food processing operations in which there is Cuban capital and technology. A portion of the earnings from these industries is returned to Cuba. *Cía. de Tasajo de Uruguay*, for example, was established in Uruguay to process jerked beef and other meat products for export to Cuba and other Latin American and African countries. A Coralsa-owned company, *Carnes del Mercosur S.A.*, located in Cuba, imports and markets the products in Cuba for the internal market.

7. *Business Tips on Cuba*, August 1996, p. 18.

8. *Anuario Estadístico de Cuba* (2002). Capítulo VIII, Sector Industria.

9. Omar Everleny Pérez Villanueva. "La inversión extranjera directa en Cuba: Evolución y perspectiva," *Cuba—Reflexiones Sobre su Economía*, La Habana, 2002 p. 90.

10. Pérez Villanueva, p. 90.

Table 1. Cuba's Food and Beverage Imports, in Thousand Cuban Pesos[a] and as Percent of Total Imports

Year	Total Imports	Food Imports[b]	Beverage Imports	Food and Beverage Imports	Food and Beverage Imports as % of Total Imports
1990	7,416,525	827,341	3,728	831,069	11.2
1991	4,233,752	825,377	908	826,285	19.5
1992	2,314,916	498,569	12	498,851	21.5
1993	2,008,215	474,176	155	474,131	23.6
1994	2,016,821	467,331	2,760	470,091	23.3
1995	2,882,530	610,883	14,068	624,951	21.7
1996	3,480,608	689,108	11,676	700,784	20.1
1997	3,987,256	724,463	27,367	751,830	18.9
1998	4,181,192	703,940	21,208	725,148	17.3
1999	4,349,090	721,168	21,508	742,676	17.1
2000	4,759,613	671,569	16,853	688,422	14.5
2001	4,787,753	754,356	16,138	770,494	16.1
2002 est.	4,838,000	—	—	832,000	17.2

Source: Anuario Estadístico, various volumes.

a. Official Cuban exchange rate is 1 Cuban peso equal to 1 U.S. Dollar.
b. Excludes imports of live animals.

FOREIGN SOURCES

Historically, before and after the revolution, imported food has been an important factor in feeding Cuba's population. During the years of favored trade with the Soviet Union and the Eastern Bloc countries, Cuba had the financial means to continue importing many of the bulk and U.S. branded food items that its consumers preferred. With the loss of Soviet aid beginning in the 1990s, food imports declined significantly in dollar value but increased dramatically as a percent of total imports.

In 1990 food and beverage imports were 11% of total imports. In the early 1990s those imports increased to 20% or more and did not recede until economic reforms were initiated in the middle 1990s. During the past three years, a decade after the loss of Soviet support, food imports have averaged about 16% of total imports. The higher percentage at the beginning of the 1990s was a result of a reduction in total imports and a continuing need for Cuba to import food to feed its people. The lower percentage at the beginning of this century is a result of the government's effort to increase food production and to feed its population with lower-value imported food products (see Table 1).

Foods sold or made available direct to consumers and the tourist industry for dollars, generally, include those products that can be classified as consumer-oriented, but may also include intermediate products. Most bulk products require processing. Grains are an example of bulk products. Processed products, such as flour and vegetable oils, are an example of intermediate products, and meats and poultry products are examples of consumer-oriented foods.

Cuba's Ministry of Agriculture is responsible for regulating importation of bulk and intermediate agricultural products. Consumer-oriented products are imported under the jurisdiction of the Cuban Ministry of Public Health (*Ministerio de Salud Pública*—MINSAP).[11]

Food and Beverage Importers: Decentralization in Cuban foreign trade started in 1992, allowing state and private enterprises, joint ventures and international economic associations, direct access to external markets. Since then, the number of foreign business-

---

11. Caribbean Basin Agricultural Trade Office of the USDA/Foreign Agricultural Service in Miami. See recent reports on food laws and the food service sector, GAIN Reports #CU2001, 2002, and 2003.

Table 2. Cuban Companies Authorized To Import Meat

Residencial Turístico Marina Hemingway, S.A.	Distribuidora CIMEX S.A.
Compañía Hoteles Cubanacán S.A.	Empresa Importadora de Abastecimientos Técnicos
Grandes Hoteles del Caribe S.A.	Gaviota S.A.
Compañía de Tiendas Universo, S.A.	AT Comercial S.A
Grupo de Exportación e Importación de la Oficina del Historiador de la Ciudad de la Habana	Empresa Cubana Exportadora e Importadora de Servicios, Artículos y Productos Técnicos Especializados
Palmares S.A.	CORATUR S.A.
Inversiones Locarinos S.A.	Empresa Cubana Importadora de Alimentos
Parque Central S.A.	SERVIMPORT
Comercializadora D' Leone	Cubanacán
Aerocatering S.A.	Servicios Comerciales Argos S.A.
Suministro Marítimo-Portuario A.C.	Comercializadora ITH S.A.
Cadenas de Tiendas TRD Caribe	CUBALSE
Firma Comercial Importadora "Pesmar"	"Importadora del Mar"
Cadenas de Tiendas Caracol S.A.	Firma Comercial Importadora EMSUNEX
Empresa Cubana Importadora y Exportadora de Productos Técnicos	Comercial Mayorista de Alimentos "Casabe"

men opening branch offices in Cuba or represented by agents has increased. Many warehouses were established and duty free zones and industrial parks were opened. Authorizations increased for companies to import food, for example 30 companies are currently authorized to import meat (see Table 2).

Meat and other consumer-oriented foods may be imported through several different agencies and companies. Most intermediate products and bulk commodities are imported through Alimport (*Empresa Cubana Importadora de Alimentos*, under the auspices of the *Ministerio del Comercio Exterior*). Consumer-oriented foods also may be imported by Alimport to supply the peso market, such as ration stores, school lunch programs, hospitals and other institutions. Alimport also imports food ingredients for the food industry sector. In addition, dollar stores and other government-owned companies may receive food products imported by Alimport.

Alimport decides who to do business with, what quantity to buy based on end customers' needs, and negotiates and fixes prices. It also decides buying terms depending on: seller, delivery terms and place, financial facilities, and freight advantages.[12]

For FAS and FOB operations, Alimport relies on a logistics group in charge of chartering vessels and monitoring the entire process of transportation from the operational standpoint. Alimport works with Cuban flag vessels, brokers, or directly with foreign flagship owners, and agrees on terms and operates with them as per international practice standards.

For other operations, the Alimport logistics group ensures shipping terms are in accordance with contract terms. It also follows up on shipment and carriage of goods until delivery at port of destination. Alimport negotiates and agrees on discharging terms with port terminal and stevedoring companies. According to Alimport's president, Alimport looks after needs of its end-customers and its purchasing strategy is based on such needs.[13]

Other official importing agencies of dollar foods include government-owned holding companies that supply retail dollar stores and government-owned companies and mixed enterprises that own or operate tourist facilities.

Food and Beverage Imports: Food and beverage imports, in terms of total value, are currently at the level of the beginning of the 1990s. Food imports in

---

12. Presentation by Mr. Pedro Alvarez Borrego, President of Alimport, Agricultural Sales Conference, Cancun, Mexico, Jan. 30-Feb. 2, 2002.

13. ibid.

1990 were $827 million and beverage imports totaled $4 million. In 2001 food imports were valued at $754 and beverage imports at $16 million. Wine at $5.7 million in 2001 accounted for 35% of the beverage imports. From 1991 to 1995 wine imports were negligible.

Increased wine imports since 1995 reflect the government's emphasis on tourism, which has become the driving force of the economy. Tourism also requires importation of higher value foods. With the return of tourism forecast, Cuba may increase the value of food and beverage imports in 2003 over the $832 million estimated for 2002.

MAJOR MARKETING OUTLETS FOR DOLLAR FOODS

There are two principal marketing outlets for food sold for dollars in Cuba. They are the dollar stores and the tourist trade. Other entities involved in the dollar food chain include in-home family restaurants known generally as *paladares*[14] and the underground or black market. The importance of the black market, which deals in both pesos and dollars, has fluctuated with the availability of food through official channels and economic reforms and regulations imposed by the government.

In-home restaurants are limited to family employment and may serve only 12 customers at one time. They may charge their customers in either pesos or dollars; however, most *paladares* request dollars for payment. *Paladares* do not import food products, but purchase those products through the retail dollar stores, state-operated agricultural markets, semi-private *agromercados*, and from other sources using both pesos and dollars. Economic impact of the private restaurants has been reported to be negligible.[15]

Impact of *paladares* on the dollar food market, however, may be of greater proportional importance than for the total economy. In addition to purchasing food for dollars at retail dollar stores, *paladares* owners may exchange dollars for pesos at CADECAs in order to purchase food in the peso agricultural markets.

Retail Dollar Stores

Retail stores selling food and beverage products for dollars are scattered throughout the country. Dollar stores are owned by the Cuban government. No foreign investment in these stores has been permitted. In all of these retail stores, food products that have been imported or produced domestically are sold for dollars.

In Havana there are approximately 300 dollar stores, and in the entire country roughly 1,000. Most of the dollar stores outside Havana are located in the tourist areas of Varadero and Jardines del Rey, Norte de Camagüey, Norte de Holguín, Santiago de Cuba, Costa Sur and Archipiélago de los Canarraeos.

Holding Companies Serving Dollar Stores: Companies servicing the dollar stores are government-owned, but operate as semi-autonomous private companies. The companies are incorporated and have the *Sociedad Anónima* (S.A.) designation. Generally, the companies control their own hard-currency revenues and can make purchases on their own account. S.A. companies must remit a monthly payment to the government. The amount is negotiated between the government and the company directors.[16]

Names of the major dollar store chains and the government corporations owning them include: 1) *Tiendas Panamericanas* (CIMEX S.A.), (2) *Tiendas Universo* (Cubanacán S.A.), (3) *Tiendas Caracol* (Caracol S.A.), (4) *Tiendas Meridiano* (CUBALSE S.A.), (5) *Tiendas TRD Caribe* (Caribe S.A.), and (6) *Tiendas Habaguanex* (Habaguanex S.A.).

---

14. *Paladar*, translated means palate or taste, but the origin of the use for Cuban family restaurants is said to be taken from a Brazilian soap opera. The main character goes to the capital and establishes a chain of small restaurants called *Paladares*.

15. Ted Henken, "Last Resort or Bridge to the Future? Tourism and Workers in Cuba's Second Economy," *Cuba in Transition—Volume 10* (Washington: Association for the Study of the Cuban Economy, 2000), p. 331.

16. *Cuba: A Guide for Canadian Businesses*. Department of Foreign Affairs and International Trade. The Canadian Trade Commissioner Service, June 1999.

Purchases and Sales of Dollar Stores: Based on data obtained pertaining to some of the dollar store purchases, it is estimated by the authors that approximately 40% to 60% of the value of food products purchased for sale in dollar stores are imported. Remaining needed supplies are provided from national production.

Prices of products sold in the dollar stores are normally higher than those offered in other internal food markets. The consumer may pay a price that is 200% or more above the imported price or the price in one of the internal food markets.[17] Products similar to those available in the dollar stores may be found at lower prices in other internal markets. Dollar stores, reportedly, sell imported products at 240% of cost, and products of national origin at 170%.

Tourist Hotels and Restaurants

Cuba rates its hotels on a star basis, ranging from one to five stars. A five-star hotel is better than a four-star, etc. The rating system does not compare facilities and services to comparable stars of hotels in other countries, but is used only to compare quality of hotels within Cuba. With current standards, most international tourism and the resulting market for dollar foods, is concentrated in three, four and five-star hotels. While two-star and one-star hotels provide a limited market for imported dollar food products, the major source of food for these hotels is the domestic market.

Cuba has approximately 300 tourist properties with about 40,000 rooms. Five-star and four-star hotels account for approximately 40% of the hotels and 70% of room occupancy. Three-star hotels account for about 35% of the hotels and one-fifth of the rooms, while two star-hotels account for 25% of the hotels and 10% of room occupancy. Annual growth in tourism in the 1990s was more than 15%, but in 2001 the number of tourists was only slightly more

than the year before, approximately 1.8 million. A slow start for tourism in 2002 resulted in even fewer tourists, 1.7 million, than recorded each of the previous two years.

In the early 1990s, when tourists numbered some 300,000, only 12% of the products and services required for the tourist industry were provided through national production. Almost all food products needed for tourist hotels and restaurants were imported. All of the beer and bottled water served to tourists was imported. As a result of economic reforms in the mid-1990s, pursuit of a policy of import substitution, and international assistance to the food industry, the supply situation was reversed and Cuba now supports, according to a Cuban study, some 65% of the tourist hotel and restaurant needs through national production. One national brewery, a joint venture, supplies about 95% of the tourist market for beer and another joint venture supplies almost all of the bottled water.[18]

Holding Companies Serving Tourism: Several semi-autonomous holding companies service the tourist industry. They include: Corporación Cubanacán, Grupo Hotelero Gran Caribe, Horizontes Hoteles, Habaguanex, Grupo de Turismo Gaviota, Isla Azul, Grupo de Recreación y Turismo Rumbos, Compañía de Marinas Puerto Sol, and the Complejo de Convenciones. Some description of each company is given in Box 1. To some extent, all of the companies compete with each other, but they concentrate on different segments of the tourist market. No foreign investment has been introduced in the ownership of these companies.

A few foreign companies have negotiated contract agreements that permit them to import food directly for their tourist facilities. Foreign companies having arrangements under Foreign Investment Law No. 77 with the Cuban companies often operate as hotel ad-

---

17. Armando Nova González, "El Mercado Interno de los Alimentos," in *Cuba—Reflexiones Sobre Su Economía*, La Habana, 2002, p. 193.

18. Miguel Alejandro Figueras Pérez, "El turismo internacional y la formación de clusters productivos en la economía cubana," in *Cuba—Reflexiones sobre su Economía,* La Habana, 2002, pp. 111 and 112. (Cuban data on national supply, however, may consider a food product manufactured with imported food ingredients, or a repackaged foreign product as national origin.)

Box 1.   Holding Companies Supplying the Tourism Trade

Corporación Cubanacán S.A. was formed to operate four and five star hotels, restaurants, cafeterias, retail stores, water recreation centers, tourist health facilities, and tourist reception and other recreation centers. Cubanacán also produces and sells artisan handicrafts and operates a transportation company that provides tour buses and rents automobiles. Many of the tourist hotels, administered as either international economic association contracts or joint ventures, involve Cubanacan. Joint investment arrangements under Foreign Investment Law No. 77 have been developed by Cubanacán with Grupo Sol Meliá (Spain), LTI (Germany), Golden Tulip (Holland), and SuperClubs (Jamaica).

Grupo Hotelero Gran Caribe S.A. operates more than 40 hotels classified as four and five star hotels. Gran Caribe hotels have 9,500 rooms for tourists scattered throughout the country, but are located mainly in Havana and Varadero. In addition, the group operates three primary tourist attractions in Havana, the Restaurant La Bodeguita del Medio, Bar and Restaurant La Floridita and the Cabaret Tropicana.

Horizontes Hoteles S.A. is a hotel chain, mostly three and four stars, with more than 7,000 rooms. Horizontes also operates facilities with mineral water baths, treatment for stress, etc. One spa treats patients with health problems characteristic of the Caribbean.

Grupo de Recreación y Turismo Rumbos S.A. founded in 1994, has grown approximately 20% annually. It operates facilities for both national and international tourists in Cuba's major tourist cities and rustic locations. Rumbos is diversified, and has established businesses in: a travel agency; various types of restaurants, including fast food (comidas rápidas, restaurants and parrilladas); small lodges in cities, on beaches, in the country, at golf courses, airports, and marinas; and eco-tourism with 40 routes. Currently, Rumbos is planning eight new golf courses to meet the standards for both international golf amateurs and professionals.

Compañía de Marinas Puerto Sol S.A. was created to develop marinas, piers, recreational boat activities, etc. The company owns 390 two star and local hotels to meet the needs of tourists and nationals.

Grupo de Turismo Gaviota S.A. is a tourism company controlled by the Revolutionary Armed Forces. It is dedicated to operation of four and five star hotels, development of marinas, restaurants and cafeterias, recreational water facilities, and health facilities for tourists. It also operates a transportation company that offers tourist buses and rental of automobiles and taxis.

Habaguanex S.A. is part of the Office of the Historian of Havana (Oficina del Historiador de la Ciudad). It was established to develop three and four star hotels for international tourists in the Historic Center of Old Havana (Centro Historico de la Habana Vieja). Currently, it is renovating various hotels and opening restaurants in the oldest part of the city.

Isla Azul S.A. was established to develop two and three star hotels for international tourists seeking low-cost accommodations.

Complejo de Convenciones includes operation of the Palace of Conventions (Palacio de las Convenciones), Hotel Palco, the restaurants Rancho Palco and El Palenque, and Club Habana. It also administers the Sala de Exposiciones (PABEXPO), the Mansión Residencial (*Casa de Protocolo*—Protocol House), and the auto rental agency, Palcocar. Basically, the complex specializes in the development of tourist events and conventions.

ministrators and assume responsibility for food and beverage services. Some have taken equity positions in the hotels owned by the holding companies. These include, among others: Grupo Sol Meliá and Hoteles

C from Spain; Accor and Club Med from France; LTI and RIU from Germany; Delta Hotels and Resorts, Commonwealth Hospitality, Ltd., and Leisure Canada, Inc. from Canada; Viaggi di Ventaglio and Press Tours from Italy; and SuperClubs from Jamaica. About 30% of Cuba's hotels involve investments with foreign companies. There are no totally foreign owned hotels in Cuba.

Principal Supplier for Tourism: Comercializadora ITH, S.A. is the principal company importing supplies for tourist hotels and restaurants. ITH operates under the auspices of the Ministry of Tourism (*Ministerio del Turismo*—MINTUR) importing products for government-owned tourism holding companies, mixed enterprises, and individual hotels and restaurants. It is the only company supplying food and other items for tourist facilities throughout the country. Food products may be imported directly by ITH, or it may import through Alimport, or any of the official importing agencies. Products are purchased by ITH from both domestic and foreign sources.

Some joint-venture hotels have agreements under the foreign investment law to import direct, without going through a government purchasing company. At times, because of the foreign company's supplier contacts and expertise, government-owned hotels may import through the joint venture or contract agreement companies. The supply and quality of food products available through the importing company may determine which source is used.[19]

Food Purchases, Sales and Tourism Revenue: Gross revenues from tourism in 2002 from 1.7 million tourists totaled $1.5 billion, with $350 million in gross profits. Cuba has projected 3.1 million visitors in 2005, and revenue from tourism at $2.5 billion. For 2010, Cuba has projected 6.2 million visitors and $10 billion in revenue. In view of factors affecting tourism in Cuba and worldwide, it is doubtful theses figures will be achieved.

Increased tourism of this magnitude obviously would affect the demand for food, both from domestic production and imported. The proportional increase would probably favor imported food. Increased demand for imported food would impact the need for additional hard currency. With the high markup policy on food sold through tourist hotels and restaurants, however, the country may advance the foreign currency needed to import the food needed for tourism. Food is sold through tourist hotels and restaurants, generally, at 300% of the imported dollar cost. As in dollar stores, food of national origin transacted through tourism is sold at a lower price markup.

Cubanacán S.A. accounts for a large percentage of the tourist market. It is comprised of 15 companies registered in Cuba, including Cubanacán Hoteles administering 28 hotels. Other Cubanacán companies include Palmares Restaurantes, operating 50 restaurants and numerous cafeterias. Tiendas Universo owns a network of commercial centers and stores catering to the tourist trade. Cubanacán, and the mixed enterprises in which Cubanacan maintains interest, represent 34% of Cuba's tourism receipts.

VALUE OF PRODUCTS ENTERING THE DOLLAR FOOD MARKET

Complete data are not available to the authors stating the value of food, imported or produced domestically, sold for dollars through dollar stores or tourism. Estimates of the value of food distributed through dollar stores and the tourist industry are made based on both official and unofficial sources (see Table 3).

Value and Sources of Domestic Supplies

Domestic supplies of dollar food originate with the Ministry of Agriculture, the Ministry of Food Industries and mixed enterprises.

Food production, mostly fresh produce, sold through the Ministry of Agriculture to the tourist sector and dollar stores in 2001 totaled $168 million, an increase of 3.5% compared to gross revenues of US$162 million reported in 2000.[20] In 1998 and

---

19. Caribbean Agricultural Trade Office, USDA/FAS, Miami.

20. U.S.-Cuba Trade and Economic Council, Economic Eye on Cuba, March 18, 2002.

Table 3. Estimate of Annual Value of Food Sold in the Dollar Food Market, Value of Dollar Earnings from Food Sales in the Dollar Food Market, and the Sources of Food Entering the Dollar Market, Million U.S. Dollars

Source of Food Sold	Dollar Market	Value of Food at "Wholesale"	Multiplier	Value of Dollar Earnings
Imported	Dollar Stores	40 - 60	2.4	100 - 140
Imported	Tourist Industry	40 - 60	3.0	120 - 180
Ministry of Food Industries	Dollar Stores & Tourism	150 - 180	1.7	250 - 300
Ministry of Agriculture	Dollar Stores & Tourism	160 - 180	1.7	270 - 300
Mixed Enterprises	Tourist Hotels & Restaurants	5 - 10	1.7	10 - 15
Agricultural Markets	CADECAsª	5 - 10	-0-	5 - 10
TOTAL		400 - 500		750 - 950
Earnings Adjustedᵇ				650 - 800

a. CADECAs located at various agricultural markets exchange dollars for pesos. Individuals who have exchanged dollars for pesos may then purchase food with those pesos for their own private use and/or for sale through their private restaurants (paladares). Dollars exchanged through all CADECAs in 2001 earned $100 million for the government, of which it is estimated by the authors 5% to 10% was used for food. It is an indirect use of dollars to purchase food.

b. Dollar earnings adjusted to compensate for the import cost of food (bulk and intermediate) used in the manufacture of food products sold in the dollar market, and the import cost of food sold through tourism and in the dollar stores.

1999, MINAGRI reported gross revenues from marketing agricultural commodities to the tourism sector of US$59 million and US$70 million, respectively. Information is not available to explain the large increase from $70 million in 1999 to $162 million in 2000. Assuming the higher level of food supply will continue to be available for sale to the tourist industry; however, an estimated value of food produced under the auspices of the Ministry of Agriculture and sold for dollars through tourism could range from $160 million to $180 million in 2003.

Sales of processed food for the tourist sector and dollar stores in 1998 totaled $171 million, 21% more than the year before. Production was three times greater than in 1994, when the food processing industry began focusing on the dollar market. Approximately 15% of total output of the food processing industry were destined for the tourist trade and export. By 1999, the dollar market represented 20% of production sales. Processed foods sold through the Ministry of Food Industries to the tourist sector and dollar stores, assuming most of the mixed enterprise production and some of the national company production enter the dollar market, could range from $150 million to $180 million.

Data are not available on the value of food produced in Cuba, largely fresh fruit and vegetables, for the tourist market by mixed enterprises, but could range from $5 million to $10 million.

Value and Sources of Foreign Supplies

The European Union and Canada in the 1990s provided about half of Cuba's food imports, while Mexico, and Latin American (Argentina and Brazil for soybean products) and Asian countries (China, Thailand and Vietnam for rice imports) were also important sources of food imports. More than half of Europe's agricultural exports to Cuba, which totaled $185 million in 1999, consisted of wheat flour, vegetable oils and consumer-ready products, primarily dairy products and poultry meat. Wheat accounted for about 45% of the total. Canada's agricultural exports to Cuba, $115 million in 1999, were largely (83%) pulses and consumer-oriented products, such as red meat, poultry and dairy products.

Official data show food and beverage imports in recent years ranging from $700 million to $800 million. Approximately half of the food imported by Cuba meets the classifications of intermediate and consumer-ready products. The remaining half consists of bulk commodities, such as wheat, coarse grains, soybeans, pulses, and rice. Most of the bulk and some of the intermediate products imported by Alimport are for the accounts of the ration stores, institutions and food manufacturing companies. A large percentage of the imported food products clas-

Table 4. U.S. Food and Agricultural Sales to Cuba, 2001-2002, and January through May, 2002-2003 ($1,000)

Product	2001	2002	2002 Jan-May	2003 Jan-May	Percent Change (2003/2002)
Bulk Products	**2,327**	**72,774**	**38,605**	**36,099**	**-6.5**
Wheat	—	22,789	16,005	4,832	-69.8
Coarse Grains	2,327	22,739	6,538	14,746	125.5
Rice	—	6,266	6,266	8,077	28.9
Soybeans	—	20,922	9,796	8,213	-16.2
Pulses	—	58	—	230	—
Intermediate Products[a]	**—0—**	**41,316**	**7,812**	**36,796**	**373.3**
Soybean Meal	—	19,281	3,807	12,745	234.8
Soybean Oil	—	21,438	3,577	23,403	554.3
Animal Fats	—	428	428	17	-96.0
Other	—	165	0	489	—
Consumer Oriented Products	**2,247**	**25,723**	**8,554**	**15,575**	**82.1**
Snack Foods	—	176	0	83	—
Breakfast Cereal	—	41	0	0	—
Red Meats	—	254	0	32	—
Poultry Meat	1,959	22,946	7,713	13,597	76.3
Dairy Products	288	336	265	67	-74.7
Eggs & Products	—	767	267	641	140.1
Fresh Fruit	—	366	0	501	—
Fresh Vegetables	—	28	0	0	—
Processed F&V	—	189	0	92	—
F&V Juices	—	3	0	0	—
Tree Nuts	—	11	0	38	—
Wine & Beer	—	46	0	0	—
Other	—	562	308	524	70.1
Total	**4,574**	**139,814**	**54,971**	**88,650**	**61.3**

a.   Excludes live animals ($3 million in 2002). Cumulative values for major products from December 2001-May 2003 (in million dollars): soybean oil, 45; coarse grains, 40; poultry meat, 39; soybean meal, 32; soybeans, 29; wheat, 28; rice, 14; eggs and products, 1.4; and fresh fruit, 0.9.

sified as intermediate and consumer-oriented, is sold direct to consumers through dollar stores, government-owned restaurants, and tourist hotel cafeterias and restaurants.

U.S. Share of Cuba's Food Market

With changes in U.S. policy regarding food and agricultural exports to Cuba and Cuba's reduced food supply as a result of tropical storms, food imports from the United States have been initiated in the new century. In the year 2001, the United States exported $4.6 million in food to Cuba. In 2002, U.S. food exports to Cuba increased to $140 million (see Table 4).

The Cuban government has designated Alimport as the sole importer of food and agricultural products from the United States. Dollar store and tourism holding companies must obtain authorization from

Alimport before importing food from the United States. This procedure is not required for other countries.

Excluding political considerations, it is anticipated Cuba will continue buying U.S. food because of lower transportation costs and a competitive U.S. agricultural sector that wants to trade with Cuba. Another factor, less obvious, is that Cubans are familiar with U.S. brands and appreciate the quality of U.S. food products. Until 1992, soon after the loss of favored trade with the Soviet Bloc countries, Cuba purchased U.S. branded foods directly from foreign subsidiaries of U.S. based companies. With passage of the 1992 Cuban Democracy Act (the "Torricelli Act"), U.S. Treasury authority to issue licenses for most U.S. subsidiary trade with Cuba was revoked. (The Torricelli Act also banned for 180 days vessels that had entered a Cuban port from loading or unloading in U.S. ports.)

In 1996 the Cuban Liberty and Democratic Solidarity Act (the "Helms-Burton Act") further tightened the embargo. Although trade between Cuba and U.S. foreign-based subsidiaries was not legal, according to U.S. law, food products with popular U.S. brands continued to be available in Cuba throughout the 1990s. It was not until January 1999, when President Clinton announced substantial changes in U.S. commercial policy toward Cuba, before prospects improved for food and agricultural exports to Cuba.

The Executive Order President Clinton signed in 1999, although interpretation was questionable, permitted U.S. food sales in Cuba to small private farmers, private cooperatives, individual Cuban nationals, private home-based restaurants, non-government organizations (NGOs), and the government-formed Basic Units of Cooperative Production (UBPCs). Although these private sales opportunities were permitted, there were no significant sales of food to Cuba until 2001. In fact, there were no significant sales of U.S. food and agricultural products to Cuba for more than 40 years, from 1960 to 2001.

More recent action, the Trade Sanctions Reform and Export Enhancement Act (TSRA), was signed into law late in 2000. It was not until July 12, 2001, however, that the implementing regulations were published. One of the primary purposes of TSRA was to require the U.S. Government to license commercial sales of agricultural commodities to purchasers in Cuba. All sales by U.S. companies would be authorized only in U.S. dollars—no credit transactions would be permitted.

Initially, Cuba cast aside offers of U.S. food products, including donations for disaster assistance. Following Hurricane Michelle in November 2001, however, Cuba's food reserve was depleted and Cuba turned to the United States for food, especially bulk

commodities, such as wheat, coarse grains, soybeans and rice, to supply food industries, ration stores and to furnish institutional food. All purchases have been for cash.

In May 2002, the Cuban government designated Alimport as the exclusive purchasing agent for U.S. based companies that want to export food products direct from the United States to Cuba. Alimport purchases agricultural and branded food products from U.S. based companies and re-sells, or transfers, the products to other Cuba-based companies or institutions.[21]

Cuba has indicated it will continue a high level of food imports from the United States in 2003. Cuba seems to be doing this. During the first five months of 2003, Cuba has increased imports of U.S. food 61% over imports in 2002. Since exports of U.S. food to Cuba began in December 2001, Cuba has purchased U.S. food valued at $233 million (Table 4).

U.S. bulk agricultural exports to Cuba from December 2001 through May 2003 totaled $111 million, intermediate product exports were $78 million, and consumer-oriented exports reached $44 million. Major commodity exports were: soybean oil, $45 million; coarse grains, $40 million; poultry meat, $39 million; soybean meal, $32 million; soybeans, $29 million and wheat, $28 million.

With prospects for regaining a higher level of tourism, Cuba's need for high-value food may increase. A study by the Cuba Policy Foundation[22] states that expenditures of $30 per day for food by U.S. tourists would require $126 million in food imports annually by Cuba, based on 1.5 million tourists staying seven days in Cuba. Higher estimates of dollar food expenditures and larger numbers of tourists, whether from the United States or other countries, would result in higher estimates of food import needs.

---

21. On May 12, 2002, the president of Alimport reported that Alimport would be the exclusive agent in Cuba for U.S. based companies. U.S.-Cuba Trade and Economic Council, council@cubatrade.org.

22. Cuba Policy Foundation, "Estimated Agricultural Economic Impacts of Expanded U.S. Tourism to Cuba," www.cubafoundation.org, Washington, D.C., February 2003.

CONCLUSION AND COMMENTS

Combining estimates of domestic and foreign food supplies entering Cuba's dollar food market provides a total of all foods sold in Cuba for dollars at roughly $400 million to $500 million. The value of dollar earnings from food being sold for dollars could range from $750 million to $950 million. Allowing for the cost of imported food sold in the dollar market would provide adjusted dollar earnings of $650 million to $800 million.

Based on the findings, the hard currency cost of imported food appears to be offset, in general, by sales in Cuba of food for dollars. In other words, dollar earnings from sales in Cuba of imported and domestically produced food appear to be equal to or greater than the amount of foreign exchange used to import food.

Estimating the dollar value of food sales at dollar stores and tourist facilities provides a check on the value of dollar food entering those outlets. Dollar store sales totaled $1.22 billion in 2001.[23] If the level of sales continues in 2003 and half of the dollar store sales is for food, the value of dollar food sold would be about $600 million. Tourism in 2001 was reported at 1.8 million and in 2002 at 1.7 million. If tourism returns in 2003 to the 2001 level and each tourist stays seven days and spends $30 to $45 per day for food, the range in value of food sold would be $360 million to $540 million. Combined, dollar food sales in tourist facilities and dollar stores would total roughly $1 billion.

In addition to the dollar expenditures for food sold in dollar stores and through tourist hotels and restaurants, Cubans exchange dollars for pesos to buy food at the agricultural peso food markets. CADECAs often are located at or near agricultural markets to exchange dollars for pesos. The dollars then become hard currency generated from the sale of domestic food.

Growth of Cuba's dollar food market, to a large extent, is contingent on continuation of a relatively high level of remittances, and increases in tourism and foreign investment. With elevated security concern worldwide following events on September 11, 2001 in the United States, and economic recession in Canada and Europe, growth of tourism in Cuba decreased in 2002 but has risen in the first part of 2003. Foreign investment appears to be continuing on a descending trend.

With a lower rate of tourist growth and shrinkage of disposable income worldwide for tourists, as well as reduced foreign investment, Cuba's dollar food market could be affected negatively. On the other hand, if there is sustained international economic recovery, tourism increases and Cuba implements effective growth policies, the demand in Cuba for dollar food could increase. The United States, in particular, would be in a favorable position because of its competitive prices and lower freight costs.

Perhaps the greatest unknown is the future of travel restrictions for U.S. tourists to Cuba. Lifting the U.S. imposed restrictions on travel to Cuba could result in a substantial increase in the number of tourists going to Cuba. This would create an increased demand in Cuba for imported, as well as domestically produced, dollar food and beverage products.

---

23. Paolo Spadoni, "The Role of the United States in the Cuban Economy," in this volume.

U.S. TRAVEL RESTRICTIONS TO CUBA: OVERVIEW AND EVOLUTION

María C. Werlau

This paper is the first part of a larger work in progress, titled "U.S. Travel Restrictions to Cuba: Overview, Implications, and Challenges," that will provide an in-depth and comprehensive look of U.S. travel restrictions to Cuba. This paper provides the backdrop for the travel restrictions, a chronology of their evolution, and an overview of current regulations. It also recounts the growth in U.S.-based travel to Cuba beginning in 1990, when the end of massive Soviet aid prompted the development of the tourist industry in a quest for hard currency revenues. The second and third parts are in progress and will be incorporated into the larger work for future publication. The second part will look at Cuba's tourist industry—its evolution, characteristics, and prospects for growth. The third part will examine the implications of current U.S. travel restrictions, the arguments for and against them, and the policy debate.

U.S. TRAVEL RESTRICTIONS TO CUBA[1]

Travel by Americans abroad is considered by the United States government to have "significant foreign policy implications and can damage the national interest."[2] In that context, the United States currently maintains restrictions on travel on persons subject to U.S. jurisdiction to four countries: Cuba, Libya, Iraq, and North Korea. The travel restrictions do not actually forbid travel to these locations, but rather limits, in some cases, the use of U.S. passports and/or direct transportation there, and, in call cases limit the ability to spend money there unless licensed by the U.S. Treasury Department.[3] These restrictions, in fact, derive from economic sanctions that currently exist against a total of 26 countries pursuant to Presidential and Congressional mandates. Cuba is also one of seven countries—together with North Korea, Iran, Libya, Iraq, Sudan and Syria—designated by

---

1. The information for this section has been taken from the following U.S. government sources: Cuban Assets Control Regulations (Title 31, Part 515 of the U.S. Code of Federal Regulations) and "What You Need To Know About The U.S. Embargo: An Overview of the Cuban Assets Control Regulations," Office of Foreign Assets Control, Department of the Treasury; Consular Information Sheet for Cuba, Department of State, May 30, 2003, updated November 2, 2003; website of the U.S. Interest Section in Havana website; Susan B. Epstein and Dianne E. Rennack, "Travel Restrictions: U.S. Government Limits on American Citizens' Travel Abroad," Congressional Research Service Report for Congress, August 30, 2001; Mark P. Sullivan, "Cuba: U.S. Restrictions on Travel and Legislative Initiatives for the 107th Congress, Congressional Research Service Report for Congress, Update for August 29, 2002; Statement by Secretary of State Madleine Albright, U.S. Department of State, January 5, 1999; and Statement of R. Richard Newcomb, Director, Office of Foreign Assets Control, before the Committee on Foreign Relations, United States Senate, Hearings on Travel and Trade with Cuba, October 2, 2003.

2. Cuba Brief, Section on Travel to Cuba, White House, 2002.

3. Sanctions vary by country. For example, all travel transactions with Iraq are prohibited, whereas exceptions are made for Libya for travel by close family members (upon registration), journalists, and travel to arrange sales of licensed products (agricultural commodities and medicines). A 2001 Congressional Research Service report compares Cuba's sanctions to those that apply to North Korea, where the use of U.S. passports is allowed subject to certain conditions, whereas there was an additional level of sanction with respect to Iraq and Libya, where the use of U.S. passports was not allowed. See OFAC's website (op.cit.) and Epstein and Rennack (2001).

the State Department as supporting international terrorism; most of these countries are subject to comprehensive economic sanctions.[4]

The purpose of the travel restrictions is to limit transactions that would result in U.S. dollars ending up in the hands of the sanctioned government. Originally, sanctions were imposed on Cuba as a result of the Castro government's (1) uncompensated taking of American property, considered the largest by a foreign government in U.S. history;[5] (2) subversion of Latin American democracies; and (3) the Castro regime's gross human rights abuses, including the mass execution of political opponents and dissidents by the Castro regime. As a result, the stated objective of the embargo is to deny funds to the Castro regime for internal repression and international subversion and to serve as retaliation for the uncompensated confiscation of U.S. properties on the island. It has been regarded by successive U.S. Administrations as a means "to support and encourage a peaceful transition to democracy and a free market in Cuba."[6]

The U.S. Supreme Court has noted on several occasions that travel by Americans abroad can be regulated and limited within the bounds of due process and has specifically upheld the constitutionality of limitations on travel to Cuba.[7]

The Office of Foreign Assets Control (OFAC) of the U.S. Treasury Department administers the economic sanctions, including travel regulations, imposed for foreign policy or national security reasons. OFAC plays a key role in the implementation, administration and enforcement of the sanctions. Several laws provide the legal foundation for the embargo and affect travel.[8]

- **The Trading with the Enemy Act (TWEA) of 1917,** and its 1933 amendment,[9] which empower the President to regulate or prohibit all commercial transactions with a foreign nation during time of war or national emergency.[10] In 1962, President Kennedy declared a state of emergency with respect to Cuba, which has been extended repeatedly.

---

4. Written Statement of R. Richard Newcomb, Director Office of Foreign Assets Control, U.S. Department of the Treasury, Before the Committee on Governmental Affairs United States Senate, Hearings on Terrorism Financing: Origination, Organization and Prevention, July 31, 2003.

5. In 1960, the Cuban government seized more than $1.8 billion of property owned by U.S. citizens and corporations without payment of compensation. The U.S. Foreign Claims Settlement Commission evaluated and certified 5,911 claims for use in future negotiations with the Cuban government and determined that certified claimants were entitled to 6%per annum interest on the value from the date of seizure. Their current estimated value ranges from $6.4 billion (at simple interest) to $20.1 billion (at compounded interest). See "What are U.S. property claims against Cuba?," Joint Corporate Committee on Cuba Claims. (Formed in 1975, the Joint Corporate Committee on Cuban Claims is a non-profit organization of claimants that supports the U.S. policy of requiring the Cuban government to return or arrange compensation for properties seized or provide an adequate settlement before full trade and diplomatic relations are restored.)

6. Written Statement of R. Richard Newcomb Director, Office of Foreign Assets Control, United States Department of the Treasury, before the Subcommittee on Human Rights and Wellness Committee on Government Reform U.S. House of Representatives, October 16, 2003.

7. A 1996 challenge to limit travel-related transactions on grounds that the government lacked sufficient foreign policy rationale was rejected by the Ninth District Court. Zemel v. Rusk (1965) and Regan v. Wald (1984).

8. For a detailed review of the legal foundation for the embargo until 1993, see Matías F. Travieso-Díaz, "Requirements For Lifting the U.S. Trade Embargo Against Cuba," *Cuba in Transition—Volume 3*, Association for the Study of the Cuban Economy, Washington, DC, 1993.

9. Trading with the Enemy Act of October 6, 1917, amended by Public Law in 1994. (After 1977, restrictions on countries including Cuba for which a state of emergency has been declared, have been grandfathered under the National Emergencies Act (NEA) and the International Emergencies Economic Powers Act (IEEPA)n of 1977, which serves as the primary statutory authority for a Presidential declaration of a national emergency in peacetime for the purpose of imposing economic sanctions. R. Newcomb (July 31, 2003).)

10. The TWEA was amended in 1994.

- **The Foreign Assistance Act of 1961**,[11] which conferred President Kennedy the authority to impose the embargo by authorizing the suspension of all trade benefits and foreign assistance to Cuba "until Cuba demonstrates significant progress in instituting democratic reforms and compensates U.S. citizens whose properties were confiscated."

- **The 1992 Cuban Democracy Act (CDA)**,[12] also commonly known as the Torricelli Law, responded to changes in Cuba after the end of Soviet Communism and the economic support by the Soviet bloc. This law took a novel approach by defining U.S. policy as fostering a peaceful transition to democracy and economic prosperity in Cuba with a combined application of sanctions and incentives.[13] It contains a number of humanitarian exemptions on the embargo (such as donations of food, the sale of medicine and medical supplies), and authorized telecommunications' payments, direct mail delivery to Cuba, and assistance to support non-violent democratic change in Cuba. The Act also added civil penalty authority for the Treasury Department to enforce sanctions and required the creation of an administrative hearing process for civil penalty cases and the establishment of an OFAC office in Miami to assist in administering and enforcing embargo restrictions.[14]

- **The 1996 Cuban Liberty and Democratic Solidarity Act** (also know as the Helms-Burton Law)[15] codified the embargo, including the travel restrictions, and preserved the humanitarian provisions of the CDA. Section 112, "Reinstitution of family remittances and travel to Cuba," calls on the President to, "before considering the reinstitution of general licenses for travel to Cuba by individuals resident in the United States who are family members of Cuban nationals who are resident in Cuba, insist on such actions by the Cuban Government as abrogation of the sanction for departure from Cuba by refugees, release of political prisoners, recognition of the right of association, and other fundamental freedoms." Section 109 also authorized the President to furnish assistance and provide other support for individuals and independent nongovernmental organizations to support democracy-building efforts for Cuba; this included (4) Support for visits and permanent deployment of independent international human rights monitors in Cuba.

- **The Trade Sanctions Reform and Export Enhancement Act of 2000** restricted the President's discretionary authority to authorize travel-related transactions to, from, or within Cuba by restricting travel-related transactions to those twelve categories defined in OFAC's Code of Regulations related to Cuba.

Chronology

U.S. travel restrictions to Cuba have been modified on numerous occasions. Following is a brief chronology of the most significant events and changes affecting travel to Cuba.

---

11. The FAA grants the President discretion to furnish assistance to Cuba when deemed to be in the interest of the United States. (For a summary of laws regulating the embargo on Cuba before the Helms-Burton law of 1996, see Javier J. Rodriguez, Nicolas Gutierrez, Jr., and James Meyer, "A synopsis and analysis of U.S. laws relating to the economic embargo on Cuba," *International Law Quarterly*, Winter 1993.)

12. The Cuban Democracy Act, United States Code Title 22, Foreign Relations Intercourse, Chapter 69.

13. The CDA's Section 6002 (Statement of policy) reads: It should be the policy of the United States— (1) to seek a peaceful transition to democracy and a resumption of economic growth in Cuba through the careful application of sanctions directed at the Castro government and support for the Cuban people; (2) to maintain sanctions on the Castro regime so long as it continues to refuse to move toward democratization and greater respect for human rights; (3) to be prepared to reduce the sanctions in carefully calibrated ways in response to positive developments in Cuba.

14. R. Newcomb (October 2, 2003).

15. Cuban Liberty and Democratic Solidarity (Libertad) Act of 1996, P.L. 104-114, codified in Title 22, Sections 6021-6091 of the U.S. Code.

- On **February 3, 1962**, President Kennedy issued Proclamation 3447, under the authority granted by the Foreign Assistance Act of 1961, officially imposing a trade embargo against Cuba that prohibited "the importation into the United States of all goods of Cuban origin and all goods imported from and through Cuba."[16] A series of laws had been enacted from 1960 to that time that had essentially cut of all trade between the U.S. and Cuba.[17]

- On **July 9, 1963,** pursuant to the President's directive and under the Trading With the Enemy Act, the Department of the Treasury's Office of Foreign Assets Control (OFAC) issued a more comprehensive set of prohibitions, the Cuban Import Regulations.[18] These effectively banned travel by prohibiting any transactions with Cuba.

- In **March 1977** President Carter lifted the restrictions on U.S. travel to Cuba by issuing a general license for travel-related transactions and allowed direct flights to Cuba. At that time, Cuba had massive economic support from the Soviet Union and severely restricted tourists travel by all foreigners. Soon, Cuba initiated a military intervention in Africa that cooled the "rapprochement."

- In **April 1982**, the Reagan Administration reimposed restrictions on travel to Cuba, although it allowed for certain categories of travel, including travel by U.S. government officials, employees of news or film making organizations, persons engaging in professional research, or persons visiting their close relatives.

- In **June 1993** the Clinton Administration added two more categories of authorized travel under specific license from OFAC: "for clearly defined educational or religious activities" and "for activities of recognized human rights organizations."

- In **August 1994** President Clinton announced measures against the Cuban government in response to an escalation in the number of Cubans fleeing in rafts to the United States. The Administration tightened travel restrictions by prohibiting family visits under a general license and allowing specific licenses for family visits only "when extreme hardship is demonstrated in cases involving extreme humanitarian need" such as terminal illness or severe medical emergency. In addition, professional researchers were required to apply for a specific license, whereas since 1982 they had been able to travel freely under a general license.

- In **October 1995** President Clinton announced measures to ease some U.S. restrictions on travel and other activities with Cuba, with the overall objective of promoting democracy and the free flow of ideas. General licenses were allowed for transactions related to travel by Cuban Americans making yearly visits to close relatives in "circumstances that demonstrate extreme humanitarian need." This reversed the August 1994 action that required specific licenses, but required that people traveling for this purpose more than once in a 12-month period needed to apply to OFAC for a specific license. The new measures also allowed for specific licenses for free-lance journalists traveling to Cuba.

- On **February 26, 1996**, following the shootdown of two U.S. civilian planes by Cuban fighter jets, President Clinton took several measures against Cuba, including the indefinite suspension of charter flights between Cuba and the United States. Qualified licensed travelers could still go to Cuba through third countries.

---

16. 31 CFR Part 515 (the "Regulations").

17. The first sanctions were imposed in 1960 as a result of the confiscation of U.S. properties on the island. President Eisenhower placed most U.S. industrial export licenses to Cuba (excluding non-subsidized food, medicines and medical supplies) under trade restrictions and reduced the quota of Cuban sugar in the U.S. market to zero. Travel restrictions were not included. (Proclamation 3447, 27 Fed. Reg. 1085, 3 C.F.R., 1059-63 Comp., p. 157.)

18. "Treasury Dept. Cracks Down on Cuba Travel," The Associated Press, Washington, 03/24/03.

- On **March 20, 1998**, following Pope John Paul II's trip to Cuba in January, President Clinton announced several changes in U.S. policy toward Cuba, including the resumption of licensing for direct charter flights to Cuba. On July 2, OFAC issued licenses to nine air charter companies to provide direct passenger flights from Miami to Havana.

- On **January 5, 1999**, the Clinton Administration announced additional measures to increase people-to-people exchanges and support the Cuban people. These included authorizing direct passenger charter flights from additional U.S. cities other than Miami. In August of that year, the State Department announced that direct flights to Cuba would be allowed from New York and Los Angeles.

- On **May 13, 1999**, OFAC issued a number of changes that loosened restrictions on certain categories of travelers to Cuba in response to President Clinton's January 1999 announcement. Travel for professional research became possible under a general license, and travel for a wide range of educational, religious, sports competition, and other activities became possible with specific licenses authorized by OFAC on a case-by-case basis. In addition, those traveling to Cuba to visit a close family member under either a general or specific license only needed to "demonstrate humanitarian need."

- In **October 2000**, Congress approved the Trade Sanctions Reform and Export Enhancement Act of 2000 (Title IX of P.L. 106-387), that included a provision that prohibited travel-related transactions for "tourist activities." This has been interpreted as circumscribing the authority of OFAC to issue specific travel licenses on a case-by-case basis within the categories of travel already allowed by the existing regulations.

- On **July 12, 2001**, OFAC published regulations pursuant to the provisions of the Trade Sanctions and Export Enhancement Act of 2000. The following day, President Bush announced that he had asked the Treasury Department to enhance and expand the capabilities of OFAC to prevent, among other things, "unlicensed and excessive travel."

- On **March 24, 2003** the Treasury Department announced regulatory changes. No new licenses would be issued for ``people-to-people educational exchanges'' that had become a loophole for groups to travel o Cuba on "essentially tourists trips." The list of licensable humanitarian activities was enlarged to include construction projects intended to benefit legitimately independent civil society groups and educational training within Cuba and elsewhere on topics including civic education, journalism, advocacy, and organizing. The amount of money that could be taken as gifts for Cuban citizens was raised to $3,000 (equivalent to up to ten of the allowed remittances in a three month period for any individual in Cuba).[19]

Current U.S. Regulations on Travel to Cuba

Authorized ("licensed") travel: The Cuba Assets Control Regulations, issued by the U.S. Treasury Department, affect all persons subject to U.S. jurisdiction -U.S. citizens and permanent residents wherever they are located, all people and organizations physically in the United States, and all branches and subsidiaries of U.S. organizations throughout the world. Its jurisdiction extends to transactions, anywhere in the world, involving property in which Cuba or a national thereof has any interest whatsoever, direct or indirect.

OFAC authorization by way of a license is required to engage in any transactions related to travel to, from, and within Cuba. Only select categories of travelers are licensable, although, as we have seen, these have varied over the years.

OFAC has a Miami office that handles around 90% of license applications—those related to visits to close relatives. Nearly 20,000 such applications were processed during 2002. This process is handled very promptly due to its humanitarian component i.e., for

---

19. *Federal Register,* Vol. 68, No. 56, March 24, 2003.

family reunification. OFAC reports that it reviews and mails the licensing response generally within 24 hours of receipt. OFAC's national office in Washington handles the remaining categories of travel, which brought in more than 1,000 license applications in 2002. With the advent of OFAC's recently streamlined processing procedures and the assignment of additional staff, it reports processing most license applications not requiring interagency review within ten days of receipt.

U.S. citizens and residents traveling under a general or specific license from OFAC may spend money on travel in Cuba without obtaining special permission for travel-related expenses (hotels, meals, ground transportation, etc.) not exceeding the U.S. government's per diem rate, currently $166 per day. The cost of telephone calls is exempt from the per diem. Per diem rates for Cuba are based upon the "Per Diem Rate for Foreign Areas" issued by the Department of State for U.S. government officials in temporary official duty abroad. The per diem is adjusted periodically and may be checked on the internet at the Department of State website.[20] OFAC also generally authorizes the expenditure of "additional money for transactions directly related to the activities" for which a license was issued. Most licensed travelers may also spend additional money for transactions directly related to the activities for which they received their license.[21] The per diem may also be exceeded for travel-related transactions incident to the purpose of visiting close relatives (e.g. to purchase transportation within Cuba visit close relatives who live great distances from each other). Specific exemptions to the per diem authorization can also be requested from the OFAC.

Licensed travelers may also spend an additional $100 to the per diem allowance on the purchase of Cuban merchandise to be brought back with them to the United States as accompanied baggage (cigar, rums, crafts, etc.), but this $100 authorization may be used only once in any 6-month period. Purchases of services unrelated to travel or a licensed activity, such as non-emergency medical services, are prohibited. The purchase of artwork, publications, and informational materials (books, magazines, music tapes, CD ROM's, photographs, films, posters, phonograph records, microfilm, microfiche, compact disks, and newswire feed, etc.) is not limited or restricted.

In any one-year period, only $500 may be paid in fees levied by the Cuban government for travel to Cuba.

"Fully hosted" travelers whose travel and other expenses are absorbed by an individual or entity not subject to U.S. law (in Cuba or a third country) are exempt from requiring a license to travel to Cuba, but must provide supporting documentation as evidence.[22] A "fully hosted" traveler must travel to the Republic of Cuba by way of third countries. They are not subject to spending limits,[23] but are prohibited from providing any unauthorized services to Cuba or to Cuban nationals or within Cuba.

All persons on board vessels must be authorized travelers to engage in travel-related transactions in Cuba, such as purchase meals, pay for ground transportation, lodging, dockage or mooring fees, cruising fees, entertainment, incidentals, visas, entry or exit fees.[24]

---

20. http://www.state.gov/www/perdiems/index.html.

21. For example, journalists traveling in Cuba under the journalism general license may spend money over and above the current per diem for extensive local transportation and other costs that are directly related to covering a story in Cuba.

22. The U.S.-Cuba Trade and Economic Council warns of increased enforcement of travel restriction regulations with respect to travelers claiming "fully hosted" status and urges "extreme caution" if traveling under this category. (http://www.cubatrade.org/).

23. Certain restrictions apply.

24. The U.S. Coast Guard requires that vessels traveling to Cuba obtain a $25 permit to depart the Florida Security Zone. Such notification is required under Presidential Proclamation 6867 (by President Clinton in March 1996, extended by President Bush in February 2002), which established a "security zone" around the coast of South Florida essentially to keep Cuban exiles out of high-seas confrontations with Cuban patrol boats. (See www.whitehouse.gov/news/releases/2002/02/20020227-8.html.) The Coast Guard webpage warns vessels planning to travel to Cuba of the need to comply with all existing OFAC regulations regarding expenditures in Cuba. It clarifies: "OFAC presumes that any boater who sails to Cuba has made expenditures in Cuba unless that presumption is rebutted as set forth in 31 C.F.R. 515.420 - up to $250,000 fine and ten years in prison." (OFAC Fact Sheet "Cuba: Civil Penalties Rights and Procedures," March 24, 2003.)

OFAC presumes that any boater who sails to Cuba has made expenditures in Cuba unless that presumption is rebutted as set forth in the Cuba regulations. Penalties of up to $250,000 fine and ten years in prison may be levied.

In March 2003, OFAC regulations were amended to allow licensed travelers on direct flights to carry family remittances totaling up to $3,000 (in addition to his/her per diem) regardless of the number of close relatives in Cuba to receive the funds. Children under 18 are prohibited from carrying remittances on direct flights.

General licenses: Presently, general licenses are authorized for persons whose travel falls into the categories:

- Journalists and supporting broadcasting or technical personnel (regularly employed in that capacity by a news reporting organization and traveling for journalistic activities).

- Official government travelers (traveling on official business).

- Members of international organizations of which the United States is also a member (traveling on official business).

- Persons traveling once a year to visit Cuban nationals who are close relatives. (Additional trips within one year will need an OFAC specific license).

- Full-time professionals whose travel transactions are directly related to professional research in their professional areas, provided that their research: (1) is of a noncommercial academic nature; (2) comprises a full work schedule in Cuba; and (3) has a substantial likelihood of public dissemination.

- Full-time professionals whose travel transactions are directly related to attendance at professional meetings or conferences in Cuba organized by an international professional organization, institution, or association that regularly sponsors such meetings or conferences in other countries.

- Amateur or semi-professional athletes or teams traveling to participate in Cuba in an athletic competition held under the auspices of the relevant international sports federation.

Specific licenses for academic institutions: Specific licenses may be issued by OFAC to authorize travel transactions related to certain educational activities by students or employees affiliated with a licensed academic institution accredited by an appropriate national or regional accrediting association. Such licenses must be renewed after a period of two years. The following categories of travelers affiliated with the licensed academic institution are authorized under these licenses:[25]

- Undergraduate or graduate students participating in a structured educational program as part of a course offered at a licensed college or university.

- Persons doing noncommercial Cuba-related academic research in Cuba for the purpose of qualifying academically as a professional (e.g. research toward a graduate degree).

- Undergraduate or graduate students participating in a formal course of study at a Cuban academic institution provided the Cuban study will be accepted for credit toward a degree at the licensed U.S. institution.

- Persons regularly employed in a teaching capacity at a licensed college or university who plan to teach part or all of an academic program at a Cuban academic institution.

- Secondary school students participating in educational exchanges sponsored by Cuban or U.S. secondary schools and involving the students' participation in a formal course of study or in a structured educational program offered by a secondary school or other academic institution and led by a teacher or other secondary school official. A reasonable number of adult chaperones may accompany the students to Cuba.

---

25. Persons traveling under these licenses must carry a letter from the licensed U.S. institution stating the institution's license number and how the person meets the criteria for travel with that license.

- Full-time employees of a licensed institution organizing or preparing for the educational activities described above.

- Cuban scholars teaching or engaging in other scholarly activities at a licensed college or university in the United States. Licensed institutions may sponsor such Cuban scholars, including payment of a stipend or salary, which may be remitted back to Cuba.

Specific licenses for religious organizations: Specific licenses may be issued to religious organizations, which, in turn, may authorize individuals affiliated with the organization to travel under its auspices.[26]

Other specific licenses: Specific licenses may be issued on a case-by-case basis for the following activities:

- Humanitarian projects and support for the Cuban people.

- Free-lance journalism.

- Professional research and professional meetings.

- Religious activities.

- Public performances, clinics, workshops, athletic and other competitions or exhibitions.

- Activities of private foundations or research and educational institutions.

- Exportation, importation, or transmission of information or informational materials.

- Activities related to licensed exportations (marketing, sales negotiation, accompanied delivery, or servicing of exports of food and agricultural commodities, medical products or other authorized exports).

- Family reunification exceeding the one visit per year authorized with a general license.

Travel services providers: U.S. travel service providers, such as travel agents, carriers, and tour operators, handling travel arrangements to, from, or within Cuba must also be licensed by OFAC to engage in such activities. OFAC is also charged with compliance oversight of the direct charter flights to Cuba currently authorized to carry licensed travels from Miami, Los Angeles and New York.

At present, OFAC's Miami office regulates activities of 202 entities nationwide licensed to: (1) provide travel and carrier services to authorized travelers; and (2) remit funds to Cuban households on behalf of individuals who are subject to U.S. jurisdiction as authorized under the Regulations. Almost two-thirds of these licensed entities are headquartered in Miami.[27]

Enforcement[28]

Any person subject to U.S. jurisdiction determined to have traveled to Cuba without an OFAC general or specific license is *presumed to* have engaged in prohibited travel-related transactions unless he/she can provide substantiating documentation of compliance with regulations. Failure to comply with OFAC regulations may result in civil penalties and criminal prosecution upon return to the United States.

OFAC works with the U.S. Customs Service to enforce Cuba travel restrictions. As returning Cuba travelers are identified by Customs agents and inspectors at ports of entry in the United States or at U.S. Customs Pre-Clearance Facilities in Canada or the Bahamas, those travelers who do not claim a general or specific license from OFAC to engage in Cuba travel-related transactions are routinely referred to OFAC for investigation and civil penalty action. In addition, OFAC is contacted by individuals concerned that it take enforcement action against what they view as U.S. tourist travel to Cuba. Both OFAC's Washington and Miami offices investigate alleged violations of the regulations, while the Miami office also processes enforcement referrals from the U.S. Customs Service and the U.S. Coast Guard.[29]

---

26. Ibid.

27. R. Newcomb (October 2, 2003).

28. This section relies heavily on the Statement by R. Newcomb (October 2, 2003), and two excellent overviews, Sullivan (2003 and 9/2002).

29. Newcomb, October 2, 2003.

In 2002-03, OFAC considerably enhanced the transparency of its procedural framework for the enforcement of all economic sanctions programs. On January 29, 2003 it published in the *Federal Register* the "Economic Sanctions Enforcement Guidelines."[30] These guidelines include a schedule of proposed civil monetary penalties for unauthorized travel-related transactions with Cuba as well as a schedule of proposed civil monetary penalties for unauthorized transactions involving the provision of travel, carrier and remittance services to Cuba. In addition, on February 11, 2003 OFAC also published in the Federal Register disclosure guidelines involving civil penalties.[31] This came after a process that followed the publication in June of 2002, of a proposed rule announcing a new practice of releasing certain civil penalty enforcement information on a routine basis. OFAC received thirty-two public comments on the proposed rule, including from financial institutions, law firms, trade associations, individuals, and a public interest group. Finally, in April 2003 information on civil penalty proceedings against individuals became routinely available at OFAC's website on an aggregate basis, encompassing individuals who have engaged in unauthorized travel-related transactions involving Cuba.

Enforcement, reportedly lax for many years, has been tightened since 2001, when President Bush issued a statement that he had asked the Treasury Department to enhance and expand the enforcement capabilities of the Office of Foreign Assets Control.[32] Until recently, few people seem to have been taking enforcement very seriously. A Florida man fined by OFAC speaks for numerous anecdotal accounts: "I could take you to probably fifteen boats out here in the anchorage that go to Cuba all the time. There are two guys that I know of who have children over there, wives and children. They go over all the time. There's a guy who works on my engine, a mechanic, and he takes his motorcycle over there on his boat and plays in Cuba for three or four months, and he never checks in and he never checks out."[33]

OFAC is said to have issued a total of 766 enforcement letters in 2001,[34] a steep increase from what has been reported by the media for previous years: 188 in 2000, 120 in 1999, 72 in 1998, 78 in 1997, and 46 in 1996.[35] The number of letters in 2002 and 2003 is unknown, as several calls to OFAC requesting confirmation of those numbers plus updated data on enforcement and licensing failed to produce the information. But, the websites of groups opposing restrictions have been protesting loudly the increased "harassment" and "witch hunt" by OFAC.[36] A November 2002 letter by the President of the U.S.-Cuba Sister City Association to its members refers to a rise in OFAC enforcement letters and reflects the general sentiment expressed by many of these groups: "These letters are meant to intimidate people, as well as gather information about other people they might go after, and are part of increased government harassment stepped up under this administration in its attempts to erode relations between our nations. It is not acceptable, nor is it constitutional. We will not be cowed." This is a very different tone than the description of a return from Cuba in the website for the *Venceremos Brigade*, which over the years has sent 8,000 people there: "Members and organizers of the Brigade reported only minimal or no questioning at

---

30. *Federal Register,* Volume 68, No. 19 (January 29, 2003).

31. *Federal Register,* Volume 68, No. 28 (February 11, 2003).

32. The White House, "Statement by President Bush on Cuba: Toward a Democratic Cuba," July 13, 2001.

33. Kirk Nielsen, "The Will Adams Embargo: The sad saga of how the feds hounded a senior citizen over, what else, Cuba," *Miami New Times,* January 9, 2003.

34. Sullivan (2003, p.7).

35. Information provided by Rob Nichols, Treasury's Deputy Assistant Secretary for Public Affairs. In Nielsen (2003).

36. See for example letters by by Lisa Valanti, President of the U.S.-Cuba Sister City Association, "How to respond to OFAC harassment of U.S.-Cuba Sister Cities members," November 8, 2002, and a letter to supporters of October 23, 2002, both posted on the group's website, http://www.uscsca.org/ofacharass.htm.

all by the U.S. Customs officials, who generally scanned their passports and waved them through. The few *brigadistas* who were asked such questions as "Did you spend any money in Cuba?" refused to answer—as is their legal right—and passed through without incident. No one was asked where they had been..."[37]

The prosecution of embargo violations entails a range of measures from initial letters of inquiry to settlements or the imposition of actual penalties. The Treasury Department sends out enforcement letters to suspected violators. Investigative findings are referred for civil penalty consideration with an administrative record containing the evidence of transactions involving Cuba. OFAC, however, reports giving people "an opportunity to respond and sometimes drops its case based on the explanation."[38] In fact, a settlement may be negotiated with OFAC to resolve the matter informally. Individuals who have received pre-penalty notices have the right to an agency hearing in Washington, as well as to a pre-hearing discovery, including the review of all non-privileged documents that OFAC used as the basis for issuing the pre-penalty. If a penalty and/or forfeiture is eventually imposed, individuals have the right to seek judicial review of the final agency action in a federal court.[39]

In September 2003, OFAC revised its administrative penalty procedures to afford travelers to Cuba additional opportunities to present mitigating factors for consideration before a final penalty ensues. Administrative law judges (ALJs) are to preside at the review of the penalty assessments if the right to an administrative hearing has been invoked. Until very recently it appears OFAC was unable to fully enforce this regulation for lack of staff and/or resources. A January 2003 news article reported that for ten years the Treasury Department hadn't had any administrative law judges to conduct such hearings, on staff.[40] Cubalinda.com, a Cuban tourism promotion website, in its recommendations to help Americans avoid fines for unlicensed travel posted this message: "If the record of the past five years is any guide, after a hearing is requested OFAC will then file away the case because no appeals hearings have been held, nor have any judges been appointed to hold such hearings. Through the date of this posting, October 14, 2002, the legal processing of all such cases has stopped at that stage, and therefore no fines have been imposed when the request for hearing was made on time."[41]

As of late, this problem seems to have been addressed. At an October 2, 2003, congressional hearing, OFAC's Director reported that they "have made progress ... to initiate hearings before an administrative law judge on the imposition of civil penalties for engaging in unauthorized travel-related transactions."[42] In fact, letters sent by OFAC that same month announced plans to hold hearings under the administrative law judges and inform alleged violators that they will be given the choice of an administrative trial or paying a $1,000 fine for each charge.[43] At the end of October 2003, an OFAC officer verified that two attorneys from other government agencies had been assigned as independent law judges to hear the cases, a process which would very soon actually begin.[44] As of October 2003, around 50 cases had been referred for a hearing by OFAC to the Treasury Department's Office of General Counsel.

---

37. http://www.venceremosbrigade.org/.

38. Kevin Sullivan, "Americans defy Cuba embargo," *Washington Post*, October 31, 2001, p. A23.

39. "Civil Penalties: Rights and Procedures" (3/24/03).

40. Nielsen (2003).

41. http://www.cubalinda.com/English/General_Info/G_InfoSpecialInfoUScitizen.asp. Cubalinda.com is the winner of the 2002 ICub@ prize for best business and commerce website in Cuba.

42. R. Newcomb (October 2, 2003).

43. Rone Tempest, "Curbs on Travel to Cuba Feared," *L.A. Times*, October 18, 2003.

44. Telephone interview with OFAC official (name withheld on request), October 30, 2003.

Most had the assistance of public interest legal organizations.[45]

Criminal penalties for violating the sanctions range up to ten years in prison, $1,000,000 in corporate fines, and $250,000 in individual fines. Civil penalties up to $55,000 per violation may also be imposed. In 2003, actual penalties were reportedly usually in amounts ranging from $2,000-$7,000.[46] According to a report from October 2001, attributed to a Treasury Department spokesman, the average threatened fine was about $7,500.[47]

From October 1992, the effective date of OFAC's civil penalty authority, to April 1999, the Treasury Department had collected more than $2 million in civil monetary penalties for Cuba embargo violations.[48] From January 1996 through June 2002, 6,398 travel cases were opened for investigation and 2,179 cases were referred for civil penalty enforcement action from $3,000 to $7,500, but the majority of cases are settled in amounts reflecting the mitigation range outlined in the Enforcement Guidelines. Updated information was not available at the time of this writing.

As reported by OFAC's Director to Congress: "There are a few organizations and individuals who view travel to Cuba as an act of civil disobedience…"[49] The National Lawyers Guild posts a form letter on its website for travelers to challenge OFAC penalties with the following preamble: "OFAC's regulations regarding transactions incidental to travel, and OFAC's demand for information pursuant to such regulations constitute discriminatory enforcement of the laws on the basis of national origin and political viewpoint, in violation of the First and Fifth Amendments to the Constitution of the United States."[50] Several non-profit legal organizations, such as the New York-based Center for Constitutional Rights and the National Lawyers Guild are representing clients who have received letters of inquiry or pre-penalty notices from OFAC related to travel to Cuba. The Center for Constitutional Rights, headquartered in New York city, has a Cuba Travel Project, to "defend Americans who exercise this basic constitutional right." The CCR maintains that the embargo "is a deliberate end-run around First Amendment guarantees of freedom to travel" and is said to represent from 300 to 400 individuals accused of violating the ban.[51] The National Lawyers Guild, which has a Cuba Subcommittee under its International Committee, uses its members' legal skills to "help normalize relations and end the travel restrictions and U.S. economic blockade." It has a network

---

45. R. Newcomb (October 16, 2003).

46. Sullivan (2003, pp. 8-9). Officially, the" Traveler Violations/Amounts for Prepenalty Notices" are: (1) Tourist travel-related transactions: First trip: $7,500, Each additional trip: $10,000; 2) Business travel-related transactions: First trip: $15,000, Each additional trip: $25,000; (3) Travel-related transactions involving unlicensed visits to close relatives: First trip: warning letter, Each additional trip —Prior to agency notice: $1,000, Subsequent to agency notice: $4,000; (4) Travel-related transactions where no specific license was issued but where there is evidence that the purpose of the travel fits within one of the categories of licensable activities: Each trip prior to agency notice: $3,000, Each trip subsequent to agency notice: $10,000. Federal Register, Volume 68, No. 19 , January 29, 2003.

47. The Treasury Department source also said many of those cases began during the Clinton Administration and were simply enforcing the law, not responding to political pressure. (K. Sullivan (2001).)

48. Some of the corporate penalties paid are: (1) C&T Charters, Inc. paid a $125,000 penalty settlement for allegations of acting as the operator of charter flights between Nassau and Havana without OFAC authorization, and for record keeping deficiencies found during compliance audits by OFAC; (2) Wilson International Services, Inc. paid $61,000 to settle alleged record keeping deficiencies found during OFAC audits; and (3) Harper's Bazaar paid $31,000 in settlement of allegations that it engaged in unlicensed payments for travel expenses in 1998 for a photo shoot in Cuba. (See Hearing of the Senate Appropriations Committee, Subcommittee on Treasury and General Government, Federal News Service, February 11, 2002; and Rafael Lorente, "Senator Demands End to Cuba Travel Ban; Hundreds Fined Under Crackdown," *Sun-Sentinel*, Fort Lauderdale, August 18, 2001, p. 6A.)

49. Newcomb (October 20, 2003).

50. http://www.nlg.org/.

51. The Center for Constitutional Rights' website reports representing 300 individuals (http://www.ccr-ny.org/v2/legal/cuba/cuba.asp). A *Miami New Times* article reports that number to be 400 (Nielsen, 2003).

of lawyers for legal assistance with basic training in this area and sample letters to challenge OFAC penalties.[52]

Since 2001, the Bush Administration has made several announcements that enforcement of travel and embargo restrictions would be tightened.[53] The most recent came on October 10, 2003, when the President made a special appearance at the Rose Garden to deliver a statement on the toughening of Cuba policy. As the first of three measures, he announced "strengthening re-enforcement of those travel restrictions to Cuba that are already in place."[54] The President went on to explain: "We allow travel for limited reasons, including visit to a family, to bring humanitarian aid, or to conduct research. Those exceptions are too often used as cover for illegal business travel and tourism, or to skirt the restrictions on carrying cash into Cuba. We're cracking down on this deception." In addition, he reported having instructed the Department of Homeland Security to increase inspections of travelers and shipments to and from Cuba in order to enforce the law. "We will also target those who travel to Cuba illegally through third countries, and those who sail to Cuba on private vessels in violation of the embargo."[55]

OFAC's Director, testifying before Congress a few days after the President's speech, declared that OFAC would work closely with the Department of Homeland Security's Bureau of Customs and Border Protection, at all ports, but in particular at the New York, Los Angeles Airport, and Miami airports. In addition, Homeland Security would monitor closely at other locations used by unlicensed travelers and remittance couriers to travel to and from Cuba via third countries. He also announced enhanced investigation and enforcement efforts against individuals and companies that provide travel and remittance services to Cuba without an OFAC license.[56] The Homeland Security Department issued a statement that it would increase inspection of all persons traveling directly to Cuba and arriving back directly from Cuba.[57]

The tightened enforcement of the last few years is said to have been mostly directed at travelers not of Cuban descent, while an allegedly growing number of Cuban Americans[58] are believed to be traveling more than once a year as allowed under current general licensing rules. U.S. representative Jeff Flake (R-Ariz.), claims that U.S. authorities "pay no attention to Cuban Americans even as they harass and level fines against Americans who go to the island."[59] Although current OFAC regulations do not define

---

52. http://www.nlg.org/.

53. David Phinney, "Law on Travel to Cuba Criticized," *The Miami Herald*, February 12, 2002, p. 20A, as cited in Sullivan (2003).

54. In addition to greater enforcement of travel restrictions, President Bush underscored his commitment to breaking the information blockade imposed on the Cuban people by the regime and announced two other initiatives to promote freedom in Cuba: 1. The creation of a Commission for Assistance to a Free Cuba, co-chaired by Secretaries Powell and Martinez and comprised of U.S. executive branch agency representatives, and 2. Improvements in immigration procedures to encourage safe and legal migration and an increase in the number of new migrants admitted from Cuba. (Remarks by President Bush on Cuba, The White House, Washington, October 10, 2003. Also see: "White House Outlines New Initiatives on Cuba: Restrictions on American travel to the island to be tightened," 10 October 2003, Bureau of International Information Programs, U.S. Department of State, http://usinfo.state.gov.)

55. The White House, Press Office, October 10, 2003, www.whitehouse.gov.

56. Mr. Newcomb also described other measures being taken to improve enforcement. (Oral Statement of R. Richard Newcomb Director, Office of Foreign Assets Control United States Department of the Treasury, before the Subcommittee on Human Rights and Wellness Committee on Government Reform U.S. House of Representatives, October 16, 2003.).

57. "DHS Enhancing Enforcement of Travel Restrictions to Cuba," Press release, U.S. Department of Homeland Security, Office of the Press Secretary, October 10, 2003. Distributed by the Bureau of International Information Programs, U.S. Department of State, http://usinfo.state.gov.

58. For the purposes of this paper, "Cuban-American" is used to designate all U.S. based travelers of Cuban heritage, regardless of their residence status or citizenship.

59. Larissa Ruiz Campos, "Younger travelers send number of holiday trips to Cuba soaring," *The Miami Herald*, December 25, 2002.

what "humanitarian need" should or does mean in order for a person with close relatives in Cuba to travel under a general license, Rep. Flake has stated that "their relatives always seem to get sick around the same time, like Christmas and other major holidays.[60] The National Lawyers Guild for its part, reports: "The imposition of any penalties is also discriminatory. Such conduct is arbitrary and capricious and in violation of the Administrative Procedure Act. In this respect, it is noted that substantial numbers of Cuban-Americans and others travel to Cuba with the knowledge of OFAC, in apparent violation of the Cuban Assets Control Regulations, but without consequence."[61] A report by The Lexington Institute echoes this view, declaring the October 10 presidential announcement of tighter enforcement "a signal that Cuban Americans, who have faced no penalties to date for violations of regulations governing travel and delivery of family remittances, may now be scrutinized like other travelers."[62]

Marazul Charters, the largest travel service provider to Cuba in the United States, reports a very different situation regarding their direct charter flights to Cuba from Miami, New York and Los Angeles. A Marazul Vice President clarified in late October 2003 that: "People who travel to visit family more than once a year tend to have good reason for it—to visit a relative who's sick or for some type of real family emergency. Plus, they travel with a specific license from OFAC, which they get with our help. It's a very easy and simple for Cuban Americans to get these licenses and travel legally."[63]

According to Marazul, persons of Cuban heritage traveling multiple times a year outside of regulations are mostly engaged in unlicensed business transactions and tend to travel through third countries. These persons are known as "mules," and carry cash into Cuba, presumably as family remittances that skirt the travel restrictions and remittance limits.[64] The cost of the trip is typically a deterrent for frequent travel, particularly for the most recently arrived from Cuba, who are said to have the greatest propensity to travel while having the lower income.[65] On the other hand, almost any person of Cuban heritage who travels once a year could actually be traveling for other purposes—recreational, sentimental, exploring business opportunities, and even as a "mule," carrying cash for others. Reportedly, it is very easy for persons of Cuban heritage to obtain a specific license from OFAC to travel in beyond the one visit limit.[66]

But a number of Cuban Americans are said to be traveling to Cuba more than once a year without requesting a specific license from OFAC and young

60. Tracey Eaton, "8 vow to have U.S.-style meeting in Cuba," *The Dallas Morning News*, March 11, 2003.

61. NLG Cuba Subcommittee Action Alert July 2001, "Prompt Action needed to defend the right to travel to Cuba: NLG Builds a Cuba Travel Referral Network" http://www.nlg.org/cuba/Cuba_travel_alert_7.htm.

62. "President Bush Courts Old Miami," *U.S.-Cuba Policy Report*, October 17, 2003, Lexington Institute.

63. Marazul VP Armando Garcia reports that all they have to do is sign a form letter and they usually get their license from OFAC within a week. (Telephone interview with Armando Garcia, Vice President of Marazul Chaters, Inc., from Miami, October 31, 2003.)

64. Current remittance limits allow individuals 18 or older under U.S. jurisdiction to send to any individual in Cuba or to a Cuban national in a third country "individual-to-household" cash remittances of up to $300 in any consecutive three-month period, provided that no member of the household is a senior-level Cuban government or senior-level Cuban communist party official. $1,000 per payee on a one-time basis may also be sent as an "emigration-related" remittance to enable the payee to emigrate from Cuba to the United States. A licensed traveler may carry up to ten of his or her own $300 household remittances to Cuba. ("What You Need To Know About The U.S. Embargo," OFAC, op.cit.).

65. The 2002 U.S. Census confirms that the number of Cuban immigrants arrived after 1980 in proportion to the total Cuban American population has been growing and by the late 1990's constituted two thirds of the total. Recent immigrants take time to adjust and, while doing so, have lower socioeconomic status than the average Cuban American population. The 2002 Census puts the Cuban American population at 1,241,685, with a mean income of $36,193 a year (median income of $27,000 a year) for 1997-2000. Thomas Boswell and Guarioné Díaz, "A demographic profile of Cuban Americans," The Cuban American National Council, Inc., September 2002, pp. iii, 8 and 30.

66. A. Garcia (2003).

Americans of Cuban heritage with no close relatives visiting to "discover their roots." It would take supervision inside Cuba to determine if there are actual relatives in Cuba to be visited once a year. If so, how could the U.S. government establish whether the alleged family relationship is a "close" enough relative? If a license for a second or third family visit is requested, how can OFAC corroborate the compelling humanitarian nature of the request? It seems that enforcement of Cuban American travel will continue to be particularly difficult under current regulations.

In sum, the effects of President Bush's October 10, 2003 announcement of a "strengthening re-enforcement" of travel restrictions remain to be seen. The 766 enforcement letters in 2001 constituted a 76% jump from the year before, but were still only 1.9-3% of the estimated 25,000 to 40,000 U.S.-based travelers skirting the licensing procedure. Although enforcement seems to have been stepped up in 2002 and 2003, it may still be a mere drop in the bucket. Nonetheless, after the most recent presidential announcement, the more visible implementation of increased enforcement measures may well have a considerable multiplier effect in the disposition to travel and actually risk penalties, both by Cuban Americans and travelers not of Cuban heritage.

Legislative efforts to eliminate travel restrictions[67]

In recent years, several legislative initiatives have sought to change or altogether eliminate travel restrictions to Cuba. Following are some of the highlights:

106th Congress: The Senate took up the issue of travel to Cuba in a June 1999 floor action on the 2000 Foreign Operations Appropriations bill, when an amendment introduced by Senator Dodd (D-CT)

to end the travel restrictions to Cuba was defeated by a 55-43 vote. On November 10, 1999, Senator Dodd introduced identical language as the Freedom to Travel to Cuba Act of 2000 (S. 1919), but no action was taken on the bill.

In the House of Representatives, two initiatives related to travel did not prosper. In January 1999, Congressman (Serrano, D-NY), introduced a bill to allow travel and cultural exchanges between the United States and Cuba. On July 20, 2000 an amendment to the 2001 Treasury Department appropriations bill was approved (232-186) to prohibit funds in the bill from being used to administer or enforce the Cuban Assets Control Regulations with respect to any travel or travel related transaction. Subsequently, the language of the amendment was dropped from the 2001 Treasury Department appropriations bill. A number of other bills introduced in the House to ease the embargo that would have eliminated travel restrictions did not prosper.[68]

The only legislation passed by the 106th Congress related to travel to Cuba tightened the restrictions while allowing agricultural sales to Cuba. On May 4, 2000, the Trade Sanctions Reform and Export Enhancement Act was reported out of the Agriculture Subcommittee of the House Appropriations Committee as an amendment to the FY01 Agriculture Appropriations Act. The Act lifted all existing unilateral food and medicine sanctions (to Iran, Libya, Sudan, and Cuba) 180 days after enactment if the President and the Congress did not agree to re-impose sanctions and required that any future sanctions on food and medicine obtain Congressional consent.[69] The bill also prohibited U.S. financing of any sales to Cuba. The same bill also made travel restrictions subject

---

67. This section relies heavily on Sullivan (2003, p. 15).

68. Sullivan (2000), http://www.fas.org/man/crs/crscuba.htm#Legislative%20Initiatives%20in%20the%201.

69. On October 28, 2000, President Clinton signed it into law the Agriculture, Rural Development, Food and Drug Administration, and Related Agencies Appropriations Act, 2001 (HR4461—PL 106-387). Title IX is known as the Trade Sanctions Reform and Export Enhancement Act of 2000. It contains the measures authorizing agricultural sales to Cuba and other countries then facing sanctions. The Treasury and Commerce Department later enacted regulations to reflect the provisions of the Act. (See *Federal Register*, July 12, 2001, Department of Commerce, Bureau of Export Administration, 15 CFR Part 740, et al; and Department of the Treasury, Office of Foreign Assets Control, 31 CFR Part 515, et al. Exports of Agricultural Commodities, Medicines, and Medical Devices to Cuba, Sudan, Libya, and Iran; Cuba Travel-Related Transactions; Final Rules.

to Congressional prerogative and expressly prohibited travel-related transactions for "tourist activities" not authorized in the Code of Federal Regulations, thus restricting travel to the categories already contemplated in the regulations.

107th Congress:[70] Several measures introduced in the 107th Congress would have eliminated or eased restrictions on travel to Cuba. The House approved in the FY 2002 Treasury Appropriations bill a prohibition on the Treasury Department to use funds to administer or enforce the Cuban embargo with respect to travel or travel-related transactions. The Senate version of the bill, however, did not include this provision, nor did the House-Senate conference report on the bill.

During consideration of the 2003 Treasury Department appropriations bill, the travel issue was part of debate. Secretary of State Colin Powell and Secretary of the Treasury Paul O'Neill stated that they would recommend that the President veto legislation that included a loosening of restrictions on travel to Cuba (or a weakening of restrictions on private financing for U.S. agricultural exports to Cuba). The White House also stated that President Bush would veto such legislation. On July 24, 2002, the House approved the 2003 Treasury Department Appropriations bill containing three amendments that would ease embargo restrictions on Cuba. One was an amendment introduced by Representative Jeff Flake (R-AZ), which passed by a vote of 262-167, that would provide that no funds in the bill could be used to administer or enforce the Treasury Department regulations with respect to travel to Cuba. On July

17, 2002, the Senate Appropriations Committee had reported out its version of the Treasury Department Appropriations bill, with a provision similar to the Flake amendment. Congress did not complete action on the FY2003 Treasury Department appropriations measure before the end of the 107th Congress, so action was deferred until the 108th Congress. Several other legislative initiatives were introduced in the 107th Congress to ease travel restrictions, but no action was taken.[71]

108th Congress: A number of legislative initiatives on Cuba have been introduced during the current 108th Congress, in both the Senate and the House.

On September 9th 2003, the House of Representatives voted in favor of two amendments to the Treasury and Transportation Appropriations bill (H.R. 2989) that would bar the Treasury Department from enforcing travel restrictions. An amendment to prevent enforcement of the travel ban, introduced by Representatives Flake and McGovern (D-MA), passed on a vote of 227-188. An amendment that would stop the implementation of new restrictions on "people-to-people" educational travel, introduced by Rep. Davis (D-FL) passed by 246-173.[72] This came just a few days after a statement of the Office of Management and Budget on the Treasury and Transportation Appropriations bill that contained a clarification of the Administration's position against weakening Cuba travel sanctions that included the following: "If the final version of the bill contained such a provision, the President's senior advisors would recommend that he veto the bill."[73] Representative Flake's amendment received 35 fewer votes in

---

70. Sullivan, Initiatives in the 107th Congress (August 29, 2002).

71. Several bills were introduced that would have lifted all sanctions on trade, financial transactions, and travel to Cuba: The Cuban Reconciliation Act, introduced January 3, 2001 by Representative Serrano, (H.R.174); identical bills by Senator Baucus and Representative Rangel, the Free Trade with Cuba Act, introduced February 27-28, 2001; and Senator Dodd and Congressman Serrano introduced the Bridges to the Cuban People Act of 2001 (S. 1017 and H.R. 2138) that included removal of all restrictions on travel to Cuba. Several bills were introduced that would have repealed the travel restrictions of the Trade Sanctions Reform and Export Enhancement Act of 2000, e.g, identical bills introduced on February 27-28, 2001, by Senator Baucus (S. 402) and Congressman Rangel (H.R. 797), the Cuban Humanitarian Trade Act of 2001; and Senators Dorgan and Hagel introduced the Cuba Food and Medicine Access Act of 2001 on January 24, 2001. See Sullivan (2002).

72. A third amendment was also introduced by Representatives Flake and Delahunt (D-MA) to end funding for the enforcement of caps on remittances that may be sent to Cuba. It was passed by a vote of 222-196.

73. "Legislative Alert," *U.S.-Cuba Policy Report*, September 25, 2003, p.3.

2003 than the previous year (262 votes in favor in 2002, 227 in 2003). Some lawmakers who voted in favor in 2002 refrained from voting in 2003[74] and the newly-elected House Republicans considerably refrained from supporting the measure.[75] This may indicates a relative weakening of support in the House for lifting travel restrictions in the wake of a crackdown unleashed by the Cuban government on peaceful democracy advocates which has elicited worldwide condemnation.

A few weeks later, on October 23, the Senate unexpectedly began debating the 2004 Transportation-Treasury Appropriations bill and Senator Byron Dorgan (D-ND), along with Senators Craig, Hagel, Enzi, Baucus, Dodd, and Roberts, offered an amendment ending the ban on travel to Cuba with identical language as the Flake travel amendment that had passed the House in September. During the debate, Senator Ted Stevens (R-AK), chair of the Senate Appropriations Committee, made a motion to table the Cuba travel amendment. The roll was called on the motion to table, which was defeated by a vote of 59-36. Subsequently, the Dorgan amendment, barring the use of government money to enforce current travel restrictions, was passed by voice vote.[76]

The Senate had last rejected an easing of travel restrictions in 1999, by a vote of 43 to 55. But, thirteen senators who voted against easing the restrictions four years ago switched sides and voted for it this time.[77] Several influential Republican senators voted against the President's position, including John W. Warner of Virginia, Chairman of the Armed Ser-

vices Committee, Pat Roberts of Kansas, Chairman of the Intelligence Committee, and many conservatives from farm states—including Senator Inhofe of Oklahoma, Senator Brownback of Kansas, and Senator Hutchison of Texas.[78]

The Senate vote came less than two weeks after President Bush had delivered a special statement on Cuba where he promised to tighten the enforcement of travel ban in an attempt to halt unlicensed tourism there, as it "provides economic resources to the Castro regime while doing nothing to help the Cuban people."[79] Senator Max Baucus, co-sponsor of the amendment, said the Senate vote was "a strong repudiation of the president's recent announcement that his administration plans to tighten and increase the travel restrictions."[80]

The House and Senate amendments do not legalize travel to the island, but rather strip the Treasury Department of its ability to enforce the travel restrictions. Yet, they loudly express where the Congress stands with respect to travel restrictions to Cuba. Nonetheless, neither the Senate nor House votes received the two-thirds margin needed to overturn a presidential veto. But, the bill with the amendments contains vital money for highways, law enforcement and anti-terrorism; the President has a lot of political capital and credibility at stake. Moreover, before Congress adjourns in early December, the bill with the Cuba provisions may become part of a huge omnibus bill. Thus, the Senate action has placed the President and Republican Members of Congress in a potential confrontation.

---

74. See www.thomas.loc.gov and Ana Radelat, "Lawmakers won't succeed in latest bid to end travel ban, *CubaNews*, Vol. 11, No. 10, October 2003, p. 2.

75. Rep. Mario Diaz-Balart (R-FL) declared: "I wish to thank the Republican freshman class for their solid support for freedom in Cuba." *U.S.-Cuba Policy Report*, 9/23/03, op.cit., p. 1.

76. "Senate Passes Cuba Travel Amendment," Website of the Latin American Working Group, http://www.lawg.org/pages/new%20pages/countries/Cuba/senate_vote_article.htm.

77. Christopher Marquis, "Senate Approves Easing of Curbs on Cuba Travel," *The New York Times*, October 24, 2003.

78. Ibid.

79. The White House, Remarks by President Bush on Cuba, October 10, 2003.

80. For more on the votes see, for example, Frank Davies, "Lifting of ban on travel to Cuba faces obstacles," *The Tribune*, September 10, 2003; and Jim Abrams, "Senate Votes to End Limits on Cuba Travel," The Associated Press, October 10, 2003.

A "senior Administration official" reiterated that the President's advisers would recommend a veto if the bill emerges from a House-Senate conference committee with the amendment.[81] But advocates of easing travel restrictions said they had taken steps to prevent the amendment from being stripped away in the Conference Committee.[82] The Latin American Working Group, a coalition of anti-embargo groups, declared not believing "the House and Senate leadership will let it go through easily. At the very least, it will be much more difficult for the measure to be changed or taken out of the final version of the bill negotiated by the conference committee before it is sent to the President for his signature. And it is possible that a bill with Cuba travel language will reach the President's desk." They also pointed out that "because the language that passed the Senate is identical to the amendment that passed the House, it is technically not conference-able."[83] Nonetheless, the Senate's Republican leadership has reported that it will not allow the bill to get past the Conference Committee.[84]

In addition to the above-described amendments to the Treasury Appropriations bill, the following bills that would affect Cuba travel are pending action:

- **Senate:** In February 2003, Senator Max Baucus (D-MT) introduced the United States-Cuba Trade Act of 2003 (S. 403) to lift the trade embargo on Cuba. Section 5 specifically calls for the elimination of prohibitions on transactions incidental to travel.

- **Senate:** In April of 2003, Senator Michael Enzi (R-WY) introduced the Freedom to Travel Act (S. 950), which was referred to the Committee

on Foreign Relations. As of the end of October 2003, it had 31 co-sponsors.

- **House:** In May of 2003 Representative Jeff Flake introduced the Export Freedom to Cuba Act (H.R. 2071) to allow unrestricted travel to Cuba. Referred to the House Committee on International Relations; as of the end of October 2003, it had 78 co-sponsors.

In the United States Congress, the support of the leadership of the majority party is vital for a bill to reach the stage where a hearing and a committee mark-up are held, two necessary steps to reach the floor for debate and vote. The Republican leadership of the Senate has agreed to allow the Freedom to Travel Act (S. 950) to reach the floor for a vote. Reportedly, Senator Richard Lugar (R-IN) struck a deal with Senator Baucus, the bill's sponsor, to let this happen after Sen. Baucus had placed a hold on the nomination of Roger Noriega for Assistant Secretary of State for Western Hemisphere Affairs.[85] Ambassador Noriega was confirmed and the bill is expected to come up for a vote before the year's end.

CUBA'S TRAVEL RESTRICTIONS[86]

General Rules for U.S.-Based Travelers

Visas: Cuba requires a valid passport and an entry permit or visa issued by the Cuban government for all travelers from the United States, both licensed or not. Entering Cuban territory, territorial waters, or airspace (i.e., within 12 miles of the Cuban coast) without prior authorization from the Cuban government may result in arrest or other enforcement action by Cuban authorities. Violators are subject to prison terms of one to three years for illegal entry.[87]

---

81. Marquis (2003).

82. Ibid.

83. "Senate Passes Cuba Travel Amendment," www.lawg.org,

84. Lolita Baldor, "GOP Will Keep Cuba Travel Ban Intact," The Associated Press, October 29, 2003.

85. *U.S.-Cuba Policy Report*, September 23, 2003, p. 7.

86. Information for this section was obtained from the following sources: website of the Cuban Interests Section at Washington DC, http://www.geocities.com/Paris/Library/2958/espanol/index-espanol.htm; website of Cuba's Customs Agency, http://www.aduana.is-lagrande.cu/prohi.htm; and the website of the U.S. Cuba Trade and Economic Council, http://www.cubatrade.org.

87. Cuban Penal Code, Law No. 62, Chapter XI Art. 215.

The cost of visas and entry permits has changed slightly over time. Travelers born outside of Cuba, of Cuban heritage but who emigrated before 1970, and who are not traveling in the company of persons who will be visiting family in Cuba are issued A-2 visas. These are valid for "tourism only," and allow one entry and a maximum stay in Cuba of 21 days. The cost of this visa is US$50 and is the same regardless of whether travelers are licensed or not by the U.S. government.

A Travel Validity Document (*Vigencia de Viaje*) may be issued for individuals who request multiple entries into Cuba for tourism with a 90-day maximum stay per visit. It is renewable every two years up to six years.

An official visa is used for individuals subject to United States law who are traveling to Cuba for any purpose other than tourism. Visas can be obtained from the Cuban Interests Section in Washington, D.C. A tourist visa can also be obtained from: (1) a travel agent licensed by the OFAC; (2) a non-United States-based travel agent;[88] (3) at the ticket counter of a non-United States-based airline providing travel to the Republic of Cuba from a country other than the United States; or (4) in some cases, upon arrival at an airport in Cuba.

Departure tax: In addition to obtaining visas to enter the country, all visitors to Cuba must pay US$20 airport tax at the time of departure.

Customs regulations:[89] Visitors may bring into the country exempt of duties only their personal effects "in reasonable quantities relative to their length of stay" and up to 44 pounds. Excess baggage is subject to a $2.00 per pound custom duty if it is allowed in as personal effects. Up to 10 kilogram of medicines, in original containers, may also be imported free of duties. Any additional imports considered as gifts, are allowed up to US$250 per year subject to payment of a surcharge of 100% of the value after the first US$50. Technically, computers are not on the list of forbidden articles for importation, but their value exceeds the US$250 limit allowed into the country. There is a list of electronic items that may not be imported, including VCRs, DVD players as well as "any article, including literature, that attempts against the internal order and security of the country." In addition, the following articles must be pre-approved for importation by the Ministry of Communications for visitors who wish to take them into the country: radios and related equipment; faxes, telephones and related equipment; GPS—Guidance Positioning Systems—and satellite antennas, dishes, and other related equipment.

Special Rules for Travelers of Cuban Heritage[90]

Cuba does not allow entry for five years to citizens who have left the country without government authorization (considered an "illegal exit"), including those who left on official missions but remained in third countries under different circumstances than the ones under which they were authorized by the Cuban government.

All Cuban-born residents of the United States, together with U.S. citizens who left Cuba after 1970 are issued an A10 or "PRF" (*Permiso de Reunificación Familiar* or "Family Reunification Permit") at a cost of $100,[91] twice the $50 charged to U.S. citizens and Cubans who left before 1970. This permit is valid for one entry, allows a maximum stay of 21 days stay, and is valid for 90 days from the approval date. The

---

88. Travel agents tend to mark up the cost of the visa for administrative handling. Marazul charges $65 for the visa, of which $50 is payable to the Cuban government. A portion of this amount is non-refundable if the visa is not approved. Armando García (2003).

89. Information obtained at the website for Cuba's Customs Agency, http://www.aduana.islagrande.cu.

90. Website data and telephone information obtained from Marazul Charters, Inc. and the website of the Cuban Interests Section at Washington, D.C.

91. Marazul charges $115, recently lowered from $125 (Armando García, 2003, plus information provided by telephone by Marazul Charters, Inc. on December 16, 2002, and fact sheet provided by Marazul in 1998).

$100 fee is unusually high for Cuba, where the average annual salary is equivalent to $113.[92]

A special permit (P59) is issued for Cubans who emigrated before 1959 and have original proof of emigration date. This visa costs $121, is valid for one entry, allows a maximum of 30 days' stay, and is valid for 30 days from the approval date.[93]

The Cuban government considers all Cuban-born U.S. citizens who left Cuba after December 31, 1970, to be solely Cuban citizens and requires them to enter and depart Cuba using Cuban passports. These cost $280 (for a person who has never had a Cuban passport or has a very old one) and are valid for six years from their issuance date but must be renewed every two years (at a cost of $146). These fees are disproportionately high—equivalent to 2.5 to 1.3 times the average annual salary of a Cuban worker. From the perspective of the United States, using a Cuban passport to enter Cuba does not jeopardize the person's U.S. citizenship, but a U.S. passports must be used to enter and depart the U.S. and to transit any countries en route.

U.S. citizens traveling to Cuba with a Cuban passport (and an A10 entry permit) may be subject to a range of restrictions and obligations, including military service in Cuba. Cuba does not recognize the right or obligation of the U.S. government to protect Cuban-born American citizens, whom the Cuban government views as only Cuban citizens, and consular access is regularly denied to them. Cuban authorities consistently refuse to notify the U.S. Interests Section of the arrest of Cuban-American dual nationals and deny U.S. consular officers access to them. They also withhold information concerning their welfare and proper treatment under Cuban law. The U.S. Department of State reports that there are known cases of Cuban-American dual nationals being forced by the Cuban government to surrender their U.S. passports. Yet, Cuban-American dual nationals who fall ill may only be treated at hospitals for foreigners that charge in hard currency (except in certain emergencies).[94]

On September 27, 2003, Cuba's Foreign Minister Felipe Pérez Roque announced hat the Cuban government planned to stop requiring visas for overseas Cubans visiting the island. The Cuban Foreign Ministry issued a statement on October 2, 2003 confirming that Cubans residing abroad who had a Cuban passport would no longer need to purchase the higher cost entry permits, a decision that would go into effect after the first quarter of 2004. The Ministry, however, clarified that the measure would exclude those who "engage in repugnant or damaging activities against the interests of Cuba."[95]

Travelers not of Cuban heritage accompanying persons of Cuban heritage who travel to visit family are issued a special visa (AO3), which is valid for one entry, allows a maximum of 21 days stay. and is valid for 90 days from the approval date.[96] Its cost is $50, the same as for an A-2 tourist visa.

THE GROWTH OF U.S.-BASED TRAVEL TO CUBA

U.S. travel to Cuba became possible only when the Cuban government opened up to foreign tourism and began developing its neglected tourism industry to confront the severe economic crisis that followed the demise of massive Soviet aid to the island. In response, U.S. travel regulations have evolved to reflect the view of the U.S. government that certain travel to Cuba is a means to expose the Cuban people to dem-

---

92. The average wage in Cuba in 2001 was 245 pesos and the average monthly income of workers 349 pesos, which takes into account other compensation such as bonuses in hard currency convertible pesos, food support, clothing, shoes, toiletries and other consumer items (Oscar Espinosa Chepe, "El salario en Cuba," CubaNet, Havana, July 2002). That translates into US$9.42 and US$13.42 at the current exchange rate of 26 pesos to the dollar.

93. Information provided by Marazul Charters, October 15, 2003.

94. Consular Information Sheet, op.cit.

95. "Castro government agrees to drop visa requirement for Cuban exiles," *CubaNews*, Vol. 11, No. 10, October 2003, p. 9.

96. Armando García (2003).

ocratic values. The looser regulations have facilitated increased travel of persons from Cuba to the U.S. who qualify for entry visas and allowed for the streamlining of licensing procedures for qualified U.S. persons traveling to Cuba, including the licensing of multiple visits for qualified individuals and groups. As a result, travel to Cuba increased rapidly.[97]

There are, at present, many options to travel to Cuba from the United States. In recent years prices have also declined considerably, becoming very competitive with other Caribbean locations. The number of charter and direct flights from three U.S. cities (Miami, Los Angeles, and New York) to several different Cuban cities has increased significantly. Three direct flights leave from New York weekly and there are daily flights between Miami and La Habana and on a less frequent schedule to Holguín, Santiago, Cienfuegos and Camagüey. According to a Cuban government tourism official, U.S.-Cuba direct flights increased by 38% from 1999 to 2003.[98]

Travel to Cuba through a third country is also relatively easy—there are daily flights from Cancún and Nassau, as well as regular flights from other Central American and Caribbean destinations.

Most U.S.-based visitors reportedly travel on the direct charter flights. Technically, all visitors who take the direct flights from the U.S. must provide evidence that they have a specific license or are authorized under a general license. Travelers without a license generally defy the travel restrictions by going through third countries such as Mexico, Jamaica, and Bahamas. As a general rule, in order to encourage tourist earnings, Cuban immigration authorities do not stamp these visitors' passports, a practice that is advertised in tourist promotion websites of Cuban tourism enterprises and of U.S. or Canadian groups associated with Cuban entities.

The U.S. government does not have data on the actual number of U.S.-based travelers who visit Cuba. The State Department does not collect statistics on Americans traveling to Cuba and OFAC maintains that there are so many general licenses (for which individuals do not have to apply) that it is not possible to arrive at an accurate number. In addition, specific licenses may be granted for travel that is never completed. This may explain the discrepancy in estimates by U.S. government officials. For example, in congressional testimony in February 2002, OFAC Director Richard Newcomb estimated that 150,000-200,000 Americans traveled to Cuba in 2001, about one-third without permission from OFAC.[99] Yet, in October of 2003, Roger Noriega, Assistant Secretary of State for Western Hemisphere Affairs, reported that about 200,000 Americans—half of them Cuban-Americans visiting their families—traveled legally to Cuba in 2002.[100]

Data from Cuban Sources

There are many discrepancies in Cuban government statistics regarding U.S.-based travel to Cuba. This is a common occurrence when researching any other economic sector in Cuba.

A University of Florida Cuba expert who travels to the island and has access to government sources estimates that since 1994, the number of individuals subject to U.S. law traveling to Cuba without OFAC licenses increased on average 19% to 21%, while legal visits rose by 9% to 11%.[101]

---

97. Part II of the greater work on travel restrictions will examine in greater detail diverse aspects of the growth in all categories of travel by U.S., including people-to-people exchanges and travel by Cuban Americans.

98. Reported by Berto Pérez, head of Havanatur, in "Vuelos desde EEUU a Cuba han crecido un 38 por ciento por año," EFE, La Habana, 4 octubre 2003. It should be noted that the same Cuban government official stated that the number of U.S. travelers to Cuba grew at a rate of 61% per year in the last five years, which is not consistent with information given by other Cuban government representatives.

99. Hearing of the Senate Appropriations Committee (February 11, 2002).

100. A. Radelat (2003).

101. Paolo Spadoni, "The Role of the United States in the Cuban Economy," (2003), in this volume.

Table 1. Data from Cuban Officials on U.S. Visitors to Cuba in 2002

Source	Not Cuban-Americans	Unlicensed Not Cuban-Americans	Cuban-Americans	Total
Prensa Latina, December 2001	70,000	N/A	130,000	200,000
Prensa Latina, February 2002	78,800	N/A	107,000	185,800
Granma, January 2003	N/A	50,000	N/A	180,000
EFE (Min. Tourism), October 2003	80,000	40,000	N/A	N/A
AP (Min. Tourism), October 2003	77,000	35,000	N/A	N/A

In 1999, an estimated 182,000 U.S. citizens (about 120,000 Cuban Americans) are reported to have traveled to Cuba. If this figure is correct, the United States accounted for more travelers to the island than any other country, except Canada.[102]

For 2000, Cuban Foreign Minister Felipe Pérez Roque reported that 120,000 Cuban Americans and 80,000 Americans of non-Cuban origin traveled to Cuba.[103] The U.S.-Cuba Trade and Economic Council reported that approximately 22,000 U.S. citizens visited that year without OFAC authorization.[104]

For 2001, news agency Reuters reported that around 176,000 Americans visited Cuba (the breakdown for Cuban Americans is not available), with an estimated 25,000 visiting without licenses traveling through third countries.[105] The Economist informed of approximately 125,000 Cuban Americans and 79,000 U.S. citizens of non-Cuban origin visiting that year, representing about 11.5% of total arrivals to the island. About 50,000 were tourists who traveled via third countries, with or without their government's authorization.[106] For U.S. citizens not of Cuban de-

scent, the number of arrivals peaked at about 90,000.[107]

For 2002, public statements about the number of U.S. visitors by Cuban government officials have become more common, yet discrepancies still abound. For example, the Cuban official newspaper Granma reported that in December 2002, at least 26,500 passengers reserved seats in 260 flights from Miami, compared to 144 flights in November.[108] A large increase in flights is typical for December, the month when travel agencies report their highest volume of travelers as Cuban-Americans visit family and other travelers take holiday vacations. But, a very similar report in El Nuevo Herald, based on the same travel agency sources, puts the number of flights in December at 240, twenty fewer than reported by Granma, a difference that results in 3,820 fewer passengers for the month of December.[109] This is a typical problem with data coming from Cuban official sources. Table 1 illustrates the discrepancies in the data provided by different official sources.

Working with the figures cited by Cuban sources can be a dizzying proposition. Prensa Latina, the news agency of the Cuban government, reported in December 2002 that 70,000 Americans of non-Cuban

---

102. Spadoni (2003).

103. Andrew Cawthorne, "Cuba's economic linchpin, tourism, up 10.7 percent," Havana, Reuters, July 3, 2001.

104. U.S.-Cuba Trade and Economic Council (USCTEC). *2002 Commercial Highlights* http://www.cubatrade.org/2002Lst.pdf.

105. "U.S. travel agents scope out Cuba tourism," Reuters, Havana, November 22, 2002. (Reuters has journalists in Cuba with access to government officials.)

106. "Embargo or not, US is now Fidel Castro's economic partner," *The Economist*, January 7, 2003.

107. Spadoni (2003), citing interview with a Cuban economist in Havana, May 27, 2003.

108. Jean Guy Allard, "Record de visitantes procedentes de EE.UU," *Granma Internacional*, January 7, 2003.

109. This calculation uses the 93% capacity of flights that carry 206 passengers, as reported by one of the travel agencies running direct charters to Cuba, C&T Charters. Ruiz Campos (2002).

origin and more than 130,000 Cuban Americans had visited in 2002,[110] bringing the total number of U.S. visitors to 200,000. Yet, a Prensa Latina report a few months later cites Foreign Minister Pérez Roque as stating that 78,800 Americans and 107,000 Cuban-Americans traveled to Cuba in 2002 (a total of 185,800).[111] *Granma*, Cuba's official news daily, meanwhile, indicated in January 2003 that around 54,000 Americans traveled to Cuba in 2002, of which 50,000 went through third countries in violation of travel restrictions.[112] Meanwhile, a University of Florida researcher interviewed a Cuban economist in Havana in May of 2003, who reported 216,000 U.S. visitors in 2002 (equivalent to 12.8% of arrivals from all countries).[113] The Ministry of Tourism reported to the Spanish News Agency EFE that 80.000 U.S. tourists arrived in 2002, half of which (40,000) were not licensed.[114] Presumably this figure is only for Americans not of Cuban heritage. Miguel Figueras, adviser to Cuba's Tourism Ministry, for his part stated that some 77,000 U.S. citizens not of Cuban heritage visited the island in 2002—half (35,000) considered to have done so illegally with respect to the U.S. government.[115] Taking all these figures together, we can estimate that around 80,000 Americans not of Cuban heritage traveled to Cuba in 2002, 35,000 to 50,000 without authorization from OFAC. The total number of U.S.-based travelers ranged between 180,000 and 200,000, bringing the total of Cuban-American travelers between 100,000 to 120,000.

For 2003, Tourism Minister Ibrahim Ferradaz reported in October that Cuba will have received 230,000 annual visitors from the United States by the end of the year—150,000 of Cuban heritage and nearly all of the remaining 80,000 skirting U.S. licensing regulations. This, he stated, would make up 12% of all tourists traveling to Cuba, expected to amount to 1.9 million at year-end 2003.[116] It is not entirely clear if he was citing projected numbers for 2003, but it can be assumed that was the case.

U.S. travel to Cuba declined in 2001 and 2002 with respect to the level reached in 2000, arguably due to the overall decline in international tourist travel connected with the economic downturn and the September 11 terrorist attacks. But for 2003, Cuban government officials are anticipating a 15% rise from 2000 arrivals. This may be in part because some travelers are trying to travel before December 31, ahead of the expiration on that date of licenses for non-accredited educational exchanges (as per Treasury Department change in regulations of March of 2003).[117]

Regardless of the discrepancies, if the numbers from Cuban official sources are fairly accurate, there has been a steady and significant increase in U.S.-based travel to Cuba in the last decade, irrespective of travel restrictions aside, involving both legal and unlicensed travel, and travelers of Cuban heritage and not.. From 1990 through year-end 2003, 1.3 million U.S.-based travelers will have visited Cuba (almost 67% of them will have been of Cuban heritage), out of total reported tourist arrivals of a little over 15 million (Table 2). U.S. travelers accounted for 2.9%

---

110. "Aseguran que fracasará política EEUU para aislar a Cuba La Habana," Prensa Latina, 26 de diciembre de 2002.

111. "Cuba demanda sustitución de organismos financieros internacionales," Prensa Latina, La Habana, 5 de febrero de 2003.

112. Allard (2003).

113. Spadoni (2003).

114. "Vuelos…"(EFE, 2003).

115. John Rice, "Industry Group Pushes Freer Travel to Cuba," Cancún, Mexico, The Associated Press, October 18, 2003.

116. Pablo Alfonso, "Vital para Cuba el turismo norteamericano," *El Nuevo Herald*, 19 de octubre de 2003.

117. OFAC eliminated non-accredited educational travel approved since 1999, which had grown to the point that any person who enrolled in and paid for a program or tour organized by a licensed educational or cultural institution could travel. The licenses already granted would not be renewed and would be allowed to expire—all by December 31, 2003. OFAC issued a statement that said these trips were "involving minimal substantive contact with Cuban nationals" and were being abused, consisting primarily of tourist travel that was undercutting the intent of the regulation. R. Richard Newcomb (10-16-03).

Table 2.   U.S. Visitors as a Percentage of Total Visitors to Cuba: 1990-2003

	U.S. Visitors			Total Visitors (thousands)	U.S. Visitors as % of Total Visitors
	Total	Not Cuban-Americans	Cuban-Americans		
1990	9,975	7,375	2,600	340.3	2.9
1991	15,833	11,233	4,600	424	3.7
1992	24,650	10,500	14,600	460.6	5.4
1993	34,511	14,715	19,400	544.1	6.3
1994	51,437	17,937	33,500	617.3	8.3
1995	59,972	20,672	39,300	745.5	8.0
1996	85,413	27,113	58,300	1,004.30	8.5
1997	106,656	34,956	71,700	1,170.10	9.1
1998	141,678	46,778	94,900	1,415.80	10.0
1999	N/A	N/A	N/A/	1,602.80	N/A
2000	200,000	80,000	120,000	1,773.90	11.2
2001	176,000	50,000	126,000	1774.5	9.2
2002	185,800	78,800	107,000	1,680	11.1
2003	230,000	80,000	150,000	1,900	12.1
Total	1,321,925	480,079	841,900	15,453	

Note: For simplification, "Not Cuban-American" refers to U.S.-based travelers not of Cuban heritage, while "Cuban-American" is used to designate all U.S. based travelers of Cuban heritage, regardless of their residence status or citizenship.

Source: Sources: For 1990-1998: Cited in Spadoni (2003). Based on Oficina Nacional de Estadísticas, *Anuario Estadístico de Cuba*, 1996, 1998, and 2000; Alvarez A. and Amat D., "El mercado emisor turistico estadounidense hacia el Caribe," Facultad de Economía, Universidad de la Habana, Trabajo de diploma, 1996; World Tourism Organization; *Yearbook of Tourism Statistics*, 2003 and previous editions. For 2000-2002: Information from diverse Cuban officials, as cited elsewhere in this paper. For 2003, estimated; see text.

of all visitors in 1990, 8.3% in 1994, and 12.1% in 2003. By 1995, the United States was already the fourth largest source of visitors to the island (after Canada, Italy, and Spain).[118] In 2003, the United States was the third largest source of visitors to Cuba.[119]

Data from Licensed Travel Service Providers in the U.S.

The Miami Herald ran a December 25, 2002 article that cites interviews with travel agencies providing service to Cuba from the Miami International Airport as well as airport authorities. They all reported a steep increase in the number of travelers to Cuba in 2002.[120] Following is some of the information disclosed:

- At least 26,500 passengers were booked on 240 flights out of Miami in December 2002.

- At Miami International Airport, a total of 99 flights left between December 16 and 24, and an additional 11 were scheduled for Christmas Day.

- A total of 144 flights left from Miami to Cuba in November 2002.

- C&T Charters, one of the travel agencies interviewed, reported 27 flights to Cuba in December 2002 compared to its average of 16 monthly flights, flying about 5,000 travelers in December, up from the average of 3,200 passengers per month in January-November. For the whole month of December, C&T reported a 93 percent capacity in airplanes that have 206 seats.

- Reservations for December 2002 were up an estimated 35 percent to 40 percent compared to December 2000, when Miami experienced its highest level of bookings since 1959.

---

118. In 1995, Canada (143,541) was the most important source of visitors to Cuba, followed by Italy (114,767), Spain (89,501), and the United States (59,972). In 1998, Canadian travelers to Cuba were 215,644, followed by Italians (186,688), Germans (148,987), and persons from the United States (141,678). See Spadoni (2003).

119. Spadoni (2003).

120. Ruiz Campos (2002).

The above allows us to indulge in an exercise that, admittedly, is not based on verifiable data or proven assumptions, but may point to under-reporting of the total number of U.S-based travelers by Cuba. Following are a few inferences from the above information:

- An average of 8.4 direct charter flights left from Miami to Cuba daily in December 2002. An average of 4.6 direct charter flights left from Miami to Cuba in November 2002. An average of 110 passengers traveled in December from Miami (26,500 passengers in 240 flights).

- C&T Charters reported a number of passengers that matches the number of flights at the cited capacity both for the average month of the year (January to November) as well as for December.[121] From these data we can calculate that C&T Charters had a 19% share of the direct charter market from Miami in December 2002 (5,000 passengers out of a total of 26,500).

- If the same 19% share is assumed for the months of January to November,[122] the total number of travelers in direct flights just from Miami for the year 2002 would amount to 203,767.[123]

- If 26,500 passengers for December are added to an equivalent share of passengers per flight for November (144 flights at an average of 110 passengers per flight), times eleven months for the period January–November, a total of 200,740 passengers would have traveled in direct charter flights in 2002 just from Miami.

All of the above calculations for travelers going directly to Cuba in charter flights from Miami suggest levels that exceed the total number of visitors from the U.S. (both of Cuban heritage and not), coming from all three U.S. cities offering direct charter flights plus all third country flights (which, as we have seen, was reported by Cuba as ranging between 180,000 and 200,000).

If the information provided by Miami travel agents is roughly accurate, the figures provided by the Cuban government for U.S.-based travel seem to underestimate actual flows. Two scholars who have done in-depth research on the subject had already pointed this problem regarding the statistics on Cuban-American visits to Cuba. They pointed out that, while Cuban sources report that individuals of Cuban descent visiting the island between 1994 and 1996 were about 20,000 per year, U.S. sources estimate the number at approximately 40,000 in 1994 and 100,000 per year between 1995 and 1999.[124]

Revenues derived by Cuba from U.S. based visitors

At present, travelers from the U.S. reportedly spend about $200 million a year in Cuba,[125] or around 11% of Cuba's total gross revenues from tourism. It is not known how this figure, provided by a Cuban government official, was derived or what it includes. But, it would represent around 200,000 U.S.-based visitors spending an average of $1,000 per trip, which is on the low side ($200 per day if the average stay is 5 days, $143 per day for a 7-day stay). By our calculations, between 1990 and 2003 Cuba has received approximately $1.5 to $1.7 billion in gross

---

121. Approximately 93% capacity corresponds to the figures provided by C&T (3,200 passengers in 16 flights in November and 5,000 passengers in 27 flights in December).

122. The monthly passengers data provided by C&T Charters seems to match the number of passengers reported vis-à-vis the number of flights both for November and for December. The same 93% capacity holds true (3,200 passengers in 16 flights in November and 5,000 passengers in 27 flights in December).

123. C&T's 3,200 passengers for November represent 19% of a total 16,132 travelers per month. This monthly average times eleven months equals 177,452 passengers, plus 26,315 in December, brings the total number to 203,767.

124. Susan Eckstein and Lorena Barberia, "Cuban-American Cuba Visits: Public Policy, Private Practices," Mellon-MIT-Inter-University Program on Non-Governmental Organizations (NGOS) and Forced Migration, 2001, note 8, p.13.

125. Quote attributed to John Kavulich, President of the U.S.-Cuba Trade and Economic Council. In Andres Oppenheimer, "U.S. may tighten Cuba travel," *The Miami Herald*, December 15, 2002.

revenues from U.S-based visitors, estimated conservatively.[126]

There are three general types of U.S. based travelers considered "tourists" for the purposes of this paper. The data used by the Cuban government and travel agencies, refers to all visitors as "tourists." But, there are traditional tourists, tourists on family visits, and tourists traveling for professional reasons. Cuban-Americans generally exhibit significantly different itineraries and expenditure patterns, as they tend to stay longer, travel more to all parts of the island, some stay with relatives rather than at hotels, they have much more direct contact with the locals, undertake activities less associated with the tourist market, make dollar purchases on the island for their relatives, and carry remittances to leave behind. Thus, the revenues derived from travel by Cuban-Americans are probably much higher than is being reported. The same may be true, to a lesser degree, for professionals who must incur higher costs for transportation or other business-related services.

There is no limit to the amout of cash that can be brought into Cuba, although the use of credit cards by U.S. based travelers is not possible. Cuban-Americans have found it increasing easy to spend their dollars in services and purchases of Western goods for their relatives at the well-stocked state-owned dollar stores, which have the telling name of "tiendas de recuperación de divisas" or "stores to recover hard currency." Strict Customs regulations regarding what can be imported into the country as gifts for relatives promote purchases at these hard currency stores, said to mark up items at up by an average of 240%. This is likely not included in Cuban official data of revenues from tourism.

Revenues from U.S.-based Cuban NGO's co-sponsoring educational exchanges are also in all likelihood not represented in revenues from tourism.

Revenues from fees charged to U.S. tourists for visa applications, passport fees for persons born in Cuba, Customs duties, and departure taxes would also bring the amount of total revenues up. These fees are likely to be excluded from reported revenues per tourist and, instead, incorporated into the budgets of state agencies such as Customs, the airport, and the Ministry of Foreign Affairs. If we use the amount estimated for these fees, of an average of $233 per tourist, an additional roughly $308 million will have been collected from U.S. travelers by the Cuban government between 1990 and 2003. For 2003 alone, we can estimate that Cuba will receive about $53.5 million in fees from 230,000 visitors (see Table 3).

There are three other potential side effects of travel that may be generating additional hard currency revenues for Cuba. Determining whether or not this hypothesis holds true and, if so, the approximate dollar amounts, is outside the bounds of this study. But their economic impact may be considerable.

First, when visiting family members become aware of their relatives' need, they also tend to make purchase at stores on the island selling goods in hard currency. What percentage of the sales of these stores is attributable to visitors from the United States is unknown. Others also have access to those stores: Cubans receiving remittances, those employed in the foreign sector with access to dollar tips and bonuses, visiting or resident foreigners and others with access to hard currency.

Second, visits to the island to see relatives expose Cuban Americans to the stark living conditions of their loved ones. Both logic and observation lead to the

---

126. If we were to apply the $166 per diem rate used by the State Department, a 5-day stay would bring expenditures to $830 per traveler and a 7-day stay would generate $1,162, with $966 the average of the two. This would translate into $1.5 billion in expenditures for the number of U.S. tourists reported in Table 2 above. Yet, it must be considered that OFAC regulations recognize and contemplate the higher expenses required by professionals and those visiting family who must travel within the island—that would raise the expenditure per visitor. In fact, gross revenues per tourist per year for Cuba were reported by the U.S.-Cuba Trade and Economic Council (*Economic Eye on Cuba*, 20 January 2003 to 26 January 2003) to have increased from $948 in 1991 to $1,475 in 1995, decreasing steadily until 2001, to $1,037, and then rising to $1,049 in 2002. If an average of $1,262, the higher range points ($1,475 and $1,047), is instead applied to calculate the expenditures per tourist from the U.S., it would translate into around $1.7 billion.

Table 3. Estimated Annual Revenues in Fees Collected by Cuba from U.S.-based Travelers (2003 Projected) U.S. dollars

	Cuban-Americans	Not Cuban-Americans	Total
Number of Travelers	150,000	80,000	230,000
Visa applications[ab]	11,767,500	4,000,000	15,767,500
Passport fees[c]	18,179,500		18,179,500
Departure taxes[d]	3,000,000	1,600,000	4,600,000
Customs' duties[e]	15,000,000		15,000,000
Totals	47,947,050	5,600,000	53,547,050

a. Entry fees for Cuban Americans were calculated based on 2000 U.S. Census data that indicates that almost two-third of Cubans are foreign born and 54.6% arrived before 1970, from Boswell and Díaz, "A demographic profile of Cuban Americans," The Cuban American National Council, Inc., September 2002, p. 8 and Table 11 (p. 32). 45.4% of Cuban Americans traveling to Cuba were assigned the $100 entry permit fee corresponding to those who left after 1970 and 54.6% were assigned the $50 visa fee corresponding to those who left before 1970.

b. Non-Cuban Americans were all assumed to have paid a $50 visa fee.

c. Passport fees were calculated based on the same Census data, based on the requirement that all Cuban American visitors who left after 1970 (45.4% of all Cuban Americans) must enter the country with a Cuban passport. For estimation purposes, this was simplified to assume that each visitor is only a one-time visitor for the year and would require either a new passport or a renewal. Thus, an average passport fee of $213 was assigned for estimation purposes (the range in fees is $280 for a new passport valid six years and $146 for renewals required every two years). All remaining travelers from the U.S. were not assigned a passport fee, as they are assumed to enter Cuba with their U.S. passport.

d. Departure tax is US$20 for all visitors.

e. Up to $250 in gifts may be brought into the country per year; the first $50 free of duties, the remaining $200 taxed at 100%. For the purposes of the calculation, 50% of Cuban American visitors were considered as paying the $200 duty to bring in gifts for relatives.

hypothesis that this encourages economic support, which possibly translates into future remittances, either in a steadier and/or higher level if remittances were being sent before travel took place and starting if they were not, or by widening their reach to additional family members or households.[127] In 1993, the Cuban government legalized the holding of dollars, which until then had been punishable with prison. In addition, the severity of the economic crisis had a devastating effect on the population, generating extreme hardship and need for humanitarian support. Remittances were temporarily suspended by President Clinton in 1996 after the downing of two U.S. civilian aircraft, but were restored in 1998.[128] Although during the time they were suspended it is said that remittances were still being sent illegally with travelers or via third countries, the reauthorization eased the logistics and make remitting money to Cuba a very common occurrence. As a result, remittances to Cuba from the U.S. are estimated between around $500 million to $1 billion annually. That would translate into around $3 to $6 billion respectively for the 6 years 1998 to 2003. If our logic applies, a percentage of this total could be attributed to increased travel by Cuban Americans.

Third, the reunification with family and friends and the reaffirmation of sentimental ties tends to encourage more frequent telephone contact with loved ones on the island or new telephone communications with a wider circle of people with whom the traveler became acquainted or in closer contact during the trip to Cuba. Also, planning family visits requires communications. Almost all calls originate in the U.S., as Cubans generally lack the economic means to pay for outgoing long-distance calls. From September 1996 to September 2003, payments to Cuba by U.S. telecommunications companies have amounted to $482,616,162, almost half a billion dollars.[129] Although we cannot determine what percentage of that income might have been generated by an increase in calls from the U.S. to Cuba as attributable to travel, it may be significant.

127. To confront the severe economic crisis, in 1993, the Cuban government legalized the holding of dollars, which had been illegal until then and was penalized with jail, oftentimes for years. This prompted a steep rise in remittances (estimates by economists and reports from Cuba vary widely).

128. At present, OFAC regulations permit any person under U.S. jurisdiction to send remittances of up to $300 every three months to any one household in Cuba. (Cuban Assets Control Regulations, op.cit.)

129. The 1996 Cuban Liberty Act requires that U.S. telecommunications companies report their revenues paid to Cuba bi-annually (U.S. Cuba Policy Report, September 30, 2003.)

THE ROLE OF THE UNITED STATES IN THE CUBAN ECONOMY

Paolo Spadoni[1]

The collapse of the Soviet Union and its European proxies in the early 1990s inaugurated a very difficult period for Cuba and an unprecedented economic recession that seriously threatened the survival of the Castro government. The Cuban authorities were forced to loosen up their centrally planned economy, establish more developed relations with the capitalist world, and introduce limited market reforms in areas including trade, foreign investment, and tourism. Given the emergency situation of the Cuban economy, the end of Cuba's active support of revolutionary forces in Africa and Latin America as well as the end of its close ties with the Soviet Union, one could have expected the beginning of friendlier relations between Washington and Havana. Instead, the United States tightened the embargo against the island with the enactment of the Torricelli law in 1992 and the Helms-Burton law in 1996. As noted by Jorge Domínguez, "The Cold War had turned colder in the Caribbean. Cuba was the only country governed by a communist party whose domestic political regime the United States was still committed by law and policy to replace, albeit by peaceful means."[2]

Although one of the reasons for additional sanctions was to stimulate democratic reforms in Cuba, the whole point of U.S. policy was to exert economic pressure on the Castro government (and eventually hasten its demise) by stemming the flow of hard currency to the Caribbean island. A spokesman for the U.S. Treasury Department has recently admitted that sanctions against Cuba were mainly intended to "deprive the Castro regime of the financial wherewithal to oppress its people."[3] We can also add that the United States tried to capitalize on Cuba's economic dilemma and frustrated economic adjustment. Up to 1989, the embargo placed conditions on the 15% of Cuba's international trade that fell outside the socialist market. However, after 1991, the embargo placed conditions on more than 90% of that trade.[4] Under these circumstances, it appears obvious that U.S. policymakers had an unparalleled opportunity to finally get the most out of economic sanctions that had failed for thirty years to overthrow the rule of Fidel Castro in Cuba.

There has been considerable debate about just how effective U.S. economic sanctions against Cuba have been in denying hard currency earnings to the Castro government. In light of the available information, it could be argued that the United States has not only been unable to foster fundamental political reforms in Cuba, but has actually contributed to the recovery of the island's economy from the deep recession of

---

1. This paper is mostly based on field research conducted in Cuba during the summer of 2003. The Center for Latin American Studies at the University of Florida and a Wilgus Research Grant financially supported travel to Cuba and the preparation of this paper. The author alone is responsible for the content and interpretations.

2. Domínguez, Jorge I. "U.S.-Cuban Relations: From the Cold War to the Colder War." *Journal of Interamerican Studies and World Affairs*, v. 39, n. 3, Fall 1997, p. 49.

3. Kirkpatrick, David D. "U.S. Halts Cuba Access by Educational Groups." *The New York Times*, May 4, 2003.

4. Schwab, Peter. *Cuba: Confronting the U.S. Embargo.* New York: St. Martin's Press, 1999, pp. 71-72.

the early 1990s. The purpose of this study is to demonstrate that, in spite of the tightening of the embargo, the United States has played and continues to play quite an important role in the Cuban economy. More specifically, significant amounts of hard currency have been channeled into the Cuban economy through U.S. visitors (including Cuban-Americans), remittances sent by Cuban exiles to their families in the island, American food exports (sold in government-owned dollars stores), and U.S. investors who hold publicly traded shares of major foreign firms engaged in business activities with the government of Fidel Castro. The study also intends to demonstrate that a significant share of hard currency reaching Cuba is in violation of U.S. regulations, thus providing some evidence for the inability of the U.S. government to obtain compliance from its own citizens.

The importance of this work resides in the attempt to enrich the general debate on the role and usefulness of economic sanctions and shed light upon a specific aspect that has been generally neglected by scholars of international relations and by the literature on the Cuban embargo. While many scholars tend to evaluate the utility of sanctions by analyzing the behavior of the target government, this study focuses on the citizens of the coercer state. Far from downplaying the importance of economic adjustments devised by the target country to cope with sanctions, the contention of this paper is that U.S. citizens' economic activities (both legal and illegal) have mitigated the impact of the Cuban embargo and undermined its main goal. The study begins with an analysis of international tourism in Cuba and the presence of U.S. visitors in the island. It continues with an examination of the importance for the Cuban economy of remittances sent from U.S. residents (Cuban exiles) after Cuba's legalization of dollar holdings in August 1993. Finally, it provides a brief review of recent developments in U.S. food sales to Cuba and American investments in foreign companies that operate in the

Cuban market. The conclusion summarizes the main findings of the research and offers some suggestions for a more effective U.S. policy toward the government of Fidel Castro.

INTERNATIONAL TOURISM AND U.S. VISITORS TO CUBA

Since the late 1980s, Cuba has targeted tourism as a priority sector because of its ability to generate foreign exchange. International tourism is today, at least in gross terms, the single most important source of hard currency for the Cuban government. Cuba is again emerging as one of the Caribbean's most popular holiday destinations. The tourism industry, which was relatively small prior to 1990, has grown at an astounding 18.5% annually since the legalization of the dollar sector of the economy in 1993, with a period of decline following the September 11, 2001, terrorist attacks on the United States. Even more important, there has been a significant improvement in the integration between local industries and the Cuban tourist sector. The proportion of domestically produced goods provided to the tourist industry has increased from 12% in 1990 to 68% in 2002.[5] While ten years ago practically all products for hotels and restaurants were imported, local corporations and joint ventures with foreign firms currently supply a wide range of products such as mineral water, soft drinks and alcoholic beverages, processed meat, omnibuses, air conditioners, telephones, and electronic equipment.[6]

Figure 1 shows data on gross revenues from tourism, number of tourist arrivals and gross revenues per tourist for the period 1993-2002. According to official figures, arrivals rose from 546,000 in 1993 to over a million in 1996 and reached around 1.68 million at the end of the year 2002. Similarly, gross revenues from tourism increased from $720 million in 1993 to more than $1.9 billion in 2000, making the tourist industry, as Cuban officials often describe it, the "engine" of the island's economy. For 2002, the

---

5. Brundenius, Claes. "Tourism as Engine of Growth. Reflections on Cuba's New Development Strategy." Paper presented at the 2003 meeting of the Latin American Studies Association (LASA), Dallas, Texas, March 27-29, 2003.

6. Figueras Pérez, Miguel Alejandro. "El Turismo Internacional y la Formación de Clusters Productivos en la Economía Cubana." In *Cuba. Reflexiones Sobre su Economía*. Universidad de La Habana, 2002, p. 112.

Figure 1. International Tourism in Cuba, 1993-2002

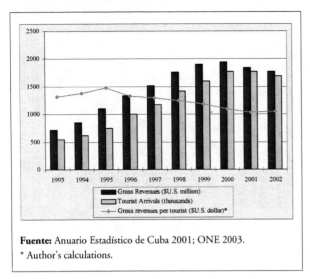

Fuente: Anuario Estadístico de Cuba 2001; ONE 2003.
* Author's calculations.

National Statistical Office (ONE) reported a slight decrease in gross revenues from tourism in comparison to 2001 ($1.77 billion and $1.84 billion, respectively), but other sources indicate that the decline could have been more pronounced. For instance, the U.S.-Cuba Trade and Economic Council reported that gross tourism revenues were about $1.5 billion in 2002, representing a decrease of approximately 18% from 2001.[7] In terms of tourist expenditures, gross revenues per tourist per year increased from $948 in 1991 to $1475 in 1995. However, since then, they decreased steadily and in 2001 they were $1037, just 9% above the 1991 level. This suggests that, if there are not other avenues for the economy to grow in the future outside tourism, the Cuban economy might plateau once the tourist sector reaches its maturity. In 2002, gross revenues per tourist were approximately $1049, only 1.2% above the 2001 level.

Restrictions on travel from the United States to Cuba have been a key component of U.S. policy toward the Castro government for most of the last 40 years, although they have changed many times since 1963. During the 1990s, president Clinton made repeated changes to travel regulations in response to actions by the Cuban government. As a reaction to the *balsero* crisis of the summer of 1994, he banned family visits by Cuban-Americans (who were previously allowed to visit their close relatives in the island) except in cases of "extreme humanitarian need." In 1996, after the shooting down of two U.S. planes flown by Cuban exiles, he suspended direct flights between the two countries.[8] However, in 1999, as part of a new policy aimed to promote people-to-people contacts, he streamlined travel procedures for students, athletes, artists, and other groups and individuals to visit Cuba. Clinton's policy, inaugurated in the wake of the Pope John Paul's historic visit to Cuba, also allowed resumption of charter flights from Miami to Havana as well as new direct flights from New York and Los Angeles. These changes were mainly intended to facilitate family reunions between Cuban-Americans and their families in the island.[9]

In order to travel to Cuba, individuals subject to U.S. law must be authorized by a general license (which requires no written authorization) or a specific license (which requires approval) from the Office of Foreign Assets Control (OFAC) of the Department of the Treasury. The majority of individuals traveling under a general license are Cuban-Americans who can visit immediate family members once a year for a self-defined "humanitarian purpose," such as a sick or dying relative. Others who can travel without specific documentation from OFAC include U.S. government officials, full-time journalists, professional researchers, and academics. A specific license is instead required for businessmen, free-lance journalists, members of religious organizations, and Cuban-Americans who want to visit their families more than

---

7. U.S.-Cuba Trade and Economic Council (USCTEC). *Economic Eye on Cuba* (20-26 January 2003).

8. Robyn Dorothy, Reitzes James D. and Church Bryan. "The Impact on the U.S. Economy of Lifting Restrictions on Travel to Cuba." *The Battle Group*, Center for International Policy, Washington D.C.: July 15, 2002, p. 2.

9. Eckstein Susan and Barberia Lorena. "Cuban-American Cuba Visits: Public Policy, Private Practices." Report of the Mellon-MIT Inter-University Program on Non-Governmental Organizations and Forced Migration, Center for International Studies, Massachusetts Institute of Technology, January 2001, p.12.

Table 1.   U.S. Visitors to Cuba, 1990-1998

	1990	1991	1992	1993	1994	1995	1996	1997	1998
U.S. citizens not of Cuban descent	7,375	11,233	10,050	14,715	17,937	20,672	27,113	34,956	46,778
Cuban-Americans*	2,600	4,600	14,600	19,400	33,500	39,300	58,300	71,700	94,900
Total	9,975	15,833	24,650	34,115	51,437	59,972	85,413	106,656	141,678
Rank**	7	7	6	6	5	4	4	4	4

Source: ONE 1996, 1998, and 2000; Alvarez A. and Amat D. "El mercado emisor turistico estadounidense hacia el Caribe." Facultad de Economía. UH. Trabajo de diploma, 1996; World Tourism Organization. *Yearbook of Tourism Statistics*, 200 and previous editions.

* Author's estimates.   ** The rank refers to the position of the United States among nations whose citizens visit Cuba

once a year. In March 2003 the Bush Administration introduced new regulations on travel (and remittances) that allowed more Cuban-Americans to visit relatives on the island and forbid trips to Cuba that combined non-credit educational activities with people-to-people contacts (which ended up becoming a loophole for groups to travel to Cuba when the educational aspect was barely evident). The new rules eliminated the requirement that visits take place only in cases of "humanitarian need," thus easing the conditions under which U.S. citizens of Cuban descent can travel to Cuba.[10]

Table 1 reports data on U.S. visitors to Cuba for the period 1990-1998. Notwithstanding the travel restrictions, the number of U.S. visitors to the island has increased significantly during the 1990s. According to Cuban official statistics, which include only U.S. citizens of non-Cuban origin, travelers from the United States rose from about 7,000 in 1990 to more than 46,000 in 1998. Regarding Cuban-Americans, the actual number of visitors grew from approximately 2,600 in 1990 to almost 40,000 in 1995. Between 1996 and 1998 (when the Clinton administration banned direct travel), Cuban-American visits to Cuba almost doubled from 58,300 to 94,900.[11] In short, whereas in 1990 about 10,000 U.S. citizens

traveled to Cuba, representing the seventh largest group among foreign travelers, in 1998 this number had jumped to more than 140,000. By 1995, the United States was already the fourth largest source of visitors to the island after Canada, Italy, and Spain.[12]

In the last few years, the presence of the United States in the Cuban tourist market has become increasingly important. Table 2 presents data on arrivals to Cuba from selected countries for the period 1999-2002. In 1999, an estimated 182,000 U.S. citizens (about 120,000 were Cuban-Americans) traveled to Cuba, more than from any other country except Canada. Since then, visits from the United States have increased constantly, consolidating U.S. citizens as the second largest group among foreign travelers. For instance, tourists from Germany, Italy, and Spain have declined significantly since 2000. Instead, approximately 125,000 Cuban-Americans and 79,000 U.S. citizens of non-Cuban origin visited Cuba in 2001, representing about 11.5% of total arrivals to the island. About 50,000 were tourists who traveled via third countries, with or without their government's authorization.[13] As noted by a Canadian official, "U.S. tourists are quite visible among visitors arriving in Cuba on flights from Montreal, Tor-

10. Lexington Institute. "Cuba Policy Report: The Bush Administration Unveils its Travel Policy." April 7, 2003.

11. Susan Eckstein and Lorena Barberia argue that there is contradictory information about Cuban-American visits to Cuba. According to them, while Cuban sources report that individuals of Cuban descent visiting the island between 1994 and 1996 were about 20,000 per year, U.S. sources estimate that the actual number was approximately 40,000 in 1994 and 100,000 per year between 1995 and 1999. Eckstein and Barberia (2001). See note 8, p.13.

12. In 1995, Canada (143,541) was the most important source of visitors to Cuba, followed by Italy (114,767), Spain (89,501), and the United States (59,972). In 1998, Canadian travelers to Cuba were 215,644, followed by Italians (186,688), Germans (148,987), and individuals from the United States (141,678).

13. The Economist. "Embargo or not, US is now Fidel Castro's economic partner." January 7, 2003.

Table 2. Tourist Arrivals by Origin, 1999-2002

	1999	%	2000	%	2001	%	2002(e)	%
Canada	276,346	17.2	307,725	17.3	350,426	19.7	348,468	20.7
United States	182,445	11.4	200,298	11.3	203,989	11.5	216,000	12.8
U.S. citizens (ncd)*	62,345	3.9	76,898	4.3	78,789	4.4	90,000	5.3
Cuban-Americans**	120,100	7.5	123,400	7.0	125,200	7.1	126,000	7.5
Germany	182,159	11.4	203,403	11.5	171,851	9.7	152,662	9.1
Italy	160,843	10.0	175,667	9.9	159,423	9.0	147,750	8.8
Spain	146,978	9.2	153,197	8.6	140,125	7.9	138,609	8.2
France	123,607	7.7	132,089	7.5	138,765	7.8	129,907	7.7
United Kingdom	85,829	5.4	90,972	5.1	94,974	5.4	103,741	6.1
Mexico	70,983	4.4	86,540	4.9	98,495	5.5	87,589	5.2
Others	373,591	23.3	424,095	23.9	416,493	23.5	361,436	21.4
Total	1,602,781	100.0	1,773,986	100.0	1,774,541	100.0	1,686,162	100.0

Source: *Anuario Estadístico de Cuba 2001*; ONE 2003; EIU 2001 and 2003; U.S.-Cuba Trade and Economic Council, 2002; Guy Allard, Jean. "Record de visitantes procedentes de EE.UU." *Granma Internacional*, January 7, 2003; Cuban Ministry of Tourism, 2003; World Tourism Organization. *Yearbook of Tourism Statistics*, 2003 edition.

(e) Preliminary estimates   * Individuals not of Cuban descent (ncd)   ** Author's estimates

onto, Kingston, Nassau, and Mexico City."[14] What's more important, U.S. travelers are believed to spend about $200 million a year in Cuba.[15] Thus, even with sanctions in place, the United States is an important source of hard currency for the Cuban tourist industry, providing almost 11% of its total gross revenues in 2001. While the total number of tourists to Cuba in 2002 declined by 5%, preliminary estimates from Cuban sources report a record presence of 216,000 U.S. visitors last year, constituting 12.8% of arrivals from all countries. For U.S. citizens not of Cuban descent, the number of arrivals peaked at about 90,000 (an increase of 14.2% over 2001),[16] with an additional 126,000 Cuban-Americans visiting their families in 2002.[17]

There is no doubt that the increasing number of U.S. visitors to Cuba in the last few years has been triggered by Clinton's people-to-people contacts policy inaugurated in January 1999. However, it is important to take into consideration that many individuals from the United States visit Cuba through third countries without U.S. travel permits, thus being technically in violation of U.S. economic sanctions prohibiting spending money for unlicensed purposes (licensed travelers are currently allowed to spend up to $166 per day for hotels, meals, ground transportation, etc.). Since 1994, the number of individuals subject to U.S. law traveling to Cuba, but not authorized from OFAC to do so, has increased on average 19% to 21%, while legal visits rose just by 9% to 11%. For instance, it is reported that approximately 22,000 U.S. citizens visited Cuba in 2000 without authorization from OFAC.[18] Other estimates put the number of U.S. illegal visits to Cuba between 40,000 and 50,000 per year, representing up to one fourth of total U.S. travel to the island. Cuban authorities, eager to accept U.S. visitors paying in dollars, do not stamp the passports of Americans, leaving no official trace of their presence.[19] One 33-year old artist from Minneapolis said she was visiting Toronto when she saw there was a flight to Havana. So she bought a

14. United States International Trade Commission (USITC). *The Economic Impact of U.S. Sanctions With Respect to Cuba.* February 2001.

15. Oppenheimer, Andres. "U.S. may tighten Cuba travel." *The Miami Herald*, December 15, 2002.

16. Interview with a Cuban economist in Havana, May 27, 2003.

17. Guy Allard, Jean. "Record de visitantes procedentes de EE.UU." *Granma Internacional*, January 7, 2003.

18. U.S.-Cuba Trade and Economic Council (USCTEC). *2002 Commercial Highlights* http://www.cubatrade.org/2002Lst.pdf (hereinafter "USCTEC 2002").

19. Sullivan, Kelly. "Americans defy Cuba embargo." *Washington Post Foreign Service*, October 31, 2001.

ticket and spent a week touring the city. Another U.S. citizen from Minneapolis said he headed illegally for Cuba by way of Cancun, Mexico, bringing gifts for locals and spending about $2,000 in cash during his stay because the travel ban prohibits Americans from using credit cards in the island.[20]

Since President George W. Bush took office in 2001, OFAC has been cracking down on those who travel to Cuba without permission. During the Clinton Administration, OFAC took steps to levy fines (the average fine is $5,500) on 46 to 188 Americans a year. That figure jumped to 700 in 2001.[21] However, these fines affect fewer than 3% of the total number of violators per year, and they target primarily U.S. citizens of non-Cuban descent. As noted by U.S. representative Jeff Flake (R-AZ), U.S. authorities pay no attention to Cuban-Americans even as they harass and level fines against Americans who go to the island. While being allowed to travel for a self-defined humanitarian need, "their relatives always seem to get sick around the same time, like Christmas and other major holidays."[22] In addition, there are several cases of Cuban-Americans who are able to visit Cuba twice a year without asking OFAC for a specific license. Asked to comment about how she was able to visit Cuba twice in 2000 to meet a newborn nephew and to take a vacation on the beach, a Cuban-American replied: "Coming to Havana is very easy. Although I am a U.S. citizen, I am required to have a Cuban passport. So I use my (U.S.) passport to enter and leave the United States and the third party country, while using my Cuban passport for the rest of the journey."[23] In short, whether they target U.S. citizens of non-Cuban descent or Cuban-Americans, travel restrictions are unable to stem illegal travel to Cuba. Even admitting that the threat of prosecution might have discouraged some potential travelers, it is virtually impossible for the U.S. government to prevent its citizens from visiting Cuba and spending money there in violations of U.S. regulations.

REMITTANCES TO CUBA

As a result of the deep economic recession that threatened Cuba's survival in the early 1990s, the Castro government decriminalized both the possession and the use of hard currency (especially U.S. dollars) in August 1993. In addition, the government legalized dollar-denominated remittances under its 1994 monetary reform program. Since then, family remittances mainly sent from Cuban-Americans have become an important source of supplemental income for many Cubans. Even more important for the purpose of this study, these practices have significantly boosted the domestic dollar market in Cuba. As observed by Ana Julia Jatar-Hausmann, the legalization of the use of foreign currency encouraged more family remittances, and the high prices at government-owned dollar stores acted as a hidden sales tax on remittances, effectively allowing the Cuban authorities to obtain access to that money.[24] In light of this development, several scholars contend that money sent from abroad has been the single most important factor in reactivating the Cuban economy in the second half of the 1990s.

Pedro Monreal, an academic from the island, argues that Cuba has become in recent years increasingly dependent on remittances and donations from abroad. He specifies that, in strict terms, the Cuban economy cannot be qualified as an economy that depends fundamentally on remittances because other important activities such as tourism and mining have emerged. Nevertheless, he concludes that the importance of money sent from abroad is beyond question. In fact, in net terms, remittances are the biggest source of foreign exchange for the country, more than tourism and sugar.[25] Many of those who analyze data on reve-

20. Moreno, Jenalia. "Cuba back into game of tourism." *The Houston Chronicle*, February 28, 2003.

21. "Americans who make trips to Cuba without OK could be prosecuted." *The Houston Chronicle*, March 9, 2003.

22. Eaton, Tracey. "8 vow to have U.S.-style meeting in Cuba." *The Dallas Morning News*, March 11, 2003.

23. "Forbidden fruit of Cuba lures U.S. travelers." IPS. November 1, 2001.

24. Jatar-Hausmann, Ana Julia. "Cuba: Is America Business Missing Out? Sí, A Bright Future." *Across the Board*, July-August 2000.

25. Monreal, Pedro. "Las Remesas Familiares en la Economía Cubana." *Encuentro de la Cultura Cubana*, N.14, Otoño de 1999.

nues from tourism ($1.8 billion in 2001) believe that the tourist industry is the main generator of hard currency for the Cuban economy. However, it must be noted that these are gross figures. In net terms, revenues are significantly lower. In March 2001, Carlos Lage estimated the cost per dollar of gross income from tourist activities at $0.76.[26] This indicator is very high and refers only to the direct cost in dollars, not the indirect cost incurred by the state in the tourist sector. Also consider that domestically-produced goods for tourism have an imported (indirect) component in dollars, which implies that the cost per dollar of gross income would be even higher. Direct and indirect cost per tourism dollar have been estimated by some economists at more than $0.80, which would mean for the country a net result of just $0.20 for every dollar of gross income from tourist activities.[27] Such an estimate has been recently confirmed by Cuban vice-minister of tourism Marta Maiz. In May 2003, in an interview for the Cuban magazine *Bohemia*, she said that the last year "income from tourism was $52.2 million less than in 2001, with a cost of USD 80 cents for every dollar captured by the country."[28]

Americans can send no more than $300 every three months to friends and relatives in Cuba. Prior to the new OFAC regulations regarding travel and remittances to Cuba enacted in March 2003, a cap of $300 in remittances was also applied to licensed travelers to Cuba, who were required to report the visa recipient's full name, date of birth, and the number and data of issuance of the visa or other travel authorizations issued. A licensed traveler was authorized to carry only remittances that he or she was authorized to remit and could not carry remittances being made by other persons. Since 1999 the U.S. government has also authorized several companies in the United States to legally transfer money to Cuba by relying on local individuals in Cuba who are contracted to deliver the money. The three most established businesses are Western Union, MoneyGram, and *El Español*. Within the limit of $300 per trimester, senders in the United States (who must be at least 18 years old) can send smaller amounts, such as $100, more than once in that period. However, they have to pay a fee (around $27 dollars in June 2002) each time the money is transferred. The new OFAC regulations of March 2003 allow U.S. authorized travelers to Cuba to carry as much as $3,000 in household remittances, up from $300 each quarter. The increased amount of remittances is intended to help up to 10 households per traveler.[29]

Estimating the flow of remittances to Cuba is difficult, given the lack of reliable information. Official figures (as reported by the Economic Commission for Latin America and the Caribbean, or ECLAC) make inferences from "net current transfers" in Cuba's balance of payments, which are mostly made up of remittances and, to a lesser extent, of donations. However, it is unclear how the Cuban government records remittances under net transfers. For instance, some Cuban economists argue that these figures include only transactions thorough official mechanisms (such as Western Union, Transcard,[30] and other

---

26. Lage, Carlos. Declaration on Cuban National Television (Noticiero Nacional de la Television Cubana), March 18, 2001.

27. "Cuba: economía y turismo." Economics Press Service. N .10, May 31, 2001.

28. Fariñas, Gilda and Tesoro, Susana. "Turismo: Monedas al aire." *Bohemia*, Año 95, No. 10, May 16, 2003.

29. San Martin, Nancy. "Rules changed on Cuba trips." *The Miami Herald*, March 25, 2003. The OFAC amendments not only increase the limit on the number of remittances that can be carried to Cuba by an authorized traveler, but also introduce the following technical changes: (a) authorize licensed remittances to be made from blocked inherited funds; (b) restrict quarterly remittances from being sent to senior-level Cuban government officials or senior-level Cuban Communist Party officials; (c) simplify rules on authorization for certain emigration-related remittances. For further information see OFAC (U.S. Department of the Treasury). "New regulations impacting Cuban travel." March 24, 2003. http://www.treas.gov/offices/enforcement/ofac/legal/regs/fr68_14141.pdf

30. An ever-increasing number of Cubans are turning to the Transcard (a Canadian company) as a fast, efficient, and less costly alternative to receiving remittances via Western Union. Individuals outside of Cuba can establish accounts in any Transcard office throughout the world and designate a Cuban national as the beneficiary, who is issued a credit card to access the account and make purchases. See U.S.-Cuba Trade and Economic Council (USCTEC). *Economic Eye on Cuba*, 27 October 1997 to 2 November 1997. It must be noted that transactions with Transcard are routed via Canadian banks, thus avoiding control from U.S. authorities.

Figure 2. Main Sources of Hard Currency and Possible Uses for the Cuban Population

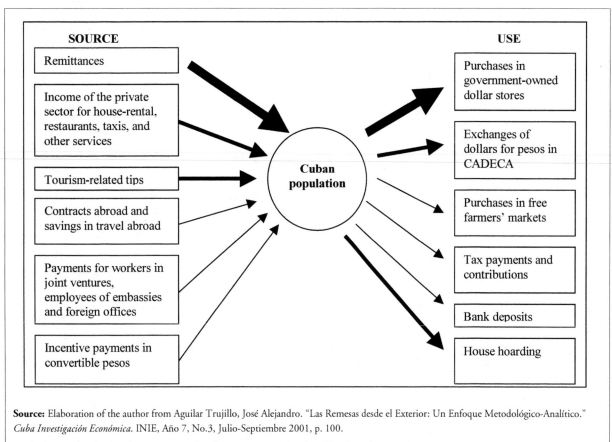

Source: Elaboration of the author from Aguilar Trujillo, José Alejandro. "Las Remesas desde el Exterior: Un Enfoque Metodológico-Analítico." *Cuba Investigación Económica*. INIE, Año 7, No.3, Julio-Septiembre 2001, p. 100.

* A thicker arrow indicates a larger amount of hard currency received and used by the Cuban population

money transfers services), excluding a variety of informal money transfers from abroad carried out through entrusted entrepreneurs ("mulas") as well as friends and relatives visiting the island.[31] Other economists, instead, contend that Cuban authorities use formal transfers only as a reference, to which they add estimates derived from sales in dollar stores, exchange activity of dollars for pesos in "money exchange houses" (CADECA), hoarding (money that people keep at home for preservation or future use), etc. Nevertheless, they quickly recognize that figures should be interpreted with caution. According to them, calculations exclude sales in tourist dollar stores (where Cubans also buy products) and make use of unreliable surveys to estimate the level of hoarding in Cuba.[32] Finally, some scholars simply claim that recorded figures under net transfers are calculated as the turnover of dollar shops minus dollar earnings accounted for by official payments of dollars (mainly through incentive schemes).[33]

Whatever the method used by the Cuban government to record transactions under "net current transfers," it appears that official counts of remittances highly underestimate the amount of money sent from Cubans abroad to their families in the island. Although it is virtually impossible to provide accu-

31. Interview with a Cuban economist in Havana, June 9, 2003.

32. Interview with a Cuban economist in Havana, May 20, 2003.

33. Barberia, Lorena. "Remittances to Cuba: An Evaluation of Cuban and U.S. Government Policy Measures." The Rosemarie Rogers Working Paper Series, The Inter-University Committee on International Migration, Massachusetts Institute of Technology, September 2002, p. 13.

rate estimates of remittances to Cuba, the best way to proceed is to analyze the main sources of hard currency for the Cuban population and its possible uses, as described in Figure 2. Remittances are believed to benefit as many as 30% of Cuba's 11 million citizens and constitute without any doubt the most important source of hard currency for the population of the island.[34] Several jobs in the tourist sector can also bring significant amounts of dollars tips to Cuban workers such as cab drivers, waiters, bartenders, and hotel employees. Similarly, Cubans in the private sector can earn hundreds of dollars per month for services of house-rental, restaurants, taxis, etc.[35] Finally, relatively small payments in dollars or eventually in convertible pesos are received by Cubans who work in joint ventures, embassies, foreign offices, or in certain industries that generate hard currency such as tourism, tobacco, and oil extraction among others. In short, jobs that can earn dollar salaries or tips from foreign businesses and tourists have become highly desirable in Cuba. Regarding the possible use of hard currency, the large majority of Cubans use dollars to make purchases in government-owned dollar stores (mainly for food and clothes) or exchange them for pesos in CADECA. Smaller amounts are utilized to make purchases in free farmers' markets, tax payments and contributions, and eventually to open dollar accounts in local banks. The level of hoarding also may be quite significant, but the lack of information makes it impossible to reliably assess the extent of this practice.[36]

Using available information on sales in dollar stores and dollar purchases by CADECA (where Cubans utilize the vast majority of hard currency they receive), it is possible to estimate the level of remittances to Cuba. As I said before, remittances are the most important source of dollars for the Cuban population, but they are not the only one. Thus, in order to estimate the amount of money sent from Cubans abroad to their families in the island, we must consider other ways through which Cubans enter in possession of dollars. Table 3 offers a calculation sample of remittances for the year 2001. Figures for sales in dollar stores are official data provided by the Cuban government, while the other amounts are estimates based on conversations with Cuban economists. Total sales in dollar stores in 2001 were about $1.2 billion, with an additional $100 million of dollar purchases by CADECA. From this amount, we must deduct the dollar income of Cubans who provide services of house-rental,[37] restaurants, taxis, etc. (about $70-80 million), tourism-related tips (assuming that direct workers in the tourist sectors earn on average 4-5 dollars a day, the total amount would be approximately $145-180 million), contracts abroad, and incentive payments in dollars and convertible pesos (about $25-30 million).

As shown in Table 3, total remittances to Cuba in 2001 were an estimated $1,030 to $1,080 million, significantly higher than the amount reported by sources like ECLAC that rely on Cuban government balance of payments data. If ECLAC figures ($730 million for 2001) are correct, then the level of transactions in dollar stores and CADECA ($1,320 million) imply that, in addition to remittances, Cubans receive about $600 million a year in hard currency revenues. This is highly improbable. Admittedly, hard currency sources not related to remittances may not be negligible, but they can hardly make up for the difference between the amount of money trans-

---

34. Johnson, Tim. "U.S. action after Cuba crackdown debated." *The Miami Herald*, May 5, 2003.

35. It must be noted that Cubans with contracts abroad such as musicians, technicians, and other professionals may also obtain payments in hard currency. However, very few people are included in this category and the amount of dollars generated by these activities, while significant at the individual level, remains overall almost negligible.

36. Interestingly, some Cuban economists argue that the level of hoarding in Cuba could be as high as $500 million. Interview with a Cuban economist in Havana, May 20, 2003.

37. It is reported that there are currently 2,705 people with licenses who rent (charging dollars) rooms to foreigners in Havana, where 80-85% of all Cuba's dollar renters are located. In addition, there are an estimated 5,200 unlicensed renters around the country who charge dollars or other foreign currencies. See Grogg, Patricia. "Landlords on the verge of a nervous breakdown." Inter Press Service (IPS), July 4, 2003.

Table 3. Calculation Sample of Remittances in 2001 ($U.S. million)

Sales in dollar stores	1,220
Dollar purchases by CADECA	100
Total	**1,320**
From this amount we deduct:	
Income of the private sector (of which) • House-rental	70-80
• Restaurants, taxis, and other	45-50
services	25-30
Tourism-related tips	4-5 dollars a day x 100,000 direct workers in the tourist sector 145–180
Contracts abroad, workers payments, incentive payments in dollars and convertible pesos, etc.	25-30
Total remittances	**1,030-1,080**

Source: ONE. "Ventas de la producción nacional con destino a tiendas y turismo", 2002; Estimates of the author based on conversations with Cuban economists

fers calculated by ECLAC and sales in dollar stores plus transactions in exchange houses. Cuban economists estimate that foreign exchange income from activities not related to remittances can at best represent about 20% of all dollar revenues for the Cuban population.[38]

Using sales in dollar stores and dollar purchases by CADECA as a reference, Table 4 provides estimates of remittances to Cuba for the period 1995-2002. Figures from ECLAC are also included in order to make a comparison. Since the legalization of dollar holdings in 1993, remittances to Cuba have increased significantly. ECLAC reports that individuals of Cuban descent sent more than $500 million to their relatives in the island in 1995, while this figure topped at $740 million in 2000. Almost 90% of remittance dollars received came from the United States.[39] Sales in dollar stores have experienced a sim-

ilar expansion, but they increased at much higher rates between 1997 and 2001. In 1997 the total value of sales in dollar stores was $867.4 million, while in 2001 they reached $1,220 million. This suggests that the actual amounts of remittances to Cuba for the period 1997-2001 might have been much higher than those reported by ECLAC. Whereas remittances as calculated by ECLAC increased only by 9% during this period, sales in dollar stores rose by more than 40%. Transactions at CADECA also grew by approximately 25% between 1998 and 2001.

The author estimates that remittances were $750 million in 1997, $950 million in 1999, and more than $1 billion since 2000. The assumption of significant undercounts in the calculation of remittances is also consistent with the growth of Cuban-American visits to the island after Clinton's inauguration of the people-to-people contacts policy in early 1999 (see Table 2). We should remember that a large part of money transfers is undertaken in the "gray area" of the informal tourist sector. Preliminary estimates for 2002 put total sales in dollar stores at $1,350 million and remittances to Cuba at about $1,150 million (more than 10% over the previous year). As evidence of such an increase, it is reported that many new items were sold in dollar stores last year, including construction materials (mainly cement), freezers, food products, etc. Only CIMEX, the corporation that runs the largest number of dollar outlets announced sales of about $600 million in 2002.[40] CIMEX officers also revealed that Western Union, which provides services of money transfers to Cuba only from the United States, registered a record of $50 million in remittance transactions in December 2002 alone.[41]

Accurate estimates of remittances to Cuba are inevitably complicated by the existence of well-developed

---

38. Interview with a Cuban economist in Havana, June 3, 2003. If remittances represent about 80% of all dollar sources for the Cuban population, then they would be approximately $1,050 million in 2001.

39. Orozco, Manuel. "Challenges and Opportunities of Marketing Remittances to Cuba." Inter-American Dialogue, Washington D.C., July 27, 2002, p.1 (hereinafter "Orozco 2002").

40. Interview with a Cuban economist in Havana, June 18, 2003.

41. Interview with a Cuban economist in Havana, May 20, 2003.

Table 4. Sales in Dollar Stores, Dollar Purchases by CADECA and Remittances to Cuba, 1995-2002 ($U.S. Million)

	1995	1996	1997	1998	1999	2000	2001	2002*
Sales in dollar stores	537	743.9	867.4	1,027	1,108.8	1,203.4	1,220	1,350
Dollar Purchases by CADECA**	—	—	—	75	82	90	100	100
Net Current Transfers	646	744	792	813	799	740	813	—
Remittances (ECLAC estimates)	537	630	670	690	700	740	730	—
Remittances (author's estimates)	537	640	750	880	950	1,030	1,050	1,150

Source: ONE. "Ventas de la producción nacional con destino a tiendas y turismo." 2002 and earlier editions; ECLAC. "Cuba: Evolución Económica Durante 2001." June 6, 2002; Cuban Central Bank, 2002.

* Preliminary estimates

** Estimates of the author based on conversations with Cuban economists

informal mechanisms for money transfers. Instead of making use of formal wire transfer services (fees charged by U.S. based companies remitting to Cuba are the highest among all operators engaged in legal money transfer to Latin American countries), U.S. citizens of Cuban descent tend to rely on relatively inexpensive and more user-friendly informal remittance channels.[42] It is well known that a huge flow of remittances arrive on the island in the luggage of friends, relatives, or entrusted agents. The latter, usually referred to as "mulas," are entrepreneurs who travel frequently to the island as tourists and without a license to operate as a business. They carry both money and packages of goods to Cuban relatives of the senders for cheaper fees than the ones charged by official agencies. A November 2001 survey carried out by the Inter-American Development Bank shows that only 32.1% of U.S. citizens of Cuban descent make use of Western Union to transfer remittances, while more than 46% prefer to send money with persons who are traveling to the island. In terms of the volume of the economic transactions, it is estimated that informal mechanisms capture up to 80% of the total flow of money transfers to Cuba from the United States.[43]

Some analysts have attempted to estimate the amount of remittances sent to Cuba by tracking the activities of money transfer companies operating in the island from the United States and Canada, and by carrying out extensive interviews with officials of those companies, travel agents, and other entrepreneurs. Recent figures from the Inter-American Development Bank (IADB), which do not differ significantly from the author's estimates, put the total amount of remittances to Cuba at $930 million in 2001 and $1.138 billion in 2002, an increase of about 22% over the previous year.[44] These findings are extremely surprising in light of the economic downturn of the U.S. economy following the terrorist attacks of September 2001. The November 2001 IADB survey estimated that about 67% of U.S. citizen of Cuban descent over age 18 sent remittances back home.[45] Using data from the 2000 U.S. Census on the Hispanic Population in the United States, the total number of Cuban-Americans sending remittances to Cuba would be more than 700,000. Whereas more than 50% of Cuban respondents in the survey said they sent less than $100 per transaction, interviews with "mulas" say that, on average, they carry more than $200 per individual package.[46]

---

42. Eckstein, Susan. "Diasporas and Dollars: Transnational Ties and The Transformation of Cuba." The Rosemarie Rogers Working Paper Series, The Inter-University Committee on International Migration, Massachusetts Institute of Technology, February 2003, p. 15 (hereinafter "Eckstein 2003").

43. Orozco 2002, pp.4-5.

44. Inter-American Development Bank (IADB). "Sending Money Home: An International Comparison of Remittance Markets." February 2003.

45. Orozco 2002, p.1.

46. Personal conversation with Manuel Orozco, April 5, 2003.

Given that most of the "mulas" travel twice a month using different routes, it is likely that money transfers using these entrepreneurs violate the annual limit of $1200 in remittances for U.S. citizens. As further evidence, if we divide the author's estimates of remittances (to be more precise, we can deduct 10% because not all remittances come from the United States) by the estimated number of Cuban-Americans who regularly send money to their families (700,000), we can see that money transfers to Cuba from the United States were on average $1,350 per person in 2001 and $1,478 per person in 2002.

It is well known that many Cuban-Americans use services in foreign countries to engage in "special" transactions that circumvent the cap on remittances. Asked to comment about his remittance activities, a Cuban exile from New Orleans revealed in 1997 that he had sent $200 dollars back home to Cuba every month for the past 15 years using a Canadian company.[47] Unlimited informal transactions are currently facilitated by the emergence of a new web-based money transfer service (Cash2Cuba) that reduces commissions and increases the speed of transfers to Cuba. The service, which is based in Canada, facilitates informal practices by providing registered Cuban recipients a card to make cash withdrawals. More specifically, the remitter can send money that the recipient in Cuba withdraws in cash at banks or official exchange businesses with a local credit card issued by the Cuban corporation CIMEX. Merchandise can also be purchased by credit card in Cuba's retail stores in hard currency.[48] In its first month of operation in December 2002, Cash2Cuba reported a volume of transfers of $320,000 dollars and 10,000 registered users.[49]

Limitations on remittances are perhaps the most contradictory element of current U.S. policy toward Cuba. While being part of a series of U.S. restrictions intended to squeeze the Castro government economically, remittances have been Cuba's fastest growing

hard currency source during the 1990s. To put things into perspective, Figure 3 provides rough estimates of Cuba's four largest sources of hard currency revenues (net figures) in 2001 and 2002. The total amounts are based on the author's data, figures released by the Cuban vice-president Carlos Lage and Cuban vice-minister of tourism Marta Maiz, and calculations of some Cuban economists.

Figure 3. Cuba's Main Sources of Hard Currency in 2001 and 2002 (net revenues in $U.S. million)

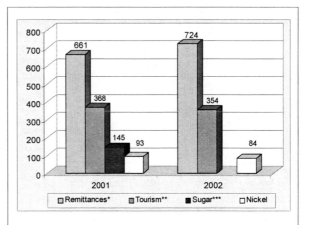

Source: Author's estimates based on Nova González, Armando. "Continuará la Dolarización?" Economics Press Service, 2001; Declaration of Carlos Lage on Cuban National Television, March 18, 2001; Economics Press Service. "Cuba: economía y turismo." N.10, May 31, 2001; Declaration of Carlos Lage in Mayoral, Julia María. "El país tiene confianza en su avance social y económico." *Granma Internacional*, April 5, 2003; Declaration of Marta Maiz in Fariñas, Gilda and Tesoro, Susana. "Turismo: Monedas al aire." *Bohemia*, Año 95, no. 10, May 16, 2003

* Net revenues are calculated as 63% of total transfers from abroad ($1050 in 2001 and $1150 in 2002)

** Assuming the cost per dollar of gross income from tourist activities at $0.80 or 80 cents.

*** Net revenues from sugar in 2002 are significantly lower than in 2001

Remittances are a source of fresh capital for the Cuban population but, in terms of revenues, they do not constitute a net benefit for the Castro govern-

47. Hegeman, Roxana. "Exiles prop up Cuban economy by sending money to families." Associated Press, November 28, 1997.

48. Arreola, Gerardo. "Canadian company exploits family remittances exceeding $1 billion yearly." *La Jornada*, November 27, 2002.

49. Economist Intelligence Unit (EIU). "Remittances flows become easier." *Country Report: Cuba*, February 1, 2003.

ment. The latter obtains access to remittances mostly through sales in dollar stores, and obviously there are costs involved in procuring the goods exchanged in these transactions. In selling products at dollar stores, the Cuban government applies an ideal mark-up (hidden tax) of 240%. This means an item that costs $100 dollars to produce domestically (or import), with a 240 percent tax, would sell for $240 dollars.[50] Therefore, net revenues of dollar stores are about 58% of total sales. We must also consider that some remittances end up in CADECA, free farmers' markets, hoarding, etc. Nova González, an economist from the island, has estimated that net revenues from remittances are about 63-64% of the total amount of money sent to Cuba.[51] From Figure 3, we can see that remittances in 2001 generated more hard currency revenues for the Cuban government than any other source, totaling approximately $660 million. In net terms, profits from money transfers were almost 80% more than tourism revenues ($368 million), four and a half times the amount of sugar revenues ($145 million), and more than seven times the value of nickel revenues ($93 million). Figures for 2002 are even more striking. In 2002, net profits from remittances ($724 million) were more than twice the level of revenues from tourism activities ($354 million), and exceeded nickel revenues ($84 million) by more than eight times. Regarding sugar, we can fairly assume that net revenues in 2002 were significantly lower than in 2001. Although Cuba reached a production level of 3.605 million tons of raw sugar in 2002 (2% higher than the previous year), low sugar prices in the international market meant losses of approximately $120 million in export revenues in 2002 compared to 2001.[52] In sum, the importance for the Cuban economy of money sent from abroad appears quite evident. Even if they are intended to provide the Cuban population a much-needed source of additional income, remittances end

up in the hands of the Cuban government, thus allowing the latter to meet the most urgent needs of the country and pay unavoidable short-term debts with high interest rates.[53]

AMERICAN FOOD SALES TO CUBA

In the last few years, economic sanctions against Cuba have been under fire in the U.S. Congress. As a result of growing skepticism on the utility of economic coercion as well as lobbying efforts by U.S. business and agricultural communities (in particular food exporters), an increasing number of lawmakers has pushed for a relaxation of the 40-year old embargo and the beginning of a new trade relationship with the Castro government. In October 2000, the U.S. Congress passed the "Agriculture, Rural Development, Food and Drug, Administration, and Related Agencies Appropriations Act, 2001." Title IX of the bill, signed into law by President Clinton a few weeks later, includes provisions that allow sales of U.S. food and agricultural products (and medicines) to Cuba for the first time in nearly forty years. It should be noted that a clause inserted in the final version of the bill prohibits U.S. companies and financial institutions from providing credits for such transactions, thus obligating the Cuban authorities to complete their purchases only with cash payments or through financing provided by third-countries' companies. Enraged by that restriction, the Cuban government initially said it would not buy any food until the embargo was completely lifted.

Indeed, for about a year after the passage of the U.S. law, Cuba refused to buy "a single grain of rice" from the United States. However, after hurricane Michelle caused widespread damage to the island in November 2001, the Castro government began to take advantage of the law and buy American food to replenish its reserves. The first contract between a U.S. firm and the Cuban government, worth about $40 mil-

---

50. Eckstein 2003, p.17.

51. Nova González, Armando. "Continuará la Dolarización?" Economics Press Service, 2001.

52. Triana Cordoví, Juan. "Cuba; Desempeño Económico en el Primer Semestre del 2002." Centro de Estudios de la Economía Cubana (CEEC), Havana, 2002. Sugar prices dropped by 27% in the first six months of 2002.

53. Interview with a Cuban economist in Havana, June 5, 2003.

lion, was signed on December 16, 2001. Since then, Cuba has purchased approximately $200 million of American food products.[54] Table 5 reports the value of Cuba's food imports from the United States in 2002 compared to total Cuban imports of the same products in 2001.

Table 5. Cuba's Food Imports from the United States in 2002 ($U.S. million)

Product	From United States 2002	Total 2001	U.S. vs Total*
Wheat	22.8	119.2	19%
Corn	22.7	19.5	116%
Poultry	21.6	62.0	35%
Soybean Oil	21.4	19.3	111%
Soybeans	20.9	15.4	136%
Soybean Oil Cake	19.3	26.7	72%
Total Imports	138.6	827.8	17%

Source: Sources: U.S.-Cuba Trade and Economic Council, 2003; García Alvarez, Anicia. "Sustitución de Importaciones de Alimentos en Cuba: Necesidad vs. Posibilidad." CEEC, March 2003.

* Cuba's imports from the United States are for 2002 while total imports from all countries are for 2001.

The United States is becoming an increasingly important trading partner for Cuba, ranking first among the island's sources of imported food in 2002.[55] In 2002, according to the U.S.-Cuba Trade and Economic Council, the Cuban government bought $138.6 million worth of American food products, including wheat ($22.8 million), corn ($22.7 million), poultry ($21.6 million), and soybean products ($61.6 million). One company alone, Illinois-based Archer Daniels Midland, reported agri-

cultural exports to Cuba valued at $70 million in 2002.[56] However, Cuba has signed contracts with 84 other U.S.-based firms from 24 different U.S. states. It is important to note that, since restrictions on agricultural trade were eased in October 2000, the United States has provided 17% of Cuban food imports from all countries (using 2001 as a reference). Preliminary figures for 2002 show that U.S. food sales could have represented more than a quarter of Cuba's total agricultural goods imports in 2002.[57] Cuban officials estimate that the U.S. share could rise to about 60% with a complete lifting of the embargo.[58]

To some extent, the Castro government's decision to buy products from the United States may be seen as part of a political attempt to encourage anti-embargo forces in the U.S. Congress. However, Cuba's economic considerations in terms of price competition have also been a factor in such a decision. As recognized by a senior official in Havana, "the proximity of U.S. Gulf ports saves freight and warehousing storage costs, which give U.S. exporters the equivalent of up to 20% price advantage."[59] American food sales to Cuba have already affected the island's key trading partners, among them Canada, France, and Spain. For instance, Canada's official statistics report that poultry and wheat exports to Cuba were down, respectively, by 60.9% and by 79.2% in 2002. More specifically, Canada exported to Cuba about $12.4 million of poultry and $14.9 million of wheat in 2001. In 2002, Canadian sales of poultry and wheat dropped to $4.8 million and $3.1 million, respectively.[60] Similarly, the French government declared that food and agricultural sales to the island (71.2 million

---

54. Frank, Marc. "US-Cuba trade group wants Havana food show to go on." *Reuters*, June 20, 2003.

55. Snow, Anita. "United States become Cuba's No. 1 source of imported food." *Associated Press*, March 2, 2003 (hereinafter "Snow 2003").

56. U.S.-Cuba Trade and Economic Council (USCTEC). *Economic Eye on Cuba*, February 17-23, 2003. It must be noted that Cuban authorities estimated American food purchases in 2002 at $189 million, because they include transportation, taxes, and other additional costs.

57. Economics Press Service. "Las compras en números." March 15, 2003, p. 10. Preliminary statistics from the U.S. Department of Agriculture's Foreign Agricultural Service indicate that Cuba imported about $452 million worth of farm products in 2002.

58. Jordan, Pav. "U.S.-Cuba Trade Grows Despite Restrictions." *Reuters*, February 17, 2003.

59. Frank, Marc. "Cuba slashes imports amid ongoing cash crunch." *Reuters*, October 15, 2002 (hereinafter "Frank 2002").

60. For further information see Statistics Canada, June 29, 2003 at: http://strategis.ic.gc.ca/sc_mrkti/tdts/tdo/tdo.php.

euros in 2002) decreased by 39.3%.[61] French wheat sales were down by approximately 40% in the first six months of 2002.[62] As shown in Table 5, the value of U.S. wheat and poultry sales to the Castro government ranked first and third among all U.S. agricultural products exported to Cuba in 2002. Using again 2001 as a reference, we can see that the United States has already captured a significant share of Cuba's wheat (19%) and poultry (35%) markets. Finally, the total value of all exports to Cuba from Spain dropped by 23.7% in 2002. The Spanish government reports that exports to the island were 625 million euros in 2001 and 476.6 million euros in 2002.[63] Regarding food products, Cuba's purchases from Spain plunged by 43.1% in the first nine month of 2002. Food sales by other traditional Cuban trading partners also decreased during the same period, including drops of 40.5% for Brazil, 39.6% for Mexico, and 81% for Argentina.[64]

How do U.S. food sales generate hard currency revenues for the Cuban government? This is quite simple. Although the majority of U.S. commodities exported to Cuba go into ration stores, almost 10% end up in local dollar shops.[65] Just as an example, it is reported that products exported to Cuba by Indiana-based Marsh Supermarket and sold at government-owned dollar retail stores continues to rise. Since October 2002, Marsh brand cereals, gelatin desserts, instant pudding, pie filling, and hot cocoa mix have been available in Cuba, with additional items reaching the local hard currency market since January 2003.[66] As stated previously, the price mark-up for imported food in government-owned dollar stores is about 240%. Therefore, the 10% of U.S. food sales ($200 million since December 2001) worth approximately $20 million that reached Cuba's dollar stores would sell for about $48 million, thus generating as much as $28 million in hard currency revenues for the government of Fidel Castro. Given that Castro has promised to increase food imports from the United States in 2003, a growing amount of foreign exchange revenues (once generated by products imported from other countries) will be generated by U.S. trade activities with Cuba. American food sales to the island were up by more than 39% in the first six months of 2003 (as compared to the same period in 2002),[67] and they are projected to increase by nearly 20% this year, for a total value of about $166 million.[68]

U.S. INDIRECT INVESTMENTS IN CUBA

This section provides a brief overview of an increasingly important and largely unexplored aspect of U.S.-Cuba economic relations, that is, the presence of American investors in foreign firms that trade with or invest in Cuba. More specifically, the U.S. Department of the Treasury authorizes individuals and firms subject to United States law to invest in a third-country company that has commercial activities in Cuba, as long as they do not acquire a controlling interest of that company and provided that a majority of the revenues of the third country company are not produced from operations within Cuba.[69] Thus, if the investment is an indirect one, a U.S. entity

---

61. Douanne Francaises. "Echanges commerciaux bilateraux en 2002." Statistics of the French Embassy in Havana, May 2003.

62. Frank 2002.

63. Europa Press. "La balanza comercial de España con Cuba registró un saldo positivo de 316 millones de euros en 2002." June 13, 2003.

64. Snow 2003.

65. Personal conversation with John Kavulich, president of U.S.-Cuba Trade and Economic Council, April 11, 2003.

66. U.S.-Cuba Trade and Economic Council (USCTEC). *2003 Commercial Highlights*. http://www.cubatrade.org/2003Lst.pdf (hereinafter USCTEC 2003).

67. U.S.-Cuba Trade and Economic Council (USCTEC). *Economic Eye on Cuba*, August 11–17, 2003.

68. Huettel, Steve. "Tampa port officials will travel to Cuba." *St. Petersburg Times*, June 12, 2003.

69. U.S.-Cuba Trade and Economic Council (USCTEC). *2000 Commercial Highlights* http://www.cubatrade.org/ (hereinafter "USCTEC 2000").

Table 6. U.S. Investments in Selected Foreign Companies Operating in Cuba

Year	Company	Country	Type of Operations in Cuba	Presence of U.S. Investors (%)	Major U.S. Investors
2000	Hotetur	Spain	Management contracts in 3 hotels	26%[a]	Florida-based Carnival Corporation
2000	Iberia Airlines	Spain	Two joint ventures (cargo terminal and aircraft maintenance)	2%	Texas-based American Airlines Inc.
2000	Mitsubishi Motors	Japan	Exporter of vehicles	10.41%	California-based Capital Research and Management Co.
2000	Nestle	Switzerland	Mineral water and soda-bottling joint venture	14%	—
2000	Sol Meliá	Spain	22 Management contracts and 4 equity investments in Cuba's tourist sector	16%	—
2000	Telecom Italia	Italy	Joint venture in telecommunications	3%[b]	New York-based Lehman Brothers Holdings Inc.
2001	Alcan	Canada	Exporter of aluminum products	23%	—
2002	Fiat Group	Italy	Exporter of vehicles	20%	Michigan-based General Motors Corporation
2002	Leisure Canada	Canada	Developer of luxury multi-destination resorts	30%	California-based Robertson Stephens Inc.
2002	LG Electronics Investment	South Korea	Exporter of refrigerators, washing machines, air conditioners, televisions	6.6%	New-York based The Goldman Sachs Group
2002	Accor	France	Several management contracts in Cuba's tourist sector	16.7%	—
2003	Souza Cruz	Brazil	Joint venture in tobacco sector	5.1%[c]	—

Source: Compilation of the author from data of U.S.-Cuba Trade and Economic Council (2000-2002) and financial reports of individual companies.

a. In 2000, Carnival Corporation owned 26% of U.K.-based Airtours PLC, which owned 50% of Hotetur.

b. In 2000, Lehman Brothers owned 3% of Italy-based Olivetti S.p.A. Telecom Italia is a subsidiary of Olivetti.

c. In March 2003, U.K.-based British American Tobacco (BAT), which also has U.S. capitals, held 75.3% of the shares of Souza Cruz.

should have no problem in building a Cuba-related stock portfolio.

In order to give a sense of the importance of U.S. indirect business connections with Cuba, Table 6 provides data on the presence of U.S. shareholders in selected foreign companies that operate in the island's market. As observed by John Kavulich, "American companies have affiliations with and U.S. citizens have investments in Sol Meliá, Unilever, Accor, Alcan, Fiat, Daimler Chrysler, and Nestlé among many other companies, which have commercial activities within Cuba." He also notes that, "most of the largest U.S. financial institutions and investment banks provide services for companies that have commercial activities within Cuba."[70] Obviously, Table 6 is just a sample based on public information, and the presence of American investors in certain companies could be higher than that reported. The key aspect is that, in an increasingly globalized world, the nationality of a specific firm may become almost irrelevant. The following are some details of specific U.S. indirect links with Cuba as reported by the U.S.-Cuba Trade and Economic Council and by financial reports of individual companies.

• In 2000, individuals subject to United States law held approximately 16% of the shares of Spain-based Sol Meliá and 14% of Switzerland-based Nestlé.[71] Sol Meliá is the largest hotel company

70. "U.S. goods, people, cash pour into Cuba." *Reuters*, July 28, 2001 (hereinafter "*Reuters* 2001").

71. USCTEC 2000.

in Spain and the leader in Cuba's tourist sector with equity interests in 4 hotels and 22 management contracts.[72] Nestlé owns several mineral water bottling plants in Cuba and has a joint venture (Los Portales S.A.) with the Cuban company Coralsa that produces and markets the best selling soft drinks and mineral waters in the island.[73]

- In 2000, Texas-based American Airlines Inc. owned 2% of Spain-based Iberia Airlines and California-based Capital Research and Management Co. owned 10.41% of Japan-based Mitsubishi Motors.[74] Iberia Airlines has a joint venture (Empresa Logística de Carga Aérea S.A.) with the Cuban company Aerovaradero S.A. involving a new freight terminal in the vicinity of the José Martí International Airport, and another joint venture (Empresa Cubano-Hispana de Mantenimiento de Aeronaves IBECA S.A.) for aircraft maintenance.[75] Mitsubishi sells automobiles, spare parts, and accessories to Cuba through the Panamanian company Motores Internacionales del Caribe S.A.

- In 2000, New York-based Lehman Brothers Holdings Inc. purchased 3% of the shares of Italy-based Olivetti S.p.A. Telecom Italia S.p.A., a subsidiary of Olivetti, has a joint venture (ETECSA) with the Cuban telephone company EMTEL for the modernization and expansion of Cuba's telephone system. In terms of capital invested, ETECSA is one of the most important joint ventures operating in Cuba. Also in 2000,

Florida-based Carnival Corporation increased indirect minority presence in Cuba through the purchase by United Kingdom-based Airtours PLC of 50% of Spain-based Hotetur Club S.L. Carnival Corporation owns 26% of the shares of Airtours PLC.[76] Hotetur Club has management contracts in three hotels in Cuba, the Deauville in Havana, the Hotetur Palma Real and the Hotetur Sun Beach in Varadero.

- In 2001, U.S. investors held approximately 23 percent of Alcan of Canada, which exports aluminum products to Cuba.[77]

- In 2002 New York-based The Goldman Sachs Group had a 6.6% interest in South Korea-based LG Electronics, Michigan-based General Motors Corporation had a 20% interest in Italy-based Fiat Group, and California-based Robertson Stephens Inc. owned about 30% of the shares of Canada-based Leisure Canada.[78] U.S investors also held 16.5% of the shares of the French group Accor.[79] LG Electronics has a strong presence in the Cuban market. A variety of its products, including refrigerators, washing machines, air conditioners, and televisions among others, are assembled and sold in the island. The Fiat Group has established in 1995 a dealership in the island (Agencia Cubalse Fiat) in conjunction with Cuba's government-operated Cubalse S.A. Since then, the Italian company has sold thousands of vehicles every year in Cuba, including automobiles, industrial vehicles, and agriculture machinery. Leisure Canada is developing five-

---

72. Spadoni, Paolo. "Foreign Investment in Cuba: Recent Developments and Role in the Economy." In *Cuba in Transition—Volume 12*. Association for the Study of the Cuban Economy (ASCE), 2002, p.170 (hereinafter "Spadoni 2002").

73. Pérez Villanueva, Omar Everleny." El Papel de la Inversión Extranjera Directa en el Desarrollo Económico. La Experiencia Cubana." Centro de Estudios de la Economía Cubana (CEEC), March 2003, p. 91.

74. USCTEC 2000.

75. Comellas, Miguel. "Iberia and Aerovaradero establish joint venture." *Granma International*, April 10, 2002.

76. U.S.-Cuba Trade and Economic Council (USCTEC). *2001 Commercial Highlights* http://www.cubatrade.org/.

77. *Reuters* 2001.

78. USCTEC 2002.

79. Interestingly, U.S. entities hold more shares (16.7%) of the French group Accor than any other international investor. Major shareholders are also from the United Kingdom (16.3%), Germany (5.2%), Belgium (3.7%), Luxembourg (2.9%), and Switzerland (2.5%). The complete list of Accor shareholders by country as of December 31, 2002 can be found at: www.accor.com.

star hotels, timeshare condominiums and PGA golf courses in Cuba, with an estimated investment plan of $400 million. Curiously, Leisure Canada announces in one of its brochures that the company is positioned to capitalize on the current growth of Cuban tourism, and the future growth fueled by the United States, following the inevitable normalization of U.S.-Cuba relations. It also specifies that it is perfectly legal for U.S. potential investors to purchase shares of the Canadian company, and that U.S. investment banks already control over 20% of Leisure Canada.[80] Finally, France's Accor group manages several hotels in Cuba with establishments that operate under the Novotel, Sofitel, Coralia, and Mercure Brands. For instance, Accor runs the Sofitel Sevilla hotel in Havana, the Mercure Cuatro Palmas hotel in Varadero Beach, and the Sofitel Casa Granda Hotel in Santiago de Cuba. The French group, which will complement its actions with the Coralia Club Bucanero Hotel in Santiago de Cuba, expects to run over 15 facilities in the island under the consortium's different brands.[81]

- In March 2003, individuals subject to United States law held approximately 5% of the shares of Brazil-based Souza Cruz. U.K.-based British American Tobacco (which also has significant U.S. capital) owned 75.3% of the Brazilian company.[82] In April 1995, Souza Cruz created a joint venture (BrasCuba S.A.) with Cuba's Unión del Tabaco. With an initial investment of $7 million, BrasCuba renovated an existing cigarette factory in Havana and started producing and selling several brands of cigarettes for the domestic market as well as for external markets. Today, after eight years of operations in the island, Brascuba has the virtual monopoly of cigarettes in Cuba's dollar stores and for exports.[83]

It is quite difficult to offer a comprehensive analysis of U.S. indirect business connections with Cuba, given that private companies are not required to make public the list of their shareholders. Such an endeavor is also complicated by the fact that, with millions of dollars moving around the world every second via electronic transactions, the real origin of financing for specific business operations is often unknown. As Everleny Pérez reminds us, "there are many companies in Cuba that are based in the Bahamas, other Caribbean islands, Spain or Britain, and you really can't tell if these companies receive U.S. funds attracted by the high interest rates we (Cubans) pay."[84] Nevertheless, the information presented in Table 6 shows that American entities hold publicly traded shares of several major foreign firms engaged in business activities with the government of Fidel Castro. While profits from the Cuba-related stock portfolio may not be particularly significant for some U.S. investors in terms of their global revenues, American investments in foreign companies that operate in the island are just another example of gaping holes in the United States' effort to isolate Cuba economically. If we consider that some of these foreign firms have provided Cuba much-needed capital, technology, management expertise, and new markets for its main exports, then the importance for the Cuban economy of U.S. indirect business operations in the island appears evident.

---

80. On June 11, 2003, Leisure Canada reported that the company had created a hotel brand (Mirus Resorts and Hotels) to use on properties within Cuba. The Canadian firm has been given the right to manage the Monte Barreto hotel in Havana under the new brand. According to the company, "the development of a hotel brand that can quickly transfer to a North American hotel chain, once the doors to Cuba open, further establishes Leisure Canada's vertically integrated gateway to Cuba." USCTEC 2003. For further information also see: www.leisurecanada.com.

81. "Accor: Big groups turn eyes toward Cuba." DTC News. Directorio Turístico de Cuba, 2003. It is reported that the Novotel Miramar in Havana, run by Accor since 2000, is now managed by the Spanish group Occidental Hotels & Resorts. For further information see "Hoteles-Occidental entra en Cuba y baja ventas un 11% en 2002." *Granma Internacional*, June 9, 2003.

82. The list of Souza Cruz shareholders is available at: www.souzacruz.com.

83. Spadoni 2002, p. 167.

84. *Reuters* 2001.

CONCLUSION

From the analysis presented in this paper, we can argue that, in spite of the tightening of the embargo, the United States has contributed in a significant way to the recovery of the Cuban economy following the deep recession of the early 1990s. While intended to stimulate democratic reforms and exercise pressure for regime change in Cuba by stemming the flow of hard currency to the island, U.S. economic sanctions have achieved neither of these goals. Admittedly, the role of the United States in the Cuban economy would have been much more important in the absence of sanctions. However, even with restrictions in place, significant amounts of hard currency have been channeled into Cuba through direct and indirect means of travel, remittances, food sales and secondary investments. Washington's policy toward Havana ended up throwing a lifeline to the same government it was supposed to undermine.

Even more important, formal and informal activities by the Cuban-American community, the most vocal group in the United States in favor of the embargo, have been a major factor in keeping afloat the economy of the Caribbean island. For instance, of approximately 200,000 U.S. citizens who traveled to Cuba in 2001 with or without their government's approval (they were the largest group of visitors after Canada), about 125,000 were Cuban-Americans. In addition, remittances to the island sent from U.S. citizens of Cuban descent mostly through informal mechanisms have been, in net terms, Cuba's most important source of foreign exchange. As argued by Susan Eckstein, "the remittance economy reflects a society that is transnationally grounded, able, willing, and wanting to operate according to its own networks and norms, in defiance both of U.S. and Cuban official regulations that interfere."[85]

In light of this situation, two possible options are available to U.S. decision-makers for a more successful policy toward Cuba. The first option is to strengthen current restrictions on travel and remittances by significantly reducing the number of U.S.

citizens authorized to visit the island and the amount of money that Cuban-Americans can send legally to their families. In order to be effective, these measures should increase the level of scrutiny for potential violations on travel and money transfers as well as hold citizens of Cuban descent to the same standards as any other American. While such a policy may be unpopular and quite expensive to implement, it makes no sense to make exceptions for a specific group of U.S. citizens that channel into Cuba more hard currency than any other group.

Recent changes of rules on travel and remittances introduced by the Bush administration in March 2003 do not help much in this regard. The new regulations put an end to "people to people" exchanges (travel permits no longer will be granted to numerous organizations that had allegedly used the licenses to build tour-operator businesses), facilitate Cuban-American visits to their families in the island by eliminating the requirement for "humanitarian need," and allow travelers to carry up to $3,000 in remittances for 10 households, up from $300. Although these measures may appear expansive at a first glance, they simply legalized what could not be prevented and may well lead to an increase in the flow of hard currency to Cuba. In single trips, "mulas" and other entrusted agents already carried thousands of dollars in remittances to be distributed to many different households in Cuba. While U.S. citizens can now carry more money with them, there is no guarantee that informal practices will be reduced. In addition, the new rules will probably trigger a rise of both illegal trips to the island by U.S. citizens not of Cuban descent and Cuban-American visits to their families. At any rate, it should be noted that so far U.S. authorities have taken no enforcement actions against Cuban-Americans for violations on travel. The general requirement for "humanitarian need" was so broad that it was hardly worthwhile to scrutinize.

A second option, which is not necessarily more viable politically but certainly less expensive than the first one, is to promote a rapprochement with Havana

---

85. Eckstein 2003, p. 16.

and a gradual removal of the embargo in recognition that economic sanctions have not achieved their main goals. A policy that respects the rights of Americans to trade with, invest in, and travel to the island may more effectively serve U.S. interests in post-Soviet Cuba by defending human rights, helping the Cuban people, and spreading the values of the American society.[86] It would also increase pressure on the current government in Havana by preventing Fidel Castro from using his traditional argument that the United States promotes economic deprivation in Cuba and seeks to constrain Cuban sovereignty.

In short, unless significant steps are taken in one of the suggested directions, the United States will have no choice but to wait until Castro passes from the scene by natural causes, and hope his successor will be less resilient than him, or perhaps more inclined to introduce extensive democratic reforms. To conclude, consider a recent quote by U.S. president George W. Bush that exemplifies the great irony of economic sanctions with respect to Cuba. In May 2002, Bush stated: "The sanctions the United States enforces against the Castro regime are not just a policy tool, but a moral statement. It is wrong to prop up a regime that routinely stifles all the freedoms that make us human."[87] If this is the case, then the findings of this paper demonstrate that U.S. policy toward Cuba in the post-Cold War era has been nothing else than a "wrong" policy.

86. Peters, Philip. "A Policy toward Cuba that Serves U.S. Interests." Washington D.C.: The Cato Institute, November 2, 2000.

87. U.S. Department of State. "The United States and Cuba." International Information Programs. http://usinfo.state.gov/regional/ar/us-cuba/.

EL REMITENTE CUBANO:
ALGUNAS CARACTERÍSTICAS PARTICULARES

Joaquín Pérez Rodríguez

Durante el año 2002, y según cifras del Banco Interamericano de Desarrollo, hacia Cuba fueron $1,138 millones por concepto de remesas. Esto coloca a Cuba como el décimo receptor de divisas del continente latinoamericano. Es de hacer notar que, según la misma fuente, durante el año 2001, Cuba ocupaba el séptimo lugar, con un monto global de $930 millones. No ha sido una disminución de los envíos a Cuba, ya que la cantidad de remesas enviadas se incrementó en $208 millones. Ha sido el aumento del flujo hacia otros países como Colombia, Guatemala o Perú lo que ha creado esta situación. Por tanto, el exilio cubano sigue destinando parte, una buena parte, de sus ahorros hacia la Isla.

CARACTERÍSTICAS DEL EXILIO DE MIAMI

En el mes de diciembre del año 2000, para el Cuba Study Group, Bendixen y Associados realizó una investigación de opinión pública entre la población cubana de Miami Dade. Las condiciones, para alguien ser entrevistado, consistían en tener más de 18 años de edad, considerarse cubano o cubano americano y estar interesados en los problemas de Cuba y del exilio. La muestra incluyó 837 entrevistas. De ese estudio fueron muchas las conclusiones que se extrajeron.

De acuerdo a las características previamente estipuladas para que un sujeto fuese encuestado, se entrevistó un 7% de personas nacidas en Estados Unidos. El resto lo conformaba personas nacidas en Cuba y que habían ido llegando a los Estados Unidos de la siguiente forma: un 26% indicaba haber llegado al exilio durante la década del 60, un 14% durante la década del 70, un 20% durante la década del 80 y un 33% durante la década de los 90.

- El exilio, de acuerdo a las cifras obtenidas en ese estudio, era un exilio **poco educado.** Solamente un 22% había culminado la universidad o poseían algún postgrado, pero el 55% manifestó poseer un título de secundaria o menos.

- Era un exilio **de edad avanzada.** El 57% dijo tener más de 50 años de edad y solamente 17% dijo tener menos de 35 años.

- Era un exilio **pobre.** El 70% indicó que la entrada familiar promedio, antes del impuesto, era inferior a los $40,000.

Al realizar un cluster analysis sobre el total de la muestra, surgían dos grupos perfectamente definidos. Numéricamente equivalentes, ya que constituían cerca del 25% de la muestra cada uno, distaban uno de otro en otra serie de aspectos.

Uno de los grupos, compuesto por el 28% de la muestra, era de reciente llegada. Se componía de personas que arribaron en las décadas del 80 y el 90. La edad promedio de este grupo era menor. El 50% había tomado la ciudadanía norteamericana y sus posiciones con respecto al tema cubano eran más moderadas, con deseos manifiestos de cambiar la política que el exilio había mantenido con relación al gobierno cubano y más propensos a viajar a Cuba o a enviar remesas.

El otro grupo, que era el 23% de la muestra, no quería cambio alguno en la estrategia del exilio, arribó en la década de los 60, la edad promedio de este grupo era superior a los 50 años y el 74% habían tomado la ciudadanía norteamericana. No querían viajar a Cuba y si enviaban remesas, no lo manifestaban públicamente.

Un tercer grupo, sin características especiales, constituía la gran mayoría cuyas opiniones fluctuaban de acuerdo a los temas, a veces coincidiendo con uno u otro de los dos grupos antes definidos.

¿QUE OPINA EL EXILIO DE MIAMI-DADE SOBRE LAS REMESAS A CUBA?

En el mes de abril del 2002, de nuevo con el patrocinio del Cuba Study Group, Bendixen y Associados realizó otra investigación de campo en el área de Miami-Dade sobre el mismo universo previamente definido como del "exilio cubano de Miami-Dade."

En ese estudio se revisaron, entre otros, temas que han sido tradicionalmente controversiales, tales como el del embargo, los viajes a Cuba o el envío de remesas.

- En el tema del embargo, por el ejemplo, los entrevistados indicaban su posición favorable al mismo (61%), aunque las opiniones se dividían a la hora de calificar su eficacia, ya que el 46% consideraba que el embargo había funcionado y el 45% consideraba que no había funcionado.

- Los viajes a Cuba, en ese momento, eran aprobados por el 54% del exilio y desaprobados por el 40%, pero los viajes a Cuba, permitidos por el gobierno norteamericano a ciudadanos americanos, sin restricciones, solamente recibían la aprobación del 46% de los entrevistados, mientras eran reprobados por el 47%.

- El tema de las remesas también fue investigado en esa oportunidad. Consultados sobre el apoyo o rechazo, que el gobierno norteamericano debía brindar al envío de remesas por parte de los cubanos, el 65% estuvo de acuerdo con el envío de remesas a Cuba, mientras un 31% se manifestó en contra y un 4% se abstuvo de opinar. Cuando la pregunta se amplió en el sentido de que no existiera ninguna limitación en el monto de la remesa enviada, el apoyo disminuyó al 53% y el rechazo aumentó al 43%, lo que demuestra cierta sensibilidad al tema. De acuerdo a estos resulta-

dos, la mayoría del exilio cubano de Miami-Dade aprueba el envío de remesas a Cuba, pero una minoría importante considera que las mismas deben ser limitadas en cuanto al monto.

¿QUIENES ENVIAN Y QUE PIENSAN LOS QUE ENVIAN REMESAS A CUBA?

Durante del mes de Julio del 2002, Bendixen y Asociados, esta vez por indicaciones del Banco Interamericano de Desarrollo y Pew Hispanic Center, realizó un estudio sobre personas que envían remesas en las ciudades de Miami y Los Angeles. El estudio consistió en 300 entrevistas con remitentes de remesas, 150 se hicieron en Miami y 150 en Los Angeles.

En el grupo de Miami, se incluyeron 27 cubanos. Aunque el número de personas entrevistadas, en el caso de los cubanos, no es válido desde un punto de vista cuantitativo, cualitativamente nos puede indicar ciertas tendencias y patrones de comportamiento interesantes a los fines de conocer la manera de pensar o actuar de los remitentes de remesas desde Miami hacia Cuba.

- En primer lugar, la mayoría de los entrevistados eran personas de larga residencia en los Estados Unidos. Un 56% alegaba haber vivido por más de 10 años en este país.

- El 33% del grupo indicó que enviaba remesas una vez al mes, mientras que el 48% dijo hacerlo cada dos o tres meses.

- Los entrevistados enviaban $100 promedio por envío.

- De acuerdo a lo expresado por los sujetos entrevistados, el 41% utiliza los servicios de Western Union para canalizar sus envíos. Un 51% utiliza otras empresas o personas que viajan y un 8% manifestó que utilizaban otras vías.

- El 100% de lo enviado se utiliza en Cuba para pagar gastos. Nada es invertido o ahorrado. De estas cantidades, un 11% manifiesta controlar ese gasto desde aquí, mientras que el 89% restante indica que no tienen control alguno sobre cómo se gastan esos fondos remesados. Sin embargo, existe algún compromiso previamente pactado o alguna planificación previa de la razón del gasto, ya que el 44% de los entrevistados dice que las remesas se emplean en aquello que fue programado, aunque hayan expresado previamente que no tenían control sobre el gasto. Por estudios similares, hechos en otros paises, cuando hay control, hay inversión y cuando hay programación en el gasto de lo enviado, una parte es porque se destina a inversión o al ahorro. Por tanto, es probable que parte de esas remesas se estén invirtiendo de alguna forma como puede ser en permutas, paladares, en la adquisición de animales, vehículos o en otros activos.

- La decisión de mandar, el cómo y el cuánto, está en manos del que remesa en un 89% de los casos. En un 4% de los casos lo decide un familiar que vive en Miami y en un 7% de los casos la decisión corresponde al que recibe la remesa en Cuba.

- Un 11% de los entrevistados indicó que los montos enviados son depositados allá en cuentas bancarias. Un 82% manifestó que no se depositan, mientras el 7% no sabe si se depositan o no.

- Del grupo entrevistado, el 11% dijo saber que las personas que reciben las remesas tienen cuentas bancarias en Cuba. El 67% dice que no tiene y el 18% no sabe. Un 22% indica que algún familiar en Cuba tiene cuenta bancaria, un 56% alega que ningún familiar tiene cuenta y un 22% no conoce de algún familiar que tenga cuenta bancaria en Cuba.

- Se le explicó al entrevistado que existen tres niveles de prioridades en el envío de las remesas. La primera prioridad viene dada por el hecho de mandar el monto estipulado a Cuba antes que cualquier gasto que se vaya a realizar aqui. El segundo orden de prioridades viene dado por el envío de la remesa una vez cancelados los gastos elementales aqui. El tercer nivel es cuando la remesa se envía con lo que sobra, después de gastar

lo esencial y los superfluo aqui. Solamente el 14% indica que la prioridad de las remesas a Cuba es del primer orden. El 71% manifiesta que es del segundo orden y el 15% restante envía las remesas con el dinero sobrante.

CONCLUSIONES

Aunque no conocemos el número exacto de personas que envían remesas a Cuba, sabemos que la opinión mayoritaria del exilio de Miami está a favor de enviar remesas a los parientes que han quedado en Cuba.

Existe un segmento de la población de ese exilio que no está de acuerdo con enviar dinero a Cuba, pero la mayoría si lo está y de hecho envía dinero constantemente.

Las remesas enviadas tienen una gran periodicidad y se encuentran en el orden de los $100 por envío.

El monto de los envíos de remesas a Cuba es de una magnitud importante para la economía del exilio de Miami y la de Cuba.

Las remesas se emplean en gastos de vida y ni se invierten, ni se ahorran. La gran mayoría indica no controlar en qué se gastan esas remesas pero casi la mitad manifiesta que se gastan de acuerdo a lo programado. Puede haber una inversión oculta que se hace en algunos casos con parte de las remesas enviadas.

Si suponemos que el exilio que envía dinero a Cuba alcanza el medio millón de personas y si cada una manda $100 por mes, que en realidad el promedio es menor al envío mensual, la suma total de las remesas sería de $600 millones, algo más de la mitad de los $1,138 millones que Cuba alega recibir por concepto de remesas. Sería interesante seguir investigando para determinar la razón de esta inconsistencia numérica.

REMESAS FAMILIARES Y LA POLÍTICA PÚBLICA CUBANA

Ricardo A. Puerta

En un régimen estadocentrista como el cubano las remesas familiares recibidas desde del exterior en la Isla representan un hecho positivo para la economía nacional, pero a su vez, fomentan incómodas opciones para el Gobierno cubano en el ámbito local, por sus efectos sociales y políticos. Las remesas contribuyen a estabilizar la macroeconomía cubana. Pero conllevan, al mismo tiempo, poner a la disposición de individuos y hogares montos significativos de dinero, no generados por la economía estatal, que en sus posteriores usos los ciudadanos, y no el Estado, tienen bajo su mando y control.

Este trabajo complementa "El remitente cubano: Algunas características particulares," valioso aporte de campo del investigador Joaquín Pérez Rodríguez, incluido también en este volumen. Consciente de esa vinculación, se limita a comentar los montos de remesas que llegan a Cuba, con notas críticas a los mismos; compara dichos montos con los recibidos por países latinoamericanos que guardan cierta similitud con Cuba y destaca la significación que tienen las remesas en el contexto de la economía cubana, bastante parecida a otros países al nivel macro, pero con marcadas diferencias al nivel micro, sobre todo en el ámbito local, familiar e individual. Al final de trabajo se explica porqué Cuba, a pesar de tener una comunidad de remitentes más prospera, se mantiene baja en montos enviados, comparada con otros países latinoamericanos, hecho que pone de manifiesto las políticas regresivas, de contención y antidesarrollistas del actual régimen cubano.

MONTOS

Cuba recibió en 1999 unos 800 millones de dólares anuales por remesas que envían los cubanos que viven en el extranjero a sus parientes y amigos de la Isla. Su mayor parte proviene de Estados Unidos, donde viven 1.2 millones de emigrados de origen cubano.[1] Al monto anterior habría que sumarle 300 millones de dólares que la Isla también recibe de Estados Unidos de ayuda humanitaria en especie: ropa, comida, medicinas, etc. En total son unos 1,100 millones de dólares anuales de ayuda—en efectivo y en especie—que se redujo en el 2001 por los sucesos del 11 de septiembre, y volvió a recuperarse a partir del 2002.

La cifra de 800 millones no es del todo aceptable entre los estudiosos de la situación cubana. Ernesto Betancourt la considera "matemáticamente imposible y políticamente inviable" y lo explica. La cantidad sale de una cínica manipulación hecha para encubrir una verdad incómoda: Castro esta recurriendo al tráfico de drogas y al lavado de dinero para financiar la brecha que tiene (desde 1990) en la balanza de pagos (Betancourt, 2000). Sergio Díaz-Briquets, sin llegar a las conclusiones de Betancourt, estima un máximo de 400 millones de dólares anuales (Betancourt, 2000). Manuel David Orrio, espía confeso e informante al régimen sobre periodistas y economistas indepen-

---

1. Este número podría elevarse a 2.5 millones si sumáramos también los hijos y nietos de los emigrados, es decir, los actuales ciudadanos norteamericanos, nacidos o naturalizados en Estados Unidos, de padres o abuelos originarios de Cuba. Ambas cifras se vuelven estratégicas al definir la actual nación cubana.

dientes calcula, "de modo más conservador," unos 900 millones de dólares en remesas familiares (Orrio, 2000). Mesa-Lago (2001) es el más coincidente con la cifra de los 800 millones. Declara que las transferencias netas en el sector externo, en su mayoría remesas a la Isla de cubanos en el extranjero, creció de cero en 1989 a 799 millones de pesos en 1999 y 842 millones en 2000. Las cifras de Mesa-Lago también coinciden con las dadas sobre el mismo tema por la Comisión Económica para América Latina y el Caribe (CEPAL).

Los voceros del régimen cubano en sus escritos nos recuerdan que los montos citados sobre remesas familiares deben ser tomados "como estimados conservadores." Esto nos pone en duda con respecto a cualquier cifra "a la alza" que se sugiera, y también deja la puerta abierta para justificar en el futuro cualquier monto superior que aparezca en el debate.

COMPARACIÓN

El factor remesas no es exclusivo al caso cubano en esta era globalizada de comercio, finanzas, migración, tecnología, cultura y de derechos humanos occidentales. El envío de remesas a sus respectivos países de origen por nacionales emigrados a países desarrollados se ha convertido en uno de los principales renglones de las economías latinoamericanas. Un fenómeno de grandes magnitudes a nivel mundial. Según la revista británica *The Economist*, el dinero enviado a sus países por emigrantes latinoamericanos es uno de los lados positivos que ha tenido el persistente desangre de ciudadanos productivos de esta parte del mundo.

Un estudio realizado por el Banco Interamericano de Desarrollo (BID) revela que América Latina recibirá en el 2003 cerca de 40 mil millones de dólares en remesas familiares desde Estados Unidos, 8,000 millones más que los recibidos en 2002. Ello representa un aumento del 25% con respecto al 2002, y un 50% por encima de la inversión extranjera directa prevista para ese año. Mundialmente, esta cantidad equivale al 23 % del total de remesas que reciben al año los

países en desarrollo desde naciones del primer mundo.[2]

El monto de remesas que llega a Cuba por año desde Estados Unidos no es de los mayores en comparación a otras naciones latinoamericanas. Más bien es bajo, contrario a lo esperado de una emigración como la cubana, de casi cuatro décadas, con fuertes flujos en la década de los 90, e integrada por personas y hogares que generan el mayor ingreso promedio entre las comunidades de emigrantes latinoamericanos en Estados Unidos. Sin embargo, esta afluencia de ingresos en la comunidad cubana no se traduce en el envío de remesas. Mientras que el emigrante latinoamericano en EEUU manda mensualmente entre 200 y 300 dólares a sus familiares, para Cuba esa cantidad fluctúa entre $50 y $100 por envío, y no por mes, sino cada dos o tres meses.

El uso de canales informales, de "mochileras" o "mulas," con entrega de remesas de mano a mano, en adición a turistas o visitantes nacionales o extranjeros, es predominante en el caso cubano.[3] Es la opción más barata, segura y personalizada del mercado. Esta práctica también esta muy difundida en otros emigrados latinoamericanos, especialmente los que tienen una gran proporción de "indocumentados," "ilegales" o "sin papeles" en su corriente migratoria, como es el caso de los hondureños en Estados Unidos. Pero no debería ser así entre los cubanos porque son inmigrantes, en su gran mayoría, debidamente documentados en Estados Unidos, a causa principalmente, de las generosas leyes migratorias estadounidenses que desde 1960 se aplican a sus casos.

Los cubanos prefieren los canales informales para enviar remesas no para permanecer en el anonimato o evadir "la vigilancia de la Migra y otras autoridades norteamericanas," como es el caso entre los latinoamericanos indocumentados, sino por razones políticas con referencia a las autoridades cubanas. La informalidad en las transferencias de remesas existe para que el Gobierno cubano "no sepa" quién recibe la re-

---

2. *El Diario de Hoy*, San Salvador, El Salvador, 28 de Octubre, 2003, Edición Virtual.

3. Orozco (2003) explica los canales utilizados. Las "mulas" representan el 46% del total, seguidos por la empresa remesadora Western Union (30%) y las cooperativas de crédito (11%).

mesa en Cuba, hecho con potenciales de represalias políticas, económicas y sociales al receptor de la remesa por parte del Gobierno cubano—principalmente por acciones de los aparatos de seguridad, de las instancias locales del Partido (Comunista) y de los órganos "ciudadanos" de vigilancia vecinal (Brigadas de Respuesta Rápida, de Repudio y de los Comités de Defensa de la Revolución).

Hay diferencias significativas entre Cuba y otros países similares en los montos anuales enviados. Por ejemplo, El Salvador, con ingresos medios menores que los cubanos, con una diáspora casi igual en número a la cubana y con una población nacional que es la mitad de la censada en la Isla, en el 2002 recibió 2,206 millones de dólares por concepto de remesas. También una cantidad mayor que la cubana recibieron los ecuatorianos en el 2002—1,575 millones de dólares—aún cuando su población nacional y diáspora son casi igual a la cubana, cuentan con una economía nacional mucho más productiva que la cubana y sus emigrados generan ingresos en el exterior menores al de los cubanos en Estados Unidos.

Pero aún fuera de Cuba, los cubanos remitentes de remesas están sometidos a las reglas del gobierno cubano a las transferencias realizadas. Mientras que los costos de enviar dinero desde Estados Unidos a países latinoamericanos promedian entre el 6% y 8% porciento del monto enviado, para Cuba ese promedio se dispara al 17%, el porcentaje más alto cobrado en América Latina.[4] Ello sucede, en parte, por "la tajada" que va a parar al Gobierno en la operación realizada, expresada en gravámenes a las casas remesadoras y de envíos de paquetes, y también por los intermediarios que tiene colocados el Gobierno en la cadena del negocio, generalmente "empresarios nacionales." A esto, habría que sumarle los costos de

gestión en los que tienen que incurrir los receptores de remesas en Cuba para llegar a tener en sus manos los fondos remitidos por canales formales, monto no estimado en Cuba pero que en países latinoamericanos fluctúa entre diez y veinte dólares adicionales. Entre los costos de gestión están las llamadas telefónicas internacionales y nacionales, correos electrónicos, viajes locales, gastos de estadías, de espera, de trámites, etc. Entre los mismos sobresalen las tarifas telefónicas internacionales, las más altas en los mercados americano y europeo. Y las razones son conocidas. En el costo de las comunicaciones globales con Cuba no sólo interviene el monopolio estatal cubano, sino también los altos impuestos cargados al usuario por la llamada o conexión, y los numerosos intermediarios, que por razones de vigilancia y monitoreo del Gobierno cubano, participan en la conectividad disponible.

Pero el 17% del total de la transferencia enviada no es la opción más cara del mercado para recibir remesas en Cuba. Por encima de ella operan, al 19%, "los bancos de dólares," operaciones informales "del mercado negro," accesibles localmente en muchos vecindarios cubanos. Esta operación supone un "banquero" en Cuba, que localiza y entrega la remesa al destinatario, y un agente colector en Estados Unidos, que capta los envíos hechos por los remitentes y les cobra los gastos por transacción. El colector de Estados Unidos y el banquero de Cuba se comunican por teléfono, o por Internet, usando "clandestinamente" servidores estatales porque en Cuba no están autorizados servidores privados.[5] De hecho, los fondos transferidos a Cuba no suponen de inmediato envío alguno de dinero en efectivo a la Isla. Son realmente "dinero telefónico o electrónico," bits de transacciones. Habitualmente el dinero remitido queda depositado en cuentas bancarias del país donde se origina la

---

4. Los dos países donde cuesta menos el envío son Ecuador y El Salvador, sólo el 4% del total remitido. Ambos tienen economías totalmente dolarizadas. Los países que siguen a Cuba con costos mayores son Venezuela (el 14% del total enviado) y Nicaragua y Haití (cada uno con el 10% del total enviado).

5. En Cuba el acceso a Internet se define "en función de los intereses del país," con lo cual sólo resulta (legalmente) accesible a los dirigentes del Gobierno y a los extranjeros. Los proveedores de acceso son estatales y la compra del módem o del ordenador deben ser "autorizadas," con lo cual los ciudadanos sólo pueden acceder a los servicios del Internet desde algún lugar controlado o un cibercafé, con precios abusivos. Los internautas tienen páginas bloqueadas y son vigilados por policías especializados en controlar también mensajes de los teléfonos móviles. (Tagliavini, 2003).

operación, en este caso Estados Unidos. Los dólares que necesita el banquero local para operar en Cuba tampoco hay que remesarlos previamente. Generalmente es un capital semilla que proviene de ganancias inversiones en dólares que "alguien" hizo en Cuba, ingresos netos de compra-ventas efectuadas en el mercado dolarizado de la Isla, muchas "ilegales" o de mercado negro, de acuerdo a las leyes cubanas vigentes.[6]

Detrás de estos negocios de transferencia, cambio e informática—altamente lucrativos—se encuentran conocidos miembros de la *nomenklatura* cubana, en capacidad de empresarios, protegidos por los aparatos cubanos de seguridad y justicia, y con ramificaciones mercantiles o de parientes en otras empresas donde figuran altos dirigentes del Gobierno y el Partido. Cualquier operación lucrativa y sostenida de mercado dolarizado, tiende a desembocar en el Grupo de Administración Empresarial/ GAESA, un auténtico imperio económico en Cuba de empresas anónimas montadas sobre las empresas y organismos estatales, y estratégicamente ubicado en los sectores más productivos de divisas. Factura casi mil millones de dólares al año. Su junta directiva esta encabezada por el General de División Julio Casas Regueiro, primer sustituto de Raúl Castro y su hombre de confianza.

Teóricamente, GAESA pertenece a las Fuerzas Armadas con el fin de recaudar divisas. Pero nada tiene que ver con lo que se podría llamar el *holding estatal*. Esta controlada directamente por su director general con poder ejecutivo, Luis Alberto Rodríguez López Calleja, casado con Déborah Castro Espín, la hija mayor de Raúl (Fernández, et. al. 2001).

SIGNIFICACIÓN

Las remesas recibidas en Cuba son propinas para la economía nacional. Es el mayor contribuyente de recursos externos en la segunda mitad de la década de los 90 (Pérez-López, 2000). Supera los ingresos que en forma combinada reciben las industrias turística y azucarera, los que a su vez representan más de las dos terceras partes de todos los ingresos percibidos por el gobierno cubano. Suponen entradas a Cuba de capital fresco, generado por el sector externo de la economía, sin que ningún cubano de la Isla tenga que producirlo. Equivalen a montos de divisas, mayormente expresados en dólares norteamericanos. Alivian el flujo de caja del Banco Central. Aumentan los fondos para pagar importaciones, comprar "al cash" y "derrotar al embargo" en el mercado internacional. Expanden las ofertas del mercado interno, en los "shopping de dólar" y "los shopping de trapos."[7]

El economista Pedro Monreal, del Centro de Investigaciones de la Economía Internacional (CIEI) en la Universidad de La Habana, reconoce que "el bienestar económico de los cubanos dependería así en grado considerable de las rentas familiares remitidas del exterior, las cuales permitirían mantener niveles de consumo superiores a los que cabría esperar del funcionamiento exclusivo de la "economía interna." En la práctica, las remesas han actuado desde la primera mitad de la década del noventa como uno de los componentes de la "nueva economía" del país"[8] (Monreal, *Futuro de Cuba*). Y al replantearse el problema del desarrollo del país agrega: "hipotéticamente, los mercados internos (de Cuba) en divisas pudieran actuar como 'trampolín' para la generación de exportaciones, pero esa posibilidad apenas se ha ma-

---

6. Aunque las mayores pérdidas económicas se centran en el sector que opera con divisas, no hay empresa estatal que esté exenta de robos, desvíos y faltantes de sus bienes económicos. En un millón de pesos se calculan las pérdidas diarias en el sector estatal por concepto de malversación, desvío de recursos y faltantes económicos, declaró un inspector popular en el municipio Cerro. La millonaria cifra se dio a conocer en una de las reuniones de instrucción a los funcionarios que participarían en los controles gubernamentales dirigidos contra las empresas del estado en la capital. Un por ciento elevado de las pérdidas económicas son muy difíciles de detectar porque se legitimizan por los directores, administradores y almaceneros de las entidades "de la Gubernamental," por medio de transferencias; vales de entradas, salidas o devoluciones y otros (Cubanet, 2003).

7. Antes conocidas por "diplotiendas." Muchas de ellas funcionan en los establecimientos "heredados" del antiguo régimen (Almacenes Ultra, Precios Fijos, La casa de los Tres Kilos, etc.). Prácticamente hay un complejo comercial de "área dólar" en cada ciudad de Cuba. Los "shopping de trapos" también responden a una etiqueta popular. Venden ropa usada y se abastecen de las "donaciones que recibe Cuba" del exterior.

8. Los otros dos componentes, según Monreal, son la utilización intensiva de recursos naturales y el ingreso limitado de capitales de préstamos e inversión.

terializado en la experiencia reciente de la industria cubana" (Monreal, 2003).

La experiencia cubana con las remesas ayuda a repensar el transnacionalismo, como nos sugiere Duany (2001). Los vínculos transnacionales entre Cuba y EEUU se han mantenido e incluso fortalecido a lo largo de cuatro décadas, pese a la continua hostilidad entre ambos países. Cuba ha desarrollado una vertiente particular de transnacionalismo, caracterizada por sus limitados intercambios políticos, económicos y culturales con EEUU. Como refugiados políticos que no pueden regresar permanentemente a Cuba, los cubanos han desarrollado unos lazos con su país muy diferentes de los dominicanos o los puertorriqueños. Económicamente, la migración transnacional ha acelerado la reinserción de Cuba en la órbita del dólar estadounidense, sobre todo durante la década de los 90. La economía cubana difícilmente podría sobrevivir sin el influjo masivo de fondos externos enviados por los migrantes.

Por su doble papel de estabilizadoras y reactivadoras, desde 1988 se abre el espacio para que las remesas ganen relevancia en la economía cubana. En ese año Cuba pierde el aseguramiento—financiero, tecnológico y de mercado—del campo socialista (Monreal, 2003) debido a su desaparición. En 1993 se despenaliza finalmente la tenencia y uso del dólar en la Isla. Las remesas adquieren aún más importancia después del 11 de Septiembre, 2001, debido a la caída de las exportaciones cubanas y la baja del turismo extranjero en la Isla.

Del lado negativo, las remesas suponen una dependencia externa del régimen cubano. Implican recibir "dinero del enemigo," de los "gusanos" que viven en "en el imperio," como "exilados" o "emigrados políticos." Son muy pocos los cubanos que se llamarían o aceptarían ser llamados "emigrados económicos," una vez fuera de la Isla.

Las remesas que envía la diáspora cubana a la Isla contradicen además las expectativas políticas que sobre el exilio cubano, mantienen algunos analistas. Su argumento es: la mayoría (61%) de los exilados cubanos radicados en Estados Unidos favorece el embargo económico a la Isla, y en consecuencia, no deberían enviar remesas, ni realizar visitas a Cuba (Orozco, 2002).[9] Pero el corolario no se cumple entre los emigrados cubanos. De acuerdo a un estudio realizado por el Banco Interamericano de Desarrollo/BID en Noviembre, 2001, el 67% de los cubanos americanos que viven en Estados Unidos mandan remesas a Cuba (Orozco, 2003).[10] La proporción de viajeros a la Isla es mucho menor con respecto al total de los 1.2 millones de cubanos-americanos que vive en Estados Unidos, pero aún significativa en relación al total de viajeros norteamericanos que legalmente llegan a Cuba. En el año 2000, de los 156,000 norteamericanos que viajaron legalmente a la Isla, más de un 70% era de origen cubano. En 2001, el total de viajeros aumentó, con una proporción menor de cubanos entre ellos, aunque todavía siendo la mayoría en el total. De los 200,000 viajeros legales norteamericanos a la Isla, 120,000 eran cubanos, 60% del total (Robyn, 2002). Las remesas y visitas a la Isla de los cubano-americanos ubicados en Estados Unidos más bien demuestran dos planos—uno privado y otro público—en cuanto a lo que creen y hacen los cubanos emigrados dentro de la relación Cuba-Estados Unidos, y si se tomaran como interdependientes ambos planos, la mayor inconsistencia—de actitud y conducta—estaría evidenciada en las remesas.

Las remesas tienen un efecto local muy visible en Cuba. Se estima que por lo menos el 25% de los 12 mi-

---

9. Locay (2002) no ve ninguna contrariedad al respecto. Y como argumento usa la siguiente analogía: "Si manejo un automóvil que contamina el aire no puedo favorecer estándares más rígidos que aumenten la calidad atmosférica." De igual forma considera que quienes mandan remesas a sus familiares en Cuba sencillamente no relacionan sus envíos con la supervivencia del régimen. El caso más bien ejemplifica "la tragedia de lo común," donde una acción individual maximizada no necesariamente resulta en el óptimo grupal.

10. La monografía de Orozco (2002) sobre Cuba contiene un excelente análisis sobre los modos y mecanismos que usan los cubanos ubicados en Estados Unidos para mandar remesas a Cuba, los agentes de transferencia y cambio que habitualmente utilizan, y las oportunidades presentes en dicho mercado. Aunque Orozco fue invitado por ASCE a participar en el Panel de Remesas de este año 2003, no pudo asistir por cumplir con otros compromisos de viajes hechos con anterioridad.

llones de cubanos de la Isla reciben directamente remesas del exterior, y otro 25% se beneficia indirectamente de ellas. Casi todo el uso de la remesa esta destinado al consumo en el caso cubano—comida, vestido, zapatos, medicinas y adquisición de bienes duraderos para el hogar. Pero al aumentar poder adquisitivo y gastos de consumo en sus receptores, las remesas agregan diferencias socio-económicas a las ya existentes entre la población en Cuba, todavía oficialmente definida como una "sociedad sin clases" de acuerdo al relato del régimen. Por tal motivo, las remesas de hecho erosionan la prédica igualitaria del Gobierno, en medio de una carestía de bienes básicos de consumo y de un bajo poder adquisitivo, penurias que por más de cuatro décadas vienen caracterizando la vida diaria del cubano medio.

Desde mediados de los 90, en la población de la Isla se distinguen los que reciben remesas versus los que no reciben remesas. Los que las reciben han superado bastante la supervivencia diaria, con estilos de vida que es mejor no hacerlos "públicos" para evitar "pases de cuenta," celos y envidias, con frecuencia promovidos en la ideología clasista vigente. Pero existen agravantes reales. Los que no reciben remesas generalmente no tienen parientes en el extranjero y tienden a ser "simpatizantes del régimen," los "siempre fieles" y "defensores" del sistema, etc. Y dentro de tales estratos hay un alto porcentaje de población negra cubana, sin duda subrepresentada en la nación cubana emigrada. Dentro de estas complicaciones, se llega al extremo, que si un amigo o familiar manda desde el exterior "un envío" a un "Patria o muerte" en Cuba, el destinatario, en precaución a represalias, prefiere recibirlo a través de terceros para no "marcarse" públicamente ante sus "compañeros revolucionarios." En este aspecto, en Cuba, a diferencia de otros países latinoamericanos, recibir una remesa del exterior adscribe una "definición" política en el receptor. La marca política se aplica, siguiendo una escala de mayor a menor así: simpatizantes, opositores, disidentes, críticos y neutrales. En casos de sanciones, a veces sale más caro en el receptor la represalia recibida que el beneficio material logrado por recibir el envío. Este costo adicional—en esencia político—habría que sumarlo en Cuba a los de transferencia, cambio y gestión en que generalmente incurre un receptor cualquiera de remesas en un país del Tercer Mundo que no sea Cuba.

EXPLICACIÓN

Hay varios factores que explican el bajo monto y frecuencia de envío de remesas en Cuba, entre ellos, las vigentes políticas cubanas sobre herencia, traspaso y venta de activos personales, así como el "estira y encoje" que el régimen viene aplicando a los cuentapropistas o autoempleados desde hace varias décadas. Todo ello inhibe la inversión y finalmente, los montos de remesas a enviarse a Cuba. En países de economía no estatal—como son el resto de los latinoamericanos—los receptores de remesas destinan a inversiones proporciones pequeñas, pero aún significativas en monto, entre el 10% y el 20% de lo recibido, que a nivel macro, agregadamente sumaría entre 80 y 160 millones de dólares adicionalmente invertido en la economía cubana. Las inversiones preferidas en los otros países de la región latinoamericana, son para el mejoramiento y construcción de vivienda, compra de ganado, tierras, bienes raíces y de otros activos "de engorde," aumento del patrimonio personal o familiar a través de cuentas de ahorro, y compra de bonos, de acciones bursátiles, etc; reducción de riesgos por compra de seguros de educación, salud y planes privados de retiro; y sobre todo inversiones en actividades productivas, de pequeños y medianos negocios—bodegas, peluquerías, talleres, comedores, hospedajes, sitios turísticos, etc.—muchas de estas inversiones tienen una base familiar o doméstica.[11]

Casi nada de lo anterior se puede hacer en Cuba, debido a las políticas vigentes. Los dueños de paladares que han invertido en sus negocios las remesas recibidas del exterior ejemplifican mejor que nadie la acción represiva del régimen cubano frente a esas opciones, que tilda de "capitalistas." Ello no impide, sin embargo, que el mismo régimen promueva la inversión privada en Cuba, siempre que sea extranjera. La política de acoso y contención mantenida por el Gobierno cubano es sólo contra los nacionales –empresarios potenciales y actuales—pues a los extranjeros los busca, les ofrece asistencia, incentivos fiscales y de otra índole para que inviertan o no se vayan de la Isla. Ello evidencia una peculiaridad muy contraria a los tiempos en que vivimos: Cuba es el único país del mundo con una política a favor del empresario extranjero, y de casi total rechazo al empresario nacional. Ni en China o Vietnam, ambos con regímenes centralizados, dan ese trato a sus nacionales.

Además, Cuba es una economía deprimida, dolarizada en parte, pero donde no se necesitan muchos dólares para sobrevivir. Por ejemplo, una familia de 4 miembros, dos adultos y dos menores, pueden acostarse diariamente sin hambre, si disponen de 50 dólares mensuales para su alimentación. Esa cantidad no será mucha de acuerdo a estándares del exterior, o del país que origina la remesa, pero en la Isla dicho monto triplica el salario mínimo mensual de Cuba, la pensión que recibe un jubilado—en pesos cubanos unos 12 a 15 dólares al mes—e incluso sobrepasa el sueldo oficial de un médico de familia, que equivale en pesos cubanos a 30 dólares mensuales.

El mantenimiento de una economía oficial baja en crecimiento, estancada o en receso por largos períodos, con salarios deprimidos a sus trabajadores y de contención a la pequeña y mediana empresa, es una decisión hecha por el Gobierno castrista desde casi su inicio en 1959. Demuestra una sistemática oposición a la clase media cubana—a la heredada del antiguo régimen y a la emergente que por años balbucea dentro del fidelismo. Por fijaciones ideológicas, su fomento equivaldría a tolerar formas propias de vida, distintas o ajenas al oficialismo en lo cotidiano, y en definitiva, a no depender materialmente del Estado.

Si bien las remesas, por ser divisas que entran de gratis al país, refuerzan macro-económicamente el sistema, son otros sus efectos a nivel micro. Permiten crear y expandir espacios individuales, familiares y locales, de acción económica, que por sus efectos facilitan respiros, atajos, alternativas y contrapropuestas al mando y control gubernamentales. Pero no nos hagamos ilusiones. La recepción de remesas en Cuba conlleva un riesgo político. Por eso, a pesar de las fisuras y socavones que posibilitan, ningún "independiente" en Cuba, puede operar liberado, con autonomía económica, mientras persistan las políticas vigentes del actual Estado cubano.

BIBLIOGRAFÍA

Pablo Alfonso. "Castro necesita más dólares del exilio," *El Nuevo Herald*, 23 de Junio, 2003.

Ernesto Betancourt. "Cuba's Balance of Payments Gap, The Remittances Scam, Drug Trafficking and Money Laundering," en *Cuba in Transition—Volume 10*. Association for the Study of the Cuban Economy. Washington D.C. 2000. Pág. 149-161.

---

11. Recientemente, Alfonso López Michelsen, ex-Presidente de Colombia comentaba una idea interesante en un diario de su país. La alternativa consiste en atraer los capitales de los emigrantes, no sólo con el aliciente de la rebaja del impuesto (sobre remesas recibidas), sino con alguna otra forma de prima, que los mueva a adquirir bonos colombianos en el extranjero y vendérselos al Banco de la República, en pesos. Otra idea, de procedencia mexicana y salvadoreña, y antes ensayada en la reconstrucción de Alemania, es utilizar las remesas colectivas para realizar obras de infraestructura social o pública, e incluso viviendas, en las comunidades originarias de los emigrados. Bajo tales esquemas, los fondos recolectados o aportados por los emigrados del exterior palanqueen fondos públicos nacionales, en una formula de tres por uno, que ejecutan contratistas privados que públicamente licitan y todo ello sujeto a auditorias ciudadanas. Así los gobiernos centrales y municipalidades, y localidades de esos países han podido construir y mejorar calles, puentes, escuelas, centros de salud, iglesias, casas culturales, campos deportivos, parques, áreas ecológicas, sitios históricos y hasta turísticos. El afán paternalista y totalizador del Estado cubano, bajo una falsa autosuficiencia, imposibilita realizar arreglos transnacionales de este tipo, a pesar de que la sociedad civil cubana del exterior, en distintas ciudades de Estados Unidos y de otros países donde se ha asentado, ha dado suficientes muestras de interés por emprender obras comunitarias y sociales en beneficio del pueblo cubano.

"Calculan en millones pérdidas por malversación," *Cubanet Independiente*. www.cubanet.org, 20 de Noviembre, 2003.

Jorge Duany. "La diáspora cubana desde una perspectiva transnacional,"en *Nueva Sociedad*, No. 174, Julio-Agosto 2001.

G. Fernández y M.A. Menéndez. "GAESA. El poder económico de los hermanos Castro," *Diario 16* (Madrid, España), 24 de Junio, 2001. Pág. 8 y 9.

Stephen Fidler. "Nuevas migraciones estimulan el crecimiento de las remesas," *Financial Times* (Londres, Inglaterra), 17 de Mayo, 2001.

International Labour Office. *Making the best of Globalisation: Migrant Worker Remittances and Microfinance*. Workshop Report. ILO. Ginebra. 20-21 Noviembre, 2000.

Luis Locay. "A General Equilibrium Model of Family Remittances to Cuba: Or Why Is It So Expensive to Send Money to the Island," en *Cuba in Transition—Volume 12*. Association for the Study of the Cuban Economy. Washington D.C. 2000. Pág. 410-419.

Carmelo Mesa-Lago. "The Cuban economy in 1999-2001: Evaluation of performance and debate on the future," en *Cuba in Transition—Volume 11*. Association for the Study of the Cuban Economy. Washington D.C. 2001. Pág. 1-17.

Pedro Monreal. "Desde Cuba." *Futuro de Cuba*. Internet: http://www.futurodecuba.org/Pedro-Monreal.htm.

Pedro Monreal. "Cuba y la opción global: Replanteando el problema del desarrollo." Reunión Internacional sobre "Cuba: Los retos del futuro," auspiciada por la Universidad Humdbolt y el New School University de Nueva York, patrocinada por la Fundación Ford. Berlín, Alemania, del 2 al 5 de Octubre, 2003.

Emily Morris. "Interpreting Cuba's External Accounts," en *Cuba in Transition—Volume 10*. Association for the Study of the Cuban Economy. Washington D.C. 2000. Pág. 145-148.

Manuel Orozco. "Challenges and opportunities of marketing remittances to Cuba." Inter-American Dialogue. Washington, D.C., July 27, 2002.

Manuel Orozco. "Remesas a América Latina y el Caribe, 2002." Diálogo Interamericano. Washington, D.C., 2003

Manuel David Orrio. "Cuba y su economía de resistencia," en *Cuba in Transition—Volume 10*. Association for the Study of the Cuban Economy. Washington D.C. 2000. Pág. 11-18.

Manuel David Orrio. "Papel de las remesas en la sociedad civil cubana." Buró de Información del Movimiento Cubano de Derechos Humanos. Miami, Florida. 3 de Diciembre, 2000.

Jorge F. Pérez-López. "Cuba's Balance of Payments Statistics," en *Cuba in Transition—Volume 10*. Association for the Study of the Cuban Economy. Washington D.C., 2000. Pág. 136-144.

Bhargavi Ramamurthy. *International Labour Migrants: Unsung heroes of globalization*. Sida Studies No. 8. Sida Information Centre, Suecia. 2003. info@sida.se. "Las remesas familiares ayudan a las economías latinoamericanas," *Contacto* (México), 26 de febrero, 2002 "Remesas superan la ayuda externa y las inversiones,"*La Tribuna* (Tegucigalpa, Honduras), 25 de Noviembre, 2003.

Dorothy Robyn, James D. Reitzes y Brian Church. "The Impact on the U.S. Economy of Lifting Restrictions on Travel to Cuba", en *Cuba in Transition—Volume 12*. Association for the Study of the Cuban Economy. Washington D.C. 2002. Pág. 262-275.

Alejandro A. Tagliavini. "Libertad para el Internet," *El Heraldo* (Tegucigalpa, Honduras), 15 de Noviembre, 2003.

Nelson P. Valdés y Mario A. Rivera. "The Political Economy of the Internet in Cuba," *Cuba in Transition—Volume 9*. Association for the Study of the Cuban Economy. Washington D.C., 1999. Pág. 141-154.

MACROECONOMIC POLICY IMPLEMENTATION IN EARLY TRANSITION: LESSONS FOR CUBA FROM POLAND AND ROMANIA

Jennifer Gauck

It has been thirteen years since the majority of Central and Eastern Europe's centrally planned economies began a transition to a capitalist system. In that time, several alternative paths to a market economy have been pursued in different countries, with varying degrees of success. As a result, there is no one commonly agreed approach to transition. Many policymakers and academics favor a rapid adjustment, or "shock therapy" approach; others support gradual implementation. The experiences of a wide range of countries suggest that rapid implementation produces more economically efficient outcomes with fewer long-term costs in terms of growth, inflation and standards of living. Yet the *choice* of shock therapy while designing policies was not a guarantee of these results; rather, it was whether policies were rapidly *implemented* that determined outcomes.

Poland and Romania provide a lesson in the factors that determine the pace of policy implementation because both started off with relatively similar assets and disadvantages, and intended to implement the same policies, but diverged in actual implementation. Poland pursued a strategy of rapid implementation; Romania instituted gradualism. That this difference in implementation led to divergent growth outcomes is clear. Rapid policy implementation leads to more rapid growth; gradual implementation delays and can sometimes impede growth. What will emerge from this analysis is that political constraints determine the pace of policy implementation. The Polish and Romanian experiences are relevant for a Cuba in

transition because they may provide guidance to a transition government on how political constraints can be incorporated into a strategy of rapid policy implementation.

This paper will limit itself to a discussion of the first five years after transition. The focus will consequently be placed on stabilization rather than structural reform, since the latter can be seen as a medium- to long-term challenge for transition economies. In addition, stabilization is a prerequisite for sustainable growth (Gomulka 2000), and its optimal implementation is crucial for the success of later reforms. Outcomes will be largely measured by growth of GDP, inflation rates, and several economic indicators that signify general standards of living.

POTENTIAL FACTORS AFFECTING POLICY IMPLEMENTATION

Initial Conditions

This analysis confines itself to countries with similar initial conditions, because they may influence the timing and design of reforms as well as the speed of implementation. Positive initial conditions, such as the existence of a private sector or educated labor force, contribute to economic growth, while negative ones, such as over-industrialization, negatively affect growth (Balcerowicz 1997). While well-designed and strongly-implemented policies help to diminish the effects of negative initial conditions, countries that begin transition from a deeper level of economic crisis will have more difficulties in overcoming reform

441

Table 1. Selected Initial Conditions for Poland, Romania and Cuba

Indicator	Poland	Romania	Cuba[a]
GDP per head, 1989 (USD)	2165	2316	2150[b]
Share of industry in GDP, 1990 (%)	52	59	37
Years under communism, 1989	42	43	44
Exports of goods and services, 1988 (% of GDP)	22	22	20
Imports of goods and services, 1988 (% of GDP)	20	13	23
Secondary school enrolment, 1989 (% of school-aged population)	.82	.92	.97

Source: Economist Intelligence Unit 2002; de Melo, et al. (2001); UN 2002

a. Data for Cuba is for 2000.
b. Economist Intelligence Unit estimate.

inertia (de Melo, et al. 2001). Because Poland and Romania shared similar advantages and disadvantages at the outset of transition, any effect these advantages and disadvantages may have had on growth outcomes or policy implementation would be fairly equal for both countries. Cuba's current conditions should align with those of Poland and Romania just before their transitions to draw relevant lessons for a Cuban transition.

Differences in initial conditions were not significant enough to account for the divergence in policy delivery or outcomes in Poland and Romania. De Melo, et al. (2001) note that most of the variability in outcomes that could be attributed to initial conditions are explained by two clusters of factors. The first is defined by pre-transition GNP levels, level of industrialization, and share of industry in GDP. The second consists of factors such as market memory, trade dependence, and repressed inflation. Table 1 compares several of these indicators for pre-transition Poland and Romania. Pre-transition GDP per capita levels were only hundreds of dollars apart. Levels of industrialization—as determined by the share of industry in GDP—were similar. What these statistics indicate, first, is that both countries had relatively similar levels of development: they both started off

with relatively similar living standards at the beginning of transition and differences in development levels were not significant enough to affect transition outcomes. (Secondary school enrollment is included in this cluster, as an educated labor force is a sign of a high level of development as well.) Second, the two countries were not over-industrialized, which Balcerowicz (1997) points to as an initial condition that negatively affects transition.

Years under communism is an important indicator because it illustrates the level of market memory, or the amount of time since market infrastructures were last in place. The number of years under central planning can be seen as a proxy for the degree of change required, as the fewer the number of years, the smaller the degree of large-scale institutional change that will need to take place (de Melo, et al. 2001). Finally, exports and imports indicate the level of openness of an economy, and its competitiveness.[1] The levels of this variable mean a rather negative initial condition for both Poland and Romania, but because the levels were similar, the two countries were on equal footing at the start of transition. Initial conditions thus do not determine the divergence in transition outcomes.

Cuba possesses initial conditions similar to those in Poland and Romania just before their transitions, so a reasonable comparison among the countries is feasible. The Polish and Romanian data, from 1989, is matched with Cuban data from 2000[2] under the assumption that if a Cuban transition were to happen tomorrow, this is what the economic situation would look like. Based on this assumption, the Cuban data illustrates conditions just before a system-wide political and economic collapse.

Cuba's GDP and secondary school enrolment parallels Poland's and Romania's, indicating the general level of development. Share of industry in GDP is slightly lower, which may be to Cuba's advantage as it will not suffer from the negative effects of over-industrialization. Market memory still exists, as Cuba

---

1. These figures do not distinguish between trade with the West and the CMEA trade, but neither Poland nor Romania had the degree of trade with the West that, for example, Hungary did.

2. This is the latest year for which fairly complete data were available.

would have spent a similar number of years under communism as Poland and Romania. In addition, the level of openness of the economy is similar as measured by imports and exports. These similarities can be taken as an indication that Cuba may suffer many of the same post-transition problems as Poland and Romania and need to design and implement stabilization policies accordingly. If anything, Cuba is better poised for a transition, as it already suffered and adjusted to the drop in output that followed the collapse of the Council for Mutual Economic Assistance (CMEA). It must still tackle the post-transition question of creating an atmosphere conducive to rising living standards and general growth in the face of potential political constraints, however, and lessons drawn from Poland and Romania's transition could prove helpful.

Stabilization Sequence and Design

Design and sequencing of transition policies continue to be hotly debated, but the place of stabilization within the context of a reform sequence has become less of a contentious issue because of the results that have emerged from more than a decade of reform in Eastern Europe. Generally, stabilization is necessary for growth because it reduces inflation, and growth cannot be sustained at a level of inflation above 40 percent (Fischer, Sahay and Végh 1996; Gomulka 1998). In terms of its place in an overall sequence, stabilization should be instituted quickly, as early stabilizers faced early declines in output, but also experienced growth earlier (Åslund, Boone and Johnson 1996). Often, the year in which a stabilization policy is implemented is also the year when inflation falls and output ceases to decline, and two years after a stabilization policy is implemented, growth becomes positive (Fischer, Sahay and Végh 1996).

The concept of what constitutes "good" stabilization policies, or those that serve to limit inflation and create an environment conducive to growth, is trickier. Lavigne (1999) provides a detailed description of what a typical stabilization policy should (and in

some countries, did) consist: price liberalization, balancing the budget by increasing taxes, a restrictive monetary policy, at times an incomes policy, and foreign trade liberalization. Such stabilization packages were anchored through an exchange rate regime, and were complemented by two key structural changes: banking and financial sectors reforms, and privatization, either through restructuring of state-owned enterprises, or by dismantling barriers of entry and exit to foster the growth of a *de novo* private sector.

This description overlooks the significance of institutions and their role in "grounding" such policies as some authors, notably Stiglitz,[3] have pointed out. Stiglitz argues that the architects of the transition in certain countries underestimated the significance of the institutional and legal infrastructure required to create an effective market economy. This lack of infrastructure meant that certain policies, however well crafted, could not be enforced. This is a very compelling argument, and one that warrants further research, particularly on the intersection of institutions and effective policy implementation. For the purposes of this discussion, the focus remains on policies alone. It is worth noting, however, that while there were likely some key differences between Poland and Romania's institutions at the outset of transition, both countries had similar institutional capacity compared with newly independent countries like those in Central Asia. Neither Poland nor Romania had to establish state-level institutions—like a central bank—from scratch, and it is unlikely Cuba would need to do so.

This analysis confines itself to countries that aimed to implement similarly designed policies in a similar sequence so that divergent policy design can be eliminated as a possible cause of different policy implementation. On the surface, it may appear that Poland and Romania had different aims and pursued different policies. Romanian President Iliescu said early on that, while he intended to move Romania to a market economy, his version would be "market so-

---

3. See Stiglitz, Joseph E. (1999), "Whither Reform?" World Bank Annual Conference on Development Economics Keynote Address, http://www.worldbank.org/research/abcde/pdfs/stiglitz.pdf.

cialism" (Poirot 1996). However, the aims of Romania's reforms never wavered, and the fact that Romania intended to implement policies similar to Poland's is made clear by a May 1990 publication of the provisional government of Romania, entitled "Outline of Strategy for Transition to a Market Economy in Romania." The objective of the economic reforms, the report states, is a transition to a market economy, a change for which there is a national consensus. The report goes on to say that "various measures cannot be delayed because they aim at medium- or long-term purposes, for delaying them would render the tasks of the future government much more difficult, and … any delay would increase the social costs of transition immeasurably" (Demekas and Khan 1991). The 1990 policies held the same aim but suffered from a lack of coherence.

In 1991, however, Romania re-implemented stabilization in conjunction with an IMF agreement, and these policies were similar to Poland's. In Poland's 1990 and Romania's 1991 stabilization reforms, the aims included liberalization of trade, price and capital flows. Both desired financial sector reform, beginning with the breaking of the monobank system and the establishment of an independent central bank. Careful fiscal and monetary policies were meant to be pursued to ensure price stability and balance of payments equilibrium. A drive to curb the high inflation that resulted from price liberalization in conjunction with the monetary overhang was part of this. In addition, Romania placed special emphasis on social measures to ensure that living standards would be protected and start to improve. However, its planned measures included reforms that affected the entire population, not special interest groups, such as improved social insurance and a minimum wage law. Poland also aimed to circumvent privileges for special groups, and part of the theory behind its shock therapy approach was that while immediate reforms may hurt the population, they would do so evenly, ensuring that a rise in living standards would benefit the majority. The design of Poland's 1990 and Romania's 1991 stabilization policies were similar, and is thus not a sufficient explanation for the divergence of growth outcomes.

POLITICAL CONSTRAINTS AND POLICY IMPLEMENTATION
Gradual Versus Rapid Policy Implementation
Poland and Romania began their transition processes with similar initial conditions and similar policy aims in mind. Yet Poland proceeded in implementing its reforms in a rapid fashion, while Romania delayed implementation. This may appear as a deliberate choice on Romania's part, as many still contend that gradualism is a viable option in the presence of political constraints. For example, Coricelli (1996) notes that there is often a need for initial transfers to economic "losers" to create support for and foster reforms, and such transfers should be incorporated into policy design. Indeed, gradualists were not opposed to stabilization *per se*, nor were gradualists necessarily interested in keeping reforms open to reversal. Indeed, most gradualist strategies often resulted from a lack of political consensus over what to do, a desire to soften initial shocks, and fears that initial reforms that create a backlash would make future reforms politically unsustainable (Lavigne 1999).

Yet it is the potential presence of this backlash that makes the choice of rapid reform compelling. If certain reforms are implemented piecemeal, opponents have the time to mobilize and become a more formidable force of opposition. Rapid reform that utilizes the economic crisis as a window of opportunity does not meet with a "groundswell of political opposition" threatening to reverse reforms (Åslund, Boone and Johnson 1996). Windows of opportunity, in which potentially unpopular reforms can be rapidly implemented with little opposition, do exist in transition because the deeper the crisis, the more willing the public is to accept deeper reforms. Many of the initial costs of stabilization are temporary and spread over much of the population; institutional reforms such as privatization are usually those reforms that attract the most vocal rent-seeking minorities (Diamond 1995).

The Nature of Political Constraints in Early Transition
Why then, would Romania choose to implement stabilization policies gradually? The answer lies in the nature of political constraints in transition. Political

Table 2. Implemented Stabilization Measures, Poland and Romania

Reform Area	Poland	Romania
Price Liberalization	90% of prices freed January 1990	80% of prices freed by end of 1991, but prices were liberalized in 3 rounds - November 1990, April 1991, July 1991
Trade Liberalization	Import restrictions abolished January 1990	Import restrictions abolished January 1991
Exchange Rates	Fixed, then crawling peg since Ocober 1991	De facto fixed until 1997; floating rate since 1997
Incomes Policy	Tax on excess wages in state sector from 1990-1994	Tax-based incomes policy in 1991
Financial Institutions	Independent central bank established before transition	Independent central bank, December 1990
Fiscal and Monetary Policy	Tight	Loose in 1990; tighter in 1991

Source: Lavigne (1999); Demekas and Khan (1991)

constraints fall into two broad categories: *ex-ante* and *ex-post* (Roland 1994). *Ex-ante* political constraints are present at the outset of transition as feasibility constraints that block decision-making or proposals. They can be either internal, as in an inability of government leaders to achieve consensus on policy design or speed of implementation, or external, such as rent-seeking groups. An example of the latter would be a coalition favoring redistribution to workers blocking a policy that redistributed to the population at large. *Ex-post* political constraints refer to the danger of a backlash and reversal after decisions have been made and outcomes observed, and can also be internal, such as anti-reform government leaders who come to power, or external rent-seeking groups.[4] In essence, *ex-ante* political constraints *anticipate* the negative effects of reform and apply pressure accordingly, while *ex-post* political constraints *observe* negative effects and apply pressure therein.

Political constraints exert pressure on governments to design and implement stabilization policies based on political considerations instead of efficiency considerations. *Ex-ante* political constraints can affect policy design if the government cannot achieve consensus. Policy implementation can also be affected *ex-ante* by rent-seeking groups anticipating their losses from reforms, especially if reform implementation is delayed. If policies are drawn up slowly, it allows more time for rent seekers to organize opposition to anticipated reforms. Both *ex-ante* and *ex-post* political con-

straints present danger for policy implementation, as governments that have only partially or gradually implemented can face a backlash and be forced to abandon sound policies due to political pressure. If a group is vocal and a government bows to its pressure, policy design can be revised if a policy has not been fully implemented. *Ex-post*, policy implementation can be hampered if reforms have been only partially implemented. A good example comes from Russia. In Moscow in 1990, partial price liberalization triggered purchases of goods in anticipation of price increases, which led to shortages, foot riots and political pressure on the government to delay further increases (Blanchard, et al. 1991). Political constraints thus have serious potential to undermine reforms.

Policy Implementation in Poland: Effects and Causes

In Poland, a strong political consensus on the part of the first post-communist government led to a clear transition strategy and rapid decision-making process. As illustrated in Table 2, the strategy was to introduce stabilization measures as quickly as possible in a single package: crucial decisions on foreign trade, prices, subsidies, wage controls, taxes, and subsidies occurred in the space of a few weeks at the end of 1989 and beginning of 1990 (Sachs, 1992). The aim of the stabilization reforms was to reduce aggregate demand and anchor the price level through five measures: cutting subsidies and investment spending to

---

4. Political constraints can also come in the form of widespread opposition to reforms from the population as a whole, but this discussion will focus mainly on government and rent-seekers.

Table 3. Selected Economic Indicators, Poland and Romania, 1989-1995

Indicator	1989	1990	1991	1992	1993	1994	1995
Poland							
Real GDP (% annual change)	0.2	-11.6	-6.9	2.6	3.7	5.2	7.0
Consumer prices (% annual change)	633.3	224.2	60.2	44.6	37.7	29.4	21.8
Average real wages (% annual change)	n.a.	n.a.	-2.4	-5.6	-1.9	2.6	3.8
Labor costs per hour (USD)	n.a.	0.74	1.14	1.21	1.23	1.34	1.66
GDP per head (USD)	2164.9	1546.4	1999.2	2198.4	2235.4	2402.0	3291.3
Private consumption per head (USD)	948.7	741.9	1186.5	1357.1	1409.2	1545.6	1982.3
Romania							
Real GDP (% annual change)	-5.8	-5.6	-12.9	-8.7	1.5	3.9	7.1
Consumer prices (% annual change)	n.a.	n.a.	222.8	199.2	295.5	61.7	27.8
Average real wages (% annual change)	n.a.	n.a.	-13.4	-15.0	-14.9	-3.1	14.0
Labor costs per hour (USD)	n.a.	0.81	0.56	0.36	0.45	0.47	0.58
GDP per head (USD)	2316.2	1647.9	1244.1	859.1	1158.2	1323	1564.3
Private consumption per head (USD)	1362.8	1085.7	755.6	538.8	737.8	840	1057.9

Source: Economist Intelligence Unit

restore budget balance; sharply increasing interest rates to control the growth of domestic credit in the banking system; devaluing and making convertible the exchange rate so it could be stabilized at the new rate; limiting nominal wage growth through a tax-based policy; and full price liberalization save certain public utility sectors.

This rapid and comprehensive orthodox reform package resulted in swift consequences, both positive and negative. As illustrated in Table 3, inflation rose sharply and was in the triple digits in 1990 due to price liberalization, but much of that was in fact concentrated in the first few months of 1990 (Lipton and Sachs 1990). By the end of 1990, monthly inflation had dropped to double digits, and it continued its steady decline through 1995, reaching below the 40 percent level highly conducive to growth by 1993. GDP began growing again in 1992, and average real wages saw growth in 1994. As a result, living standards began to increase in Poland by 1991, after an initial drop at the start of reforms. Average real wages in Poland declined until 1992, and were positive in 1994. Labor costs per hour began to climb in 1991, and continued to grow, becoming double its 1990 level in 1995. GDP per head declined initially, but

rose in 1991, and surpassed 1989 levels in 1993. In addition, private consumption rose starting in 1991. While the initial price increase and the decline in living standards were sharper than in countries implementing reforms gradually, the recovery time in Poland was shorter, so that prices stabilized and living standards rose much faster than in gradual reformers.

In Poland, the rapid formation of a non-communist government, combined with the quick consensus achieved by the Balcerowicz team, allowed for immediate policy implementation. This meant that little or no social breakdown—which could have influenced policy design or implementation—had the chance to occur before implementation. Because the methods and design were fairly obvious to the population, an overwhelming proportion of people supported the government in this, despite the economic hardship that ensued (Przeworski 1991). In creating coherent policies and implementing them quickly, Poland negated the appearance of *ex-ante* political constraints. Because there was consensus among those creating the reforms, no internal[5] political constraints on the decision-making process existed. Externally, coalitions that might have tried to block reforms were marginal, and did not have time to become more powerful because reforms were implemented so quickly.

---

5. Internal is defined as constraints existing within the government; external as constraints coming from groups or a mass of individuals in the population.

One reason why *ex-ante* political constraints may have been minimal in Poland was the legitimacy of the Polish government. The collapse of the communist system was legitimated when a non-communist government took over in Poland, and this government utilized its window of opportunity to initiate reforms not easily reversed should hostile political conditions prevail later (Gomulka 2000). Most Poles favored the move to a different system in the immediate aftermath of transition, and the legitimacy of the Polish government played a role in this support. Funke (1993) notes that the credibility of a government, even a new one, plays a significant role in the amount of *ex-ante* opposition. If voters know the government is benevolent, its reform objectives will not be met with large opposition. If this is unknown, however, the credibility of the reform program becomes more important. If reform credibility is high, more difficult tasks, such as stabilization reforms that incur immediate, short-run costs, should be completed first. The Polish government utilized this legitimacy and implemented reforms when favor for them was high, before any costs could be fully anticipated or observed. By the time the costs were observed, reforms were imbedded to the point where anti-reform politicians, even if they came to power on the issue of reversing reforms, would find it difficult to do so.

Policy Implementation in Romania: Effects and Causes

Romania, in contrast, implemented its reforms piecemeal; it did not begin with the same sort of consensus that Poland did. First, its political transition occurred at the end of 1989, whereas Poland already had a non-communist government in power in 1989. In addition, there was more social disorganization at the beginning of Romania's transition, exemplified by a breakdown in law and order, which did not afford the provisional government the luxury of a pre-reform period in which a broad consensus on strategy could be reached before reforms were implemented (Demekas and Khan 1991). As a result, many reforms had to be modified or replaced later. In addition, although their stated purpose was to move toward a market economy, much of the 1990 reforms were geared more toward crisis management and ap-

peasing vocal demands from the population. In particular, expansionary fiscal and monetary policies were pursued; revenues declined while expenditures on subsidies, pensions and transfers increased; and food exports were banned to improve the domestic availability of food. The authorities pursued these policies because they considered them necessary to ensure social peace *vis-à-vis* improving living standards (Demekas and Khan 1991). All of these measures contributed to a deteriorating macroeconomic situation in 1990, one that led to a reconsideration of reform priorities and an emphasis on macroeconomic stabilization in conjunction with an IMF stand-by arrangement that became operative in April 1991.

In 1991, Romania began to implement a package of reforms that was similar to Poland's. The new reform strategy consisted of price and trade liberalization, tax reforms and an incomes policy similar to Poland's. Yet price liberalization was implemented gradually, in three stages (November 1990, April and July 1991), and other measures went slowly as well, such as subsidy reductions. As a result, the Romanian economy performed more poorly than Poland's in terms of growth. Romania did not experience positive growth until 1993. Its inflation rate did not peak at as high a level as Poland's, but it stayed in the triple-digit range for three years. More importantly, it did not achieve the threshold below-40 percent inflation rate so crucial for growth as quickly as Poland. In 1994 inflation finally fell to double digits, but it was well above the 40-percent mark, while Poland's was below that mark in 1994. Finally, living standards were roughly half those of Poland. In Romania, average real wages declined until 1993, and did not become positive until 1995. Labor costs per hour declined until 1992, but by 1995 were still less than its 1990 level. GDP per head declined until 1992, when it began steadily rising. However, by 1995 GDP per head in Romania was much lower than its 1989 level and half the level of Poland's in 1995. Private consumption in Romania declined until 1993, and in 1995 was also half that of Poland. Ironically, the Romanian program emphasized its desire to maintain living standards as the reason it chose gradual implementation over shock therapy.

Romania did not have political consensus on how reforms should be pursued, and had little time to draw up a coherent set of reforms before social unrest became a factor influencing the reforms. Iliescu, a former party member, came to power in December 1989 in a coup that overthrew the Ceausescu government. Immediately, the Iliescu government lacked the legitimacy of the Polish government because of Iliescu's ties to the old regime. This narrowed the potential for a window of opportunity, although this still could have been utilized had there been a very strong consensus on the part of politicians and policymakers. However, such consensus did not exist. As economic policy was being discussed, a breakdown of law and order was occurring, and the anticipation of the negative consequences of reform was becoming palpable as output declined. Social unrest increased due to this, and *ex-ante* political constraints emerged. In February 1990, for example, a large group of coal miners converged in Bucharest to demand that the government protect their standard of living (Poirot 1996). Iliescu gave into their demands with large pay increases, at a time when fiscal policy should have been tightened. The failure to resist such demands, and the willingness of the government to incorporate *ex-ante* political costs into its reform policies, led to poor policy being haphazardly drawn up and implemented throughout 1990. Internally, decision-making was blocked by a lack of consensus, and externally, political groups had the time to gather momentum because reforms were not implemented strongly and immediately.

In 1991, when a solid, coherent reform package was designed and began to be implemented, the effects of incorporating *ex-ante* political constraints became apparent. The Romanian population would likely not tolerate harsh reforms; the window of opportunity had passed. Romania was forced to implement many reforms gradually. A key example is price liberalization. Instead of liberalizing the majority of its prices immediately, Romania did so in three stages from November 1990 to July 1991. Gradual price liberalization can be very dangerous, as noted previously with the Russian example. In addition, gradual price liberalization prolongs the period of high inflation, imposing long-term costs on the population. Yet the

greater long-term costs were borne for short-term political acceptance. Such acceptance is unstable however; gradual implementation can lead to a backlash that forces governments to abandon sound policies. Such a backlash would be an example of *ex-post* political constraints. By incorporating *ex-ante* political constraints into its early reforms, Romania was forced to implement further reforms gradually, making it more vulnerable to *ex-post* political constraints.

IMPLICATIONS FOR A CUBAN TRANSITION

These vastly different experiences point to the degree of significance political constraints have for transition paths. Gradual implementation of stabilization policies is not a feasible option in the presence of political constraints as it can lead to policy redesign based on political considerations instead of efficiency considerations. This in turn can lead to less-than-optimal outcomes in terms of slower, lower growth and delayed increases in living standards. Poland utilized its window of opportunity to bypass *ex-ante* political constraints, and embedded its reforms so that any potential anti-reform governments that came to power would have difficulty undoing key reforms. Romania implemented its reforms gradually, allowing *ex-ante* political constraints to anticipate negative effects of reforms and build momentum in opposition. Thus the government had trouble continuing to implement the rest of its reforms as the negative effects were observed. A vicious cycle in which *ex-ante* opposition gathered momentum and fed into *ex-post* opposition was created. The key question, then, is how can a post-transition, pro-reform Cuban government implement and make irreversible such reforms in the face of political pressure?

Cuba should follow the path of Poland to negate such a cycle from occurring in its post-transition environment. Rapid implementation of stabilization policies can be achieved in several ways despite the threat of political constraints. First, a government can draw on the evidence showing the benefits of rapid implementation to quell any *ex-ante* rent-seekers' protestations by utilizing its window of opportunity. Second, governments can create the basis for a liberalized *de novo* private sector, thus providing alternatives for those potentially made redundant by stabilization measures. To negate the effects of *ex-post* rent seekers, governments can embed reforms with macroeconomic "poison pills" (Boone and Hørder 1998) to constrain future governments and make reforms more palatable by obtaining conditional assistance from external actors.

Consensus and the Window of Opportunity

If there is an internal consensus on which stabilization policies will create a pro-growth environment, those policies are best implemented while a window of opportunity exists. Cuba will have the benefit of ten-plus years of transition in Eastern Europe to draw on; this may negate the possibility of a lack of consensus. That is, if those policymakers in charge of a Cuban transition are well informed about "best practices" such as the Polish path of stabilization, there may be little need for discussion over what the policy should be. The specifics of the macroeconomic situation in Cuba, as well as some differing initial conditions, will mean that policies will not be an exact replica. However, it is a reasonable assumption that Cuba might choose policies that look much like Poland's. If this is so, one *ex-ante* political cost—a lack of consensus—will be negated.

Cuba can negate the other potential *ex-ante* political costs by utilizing the window of opportunity. The key concern of a government in doing so is that the pain associated with reforms will result in voters ousting the government. Yet there is quite a bit of evidence to the contrary on this. Balcerowicz (1997) notes that the normal predisposition of voters is to judge a government by a change in their life situation, but in times of special conditions voters are aware that negative conditions are unavoidable and due to external forces, and may respond accordingly. Hence he states that the window of opportunity represents a "period of extraordinary politics." To take price liberalization as an example, early and decisive price liberalization signals to the public that a new government is intent on making a fundamental break with the past (Roberts 1994). This in turn lends credibility to other reform and stabilization efforts.

Creating a *De Novo* Private Sector

Typically, *ex-ante* groups are labor groups anticipating a negative change in their lifestyle due to reforms.

Indeed, Fidrmuc (1996) notes that voters in regions hit hard by unemployment are more inclined to vote for parties opposing reforms. The policy implication is that economic reforms should be designed in such a way that they avoid excessive unemployment. Unemployment will be a likely effect of reforms in Cuba, but a government can combat *ex-ante* groups by implementing reforms that have an immediate, positive short-term effect, such as liberalizing legislation on small- and medium-sized private enterprises. In Cuba, for example, a potentially large service sector of *paladares* (home restaurants) and *casas particulares* (private lodgings) are continually repressed by the current government (Castañeda and Montalván 1993). Legalizing such enterprises would create a base of support for reforms, and the potential for workers displaced from industry and agriculture to find new employment in the service sector.

Creating Irreversibility: Poison Pills and International Aid

If *ex-ante* costs are negated, many *ex-post* costs will not arise. However, those that do should not be able to undermine key reforms. There are several measures a democratic Cuban government can take to embed its reforms and create irreversibility. First, immediate stabilization and a government committed to it will itself be politically self-sustaining. As Åslund, Boone and Johnson (1996) note, when stabilization is launched, the industrial lobby "cries out." Yet its resistance is dependent upon the response and credibility of the government, and eventually managers will begin adjusting when they realize subsidies will no longer be coming their way. The industrial lobby will break up, eliminating one *ex-post* political constraint to reform.

Another measure is what Boone and Hørder (1998) call a "macroeconomic poison pill." Poison pills are essentially reforms embedded with some measure that changes the incentives of reform reversal for future governments. An example is Estonia's currency board, which has stringent rules about foreign currency sales and a pegged exchange rate; any change in the rate requires the approval of parliament, which would likely result in a run on foreign reserves. This changes the incentives structure for reversing reforms because the penalty of policy reversal is greater than the net gain. This can only work in certain cases, but it is worth considering in the face of strong *ex-post* political constraints.

A final measure that both Diamond (1995) and Boone and Hørder (1998) mention is conditional assistance. Usually this comes in the form of aid or technical assistance, the key example being the IMF. What role the United States may play in a Cuban transition is unclear; certainly some assistance will likely come from either the U.S. government or the many Cuban exile groups waiting for an end to the Castro regime. An IMF loan, in contrast, would be based more Cuba's fiscal and economic policies and performance than on domestic U.S. politics. Although problems with some aspects of IMF lending have recently emerged, it does, for better or worse, provide compelling incentives for countries that need its help. If a government does not demonstrate commitment in pursuing reformist policies, the IMF will suspend its loans. While this has not guaranteed non-reversal in the past—in Romania, there was policy reversal after 1995 despite its IMF loan—it does act as an incentive, and a government that is contemplating undermining reforms because of political pressure will need to consider conditional assistance in its cost-benefit analysis.

CONCLUSION

Stabilization is a prerequisite for growth. As part of an overall package of reforms designed to move economies from central planning to the market, stabilization policies should be instituted early to create a growth-conducive environment. While many policymakers favor gradual implementation of stabilization policies, the evidence of a decade of transition suggests that rapid implementation leads to faster recovery of growth and a greater rise in living standards. Yet gradual implementation is often pursued due to political constraints. Achieving rapid implementa-

tion in the face of political constraints is difficult, but not impossible.

Poland was able to implement its stabilization polices rapidly, with little internal government opposition or opposition from the population, for several reasons. It quickly drew up a stabilization policy, in a few weeks, with consensus on the part of policymakers; it employed the window of opportunity created by the severe economic crisis to push through potentially unpopular reforms; and it utilized its legitimacy as an ex-communist government to make the reforms credibility and thus difficult for future governments to reverse.

In contrast, Romania initially suffered from a lack of consensus on the part of policymakers in creating stabilization policies, which led to delayed implementation and the appearance of rent-seekers applying pressure on the government to modify its policy design. By failing to quickly design a stabilization policy, Romania lost the window of opportunity in which to apply it. This in turn made it difficult for Romania to rapidly implement future policies.

The lessons for a transition in Cuba are twofold: any Cuban government instituting stabilization policies must incorporate *ex-ante* and *ex-post* political constraints into its policy implementation. First, *ex-ante* political constraints can be circumvented by utilizing the window of opportunity present at the outset of transition. Second, *ex-post* political constraints can be avoided by embedding reforms; in this way, the net political costs of undoing reforms is too great for it to be considered a viable option. Additionally, by developing the basis for a *de novo* private sector that could absorb unemployed persons, governments can minimize the pool of rent seekers concerned about redundancies that are the result of reforms. By anticipating and responding to these constraints, Cuba may be able to avoid gradual implementation and the negative economic outcomes that follow.

SOURCES

Åslund, A., Boone, P. and Johnson, S. (1996). "How to Stabilize: Lessons from Post-Communist Countries," *Brookings Papers on Economic Activity*, Vol. 1996, No. 1.

Balcerowicz, L. (1997). "The Interplay Between Economic and Political Transition," in Zecchini, S. (ed.), *Lessons from the Economic Transition* (London: Kluwer Academic Publishers).

Blanchard, O., Summers, L., Dornbusch, R., Layard, R. and Krugman, P. (1991). *Reform in Eastern Europe* (Cambridge: MIT Press).

Boone, P. and Hørder, J. (1998). "Inflation: Causes, Consequences and Cures," in Boone, P., Gomulka, S., and Layard, R. (eds.), *Emerging from Communism: Lessons from Russia, China and Eastern Europe* (Cambridge: MIT Press).

Castañeda, R. and Montalván, G. (1993). "Transition in Cuba: A Comprehensive Stabilization Proposal and Some Key Issues," *Cuba in Transition—Volume 3*.

Coricelli, F. (1996). "Fiscal Constraints, Reform Strategies, and the Speed of Transition: The Case of Central-Eastern Europe," Center for Economic Policy Research, Discussion Paper No. 1339.

De Melo, M., Denizer, C., Gelb, A. and Tenev, S. (2001). "Circumstance and Choice: The Role of Initial Conditions and Policies in Transition Economies," *The World Bank Economic Review*, Vol. 15, No. 1, pp. 1-31.

Demekas, D. and Khan, M. (1991). "The Romanian Economic Reform Program," International Monetary Fund Occasional Paper No. 89.

Dewatripont, M. and Roland, G. (1992). "The Virtues of Gradualism and Legitimacy in the Transition to a Market Economy," *Economic Journal*, Vol. 102, No. 411, p. 291-300.

Diamond, L. (1995). "Democracy and Economic Reform: Tensions, Compatibilities and Strategies for Reconciliation," in Lazear, E. P. (ed.), *Economic Transition in Eastern Europe and Russia. Realities of Reforms.* (Stanford, CA: Hoover Institution Press).

Economist Intelligence Unit Country Data, http://www.eiu.com.

Falcetti, E., Raiser, M. and Sanfey, P. (2000). "Defying the Odds: Initial Conditions, Reforms and Growth in the First Decade of Transition," EBRD Working Paper No. 55.

Fidrmuc, J. (1996). "Political Sustainability of Economic Reforms: Dynamics and Analysis of Regional Economic Factors," Center for Economic Research, Tilburg University, Discussion Paper No. 74.

Fischer, S., Sahay, R. and Végh, C. (1996). "Stabilization and Growth in Transition Economies: The Early Experience," International Monetary Fund Working Paper No. 31.

Funke, N. (1993). "Timing and Sequencing of Reforms: Competing Views and the Role of Credibility," *Kyklos*, Vol. 46, No. 3, pp. 337-362.

Giuriato, L. (1997). "Dynamic Constraints to Economic Transformations: An Evolutionary Perspective," *Journal of International and Comparative Economics*, Vol. 5, No. 2, pp. 177-98.

Gomulka, S. (1998) "Output: Causes of the Decline and the Recovery," in Boone, P., Gomulka, S., and Layard, R. (eds.), *Emerging from Communism: Lessons from Russia, China and Eastern Europe* (Cambridge: MIT Press).

Gomulka, S. (2000). "Macroeconomic Policies and Achievements in Transition Economies, 1989-1999," London School of Economics, Centre for Economic Performance Discussion Paper No. 475.

Lavigne, M. (1991). *The Economics of Transition* (New York: St. Martin's Press).

Lipton, D. and Sachs, J. (1990). "Creating a Market Economy in Eastern Europe: The Case of Poland," *Brookings Papers on Economic Activity*, Vol. 1990, No. 1, pp. 75-133.

Poirot, C. (1996). "Macroeconomic Policy in a Transitional Environment: Romania, 1989-1994," *Journal of Economic Issues*, Vol. 30, No. 4, pp. 1057-75.

Przeworski, A. (1991). *Democracy and the Market: Political and Economic Reforms in Eastern Europe and Latin America* (Cambridge: Cambridge University Press).

Roberts, B. (1994). "Inflation and the Monetary Regime During the Cuban Economic Transition," *Cuba in Transition—Volume 4* (Washington: Association for the Study of the Cuban Economy).

Roland, G. (1994). "The Role of Political Constraints in Transition Strategies," *The Economics of Transition*, Vol. 2, No.1, pp. 27-41.

Sachs, J. (1992). "The Economic Transformation of Eastern Europe: The Case of Poland," *The American Economist*, Vol. 36, No. 2, pp. 3-11.

Shleifer, A. (1997). "Government in Transition," *European Economic Review*, Vol. 41, No. 3-5, pp. 385-410.

UN Statistics Division Social Indicators, http://unstats.un.org/unsd/demographic/social/default.htm.

¿SOCIALISTA O SUBDESARROLLADO?: UNA PROPUESTA SOBRE LA TRANSICIÓN ECONÓMICA DE CUBA

Alfie Antonio Ulloa Urrutia[1]

Pronto se cumplirán quince años del fin de los sistemas socialistas que orbitaban en torno a la Unión Soviética, un acontecimiento que desenmascaró los íconos de la publicidad y la fábula del obrero todopoderoso y al que cada país aportó dictaduras y violaciones, déficit y distorsiones, enormes e ineficientes aparatos estatales. Sin distinguir latitudes ni poderío, se evidenció la incapacidad económica de la Planificación y la incapacidad política de la Socialización, el caso cubano es sólo otro de los fracasos.

Como a sus antiguos socios, la crisis del experimento socialista implicó un costo gigantesco y será una pesada carga en el futuro cubano, una carga que descansa mayoritariamente sobre un pueblo indefenso respecto de sus gobernantes. Luego de treinta años de distorsiones subsidiadas y trece de *período especial,* la isla tiene destruida su capacidad productiva, desempleada una enorme población y comprometida dos décadas de exportaciones en el pago de su deuda externa, sólo mencionando algunos de sus padecimientos. Para el necesario debate sobre su reconstrucción económica es vital diagnosticar su estado actual y sus alternativas de desarrollo futuras, dado que cualquier programa de transición que se haga deberá reconocer el largo plazo que exige su aplicación. La hipótesis central de este escrito es que en el diagnóstico de la Cuba de hoy y más aún el de la futura e inminente transición, estará más marcado por los últimos 13 años de *período especial* que por los 30 años de Planificación que le antecedieron. Esta hipótesis se sustenta en varias razones, pero principalmente en reconocer que si algo tuvo de *especial* este *período*, es haber enseñado al cubano que su sobrevivencia y bienestar depende de su capacidad y gestión, más que de la asignación oficial.

La primera sección de este documento refiere el punto de partida de la transición cubana. La segunda parte escoge hechos fundamentales del proceso de transición. Las conclusiones se entregan en la tercera y última parte.

LA HERENCIA SOCIALISTA

El debate sobre le economía planificada antecede su propia existencia. Desde el inicio se argumentó a su favor la superioridad moral del objetivo y se la rebatió por la supresión de libertades individuales que requería. Luego apareció el socialismo con gentilicio, mientras cada país "adherido" pretendía aporte y renovación. Detrás de diferencias cosméticas es posible sintetizar su argumento esencial: dualidad monopólica del Partido Comunista, concentrando los activos económicos y el poder de coerción legal.

Para Kornai (2000), no es posible comparar socialismo y capitalismo en igualdad de condiciones, porque exagerariamos la importancia de un sistema que no pasó de ser "una aberración temporal al curso de los eventos históricos." El autor propone en cambio

1. El autor está en deuda con los comentarios y recomendaciones recibidos de Antonio Gayoso y Jorge Pérez-López. Los errores u omisiones, así como las opiniones aquí recogidas, representan únicamente al autor y son de su exclusiva responsabilidad, y en ningún caso de las instituciones en las que se desempeña.

(Cuadro No. 1) que comparemos sus bases prácticas fundamentales, no la aproximación teórico-normativa de una organización que cree y aplica las ideas socialistas, sino del sistema que efectivamente se instaló por la fuerza en "26 países y se llamó a sí mismo Sistema Socialista."

Cuadro 1.

Sistema Socialista	Sistema Capitalista
1.- Poder político indivisible, no desafiable y único del Partido Comunista. Concentración de poderes.	1.- Poder político fraccionario, desafiable y competitivo. Equilibrio de poderes.
2.- Dominio de la Propiedad Estatal	2.- Dominio de la Propiedad Privada
3.- Dominio de la coordinación burocrática en la asignación: criterio planificador, precios fijos. El Partido decide.	3.- Dominio del mercado en la asignación: criterios de uso alternativo, precios libres. El Estado regula.
4.- Indisciplina presupuestaria. Subsidios.	4.- Presupuestos restrictivos. Quiebra.
5.- Mercado orientado al vendedor. Escasez crónica. Desempleo en el puesto.	5.- Mercado orientado al comprador. Desempleo "natural." Ciclo económico fluctuante.

Fuente: En base a Kornai (2000).

Fuente: Los tres primeros definen la estructura, el resto aparecen como efecto. La propiedad estatal sobre los medios de producción,[2] que reparte planificadamente beneficios y costos, define el sistema económico socialista; mientras la propiedad privada y la asignación por el mercado, el capitalista. La planificación intentó suprimir al mercado (punto 3) porque un planificador que conozca precios relativos y relaciones de escasez de cada producto, en cada momento del tiempo y para cada individuo, teóricamente es capaz de hacerlo. La práctica en cambio lo desechó, porque no es posible sujetar los supuestos ni emular al mercado en la formación y trasmisión de precios, tampoco conocer centralizadamente gustos y necesidades a cada instante. Adicionalmente, basta que la política entre en juego para que la planificación pierda el objetivo de eficiencia e intente cumplir otros, publicitariamente más aventajados o políticamente más atractivos.[3]

La tragedia económica del socialismo es considerar la escasez como un problema político; hasta la inflación resulta de un acto intencional de capitalista para exprimir al trabajador. Note en la propaganda que la escasez exclusivamente es responsabilidad del obrero que no asume su papel de vanguardia, del campesino o intelectual pequeño burgués, del sabotaje capitalista o del embargo, jamás del Partido-propietario. Hoy, sin embargo, ya conocemos el fin de la "tragedia de los comunes" y sabemos que el consumidor (familia o empresa) que tiene asignado un vendedor, no puede evitar que este ejerza poder monopólico vía cantidad o calidad, dado que los precios están fijos. Eso es la economía orientada al proveedor, donde el oferente (Estatal y asignado) "hace un favor" al demandante, un favor que es la diferencia entre el precio real (de mercado negro) y el oficial.

Los planes económicos decidían qué, cuándo y cuánto consumiría cada persona, y determinaban la cantidad de insumos requeridos, todo calculado matemáticamente.[4] Cumplir el plan aseguraba la canasta y era la medida de eficiencia, sobrecumplirlo era un "exceso" de eficiencia y una buena oportunidad política para discursar. Considere los problemas agenciales: los únicos incentivos son políticos, los salarios no dependen del desempeño y están fijos; el pleno empleo está asegurado, de modo que no habrá interés ninguno en aumentar productividad o esfuerzo y sí para reducirlos. A pesar de esto, el exceso de empleo inútil se contrasta con la falta de mano de obra en sectores claves, algo anticipable considerando que el exceso no se mueve hacia la escasez, por salarios que

---

2. El Partido controla el capital, la banca, la industria y la capacidad técnica de investigación, también la tierra y hasta el ganado, la producción de todos lo insumos, los mercados y así sucesivamente. El control sobre el trabajo, el capital humano y los factores inactivos, es completo a través de la educación, el sindicato único y el monopsonio del empleo.

3. En tiempos de Marx la oferta constituía el único instrumento de economía teórica, pues la función de demanda se formalizó a fines del siglo XIX y no fue incorporada a la doctrina monolítica comunista. Hay mayores complejidades, pero nunca dijo Marx que el hombre nuevo sería "bueno" por leerle, es la planificación lo que permite al "ser novedoso" el goce de satisfacción plena.

4. Definido el nivel de consumo deseado y conocida la función de producción, la matriz insumo-producto determina el requerimiento de insumos. De modo que la planificación es teóricamente razonable.

lo desincentivan o leyes que lo prohíben. En la fijación del salario el gobierno ejerce su poder monopsónico pagando salarios bajos, en los que implícitamente cobra las "regalías" que entregará. Porque el trabajo no tiene usos alternativos no hay desempleo, pero sí muchos inactivos que prefieren gastar su tiempo en otras actividades más rentables, habitualmente ilegales. Por último, no importa si los salarios se financian con emisión o subsidios, el gobierno no escatima porque a través del empleo logra control político absoluto.

Si la transición cubana se iniciara en 1989 esta descripción aplicaría a toda su economía y en detalles sería diferente de sus antiguos socios del Este Europeo, hoy en cambio los principales sectores económicos funcionan lejos del Plan. Tras el fin del subsidio externo el país debió forzadamente ajustar y rigidizar sus presupuestos, reviviendo olvidadas prácticas contables, reduciendo el sobrempleo y limitando la emisión. Como resultado: cerró plantas y abrió espacios privados, limitó la producción, elevó los precios y mantuvo los salarios. El cambio definitivo fue la legalización del dólar, que atrajo remesas y capitales extranjeros, abriendo oportunidades al mercado. Como en el capitalismo, la escasez dejaba ser un problema de abastecimiento y pasaba a ser un problema de ingresos. En la Universidad reapareció el clásico texto de Samuelson.

Nuestro análisis sobre el futuro económico cubano considera cuatro observaciones fundamentales, que hacen el sustento para la hipótesis inicial. Primero, no es lo mismo la propiedad estatal soviética, con 70 años de comunismo construido sobre un sistema feudal, o la reconstrucción europea sobre las ruinas de posguerra, que el socialismo cubano. El gobierno de 1959 heredó una economía golpeada por tres años de conflicto civil y guerrillero, pero a la cabeza en la competitividad regional. Además, los años de dictadura

política han sido variables en economía, porque hubo propiedad privada hasta fines de los sesenta[5] y reaparecieron algunos mercados a fines de los ochenta. A ratos pareciera que esta cercanía temporal ha mantenido el espíritu empresarial y la capacidad de gestión privada latente, a juzgar por la proliferación de pequeños negocios, por como se forzó la liberalización del dólar o la capacidad de un reducido número de pequeños agricultores para mantener abastecido el mercado paralelo.

En segundo lugar, más de un millón de cubanos han abandonado la isla, creando una masa critica de cubanos insertos en un mundo de mercado y democracias. El Exilio puede contribuir de manera fundamental en la transición, no solo con su reincorporación a la fuerza laboral, también aportando capital, tecnología, prácticas empresariales, contactos de negocios, etc., y aún sin regresar masivamente habrán de estar presentes en esta transición.

El tercer factor es el geográfico. Si la antigua maldición de estar "tan lejos de Dios y tan cerca de EEUU" es hoy el principal activo mexicano, lo será también de Cuba en el futuro.[6] Esto debe fortalecerse económica y políticamente, pero es desde el inicio una ventaja de localización. La isla también está muy cercana a Europa y a otros mercados latinoamericanos, pero sin dudas la relación comercial con Estados Unidos marcará el paso de la recuperación local.

Finalmente, los años sin "muro" no han pasado en vano. La principal causa recesiva de los países socialistas fue la desaparición del bloque comercial en torno a la URSS,[7] un impacto que la isla ya sufrió con caídas de 35-45% del PIB entre 1989 y 1993,[8] que provocaron a pesar de encuentros violentos entre política y reactivación, la aventura reestructuradora y el desarrollo del "área dólar." El violento escenario político de la caída soviética, la llegada del turismo, el éxodo

---

5. Aunque a fines de los sesenta el Estado controlaba ya toda la economía, podríamos considerar a partir de la Constitución Socialista de 1976 el inicio "oficial" del socialismo real cubano, aunque antecedido por 15 años de preparación errática, nacionalización y sociabilización forzosa.

6. Mantenerse autárquico dentro del bloque socialista generó una enorme distorsión en la economía cubana. Montenegro y Soto (2000) estimaron que un 80% del intercambio comercial pasaría a EEUU cuando el embargo se elimine.

7. Tomando las antiguas Repúblicas de la URSS, Europa del Este y Mongolia (26 países) el promedio de crecimiento de los 80's fue de 2.9%, mientras entre 90-97 la caída fue de—5,7%. Banco Mundial.

8. Mesa-Lago (2001).

desesperado y la dependencia de las remesas, han destruido los cimientos ideológicos y de paso han dividido la isla en dos mundos económicos. El prospero, el del "área dólar" vivió una pre-transición al liberarse del plan e independizarse de los subsidios, también ha sabido controlar y convivir con la cúpula y está en mejor situación para la transición siguiente; la paupérrima "área en moneda nacional," aunque traumatizada, está rezagada y demandará ajustes mayores y radicales.

Estos antecedentes condicionan el proceso y cubanizan la transición, separándola de los procesos similares que los antiguos socios políticos siguieron en su huída hacia la democracia. No se trata de expulsar a los Asesores ni ignorar la economía, sino de hacer el mejor análisis de donde estamos y donde queremos llegar. Sabemos que el diagnóstico de la situación cubana es de gravedad extrema: una sociedad sin derechos y una economía sin derechos de propiedad; distorsionada por la protección sectorial, los privilegios y la intervención; informal y de subsistencia; con autoridades débiles, subordinadas y políticas; un Estado productor hipertrofiado e interventor, de arcas deficitarias y seguridad social sobreutilizada, con un ejército de burócratas y sin sociedad civil.

Profundizando sobre la hipótesis inicial y buscando las similitudes cubanas, el diagnóstico que creemos más realista es que Cuba, con su nula democracia, mal mercado y fragilidad institucional, está más cerca hoy del pasado latinoamericano, que del antiguo Este planificado y Europeo.

HECHOS FUNDAMENTALES DE LA TRANSICIÓN

¿Qué Hacer?

Para Cuba anhelo un Estado democrático, con separación de los tres poderes y economía de mercado. Un sistema donde la iniciativa y responsabilidad individual determinen la acción de los agentes, circunscritos a un sistema legal de garantías y obligaciones Constitucionales, donde el Estado provea bienes públicos, asegure igualdad ante la ley y de oportunidades, teniendo al bienestar de la población como objetivo.

Entonces, la transición debe comenzar con una Constitución distinta de la actual, que resguarde los derechos y modifique el aparato gubernamental, generando un poder político equilibrado en su estructura y desafiable en las urnas. Entonces podrá iniciarse la urgente reforma micro y macroeconómica, con responsabilidad y acción coordinada en los tres Poderes del Estado. Evito el uso de la palabra, pero esto será ciertamente una revolución. En este proceso de gestación y renacer legal, las autoridades económicas y políticas tienen la obligación de validar el modelo y crear las condiciones para que aparezca y se desarrolle el mercado. Es necesario limitar el papel a crear las condiciones y evitar la tentación de crear los mercados.

¿Cómo Hacerlo?

En tamaña reforma es imposible la "sintonía fina," el retoque especial que cataliza un sector, elimina la traba innecesaria o la décima excesiva, y será necesario aceptar el sacrificio de varios niveles de eficiencia y ortodoxia los primeros años, a cambio de la paz social, la consolidación del sistema y del nuevo gobierno. La teoría de laboratorio no es aplicable, ni aún es deseable a este nivel de reforma, porque en este proceso lo perfecto se enemista de lo bueno, cuando se incorpora el factor de economía política. Cualquier medición de eficiencia es subjetiva y por ende la duración de los plazos dependerá del proceso mismo y aunque suene tautológico, el plazo será el inverso de la velocidad a la que sea posible hacer las reformas, lo que dependerá a su vez del proceso de aprendizaje de agentes, políticos y reguladores. En resumen, habrá que hacerlo con cautela, lo que equivale a decir gradualmente.[9]

---

9. Es evidente que un proceso acelerado será más errático, lo que arriesga la venta masiva del país, la captura de los sectores por los actuales jerarcas y al máximo nivel de incertidumbre y descontento por parte de la población.

Cuadro 2. Etapas de la Transición

Corto Plazo	Mediano Plazo	Largo Plazo
Facilitar la reasignación de recursos y la creación del mercado interno.	Consolidar el mercado y su desarrollo autónomo.	Perfeccionar el mercado y eliminar las distorsiones.
Sostener los ingresos de los desempleados	Facilitar la inserción internacional y la apertura de mercados.	Consolidar la participación en mercados extranjeros.
Se mantienen subsidios y participación estatal.	Mejorar la focalización de los subsidios y minimizar la participación estatal.	Transformar el subsidio de desempleo en un seguro.
Un 60% de eficiencia[a] será una meta aceptable para el primer gobierno.	Meta 85% de eficiencia.	Objetivo y dirección de la eficiencia máxima.

a. Algún indicador mixto que creemos para evaluar la evolución.

¿Cuándo Hacerlo?

El gusto por la intervención del Estado se ha difundido incluso en los países con fuerte respeto por la propiedad privada y orientación al mercado y su maduración hacia la eficiencia ha estado más influida por el avance del mercado que por su propia reflexión. Por esta razón es importante enfrentar el proceso cubano con una fórmula real, aceptando desde el inicio que este tránsito en dirección al mercado ha sido un proceso complejo, que se ha impuesto en el mundo luego de 50 años de lenta consolidación y complejas negociaciones.

El Cuadro No. 2 resume brevemente los objetivos de cada etapa, según los niveles de eficiencia a los que el equipo económico debería aspirar a conseguir. Como ya hemos expuesto, en el corto plazo es impracticable una liberalización plena o aspirar a la eficiencia máxima que promueven los terapeutas a través del "choque," puesto que el Gobierno estará obligado a participar activamente en la consolidación del mercado y a mantener importantes niveles de subsidio a los servicios sociales, al mismo tiempo que sigue siendo accionista mayoritario en los proyectos de asociación que hoy mantiene con los inversionistas extranjeros. Mientras el mercado se desarrolle internamente y el país sea capaz de atraer inversión extranjera, especialmente a los servicios públicos, el gobierno podrá reducir el nivel de subsidios y al mismo tiempo focalizar mejor aquellos que aún mantenga. La normativa de los sectores regulados (tarifados) debe ya permitir que los capitales internacionales inviertan en los sectores monopólicos del gobierno y los servicios sociales. La banca privada, domestica y externa, estarán limitados en sus operaciones de flujos de capitales, al menos en los movimientos trasnfronterizos de corto plazo.

No antes de diez años, cuando el gobierno haya madurado y perfeccionado su componente técnico, y consolidado un Estado Democrático de Derechos validado por las urnas y equilibrado por los otros poderes, entonces estará en posición de liberar el mercado hasta el nivel máximo que sea posible. Esto significa que las cargas sociales a cuenta de los fondos públicos se reducirán, porque ya los capitales extranjeros estarán en condiciones de invertir con garantías plenas y también con responsabilidades claras, los seguros personales y las cuentas de capitalización individual deben sustituir al menos en parte a los servicios públicos de reparto. A esta última etapa corresponde también la apertura y liberalización del mercado financiero y la cuenta de capitales, siempre manteniendo las capacidades de la autoridad monetaria para la intervención, así como la de otras entidades reguladoras. Es el momento para llevar al mínimo los aranceles a las importaciones (tal vez un 5% parejo) y comenzar el cierre de los subsidios.

Microeconomía

Mercados

Los primeros diagnósticos sobre el surgimiento del mercado en las economías socialistas padecía exceso de optimismo y algo de inocencia. Enfocándose en los esfuerzos enormes que sus gobiernos debieron desplegar para contener los mercados no planificados, se decía que una fuerza latente resistía la represión del sistema y que bastaría omitir esos esfuerzos para develar el mercado que luchaba por nacer, encabezado por nuevos capitalistas que surgirían espontáneamente de obreros y profesionales socialistas.

Ahora tenemos información para evaluar esta idea, tan platónica como la del antiguo hombre nuevo socialista. Los mercados reprimidos dejaron de ser rentables a precios reales, mostrando que la intensa actividad subterránea es mayormente arbitraje entre precios oficiales y de mercado negro, tráfico de bienes robados al gobierno y los inversionistas o intermediación por información y derechos especiales. Cuando precios y salarios se liberan, las normas absurdas se eliminan y las leyes se aplican, el mercado negro pierde rentabilidad y desaparece, la asignación planificada y la economía del oferente también caen y no se necesita mayor privilegio para adquirir un bien que estar dispuesto y en capacidad de pagarlo. Estos efectos se refuerzan con el *shock* competitivo que implica abrir la economía a proveedores internacionales.

Vamos al cuadro cubano. Varios negocios *cuentapropistas* aparecieron en la isla, siempre pequeños servicios enfocados al turismo y a la demanda local en dólares. Para el Partido eran de máxima peligrosidad política, pero debió tolerarlos como paliativo tras el corte de las transferencias soviéticas, también resultaron una amenaza económica para el gobierno y sus socios extranjeros, que pronto reclamaron competencia desleal.[10] A pesar de estar contenidas por impuestos y prohibiciones y ser vistas como un mal amenazante, subsisten más de un centenar de miles. Algunas de estas tienen potencial, que reforzarán cuando se levante el ambiente hostil y constituirán el sector de pequeña y mediana empresa (PYME) cubano, típicamente familiar y capitalizado por remesas, que competirá por precios en el sector turístico y podrá abastecer algo de la demanda interna. Su futuro dependerá de la apertura comercial y de la política nacional de soporte.

Aunque una parte del sector estatal permanece en el invernadero de la planificación subsidiada, otra ha entrado al mercado aprovechando la liberación del dólar, que le permitió al gobierno consolidar nuevas sociedades con extranjeros para vender al pueblo la antigua canasta oficial garantizada.[11] Este sector presenta características de mercado, aunque padece regulaciones y distorsiones, protección y colusión y muchos de ellos operan en base a privilegios, explotando al Ejército Juvenil del Trabajo o el Servicio Militar. Algunas están en buen pie para enfrentar la transición, porque se han fundado por criterio de rentabilidad y tienen activos importantes, luego podrán optimizar y aumentar su productividad al liberarse de la intermediación estatal, reducir sus gastos en corrupción y sus pérdidas por robo, o mientras puedan importar sus insumos.

La transición entonces será un proceso de reasignación entre los mercados que se consolidan, crean o destruyen. Este proceso es necesario y deseable, pues con solo eliminar las distorsiones artificiales e imponer un criterio de rentabilidad, se estará ganando en eficiencia y los beneficios posteriores serán enormes. Pero también lo serían los costos sí la creación de empleo es menor que la destrucción, como podemos razonablemente anticipar.

A mediano plazo es posible eliminar el sector estatal mientras se expande el privado, a corto plazo no hay tal alternativa: se subsidia a la empresa o al desempleado mismo. Esto es discutible, pero dentro del proceso en que estaremos me parece preferible subsidiar al desempleado y no a la empresa, primero porque resulta menos oneroso para las arcas fiscales, siendo más eficiente y más barato, pero también porque dentro del proceso de reasignación es necesario destruir los empleos ineficientes, en tal sentido este sub-

---

10. Ellos tributan cargas variadas y asumen fuertes costos al importar prácticamente todos sus insumos y cubrir su plantilla salarial en divisas. Pagan salarios fijos en dólares a la oficina estatal, que luego paga en pesos cubanos al trabajador a la tasa oficial de uno por uno, como el tipo de cambio real es un dólar por veinte pesos, las empresas pagan a sus trabajadores 200 dólares y reciben productividad por 200 pesos, es decir por 10 dólares. En tanto, los negocios cubanos comenzaron clandestinos, no tributaban y pagaban salarios no intermediados. Además, los negocios cubanos se mantenían en sus orígenes a base de productos robados.

11. Leche, pasta dental, pan, aceite, todas las conservas, las únicas proteínas posibles de adquirir, ropa, calzado y medicinas se venden exclusivamente en dólares. Y es que mas que bienes suntuarios, las empresas mixtas producen para la canasta básica, los mismos bienes que antes se entregaban racionados, como parte de aquel contrato socialista: canasta, salud y educación "gratis" por la renuncia de los derechos cívicos.

sidio se justifica por mantener el ingreso y no el empleo. Esto es necesario para garantizar a la sociedad algún grado de certeza respecto del nivel de vida, lo que requiere también de un plan de retiro y algún nivel de soporte a los actuales beneficios sociales. Capacitación y reconversión son medidas muy oportunas en este período, no solo eleva la probabilidad de reinserción, también compensa los efectos morales del desempleo. En resumen, con la reforma inicial es necesario generar las condiciones para una solución "Pareto Superior," que a lo menos mantenga un nivel de vida igual o mejor que el actual, que sumado a los intangibles de democracia y libertad, reduzca la oposición interna y permita la consolidación del proceso. Esto no es tan eficiente como quisiéramos, pero otra cosa no es factible políticamente.

Recursos

Si la transición es reasignación, junto a permitir el movimiento de factores hay que anticipar el impacto de las políticas. Los capitales buscarán rentabilidad,[12] lo que depende del mercado interno y la proyección externa, pero también de impuestos,[13] regulaciones y garantías de propiedad (uso y transferencia), entre otros. Los trabajadores buscarán el mejor salario, emplearse depende de las alternativas disponibles y estas de la legislación laboral. La legislación laboral incluye al menos: salario mínimo, normas de contratación y despido, seguridad, jubilación, indemnización y una enorme cantidad de detalles. Costos asociados a la contratación o el despido encarecerán la mano de obra, con el consiguiente efecto en el desempleo; normas laxas permitirán a los empresarios ejercer su posición dominante sobre los trabajadores con el consiguiente efecto social. Para que el capital fluya es imprescindible la legislación de quiebra, esta obliga

asumir un criterio puro de rentabilidad y envía el mensaje claro y nuevo de responsabilidad privada, pero también permite que el capital y el capital humano de los empresarios fluya, una mala legislación de quiebra hace incierta la inversión, aumenta el riesgo y el costo del capital, o impide que el empresario salga del ciclo de pérdidas y logre reiniciar otra actividad.

Si el objetivo es conseguir que los recursos abandonen los sectores no productivos hacia los rentables, entonces la legislación, las instituciones y el esfuerzo inicial del gobierno deben facilitar este movimiento, ayudando al desempleado resultante a través de algún mecanismo.[14] A mediano plazo el nivel de desempleo dependerá de la legitimación del mercado y la propiedad, que junto al devenir general de la economía determinarán la capacidad de crear empleos. Luego podrá revisarse el subsidio y las otras regalías, para hacerlos más eficientes y focalizados, pasar de un subsidio a un seguro de desempleo y de un plan de retiro (reparto) a uno de capitalización individual con ahorro forzoso.

Sabemos por la experiencia del Este europeo[15] y de América Latina, que si las instituciones del Estado se resisten al cambio, la recuperación económica será más lenta, corrupta y distorsionada, sesgada hacia empresas extranjeras y costosa en términos políticos, con un efecto que predestina el modelo de desarrollo futuro.[16] Durante el primer gobierno cubano, toda la legislación y las autoridades estarán en medio de un proceso de gestación y transformación, con problemas de información, aprendizaje y credibilidad en instituciones (y su personal) claves en la formación, trasmisión y comprensión de señales relevantes para el mercado, así como en toda la gama de entes regula-

---

12. Buscarán rentas económicas ejerciendo poder de mercado mientras la regulación de competencia no esté establecida.

13. El sistema impositivo y los mecanismos de ingresos fiscales deben definirse en una etapa temprana. La estructura impositiva a las empresas influirá radicalmente en la consolidación de inversiones y mercados. Un impuesto al valor agregado parece la mejor opción como principal fuente del ingreso fiscal, es un sistema simple y fácil de administrar y con una buena política de focalización del gasto se reduce sus regresividad.

14. Naturalmente que la teoría ayuda en estos casos, se conocen las reglas generales que debe cumplir un subsidio para ser pro empleo, siendo decreciente en el tiempo, para hacerse cero en un período razonable.

15. Aslund (1998).

16. Ekelund y Tollison (1995).

dores y de competencia. Si los agentes visualizan la dirección, irán mas allá de la contingencia. Por esta razón las cláusulas de adhesión a la Comunidad Europea resultaron un excelente mapa para las economías post socialistas que aspiraban integrarla.[17] Esto permitió a los inversionistas anticipar el tipo de regulaciones y el objetivo de las políticas, al menos las cotas mínimas que debían respetar.

Cuba tiene la opción de un acuerdo amplio con EEUU para delinear el futuro marco de su política económica, eso en la práctica son los acuerdos comerciales de hoy, una forma de converger a disciplinas y principios que limiten la imaginación de autoridades creativas y aseguren consistencia (del ejecutivo y legislativo) a largo plazo. Un Acuerdo de esta amplitud es imposible de concretar inmediatamente, pero a nivel de expectativas basta un anuncio y la creación de una comisión mixta previa que avance en temas bilaterales mientras se consolida el aparato de gobierno en la isla y se crean las condiciones mínimas.

Propiedad

Un tema muy complejo será el reclamo de las propiedades confiscadas por el actual gobierno fáctico. Esto contamina la relación entre exiliados y locales, pero también enrarece el ambiente de atracción de inversiones y es un desafío de política fiscal e internacional. Las alternativas extremas serían: devolución con compensación por lucro cesante, o una ley de punto final que no reconozca y declare prescritos los derechos de los antiguos propietarios. La primera dejaría al Estado en la quiebra, la segunda ocasionaría un problema político y social de magnitudes, ninguna es eficiente *ex-ante*. La alternativa intermedia sería activar los mecanismos jurídicos internos o acudir a un tribunal internacional para evitar la demora que exige la maduración de un Poder Judicial serio y respetable en la isla, que cada parte defienda en los tribunales sus derechos y los montos de compensación.

Debe ser entendido que las compensaciones pagadas por el gobierno democrático irán directamente a reducir los fondos del gobierno para otras actividades,

de modo que en este juicio las contrapartes serán el gobierno democrático y los antiguos propietarios que reclaman. Es evidente que no se puede aislar el efecto fiscal de una operación que compense a todos los reclamantes.

Lo importante en este proceso es que el gobierno asuma el costo de los reclamos y aleje la probabilidad de demanda sobre los privados que desean invertir o participar en los procesos de privatización sobre estos activos. Algunos sectores clave deben privatizarse inmediatamente (telefonía, energía, viales, etc.) y ello sólo es posible si la amenaza de demandas compensatorias está despejada. Para poder avanzar en el proceso de privatizaciones y reconstrucción de la infraestructura del país, la devolución de los activos no puede ser una opción al final de estos juicios. Es decir, el proceso judicial terminará con una transacción por la compensación a cargo del Tesoro Público, en un monto definido por un juicio y en ningún caso con el reintegro de los bienes.

Privatizaciones

El valor de una empresa depende a lo menos de dos factores: activos corrientes y flujo esperado. Por eso privatizar es una forma de acelerar el proceso de reasignación, los activos se mueven hacia quien los valora y anticipa ingresos de su explotación. La receta inicial daba a las privatizaciones preeminencia, urgencia sobre cualquier otra medida, porque cumple una variedad de objetivos simultáneos: genera sentimientos de propiedad mientras desarma el aparato estatal y alivia el déficit, atrae inversión extranjera que ayuda la balanza de pagos, la renovación tecnológica y las exportaciones; también es una alternativa de continuidad a la empresa, que de otra forma debería ser subsidiada o desaparecer. Sin embargo, la urgencia se basó en razones políticas más que económicas y privatizar se transformó en el fin, mas que en el medio para desarrollar el mercado interno y consolidar el modelo. Hoy sabemos que ciertos métodos son superiores, tras comprobar que el mecanismo predestina la viabilidad y el resultado futuro de la empresa[18] y

---

17. Gomulka (2000).
18. Frydman (1999).

también que la urgencia no trae ningún beneficio económico.

La forma más fácil de privatizar es entregar la empresa a sus trabajadores (el "capitalismo popular"). Un mecanismo sin costo de búsqueda ni espera, con ganancia política neta y simpatía inmediata. Esta alternativa no es desechable, aunque sólo puede aplicarse a ciertas empresas pequeñas y de poco capital, a cambio de un mínimo de requisitos (formalización, algún pago o un proyecto específico). Su valor actual depende de sus ingresos futuros, lo que da a los trabajadores el incentivo correcto, pero un sistema de apoyo en capacitación y upgrading tecnológico, enmarcado dentro de la política PYME nacional, son necesarios para dar viabilidad futura real.

La forma más amplia y versátil de privatizar es a través de *vouchers*, donde el gobierno reparte la propiedad con acciones de una empresa, o de un fondo que agrupa varios activos estatales. Para formar un fondo mixto hay buenas razones, especialmente los subsidios cruzados entre sectores. La principal ventaja de este mecanismo es su flexibilidad, las acciones pueden depositarse en cuentas de capitalización para pensiones, como desahucio tras el despido, venderse en el mercado de valores o mantenerse en un porfolio estatal mientras un staff de profesionales *ad hoc* administra las empresas. El principal riesgo es diluir la propiedad en exceso y no definir claramente al controlador. La distribución (exilio vs locales) requiere un acuerdo político mayor. Empresas turísticas y algunas de rubros competitivos cabrían en este mecanismo, mientras el Estado salga de las decisiones y se mantenga un controlador capaz de operar con eficiencia.

Un método conflictivo, pero también el más promisorio es privatizar hacia afuera, licitando, concesionado o vendiendo internacionalmente. Los *outsiders* son superiores en capacidad empresarial, acceso a capital, conocimiento, el manejo de recursos humanos, etc.

Incluso se ha mostrado, que tras la venta a extranjeros los despidos son menores a lo esperado[19]. Esta es la forma de conseguir capacidad empresarial y solidez de largo plazo, porque los capitales extranjeros son los únicos capaces de absorber los monopolios estatales o enfrentar los grandes proyectos económicos que requiere la reconstrucción de infraestructura, u otros donde el capital y la escala son un factor relevante.

En cualquier caso, si la velocidad se impone como el factor determinante se condena el proceso. Para Cuba debemos diseñar un plan de eliminación paulatino de subsidios, seriedad presupuestal y privatización, en conjunto a una estrategia de desarrollo de mercado PYME, sin generar inmediatamente la destrucción del aparato productivo heredado. Para el éxito de este plan es determinante la institucionalidad a cargo, la coordinación de las autoridades y la voluntad política: transparencia, costos de operación e información y otros detalles vitales hacen recomendable un modelo similar al Húngaro, con un ente privatizador único, profesionalizado, autónomo por ley y guiado por un Directorio de composición mixta. Esta entidad (bauticémoslo Sistema Administrador de Empresas, SAE) posee todos los activos estatales enajenables y mantiene las empresas en operación, mientras dedica tiempo a la búsqueda de socios estratégicos.[20]

En resumen, la diversidad de empresas obliga considerar varias alternativas en el proceso mismo y también en los plazos. El Cuadro No. 3 sintetiza esta idea, cada etapa esta en consonancia con las respectivas del Cuadro No. 2. Las empresas más simples y pequeñas, en términos de personal y de activos, pueden ser privatizadas de inmediato, ellas son parte del proceso de consolidación del mercado y sirven para contener el desempleo, la libertad de ejercicio de los profesionales sustenta la privatización inmediata de los servicios.

---

19. Frydman (1999) muestra que los extranjeros logran acuerdos pro empleo. Las empresas transnacionales tienen mayor horizonte de recuperación de la inversión y pueden mantener mejores condiciones laborales que empresas pequeñas y descapitalizadas.

20. Hungría atrajo a: Audi, GE, Ford, IBM, SIEMENS y otras. La misma institución, vinculada a la política PYME del gobierno, tiene economías de escala en la entrega de capacitación y asesorías y se relaciona a la política turística y de exportaciones que se determine.

Cuadro 3. Etapas de la Privatización

Corto Plazo	Mediano Plazo	Largo Plazo
Empresas clave de infraestructura energética (generación, trasmisión y distribución) y de transporte (vial, portuaria, transporte, etc.) y comunicaciones (telefonía, correos), que determinan la capacidad de desarrollo del país y operan en monopolios naturales. La licitación abierta es el mejor método, buscando capitales extranjeros.	Las que pueden operar en eficiencia porque están guiadas por algún controlador con objetivos privados y capacidad competitiva a nivel internacional. Las nacidas al alero de la Ley de Inversiones estarían en este caso.	El remanente de los procesos anteriores. La banca estatal. La seguridad social: salud, educación y pensiones, para lograr un sistema mixto público-privado.
Empresas pequeñas y de poco capital, servicios varios y profesionales, las escindidas de las "consolidadas" estatales.	Los recursos naturales. Un sistema mixto de *vouchers*, venta internacional y socios estratégicos, que permita al Gobierno maximizar los ingresos y la viabilidad del sector.	Objetivo: reducir la participación del Estado, recaudar y aumentar la eficiencia.
Objetivo: crear condiciones de mercado y propiedad para disminuir el desempleo.	Objetivo: recaudar.	

Respecto de las empresas o los proyectos de mayor tamaño, y teniendo en mente que el objetivo de corto plazo es el desarrollo de las condiciones de mercado, deberán centrarse los esfuerzos en pasar a manos privadas todos aquellos sectores que impactan directamente en la capacidad competitiva del país, principalmente los de energía, transporte y comunicaciones. Lograr esto exigirá enormes esfuerzos y coordinación de los tres Poderes del Estado, conjuntamente con nuestra entidad privatizadora, de esta primera etapa dependen muchas cosas, no solo respecto del funcionamiento de los sectores liberados, pero también de la forma técnica y la reputación del aparato público.

Esto no significa que todos los servicios médicos o de educación deban ser públicos. El derecho a la educación, que es un derecho Constitucional, debería incluir el derecho a recibir educación tanto como el de proveerla. De modo que bajo la supervisión de los entes respectivos, servicios educacionales o médicos privados pueden surgir desde el primer momento.

Es importante que en esta primera etapa no se intente despojar al gobierno de todos sus activos. No solo es descabellado, es también innecesario. Todas aquellas empresas que estén en manos de un controlador que las administre eficientemente, incluyendo todos los *joint ventures* y las empresas mixtas con capital extranjero pueden mantenerse en operaciones dejando al gobierno como accionista e integrante del Directorio.

Una segunda etapa de privatizaciones debe estar orientada a recaudar. Aquí el Gobierno lo que pretende es vender al mejor postor su paquete accionario y su participación en empresas turísticas o de cualquier índole. Con la legislación en funcionamiento y el equipo regulador con experiencia adquirida, también puede despojarse de los enormes recursos naturales que posee el Gobierno, incluyendo tierras, minas, etc., esta etapa también puede asignar anchos de banda para telefonía, cuotas de pesca y toda serie de trasferencia de derechos que deben normarse. La metodología dependerá de las empresas y de las posibilidades disponibles, en este caso los *vouchers* permitirían a los cubanos de la isla recibir parte de estos beneficios, en algún tipo de "capitalismo popular" que mantenga una parte minoritaria de las acciones los cubanos que trabajen para las empresas o bien como parte de un fondo accionario que están en las cuentas de capitalización personales.

A largo plazo el Estado debe tender a dedicarse a su rol subsidiario y regulador, lo que significa que debería reducir al mínimo su participación como ente proveedor o empresarial. Quedará para la tercera etapa todo el remanente de las anteriores, así como una serie de activos y funciones que el Estado debe traspasar a los privados, incluyendo la seguridad social, que el gobierno puede subsidiar, pero que no necesita proveer directamente.

Este último impulso al mercado intentará dotarle de más eficiencia, reduciendo la intervención pública.

En cualquier caso, no se trata de un fanatismo reductor del aparato público, sino de llevar a un paso las recomendaciones que la economía moderna y la experiencia entregan, junto a la voluntad de las urnas y del Congreso cubano.

La política de privatizaciones debe supeditarse a otros objetivos y no tener como único foco la desintegración de la economía anterior, por esta razón la velocidad no es la mejor recomendación para este proceso y si el análisis de los detalles y las alternativas. En cualquier caso, lo más importante sigue siendo promover el surgimiento de nuevas empresas en todos los sectores.

Macroeconomía

Política Económica

Ninguna explicación coherente puede darse sobre la profundidad de la crisis económica en las transiciones (y en general), ignorando el mercado monetario, las intervenciones de política y las expectativas de los agentes. Incluso en países con mercados maduros, agentes informados y autoridades reputadas, los manejos de la política macroeconómica despiertan controversia y diferencias.

Una síntesis teórica de consenso reconocería al menos cinco proposiciones fundamentales: (1) el efecto de la política fiscal, incluso a largo plazo; (2) que un déficit exagerado desincentiva la acumulación de capital y reduce el producto de largo plazo; (3) el efecto transitorio de la política monetaria y sus riesgos inflacionarios; (4) que ambas políticas resultan de un juego estratégico entre autoridades y agentes, donde las expectativas juegan el papel primordial; y (5) la persistencia del nivel "natural" de producto, modificable por acumulación de capital —físico y humano— y el progreso tecnológico.

Las recomendaciones más importantes recalcan la necesidad de coordinación fiscal-monetaria y coherencia entre políticas macro, micro y comerciales. Pero en los países en transición, la disciplina y la madurez institucional son el factor más relevante.[21] Coordinar micro y macro implica cerrar el déficit público o al menos dar la señal creíble de tal prioridad. Lo elemental es acortar el déficit, limitar subsidios, generar mercados, tributación y capitalizando vía privatizaciones. Aun cuando esto demore, es básico que se perciba la dirección y el empeño, siendo las expectativas el canal más poderoso de hacer política macro, mientras se use el aparato estatal de locomotora,[22] se arrastrará la carga de subsidios, déficit y una moneda débil.

El mercado monetario enfrenta traumáticos cambios en transición. Con ingresos y precios fijos, sin banca ni mercado financiero, sin un referente nítido de autoridad y con la brecha entre valor oficial y real de la moneda, así llegaron los países socialistas ante las ruinas del muro. Puesto que el mercado ajusta primero por precios, inmediatamente las monedas socialistas perdieron valor de manera estrepitosa y la inflación se convirtió en la medida de todas las cosas y el desafío mas grave, general y persistente que debieron enfrentar.

El Banco Central juega el papel protagónico en esta sección. Su desempeño previo no es indicativo de su capacidad futura, que sí depende de su configuración institucional y principalmente de los mecanismos de trasmisión entre la política monetaria y la inflación. La amplia literatura en el tema reconoce al menos cinco canales de trasmisión disponibles: (1) tasa de interés; (2) precio de los activos; (3) tipo de cambio; (4) crédito; y finalmente (5) expectativas. Con mercados superficiales y poco desarrollados, serán la tasa de interés y las expectativas los canales más activos para trasmitir las decisiones de política.

Emplear activamente la política de tasas para contener la inflación tiene impactos sobre la actividad económica, anticipable una vez que las autoridades hayan determinado la "razón de sacrificio" que sean capaces de aceptar. La efectividad de este mecanismo dependerá de la capacidad efectiva de la autoridad para afectar la tasa de interés real y también de la sensibilidad de la inversión y el consumo a esta variable,

---

21. Berg (1999).

22. Carranza (1995).

entonces la elasticidad de la demanda agregada a la tasa de interés determinará la velocidad y el impacto de las políticas sobre la economía. En cualquier caso, modelar las expectativas reduce el costo (*trade off*) entre las políticas antiinflacionarios (contractivas) y el nivel de actividad económica.

Utilizar las expectativas como política antiinflacionaria exige de la autoridad credibilidad y reputación sólida. Esto es parte de un proceso y poco puede hacerse en el origen mismo, salvo seleccionar adecuadamente los miembros del Directorio y dotar al Banco Central de autonomía la que además debe ser respetada desde un comienzo. Las políticas basadas en "metas de inflación" han demostrado efectividad y parecen adecuadas para alinear las expectativas, pero requieren de sólida posición fiscal y capacidad real de anticipación de los indicadores económicos

Política Cambiaria

El canal del tipo de cambio ha sido ampliamente discutido y cualquier estudio entre los países del antiguo bloque comunista o de nuestra América Latina mostraría un patrón similar: tipos de cambio anclados a divisas duras y monedas locales subvaluadas, para luego devaluar y flexibilizar, en el mejor de los casos, o cerrar el Banco Central y dolarizar en caso contrario. La teoría aun no define el mejor sistema y aunque avala la secuencia (fijo a flexible), la amenaza de ataques especulativos hace que sólo los extremos sean viables.

Si la inflación lo permite, el "primer mejor" sería un mercado cambiario libre, donde la moneda refleje su valor relativo, el Banco Central haga política monetaria, actúe como regulador del sistema de pagos y prestamista de última instancia. El valor simbólico y el costo político de perder el peso cubano refuerza esta opción. Un Banco Central autónomo y bien constituido, con mandato claro de estabilidad de precios y un nivel aceptable de reservas, podría explorar un sistema que combine bandas cambiarias y restricción al movimiento de capitales de corto plazo (permanencia o encaje), para consolidar su reputación antes de exponerse a la especulación mundial. Minimizar el impacto cambiario sobre la inflación y el riesgo de ataques, permite a mediano plazo la apertura de la banda y finalmente la liberalización de la moneda.

Esto naturalmente exige la coordinación de las autoridades económicas y principalmente un férreo control del presupuesto fiscal.

Dolarizar es una opción real. La experiencia ha demostrado la debilidad innata del Banco Central en transición, no es creíble que puedan mantener la tasa de cambio fijada, pronto sus reservas se ponen a prueba por los especuladores y los agentes se refugian en monedas de valor. La adopción del dólar es entonces una alternativa razonable, pero una solución de "segundo mejor" que responde a la renuncia (fracaso) de la política monetaria e implica la desaparición del Banco Central. Esto dejaría al país a merced de una muy limitada capacidad fiscal, como única herramienta de política. Un factor a considerar contra la dolarización es su irreversibilidad.

Resumiendo respecto de la autoridad monetaria, la estabilidad de precios debe ser su única responsabilidad y la efectividad de su gestión dependerá de su institucionalidad y del apoyo de la autoridad fiscal en un manejo serio. La apertura financiera hacia los flujos internacionales debe supeditarse a la real capacidad de control del Banco Central, aunque esto no impide que la propiedad bancaria se abra a los inversionistas internacionales. La misma recomendación microeconómica de crear las condiciones para que nazcan mercados, propietarios e incentivos correctos resulta siempre vital, porque moldea las expectativas y le agrega grados de libertad a la gestión monetaria al entregarle otros canales de trasmisión de su política.

Integración Económica

Dado el carácter monopólico del comercio estatal, la apertura es otra de las reformas habituales en transición. Las importaciones liberan los precios internos, aumentan la variedad de bienes e insumos y evitan que el "salto" de demanda se transforme en inflación neta. Las empresas se obligan a competir y se motiva la creación de nuevas empresas y la reorientación de otras a la exportación, el capital se abarata, se amplía la opción de insumos y el valor agregado crece con la densidad tecnológica, adicionalmente el mercado internacional permite aprovechar las economías de escala y una demanda infinita. Sobre los costos de la apertura hay poco consenso, incluso es debatible si estos son indeseables, aunque sean inoportunos en los primeros momentos sobre el empleo.

La recomendación inmediata es eliminar las distorsiones y barreras, llevando todo a una tarifa plana ad valorem, más transparente, fácil de implementar y administrar.[23] La apertura comercial unilateral puede consolidarse posteriormente reduciendo la tasa, para reducir la desviación de comercio si el país negocia Acuerdos Preferenciales Bilaterales o facilitar las importaciones. Esto puede ser muy importante en cuanto a la recaudación fiscal, mientras el sistema impositivo definitivo se consolida, sin embargo, a mediano plazo la recaudación fiscal no debería depender de las aduanas.

Cuba debe solicitar su inclusión entre los beneficiarios del Sistema Generalizado de Preferencias (SGP), eso le permitiría competir con otros países pequeños que se benefician del SGP actualmente. Lo antes posible también debe regularizar las materias impositivas respecto de las remesas del exilio, principalmente con EEUU. Ya mencionamos la importancia de negociar un acuerdo comercial amplio entre Cuba y EEUU, por los impactos reales del comercio y también por las expectativas y la consolidación del modelo, la isla estará en la posición política de hacerlo aun sin que el Presidente norteamericano recibe una autorización del Congreso (el Trade Promotion Authority que permite al Presidente negociar acuerdos comerciales). El objetivo sería lograr un acuerdo amplio y beneficioso para la isla, idealmente el trato de Nación Más Favorecida en acceso y otros beneficios que le permitirán competir en su principal mercado de destino, sin que eso signifique para Cuba la imposición de cláusulas inoportunas o coarte la capacidad real de regulación e intervención de las autoridades y los legisladores.

Si esperamos que las exportaciones se transformen en un aporte al crecimiento económico del país es necesario invertir en la capacidad de orientación al exterior de nuestras empresas, aquí se requieren medidas tan amplias como invertir en el capital fito y zoosanitario, imagen internacional de nuestros productos y el conocimiento de prácticas internacionales. Mantener una participación activa en la Organización Mundial del Comercio (OMC) es siempre positivo por el mecanismo de solución de controversias que la institución posee, es posible anticipar reacciones proteccionistas de varios países y acusaciones de practicas desleales una vez que la isla comience su despegue exportador.[24] La política internacional y diplomática debe activamente contribuir a facilitar la inserción internacional, esto tradicionalmente ha sido una responsabilidad compartida por las autoridades y los privados.

Habrán de evaluar las autoridades del momento el beneficio de incorporase al Acuerdo de Libre Comercio de las Américas. Esta sería una opción atractiva únicamente si un Acuerdo amplio con EEUU es imposible, de lo contrario serían los mismos beneficios por mayores costos.

CONCLUSIONES

Se ha descrito parcialmente la amplitud del desafío cubano en transición. Un proceso complejo de reformas simultáneas y consecutivas, orientadas por un objetivo de largo plazo de crecimiento con estabilidad, ajustadas en velocidad e intensidad por sub-objetivos de consolidación política y económica.

Puesto que la hipótesis central del escrito alejaba al caso cubano de sus antecesores en transición, los países de Europa Oriental y las antiguas Repúblicas soviéticas, y en cambio lo situaba en un plano más latinoamericano y de país subdesarrollado, el set de recomendaciones propuestas no provienen de las antiguas economías socialistas, en cambio han sido aplicadas exitosamente por un país latinoamericano. De hecho, la única recomendación fundada en Europa es el SAE, la entidad privatizadora que se encargará de administrar y vender los activos del Estado, y que si-

---

23. Brodman (2000) muestra que el tipo de medidas (v.g. cuotas, licencias u otras) determinan el nivel de corrupción.

24. Sin dudas que escucharemos sobre el "dummping" que los exportadores cubanos harán, principalmente los agricultores, cuando sus competidores reclamen por las políticas de soporte que el gobierno de transición hará o bien por la "entrega" de propiedades estatales, que serán consideradas subsidio por otros socios.

gue el modelo Húngaro. El resto y términos generales, es la batería de medidas que hicieron de Chile la economía más exitosa del vecindario: liberación micro absoluta pero con apoyo social, privatización activa pero paciente, consolidación del modelo exportador basado en ventajas propias, apertura comercial agresiva pero apertura financiera administrada, Banco Central con capacidad activa y autonomía de intervención, autoridad fiscal férrea.

Cuando la isla estableció el *período especial*, Chile regresó a la democracia, recibió al exilio y se abrió a los mercados. Equilibrios muy similares en lo político y lo social debieron mantenerse y desafíos comunes se lograron con éxito. Recomendar a Cuba las medidas chilenas parece descabellado, sin embargo, reconocer que Chile en 1989 no tenía Banco Central autónomo, mostraba fuerte participación del Estado en empresas productivas, era un paria internacional en comercio e Inversión Extranjera, estaba en medio de una transición política delicada, absorbiendo al exilio y lidiando con la herencia de violaciones humanas internas, reformando el sistema impositivo, las leyes, el Parlamento, etc., permite comparar las situaciones. Que la dictadura anterior haya sido una pro mercado importa poco hoy, cuando las autoridades cubanas han olvidado la planificación y no cuentan con el respaldo de los subsidios soviéticos.

Que hay diferencias importantes en Chile y Cuba es también evidente, principalmente la ausencia de sociedad civil que aqueja a la isla y que fue más atenuada durante la dictadura del Gobierno Militar chileno, mi opinión sin embargo es que el exilio cubano tiene la capacidad de asumir esa brecha y debe hacerlo. Esto no era posible en Europa del Este porque la imposición del socialismo vino inmediatamente después de la Segunda Guerra Mundial, antecedida a su vez por siglos de una fuerte tradición monárquica, y al momento de la transición la memoria histórica civil e institucional se había perdido. El caso cubano es distinto, el exilio, principalmente en Miami, ha logrado mantener las tradiciones e incluso mantiene vigentes una serie de instituciones sociales que pueden permutarse a la isla. Lo importante es que esa masa critica aparezca en el momento de la transición y haga su válido aporte.

Para el autor, una transición económica positiva será la que cumpla tres condiciones mínimas: esté diseñada en base a las especificidades y necesidades de la isla, sea pacifica en términos sociales y productiva en términos de crecimiento económico. Con esto en mente, creo sinceramente que Chile es un ejemplo válido para el caso cubano.

REFERENCIAS

Aslund, Anders; Boone, Peter; y Johnson, Simon. "Escaping the Under-Reform Trap." *A Decade of Transition*, CEIP, enero 2000.

Aslund, Anders. "Possible Future Directions for Economies in Transition." *Transforming Post-Communist Political Economies*, 1998.

Banco Mundial. *World Development Report*. Varios años.

Berg Andrew; Eduardo Borensztein; Ratna Sahay; y Jeromin Zettelmeyr. "The Evolution of Output in Transition Economies: Explaining the Diffe-

rences," FMI, Working Papers WP/99/73, mayo 1999.

Betancourt, Roger. "Cuba's Reforms: A New Institutional Economics Perspective." *Perspectives on Cuban Economic Reforms*, Special Studies No. 30. Arizona State University Press, 1998.

Betancourt, Roger. "Las Reformas de la Economía Cubana y el Siglo XXI." Universidad de Maryland, abril 2000.

Blanchard, Olivier. *The Economics of Post-Communist Transition*. Oxford University Press, 1997.

Broadman Harry y Rocanatini Francesca: "Seeds of Corruption—Do Market Institutions Matter." Banco Mundial, Policy Research Working Papers N2368, junio 2000.

Carranza, Julio; Gutiérrez, Luis; y Monreal, Pedro. *Cuba, la restructuración de la economía*. Ed. Ciencias Sociales, Habana 1995.

Ellman, Michael. "Socialist Planning," en *The New Palgrave*, Problems of the Planned Eonomy. Macmillan, 1990.

Ekelund, Robert y Tollison, Robert. "Mercantilism as a Rent-Seeking Society." IMF Staff Papers, 1995.

Frydman R.; Gray C.; Hessel M.; y Rapaczynski A. "When does privatisation work? The impact of private ownership on corporate performance in the transition economies," Stokholm School of Economics, Working Paper N° 142, enero 1999.

Gomulka, Stanislaw. "Macroeconomic Policies and Achivements in Trasition Economies, 1989-1999." *Economic Survey of Europe*, United Nations, diciembre 2000.

Havrylyshyn, Oleg y McGettigan Donald. "Privatization in Transition Countries: A Sampling of the Literature." FMI, Working Papers WP/99/6, enero 1999.

Kornai, János. "What the Change of System From Socialism to Capitalism Does and Does Not Mean." *Journal of Economic Perspectives*, V.14, N°1, winter 2000.

Mesa-Lago, Carmelo. *Breve historia económica de la Cuba Socialista. Políticas, resultados y perspectivas.*" Alianza Editorial, Madrid, 1994.

Mesa-Lago, Carmelo. "The Cuban Economy in 1999-2001: Evaluation of Performance and Debate on the Future," *Cuba in Transition—Volume 11*, Washington, ASCE, 2001.

Montenegro, Claudio y Soto, Raimundo. "How Distorted is Cuba's Trade? Evidence and Predictions from a Gravity Model," *Journal of International Trade & Economic Development*, V.5, N°1, March 1996.

OECD, Centre for Co-Operation with Non-Members. "A decade of trade liberalisation in transition economies." Paris, Mayo 2001.

REFORM OF THE ARMED FORCES
IN A POST-CASTRO CUBA

Armando F. Mastrapa III[1]

Cuba's Revolutionary Armed Forces (*Fuerzas Armadas Revolucionarias de Cuba*—FAR) have undergone over the years a dynamic change in their role and doctrine as a defense institution, from their genesis of the Rebel Army who fought the Batista dictatorship. Army General Raúl Castro has called the FAR a "vanguard of the state,"[2] ready to defend the socialist state and its revolutionary achievements.

The armed forces have achieved a level of professionalism[3] and autonomy, e.g., by the training the officer corps received in Soviet military academies that taught them about Soviet military doctrine and their international campaigns in Africa (e.g. Angola and Ethiopia) and in the Middle East (e.g. Iraq and Syria) in the 1970s and 1980s. However, the professionalism and autonomy of the FAR brought concern to the regime's leadership. The leadership perceived the FAR to be a potential rival power whereas their main mission was to defend the state.

As a result of the Soviet Union slashing subsidies to the island, an economic crisis occurred in the early 1990s known as the Special Period (*Período Especial*) that gave the regime leadership an opportunity to re-adjust the FAR's mission: a new role that emphasized participation in the economic survivability of the communist state. The Cuban Communist Party (*Partido Comunista de Cuba*—PCC) and the population, through a new doctrine called the War of All the People (WAP) (*la guerra de todo el pueblo*), were also included in defending the regime by diversifying the responsibility and not depending on a single institution for the country's defense. WAP was a check and counterbalance to the perceived autonomy of the FAR.

The objective of this essay is to discuss the role and mission that the armed forces will have in post-Castro Cuba, principally in a transition to democracy, not in a succession perpetuating the *status quo*. The essay is composed of four parts: first, a review of civil-military relations in Cuba; second, the theories and trends of civil-military relations in post-communist states; third, the role and mission of the armed forces in a post-Castro Cuba; and finally, a conclusion.

---

1. An earlier version of this paper was presented at the 57th Annual Conference of the New York State Political Science Association, Wagner College, Staten Island, New York, April 12, 2003.

2. See Juan Carlos Espinosa, "Vanguard of the State: The Cuban Armed Forces in Transition," *Armed Forces and Society*, 48:6, 2001, 19-30.

3. Civilian control in the objective sense is the maximizing of military professionalism. More precisely, it is that distribution of political power between military and civilian groups which is most conducive to the emergence of professional attitudes and behavior among the members of the officer corps. See Samuel Huntington, *The Soldier and the State: The Theory and Politics of Civil Military Relations* (Cambridge, Mass: Harvard University Press, 1967), p. 83; Alfred Stepan, *The Military in Politics: Changing Patterns in Brazil* (Princeton, NJ: Princeton University Press: 1971).

CIVIL-MILITARY RELATIONS IN CUBA

The relations between the civil government and of the military in Cuba can be categorized in two historical periods. Frank Mora classifies Cuba's civil-military relations into *Fidelismo* and *Raulismo*.

- *Fidelismo* is the period of civilian control from 1959 to 1979, characterized by a policy or pattern of civilian control similar to what Samuel Huntington described as subjective control of the military.[4] Huntington writes: "Consequently, the maximizing of civilian power always means the maximizing of the power of some particular civilian group or groups. This is subjective civilian control. The general concept of civilian control is identified with the specific interests of one or more civilian groups. Consequently, subjective civilian control involves the power relations among civilian groups. It is advanced by one civilian group as a means to enhance its power at the expense of other civilian groups."[5]

- *Raulismo* is the period from 1989 to the present, characterized by a new policy of civilian control based on restructuring the FAR and transforming it into an instrument of Raúl Castro's political and economic objectives.[6]

When the Rebel Army was being transformed from a group of rebels into a standing army (the FAR), there was discussion within the leadership as to how the new army would be fashioned. Damián Fernández suggests, "Two options for the army were debated in 1959 and early 1960s: (1) the army would be composed of the armed Cuban people; or (2) a professional army would function as a traditional military establishment. [Che] Guevara favored the former, while Fidel hesitated between the two. For the Castro brothers the most significant concern was control over the military institution to guarantee their survival in power."[7] Fidel Castro knew that supreme control of the military establishment would ensure that a vital instrument such as the armed forces would perpetuate his power as the process of consolidating the government and power structures was taking place. Fidel Castro's role both as leader of the Cuban Revolution and virtual founder of the FAR and the ruling Cuban Communist Party (PCC) acted both to maintain control over and insure the loyalty of the armed forces. His ties with many senior officers, dating back in many cases to the insurgent struggle against the dictatorship of Fulgencio Batista in the 1950s, not to mention the role of his brother Raúl as defense minister, provided yet another level of control absent in most Latin American military establishments.[8]

However, Army General Raúl Castro has structured and crafted a doctrine and mission for the armed forces through a process of reorganization that attempts to guarantee a smooth succession of power in the event that his brother, Fidel is no longer the *maximum leader* due to death or incapacitation. Frank Mora further expands on this:

> When in 1991 [Fidel] Castro stated that "one of the tasks of the armed forces is to help the economy of the country during the Special Period," it was clear that the future role of the post-Cold War, post-internationalist FAR had been defined. It was Raul Castro, however, who took over the process of reorganizing the FAR. His goals were to enhance the role and contribution of the military to the national economy and to reassert control of the military in the aftermath of the Ochoa case...Raul played a pivotal role in restructuring the economy and military, enhancing his profile and visibility (and that of the FAR) in an effort to

---

4. Frank Mora, "From Fidelismo to Raulismo: Civilian Control of the Military in Cuba," *Problems of Post-Communism*, 46:2, 1999, p. 25.

5. Huntington, *The Soldier and the State*, p. 80.

6. Mora, "From Fidelismo to Raulismo," p. 31.

7. Damián J. Fernández, "Historical Background: Achievements, Failures, and Prospects," in Jaime Suchlicki. ed. *The Cuban Military Under Castro*. (Coral Gables: University of Miami, 1989), p. 7.

8. Richard L. Millett, "From Triumph to Survival: Cuban Armed Forces in an Era of Transition," in Richard L. Millett and Michael Gold-Bliss, eds. *Beyond Praetorianism: The Latin American Military in Transition*. (Coral Gables: North-South Center, 1996), p.134.

secure the survival of the regime and his position as Fidel's heir apparent.[9]

While Paul Buchanan suggests,

The FAR leadership under Raúl Castro has been able to do five things simultaneously. First, they have been able to steer the Cuban economy more firmly in the direction of fundamental market-oriented reform, albeit with a heavy state managerial presence. Second, they have now made the FAR a direct source of employment and opportunity for the civilian population, which along with the mass citizen-soldier training provided under the strategic umbrella of the "War of All the People," has expanded the leading mobilizational role it has played since the early days of the revolutionary regime. Third they have reaffirmed the FAR's image as an institution that can get things done at a time when virtually all of Cuba's major institutions—the Communist Party, civilian bureaucracy, Peoples Popular Assemblies, etc.—are viewed with outright skepticism, when not disdain. Forth, they have committed the armed forced to their most far-reaching post-internationalist mission, one whose importance to national survival restores the military's institutionally prestige while simultaneously reaffirming its reason d'etre. Finally, by assuming direct control of economic management, the FAR has distanced—and insulated—Fidel Castro and his chosen successors from criticism of the social costs, pace, scope and potential failures of the reform program.[10]

Not only has Raúl Castro set an institutional pattern of loyalty, but he has placed several *Raulistas* in key positions within the military and economic institutions to ensure total loyalty from these establishments, e.g. General Abelardo Colomé Ibarra, Ministry of Interior (MININT); General Ulises Rosales del Toro, Ministry of Sugar; and General Luis Pérez Róspide, Gaviota Enterprises, S.A.

CIVIL-MILITARY RELATIONS IN POST-COMMUNIST STATES

A consensus of research (Espinosa 2001; Latell 2002; Mora 1999 and 2002) views the likelihood of the eventual transition in Cuba to be one of succession (from Fidel to his brother Raúl) rather than a democratic one in the short-term. However, it remains to be seen how the FAR will address the democratic change in a transition. They have the organizational structure to oversee and participate in such transition, but can they reorganize themselves to fit a democratic model?

The FAR have been in the past, are now, and may continue to be for the foreseeable future, the most cohesive, influential, prestigious, and strongest institution of the ruling system in Cuba. One important feature is their proven ability to survive, which gives them the great potential to play a role in any government project involving reforms, changes, or transition processes that may occur.[11]

Post-totalitarian regimes realize that one of the key components of political democracy is civilian control of the military. Successor regimes, by coincidence or design, appear to rely on Huntington's theory that professionalism, as understood and practiced in Western democratic societies, renders the military politically neutral and an sterile servant of the legitimate state authorities. Toward this goal they emphasize three complementary, interrelated, and even overlapping strategies: depoliticization, departization, and democratization. A cursory review of civil-military relations in former Eastern bloc countries reveals that with the exception of the three Baltic republics, Soviet successor states have yet to achieve de-

---

9. Frank O. Mora, "A Comparative Study of Civil-Military Relations in Cuba and China: The Effects of Bingshang," *Armed Forces and Society*, 28:2, 2001, p.197.

10. Paul G. Buchanan, "The FAR and Cuban Society," in International Research 2000, Inc. *The Military and Transition in Cuba: Reference for Policy and Crisis Management* (Washington: Report prepared for the Department of Defense. March, 1995), p. III-4-1 and 2.

11. Humberto León, "Impact of the Economic Crisis on the Cuban Revolutionary Armed Forces (FAR)," in International Research 2000, Inc., *The Military and Transition in Cuba: Reference for Policy and Crisis Management* (Washington: Report prepared for the Department of Defense. March, 1995), p. III-6-3.

sirable levels of depoliticization, departization, and democratization in civil-military relations.[12]

It remains to be seen what path Cuba will take in a transition to democracy. James Burk has set out two theories of democracy:

- *liberal theory* argues that the first priority of the democratic state is to protect the rights and liberties of individual citizens; and

- *civic republican theory* contests the liberal notion that the first priority of the democratic state is to protect individual rights and liberties. It argues instead that priority should be placed on engaging citizens in the activity of public life.[13]

Will Cuba model its government based on elements of the 1940 Cuban Constitution as it has been suggested[14] following a progressive view of individual rights?

Douglas Bland stresses, "If civil-military relations in emerging democracies are to be constructed from a western-liberal democratic regime of civil military relations, then this regime must be spelled out in explicit terms. Civil-military relations as practiced in each liberal democracy are based on cardinal principles, norms rules, decision-making procedures; a national regime that has evolved from the cultural, political, political, social, and military history of each state."[15]

Moreover, there will be several transitional issues arising for the regime's leadership and for the armed forces in a post-Castro Cuba. For example, Juan Carlos Espinosa sets out four propositions regarding the armed forces in a post-Castro future:

- the FAR will have a central role in regime change or re-equilibration;

- the FAR is not a unitary actor and the Cuban regime is not monolith—factions and interest groups will emerge within the regime and the military;

- the current process of reform, including the (*sistema de perfeccionamiento empresarial*—SPE)[16] has had its winners and losers, generating an undercurrent of jealousy and resentment fueled in part by the internalized values of egalitarianism and by the brazenness of nepotism, *sociolismo*, and corruption; and

- the military's involvement in non-traditional economic activities is a stabilizing element in the short-term for the regime, the FAR, and the national economy, but it may become a source of instability in the medium and longer terms.[17]

ARMED FORCES' STRUCTURE, ROLE AND MISSION

As a result of the economic crisis of the early 1990s, the regime's leadership faced the necessity of reducing and re-adjusting its total armed forces. In 1998, Cuba's total armed forces were at 60,000, and by 2002 they had fallen to 46,000 (Figure 1). For 1998, the active army was at 38,000, and in 2002 at 35,000. Meanwhile, Cuba's active navy (charged with the coastal defense of the island) fared worse in terms of personnel reductions: in 1998 it was at 5,000 and in 2002 at 3,000. Surprisingly, the air

12. Costas Danopoulos and Daniel Zirker, "Civil-Military Relations Theory in the Post Communist World," *Geneva Centre for Democratic Control of Armed Forces (DCAF)*, Working Paper Series No. 38, 2002, p. 12.

13. James Burk, "Theories of Democratic Civil-Military Relations," *Armed Forces and Society*, 29:1, 2002, p. 9-10.

14. See Néstor Carbonell Cortina, "La Constitución de 1940: Simbolismo y Vigencia," in *Cuba in Transition—Volume 7* (Washington: Association for the Study of the Cuban Economy, 1987); Jorge A. Sanguinetty, "Los nuevos debates sobre la constitución del 40," *Cuba Futuro*, available at http://www.cubafuturo.org/Temas_Constitucionales/Nuevosdebates.pdf.

15. Douglas L. Bland, "Patterns in Liberal Democratic Civil-Military Relations," *Armed Forces and Society*, 27: 4, 1999, p. 529.

16. See Armando F. Mastrapa III, "Soldiers and Businessmen: The FAR During the Special Period," in *Cuba in Transition—Volume 10* (Washington: Association for the Study of the Cuban Economy, 2000).

17. Juan Carlos Espinosa, "Vanguard of the State: The Cuban Armed Forces in Transition," *Armed Forces and Society,* 48:6, 2001, p. 25.

Figure 1.   Cuba: Total Armed Forces (1998–2002)

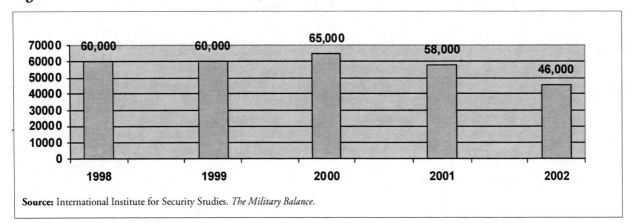

Source: International Institute for Security Studies. *The Military Balance.*

force exceeds the navy in active forces: 10,000 in 1998 and 8,000 by 2002.[18]

The navy (coast guard) has a handful of coastal boats to patrol a very vast coastal territory, and in 1998 their Cienfuegos submarine base was converted into a tourist facility.[19] According to Brigadier General Rafael del Pino—the highest-ranking military officer to defect from Cuba—fuel shortages have caused the army to roll their tanks up hills and let gravity start them, and the air force has had to cannibalize its fleet for spare parts due to the engine's maintenance expiration date.[20] The economic crisis has left the armed forces ill equipped and with shortages of their aged Soviet equipment. In a post-Castro Cuba, the armed forces must strengthen their naval forces to meet the challenges of future security concerns.

Will the armed forces role change in a post-Castro Cuba? Claude Welch and Arthur Smith define the role of the military as follows:

> Social organizations are made up of structures (or institutions), which are patterns of interacting roles…Thus, for example a military organization is made up of roles and structures of roles…The mili-

tary does not exist in a vacuum…It is a part of the larger social system, and both affects and is affected by the roles and structures of other organizations.[21]

The Cuban armed forces share their role with other institutions. For example, the PCC was also charged with defending the homeland, as was the population through the doctrine of the War of All the People. The sharing aspect of the military's role is evident in the National Defense Law (*Ley de la Defensa Nacional*):

> The national defense corresponds to Cuban military doctrine. It is prepared and executed under the direction of the Cuban Communist Party as a superior guiding force in society and the State; and according to the decisions made within the limits of their respective abilities by the superior organs of Popular Power.[22]

By dividing the responsibility of defense among institutions the regime reigned in the professionalism and autonomy of the FAR. The armed forces must take the central role again as the primary defense institution. In a post-Castro Cuba transitioning to a democracy, the FAR must take up its central role as the

---

18. International Institute for Security Studies. *The Military Balance* (Oxford University Press. 1997-2002).

19. *Cuban Armed Forces Review*, "Navy: Intel," March 28, 1998, available at http://www.cubapolidata.com/cafr/cafr_navy.html.

20. Brigadier General Rafael Del Pino, Conversation, Winter 2002.

21. Claude E. Welch and Arthur K. Smith, *Military Role and Rule: Perspectives on Civil-Military Relations* (Belmont, California: Duxbery Press, 1974), p. 40.

22. Asamblea Nacional del Poder Popular de la República de Cuba, *Ley de la Defensa Nacional*. December 21, 1994, Available at www.uh.cu/infogral/areasuh/defensa/ldn.htm.

guardian of the state, constitution, civilian control and the individual rights and freedoms of citizens.

In the span of the Castro regime's existence, the FAR have seen their mission change. The military mission of the Cuban military has been to provide for external defense and to suppress internal challenges to government rule. The military doctrine of the FAR has long insisted that the national defense is, at root, a Cuban responsibility.[23]

A mission that could be strengthened is enforcing the prevention of transshipment of narcotics in the Caribbean basin,[24] a problem that will pose a threat to a post-Castro Cuba. Apart from trading their own marijuana in the United States, some Caribbean countries have become important transshipment centers for South American cocaine, heroin, and marijuana bound for Europe and North America. Drug operations also have generated increased violence both political and nonpolitical.[25] Perhaps Cuba's navy and coast guard (restructured to a larger force), in cooperation with the United States, could address such a security concern and problem be facing both countries.

Another mission for the FAR could be the rapid mobilization and response to natural disasters occurring in Cuba. Hurricane Michelle, the most destructive hurricane in Cuba's history, battered the island in early November 2001, affecting 45 percent of the country's territory (eight provinces) and the homes of 53 percent of the population.[26] An expansion in the FAR's role in a civil disaster is possible by creating an air regiment[27] that not only would oversee the skies of Cuba but quickly assist civil defense in an event of a weather disaster.

Finally, as Brian Latell suggests, "personnel at all levels should receive international training in counter-terrorism and counter-narcotics missions that ought to be among the principal new preoccupations of the country's post-Castro armed forces."[28] The counter-terrorism aspect is important in the event that political violence should arise in a transition to a democracy and its aftermath, should rely on such violence to challenge the new government.

CONCLUSION

Cuba's armed forces face many challenges in a post-Castro Cuba. First, their role and mission were changed to counter the professionalism and autonomy they developed through training and internationalist campaigns. To gain greater control of the military institution, the regime leadership under Raúl Castro decided to restructure the role and mission of the armed forces. The *Special Period* brought the armed forces into the economy in order to ensure the survivability of the state. Preparing the transition process, Raúl Castro turned to key loyalists and placed them in important positions within the state's and military's enterprises—enriching them and assuring their loyalty.

The defense role of the FAR was further diluted by adding the PCC and the population at large (through the doctrine of the WAP) as a counter-balance to any potential threat that the FAR may pose as a rival to the regime's leadership. The FAR's post-Castro role should be to take center stage as the primary defense institution. Its missions should also encompass an ar-

---

23. Jorge Domínguez, "Institutionalization and Civil-Military Relations in Cuba," *Cuban Studies*, 6:1, 1976, p. 42.

24. STRATFOR contends that U.S.-led crackdowns on Pacific coast and Caribbean smuggling routes have changed and Cuba could pose a strategic asset to smugglers exploiting a security vacuum with the genesis of a new government in Havana. See "Colombian Chaos Bridges Geopolitical Divides in South America," May 15, 2003, Available at www.stratfor.com.

25. Ivelaw L. Griffith, *Drugs and Security in the Caribbean: Sovereignty Under Siege* (University Park, Pa.: Pennsylvania State University Press, 1997), p. 8.

26. Orlando Oramas, "Michelle: The most destructive hurricane the island has ever seen," *Granma International Digital*, November 9, 2001, Available at www.granma.cu/ingles/noviem1/46lage-i.html.

27. General Rafael del Pino, Conversation. Winter 2002.

28. Brian Latell, "The Military in Cuba's Transition," *Cuba Transition Project*. University of Miami, August, 2002, p. 38.

ray of new security challenges from counter-narcotics to counter-terrorism.

However, the legacy of Fidel and Raúl Castro's civilian-military relations is the corrupting effect of the military in the economy. By tying the military to economic entrepreneurship, their institutional mission has become the pursuit of profit, instead of military professionalism and preparedness. A new oligarchy has been created that will be play a key role in any transition scenario and may have an effect on the democratic process of transition in the long-term.

Appendix A
Authors and Discussants

B. E. Aguirre is Professor, Department of Sociology and Criminal Justice, University of Delaware.

José Alvarez is Professor, Food and Research Economics Department, Institute of Food and Agricultural Sciences, University of Florida, where he works as the Area Economist at the Everglades Research and Education Center, Belle Glade, Florida. He has traveled to Cuba in the last few years as one of the principal investigators in two grants from John D. and Catherine T. MacArthur Foundation to study Cuban agriculture and the potential economic impact on the agricultural economies of Florida and Cuba after lifting the U.S. economic embargo. He earned a B.A. in economics (1971) and M.S. (1974) and Ph.D. (1977) in Food and Resource Economics from the University of Florida.

Domingo Amuchástegui es Profesor de Conflictos Regionales, investigador independiente y especialista en Estudios Cubanos.

Ricardo Bofill es Presidente del Comité Cubano Pro Derechos Humanos.

Joel Brito, economista de profesión, ha dirigido el proyecto sobre Sindicalismo Independiente en Cuba por los últimos cinco años. También ha trabajado de investigador auxiliar en el Center for Labor Studies de Florida International University. Fue Jefe del Departamento de Auditoría de la CTC Nacional y miembro del Comité Central de la CTC, atendiendo la esfera económica y laboral.

Rolando H. Castañeda es consultor económico. Se retiró del Banco Interamericano de Desarrollo donde fue funcionario por 27 años, siendo su última asignación como Especialista Principal de Proyectos en Santiago, Chile, en 1996-2001.

Alejandro A. Chafuen, Ph.D., is the President and CEO of the Atlas Economic Research Foundation (Fairfax, VA), President of the Hispanic American Center for Economic Research (Fairfax, VA) and a member of the Board of Advisors for the Center for Research into Post-Communist Economies (London, United Kingdom). He has written and lectured on numerous topics including economics, religion and ethics. He is the author of *Faith and Liberty: The Economic Thought of the Late Scholastics* (Lexington Books, 2003).

Isaac Cohen is President, INVERWAY LLC, and former director of the Washington Office of the United Nations Economic Commission for Latin America and the Caribbean (ECLAC).

Nicolás Crespo is President, The Phoenix Hospitality and Consulting Corporation, Miami, Florida.

Larry Daley (García-Iñiguez Enamorado) holds BSA and MSA degrees from the University of Florida and a Ph.D. from the University of California, Davis. He is currently Professor of Biophysics and Biochemistry of Plant Germplasm at the Department of Horticulture, Oregon State University, Corvallis, Oregon.

Sergio Díaz-Briquets is Vice President of Casals & Associates, Inc. (C&A), a Washington area-based consulting firm.

Daniel P. Erikson is director of Caribbean programs at the Inter-American Dialogue, a leading policy forum on Western Hemisphere affairs in Washington, D.C. His current work is focused on the Cuban economy, hemispheric security issues, and U.S. foreign policy in Latin America. Prior to the Dialogue he was a Fulbright scholar to Mexico and research associate at Harvard Business School.

María Antonia Fernández Mayo is a Research Associate with GECYT, a Government of Cuba consulting enterprise in Havana. Her work focuses on marketing, trade and foreign investment. Prior to joining GECYT in 2001, she was an economist with the government's Center for Research on the World Economy (CIEM).

Manuel García Díaz is Professor in the Department of Applied Economics, Universidad de Granada, Spain. He holds a Licenciatura in Economics from the Universidad de La Habana and a Doctorate in Economic Sciences from Moscow State University, M. V. Lomonosov.

Jennifer Gauck is a Program Associate at the American Bar Association Central European and Eurasian Law Initiative (ABA/CEELI), where she works on anti-corruption issues and provides technical assistance to programs in Bosnia, Bulgaria and Slovakia. In 2002, she received a MSc in European Political Economy of Transition from the London School of Economics and Political Science. She also studied Cuban politics and economics at the University of Havana in January 1999.

Dominga González Suárez is Professor in the Department of Social Psychology and Methodology of the Behavioral Sciences, Faculty of Psychology, Universidad de Granada, Spain. She received a Licenciatura in History from the Universidad de La Habana and a Doctorate in Psychology from the Universidad de Granada.

Armando M. Lago has both a Ph.D. and an M.A. in Economics from Harvard University. Among other publications, he co-authored the landmark study *The Politics of Psychiatry in Revolutionary Cuba* (1991). After a distinguished career as owner of a firm dedicated to econometrics and international transportation issues, he is finishing a book on the victims of the Cuban Revolution and is Vice-President of the Free Society Project, Inc.

Alberto Luzárraga es Doctor en Derecho Civil Summa Cum Laude por la Universidad de Villanueva, estudió Ciencias Comerciales en la Universidad de la Habana y obtuvo un MBA en The University of Miami. Como banquero internacional fungió como Chairman de Continental Bank International en New York. Hoy dirige su propia empresa.

Argelio Maldonado, a graduate of the University of Florida and Columbia University, has enjoyed a multi-industry international business career with Procter & Gamble, Citibank, IBM, and Charles Schwab. Last year, after a near death experience, he gave up corporate job security, converting his avocation for environmental preservation into a vocation by accepting an assignment as a Senior Fellow with the World Wildlife Fund. Recently, he left WWF and is currently organizing a Cuban Conservation Trust Fund.

Armando F. Mastrapa III is the editor and publisher of the *Cuban Armed Forces Review* Internet Site. He received his M.A. in Government and Politics from St. John's University.

George Plinio Montalván es Analista Gerencial Principal en el Banco Interamericano de Desarrrollo.

Armando A. Musa, Esq., holds a J.D. from Harvard Law School (2003) and a B.A. from the University of Pennsylvania (2000).

Art Padilla is Associate Professor, Department of Business Management, North Carolina State University.

Daniel J. Perez-Lopez is a graduate student in the Department of Statistics at Virginia Tech. He earned a B.A. in Economics and International Studies from the College of William and Mary.

Jorge F. Pérez-López is an international economist with the Bureau of International Labor Affairs, U.S. Department of Labor. He is the author of *Cuba's Second Economy: From Behind the Scenes to Center Stage* (Transaction Publishers, 1995), co-editor of *Perspectives on Cuban Economic Reforms* (Arizona State University Press, 1998), and co-author of *Conquering Nature: The Environmental Legacy of Socialism in Cuba* (University of Pittsburgh Press, 2000). He received a Ph.D. in Economics from the State University of New York at Albany.

Ricardo A. Puerta is a Sociologist with 30 years of experience in development projects in Latin America.

He holds a Ph.D degree in Development Sociology from Cornell University. He served as Chief of the Pan American Agricultural School's Rural Development Program and as Assistant Director of the Latin American Program at Private Agencies Collaborating Together (PACT), an international NGO consortium based in New York. He has been a trainer in project design for the Central American Bank for Economic Integration (BCIE) and also in project evaluation for the Inter-American Development Bank (BID). Currently he is the principal Advisor to the Remittances Group in Honduras and a Consultant to several international development agencies.

Matthew McPherson is an economics Ph.D. student at West Virginia University doing work on international trade issues. He spent part of the summer of 2003 in Cuba working with an economist at the University of Havana on a trade-related project.

Joaquin Pérez Rodríguez fue Vice Ministro de Información y Turismo del gobierno de Venezuela y presidente del Consorcio Azucarero de ese país. Hizo un Master en Administración Pública en la Escuela Kennedy, de la Universidad de Harvard e hizo un MSM en el MEI de Arthur D. Little. Fue por quince años profesor en la Escuela de Ciencias Políticas y Sociales de la Universidad Central de Venezuela. Es socio y Vicepresidente de Bendixen and Associates, empresa de Miami especializada en el universo hispano de Norte, Centro y Suramérica. Desde hace dos años coordina una investigación sobre las remesas para el Banco Interamericano de Desarrollo y Pew Hispanic Center.

José M. Ricardo earned the degree of Ingeniero Agrónomo from the Universidad de la Habana in 1948. He also earned the M.S. and Ph.D. degrees in Agricultural Economics from the University of Mayland in 1967 and 1976, respectively. From 1955 to 1960, he was the local assistant to the Agricultural Attache, U.S. Embassy, La Habana. He also worked for the U.S. Department of Agriculture's Foreign Agricultural Service during 1961-70 and for the Census Bureau, assigned to the U.S. Agency for International Development under a PASA until his retirement in 1986

James E. Ross, Courtesy Professor at the University of Florida and retired foreign service officer, has over 40 years' experience in international agricultural trade, agribusiness investment, and economic development. Since 1993, he has specialized on studies of Cuba's food and agricultural situation and the potential market for U.S. agribusiness.

Christopher Sabatini is the Senior Program Officer for Latin America and the Caribbean at the National Endowment for Democracy, a position he has held since 1997. Mr. Sabatini has written and published articles on a number of themes concerning Latin America, democratization, security and defense, political parties, and the effectiveness of international programs to support democratic development. His most recent work includes "Lost Illusions: Decentralization and Political Parties" (*Journal of Democracy*, April 2003) and "The Decline of Ideology and the Rise of 'Quality of Politics' Parties in Latin America" (*World Affairs*, Fall 2002). Mr. Sabatini has testified before the House Sub Committee on the Western Hemisphere on the status of democracy in Latin America and before the House International Relations Committee on human rights in Cuba and has a Ph.D. in Government from the University of Virginia.

Juan Tomás Sánchez es Secretario General de la Asociación de Colonos de Cuba, en el exilio.

Paolo Spadoni is a PhD student in the Department of Political Science at the University of Florida. He holds a Master in Latin American Studies from the Center for Latin American Studies at the University of Florida.

Matías F. Travieso-Díaz is a partner in Shaw Pittman LLP, a law firm with offices in Washington, D.C., London, New York City, Los Angeles and Northern Virginia. He is the author of *The Laws and Legal System of a Free-Market Cuba* (Quorum Books, 1996) and numerous law review articles, papers and newspaper columns on matters related to Cuba's transition to a free-market, democratic society. He holds B.S. and M.S. degrees in Electrical Engineering from the University of Miami and a Ph.D. in Electrical Engineering from Ohio State University. He earned a J.D. degree from Columbia Law School.

William N. Trumbull is Director, Division of Economics and Finance, College of Business and Economics, West Virginia University. He received his Ph.D. in economics at the University of North Carolina and his BBA at the University of Miami. His teaching and research interests include comparative economic systems and he teaches a course on the economics of Cuba that includes a field trip to Cuba.

María C. Werlau is a consultant residing in the greater New York city area and author of numerous papers on Cuban affairs. She is also President of the Free Society Project, Inc., a non profit organization dedicated to human rights' research that is currently archiving the loss of life during the Cuban revolutionary process.

Alfie Antonio Ulloa Urrutia es cubano residente en Chile, Economista de la Universidad de Chile, donde además es Profesor. Adicionalmente se desempeña como Asesor Económico del Ministerio de Hacienda de Chile.

Appendix B
Acknowledgements

We want to take the opportunity to acknowledge the continued financial support provided to ASCE's activities by the following sponsoring members:

José Alvarez
Walter Arensberg
Victor Batista
Ernesto Betancourt
Beatriz Casals
Rolando Castañeda
Nicolás Crespo
Alfredo Cuzán
Maria Dolores Espino
John Fanjul
Matías Fernández
Emilio Fernández
Carlos Fernández
Antonio Gayoso
Juan Carlos Ginarte
Ariel Gutiérrez
Alfredo Gutiérrez
Salvador Juncadella

Luis Locay
Luis R. Luis
Alberto Luzárraga
Terry Maris
René Monserrat
National Association of
     Mill Owners of Cuba
Jack Otero
Lorenzo Pérez
Jorge Pérez-López
Joaquín Pujol
Mario Roque de Escobar
Nicolás Sánchez
Juan Sánchez
Federico Sánchez-Febles
Jorge Sanguinetty
Maria Werlau

Heterick Memorial Library
Ohio Northern University

DUE	RETURNED		DUE	RETURNED
1. FEB 17 2006	JUL 14 20		13.	
2.			14.	
3.			15.	
4.			16.	
5.			17.	
6.			18.	
7.			19.	
8.			20.	
9.			21.	
10.			22.	
11.			23.	
12.			24.